The Air War:

1939–1945

21

The Air War:

1939–1945

by

Janusz Piekalkiewicz

Translated from the German by Jan van Heurck

BLANDFORD PRESS
POOLE · DORSET

Originally published as *Luftkrieg 1939–1945*

Historical Times, Inc., Harrisburg, PA 17105

 Published 1985
Printed in the United States of America
93 92 91 90 89 88 87 86 85 9 8 7 6 5 4 3 2 1

First published in English in the UK 1985 by Blandford Press,
Link House, West Street, Poole, Dorset, BH15 1LL

Distributed in the United States by
Sterling Publishing Co., Inc.
2 Park Avenue, New York, NY 10016

Contents

Library of Congress Cataloging in Publication Data

Piekalkiewicz, Janusz.
The air war, 1939–1945.

Translation of: Luftkrieg, 1939–1945.
Bibliography: p.
Includes index.
1. World War, 1939–1945 – Aerial operations. I. Title.
D785.P5313 1985 940.54'4 85-779
ISBN 0-918678-05-6

Typeset by Duncanphototype, Camp Hill, PA 17011
Printed by Kingsport Press, Kingsport, TN 37662
Manufactured in the United States of America

A Word of Thanks

I want to express my sincere thanks to:

Dr. M. Haupt, Bundesarchiv Koblenz
Dr. Fricke, Dr. Wieseotte, Militärgeschichtliches Forschungsamt Freiburg
Dr. M. Lindemann, Institut für Zeitungsforschung, Dortmund
Professor Dr. J. Rohwer, W. Haupt and their colleagues, Weltkriegsbücherei, Stuttgart
Dr. Sack and his colleagues, Zentralbibliothek der Bundeswehr, Düsseldorf
Colonel De Rill and C. Kesteloot, Belgian Embassy in Bonn
Colonel E. Raunio, Finnish Embassy in Bonn
Brigadier General Sionta, Greek Embassy in Bonn
Colonel R. Aoto, Mr. Opiolka, Japanese Embassy in Bonn
Colonel A. Viviani, Italian Embassy in Bonn
I. Ivanji, Mrs. D. Alavantic, Yugoslavian Embassy in Bonn
Lt. Col. R. Kristiansen, Norwegian Embassy in Bonn
Alan Dodds, Mrs. I. Köpf, U.S. Embassy in Bonn
Dr. H.R. Kurz, Eidgenössisches Militärdepartement, Bern
Colonel J.-J. Willi, Eidgenössisches Militärdepartement, Bern
Dr. O. Gauye, E. Tschabold, Bundesarchiv Bern
Dr. F.G. Maier and his colleagues, Schweizerische Landesbibliothek, Bern
J.S. Lucas, P.H. Reed, Imperial War Museum, London
Everyone in the Photographic Library, Imperial War Museum, London
A.D. Walton, University of Keele
Commander B. Wronski, Capt. W. Milewski, Capt. R. Dembinski, Capt. S. Zurakowski, Engineer K. Barbarski, Sikorski Institute, London
Bertil Lagerwall, Flygstaben Stockholm
P.R.A. van Iddekinge, Gemeentearchief Arnhem
Lt. Col. F. Dou, Service Historique de l'Armée de l'Air, Château de Vincennes
Lt. Col. P. Dousset, P. Rolland, Établissement Cinématographique et Photographique des Armées, Fort D'Ivry
Maj. F.C. Lepore, Dept. of the Army, US-Army Audio-Visual Activity, Pentagon, Washington D.C.
Mrs. M.B. Livesay, Dept. of the Air Force, 1361st Audiovisual Squadron, Arlington/Virginia
W.H. Leary, National Archives, Washington D.C.
P.M. Maddocks, Library and Photographic Services, United States Naval Institute, Annapolis/Maryland
Col. B.J. Morden, Center of Military History, Dept. of the Army, Washington D.C.
A.F. Hoover, Photographic Section Naval History Division, Washington D.C.
Brigadier General E. Simmons, Marine Corps History and Museum Division, Navy Yard, Washington D.C.
B. Lindsey Command History, John F. Kennedy Center for Military Assistance, Fort Bragg/North Carolina
W.J. Armstrong, Ph.D., History Office, US Naval Air Systems Command, Washington D.C.
J. Koontz, Operational Archives Branch, Naval History Division, Dept. of the Navy, Washington D.C.
M.P. Mariana, Archivio Centrale dello Stato, Rome
Col. E. Ripamonti, Stato Maggiore dell'Aeronautica, Rome
Co-Admiral R. Fadda, Stato Maggiore della Marina, Rome
(German) Veterans' Association of the "Immelmann" Dive Bomber Wing
(German) Brotherhood of Former Transport Fliers
F. Neubert
Retired Colonel W. Hedderich
Retired Colonel Dr. C.H. Hermann
Retired Colonel Dr. H.-A. Koch
P. Mahle
K. Reichert
K. Kirchner
Colonel W.D. Kasprowicz, C.O.M., London
Engineer J.B. Cynk, London
Hannes Limmer, Munich
U. Schefold, H.-P. Piehl, Mrs. B. Thauer, Südwest Verlag, Munich

Bibliography

Air Force Combat Units of World War II, USAAF Historical Division, New York, 1963

Air Ministry, *Recognition Handbook of British Aircraft*, Section A-4 Issue 2, London, 1944

Barker, R., *Aviator Extraordinary*, London, 1969

Collier, B., *The Defense of the United Kingdom*, H.M.S.O., London, 1957

Craven, W.F./Cate, J.L., *The Army Air Forces in World War II*, 7 vol., Chicago, 1945/49

Cynk, J.B., *History of the Polish Air Force 1918–1968*, London, 1972

Douhet, Giulio, *Luftherrschaft*, Berlin, 1935. [Trans. of *Il dominio dell'aria*, 1921; Eng. trans. *The Command of the Air*, 1943]

Effects of Strategic Bombing on the German War Economy, ed. by the US Strategic Bombing Survey, Overall Economic Effects Division, 1945 ff.

Feuchter, G.W., *Der Luftkrieg*, Frankfurt am Main, 1964 [The Air War]

Frankland, N./Webster, Sir Charles, *The Strategic Air Offensive against Germany*, 4 vol., London, 1961

Fuchida, M./Okumiya, M., *Midway, the Battle that Doomed Japan*, Washington, 1955

Fuller, J.F.C., *The Second World War*, London, 1948

Galland, Adolf, *Die Ersten und die Letzten*, Darmstadt, 1953 [Eng. trans. *The First and the Last: The German Fighter Forces in World War II*, London, 1955]

Goyet, P. Le, "Évolution de la doctrine d'emploi de l'aviation française entre 1919 et 1939" in: *Revue d'histoire de la deuxieme guerre mondiale*, No. 73, 1969 [Evolution of Operational Doctrine in French Aviation 1919–1939]

Harris, Sir, A., *Bomber Offensive*, London, 1947

Karis, W., *Battle Report*, 5 vol., New York, 1944/49

Kens, K./Nowarra, H.J., *Die deutschen Flugzeuge 1939–1945*, Munich, 1964 [German Aircraft 1939–1945]

Kirchner, K., *Flugblätter: Psychologische Kriegsführung im Zweiten Weltkrieg in Europa*, Munich, 1974 [Air Leaflets:

Psychological Warfare in World War II Europe]
KOCH, H.-A., *Flak: Die Geschichte der deutschen Flakartillerie*, Bad Nauheim, 1965 [Flak: The History of German Flak Artillery]
LEVRAULT, B., *Les forces aériennes françaises de 1939 à 1945*, Paris, 1949 [The French Air Force 1939-1945]
LOCHNER, L.P. (ed.), *Goebbels-Tagebücher aus den Jahren 1942/43*, Zürich, 1948 [Eng. trans. *The Goebbels Diaries*, London, 1948, *see* years 1942/43]
MACMILLAN, N., *The Royal Air Force in World War II*, 4 vol., London, 1942-1950
MORISON, S.E., *History of United States Naval Operations in World War II*, 15 vol., New York, 1947/62
OKUMIYA, M./HORIKUSHI, J., *The Story of the Japanese Navy Air Force 1937-1945*, London, 1957
PIEKALKIEWICZ, JANUSZ, *Secret Agents, Spies and Saboteurs: Secret Missions of the Second World War*, Newton Abbot, 1974 [Trans. of *Spione, Agenten, Soldaten—Geheime Kommandos im Zweiten Weltkrieg*, Munich, 1969]
———, *Die Ju 52 im Zweiten Weltkrieg*, Stuttgart, 1976 [The Ju 52 Aircraft in World War II]
———, *Fieseler Fi 156 Storch im Zweiten Weltkrieg*, Stuttgart, 1977 [Fieseler Fi 156 Stork Aircraft in World War II]
———, *Stalingrad—Anatomie einer Schlacht*, Munich, 1977 [Stalingrad: Anatomy of a Battle]
———, *Schweiz 39-45: Krieg in einem neutralen Land*, Stuttgart, 1978 [Switzerland 1939-1945: War in a Neutral Country]
PLAYFAIR, I.S.O., *The Mediterranean and Middle East*, 4 vol., H.M.S.O., London, 1960
RICHARDS, D./SAUNDERS, H., *Royal Air Force 1939-1945*, 3 vol., H.M.S.O., London, 1953/55
RUMPF, H., *Das war der Bombenkrieg*, Oldenburg, 1961 [The Bombing War]
SALESSE, LT. COL., *L'Aviation de chasse française en 1939-1940*, Paris, 1948 [The French Fighter Air Force 1939-1940]
SANTORO, G., *L'Aeronautica italiana nella seconda guerra mondiale*, 2 vol., Rome, 1957 [Italian Aviation in World War II]
SCHRAMM, P.E., *Die Niederlage 1945*, Munich, 1962 [The 1945 German Defeat]
SOVIETSKIYE VOYENNO VOZDUCHNOYE SILY V VIELIKOI OTIECHESTVIENNOI VOINIYE 1941-1945 (compilation), Moscow, 1968 [The Soviet Military Air Forces in the Great Patriotic War 1941-1945]
SPEER, ALBERT, *Inside the Third Reich: Memoirs*, New York, 1970 [Trans. of *Erinnerungen*, Berlin, 1969]
TAMURA, Y. (ed.), *Hiroku Daitoa Senshi*, 7 vol., Tokyo, 1953 [Secret Documents of the Great-Asian War]
TEDDER, LORD, RAF MARSHAL, *Air Power in War*, London, 1946
TRUELLE, J., "La production aéronautique militaire française jusqu'en juin 1940" in: *Revue d'histoire de la deuxième guerre mondiale*, No. 73, 1969 [French Military Aircraft Production up to June 1940]
VINOGRADOV, R.I./MINAYEV, A.V., *Samoliety SSSR*, Moscow, 1961 [USSR Aircraft]
WINTERBOTHAM, F.W., *The Ultra Secret*, London, 1974
WYKEHAM, P., *Fighter Command: A Study of Air Defense 1914-1960*, London, 1960
YAKOVLEV, S.A., *50 Liet Sovietskovo Samolietostroyenie*, Moscow, 1967 [Fifty Years of Soviet Military Aircraft Development]

Also, the following German archival materials pertaining to Reich internal security and war propaganda:

Geheime Berichte des Sicherheitsdienstes der SS zur innenpolitischen Lage: Meldungen aus dem Reich, Berichte zur innenpolitischen Lage, SD-Berichte zu Inlandsfragen [Secret Annals of the SS concerning internal political affairs in the Third Reich]; Bundesarchiv, Koblenz: R 58 Reichssicherheitshauptamt, Nos. 160-178; Boberach, H., *Meldungen aus dem Reich* [Official Reich Reports]; *Tagesparolen des Reichspressechefs* [Daily Keynotes from the Reich Press Chief], Reichspropagandaamt Hessen-Nassau, Frankfurt am Main; *Sammlung Oberheitmann*, Bundesarchiv, Koblenz; Krümmer, K., *Aufzeichnungen über Teilnahme an den Ministerkonferenzen*, vols. 1 and 2 [Notes on Ministerial Conferences]; Politisches Archiv des Auswärtigen Amtes, Bonn; Boelcke, W.A., *Kriegspropaganda 1939-1941: Geheime Ministerkonferenzen im Reichspropagandaministerium* [Secret Ministerial Conferences in the Reich Ministry of Propaganda], Stuttgart, 1966; Boelcke, W.A., *Wollt Ihr den totalen Krieg?* [The Question of Total War], Stuttgart, 1967

Newspapers and Periodicals:

Aviation Magazine International—Basler Nachrichten—Der Adler—Das Reich—Flugwehr und Technik—Forces Aériennes Françaises—Frontnachrichtenblatt der Luftwaffe—Journal de Genève—Le Figaro—Pravda—Revue de L'Armée de l'Air—Rivista Aeronautica—Royal Air Force Flying Review—Stockholm Tidningen—Svenska Dagbladet—Völkischer Beobachter—Wojskowy Przeglad Lotniczy

Archives:

Britannic Majesty's Stationery Office, London—Bundesarchiv, Bern—Bundesarchiv, Koblenz—Bundesarchiv, Militärarchiv, Freiburg—Institut für Zeitungsforschung, Dortmund—National Archives, Washington D.C.—National Central Archive of the Soviet Army, Moscow—Weltkriegsbücherei, Stuttgart—Zentralbibliothek der Bundeswehr, Düsseldorf—Service Historique de l'Armée de l'Air, Château de Vincennes

Photograph Sources

Bundesarchiv Koblenz, 38—Établissement Cinématographique et Photographique des Armées Fort Ivry, 19—Imperial War Museum, 80—National Archives, 2—Navy Department (National Archives), 5—Official US Air Force, 8—Official US Marine Corps, 5—US Air Force, 22—US Army, 10—F.Bordoni Archive, Rome, 15—M.R. de Launay Archive, Paris, 45—J.S. Middleton Archive, London, 32—A. Stilles, Archive, New York, 18—J.K. Piekalkiewicz Archive, 79

Prologue

The aged Marshal Foch was right when he said at Versailles in 1919: "This isn't peace, it's a twenty-year truce."

The Versailles Peace Treaty dealt a hard blow to German aviation. Germany had to destroy all war planes which were not yet in Allied hands and was strictly forbidden to rebuild an air force; it was sent back virtually to the days of the Montgolfier hot air balloons. The treaty stopped just short of banning gliders and the construction of light sports planes. To keep pace with technological developments, a number of German aviation firms soon went abroad to carry on their work on new aircraft designs.

The Paris Air Agreement of May 1926 allowed Germany not only to build aircraft but also to found an air raid early warning system. By 1931/32 the Reich's air warning organization was—at least theoretically—ready for deployment. Officially its purpose was to warn the populace and industry in the event of attack; but secretly, it was already preparing the way for planned antiaircraft artillery ("flak") and an anticipated fighter plane defense.

Meanwhile the Aviation Department of the Reich Ministry of Transport, the German Scientific Society of Aviation, and the German Aviation Research Institute were working tirelessly on the problems of air combat. When Hitler seized power in January 1933 and at last the right conditions were created for a strong air force, it was based on the groundwork laid by these organizations.

Back in 1921, in his book *Il dominio dell'aria* (Eng. trans. *The Command of the Air*, 1943), the Italian military theoretician General Giulio Douhet (1869–1930) had developed the controversial thesis that massive bomber offensives could bring an enemy to his knees virtually without the aid of the other armed forces.

Douhet summed up his clear and convincing doctrine of air domination, in the lapidary sentence: "Resist on the ground, and look to the air for a decision!"

General Douhet perceived that unity and cooperation between the front line and the home front had become a critical factor in war, and he concluded from this that in a future war, the main target would be not the armed forces but the territory deep behind the lines.

He believed that once command of the air was achieved, no people could withstand aerial attacks on cities and industrial centers for any length of time. In his view the destruction of a few large towns would be enough to force settlement of a war.

This theory of the essential role of strategic bomber operations, was eagerly debated by the general staffs of all nations; but nowhere was it accepted completely, nor was it implemented in air mobilization programs. Military analysts, among them British World War I. Captain B.H. Liddell Hart, warned: "You can't surrender to a bomber in the sky."

In Germany, General Walther Wever, the first general staff chief of the German Luftwaffe, was a convinced advocate of Douhet's theory; but at the same time he was enough of a realist to recognize that the German Reich would most likely never be able to afford the strategic bomber fleets of a world power. In 1936 Wever died in a fatal plane crash, and his successors did not have his foresight: They underestimated the importance of strategic air combat and abandoned the plans Wever had underway for heavy bomber units.

At the end of April 1937, Göring halted further development of experimental prototypes of the four-engined combat planes, the Do 19 and the Ju 89. In 1938, the Heinkel firm actually did design a four-engined bomber (with two twin engines), the He 177 Greif (Griffin), which was designed to be at the same time a long range reconnaissance aircraft and a long range and dive bomber. Ultimately this monster would cause the German Luftwaffe more grief than any other aircraft: The Luftwaffe lost more He 177s through construction flaws than through enemy action.

The German Luftwaffe arose as if by magic in a mere four years' time, partly using remodelled passenger aircraft. The advantage of this lightning-fast buildup was that the industry developed unencumbered by antiquated plane designs. But the new Luftwaffe suffered from the lack of qualified personnel familiar with the problems of aerial combat. Because of this, irreparable wrong decisions were made during the crucial years of rearmament. Later, during the war, their effects proved fatal.

Hitler himself was a layman and completely dependent on his air force experts in all questions relating to the complex field of aeronautics. Göring on the other hand had been a fighter pilot in World War I, as had his closest assistants Udet and Jeschonnek. As a politician he had neither time nor opportunity to acquire a well-founded knowledge of strategy. Of the seven bureau chiefs in his Ministry of Aviation, four were army officers who had not had the slightest contact with aviation before.

Thus under the influence of a dominant army, German strategists created an air force which, in direct contradiction to Douhet's theory, was mainly intended for the tactical support of ground troops.

The air force leadership, aware of the Luftwaffe's limited potential and oriented toward quick successes, planned the war to depend on an initial powerful and lightning-fast air strike.

At the same time that the Germans were emphasizing development of tactical, twin-engined medium range bombers, the British and Americans were working to produce heavy strategic bombers.

The German air force leadership failed to perceive another, no less important move on the part of their later foes: In 1935 the British physicist Robert Watson-Watt handed in a memorandum about the "detection and location of an aircraft by radio methods."

Also in 1935, the British War Office founded the Tizard Committee for research into the scientific surveillance of air defense. The committee recognized the value of Watson-Watt's thinking and immediately set the first experiments in motion. This marked the beginning of the British development known as "radio direction finding," later called Radio Detecting and Ranging—radar. Its purpose: to use radiotelephony to pinpoint the position of attacking bombers from the ground, and to lead the defending fighter planes to them.

By August 1935 the British were already able to locate a flight target 6,500 feet up and 35 to 50 miles away (60–80 kilometers), using 65-foot-high towers on a 12-meter wave length. By the time of the Sudetenland crisis in September 1938, the first five British radar stations were in operation. In the so-called Biggin Hills Experiments, new tactics of fighter-plane guidance were tested and a comprehensive reporting and guidance system set up.

When the Germans marched into Prague on Good Friday, 1939, the alarm sirens sounded on the English coast and the continuous receivers of the Chain Home radar station chain were switched on so that not one plane could fly in undetected anywhere along the southeast coast.

Germany never overtook England's lead in high frequency technology.

The Luftwaffe paraded its strength to the world for the first time when Austria was annexed to the German Reich. On the afternoon of 15 March 1938, Hitler, accompanied by generals von Brauchitsch and Milch, reviewed the German and Austrian troops in Vienna. When the army review ended a few minutes prematurely and von Brauchitsch ironically queried whether the air force was ever going to arrive, Milch pointed to his watch: "Still five minutes too early." Half a minute before the appointed time the air trembled with the roar of engines.

The Organization of an Aerial Review

The German publication *Der Adler* carried the following account of the aerial review of March 1938:

A few days before the review a flight (3 planes) is repeatedly timed with a stopwatch and average times are laid down for starting the engines, rolling up for takeoff, the takeoff itself, the approach flight to the assembly ground, and finally the approach to the review point.

The crews sit in the planes ready for takeoff. The

rigger mechanics are posted beside the machines with their compressed air cylinders so that they can start the engines immediately on the takeoff signal. The command post on the review ground knows precisely which army troop unit will march past twenty-five minutes before the end of the ground parade. When this troop crosses a certain line, the takeoff signal will be transmitted to the airfield by radio and telephone.

To transmit the approach order to all aircraft at the same time, a large cloth X is spread out on the ground and a flare fired off to explode in the air. A signal rocket drops from the lead plane – Attention! The wing commander sends his fast, maneuverable single-seater steeply upward, wings over so that he can be seen by all the crews; and then squadron after squadron, uniformly losing altitude, moves onto the review path.

The last tanks are just roaring past. Then thunder rages over the houses of the city; from the front it looks like a swarm of bees. The squadrons fly past at a uniform height, in an impeccably dressed V-formation, and hearts vibrate in harmony with the thundering engines, the iron song of the German Luftwaffe.

"Two years' war experience have proved more useful than ten years' peacetime training," General von Reichenau stated in a talk to the German military in the summer of 1938: He was speaking of the civil war in Spain which, he said, was the military academy of Germany.

The German air forces, who fought on Franco's side, and the Soviets, who supported the Spanish Republicans, benefited particularly from their military experiences in Spain. For example, the German ace Werner Mölders, who with 14 aerial victories was one of the most successful fighter pilots to take part in the Civil War, developed new aerial combat tactics once he had experienced the maneuverability of the Soviet Polikarpov I-16 Rata fighter plane. In the past, fighters had flown in a fixed three-plane flight formation. Now this was replaced by the two-plane pack in which the lead plane maintained a distance of approximately 650 feet (200 meters) from a companion craft known by a Russian nickname. When several packs grouped into flights, the lead pilots – confident in the assurance that their backs were covered – were able to concentrate completely on the target. This new tactic proved its superiority in countless fights and is one of the most important things the German Condor Legion learned from the Spanish Civil War. The new combat technique was adopted by both the RAF and the US aerial forces in World War II. Two items of practical knowledge gained by German pilots under Spanish skies, were the effectiveness of tactical air operations to support the land army, and the role of flak (antiaircraft artillery) in ground battle. However, the Soviet Union converted this knowledge into action the most consistently. By 1937, General Alksnis, the supreme commander of the Red Air Force, had already recommended development of a well-armored, heavily armed low-level ground attack aircraft. At his instigation, S.V. Ilyushin designed what was probably the best and the most-produced plane of World War II (36,163 were built): the famous Ilyushin Il-2 Sturmovik.

The Soviet leadership drew a further inference from the war in Spain. They began at top speed to reequip their air force for a completely new technique of warfare, because their fighter planes were not equal to the modern German aircraft, particularly in speed and weaponry.

One year before war broke out, the sky over Germany became the showplace for an adventure that would do credit to James Bond.

On Saturday 10 September 1938, Göring, who had been appointed Field Marshal in the middle of peacetime, declared the border between Luxembourg and Switzerland off limits to civilian aircraft, and only international airlines were allowed to use certain air corridors, following clearly-defined routes. Naturally this surprising order attracted the special interest of the very parties whom it was no doubt intended to keep away: the British and French secret services. As it happened they knew very little about the works along the Siegfried Line, as they called the German western fortifications, and now they hatched out a daring plan: A spy plane, disguised as a commercial aircraft, would take aerial photographs of the prohibited zone. That same month they found a suitable pilot for the enterprise – Sidney Cotton, an Australian aerial photography specialist with a passionate devotion to flying. By main profession the director of an international firm for the commercial exploitation of the Dufaycolor color-filmmaking process, Cotton was a very popular figure in European amateur aviation.

A high-powered plane fresh off the factory floor, the twin-engined passenger flier Lockheed 12A, registration number G-AFKR, was placed at Cotton's disposal in January 1939. He was told to use the plane as often as possible in order to lend credence to the story that it was a privately owned British commercial aircraft.

Cotton's first mission to the Rhine began at the

start of February 1939, when he took off from the small French airfield of Toussous-le-Noble about fifteen miles southwest of Paris. On board with him were a French secret serviceman, a certain Monsieur Bois, and several cameras. Reports had been received of new airfields and munitions plants around Mannheim, and Cotton's mission was to take aerial photographs of the region. He was ordered to approach the city along the same route and at the same time as the scheduled passenger aircraft travelling from Strasbourg to Mannheim. Provision was made to jettison all the cameras and other incriminating materials in the event that the Lockheed craft was forced to land. Later Cotton described how they approached Mannheim from the southwest at an altitude of 23,000 feet (7,000 meters), often having to change their heading to follow the course of the Rhine. Visibility was so good that even from that height they were able to see the Siegfried Line clearly.

Over the next few days Cotton undertook several undetected flights along the German western for-

Above: A German Messerschmitt Bf 109 (Me 109) is being tested in a wind tunnel. At the time of the Spanish Civil War it was the fastest fighter plane in the world.

Below right: The Heinkel He 111, the Luftwaffe's most important standard bomber, was designed in 1934 as a high-speed passenger aircraft for German Lufthansa.

tifications down to the Swiss border and to the northern part of Lake Constance.

In April Cotton was ordered to Tunis; now his plane was given the French registration F-ARQA. During several missions he photographed the Italian airfields in North Africa. In May, back in Great Britain, Cotton was given a new plane of identical type, bearing the registration code G-AFTL. Its built-in auxiliary fuel tanks doubled the Lockheed 12A's range to 1,500 miles. Cotton's first mission with his new plane led him to Italian Somaliland in June, accompanied by an RAF pilot named Bob Niven. On June 25 they returned to England, where the story went that they were returning from a flight rally in Hungary.

At the beginning of July, Cotton met a German named Schöne who was interested in developing a German market for the Dufaycolor film. Schöne, a former member of the Richtofen Fighter Wing and therefore well acquainted with Hermann Göring, but nevertheless (he claimed) an opponent of National Socialism, was hired by Cotton as his sales agent in Germany. A week later Schöne telegraphed to say that his commercial efforts were prospering and asked Cotton to come to Berlin.

On Wednesday 26 July 1939, Cotton left Heston airfield with Bob Niven and flew to Berlin. The very next day, July 27, the two men returned to England

„Legion Condor"

Illustrierter Beobachter

Deutsche Flieger an der nationalspanischen Front

General Frhr. v. Richthofen vor einem Frontflug im Gespräch mit seinem Beobachter.

General Frh. v. Richthofen will sich über den Verlauf der Kampfhandlungen und die dadurch geschaffene Lage orientieren. Er steuert dabei seine Maschine stets selbst.

with screen tests filmed by the Tobis Film Company, and an invitation from Herr Böttger, the director of Berlin's Tempelhof airport, to take part in an international amateur pilots' rally in Frankfurt. Cotton then had two Leica motor-driven cameras installed in his wings which he could activate by pressing a button under the pilot's seat. This button, linked to the motor of an automobile windshield wiper that automatically opened and closed the concealed guard plates under the Leicas, also started up the cameras with their 250-exposure rolls of negative film.

In Frankfurt the so-called "giant Lockheed" was the number one conversation topic, and when the attending director of Tempelhof airport asked Cotton to take him along on one of his flights, the Englishman suggested a trip "along the beautiful Rhine to Mannheim, which his aunt raved about so." And while the unsuspecting airport chief admired the Rhine panorama, Cotton busily pressed the button under his seat.

On his flight home, defying strict instructions to take a particular flight route which naturally lay outside any military sites, Cotton took advantage of the heavy cloud cover to head off toward the German Siegfried Line and follow it northward. Not until he reached Aix-la-Chapelle (Aachen) did he change direction and head for Brussels. This time too the concealed Leicas did not let him down. "Real high-quality German workmanship," said Cotton.

On Thursday 17 August 1939, Cotton again took off for a business conference in Berlin. Incidentally, he had also been commissioned by the secret service to take aerial photographs of airfields in the

Above: A burning Soviet fighter plane, the Polikarpov I-16 Rata. Some 475 of these aircraft flew in the Spanish Civil War on the Republican side. The I-16 was the first cantilever monoplane in the world with a retractable undercarriage.

Above left: The 265-foot-high towers of the British Chain Home early warning air raid defense system. The word "radar" developed later as an abbreviation of "Radio Detection and Ranging System."

Below left: A German newspaper illustration shows German fliers of the Condor Legion who fought on the side of the Spanish Nationalists. General Baron von Richtofen is discussing operations with his on-board observer; he always flew his own plane.

Below right: Map of the secret reconnaissance flights of Sidney Cotton and his team from February to September, 1939.

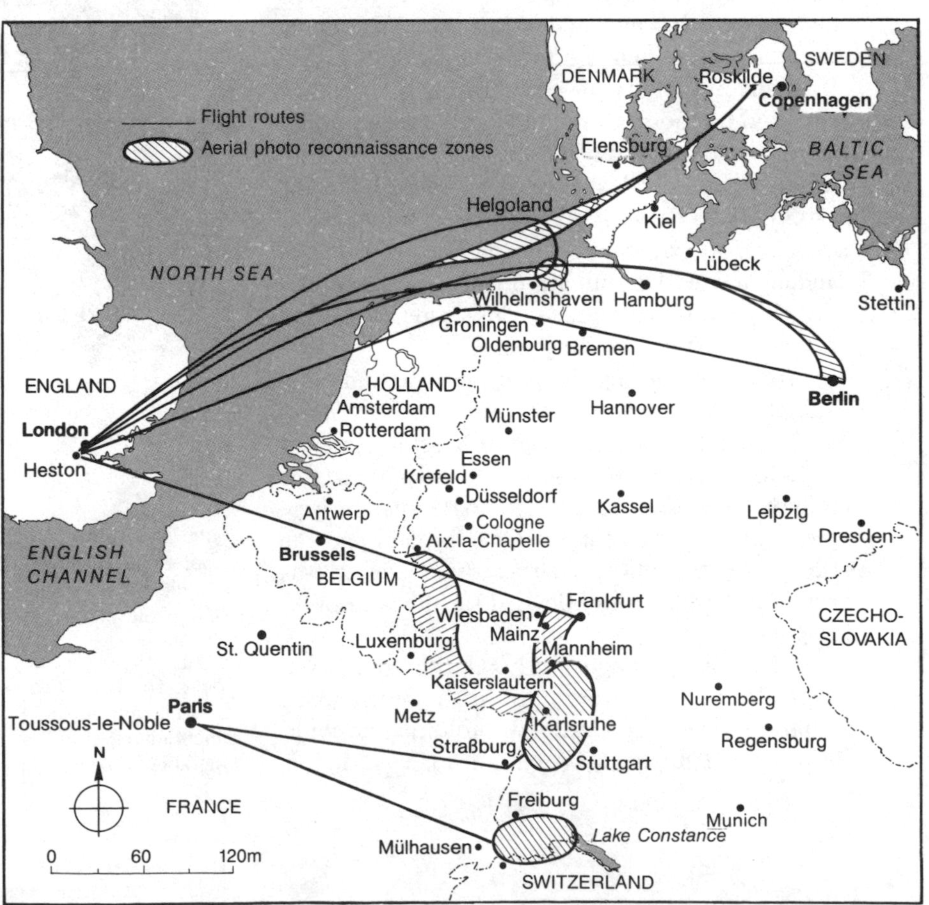

north of the German capital. At Karinhall, Göring's magnificent residence where Schöne was exhibiting another series of Dufaycolor screen tests, the master of the house was away, and Cotton managed to get a look behind the screens surrounding a building site. Here he found nothing less than the Field Marshal's private air raid shelter, just then undergoing construction. When Cotton and Schöne talked about the possibility of war breaking out, Schöne remarked on Göring's doubts that England would intervene if Germany were to march into Poland. Cotton reported: "I suggested to Schöne that he ask Göring to fly with me to England as my guest. Because if we could convince the Field Marshal of England's true determination, then he would certainly inform Hitler at once. This seemed to me the only hope left of avoiding war."

Surprisingly, Göring accepted the invitation to fly to England with Cotton one week later, on Thursday 24 August. Back in London, Cotton reported to the head of the secret service his idea that Göring should come to visit England. After matters were agreed with Prime Minister Chamberlain and the Foreign Secretary Lord Halifax, the invitation was drafted and an itinerary devised for the high-ranking guest.

On Tuesday 22 August 1939, Cotton and Niven flew to Berlin to forward the British government's invitation to Göring. Cotton was told that he could fly home to Thursday 24 August at 10:00 A.M., this

Center: The cockpit of Sidney Cotton's plane. At the lower edge of the pilot's seat on the left is the trigger button for the two Leica cameras concealed under the wings.

Right: The Rhine Bridge at Strasbourg, one of the countless aerial photographs that Sidney Cotton brought back from his hazardous flights, and that helped the RAF to complete its German target file.

Above: The Lockheed model 12 A, the plane which the British secret service turned over to Sidney Cotton. It was almost identical to the Lockheed 12 A Electra, the best known passenger plane of the time.

time accompanied by Göring. He was to fly out of Munich because the Field Marshal was in Berchtesgaden in Bavaria at the time. The Führer himself (Cotton was told) had given the Englishman special permission to land in Munich, and Hitler's personal pilot was to accompany Cotton from Berlin.

While Cotton and his copilot Bob Niven received the VIP treatment, awaiting their great hour in Berlin's sumptuous Adlon Hotel, behind-the-scenes political events accelerated steadily. The following day, Wednesday August 23, von Ribbentrop signed Germany's pact with Stalin in Moscow. The situation had changed, and now the Nazi leaders were more interested in blowing up the coalition of Great Britain, France and Poland, than in any on-the-spot verification that London was determined to go to war. On Thursday August 24, the two Englishmen passed anxious hours at Tempelhof when instead of Hitler's personal copilot whom they were expecting, an order arrived strictly forbidding them to take off. They heard nothing from Göring, and only after a long spell of uncertainty could they heave a sigh of relief: At 11:15 A.M. they received permission to take off for England. Cotton reported how Schöne gave him a piece of paper exactly marking out the Englishmen's route. They were supposed to fly at an altitude of 975 feet and not deviate from their heading: otherwise they would be shot down, Schöne warned them as they said goodbye. The Lockheed G-AFTL was the last privately owned British aircraft to leave Berlin before war broke out.

On the return flight they kept seeing German air force combat units on the way to their operational bases in East Germany. Approaching the Dutch border near Groningen, they saw German naval units on the Schilling Roads (Schilling-Reede straits) outside Wilhelmshaven, the main German naval base in the North Sea. Cotton made some photos. At that moment he did not suspect that these very photographs would motivate the RAF to launch their first raid on German shipping.

Above: Waiting for war. Somewhere along the Polish border, the German crews of tree-camouflaged He 111 bombers are sunning themselves by the roadside on the last day of August, 1939.

Below: British photointerpreters (PI's), whose job it was to analyze and classify the photographs supplied by Sidney Cotton.

Two days later, on Saturday August 26, Cotton was flying over Germany again, or more precisely over the island of Sylt, this time on a top secret photographic mission for the British Admiralty.

On the morning of Thursday 31 August 1939, Hitler ordered the execution of Plan White, the attack on Poland. By 1:00 P.M. all units had received the necessary orders. Everything was ready for war to begin the following day.

The Poles had only 463 combat-ready front-line aircraft to deploy against the 2,093 German aircraft. The Polish force included 150 fighters, 86 bombers and 154 reconnaissance planes; all completely antiquated and weakly armed except for 36 modern Los-model bombers. In addition, the Polish generals had no plan at hand for directing this modest air force in case of war. The six Polish flier regiments had been dissolved in June 1939, and turned into one bomber and one fighter brigade under orders of the commander-in-chief of the Polish army. Air force squadrons were also attached to individual land armies and operational units.

The partitioning of the small Polish air force contributed to its annihilation and ruled out the possibility of any successful deployment.

Another action of the Polish high command banned the chances of the weak air force from the outset. To obtain the necessary cash to equip the

Above right: A Polish medium all-metal PZL P-37 Los (Elk) bomber, in a row with standard Polish PZL P-11a and 11c fighter planes at Okecie airfield near Warsaw, the base of the First Flier Regiment.

Below: The last hour of peace. Pilots of the Polish Bomber Brigade at the edge of a camouflaged unprepared airfield on 31 August 1939. In the background are PZL P-23 Karas (Carp) light bombers.

army, they sold off the most modern types of Polish combat aircraft to foreign nations grade by grade, so that by September 1939 the best Polish planes were all in the hands of the Rumanian, Bulgarian, Greek, Turkish, Greek and other air forces: the Polish pilots knew what they looked like only from photos. Due to various misguided actions, in the summer of 1939 the largest Polish PZL-1 aircraft plant in Warsaw, worked only three days a week. Half the staff were sent away on vacation.

The Polish flytroop under General Zajac, like the other Polish combat forces, suffered considerable delay before beginning their mobilization, and there was no longer time enough to call up all the ground personnel, which also reduced Polish combat readiness.

The fliers spent exhausting hours because up until the very last moment the Polish high command hesitated to transfer the front-line aircraft from their known peacetime air bases to secret advanced airfields, "so as not to provoke Berlin unnecessarily." Admittedly all the first-line aircraft were successfully transferred to well-camouflaged advanced airfields by the evening of August 31, but all the equipment of the peacetime air bases got left behind.

1939
September to December

Friday 1 September 1939, Warsaw
The *Polish Supreme Command Staff* announced in their Number One Communiqué:

In the early hours of this morning the Germans invaded our country in a surprise attack by their air force and ground troops, without a declaration of war. The German Luftwaffe carried out a number of attacks on individual targets throughout the territory of Poland.

The Polish *PAT* News Agency reported:

The first hostilities were initiated from the German side in the wee hours of Friday morning. Bomber wings attacked the Polish coastal town of Puck (German *Putzig*) near Gdynia (German *Gdingen*) to destroy the airfields there; but they did no damage. Bombs were also dropped on Gdynia itself, however they caused no damage. Chelmno (German *Kulm*) in Eastern Pomerania was also bombed. Another air assault aimed at airfields near Biala, missed its target.

The evening of 1 September 1939
The German *Wehrmacht High Command* announced:

Today, in a series of vigorous operations, the German Luftwaffe attacked and destroyed the military installations on numerous Polish airfields including Rumia, Puck, Grudziadz, Poznan, Plock, Lodz, Tomaszow, Radom, Ruda, Katowice, Krakow, Lvov, Brest, Terespol. In addition, several air combat wings are effectively supporting the advance of the army. Thus the German Luftwaffe today fought for and won command of the air over Poland, even though powerful German forces were held back in central and western Germany.

The First Assault

The Nazi newspaper *Völkischer Beobachter* carried the following descriptive account in September 1939:

We are in Silesia about fifty miles from the Polish border. Our brave Do17s stand ready for takeoff, with bomb magazines loaded, in the squadron hold. Every morning the engines are started; there is just a trace of light in the east and already we hear our flight mechanics and first lookouts revving up their machines.

That has been the pattern day after day. The bomber technical sergeant says to me, "Let's hope we don't have to unload the machines again." Every crew has already studied every detail of the maps, every man knows by heart the flying time to the Warta and the Pilica rivers. Every man knows the prominent features of Warta Bay west of Dzialoszyn. And yet we must continue to be patient.

August 31 ends uneventfully for us just like the previous days. As always we spend our free hours sitting around the loudspeaker, hoping to hear a special announcement. – Then the telephone rings shrilly. We all read the announcement from the adjutant's face: "Be ready to take off tomorrow morning at 4:20 A.M." Rapidly the needed instructions are passed to the squadrons: "Wake-up time 2:00 A.M. Breakfast 2:30, flight briefing at 3:15, crews man their planes at 4:00. Machines warmed up at 4:10. Now everyone go to sleep at once!"

A cool morning greets us as we go to our flight briefing. Everyone is keyed up to the highest pitch. Then we hear the clear command of our wing commander, ordering our combat group into our first enemy action: "The group is going to make a ground attack on Krakow Airfield! Attack time 5:45 A.M." The target sheets show us everything clearly: the hangars—the depots—the repair hangar—the radio-telegraph installations. Focus of the attack: recognized enemy aircraft on the field. Data follow on probable Polish air defense.

We must not fail to arrive at our target at exactly the appointed time, to avoid getting caught by the bombing effects of other squadrons. The raid is to be made from the east. Everything is cleared for action, watches are synchronized down to the minute.

The old soldier's cry, thrice repeated, rings out strongly in the dusky morning of September 1: a greeting to our beloved Führer. In the pale light of the rising sun we see the exhaust flames lick out of the running engines. The machine guns are operational, the drums are mounted. The first squadron takes off—two minutes later.

Warsaw, 1 September 1939: Citizens of the Polish capital building air raid trenches. Soon they will be among the first to suffer the full cruelty of the air war.

We are on course. At first it is hard to keep our bearings in the thick morning haze. We know that at this same moment our comrades on the ground are tearing down the boundary posts and beginning their attack . . . Slowly it gets light, visibility is good now. We are flying over enemy land. We leave Tschenstochau [Czestochowa] to our left to follow an eastward heading and then, travelling a course south and west along the river Vistula, we set upon Krakow. Soon we do not need a map to tell that we are flying in Poland. Large uncultivated expanses, fallow wastes lie beneath us, interspersed with dirty farmhouses. We fly at an altitude of 150 to 350 feet. In each one of us the excitement mounts from moment to moment.

Another squadron is flying to our left: we see that it is being fired on. Then a cloud of black smoke on the horizon shows us our target. We are alongside, we see fire, smoke, more fire and explosion after explosion. We nose our aircraft to 150 feet so that the bombs will bite on impact. Then a short distance ahead at the edge of the airfield, we see a neatly-arranged string of Polish fighter planes. The bomb trail is launched. The bombs batter our enemy to pieces. Red explosions are bursting all over the ground, the threads of enemy antiaircraft shells pull around us. Our machine-gun barrels are hot; probably the turrets have never been rotated so fast. Then, pressed close to the ground, we race off on the course for home.

The evening of Saturday 2 September 1939
The *Wehrmacht High Command* announced:

After today's successes we can conclude that the gravest blow has been dealt to the effective strength of the Polish flytroop. The German Luftwaffe has unlimited command of the air over all of Poland and is now available for further duties in defense of the Reich.

Monday 4 September 1939, London
The British *Ministry of Information* reported:

Last night RAF squadrons carried out extended reconnaissance flights over northern and western Germany without engaging in aerial combat with enemy aircraft. More than six million air leaflets containing an appeal from England to the German people, were dropped over Germany.

4 September 1939, London
The British *Ministry of Information* reported:

This afternoon the RAF carried out a successful raid on German naval units in Wilhelmshaven and

Above: The crucial moment of attack: The bombs are released in the final phase of dive by a Stuka (German dive bomber) Junkers Ju 87—when the propeller nose is pointed straight at the target.

Brunsbüttel at the entrance of the Kiel Canal. A direct hit on a battleship near Wilhelmshaven was recorded, that severely damaged the ship. At around 1:00 P.M. attack was made on another battleship anchored at Brunsbüttel. This too was heavily damaged. The raid took place under very unfavorable weather conditions. The RAF aircraft encountered strong German aerial forces and vigorous antiaircraft artillery fire; there were several casualties.

4 September 1939, Wilhelmshaven
The *German News Bureau* (Deutsche Nachrichtenbureau) reported:

This evening at 6:00 P.M., English fighter planes of the most modern design attacked Wilhelmshaven and Cuxhaven. They met heavy defensive fire, so the bombs they dropped caused no damage. Five of the total 12 English aircraft were shot down. The attackers flew southwest in an attempt to escape the flak fire and headed for Dutch territory.

Monday 4 September 1939
The *Wehrmacht High Command* announced:

On September 3 the German Luftwaffe carried out increasing attacks on important Polish military traffic installations and large troop transports. The repeated deployment of fighter planes and dive bombers contributed substantially to the rapid success of the German troops advancing out of Silesia.

Tuesday 5 September 1939
The *Wehrmacht High Command* announced:

The Luftwaffe has command of the air. Forty Polish aircraft have been shot down, 15 of them during aerial combat. Planned retreat by the enemy is being thwarted increasingly by air assaults on their march and rail columns. At 6:00 P.M. along the North Sea coast, English fighter planes of the most modern design attacked Wilhelmshaven and Cuxhaven as well as German naval forces in the estuaries. Fighter plane and flak defense by the navy

Below: Direct hits on the Polish border fortifications north of Mlawa. The bombs are exactly on target; thick clouds of smoke surge up.

and the Luftwaffe were called out so rapidly and effectively that the attack on Cuxhaven was frustrated completely, while bombs dropped on Wilhelmshaven inflicted no damage. More than half the striking aircraft were shot down.

Wednesday 6 September 1939
The *Wehrmacht High Command* announced:
Yesterday's attacks by the German Luftwaffe have once again severely disrupted enemy transport and communication lines. The railway stations of Zdunska-Wola, Skarzysko, Tarnow and Wrzesnia are burning, countless tracks have been disconnected. With the exception of isolated fighter planes near Lodz, nothing more has been seen of the Polish flytroop.

Thursday 7 September 1939
The *Wehrmacht High Command* announced:
Yesterday the Luftwaffe made a successful ground-strafing attack on retreating enemy columns and dispersed them. The attack on railway installations, rail stations and bridges continued, and in the course of it the bridges over the Vistula south of Warsaw were severely damaged by bomb hits. Warsaw's western railroad station is on fire.

Friday 8 September 1939
The *Wehrmacht High Command* announced:
Yesterday the operations in Poland assumed the character of a military pursuit in many locations; more serious battles took place only at isolated points. Once again the Luftwaffe played a crucial role in these rapid and major successes. It was deployed massively against the retreating Polish army. Its fighter and dive bomber wings intervened directly in the ground battle. March columns were routed, paths of retreat cut off by the destruction of bridges and rail crossings, attempted enemy conterattacks smashed even as the troops were marshalling for action. The bridges on the Vistula south of Warsaw have been permanently destroyed, and in Warsaw itself the transit roads are jammed and congested with troops. The city is being rapidly evacuated. Two German aircraft were shot down over Polish territory, one aircraft is missing.

An Armstrong Whitley RAF bomber of 102 Squadron, before the night operation over Germany where the squadron dropped leaflets instead of bombs.

Saturday 9 September 1939
The *Wehrmacht High Command* announced:
All day long the Luftwaffe has concentrated its attacks on the enemy's retreat ways west and east of the Vistula. The Polish flytroop hardly made an appearance except for a few fighter planes over the Vistula bridges between Sandomierz and Warsaw.

Sunday 10 September 1939
The *Wehrmacht High Command* announced:
The Luftwaffe has led bombing assaults that blocked the roads and rails leading back from Warsaw to the east and southeast, and has attacked the remnants of the Polish ground installations in this area. In an operation against Lublin, 7 Polish aircraft in a combined fighter and bomber unit, were shot down in aerial combat, and bombs severely damaged 8 Polish aircraft on the ground. On the Western border, 3 French planes were shot down over German sovereign territory. No bomb attacks took place on Germany.

Tuesday 12 September 1939
The *Wehrmacht High Command* announced:
As on the previous day, Luftwaffe units were brought into action very successfully to support the army near Kutno and to destroy the enemy's communication lines east of the Vistula. A dive bomber group has sealed off the eastern exits from Warsaw. Yesterday no air raids were made on Reich territory.

Wednesday 13 September 1939
The *Wehrmacht High Command* announced:
Yesterday the Luftwaffe again made successful attacks on roads, bridges and rails east of the Vistula. Three trains are burning at Krystynopol rail station. Luck Airfield was badly damaged, the Biala Podlaska aircraft factory was set afire. Fourteen enemy aircraft were destroyed, 2 of them in aerial combat. No air raids were made on Reich territory.

Above: The backbone of RAF assaults on Germany in the early war years was the Vickers Wellington bomber designed by Dr. Barnes Wallis, the first bomber with a tail machine gun turret.

Center left: Warsaw, 5 September 1939: The debris of a German He 111 bomber shot down by Polish flak artillery, that crashed into the houses in flames.

Friday 15 September 1939

The *Wehrmacht High Command* announced:

The very strong Polish forces bottled up around Kutno and struggling desperately to defend themselves, tried to break out again yesterday. These stories failed like the others. Despite bad weather conditions the Luftwaffe successfully attacked rail lines and rail stations, and supported with bombing and strafing raids the Army's struggle against the enemy army surrounded at Kutno. No air attacks were made on Reich territory.

Sunday 17 September 1939

The *Wehrmacht High Command* announced:

Although the weather continued unfavorable, the Luftwaffe made repeated attacks on Polish troop assemblies and march columns east of the Vistula, thereby making it impossible for the fleeing enemy to order their units.

Monday 18 September 1939

The *Red Army High Command* reported:

Our troops crossed the Polish border on the morning of September 17 at 4:00 A.M. Central European Time. The advance ensued along the entire length of the border from Polotsk in the north to Kamenets-Podolski in the south. After overwhelming the weak resistance of Polish outposts, we

The unprepared airfield of a Stuka (German dive bomber) wing in East Prussia, September 1939. The onlookers are inhabitants of a nearby village who are getting a taste of war from the sidelines.

occupied the villages of Glebokkie, Moledeczno and others. Heading toward Baranow, we crossed the Neman river and occupied the villages of Mir and Snow and well as the important railway junction of Baranow. In the western Ukraine the advance of our army has proceeded at a remarkable pace: The cities of Rovno, Dubno, Tarnopol and Kolomyia are already in our hands. With the thrust at Kolomyia our troops have already cut off most of the border between Poland and Rumania. In addition, 7 Polish fighter planes and 3 Polish bombers have been shot down by the Soviet Air Force.

18 September 1939
The *Wehrmacht High Command* announced:
The campaign in Poland is approaching its end. The Luftwaffe made an effective attack on the Polish forces surrounded southwest of Wyszogrod. No further sign has been seen of Polish air forces anywhere on the front. Thus the German Luftwaffe has substantially completed its duty in the East. Numerous units of the German Flytroop and antiaircraft artillery have massed their forces and are ready to be deployed elsewhere. No air attacks were made on German sovereign territory on September 17.

Tuesday 19 September 1939
The *Wehrmacht High Command* announced:
The disintegration and capitulation of the scattered or encircled remains of the Polish army, are proceeding rapidly. The Battle of the Bzura is over. Yesterday the Luftwaffe carried out only a few isolated raids. Otherwise its deployment on the Eastern Front was no longer necessary. There was weak artillery and patrol activity at isolated locations along the Western Front near Saarbrücken. Repeated observations were made of the enemy building trenchworks. No aerial combats took place.

Saturday 23 September 1939
The *Wehrmacht High Command* announced:
Weak artillery activity at only a few isolated spots in the West. A French plane was forced to land by flak fire near Saarbrücken, the crew were captured; one German plane was shot down in aerial combat.

The Last Battles

Tuesday 26 September 1939, Warsaw
Communiqué from the *Supreme Commander of the Warsaw Garrison:*
The raids on the night of the 24th and the following day were the worst our capital has suffered so far. The Germans undertook the systematic destruction of Warsaw by heavy artillery and air attacks. From dawn onward, German aircraft flew over the city in dense waves and dropped bombs over the center, starting hundreds of fires. Eight German aircraft were shot down. The Polish units standing before Warsaw, suffered less than the civilian population, against whom the air attacks were chiefly directed in order to shake their morale. It is impossible to estimate the toll of the victims. Warsaw consists of nothing but ruins. Traffic is virtually or completely at a standstill in a number of streets because of the fires or the debris.

The encircled fortress of Modlin continues to defend itself bravely. The Warsaw Garrison has beaten back an attack along the Mokotow sector. The Garrison is still holding out on the smoking ruins and defending itself heroically.

Wednesday 27 September 1939, Warsaw
The *Supreme Commander of the Warsaw Garrison* reported:
Warsaw and Modlin are continuing to defend themselves stubbornly against the German attacks. The capital has suffered an extremely violent three-hour air raid along the left bank of the Vistula. Thirteen German planes were shot down, raising the total number of German aircraft brought down in the Warsaw area to 106.

Naval Unit Attacked in the North Sea

27 September 1939
The *Wehrmacht High Command* announced:

Yesterday German air forces made a successful raid on English naval combat forces, battleships, aircraft carriers, cruisers and destroyers, in the central North Sea. One aircraft carrier was destroyed and several damaging hits were scored on a battleship. Our aircraft suffered no casualties.

27 September 1939, London
Churchill stated in response to a question in the House of Commons:

The Commander-in-Chief of the Home Fleet, Sir Charles Forbes, has wirelessed as follows: "Yesterday afternoon in the middle of the North Sea a squadron of British capital ships together with an aircraft carrier, cruisers and destroyers were attacked by about 20 German aircraft. No British ship was hit and no British casualties were incurred. One German flying boat was shot down and another is reported to be badly damaged."

27 September 1939, Berlin
The *German News Bureau* (DNB) reported:

An English report of the German air raid on a

Above: German Stukas support tank units to overcome enemy resistance. Their built-in sirens and hawk-like profiles considerably heightened the effect that their dive attacks had on morale.

Below: Nowe Brudno, a suburb of northern Warsaw, 15 September 1939. The first line of defense ran along about 1,600 yards from the bombed-out houses.

British fleet squadron states that all the bombs missed their mark. On the contrary, the Supreme Commander of the German Luftwaffe declares that an 1,100-lb bomb scored a direct hit on an English aircraft carrier. Two 550-lb bombs hit an English battleship forward and amidships. No further commentary is needed to tell what effect was achieved by these heaviest of all bombs. German authorities have determined that not one of the attacking aircraft was hit. All the aircraft are in their home shelters.

Friday 29 September 1939
The *Wehrmacht High Command* announced:
One French aircraft was shot down in aerial combat near Weissenburg, one British aircraft was brought down near Osnabrück.

Saturday 30 September 1939, London
The British *Air Ministry* reported:
British reconnaissance planes, which over the past few days have again been making aerial photographs of individual segments of the Siegfried Line, have now completed their duty, thereby procuring for the British and French general staff a precise picture of German fortifications in the West, which is indispensable for the military action now beginning. The RAF squadrons which dropped air leaflets over Germany, have likewise fulfilled the duty assigned them, and it can now be made known that the leaflet drops were by no means the sole purpose for these flights.

30 September 1939
The *Wehrmacht High Command* announced:
Two flights of British combat aircraft, a total of 12, have attempted to fly into German sovereign territory along the North Sea coast. One flight attacked destroyers in the German Bay, without any success. The British aircraft were driven away by flak fire. No bomb hits were scored. German fighter planes brought the other flight to bay near the East Frisian islands of Wangerooge and Langeroog. In the ensuing aerial combat, 5 of the 6 British aircraft were shot down. The crews of two German fighter planes were forced to make an emergency sea landing and were rescued, unhurt, by German warships.

Sunday 1 October 1939
The *Wehrmacht High Command* announced:
In the East the capitulation of Warsaw and Modlin is proceeding according to schedule. In the West, 2 French and 10 British planes were brought down; over the North Sea, 2 British combat aircraft. We lost 2 planes.

Attack on England

The German publication *Der Adler* carried the following descriptive account in October 1939:

On Monday 9 October 1939, we took off from an airfield in northwestern Germany for our first attack on units of the British navy operating in the northern North Sea. For the first time we flew for hours and hours across the sea. An autumn hurricane raced over the North Sea and lashed the waves as high as houses. It seemed as if we had become the plaything of the elements.

After several hours we were recalled by radio. Other aircraft had preceded us into the attack and the British fleet had sheered off. Unfortunately, on our return flight the wind was blowing straight into our noses. We had been underway for several hours already, and we ought to have sighted land long ago. But as far as the eye could reach, all we saw was water – water – sky – clouds – water.

My flight mechanic crawled forward to me and said frankly: "Lieutenant, I don't believe we will ever get home again. But for the time being we still have enough fuel." At least that was one comfort.

Slowly it began to get dark. Then finally a narrow dark strip cropped up on the horizon: land, land at last! Now we could begin to imagine how explorers and seafarers must have felt when they finally saw land again. It was high time too, damn it! With our last drop of fuel we landed in darkness at our base. We had gotten a small foretaste of the air war against England, the battle in the Atlantic.

Monday 16 October 1939, Berlin
The *German News Bureau* (DNB) reported:
German radio, which hitherto has concluded its news service by playing the "March of the Germans in Poland," has now made a change. After the daily news report, it will play the poet Hermann Löns' song, "We Ride against England."

Tuesday 17 October 1939
The *Wehrmacht High Command* announced:
Yesterday successful raids were again made on English naval forces. Two of the English warships lying in the Firth of Forth were hit by bombs of the heaviest caliber. We were able to score this success despite the most intense enemy resistance by flak fire and fighter planes.

Above right: The "glasshouse" glazed panel nose fuselage of a German He 111 H-11. This standard horizontal bomber, of which the Luftwaffe built 5,656, had two serious flaws: a low firing range and weak weaponry.

Below: The Firth of Forth, the most important inlet on the eastern coast of Scotland, on 16 October 1939, after the German Luftwaffe made its first raid on British war vessels anchored here. Its distinctive landmark is the Forth Railway Bridge.

Far left: First Lieutenant Frank Neubert, a German Stuka pilot (first from left) won the first air victory of World War II. He is shown here at the Steinberg glider base near Oppeln (Pol. *Opole*) in Upper Silesia, the operational headquarters of the 1st Group the Immelmann Dive Bomber Wing.

Left: Second Lieutenant Wladyslaw Gnys, Polish pilot of 122 Fighter Squadron, the first man to shoot down a German aircraft.

Above right: A flight of three British Wellington bombers. These aircraft, built with the geodetic form of lattice work construction and covered with fabric, rapidly became famous for their indestructibility.

17 October 1939, London
A joint communiqué from the British *Admiralty* and the British *War Office* stated:

Approximately one dozen aircraft took part in Monday's German aerial attack. No serious damage occurred to our warships. The cruiser *Southampton*, slightly damaged by a bomb, has three injured men, and seven men were wounded by bomb splinters aboard the cruiser *Edinburgh*. Another bomb fell near the destroyer *Mohawk* and wounded twenty-five men. At least four of the attacking aircraft were shot down, three of them by British fighter planes.

The assertion that the German bombers attacked and damaged not only the *Royal Oak* but also the *Repulse*, is pure invention.

The crew of an English trawler who rescued three survivors from one of the shotdown German bombers, reported:

"Our cutter was headed back to Port Seaton. At around 3:00 P.M." (one of the fishermen stated) "when we were on the way home, we saw a big plane approaching us fast. Two British combat aircraft were in pursuit; they circled around and opened machine-gun fire on the German plane, whereupon it crashed into the sea. The craft floated on the surface for a time and then sank. As soon as we got close enough to the plane wreck, we found three men clinging to a large life buoy. We threw ropes to the Germans and pulled them onto our cutter. Only then did we determine that they were all wounded. They told us that a fourth crew member had gone down with the plane. One of the officers drew a signet ring from his finger and gave it to us in gratitude for rescuing him."

Bombs on Helsinki

Thursday 30 November 1939, Stockholm
The Swedish newspaper *Svenska Dagbladet* reported:

Approximately ten Soviet bombers appeared over Helsinki this morning shortly after nine o'clock, and later the air raid alarm was sounded repeatedly at 12:15 P.M. On their second approach flight the Soviets dropped air leaflets, mainly into the working-class district of the capital, that called on the population to rebel against the government. It has been claimed that two of the bombers were shot down, however so far this has not been confirmed. At 7:00 P.M. renewed air attacks took place on Hel-

A Tupolev SB-2 Soviet bomber shot down in northern Finland. These medium weight standard Red Air Force bombers took part in the Spanish Civil War.

sinki. During the noon raid incendiary and high-explosive bombs caused considerable damage. A large number of houses were set afire, among them the Institute of Technology, which seems to have been completely destroyed. Nine people died in the afternoon air attack on Vyborg (Viipuri), Finland.

A Stockholm newspaper correspondent reports that the ghastly scenes which took place, were worse than anything he had experienced in Madrid or Barcelona. Countless houses were destroyed by bombs and set on fire. Hearses are driving through the streets. Part of the population spent the entire night inside air raid shelters and protective trenches. The Soviet bombers came from the Estonian airfield at Paldiski, only fifteen minutes from Finland by air.

Polish Aircraft Wings in England

Wednesday 13 December 1939, London
The Polish *PAT News Agency* commented on the British Air Ministry's decision to form a Polish air force in England:

This announcement has been heartily welcomed by members of the House of Commons. Measures have been taken to mount several Polish wings in Great Britain, commanded by Polish officers. The wings are to collaborate with the RAF.

Monday 18 December 1939, Berlin
The *German News Bureau* (DNB) reported:

On the afternoon of December 18 the English undertook a large-scale aerial assault, using 44 of the most up-to-date aircraft. The enemy unit tried to raid various points along the North Sea coast, but was scattered by Messerschmitt Me 109 German fighters north of Helgoland while it was still making its approach. Several stubborn aerial fights took place over the inner part of the German Bay. In the process, 34 British aircraft were shot down, according to reports received so far. This number does not include losses which the remnant of the planes in all probability suffered on their return flight. Debris from shotdown English planes has already washed ashore on the German isles. The crews of two British aircraft have been taken prisoner. Only a few enemy planes succeeded in penetrating as far as Wilhelmshaven. Here they came under concentrated flak fire and released 3 random bombs which fell onto the fields without effect.

On the German side two aircraft have been lost; their crews got out by parachute.

Tuesday 19 December 1939
The *Wehrmacht High Command* announced:

In the early afternoon hours, 52 British combat planes tried to attack Wilhelmshaven. The German air raid warning service recognized the attackers early on. They were held at bay by fighter and destroyer aircraft when they had gotten no farther than the north of Helgoland. Thirty-four British planes were shot down after hard battle. We lost 2 planes.

A page from the flight-book of RAF Squadron 139, reporting on the first operation of a British bomber over Germany: to take photos.

What the Germans Learned from the British Aerial Attack of 18 December 1939

Luftwaffe Front-Line Bulletin No. 3 reported:

1. Our foes were Vickers Wellington-model English bombers. The enemy flew in a squadron column, in echelons slightly graduated to the rear and below. Flight altitude 13,000 feet (4,000 meters).

2. The English pilots dropped altitude during combat so that for the most part their departure flight was taken 6 to 16 feet above the water (2 to 5 meters). Only one squadron was observed to maintain its altitude in combat and departure flight.

3. The English flying units formed close ranks during combat. Sometimes they banked opposite each other as a defensive maneuver. Some aircraft lowered a ventral "dustbin," a downward-extendable machine gun turret fitted with a double machine gun; in each case it was the outlying aircraft of the formation which did so.

4. In most cases the aircraft were observed to jettison their bombs in the sea upon attack, without the bombs exploding.

5. The coloring of the aircraft differed considerably from the German. Their dominant feature was their camouflage paint of wavy brown, green and yellow lines. For the first time we observed clearly visible national markings, printed on both sides of the fuselage.

6. Speed in horizontal flight was generally a good 180 mph; in push-down flight it was clocked at 220 to 230 mph. Our Bf 110 is easily able to catch up and overtake this English model, even in push-down flight, so that many attacks can be launched on

Appendix Appendix 4 R.A.F. Form 541.

OPERATIONS RECORD BOOK.

DETAIL OF WORK CARRIED OUT.

From 0001 hrs. 3/9/39 to 2359 hrs. 3/9/39 By 139 Sqdn. No. of pages used for day

Aircraft Type and No.	Crew.	Duty.	Time Up.	Time Down.	Remarks.	References.
Blenheim Mk. IV N6215	F/O McPherson. Cdr. Thompson. Cpl. Arrowsmith.	Photo. Reco.	1200.	1650.	Duty successful. 75 photos taken of GERMAN fleet. The first Royal Air Force aircraft to cross the GERMAN frontier.	

Above: A historic moment, 2 September 1939, 9:00 A.M. A Polish P-23 Karas light bomber of 41 Reconnaissance Squadron at Zdunowo advanced airfield, is readied for the war's first bombing raid onto German soil.

Below: The flight route of the P-23 Karas that bombed German rail installations at Neidenburg, East Prussia (Pol. *Nidzica*) on 2 September 1939.

them rapidly from either side, and they can be attacked broadside on.

7. The main fire power of the Vickers Wellington bombers is at the rear: however forward defensive guns were also observed. The English aerial gunners were good shots. Our own fighters achieved the best results by attacking from the side.

In several cases where attack had to take place from the rear, it proved possible to finish off the tail gunner with aimed long-distance fire from 1,300 feet (400 meters). In these cases it was then possible to come right alongside the aircraft without meeting resistance. In no case was resistance observed to come from the ventral turret.

8. The English aircraft flew their course smartly and could not be diverted: the formations could be broken up only after hard attack. Scattered individual English craft always tried to join ranks in a new formation as fast as possible.

9. The Vickers Wellington aircraft is highly susceptible to fire. Not only could the engine and fuel tanks easily be set alight by gunfire, but the lining fabric too caught fire. Different phenomena occurred when the engine and fuel tanks caught fire: sometimes there were explosions, sometimes a slow burn that gave off smoke. The fire continued to eat its way slowly along the wings and tail unit.

Strategy and Tactics

September to December 1939

In the dawn of 1 September 1939, a thick ground fog sheltered Polish land from the planned "great first strike" of the German Luftwaffe. The Luftwaffe had been assigned a crucial role: In keeping with the Douhet theory, its first duty was to make "strategic" attacks against the enemy air forces on the ground and after destroying them, to fly "tactical" missions in support of the land army units.

After the fog slowly dissolved, the German flying wings took off to fulfill their combat missions in gleaming autumn sunshine.

A legend created by Nazi propaganda continues to crop up again and again even today, in a wide variety of books: It says that the Luftwaffe smashed the Polish Air Force on the ground in the very first days. But really, what was destroyed almost completely was the equipment of the peacetime airfields, the reserve and training aircraft, as well as aircraft which were just then undergoing repair or overhaul. In fact, according to Polish sources, not one single front-line aircraft was destroyed on the ground during the first two days of September. Nevertheless, the qualitative and quantitative superiority of the Germans gave them unlimited command of the air from the very first hour.

The first raid was flown by 3 Squadron of the German 1st Stuka (Dive Bomber) Wing fifteen minutes before war broke out. Their bombing raid entailed a special mission: To save the strategically important Vistula river bridge at Tczew (Ger. *Dirschau*) from the Poles, who had prepared to destroy it. The Germans intended their reinforcements for the troops in East Prussia to move across this bridge. The three German Junkers Ju 87s took off at 4:26 A.M. and roared along in low-level flight, barely 30 feet above the still peaceful land. These Stukas had orders to bomb out the ignition points the Poles had prepared to explode the bridge, directly beside the Tczew rail station. At the same time a German armored train was supposed to advance to the bridge and secure it. The Stuka attack was a success; the bombs hit their targets with precision. But it was a waste of effort: the Poles mended the torn cables and at 6:30 A.M. the bridge blew up.

Shortly after 4:45 A.M., twenty-one Ju 87 Bs of the 1st Group of the Immelmann 2nd Stuka Wing, took off from Nieder-Ellguth airfield at Steinberg near Opole (Ger. *Oppeln*) in Upper Silesia. They were commanded by Major Oscar Dinort, who had made a name for himself as a glider pilot. First Lieutenant Frank Neubert, who won the first aerial combat victory of the war, flew the Ju 87 B (T6 + GK).

Frank Neubert gave this account: "Our mission was to attack Krakow airfield. After releasing the bombs we flew back toward Reich territory, gaining altitude easily. Then I saw below and to the right—it must have been in the northwest of Krakow—an advanced airfield being circled by Polish planes. Next, ahead of me I saw a Ju 87 flying solo, which was under attack by two Polish fighter planes. Immediately I determined to help my comrades, and I tried to approach one of the Polish planes and come into position to fire. Having succeeded in this I released a burst of fire which produced no visible result as far as I could tell. After a second burst of fire I was able to observe the tracer bullets from my machine gun disappear inside the fighter plane cockpit; but at first I detected no further reaction. As I set about a third attack, the aircraft suddenly exploded in the air, burst apart like a huge fireball; the fragments literally flew around our ears. I immediately directed my attention to the second attacking fighter. Just as I came into shooting position, the Polish fighter

Right: A P-11 a of the 113 Owl Squadron (Warsaw Fighter Brigade) after an unequal air fight. The Polish fighter planes were some 90 mph slower than the German 109 Es, and their top altitude was about 6,500 feet lower.

Above left: 3 September 1939, Wyton airfield (Huntingdonshire): A Blenheim Mk IV of 139 Squadron, the first RAF plane called into action over Germany, has just landed. The exposed negative had to be developed quickly.

Above right: Monday 4 September 1939, watches are being synchronized before action. Only now, four days after war began, have the crews of the Polish P-37 Los bombers finally received permission for takeoff.

withdrew, executing an elegant curve upward and to the left, and disappeared from view. Then we flew on to Nieder-Ellguth and landed there. Lieutenant Brandenburg literally embraced me on the airfield, saying: 'You saved our lives.'"

Inside the Polish fighter plane which succeeded in escaping airman Neubert's machine-gun bursts, was Polish second lieutenant Wladyslaw Gnys. Moments later he shot down the first German aircraft of the war, a Stuka from 1st Group of the Immelmann Wing.

Wladyslaw Gnys reported: "Our unprepared airfield lay at the edge of the mountain spur village of Balice, near Olkusz. The mission of our fighter squadron, the 122 attached to the Army of Krakow, was the air defense of Krakow. We had just learned by telephone that the German forces had crossed the border into Poland, and Captain Medwecki, our squadron commander, ordered me to fly patrol with him. We pushed into our P-11s and rolled up for takeoff. Suddenly, about three miles to the south, several Stukas cropped up at an altitude of no more than 975 feet (300 meters). While we slowly increased our altitude and velocity, the Stukas opened fire with machine guns. I saved myself only by making a desperate banking turn. A bright jet of flame suddenly shot out of the P-11 belonging to our squadron commander, and his plane exploded in the air. I knew that my chances of survival were slim because I was no match for the much faster and better armed Stukas. The only thing I could depend on was the maneuverability of the good old

P-11. So I rushed at one of my enemies and shot almost the whole of my gun magazine into his fuselage. The struck aircraft climbed steeply at full speed and then at once arched into a dive. I thought to myself, 'He's just trying to fool me,' cut off his path and attacked again. While curving he grazed the trees and crashed into the ground. I looked at my wristwatch automatically, it was 5:30 A.M."

At about 7:00 A.M. the Polish Fighter Brigade, flying at an altitude of 6,500 feet over the village of Nieporet north of Warsaw, encountered more than 80 German bombers, models Heinkel He 11 and Dornier Do 17, escorted by about 20 Messerschmitt Me 110 fighter planes. They were flying in a tight closed formation.

This first and no doubt greatest air battle until the summer of 1940, lasted about fifty minutes. In addition to the 54 P-11 aircraft of the Polish Fighter Brigade, 10 planes of 152 Squadron of the Army of Modlin also took part. Thus roughly 64 fighter planes fought on the Polish side against around 100 German planes, a total of 160 aircraft.

On the advanced airfields of the Polish Bomber Brigade, the squadrons of modern Polish Los bombers had been waiting with hung bombs for the takeoff order since the early morning hours. Nevertheless Polish Marshal Rydz-Smigly refused, under pressure from the Allies to approve bombing assaults by his brigade—even on targets as tempting as the German motorized columns which the Army of Krakow had reported were moving through the mountain valleys.

At noon the same day a Beechcraft-model sportsplane flew over the German naval base at Wilhelmshaven at an altitude of almost 23,000 feet (7,000 meters), undetected by German antiaircraft. Cotton's copilot Bob Niven was at the controls. His duty was to find out whether German naval units were still lying in the Schilling Roads. In fact the ships were still there. Niven took a couple of photos and returned to Heston airfield as fast as he could.

By 2 September 1939, despite repeated German air assaults on Warsaw, the Polish Fighter Brigade had not succeeded in approaching within firing range of enemy planes. That day Polish bombers went into action for the first time. Six Karas aircraft of 24 Squadron, from the operational air force attached to the Army of Karkow, attacked the 16th Panzer Corps under General of the Cavalry Hoepner, north of Czestochowa (Ger. *Tschenstochau*). All the aircraft later returned to base.

Thanks only to the energetic intervention of Colonel W. Heller, commander of the Polish Bomber Brigade, permission was obtained from his superiors for 18 P-23 Karas machines (6th Group) from his unit to attack German armored columns around Czestochowa. They released their bombs from an altitude of approximately 4,800 feet (1,500 meters) and violated a strict prohibition to fly low in order to strafe German armored cars. Five aircraft were shot down by the German ground defenses; what is more, another was brought down by Polish flak, and two badly damaged Karas planes crashed on landing at their advanced airfield. Yet the squadrons of Polish Los bombers were still waiting for takeoff orders.

In the early morning hours of September 2, Polish Second Lieutenant Malinowski of 41 Reconnaissance Squadron of the Army of Modlin, received orders to investigate the movements of the German Third Army under General of the Artillery von Küchler, in the Olsztynek-Nidzica-Wielbark area of East Prussia (Ger. *Hohenstein-Neidenburg-Willenberg*). He took off from Zdunowo advanced airfield about twelve miles north of Modlin. Under the wings of his Karas bomber he carried eight 110-lb bombs, the first that would fall on Germany.

Lieutenant Malinowski reported: "We flew across the border from Poland into Germany at 9:40 A.M. On the right was the silvery autumn sun, it was absolutely peaceful. At 10:10 we sighted the first large-

sized German unit, a cavalry detachment. At 10:25 we saw a line of cars over one mile long along the Wielbark-Chorzele highway. The Germans opened heavy fire with antiaircraft artillery. Some shots passed through our wings. We set a heading for Olsztynek, encountering heavy car traffic near they city; then we flew over the Tannenberg Monument and sheered off toward Nidzica. In the air everything continued quiet. Below, a long troop-transport train steamed along the Olsztyn section of the line [Ger. *Allenstein*] headed toward Nidzica. At 10:50 I crawled into the bay, set the bomb sights and guided the pilot to the railway station. We flew over the city, and when the railway installations appeared in the sights, I pressed the release mechanism. The eight bombs whistled to the ground. At the same time the ground flak opened fire. The bombs were precisely on target. Explosive clouds rose over the tracks and from the packed military transports. Flying low we raced toward Mlawa. Our Karas landed in Zdunowo at 11:27. Naturally I did not know that this would turn out to be the only bombing raid made onto German territory during the September Campaign."

For the first two days the operations of the German Luftwaffe had a partly "strategic" character. Besides the raids on the peacetime airfields of the Polish Flytroop, operations were aimed at transport targets, to disrupt Polish troop movements. Polish mobilization degenerated into chaos as a result, and the Polish military command apparatus was completely paralyzed in some places.

From September 3 on, the Luftwaffe had already diverted its forces to ground battle support on the front. Its cooperation with the land army extended to direct bombardment of pockets of resistance, artillery positions and troop concentrations. This close collaboration became paramount, so that henceforth the Luftwaffe was deployed only tactically.

That day the Polish flytroop commander reported

Warnung

Großbritannien an das Deutsche Volk.

Deutsche,

Mit kühl erwogenem Vorsatz hat die Reichsregierung Großbritannien Krieg aufgezwungen. Wohl wußte sie, daß die Folgen ihrer Handlung die Menschheit in ein größeres Unheil stürzen, als 1914 es tat. Im April gab der Reichskanzler euch und der Welt die Versicherung seiner friedlichen Absichten: **sie erwies sich als ebenso wertlos** wie seine im September des Vorjahres im Sportpalast verkündeten Worte: „Wir haben keine weiteren territorialen Forderungen in Europa zu stellen."

Niemals hat eine Regierung ihre Untertanen unter geringerem Vorwand in den Tod geschickt. Dieser Krieg ist gänzlich unnötig. Von keiner Seite waren deutsches Land und deutsches Recht bedroht. Niemand verhinderte die Wiederbesetzung des Rheinlandes, den Vollzug des Anschlusses und die unblutig durchgeführte Einkörperung der Sudeten in das Reich. Weder wir, noch irgendein anderes Land, versuchte je dem Ausbau des deutschen Reiches Schranken zu setzen—solange dieses nicht die Unabhängigkeit nicht-deutscher Völker verletzte.

Allen Bestrebungen Deutschlands—solange sie Andern gerecht blieben—hätte man in friedlicher Beratung Rechnung getragen.

Right: On the night of September 3/4, RAF bombers dropped these air leaflets, the first of 6.5 billion. The "Warning of Great Britain to the German People" assures Germans that the war is unnecessary because no nation was offering threat to Germany's annexation of German-speaking territories, so long as the independence of non-German peoples was not affected.

Below: The scantily camouflaged P-11cs of the Polish 113 Owl Squadron on the Fighter Brigade's advanced airfield at Zielonka, near Warsaw.

Above left: 12 September 1939 after the Battle of the Bzura: A light 40-mm antiaircraft artillery gun belonging to the Polish Cavalry Brigade, in the middle of Polish fieldworks smashed by the Germans.

a Polish bombing assault on German motorized columns at Radomsko at 10:00 A.M. These troops were the German First and Fourth Armored Divisions advancing into the thrust center of the Tenth Army under General of the Artillery von Reichenau. "Enemy losses are estimated at thirty per cent," was the Polish claim. Naturally this was a gross exaggeration, for 18 Karas aircraft could never have inflicted such losses on the enemy. Nevertheless the fact is that both German armored divisions called for air support.

The results so far of Polish raids on German motorized columns: The Polish Bomber Brigade alone had lost about 15 of its 45 Karas bomber-reconnaissance planes. Most of the losses occurred during low-level strafing of the enemy columns, which were well-equipped with light antiaircraft artillery.

London, Sunday 3 September 1939: Prime Minister Neville Chamberlain had just announced to his countrymen over the radio that England was now at war with Germany. Fifteen minutes later millions of people in London and southern England heard the howl of air raid warning sirens, and hurried into the shelters. But instead of German bombers, the intruder turned out to be just a deputy air force attaché, attached to the French Embassy in London, who was returning to his duties after a weekend trip to Le Touquet in his private sports plane. He had neglected to hand in his flight plan, and thus had triggered a false alarm.

Thanks to the photographs that Bob Niven brought back from his September 1st flight in the Beechcraft 17, the RAF knew which units of the German navy were lying anchored in Wilhelmshaven. Then, shortly before the deployment of English bombers, an RAF reconnaissance plane was ordered to confirm that the ships were still there.

At noon on September 3, a Blenheim Mk IV of 139 Squadron left Wyton airfield in Huntingdonshire on this top secret mission. The pilot, Flying Officer A. McPherson, had a naval observer as on-board passenger. The Blenheim was the first RAF aircraft to fly over enemy territory. Both men indeed sighted several heavy German war vessels and took about 75 aerial photographs of them. Setting out for home, McPherson reported to base that the ships were far enough away from Wilhelmshaven to be attacked without fear of inflicting losses on the civilian population. But his message did not get through, the radio equipment was frozen. This delayed the deployment of British bombers over Germany. Not until that night did ten Whitley machines take off, armed with leaflets instead of bombs. They released a total of thirteen tons of leaflets over the Ruhr district, Hamburg and Bremen.

The radio failed again to work on the next reconnaissance flight of September 4, so the second flight of British bombers was postponed. But later, ten aircraft flew to Wilhelmshaven, this time with bombs on board. A violent thunderstorm forced the formation to attack from an altitude of only 650 feet (200 meters). Flight Lieutenant Doran attacked the armored vessel *Admiral Scheer* and saw his bombs hit and then bounce off without detonating. He also saw an explosion on the light cruiser *Emden*, and fires in the bay; but he did not suspect that the explosion was of an English Blenheim bomber that had crashed into the *Emden*, and that the fires were the burning wreckage of four other English planes.

During this attack, German Aerial Staff Sergeant Troitsch of 77th Group, 2nd Fighter Wing made the first air kill in the West. In all, 50% of the British bomber force was lost: not a very encouraging beginning.

On Monday 4 September 1939, the Polish defense began to collapse. In the early morning hours the modern Los bombers went into action at last, for the first time since war broke out. The 10th and 15th Bomber Groups, a total of 27 aircraft, took off to attack the German 16th Panzer Corps near Radomsko. They raided German columns in flights of three planes each, at several-minute intervals. In the afternoon they repeated their assaults, this time at Kamiensk and Wielun.

Shortly before sunset the Karases of 6th Group also took off to attack motorized columns between Ciechanow and Pultusk. These five bombing raids, which resulted in the loss of 9 Los bombers and 2 Karases, were the highpoint of Polish Bomber Brigade operations during the Polish campaign. They had almost no effect on the enemy. After releasing their bombs the Polish pilots flew additional low-level strafing assaults, which they had been strictly forbidden to do in their unarmored machines. For many pilots this was their first and their last action. Moreover, the bombers were afforded no protection by Polish fighter planes, even though the fighter squadron of the Army of Krakow was stationed at Demblin.

The same day the Polish Fighter Brigade moved to new advanced airfields and lost precious time in camouflaging its aircraft. Its effective strength had been reduced to a mere 25 planes. Then the German Luftwaffe succeeded for the first time in destroying Polish front-line aircraft on the ground: 2 Los bombers of the Bomber Brigade were smashed at Kuciny, as were 3 P-11 fighter planes of the Army of Lodz at Widzew.

The lack of fresh supplies was affecting the combat readiness of the Polish fliers. For example, by the fifth day the Fighter Brigade had already run out of special components for their metal machine gun belts. "To save them, we were each time ordered to arm ourselves with only 200 machine gun bullets. This was enough for no more than 30 seconds of continuous fire."

The first "success" by British aircraft against a submarine was scored on 5 September 1939, when Avro Anson reconnaissance aircraft deployed to fight German U-boats, mistakenly attacked two British submarines with 99-lb depth charges. The submarine HMS *Snapper* received a direct hit on its command tower—that did no more than break four electric bulbs inside the boat.

The RAF Coastal Command entered the war with around 300 combat-ready land- and seaplanes. Only one of 5 planned Lockheed Hudson coastal reconnaissance squadrons had been completed. No long-range aircraft whatever were available for anti-submarine defense. At the beginning of the war, even the British Navy did not have one single anti-submarine plane. The Fairey Swordfish biplane which had been in service as a torpedo and bomber craft since 1935, ended by having to take on anti-submarine duty as well.

On Tuesday 5 September 1939, the 15th Group of the Polish Bomber Brigade—two flights comprised of three Los bombers each—made a final assault on the German 16th Panzer Corps, which having smashed the Polish defense at Petrikov, was advancing toward Warsaw meeting virtually no resistance. Growing losses among the antiquated Polish reconnaissance planes forced the Poles to deploy their remaining bombers and fighters exclusively on scout flights.

In the morning hours of September 6, two flights made up of three Los bombers each, raided the German armored units at Makow Mazowiecki. German fighter planes shot down one of the flights. The Polish high command moved their headquarters to Brest-Litovsk. Here, too, assembled the decimated Polish air forces, who by this time had lost 60% of their original combat strength. They decided on a reorganization: The operational flying forces attached to the individual land armies, were largely disbanded so that they could strengthen the fighter and bomber brigades. But at no time throughout the campaign did the Polish Flytroop succeed in coordinating the deployment of its two brigades: Not once did the Fighter Brigade fly with the bombers to afford them protection.

On the night of September 7, the Polish Fighter Brigade was transferred to the Lublin area; but it found nothing waiting but deserted advanced airfields without maintenance provisions or communications networks. Moreover there were no listening or observation posts. The pilots had their own way of dealing with the total lack of engine fuel: They flew low reconnaissance flights over the railway lines, on the lookout for fuel tankers. When they found one that they thought might contain fuel, they raced as fast as they could back to base, where they had tank cars waiting to move. Their combat duties here were unlike those at Warsaw, for now the Brigade no longer received any clearly-defined orders.

The Polish capital, without fighter plane pro-

The British Expeditionary Force, which in September 1939 took up a position along the northern border of France, had only a few fighter and reconnaissance squadrons. British medium bombers (Fairey Battles and Blenheims) were stationed in the Champagne along with a fighter plane unit, making a total of about 100 aircraft.

The remarkable thing is that the German Luftwaffe did not try to prevent transport of the British divisions across the English Channel; nor did the French and English forces interfere with the transferral of the German armies from Poland to the Western Front. The French Air Force limited itself to scout flights along the Siegfried Line and strictly opposed allowing the British Bomber Command to operate out of French bases.

Above left: Bombardier at his bomb sight, which is attached to an autopilot, making it possible for the aircraft to home in exactly on target. Course corrections occurred automatically.

Right: 18 September 1939 at Rovno, eastern Poland. A Red Army soldier stands guard over a Polish P.W.S. 26 liaison aircraft, shot down by Soviet fighter planes on its way to Rumania.

Below: An He 111 releasing its SD 550-lb bombs over Wola, the industrial district in the western part of Warsaw.

tection and stripped of the antiaircraft artillery which had been diverted east the day before, was now defenseless to the attacks of the German Luftwaffe.

The more German troops reached central Poland, the more intensively the Luftwaffe concentrated its activities on the region between the central Vistula and the Bug rivers. To neutralize preparations for the defense of Lublin and Polesye, the Luftwaffe bombed all the rail installations in this area, and the German 4th Air Fleet (under General of the Air Force Löhr), transferred most of the close-reconnaissance, fighter and dive bomber units assigned to the tactical support of the army, from Silesia to Kielce and Radom.

At first the air war in Western Europe was marked by extreme caution: In the autumn and winter of 1939, the RAF and the Luftwaffe alike released no bombs on enemy land. The Germans were still hoping to get Great Britain to conciliate; the English in turn felt they were not yet strong enough to attack. The only legitimate targets were enemy war vessels.

On Friday 8 September 1939, the German troops of the 4th Panzer Division occupied Okecie airfield in Warsaw. Approximately 120,000 Polish soldiers barricaded themselves in Warsaw in preparation for the expected street fighting. Then something amazing happened: It escaped the notice of German reconnaissance that the then strongest concentration of Polish troops was situated to the rear of the German army group which had just encircled the Polish capital. This was the Army of Poznan under Major General Kutrzeba, combined with the battered Army of Pomerania under General Bortnowski. The two armies had retreated from western Poland by night marches, sheltering in the woods of the Polish plain by day—undetected by the Luftwaffe.

The battle that broke out on September 9 and entered history under the name of the Battle of Kutno (also known as the Battle of the Bzura), was the greatest of the entire Polish campaign.

It was thanks to his reconnaissance fliers that General Kutrzeba held the battlefield initiative for two days; for the forceful general had resisted the order to liquidate his flytroop and held onto his aircraft. As a result he received continuous information about German troop movements, and when his scout planes discovered the unprotected flank of the German Eighth Army under General of the Infantry Blaskowitz, he decided to strike there. So the Poles crossed the Bzura river on September 9 with superior forces. Hard fighting lasted all day and into the following night. The cavalry and the few armored tanks that Kutrzeba had at his disposal, succeeding in making deep incursions; the German 30th Infantry Division was especially hard hit.

The situation was so grave that the German South Army Group under Colonel General von Rundstedt urgently demanded, for the first time since war began, that the Luftwaffe "deploy powerful aerial forces in the Kutno zone on September 11." Several German bomber wings which had spent the last few days mainly in making relay assaults on Warsaw and on railway and industrial targets east of the Vistula, were thrown immediately into the Battle of the Bzura. Only these massive deployments of Stukas and combat fighter squadrons, were able to stop the Polish attacks. Aerial machine gun bursts mowed down Polish soldiers and horses; a hail of fragmentation bombs rained down on them.

The tide began to turn. The German 16th Armored Division under General of the Cavalry Hoepner, had once again been forced to retreat on meeting unexpectedly heavy resistance outside Warsaw, and von Reichenau ordered it to swing around toward Kutno. At the same time the Fourth Army under General of the Artillery von Kluge reached the Vistula west of Modlin, and the Eighth Army (under General of the Infantry Blaskowitz) started to gain ground again northeast of Lodz; so the Germans encircled the two Polish armies on either side of the Bzura.

Above: Warsaw, 25 September 1939. That day the Luftwaffe flew 1,176 missions against the fiercely defended Polish capital. Seventy-two European tons of incendiary bombs and 486 tons of high-explosive bombs were dropped on the city.

Center: A hard-hit Polish P-37 Los bomber is burning outside a hangar: a scene from the Nazi propaganda film *Feuertaufe* (Baptism of Fire), made in 1939.

Left: Position of the Polish aerial forces on 16 September 1939.

Meanwhile, some 120 miles to the east in Brest-Litovsk, command of the Polish Flytroop had degenerated into complete chaos. German bombers, Stukas and fighters, enjoying brilliant weather, were free to dive on the compressed Polish armies from dawn to dusk, while meanwhile more than 120 Polish aircraft, including large numbers of fighter planes, were standing east of the Vistula doing nothing. Among them were planes which just a few days before had been taken away from the Army of Pomerania so that they could be incorporated into the two Polish air brigades. Polish communications had broken down completely, so that the air force at Brest-Litovsk knew virtually nothing about the growing disaster on the Bzura.

The following day the Polish armies of Poznan and Pomerania, comprising almost 200,000 men, were jammed inside a pocket approximately 18 miles wide and 27 miles long. Polish general Kutrzeba reported: "The vigorous air assaults on the Bzura crossings were unprecedented with respect to the numbers of aircraft deployed as well as the ferocity of the attacks and the sheer acrobatic skill of the pilots. Every one of our movements, every troop assembly, every route of march, came under a pulverizing bombardment . . . The bridges were destroyed, the fords blocked and the choked supply columns decimated."

On Wednesday 13 September 1939, the German ring closed around Warsaw. In an abandoned hangar of the old Mokotow airfield right at the edge of the city center, members of the Polish Flytroop mended a couple of damaged aircraft and two sailplanes, despite the German infantry who had already reached the western rim of the airfield. Using a P-11 fighter plane that was still fit to fly, they even undertook several assaults on German positions at Okecie. The two RWD 8-model Polish sportsplanes enabled General Rommel, the supreme commander of the besieged capital, to maintain communications with Marshal Rydz-Smigly and to supply the besieged fortress of Modlin with medicines and bandages. In all, more than 100 additional air operations were flown before the end came.

On Thursday 14 September, shortly before sunset, the Luftwaffe raided one of the most important unprepared airfields of the Polish Bomber Brigade—Hutniki near Brodow. Almost all the Polish aircraft—11 by German report—were destroyed on the ground, including Los bombers. This raid that happened exactly two weeks after war began, was in fact the first to cause serious losses to front-line air-

Norddeutsche Ausgabe

271. Ausg. / 52. Jahrg. / Einzelpreis 20 Pf.

„Freiheit und Brot!"

Norddeutsche Ausgabe

Berlin, Donnerstag, 28. September 1939

VÖLKISCHER BEOBACHTER

Kampfblatt der national-sozialistischen Bewegung Großdeutschlands

Erfolgreicher Luftangriff auf die britische Hochseeflotte

Flugzeugträger zerstört — Schlachtschiff schwer getroffen

Festung Warschau vor der Uebergabe

Berlin, 27. September.

Das Oberkommando der Wehrmacht gibt bekannt:

Im Osten nähern sich unsere Truppen der mit der Sowjetregierung vereinbarten Demarkationslinie.

Von den versprengten Teilen des polnischen Heeres, die sich noch zwischen den deutschen und den vormarschierenden russischen Truppen befinden, wurde gestern östlich Bilgoraj die 41. polnische Division und die 1. Kavalleriebrigade gefangengenommen.

Die zu Beginn der Kampfhandlungen als offene Stadt angesehene und dementsprechend respektierte Hauptstadt Polens ist durch die Maßnahmen des Kommandanten, die Wiederinstandsetzung der alten Forts und die Bewaffnung von Teilen der Zivilbevölkerung in eine Festung verwandelt worden

Britischer Selbstbetrug

Berlin, 27. September.

Für das britische Lügenministerium ist es gewiß keine sehr erquickliche Aufgabe, ‚den völligen Zusammenbruch Polens festzustellen, nachdem das englische Volk wochenlang über den wahren Gang der Dinge' im Unklaren gelassen und immer wieder ein großer Umschwung in Polen vorausgesagt wurde. Die Londoner Rückzugskanonade kann demgemäß nur denkbar kläglich sein. So erklärt der britische Rundfunk, der Krieg in Polen habe immerhin England und Frankreich gestattet, ihre Mobilmachung ungestört durchzuführen. Das mag auch Engländern, die noch über einen Rest von Erinnerungsvermögen und logischem Denken verfügen, zu denken geben. Denn schließlich wurde die englische Kriegserklärung an Deutschland damit begründet, England sei verpflichtet, Polen zu Hilfe zu kommen. Die englische Garantie war ja Polen geradezu aufgedrängt worden, und es ist daher mehr als sonderbar, wenn jetzt der Sinn dieses Abenteuers, das Polen ins Verderben gestürzt hat, so ausgedeutet wird, als ob nicht die Westmächte zur Hilfeleistung in Polen verpflichtet gewesen wären, sondern vielmehr Polen sich hätte aufopfern müssen, um seinen armen schwachen Verbündeten eine Atempause zu verschaffen.

Gegenüber diesen kaltschnäuzigen Feststellungen des Londoner Lügenministeriums wiegen die reichlichen Lobsprüche, die man hinterher dem durch englische Schuld zugrunde gegangenen Polen spendet, recht belanglos. Da offensichtlich in der englischen Öffentlichkeit die blitzschnelle Niederwerfung Polens die ernstesten Besorgnisse für den weiteren Verlauf des von England vom

Ribbentrop auf dem Wege nach Moskau

Berlin, 27. September.

Der Reichsminister des Auswärtigen, von Ribbentrop, begab sich am Mittwochvormittag um 9 Uhr im Condor-Flugzeug „Grenzmark" vom Flughafen Tempelhof aus mit dem Botschafter der UdSSR. in Berlin, Alexander Schkwarzew, und Legationssekretär Pawlow von der Sowjetrussischen Botschaft auf Einladung der Sowjetregierung nach Moskau.

Der Reichsaußenminister ist begleitet von

Aufnahme: Presse-Hoffmann

Der Führer und seine Generale beobachten die Kampfhandlungen
Links: Generaloberst Keitel, Rechts: General v. Reichenau

Deutsch-sowjetrussische Wandlungen

Von Harald Siewert

Wohl noch niemals in der Geschichte haben sich innerhalb nur eines Monats in dem Verhältnis zweier Großmächte so radikale, durchgreifende Wandlungen vollzogen wie jetzt zwischen Deutschland und Rußland.

daß Stalin bereits im März dieses Jahres auf dem 18. Parteikongreß klar und deutlich erklärt hatte, daß die Gerüchte über angebliche deutsche Eroberungsgelüste der Ukraine gegenüber nichts anderes seien als ein Köder

Above: An example of Nazi propaganda: A false newspaper account of the "sinking" of the British 22,000-ton aircraft carrier *Ark Royal*, which in reality was not hit by a single bomb during the German air assault of 26 September 1939.

craft. The following morning the German machines appeared again and destroyed another six bombers that they had failed to hit on the first raid.

That afternoon and in the morning hours of September 16, all units of the Polish Bomber Brigade which were still intact, were transferred to fresh advanced airfields farther east. Crewmen of the 15th Group landed their Los bombers on a stubble-field near Buczacz, spent the night under their planes, and next morning flew two more bombing assaults, the last Polish raids in the September Campaign. One flight of 4 Los craft bombed German armored columns at Hrubieszow, the other flight of 3 Loses bombed a motorized column on the west bank of the Bug river near Woldawa. The other 6 Los bombers no longer had enough fuel to fly.

On Sunday 17 September 1939, the Polish Air Force was alarmed by more bad news: The Soviet army had crossed over the border into Poland and already had occupied the first airfields. Since the early morning hours a handful of Polish fliers had been confronting a second overwhelming enemy. All day stubborn duels were fought between the Poles and the Red Air Force. The Soviets made surprise assaults on the easternmost unprepared airfields at Kovel, Dubno and Luck, where the remnants of the Polish bomber and fighter brigades were stationed along with the operational air force of the Army of the Carpathians. Polish fliers shot down 2 Soviet Tupolev SB-2 bombers and 5 Polikarpov I-16 Rata fighter planes. That day the Soviets reported

Below: The Luftwaffe's office for the interpretation of aerial photographs, where the British naval units in the photos are being identified with the help of models.

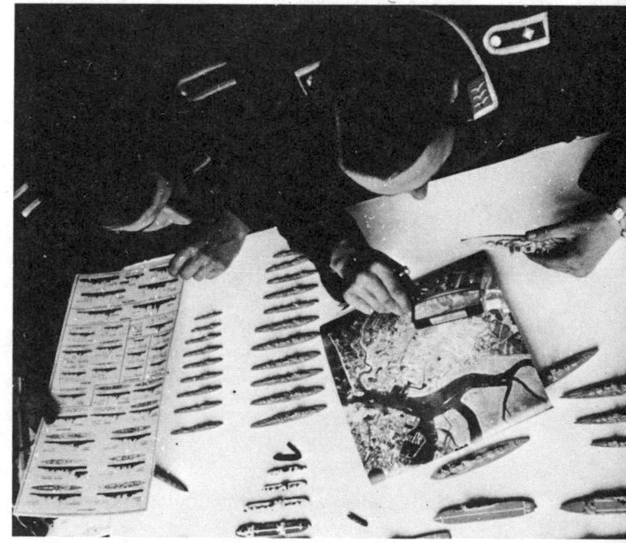

Above right: Medium Soviet bomber, the Tupolev SB-3. From September 17–27, aircraft of this model led numerous attacks on Polish troops retreating toward the Hungarian and Rumanian borders.

Below: Tactics of the German Ju 88s during dive bomb raids on shipping targets.

shooting down 7 Polish fighters and 3 bombers.

The Polish air force commander ordered all takeoff-ready aircraft to evacuate to Rumania. The remaining craft, for which there was no more available fuel, were set on fire, along with the damaged planes. Part of the crews and ground personnel tried to save themselves from the Germans and the Soviets by making a forced march to Rumania or Hungary.

That Sunday the Luftwaffe's operations against the pocket of Polish troops on the Bzura, reached their climax. The concentration of its forces at this point, forced the Luftwaffe to break off almost all other military operations. Nothing but reconnaissance flights were made over the territories east of the great bend of the Vistula.

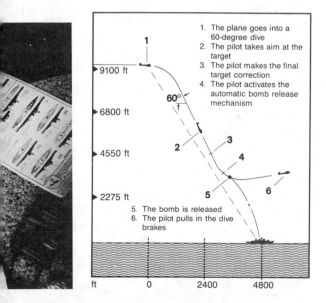

1. The plane goes into a 60-degree dive
2. The pilot takes aim at the target
3. The pilot makes the final target correction
4. The pilot activates the automatic bomb release mechanism
5. The bomb is released
6. The pilot pulls in the dive brakes

9100 ft
6800 ft
4550 ft
2275 ft
60°
ft 0 2400 4800

Almost 100 Polish military aircraft landed in Rumania on September 17 and 18. All the planes and crews were interned because of Rumanian fears of German and Soviet retaliation. The Los and Karas aircraft were impressed into the Rumanian air force and later used along the Eastern Front in the battle against the Soviet Union.

On Monday 25 September 1939, 400 German aircraft that made three or four assault flights each, dropped 486 long tons of high-explosive bombs and 72 long tons of incendiary bombs on Warsaw. There was no way to fight the fires in the city because bombs had destroyed the water pipes and the streets were blocked with debris from the collapsed houses. The situation was made completely hopeless by the absence of the fire brigade, who had been evacuated two weeks before.

On the night of 25/26 September 1939, the eve of the surrender of Warsaw, 11 Polish aircraft and 2 Polish Komar sailplanes took off from Mokotow airfield, which was lit up by the conflagrations, under rifle fire from German infantry. Among them was a P-11 fighter plane that stumbled over the takeoff field ploughed by German artilley, until it slowly gained altitude. The reason for this laborious takeoff was that the aircraft radio equipment had been removed to make a place for Air Force Lieutenant Colonel M. Izycki, later the commander

German Ju 87 Stuka dive bombers flying in flights of three, linked in squadron formation.

of the Polish Air Force in England which fought on the side of the RAF. There were no maps available, so the aircraft were guided exclusively by compass. The sailplanes got no farther than Grojec thirty miles south of Warsaw. One of the planes ran out of fuel at Kielce. The pilot landed, stripped out the compass and reached Hungary on foot.

Tuesday 26 September 1939: A German Ju 88 of the 26th Combat Wing under Airman Third Class Franke, released an SC 1,100-lb bomb in its dive on the British aircraft carrier *Ark Royal* in the central North Sea. The pilot testified that the bomb fell hard by the carrier. This raid was the first German aerial operation against the British Home Fleet in World War II. In late afternoon of the same day, Luftwaffe reconnaissance planes sighted two British battleships on a westward course—without the aircraft carrier.

The chief of staff of the German 10th Air Division, General Air Staff Major Harlinghausen, was convinced that the *Ark Royal* had formed part of the sighted unit, and thereupon ordered German reconnaissance planes to be on the lookout for oil slicks. He then very quickly received the report of a sighted oil slick, and cabled the observation to Göring.

Next day, Wednesday 27 September 1939, the Wehrmacht reported the "destruction" of a British aircraft carrier, prudently refraining from giving its name. But Hermann Göring did not want his Luftwaffe winning victories against nameless targets. The Field Marshal decided it was the *Ark Royal*. He sent his personal congratulations to Franke, immediately promoted the Airman to the rank of Second Lieutenant, and decorated him with two grades of the Iron Cross. But the truth was that the *Ark Royal* put out to sea in the south Atlantic at the beginning of October, and took part there in the months-long pursuit of the German armored naval vessel *Admiral Graf Spee*.

On the evening of Sunday 1 October 1939, 4 Whitley aircraft of the British 10 Squadron took off from Dishford airfield. Three planes reached Berlin and dropped air leaflets over the capital; the fourth Whitley got lost in flight. This was the first British unit to fly over Berlin.

Wednesday 4 October 1939: While preparations for Hitler's victory parade were starting up in Warsaw, the last large Polish unit under General Kleeburg was fighting at Kock some 66 miles to the southeast. During the Battle of Kock two RWD-8 aircraft and one PWS flew the last Polish missions against the Germans. Apart from communications and reconnaissance flights, they also carried out bombing raids—using hand grenades. On the morning of 4 October 1939 one RWD-8 came back, having used its last drop of fuel. This flight ended the operations of Polish fliers in the September War:

There was no fuel left for another takeoff.

In peacetime the Polish Air Force admittedly had well-trained flying personnel. However, only 340 aviators, 250 observers and 210 aerial gunners were able to take part in combat – the rest had no planes. Despite that, theirs was a notable achievement, along with that of the Polish antiaircraft artillery. When the German Luftwaffe drew up a balance of their losses after the Polish Campaign, the results showed: 285 aircraft totally destroyed, 279 damaged, and 734 crewmen dead. By comparison, Luftwaffe losses during the three-year-long combat in Spain (1936–1939) amounted to 96 aircraft.

A paradox of the September 1939 air war was that according to Polish sources, Polish antiaircraft shot down almost twice as many Polish aircraft as the German antiaircraft. Certainly, some 10% of the Polish Air Force was lost to friendly fire; one out of three crews died in the process. For whatever reasons, the Polish army leadership neglected to familiarize their soldiers with the profiles of their own as well as of enemy aircraft; this information was even kept on the list of classified materials! The Polish aircraft could not fly higher than 1,600 feet (500 meters) over their own territory and were slower than the Germans, so they made easy marks for the Polish antiaircraft defenders who suspected every plane of being an enemy. Even those fliers who managed to save themselves by parachuting out, felt the effects of their countrymen's anxiety psychosis. They were often beaten up because anyone who landed by parachute was regarded as a German agent.

The Polish campaign successfully combined the deployment of Luftwaffe and land army forces, and the German leadership took it as a model for future blitz campaigns – a fact that was not sufficiently appreciated by Germany's foes. On the other hand, the experiences of September also testified that the German Luftwaffe was strong enough only for short-term warfare on a single front.

Some mistaken judgments resulted from the vic-

Below right: Assault tactic of the Ju 87 Stuka dive bomber squadrons. A squadron row was formed before the assault began; then the planes dived in pairs.

Below: The skeleton of a burnt-out Wellington, the most-produced British bomber (11,461 were built). Here we see its geodetic structure, like that of an airship.

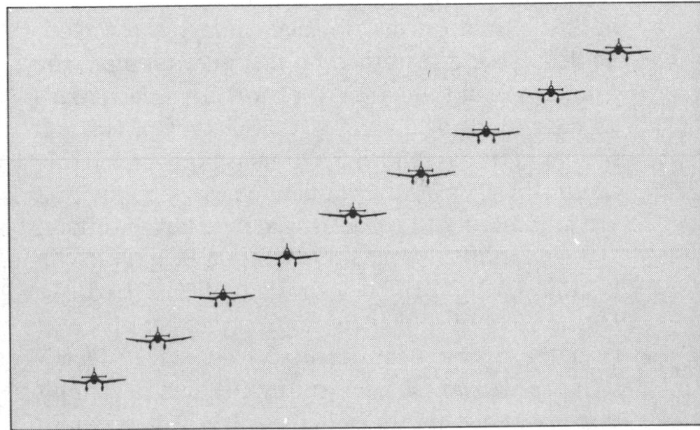

tory in Poland. One of the most serious for Germany stemmed from the success of the blitzkrieg, of the Luftwaffe's role, and above all of the Stukas and medium bombers, which misled the Germans into a policy error in the future development of their aerial forces. As a result, over the next few years they completely lacked the aircraft indispensable to the conduct of an independent strategic air war.

Sunday 8 October 1939: During a patrol flight over the North Sea, a Lockheed Hudson coastal reconnaissance plane of 224 Squadron became the first English craft to shoot down a German plane, a Dornier Do 18 flying boat. Chance decreed that on the same day at around 3:00 P.M., two French fliers named Villey and Casenobe shot down one German fighter plane each near Landau, during an aerial combat between 5 Curtiss Hawk fighters of the French "Red Devil" Squadron (4 Squadron of 2nd Fighter Group), and 4 German Messerschmitt Me 109s. These were the first French air kills of the war.

Monday 16 October 1939: The 1st Group of the German 30th Bomber Wing under Captain Pohle, carried out the first air raid on a Royal Navy base in World War II. The target was British war vessels in the Firth of Forth. Material damage and personnel losses were sustained on the *Southampton*, the *Edinburgh* and the *Mohawk*. Two German Junkers Ju 88s were shot down by two Spitfires of 602 and 603 squadrons. Another German bomber fell victim to the flak bombardment. These were the first German planes to be destroyed over Great Britain.

After another German assault on Scapa Flow in Scotland, the British Admiralty transferred the Home Fleet to safe anchorage on the remote Clyde river. This move significantly weakened the Fleet's strike effectiveness against any German naval unit that might put out to sea in the Atlantic or approach the eastern coast of England. Astonishingly, the Germans failed to act on their strategic advantage. German aerial operations against British warships in Scapa Flow and the Firth of Forth, also revealed that the German SC 550-lb bombs were ineffective, and Göring ordered the development of heavier bombs.

Thursday 23 November 1939 was a black day for the German rocket missile project which was taking shape in the remote pine forests of Usedom island in the Baltic Sea, in the town of Peenemünde, at the German Army Experimental Institute under Colonel W. Dornberger. One month before, the army supreme command had set a May 1941 completion date for the mass production of "Aggregate 4," the code name for a liquid rocket with a gross weight of 12.9 European tons which was capable of transporting its 2,200-lb explosive charge a distance of 210 miles (350 km), and which was developing under the direction of engineer Wernher von Braun.

Then on November 23, Hitler stopped the whole project because "after the victory over Poland [he] will no longer need any rockets in this war." Once the Peenemünde project lost its priority status, its men and materials were withdrawn.

On 30 November 1939, Soviet bomber wings appeared over Helsinki and bombed the city center, without a previous declaration of war. This marked the beginning of the Winter War in Finland. Finland, with a population of 3.5 million and a peacetime army of 3 divisions, set itself to make a determined defense.

In the first few days the Red Air Force ordered some 900 air machines to the Finnish front. The Finnish Air Force had a total of only 145 aircraft of which 114 were ready for action. At the beginning of the Winter War, the Dutch Fokker D-XXI was Finland's most modern fighter plane. The commander of the Finnish Air Force, General J.F. Lundquist, formed 31 aircraft into 24 Fighter Squadron, which was stationed at Immola airbase near the important power-station of Imatra, about thirty miles north of Viipuri.

On Friday 1 December 1939, the second day of the war, Finnish Captain Eino Luukkanen received the order to take off from Immola at 5:30 A.M. and to keep up a continuous patrol of two fighter planes over Vuoksenlaakso. Shortly thereafter they sighted a formation of Soviet bombers, and Captain Luukkanen made the first air kill of the Winter War when he shot down a Tupolev SB-2 bomber.

Despite its numerical inferiority, the Finnish Air Force by no means confined itself to warding off Soviet air assaults. On the contrary, it also flew missions against Murmansk, Leningrad, Kronstadt and Paldiski.

By the end of the year the Soviets had carried out countless assaults on the Finnish hinterland, plastering villages and even individual farmsteads with bombs. In their adversity, the Finns managed to turn

The RAF Bomber Command made inconspicuous preparations for the strategic air war. Here an RAF plane is shown shortly before takeoff on a "pamphlet raid."

the intense cold to their advantage: They poured water over their houses, which for the most part were only one story high, and the layer of ice that then formed, afforded good protection against incendiary bombs.

No other air assault influenced both British and German air strategy and tactics, more than the RAF armed reconnaissance mission over Wilhelmshaven on Monday 18 December 1939. In fact the British general staff numbered it among the most significant aerial combat incidents of World War II.

On the morning of December 18, 24 Vickers Wellington bombers of the 9th, 37th and 149th Wings took off from their bases in eastern England. Their mission: to patrol the mouth of the Weser river, Wilhelmshaven and the Jade Bay, and to bomb every German war vessel sighted at sea. Shortly after 1:00 P.M. the report of intruding enemy aircraft was carried by German Freya radar on the island of Wangerooge, to the command post of the German fighter wing in Jever, but it was interpreted as an observer error. The alarm was only sounded a few minutes later, when a second Freya radar report confirmed the first. For the first time, fighter aircraft were successfully guided to an enemy unit by radar, with the support of radiotelephony.

The German 10 Squadron of the 26th Fighter Group under First Lieutenant Steinhoff, was the first to reach the enemy: "We could not have wished for better weather for our first massive encounter with the RAF. A fair-weather fog layer along the ground surmounted by a blue cloudless sky with clear long-distance visibility." The English flew in compact formations, at an altitude of approximately 11,375 feet, past the German island fortress of Helgoland, and set a heading for the Jade Bay and Wilhelmshaven under fire from the Helgoland naval batteries. Airman First Class Helmayer made the first kill: "He must have been an old hand. Each time he banked opposite us at the moment we opened fire, and our gun bursts hissed away past the target. We were on our fourth attack – range 2,000 feet – 1,600 feet – 1,300 – 1,000 – then came a thud, a hiss, hits in our own aircraft, a blow to my left arm. But at the same time we saw that our assault had been successful. The Wellington was burning and crashed into the sea. We saw the impact point, the oil slick. Our cockpit was smoking and there was a smell of gunpowder. I saw splashes of blood. Ow, my arm was so heavy, suddenly my left hand felt as if it were on fire – blood,

A formation of British medium-range Wellington bombers. After 18 December 1939 these aircraft, which their crews affectionately called "Wimpeys" (after Popeye's friend J. Wellington Wimpey), were flown only on night missions.

I was wounded too! . . . We had reached Jever. We heaved a sigh of relief. The aircraft taxied to a halt, we were back on the ground. Our squadron emblem, the ladybug with its seven spots, had brought us luck once again."

The air battle lasted no more than half an hour. Shortly after 3:00 P.M. the remains of the badly-hit British bomber unit had already flown outside German fighter range. By British accounts, 15 of their 22 aircraft were lost. German sources, on the other hand, claimed that 34 out of 44 intruding enemy aircraft had been shot down.

From that day onward, 18 December 1939, the British never again carried out daylight bombing strikes in compact formations, without fighter protection. Now they switched to night bombing raids. Not until October 1944 did British Bomber Command once again dare to make daylight raids on Germany. The RAF were convinced that German industrial centers could be destroyed in night raids; for the British had encountered no effective German night antiaircraft on their night-time air leaflet drops over Germany. The RAF also recognized the need, from now on, to equip their bombers with selfsealing fuel tanks which resisted fuel loss after puncture by enemy gunfire.

The night raids by the RAF forced the Luftwaffe to set up an expensive communications defense system which pulled away men and materials from other important munitions projects. The RAF had learned the lesson that bombers could operate more safely by night and, by day, had to be protected by a fighter escort. The German command recognized this only after Germany's own heavy losses over England in the summer and autumn of 1940.

Meanwhile, night after night the Whitley bombers of the British 4th Wing ignored fog and frost to fly air leaflets to the Ruhr, to Hamburg, Berlin, Nuremberg, and even to Vienna, Prague and Warsaw. Between 10 November 1939 and 16 March 1940, German antiaircraft defense was so ineffectual that the 4th Wing did not lose a single aircraft to enemy action. However, several planes were lost by icing up, for the weather conditions posed a greater hazard to crews than German antiaircraft. Twenty to thirty aircraft that spread all across Germany to drop leaflets, provoked no particular reaction from the German side.

These "pamphlet raids" camouflaged with great cleverness the true intentions of the British. The German command succumbed to the deception and failed to notice that the night flights represented the first step in the strategic air war against Germany. At the same time the Luftwaffe failed to set up a night fighter plane defense, and by the time they started to do so, precious months had been lost and it was virtually impossible to make up this lost time.

1940

January to June

Daily Keynote from the Reich Press Chief [Otto Dietrich]
Saturday 13 January 1940:

On 10 January 1940 the Luftwaffe High Command [the OKL] instructed the German press that it was forbidden to publish any information about German Me 110, Ju 88 and Me 210 bomber aircraft, mine-laying aircraft, one-ton bombs, and the aircraft controlling and reporting service *[Flugmeldedienst].*

Sunday 14 January 1940
The *Wehrmacht High Command* [OKW] announced:

On the night of January 12, several enemy aircraft undertook reconnaissance flights over German territory. During the night an English aircraft tried to attack a North Frisian island; the bombs fell harmlessly into the sea.

From the edict of the *SS-Reichsführer and Chief of the German Police* [Heinrich Himmler] in the Reich Ministry of the Interior, dated 29 February 1940:

Re: Discovered enemy air leaflets and spreading devices.

Various confusions that have arisen in the treatment of discovered enemy air leaflets, balloons and other spreading and drop devices, have caused me to decree the following: The local police authority is to govern the search action. They are to approach the appropriate local [National Socialist] Party authorities for assistance in collecting leaflets. The police authority is to take the collected leaflets into custody and to notify the state police immediately. The latter will have the final disposition of the material brought into safekeeping, in this manner: For archival purposes, 30 copies of each leaflet will be sent here—to Office IV (II A 1)—in a single batch. Once high-ranking Party departments, and other authorities who cite a well-founded and justifiable interest in the material, have received their desired number of copies, the rest are to be reliably disposed of by an appropriate method. The purpose of the search action is the seizure of all the disseminated leaflets, leaving if possible none in circulation.

Tuesday 9 April 1940
The *Wehrmacht High Command* announced:

Operations for the occupation of Denmark and of the Norwegian coast, went according to plan on April 9. No incidents occurred anywhere during the landings and entry into Denmark. On the coast of Norway, notable resistance was offered only in Oslo; this was broken in the afternoon hours. Oslo itself has been occupied.

Parachute Drop over Narvik

The Nazi newspaper *Völkischer Beobachter* carried this descriptive account of German airborne landings in Norway, published in April 1940:

After a smooth trip—reports *Obergefreiter* [Airman 2nd Class] Dambeck—we reached Trondheim airbase. Everyone was keyed up and on the alert.

We started north to Narvik. An uncanny landscape sailed past beneath us. Nothing but mountains, snow and ice. It was also bitter cold. After several hours of flight we finally reached our drop point.

"Get ready!" Out I go! I made a smooth landing,

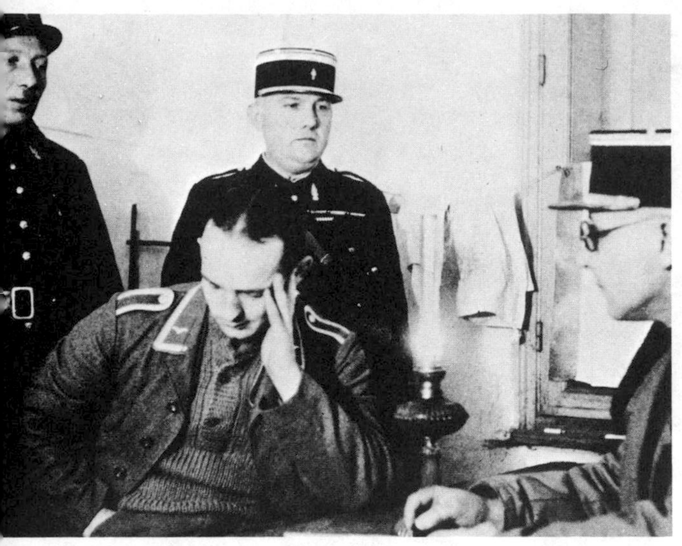

Left: The sole survivor of a Dornier Do 17 German long-range reconnaissance plane, being interrogated by the French. During the 8-months-long "sitzkrieg" or "sitting war" before the Germans launched their Western offensive, the Luftwaffe carried out large-scale reconnaissance missions over France.

Right: 9 April 1940, Operation Weserübung. German mountain troops who took part in the first airborne landing operation of the war, were transported to Norway in Junkers Ju 52s.

Below: Le Figaro warns its French readers barely 24 hours before the German airborne invasion begins. The German High Command kept strictly secret their plans to launch the war in the West with a surprise attack that came on 10 May 1940, the morning after this article appeared in print.

set down on a moss-covered expanse free of snow. Then it was on to the so-called Base Two with a Norwegian bearer column. Once up on the mountain, we were surprised and not exactly pleased to learn that we still had farther to go, that we were supposed to occupy Hill 698 with out trench mortar train. The Swedish border ran along 150 yards from our new position. So, we had to take charge of the right flank of the German front at Narvik.

Look Out for Parachutists and Transport Planes

Thursday 9 May 1940, Paris
Le Figaro reported from Paris:

The role of the German Luftwaffe in reinforcing and supplying their combat forces in Norway, has surpassed the boldest expectations.

Thus it has proved possible to supply large units with daily arms and provisions by air. These operations were greatly facilitated by the use of Danish departure bases, and the previous occupation of Norwegian landing fields. So we are justified in fearing, like the Dutch, that small groups of daring parachutists will try to seize landing fields during the night, and to sow disarray behind the lines, in the countryside or small isolated towns, acting in consort with troops subsequently dropped by transport plane.

To obviate this danger, one cannot stress too strongly that every parachutist and every transport plane that lands at night in isolated spots, should be considered suspect, regardless of what uniform or costume is worn by the occupants.

LE FIGARO. — JEUDI 9 MAI 1940

Attention aux parachutistes et aux avions de transport

Le rôle joué par l'aviation allemande en Norvège pour renforcer les effectifs ennemis et les ravitailler a dépassé les résultats que les esprits les plus audacieux auraient osé imaginer.

Des effectifs importants ont pu être ainsi transportés quotidiennement avec armes et bagages. Ces opérations étaient d'ailleurs facilitées grandement non seulement par l'utilisation des bases de départ danoises, mais par la mainmise préalable sur les terrains d'atterrissage norvégiens.

On peut donc redouter, ainsi que la crainte s'en manifeste en Hollande, que de petits groupes de hardis parachutistes s'efforcent de s'emparer de nuit de terrains d'atterrissage et ne soient suivis, peu d'instant plus tard, de gros avions de transport débarquant au sol des troupes en arrière des lignes, voire même dans des campagnes ou petites villes isolées pour y jeter la panique.

Pour obvier à ce danger toujours possible, on ne saurait trop recommander de considérer comme suspect, *a priori*, tout parachutiste ou tout avion de transport venant au sol de nuit ou dans des lieux isolés, *quelque soit l'uniforme ou le costume* revêtu par les occupants.

En semblable circonstance, prévenir immédiatement l'autorité militaire la plus proche (commandant de cantonnement, gendarmerie, etc.) est un devoir évident : mais il faut, en dépit de toutes protestations possibles, s'opposer à l'éloignement des visiteurs inconnus, en n'hésitant pas à employer s'il le faut la force en cas de rébellion de leur part. S'il s'agit véritablement d'aviateurs français ou alliés, ils seront les premiers à reconnaître la nécessité de ces mesures de sécurité. — G.

In such cases, the first duty of a citizen is immediately to notify the nearest military authority (the local army post, the gendarmerie). Moreover, the unknown persons must be prevented from leaving the landing place despite any protests they may make, and one must not hesitate to use force if they offer resistance. If they are genuine French or Allied aviators, they will be the first to understand the necessity of such security measures.

Friday 10 May 1940
The *Wehrmacht High Command* announced:

At 5:30 A.M. today, German troops crossed the borders of Holland, Luxembourg and Belgium. Enemy resistance near the border was broken everywhere by vigorous action, often with the closest cooperation of the Luftwaffe.

10 May 1940, Brussels
The French *Havas News Agency* reported:

German troops have crossed the border into Belgium. Battles are being fought along the Belgian-German border. Evers Airfield at Brussels has been bombed by the Germans. Belgium has asked France and England for help.

10 May 1940
Dutch Army Headquarters announced:

German troops began to march into Holland at 3:00 A.M. Assaults have been launched against several airfields. Our army and antiaircraft defenses are ready for action. Flooding to obstruct the German advance, is proceeding according to schedule. At least 6 German aircraft have been shot down so far.

10 May 1940, Hilversum (Holland)
The French *Havas News Agency* reported:

Dutch radio has made an appeal to the population, in which it was reported that German parachutists have landed in the Netherlands, some of them wearing Allied and Dutch uniforms. The Dutch people were urged to exercise extreme caution and vigilance.

Dawn Takeoff

The Nazi newspaper *Völkischer Beobachter* carried this descriptive account in May 1940:

Our mission is to attack and destroy flak [antiaircraft] positions at airfields in the zone of Rotterdam, The Hague and Delft. A pitch-black night swallows all the preparations.

Takeoff has been ordered for 4:30 A.M. We fly into the morning dusk of May 10. First Lieutenant Beermann's flight is ahead of me. We fly in tight formation. Slowly we ascend to our attack altitude. The sky is getting lighter minute by minute.

Before us and to one side we recognize "our" airfield. The muzzle flashes of the flak batteries blaze incessantly all around us.

We must destroy them so as to safeguard the operation of our paratroopers. I can already see the first bombs hit along the southern edge of the airfield.

I head into a dive. The target flashes up to meet me. The farmstead grows visibly in my cross spider lens. I release the bombs. At the same time, gunbursts from our heavy arms hail onto the flak position from the lowest altitude. Our aerial gunner reports: "Hurrah! Direct hit! Direct hit!"

Taking Waalhaven

Descriptive account of a German paratroop landing in Holland, from the *Völkischer Beobachter,* May 1940:

My battalion had the duty to take the Rotterdam landing field of Waalhaven and to secure it for the airborne troops to follow.

Wherever you look, around and above us, fly the transport planes carrying paratroops. The sun climbs above the horizon behind us and casts a warm glow on the men in the plane behind me. A short way from Waalhaven Airfield, gunfire starts crackling uncomfortably close to us. Despite the roar of the engines, we can hear the explosions from the very vigorous flak defense. Muzzle flashes light up all over the ground and there is a loud report in our aircraft.

The jump signal at last. In a flash we are all out of the plane and making a pike dive.

It is clear to see that the edge of the airfield is the base of the defense. The Dutch appear to have committed very strong forces to secure their most important airfield.

Running toward the field, we already hear vigorous machine gun fire mixed with the lashing wheeze of hand grenades; there is a clanging sound, and then it is German hand grenades that we hear.

The Dutch have fought bravely, harder then we expected of a people who have not waged war for a hundred years.

I realize that I needed less time than was allotted me to beat down the airfield's defenses. It is still early morning, so why not stir myself to find a cup of coffee? The coffee here in Holland is said to be especially good. At that very moment one of my men runs up and reports: "Captain, the command post has been set up and there's coffee on the table!" I go with him into the office at the edge of the field and cannot help laughing. There it is, a table set with a sumptuous breakfast. The radio is running: the mayor of Amsterdam is just now making an inflammatory speech. All I have to do is take a seat. "Boys, how did you conjure all that up so fast?" "It wasn't us, Herr Captain, it was the Dutch who got it ready!" The beautiful breakfast is interrupted by the roar of many engines. The airborne troops! I hurry out onto the field just in time to see the first plane glide in. At one window I recognize First Lieutenant von Choltitz, who waves at me with a beaming face. Only yesterday he shook his finger at me and said: "Hey guys, just you be sure you're there when I land!"

Above: German paratroops are dropped at Narvik, Norway, where they will bring aid to the hard-pressed mountain infantry under Maj. Gen. Dietl.

Right: The German medium bomber Junkers Ju 88, designed in 1935, was manufactured in large numbers. About 15,000 Ju 88s were built to serve as bombers, dive bombers, mine-laying, torpedo-carrying and photo-reconnaissance aircraft, as well as day and night fighters.

Saturday 11 May 1940

The *Wehrmacht High Command* announced:

After crossing the borders of Holland, Belgium and Luxembourg, the German West Army has repulsed the enemy border troops everywhere in Holland and Belgium and, despite the [enemy's] destruction of countless bridges, and despite obstructions of every kind, is on the offensive and advancing rapidly. Paratroops and airborne troops have landed and are about to carry out their security missions. Luftwaffe units, flying in relays, are supporting the advance of the Army by bombing fortified installations and field fortifications, march columns and troop camps, and by damaging or destroying roads, railway lines and bridges. Their sweeping reconnaissance has brought clear information about enemy army movements. Furthermore, on May 10, massed forces of the German Luftwaffe led the first grand assault on the root of the enemy air force in France, Belgium and Holland. Seventy-

two airfields were attacked, 300–400 enemy aircraft destroyed on the ground, large numbers of airfield installations and hangars destroyed by fire and explosions.

11 May 1940
The *German News Bureau* (DNB) reported:

Yesterday 3 enemy bombers attacked the open city of Freiburg-im-Breisgau, which is located completely outside our own field of operations and contains no military installations. From now on, any planned enemy bomb assault on the German population will be answered by five times the number of German aircraft bombing an English or French city.

11 May 1940, London

The British *Air Ministry* announced that the German report of Allied planes bombing the open city of Freiburg, was a pure fabrication.

The morning of 11 May 1940
The *French Army Report* stated:

During the night we continued our movements to Belgium. Despite a vigorous assault, the enemy was not able to continue his advance in the south of the Grand Duchy of Luxembourg. Nothing noteworthy occurred in Lorraine and Alsace.

On Friday, the German Luftwaffe bombardment of French territory claimed countless victims among the civilian population. The French High Command regrets having to report that we have more than 100 dead and wounded to mourn, including (especially) women and children.

Secret Weapon?

Sunday 12 May 1940, Stockholm
The Swedish newspaper *Svenska Dagbladet* reported:

A gigantic concentration of all the German armed forces has moved against Belgium and Holland, and is claimed to have used its secret weapon for the first time. This was confirmed tonight in a report by the German Wehrmacht High Command, which claims that the strongest fort held by the defensive lines at Liège (Belgium), has been seized with the aid of a new assault weapon. Strict silence is being maintained about the nature and use of the new weapon, which was strong enough to compel turnover of the fort with its 1,000-man garrison. However, the sparse reports of the operation seem to indicate that the Luftwaffe must have formed the backbone of the assault.

According to the report of the German Wehrmacht High Command (the OKW), German troops under Captain Koch landed by plane and, in a surprise raid, seized two bridges over the King Albert Canal, where they immediately built bridgeheads. The 1,000 Belgians were then encircled inside the fortress. Second Lt. Witzig is said thereupon to have directed his weapon against the center of the fortress, and the colossal blow he struck proved successful. The operation caused immense astonishment [inside the fort]; whereupon the 1,000 Belgians and their commandant were captured, despite the most violent resistance, when German Army units advancing from the north joined up with Second Lt. Witzig's detachment. Apart from this rather mysterious description, no further details are available about how the blow was executed.

12 May 1940
The *Wehrmacht High Command* announced:

On May 11 the German Luftwaffe continued the grand assault begun the day before, against the enemy air forces in France, Belgium and Holland. A multitude of airfields were attacked again and in the attacks, hangars were set afire, repair hangars destroyed, and fuel tank and ammunition depots blown up. At Vraux airfield alone 30 aircraft were successfully destroyed, at Orléans airfield 36. Fifty-two aircraft were shot down in aerial combat, 12 by flak artillery. We can accept with certainty that yesterday and the day before, a total of 300 aircraft fell victim to our offensive and to our air defense. Effective aerial raids have been made on troop assemblies and transport trains.

12 May 1940, London
The British *Air Ministry* announced:

On Saturday afternoon, the German troops advancing from the Rhine to the Meuse (Maas) were bombed again by British aircraft, as were the roads leading to Maastricht. Armored cars and troop transport vehicles were attacked and partly destroyed several miles southwest of the town, on the roads leading to Tongres.

12 May 1940, The Hague
The *Dutch General Staff* reported:

All Dutch airfields are now back in our hands. In the early hours of Saturday morning, our troops attacked the airfield at Rotterdam—the only field still occupied by the Germans—following an assault by the Koninklijke Luchtmacht (Dutch Royal Air Force). Two powerful bomber groups dropped a large number of high-explosive bombs on the air-

Right: A Fairey Fox VI of l'Aéronautique Militaire Belge, the Belgian Air Force. Some 200 of these biplanes, used as reconnaissance aircraft and light bombers, were manufactured under license in Belgium. With its 220 mph velocity and its two machine guns, it was no match for the German fighter planes.

Below left: May 1940, a French airfield after seizure by German troops. A German Me 109 is approaching for a landing. The French Morane-Saulnier 406s (of which 1,037 were built) have been destroyed on the ground. Moranes made up the bulk of the French fighter force.

field, where many German aircraft were stationed. Extensive damage was inflicted and a number of German planes caught fire. Immediately after the assault, our infantry recaptured the airfield after a violent battle costing heavy casualties. At the same time, the German paratroops who had possession of the Meuse bridge were completely encircled. The fighting was extremely bitter on both sides.

A sizeable number of German troops landed in Rotterdam harbor by seaplane and came onto land in rubber dinghies, armed with light machine guns. It proved extremely difficult to fight off these landing troops, and they were overcome only by calling in stronger forces.

On Friday the Germans conquered and lost the airfield in The Hague three times over. Not until night was it possible to destroy the German paratroops, all of whom without exception wore Dutch, British, Belgian and French uniforms.

An extraordinary achievement was that of a Dutch destroyer that sailed right up to Rozenburg Island despite a mine barrier, and opened fire on the German aircraft and crews who had landed there. The paratroops were completely wiped out in an hour and a half of artillery fire. All the aircraft were badly damaged by the gunfire and many were aflame.

12 May 1940, Brussels
The *Belgian Army* reported at Sunday noon:

Our troops are vigorously resisting the intruders, and tenaciously defending the positions assigned them in our plan of operation. The enemy forces who penetrated our fortified installations, have made no particular progress. Paratroops have been wiped out at various points. Large numbers of enemy aircraft have been shot down.

Secret Report of the *SS Secret Service*
on German internal affairs, No. 87 of
Tuesday 14 May 1940 (extract):

I. General comments: The sudden German entry into Belgium and Holland came as a surprise to the [German] population . . . Their initial enthusiasm changed to a deep solemnity after public announcement of the Führer's appeal to the soldiers of the West Army . . . The rapid seizure of the strong Belgian fort of Eben Emael, and the capture of its garrison, came as a particularly happy surprise. The bombing assaults on the open cities of the Ruhr district, and on Freiburg above all, have caused universal outrage, and in the latter case have aroused a hatred of France. There is a firm expectation that henceforth, any such action will immediately receive the compensation it deserves.

14 May 1940
The *Wehrmacht High Command* announced:
Under the overwhelming impact of German dive bomber attacks, and of the impending tank assault on the city, Rotterdam has surrendered and thus saved itself from destruction.

Saturday 18 May 1940
The *Wehrmacht High Command* announced:
Enemy air assaults have been aimed at various cities along the North German coast, especially Hamburg and Bremen, and at cities in West Germany. As in all previous instances, the attacks were made indiscriminately on nonmilitary targets, except for one military barracks. The German Wehrmacht High Command makes this point expressly, in the light of the consequences that are to follow.

Sunday 19 May 1940
The *Wehrmacht High Command* announced:
The Luftwaffe has effectively supported the Army advance. Its main stress has continued to be on the enemy's rear communications, traffic installations and paths of retreat. Bombs dropped on several airfields destroyed hangars, repair sheds and aircraft on the ground.

Tuesday 21 May 1940
The *Wehrmacht High Command* announced:
The greatest offensive operation ever to take place in the West, is achieving its first strategic success following upon a series of major individual tactical successes. The French Ninth Army on the Meuse between Namur and Sedan, whose duty it was to establish and maintain communication between the powerful enemy strategic group in Belgium, and the Maginot Line south of Sedan, has been smashed and is breaking up. The Luftwaffe has played an outstanding role in this victory march of the German Army. By its complete command of the air, its destruction of river crossings and transport installations, and its assaults on march and transport columns, it has hastened the dissolution of the French Ninth Army and nipped in the bud all attempts made so far to threaten the flanks of our breakthrough.

10 May 1940 near Egmond, Holland: A scantily camouflaged twin-fuselage Fokker G.IA bomber-interceptor of the Dutch Air Force, the Koninklijke Luchtmacht.

Wednesday 29 May 1940
The *Wehrmacht High Command* announced:

On May 28, enemy air losses totalled 24 aircraft, 16 of which were shot down in aerial combat, 8 by flak. Three German aircraft are missing. [German air ace] Captain Mölders has won his twentieth air victory.

Thursday 30 May 1940
The *Wehrmacht High Command* announced:

On the afternoon and evening of May 29, strong formations from two air corps under the command of Generals Grauert and von Richtofen, attacked British war and transport vessels in the port and sea territory of Dunkirk and Ostend, as they were trying to evacuate the remains of the British Expeditionary Force.

Operation over Dunkirk

The German newspaper *Völkischer Beobachter* carried the following descriptive account in June 1940:

Our squadrons fly toward the enemy. Along a wide circumference, the wrecks of sunk and sinking vessels stretch their masts and superstructures into the dismal sky: destroyers, freighters, troop transport vessels, large, small and tiny cutters, dinghies and boats – all random and confused like the [Allied] collapse itself.

The last free strip of coast between the pincers of the encircling German troops, has grown narrower and narrower. No wonder that the enemy antiaircraft batteries have piled up once more in the crowded space. We are densely surrounded by the black, white, sulfur-yellow-green flak missiles. Suddenly two, three, four British fighter planes dash through the dense barricades of their own flak like powerful soaring birds of prey. Banking steeply, they search for their victims. We see clearly the streamlined shapes and identifying marks of the yellow-brown Spitfires. They race past swift as an arrow. Apparently the dense fire of their own flak is making an impression on them. Skillfully and swiftly our pilot banks into the drifting clouds. Now our own fighters will face them.

Saturday 1 June 1940, Paris
This morning the French Army reported:

The French and British land, sea and air forces at Dunkirk are continuing, in full accord, their stubborn fight against the impressing German troops, and at the same time are trying to secure the evacuation.

Dunkirk: German Me 110 "destroyers" fighter bombers are shown attacking the remains of the British Expeditionary Force. (A Nazi propaganda drawing by Theo Matejko)

Grave Infringements of Swiss Air Space

1 June 1940, Bern
The *Swiss Army Staff* reported:

This afternoon in the Jura mountains, Swiss sovereign territory was violated by foreign aircraft. The Swiss Alarm Patrol immediately took up pursuit, engaged in aerial combat with a German bomber and shot down the aircraft near Lignières (Ger. *Tassenberg*). One hour later another Swiss fighter plane engaged in aerial combat with a second German aircraft over the Freiberg region (Fr. *Franches-Montagnes*). The burning German plane crashed onto French territory near Oltingen, on the other side of the Swiss border.

1 June 1940, London
This morning the *BBC* reported:

The Germans have suffered heavy losses near Abbéville. Several hundred German soldiers have been taken prisoner, and the Germans left behind considerable war material. The Allies have reconquered the area around Abbéville and crossed the Somme at one point. The disembarkation of British and French troops is continuing in English seaports. The majority of contingents of the northern Allied armies have been successfully transported to England. The troops who have stayed behind, are fighting on with undiminished courage.

Sunday 2 June 1940, London
The *British Air Ministry* announced:

During June 1 the RAF supported the retreat operations of the British Expeditionary Force, by attacking bridges, canals, troop columns and rail junctions. Forty German aircraft have already been shot down in the Dunkirk area. Thirteen British planes are missing. For the past week our coastal wings have carried on uninterrupted patrol flights to secure the evacuation of Allied troops. Large numbers of German aircraft were shot down in the numerous aerial combats fought during supervision of the transport ships on their journey to England.

Tuesday 4 June 1940, London
The London *Daily Telegraph* reported:

Measures to oppose the expected air invasion of England, are virtually completed. These include digging trenches through park grounds, sports palaces and fields, and the erection of road barricades. Furthermore, armed patrols have been organized and all road signs and place designations removed.

4 June 1940, London
The *Reuters News Agency* reported:

Today the regular twice-weekly London-Bordeaux-Lisbon air service was resumed. This line has restored air communication between England and America, because the "American Clipper" regularly flies into Lisbon.

Daily Keynote from the Reich Press Chief
[Otto Dietrich]
4 June 1940:

The German bomb assault on Paris must be depicted as a military operation that does not violate international law, and the description of its effects must be disseminated as widely as possible via the translating and interpreting service, especially in broadcasts to England and France.

Shot Down after 25 Victories

Wednesday 5 June 1940
Renowned German air ace *Werner Mölders* gave the following descriptive account in the German newspaper *Der Adler:*

Takeoff at 5:15 P.M., once again with 8 Squadron. We fly to Amiens. Our time in the air is almost up. There are aircraft overhead, we cannot make out who they are, we climb to nearly 23,000 feet. German Me's [fighter planes]! So we descend a bit lower again and gradually head off home. Suddenly we run into six Moranes [French fighters]. I set myself to attack with a rear broadside. In the middle of my approach I recognize two stranger squadrons of Me's who are engaging the same enemy from the rear and above. They were in position first, so I pull back a little and watch what happens. There is the usual dogfight while several Moranes bravely stand their ground and fight. A burning Me crashes to earth, the pilot is hanging from a parachute. I watch the fight for a while and then attack a Morane that keeps making banking turns while three Messerschmitts fire at it in vain. Briefly I get my enemy in my sights. He swings away at once, but still he has not had enough. Suddenly he pulls up underneath me; I lose him under my wing. There he is again down below, behind me and off to the side. Damn it – he's still shooting too, although very wide to be sure.

I bank briefly, then pull sharply into the sun. My enemy must have lost me, for he turns in the opposite direction and disappears deep into the south.

Down below me, two Me's are still grappling with a last Morane. I observe the fighting, which turns into a low-level flight in which the Morane can evade effective fire by continual banking. A backward look, a glance above and behind me: the sky is still full of banking Me's. I am about 2,600 feet up. Then suddenly there is a bang and flash in my cockpit so that I black out. The throttle is shot to pieces, the control stick plunges forward, we're headed straight down. Get out now, otherwise you've had it.

I grasp the airdrop lever, the cockpit sails off, then my brave bird rears up once more and gives me a last opportunity to unfasten the strap and rise out of my seat.

Me 109 fighter planes of the Swiss Air Force. Switzerland used these planes to defend its neutral sovereign territory. During the war they shot down a number of German and Allied planes.

Free – pull the rip cord, suddenly I find it has torn off in my hand – an uncanny shock goes through me – I reach up – but – the parachute has opened . . . !

Now everything is quiet and peaceful. I see my pilotless plane once again, its left wing gaping open. Just above the ground it rears up one more time as if it found it hard to believe that now, after winning twenty-five victories, it too has been vanquished; then it hits the ground vertically and burns up. I hang peacefully from my parachute. It carries me ever so gently to the ground, and the ground is still inside France: 36 miles behind the front, west of Compiègne.

I draw my pistol and release the safety catch, then stick it into my trouser pocket. Down below me two farmers pull their horses together and run off. A brief look at the landscape reveals a small patch of woods, otherwise nothing but meadows. Suddenly the ground rises up swiftly, I get into a squat position – the impact is comparatively soft. I free myself from the parachute at once and run toward the wood. Frenchmen come running from the side. At the edge of the wood a shot whistles past my head. I throw away my fur jacket and run to the other end of the thicket, arriving out of breath. There is no point in staying here because they will immediately make a systematic search of the wood. At the far edge, I stop and test the wind for a minute; I see soldiers and farmers running toward the thicket from both sides. In front of me stretches a large field of lupines. I crawl into it on my belly, trying to get as far as I can from my drop point. Suddenly I hear an explosion nearby and see a thick cloud of blue smoke rise into the air. My plane, which had already caught fire on impact, has now exploded to bits.

I belly along on my elbows and knees, sounding the landscape now and then. I am able to work my way along this way, unseen, for about an hour. But then suddenly I see that this field too is being searched and men are coming toward me from the front. I lie completely flat on the field. A farmer goes past 10 yards to my left. I believe the danger is already past, when someone calls to me from behind. Done for!

I stand up very quietly and now for the first time I see soldiers and farmers searching the whole area. As I stand up, some maddened French infantryman sends another shot past my nose without hitting me. So, hands up: Captured!

Wednesday 12 June 1940, Paris
The French *Havas News Agency* reported on the military situation:

The enemy is continuing his grand efforts to force a swift decision. The German Luftwaffe has

Second Lieutenant Pomier-Layragues, the French fighter pilot who shot down German flying ace Werner Mölders.

bombed French airfields and connections leading to Paris. French aircraft have bombed various German industrial cities and also took part in the battles in France.

Paris in Sight

The German newspaper *Völkischer Beobachter* carried this descriptive account in June 1940:

"Still six minutes yet; five; four minutes," the aerial observers said over the on-board intercom. They all knew the aerial photographs of the targets down to the last detail; the hangars, the fuel tank installations, the taxi strip of Le Bourget airport where all hell was due to break loose in a few minutes' time. There it lay before us, clearly visible through the drifting cloud cover: Paris. Never will we forget the moment when the bombs left our bays and whistled down onto the square. Then we heard a crashing sound down below, where the flights that came after us had hit their targets. Impact after impact, flash after flash, one explosive cone after another over the whole expanse of the air base – an overpowering picture of the fearful effects of mass bombing. The conflagration from a large fuel tank blazed brightly. Our wing commander had finished that off personally, and now every corner of Le Bourget was ablaze. Flights of enemy Morane aircraft appeared and chased along beneath us like dangerous hornets. The radiant city of Paris made an unreal contrast to these images of serial combat. Its battlements and towers, the bright ribbon of the Seine, the projecting Eiffel Tower, the Champs-Elysées, the straight-as-a-die avenues and the traffic star around the Arc de Triomphe, shone, glittered and glistened. But we knew that today the splendor of Paris was deceptive and that down below, the panicked and horrified populace were listening inside the cellars and air raid shelters to the thundering blows of our bombs.

The Situation in East Africa

Friday 14 June 1940, Berbera (British Somaliland)
The *Reuters News Agency* reported:

On Friday afternoon the seaport town of Berbera in the Gulf of Aden was bombed by Italian aircraft. Little damage occurred.

The War in the Mediterranean

14 June 1940, Cairo
The *British Middle East Air Force in Egypt* announced:

A single aircraft flew several times over Malta releasing bombs. A number of buildings were damaged, two British soldiers were killed and one wounded. In addition the Italians have made aerial raids on two small towns in the Sudan, inflicting little damage.

Saturday 22 June 1940, Rome
The *Italian High Command* announced:

The Italian navy and air force have stepped up

their activities in the Mediterranean. Powerful air attacks have been made on Marsa Matruh in North Africa. The enemy bombed the hospital and a military hospital in Tobruk. One English airplane was shot down. In East Africa a large number of operations have been undertaken against enemy bases in the Sudan and in Kenya. An English airplane was shot down during an enemy attack over Dire Dawa.

Sunday 23 June 1940, Rome
The *Italian High Command* announced:

The Regia Aeronautica (Italian Air Force) has continued its activity in the Mediterranean. It has successfully bombed the naval base at Alexandria, the present site of the British fleet. Italian aircraft have bombed Bizerta (Tunisia) and enemy vehicles in the eastern Mediterranean. One Italian aircraft has not returned. Our operations in North Africa have proved successful. Our aircraft took vigorous measures against armored cars. One four-engined British aircraft was shot down. The enemy bombed the city of Trapani, but inflicted damage only on civilian dwellings. There were 20 dead and 38 wounded.

23 June 1940, Cairo
The *British Middle East Air Force in Egypt* announced:

During the night of Friday to Saturday, three Italian aircraft flying over Alexandria and its environs, dropped 20 bombs at random on the city, seaport and surrounding villages; additional bombs fell into the sea.

Strategy and Tactics

January to June 1940

Bad weather all across Europe paralyzed flying activity for the first week of January. Yet it was during this same week that the Finnish Air Force achieved a record for the number of enemy planes shot down. On 6 January 1940 at 12:03 P.M., Captain Jorma Sarvanto came upon a formation of 7 Ilyushin DB-3 Soviet bombers. In the next four minutes he shot down 6 of them: 1 bomber every 40 seconds. Another Finnish pilot finished off the last of the 7 bombers.

Stalin, alarmed by the increasing losses in his air force, dispatched another 600 recently-designed aircraft to the Finnish front. Slowly reinforcements also began to arrive for the small Finnish flytroop. The first to come were 33 Gloster Gladiator fighters, 12 Hurricanes, 17 Lysanders and 24 Blenheim bombers, all from Britain; after that, 76 Morane-Saulnier and Koolhoven F.K. fighter planes arrived from France. Italy sent 17 Fiat fighters, Sweden 12 Gloster Gladiators, and the USA 44 Brewsters, of which however only 5 reached Finland in time. Even the Union of South Africa sent the valiant Finns a gift of 25 Gloster Gladiators. Pilots and ground personnel from a number of countries also volunteered to assist them.

Meanwhile the Soviet Union had increased its air force to around 2,000 machines.

On 10 January 1940, a German Messerschmitt Me 108 courier aircraft deviated from its heading due to bad weather while carrying important deployment documents, and had to make an emergency landing at Mechelen, Belgium. This loss, together with the cold, extremely snowy winter, forced the Germans to postpone their western offensive until the spring.

For a long time the German Reich had been receiving large shipments of raw materials—above all, of strategically important oil—from Moscow. This dismayed the governments in London and Paris, who realized all too well that these materials gave Hitler the ability to launch his Luftwaffe and motorized tank units in the West.

Italian Savoia-Marchetti 81 Pipistrello (Bat) bombers over Albania. Originally they were passenger aircraft, but in their later military version they took part in the Ethiopian Campaign and in the Spanish Civil War.

On Friday 19 January 1940, French premier Daladier asked General Gamelin, the Supreme Commander of the Allied Armed Forces in France, and Admiral Darlan, the Commander in Chief of the French naval fleet, to "work out a memorandum on a possible intervention to destroy the Russian oilfields."

On February 1 the Soviet armies began their attack on the Mannerheim Line [Finnish fortifications] on the Karelian Isthmus [the land bridge between Russia and Finland].

The failure of Soviet General Timoshenko's attempt to encircle Lake Ladoga (Finland) from the northeast, did not prevent him from opening his grand offensive on both sides of the railway line from Leningrad to Viipuri (Vyborg). That day paratroops were deployed for the first time in the air war. During the Soviet Army's attack on Summa, the weakest point along the Mannerheim Line, Soviet paratroops, formed into small combat groups, dropped behind the lines of the Finnish Army.

However, this operation, though it involved units of up to battalion strength, turned out to be a complete fiasco. The Finns were on guard both at the front and behind the lines. They shot some of the parachutists while they were still in descent, and captured the others immediately after landing.

On 4 February 1940, three days after the battle for Summa began, the Soviet offensive broke down under heavy losses.

A state of truce still reigned along the 250-mile-long front between Basle and Luxembourg; the air offensives expected by both sides, failed to materialize. The adversaries' aerial operations were limited to reconnaissance flights that led to isolated fighter plane clashes, and long-range reconnaissance missions conducted at very high altitudes. The Luftwaffe made occasional raids on shipping targets.

No one on the French general staff was thinking in terms of an offensive. General Gamelin's view was: "Whoever attacks, will lose."

In autumn of 1939, the French had formed two air forces and deployed them over northern and western France; but in February 1940 they were dissolved again and most aircraft, including all reconnaissance units, the bulk of the fighter planes and parts of the bomber groups, were placed under the command of the large army units. This fragmentation of the French Armée de l'Air and the attachment of its parts to individual armies, later proved a handicap to the French High Command when they needed to deploy aircraft to specific threatened sectors.

While German propaganda squadrons were pouring air leaflets onto French military positions and assuring the French by loudspeaker of their readiness for peace, the Germans were rigorously training their paratroops, airborne troops and assault engineers how to wage war against fortresses and other targets.

On 22 February 1940, General Gamelin submitted the report that Premier Daladier had commissioned him to make one month before. In his view (he said), "an operation against the Russian oil industry in the Caucasus would make it possible to strike a heavy, if not decisive blow against the military and economic organization of the Soviet Union." In a few months the Soviet Union might even get into such difficulties "that it would risk total collapse." Gamelin pointed out that of the three vulnerable

Soviet oil-producing localities, Batum and especially Baku – "by far the most important petroleum center in the Caucasus" – would be the recommended target of an attack.

On Monday 11 March 1940, an RAF Blenheim bomber that was operating solo, successfully attacked German U-boat U 31 under Lieutenant Habekost on the Schilling Roads (Schillig-Reede straits) at Wilhelmshaven. This was the first time an aircraft sank a U-boat in World War II.

12 March 1940: The Soviet-Finnish Peace Treaty of Moscow, which came as a surprise to the Allies, ended Finland's unequal struggle. Among other things, Finland had to cede important parts of Karelia to the Soviet Union.

The balance sheet of the Winter War in the air: Finnish fliers shot down 240 Soviet planes. Total Soviet losses, including aircraft destroyed by antiaircraft fire, were 684. Thirty-one Finnish Fokker D-XXI fighter planes alone, managed to destroy 120 Soviet bombers while suffering casualties of only 12 fighters and 8 pilots. Finland lost a total of 67 aircraft, 42 of them in aerial combat.

One day history may clear up the question of whether the Soviet Union's remarkably swift conclusion of peace with Finland, resulted from the threat looming to Soviet oil fields in the Caucasus. By the beginning of March 1940 at the latest, Stalin must have learned of the Allies' intentions to attack the oil fields in Baku. We know this because on

Above: Lake Saimaa (Finland), February 1940: Finnish fighter planes have forced an undamaged Soviet bomber to land on the frozen lake, and are readying it for combat.

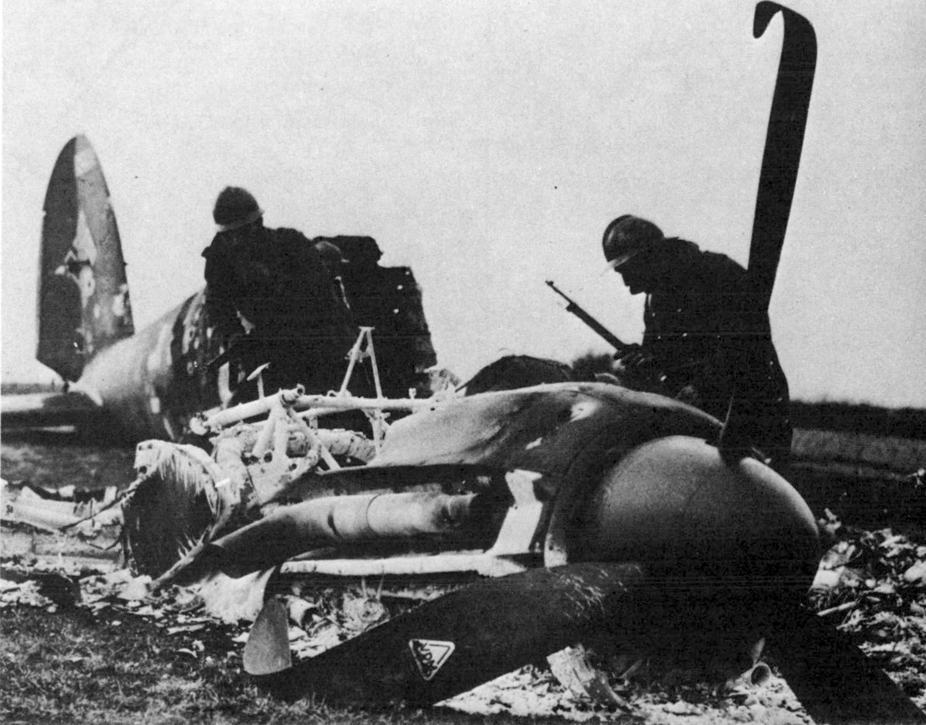

Right: March 1940, a German He 111 shot down in the French Fourth Army Zone at Châlons. During the "sitting war" German bombers were rarely deployed over France.

Above: Preparations for the British aerial reconnaissance mission over Baku. Sidney Cotton (left) is seen talking with Air Marshal Sir Arthur Barratt, the commander of the British aerial forces in France.

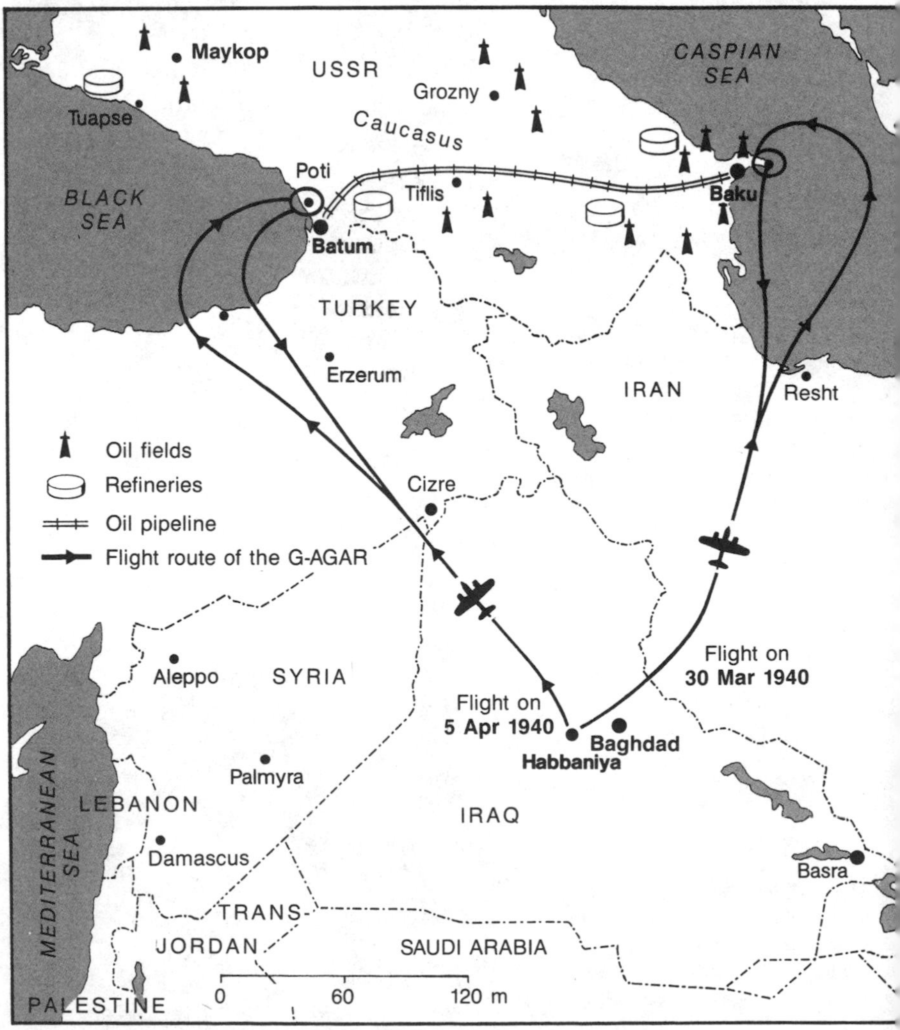

March 14 the French government learned from Ankara that the Soviets had commissioned American experts to assess "whether and how a fire in the Baku oil fields, arising from a bomb attack, could be combatted successfully." Allegedly the US experts replied that given the output of the oil fields so far, the ground must be so saturated with oil that a blaze would be bound to spread instantly to the entire neighboring region; it would be months before the fire could be put out, and years before oil production could be resumed.

At that same time, foreign embassies in Moscow reported that at the beginning of March 1940, the Soviet High Command transferred troops into the Caucasus. On 6 March 1940, Voroshilov, the People's Commissar for Defense, paid an ostentatious visit to the Caspian Sea area.

On 16 March 1940, 15 Junkers Ju 88 German bombers of 1st Group, 30th Bomber Wing [1st *Gruppe* of *Kampfgeschwader* 30], raided the British

Right: British reconnaissance flights over the Soviet oil fields in Spring 1940.

naval base at Scapa Flow, Scotland, and British civilians suffered casualties for the first time.

On 20 March 1940 the Allied air force staffs met in Aleppo, Syria to agree on their plans to launch a bombing raid on the Soviet oil fields.

When Allied strategists had settled on their plans for the attack, the British secret service called in its best aerial reconnaissance assistant for aid. Sidney Cotton, working in collaboration with F. W. Winterbotham, the Chief of MI 6, the Air Department of the Secret Intelligence Service, was asked to draw up a plan for reconnoitering the Caucasus oil fields.

On the morning of March 23, the Lockheed 12 A civil aircraft, registration code G-AGAR, left Heston airfield on a southeast heading. At the controls was Hugh MacPhail, Cotton's personal assistant. Several high-powered cameras had been built into the fuselage. After intermediate landings on Malta and in Cairo, the Lockheed reached the RAF base of Habbaniya, near Baghdad. Its identifying marks were carefully painted over and the hidden cameras were inspected.

On Saturday 30 March, shortly before sunrise, MacPhail took off with his co-pilot, Flying Officer Burton, and two RAF photographers who were detailed to take additional photographs of the target zone using hand cameras. They flew over the Iranian plateau and come out over the Caspian Sea near Resht. After they had been flying for an hour, the outlines of the Baku Peninsula, a vast oil-rich industrial area, appeared far below them wreathed in clouds of smoke. For an entire hour MacPhail circled the radiant sky at an altitude of almost 23,000 feet (7,000 meters), above the tangle of drilling derricks, oil tanks and refineries that stretched from one horizon to the other. The Lockheed flew over the Soviet oil supply center six times, unmolested either by fighter planes or antiaircraft artillery, and took dozens of photographs. That afternoon they were back in Habbaniya. They had been aloft for almost ten hours.

Six days later, on Friday 5 April, MacPhail and Burton flew their second reconnaissance mission. This time the target was Batum, the most important Soviet oil seaport on the Black Sea and the terminal point of the Baku pipeline. They flew across Turkey and approached Batum at a high altitude from the Black Sea. They had just finished their photographs and were still circling over the endless rows of oil refineries, when suddenly antiaircraft shells exploded all around them. MacPhail pulled up the aircraft and was able to escape under the protective cloud cover.

MacPhail's Lockheed 12 A shortly after takeoff from Habbaniya on its flight over the Soviet oil fields at Baku. The plane had extremely powerful engines and thus could evade the antiquated Soviet fighters.

As soon as MacPhail got home, his aerial photographs were sent at top speed to Cotton's headquarters at Wembley. By the following day the photos and accompanying evaluations were already on the desks of the British and French general staffs.

The Allied generals decided to concentrate on the refineries and oil tanks. The French Armée de l'Air was supposed to raid Batum, and the RAF to destroy the installations in Baku and Grozny. They calculated that it would be possible to destroy approximately one third of their targets in the first six days.

Allied plans provided for the deployment of 9 bomber squadrons to level 122 petroleum refineries (67 in Baku, 43 in Grozny and 12 in Batum) within a period of from 10 to 45 days. Two French squadrons of Farman 221s, 4 French squadrons of Glenn Martins, and 3 British squadrons of Wellingtons—a total of 117 bombers—stood available for the operation.

The plan was for the Armée de l'Air to take off from its main base at Cizre (Turkey) and the RAF from Mosul (Iraq). Due to the weight of their built-in auxiliary fuel tanks, the Allied aircraft could carry a total of only 70 metric tons of bombs on each flight. The RAF anticipated losses of 20 percent; the French on the other hand hoped to get away unscathed.

The two partners were united in their view that the planned operation would not only lead inevitably "to a total collapse of the USSR's war capability," but could even "decide the entire course of the war." Not even Douhet could have dreamed of such a result, and the touching naiveté of Allied hopes surpassed the optimism even of a Hitler.

On Saturday 6 April 1940, British Bomber Command halted its leaflet-drop operations over Germany which had released a total of 65 million leaflets since 4 September 1939.

At 5:00 A.M. on 9 April 1940, "Operation Weserübung" began: the German troop occupation of Denmark and Norway. Denmark was overrun in a single day.

The little Norwegian Air Force, totalling barely 80 front-line aircraft, was no worthy target for an introductory "strategic" grand assault of the kind the German Luftwaffe had mounted on Poland. Consequently the Luftwaffe was deployed only in the tactical support of the German army and navy.

At the same time that German naval units were landing at five separate target points in Norway, paratroops were dropped at two locations. The Germans occupied the Norwegian capital with the support of 6 paratroop companies and a number of airborne troops who landed at Fornebu airfield in Oslo. For the first time, paratroops and airborne troops played a decisive role in the history of the air war.

The German Luftwaffe's role in the Norwegian campaign involved 878 aircraft, including 95 fighters and fighter-destroyers [*Zerstörer*], and 240 bombers and dive bombers.

That same day, 88 bombers of the German 10th Air Corps [*Fliegerkorps*] attacked the British fleet west of Bergen, Norway. They sank the destroyer *Gurkha,* damaged the two cruisers *Glasgow* and *Southampton,* and scored a hit on the battleship *Rodney.* The British naval forces gave up their attempt to occupy Bergen.

On Wednesday 10 April 1940, 15 British Blackburn Skua dive bombers took off from the aircraft carrier *Furious* to carry out their first successful dive-bomb attack. They made three direct 562-lb bomb hits on the light cruiser *Königsberg* and sank it, losing only one plane.

On Thursday 11 April 1940, 6 Wellington bombers attacked the airport at Stavanger, Norway. According to British sources this was the first RAF bombing operation on a target in the interior: So far its air attacks had been directed only against enemy armed forces, merchant shipping or seaplane bases.

On Saturday 13 April 1940 and the days that followed, British, French and exile-Polish troops landed in Norway in the area around Narvik, Namsos and Andalsnes. Their operations were supported by carrier-based aircraft of the Royal Navy. The Skuas flew patrol, the Swordfish biplanes carried out bombing raids. But their missions were considerably handicapped by German planes that took off from Norwegian air bases.

Heavy fighting developed between aerial forces and naval units, especially at Narvik. The German troops who had landed there were now reinforced by paratroop units and aerial provisions. Meanwhile German troops supported by the Luftwaffe attacking in waves, penetrated Norway's interior.

On 17 April 1940, French General Weygand reported to Gamelin and to General Vuillemin, the commander in chief of the French Air Force, that "the preparations for the bombing of the Caucasus oil fields have advanced so far that the operation can take place shortly." The French High Command accepted Weygand's proposal and decided to attack the USSR at the end of June or beginning of July, 1940.

One of the most remarkable press appeals of the

war was made by the Paris newspaper *Le Figaro* on May 9, when it warned its readers of the impending German airborne troop landing operation which the German High Command had kept in the greatest secrecy. The warning came barely 24 hours before the surprise Western offensive was launched on the following morning. Did the Paris paper know beforehand what was going to happen?

At 5:35 A.M. on 10 May 1940, the German armed forces opened their offensive in the West, by violating the neutrality of Holland, Belgium and Luxembourg.

At the beginning of the hostilities, the adversaries commanded the following aerial forces:

On the German side—3,834 aircraft (including 1,482 bombers and Stuka dive bombers, 42 ground attack aircraft, 1,016 fighter planes and 248 *Zerstörer* fighter-destroyers).

On the Allied side, a total of 2,372 aircraft (including 1,151 fighter planes).

The Allied aircraft were distributed as follows:

Right: Crailsheim, Germany, 10 May 1940: Fieseler Storch transport planes of "Förster Group" shortly before take-off on the second wave of secret Operation Niwi.

Below: 9 April 1940 at Oslo's Fornebu Airport. Heavy machine gun fire greets the first German Ju 52s carrying in airborne troops to capture the Norwegian capital by surprise attack.

France: 1,604 aircraft (764 fighters, 260 bombers, 180 reconnaissance planes, 400 army aircraft).

Great Britain (based in France): 456 aircraft (261 fighters, 135 bombers, 60 reconnaissance planes).

Belgium: 180 aircraft (81 fighters).

Holland: 132 aircraft (including 35 fighters and 23 fighter-destroyers).

Just as in the Polish campaign, National Socialist propaganda gave birth to a tale about the Luftwaffe's "annihilating surprise strikes" that allegedly destroyed French aerial forces on the ground on the first day of fighting. These allegations, posing as "facts," have survived the Third Reich and are still to be found in many German publications today. The first German bombing assaults did in fact decimate the small air forces of Holland and Belgium. However, according to French and British sources, the German Luftwaffe destroyed only 45 French and 15 British aircraft on the ground on the first day of the Western Campaign. Throughout the day, aircraft of France and Great Britain supported the advance of Allied ground troops in Belgium, and the French fighter planes succeeded in shooting down 90 German aircraft with a loss of only 20.

On May 10 the German Luftwaffe bore the heaviest losses ever suffered by any air force on a single day: 304 machines destroyed, 51 damaged and 267 flying personnel dead.

The German offensive in the West opened with two secret airborne landing operations that few people know about today: "Operation Niwi" in the Belgian Ardennes, and "Operation Hedderich" in Luxembourg. These may have numbered among the strangest military operations of the war. The comical long-legged Fieseler Fi 156 Storch (Stork) – a German liaison aircraft that carried one pilot and two soldiers – was used to transport the airborne troops.

The plan was for Operation Niwi to prepare the way for a decisive advance by von Kleist's Panzer Corps to the Meuse river at Sedan. The 3rd Battalion (under Lt. Col. Garski) of the elite Grossdeutschland Division, and a combat engineer group – a total of 400 volunteers – were to serve as the airborne troops. They were divided into two units. The Garski Group, South Division, was given 56 Storch aircraft for its transport; and the Captain Krueger Group, North Division, had 42 Storchs. Their mission was to confuse the Belgian and French troops east of Sedan around Neufchâteau-Martelange, and to blockade the roads until the arrival of the German armored spearheads. At 4:20 A.M. the two groups took off from Bitburg and Dockendorf with the first wave of 196 soldiers. Their target: the small Belgian towns of Nives and Witry.

Punctually at 5:35 A.M., Garski Group flew across the Luxembourg border. Wolf Durian, a member of the Grossdeutschland Division who took part in the operation, reported: "We had expected to be fired on over Perlé on the Belgian border, but not one shot was fired. We flew across the Belgian lines, reached the woods where we were safe [from antiaircraft fire]. Our flight lasted half an hour, then we made a precise landing between Witry and the little hamlet of Traimont, on a meadow beside the highway. The *Oberstleutnant* (Lt. Col.) and his adjutant were the first to jump out of their plane, clutching their submachine guns in their fists. The other Storchs also approached for a landing. Four men who had landed south of the road came running up, dragging two machine guns. 'Barricade the road immediately!' ordered the *Oberstleutnant.* As the crow flies, we were already 36 miles into enemy country. We could not expect reinforcements before 8:00 A.M." Two hours later the soldiers, having landed in two waves, engaged in hard battle with the advanced guard of the 1st Ardennes Regiment and the French 5th Armored Car Regiment, until the spearheads of the German 1st Panzer Division arrived next morning.

The second German airborne landing operation, Operation Hedderich, aimed at Luxembourg. One hundred and twenty-five German soldiers of the 34th Infantry Division under 1st Lt. Hedderich, were ordered to blockade all the road junctions around Esch-sur-Alzette (Luxembourg) so as to

prevent the advance of French troops from the massively armed Maginot Line toward the Luxembourg capital, and thus to shield the south flank of the German armored wedge advancing through the Ardennes. Twenty-five Fieseler Fi 156 Storchs stood at Trier-Eupen airfield, ready for use in Operation Hedderich.

At 5:00 A.M., German Army Headquarters 1a reported to Rundstedt's Army Group A: "First wave of Fieseler Storchs have landed at their targets according to schedule." Staff Sergeant Tappert gave this account of the airborne landing: "It was still dark when I pushed into the crammed Storch cockpit. I squatted on a small makeshift seat between machine-gun ammunition belts, bundles of hand grenades and other equipment. Behind me was the bulkhead wall, in front of me was Airman 2nd Class Dreikandt, and right at the front was the pilot, 2nd Lt. König. The engine was started and we rolled up slowly to a takeoff. Far off on the eastern horizon rose a narrow bright strip: the new day was beginning – Friday 10 May 1940. The plane made a couple of skips, we were in the air and flew low over the woods in a westerly direction. The lead planes, soaring straight ahead of us, stood out dimly against the still dark sky. It got lighter in the cockpit. The mist from the valleys rose through the golden sunbeams and surrounded the hills, promising a beautiful day.

"We were over Luxembourg. Every instant we expected to be fired at from below – but nothing happened. 'Gentlemen, we're going to land,' our pilot called suddenly. He throttled the engine and made a gentle descent; the other planes were already landing a couple of hundred yards in front of us. We touched down as softly as an elevator and while the propeller was still running, we hurriedly tossed our belongings through the open doorway onto the swampy meadow.

"With engine roaring, the Fieseler rolled past us

Above: Near Witry (Belgium), May 1940: One of the floundered Fi 156 transport planes of the secret German "Niwi" detachment.

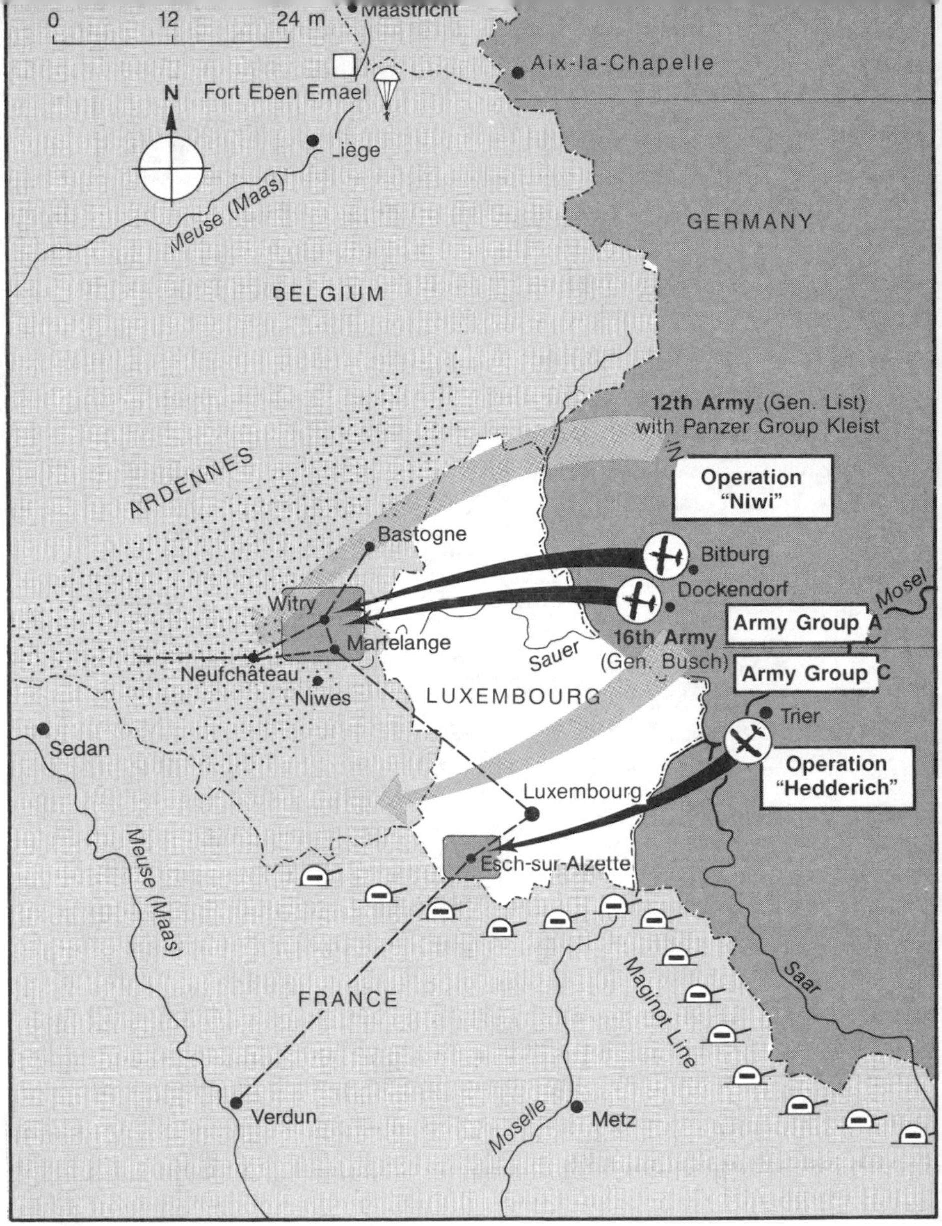

10 May 1940: The routes of German air and land forces during airborne operations "Niwi" and "Hedderich."

Below: Belgium, 10 May 1940: An Fi 156 A-1 of "Förster Group", damaged by ground fire, is forced to make an emergency landing beside the highway leading to Neufchâteau.

preparing its takeoff, its wheels almost axle-deep in the marsh. To our dismay we suddenly saw the machine tip onto its nose; the propeller cracked, the plane twisted on its own axis and turned over on its back.

"König scrambled out of the Fieseler on all fours, swearing like a taxi-driver. We stood him on his feet and discussed what to do. 'Well, according to regulations the first thing I have to do is destroy the Storch so it won't fall into enemy hands,' muttered König and fumbled at the plane. Then it made a gurgling sound and the smell of gasoline spread.

"'Come on, let's go' he called to us and threw a burning piece of paper between the wing and the cockpit, from which the Storch's long, thin stork-legs jutted into the air."

Just as the Germans had feared, French troops

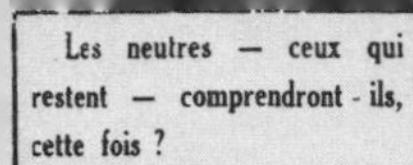
Les neutres — ceux qui restent — comprendront-ils, cette fois ?

Paris-soir

GRAND QUOTIDIEN D'INFORMATIONS ILLUSTRÉES

SAMEDI 11 MAI 1940 — 6e ÉDITION — 50 cent.

Les ALLEMANDS ont ENVAHI

ce matin à l'aube

LA HOLLANDE, LA BELGIQUE ET LE LUXEMBOURG

BRUXELLES bombardée
Grande bataille aérienne au-dessus d'AMSTERDAM

Bombardement de l'aérodrome de BRON près de Lyon

LYON, 10 Mai.

L'alerte a été donnée ce matin à 4 h. 45.

Les troupes françaises alertées au cours de la nuit

Les troupes françaises, dans l'ensemble de l'armée, ont été alertées au cours de la nuit.

LES OFFICIERS permissionnaires doivent rejoindre immédiatement leur poste

Les troupes allemandes ont franchi la frontière hollandaise ce matin à 3 heures

BRUXELLES, 10 Mai.

Le quartier général de l'armée néerlandaise communique :

« Les troupes allemandes ont franchi la frontière néerlandaise à partir de 3 heures ce matin. Des attaques aériennes ont été tentées sur quelques aérodromes. L'armée et l'artillerie antiaérienne sont prêtes. Les inondations s'effectuent selon les plans. Jusqu'à présent, d'après ce qu'on sait, six avions allemands au moins ont été abattus. »

La Belgique attaquée fait appel aux Alliés

Le Luxembourg est envahi

BRUXELLES, 10 Mai.

On apprend que des bombes ont été jetées sur l'aérodrome d'Evère, que des tirs d'artillerie ont eu lieu à la frontière belgo-allemande et que la Belgique, s'estimant attaquée, a fait appel à la France et à l'Angleterre, ses garants.

D'autre part, on apprend que le Luxembourg a été envahi.

Les Alliés apportent toute leur assistance à la Belgique et à la Hollande

LONDRES, 10 Mai.

La « Press Association » publie l'information suivante :

« On annonce officiellement que les Alliés vont apporter toute l'assistance en leur pouvoir à la Belgique et à la Hollande. »

LE ROI DES BELGES a pris le commandement de l'armée

La mobilisation générale est décrétée

BRUXELLES, 10 Mai.

L'état de siège et la mobilisation générale phase 2 ont été décrétés au moment de l'invasion allemande, ce matin vers 4 h. 30.

L'armée franco-britannique est en marche pour aller au secours de la Belgique. D'autre part, le gouvernement belge a adressé une protestation à Berlin et une note aux autres puissances.

Le roi, qui a pris le commandement de l'armée, fera par l'intermédiaire de l'I. N. R. un appel au peuple belge.

M. Pierlot se rend auprès du roi

BRUXELLES, 10 Mai.

Le Conseil des ministres réuni extraordinairement ce matin a duré peu de temps. M. Pierlot, premier ministre, et M. Spaak, ministre des Affaires étrangères, se sont rendus immédiatement auprès du roi.

A 4 h. 30, Anvers est survolée par l'armée aérienne allemande

ANVERS, 10 Mai.

La Haye est attaquée par l'aviation nazie

Une grande bataille aérienne au-dessus d'Amsterdam

Le gouvernement du Luxembourg aurait quitté la capitale

WASHINGTON 10 Mai.

Selon l'ambassadeur des Etats-Unis à Bruxelles, M. Cudahy, le gouvernement du Luxembourg, à l'exception du ministre des Affaires étrangères, aurait quitté la capitale.

C'est à l'aide de nombreuses embarcations blindées que l'Allemagne a envahi la Hollande

Les parachutistes allemands sont déguisés en soldats hollandais

C'EST M. CHURCHILL *qui remplacerait M. Chamberlain*

TELLES SONT DU MOINS LES PRÉVISIONS DE LA PRESSE BRITANNIQUE

LONDRES, 10 Mai.

La démission de M. Chamberlain est considérée comme certaine par plusieurs journaux du matin. Ils estiment probable son remplacement par M. Churchill. La décision interviendrait à bref délai en raison de la situation internationale.

Les travaillistes ne participeraient pas à un gouvernement Chamberlain

UNE ALERTE CE MATIN DANS LA RÉGION PARISIENNE

...et hier dans le Nord

...et dans le Nord-Ouest

Grand Conseil à Washington

M. Roosevelt et ses ministres fixent la nouvelle position de la neutralité américaine

NEW-YORK, 10 Mai.

Une importante conférence se tient à Washington sous la présidence de M. Roosevelt. Y assistent non seulement MM. Cordell Hull et Sumner Welles, mais aussi des chefs militaires : le chef d'état-major de l'armée, le chef d'état-major de la marine, le ministre de la Marine, ainsi que l'attorney général.

C'est pour « protéger » la Belgique, la Hollande et le Luxembourg contre les attaques alliées que le Reich les a envahis

FRONTIÈRE ALLEMANDE, 10 Mai.

Communiqué n° 498

Communiqué n° 497

Lire la suite des dépêches en page 4

Above: The DFS 230 cargo gliders of the "Granite" Assault Group have just landed German paratroops inside the Belgian fort of Eben Emael.

Left: A Paris newspaper takes an optimistic view: While announcing the German invasion, it reports that the French are marching to Belgium's aid.

Below right: Neerhepsen airfield in Belgium in the early morning of 10 May 1940: Fairey Fox aircraft are burning after a German air attack.

turned up after the landing of the Hedderich group: The 6th Algerian Spahi Regiment under Colonel Jouffrault arrived with its exotic cavalry. The two groups continued to fight until the arrival of units of the German Sixteenth Army under General of the Infantry Busch.

The charred remains of Fieseler Storch aircraft were left to mark the sites of Germany's first and only mass deployment of Fi 156s. Twenty-two aircraft were lost in these two airborne operations, most when they took off or made crash landings on marshy meadows, and were then set afire by their pilots.

Early in the morning of May 10, German airborne troops occupied the important bridges over the Belgian Albert Canal at Vroenhoven and Velwezelt near Maastricht, before the Allies could blow up the bridges. The Germans intended relief for their troops to roll across these bridges northwest of the Belgian fort of Eben Emael, as soon as German forces had captured the fort by surprise attack. Eben Emael, completed in 1935, was considered the strongest fort in Europe. It consisted of rows of reinforced concrete casemates that reached deep under the ground; its turrets were heavily armored. With its 1,200-man garrison, it was regarded as impregnable.

The German "Granite" Assault Group (under 1st Lt. Witzig) was assigned the mission of conquering the fort of Eben Emael by airborne attack. The group's transport was 11 DFS 230 cargo-carrying gliders that were to carry one assault troop per plane—an operational force of 84 men. On board the planes were 29,912 rounds of ammunition and 5,282 pounds of explosives, including the new 28-lb

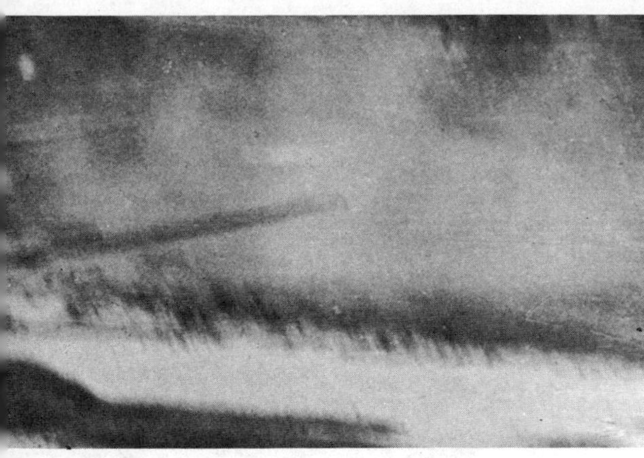

and 110-lb hollow charges that could penetrate armored domes up to 10 inches thick.

The cargo glider pilots were the best of Germany's pre-war glider pilots who had received additional training as combat engineers [*Pioniere*].

At 4:30 A.M., a number of Junkers Ju 52 aircraft took off from the two Cologne airports, Ostheim and Butzweilerhof, towing the cargo gliders. Suddenly one of the tow-ropes broke and the glider carrying the assault group's leader Lt. Witzig, was forced to make an emergency landing on a Rhineland meadow. Some time passed before a Ju 52 ordered out from Gütersloh succeeded in towing the glider out of the field. Yet another glider failed to reach its target and landed in Düren (Germany).

As the cargo gliders were released from their tow-ropes and sailed toward the fort, the high emplacements rose up out of the ground fog. Within a single minute all 9 gliders set down under light antiaircraft fire, to the complete stupefaction of the Belgian gunners. The Germans too had a surprise in store for them. The northern apex of the Eben Emael fortifications, which the attackers had taken to be the most strongly defended part, turned out to be a dummy installation with giant mock domes made of tin-plate. Two gliders that landed in this corner along with their assault troops and gear, were out of action for the time being.

Then the seven remaining assault troops, a total of only 25 men—leaderless to boot because Lt. Witzig, due to his delayed takeoff, did not land until three hours later—attacked the fort garrison. It took them only a few minutes to capture the antiaircraft machine gun positions and to apply hollow charges to blow up the armored domes and heavy cannon of the 10 defended fortifications. Then the Belgian batteries outside the fort opened fire on their own installations and impeded the further actions of the assault troops. The German 51st Combat Engineer Battalion under Lt. Col. Mikosch was advancing to relieve them but making slow progress, so the battle for the barricade fort raged until the next day. Then at 1:15 P.M. Eben Emael surrendered. The commandant, Major Jottrand, chose to commit suicide. The garrison of 1,185 men, including 24 officers and 102 non-commissioned officers, did not know until the end what had really happened on the surface of their fort. Witzig's assault group suffered casualties of 6 dead and 20 wounded. The fort garrison lost some 200 men.

The unexpected deployment of cargo gliders, the new hollow charge explosives, the Germans' success in keeping all their preparations secret, and the months of special training given the assault troops, contributed decisively to the success of the German airborne landing operations over the fort of Eben Emael and the Albert Canal bridges.

Other German airborne landings also largely succeeded. The 3rd Battalion of the 1st Paratroop Regiment under Capt. K.-L. Schulz, dropped by parachute over Waalhaven (Netherlands), and together with the 3rd Battalion of the 16th Infantry Regiment under Lt. Col. von Choltitz, conquered the tenaciously defended airfield.

The air drop of German paratroops was also successful at Moerdijk and Dordrecht. And in Rotterdam 120 German soldiers in 12 He 59 seaplanes, were able to alight on water and seize three bridges.

On the other hand, despite solid preparations and the Dutch uniforms worn by many of the German troops, airborne assault operations failed against Maastricht and Kanne, as well as The Hague, Ypenburg and Ockenburg, where the transport planes and airborne troops of the 22nd Infantry Division (under Lt. Gen. Count Sponeck) suffered heavy losses due to Dutch fighter planes and antiaircraft artillery, and soon were splintered and isolated.

On the afternoon of 10 May 1940, 45 German Heinkel 111s of the 51st Bomber Group [*Kampf-*

gruppe] under Colonel Kammhuber, took off from Landsberg air base near Augsburg, to bomb Dijon-Longvic airfield in France. Due to poor visibility, some of them deviated from course and reportedly attacked the fighter plane base of Dôle-Tavaux, their agreed-on secondary target at Dijon. At 3:59 P.M., 3 of the aircraft (under Flight Leader 2nd Lt. Seidel), flying at an altitude of nearly 5,000 feet, emerged from the stormclouds over the German city of Freiburg-im-Breisgau. Each bomber discharged its bomb load and rapidly disappeared again, leaving behind 57 dead, 22 of them children. The 3 disastrous aircraft, which had strayed over Freiburg through navigational error, were not recognized by ground defenses as German planes; so National Socialist propaganda at once laid the blame for the attack on the Allies. Henceforth Goebbels cited the Freiburg incident as the beginning of the terrorist air attacks on civilians.

Another event of that day also contributed to the further escalation of the air war. Prime Minister Chamberlain, an opponent of terror air raids on cities, stepped down from office and was replaced by Winston Churchill, who immediately pressed for the deployment of bombers over Germany. That very night, 36 bombers attacked Mönchengladbach. One of the four who died in this attack was an Englishwoman.

The chief American Red Cross delegate in Europe, Mr Taylor, arrived in Freiburg at the very moment when the Allied airmen were flying back, after having dropped about 50 bombs on the town. Speaking to the "New York Times" (see issue of May 13, 1940), Mr Taylor declared that although Freiburg must undoubtedly be considered an open town, it had been bombed by French aeroplanes. The Swiss Consul estimated the number of victims to be at least 40 killed and 150 injured, all civilians.

Freiburg was the beginning!

Since then Allied airmen have been bombing open German towns of no military importance night after night, and have claimed more and more victims amongst the civil population.

This is not war!
It is murder!

Funeral of the 8-year-old Ruth Jäger and the 6-year-old Manfred Jäger.

On 10 May 1940, 3 Dutch air crews stationed with their Fokker TV bombers at Ruigenhoek air base near Haarlem, received orders to fly a raid on Ockenburg airfield to destroy the German Ju 52s that had flown airborne troops of the German 22nd Infantry Division into Holland, and that reportedly had been assigned the duty of penetrating to The Hague to seize the royal family and members of the Dutch government. This Dutch operation, carried out without any fighter plane cover, was tantamount to a suicide mission.

Dutch 2nd Lt. G.H.J. Ruygrok said in his account: "I'm not ashamed to admit my knees were shaking, because our air defense had told us there were a lot of German fighter planes in the Ockenburg area! After takeoff we headed straight for the coast, and Japie, our pilot, pulled up our machine. He thought we would not be able to reach our prescribed altitude of nearly 10,000 feet [3,000 meters] in time, because by the time we neared Scheveningen we were only 6,500 feet up [2,000 meters]. I told him he could maintain horizontal flight. We held our heading toward the Hook of Holland [Hoek-van-Holland], and still there was not an enemy in the sky. Suddenly we saw Ockenburg airfield through the clouds, with at least 30 shimmering grey Junkers 52s crisscrossing the field. On our second approach I pressed the bomb-release mechanism and at the same time had to see to the aerial cannon, because German fighters could turn up at any moment. Meanwhile the co-pilot observed bombs striking the

Left: A German air leaflet blaming the Allies for the bomb raid on Freiburg.

Right: The German Stukas (dive bombers) had a shattering effect on morale, as these French fugitives scrambling for shelter make clear.

Left: Rotterdam, 13 May 1940. Bombs hail down on the center of the largest Dutch seaport town, here viewed from a German He 111.

Right: A Stuka formation during its approach flight. The shrill unnerving sound of the Ju 87s' dive brakes and sirens often caused panic among the assaulted troops and civilians.

center of the target. At the end we nose-dived toward the sea and banked around toward Haarlem at an altitude of 80 feet."

It was already 8:00 A.M.—three hours after the German bomb raids of French air bases—when General d'Astier de la Vigerie, commander of the French air force attached to the 1st Army Group, received his first orders. The French 1st Army Group under General Billotte, was deployed along the Franco-Belgian border where the Germans were making their main thrust. Yet the orders that d'Astier de la Vigerie received from the headquarters of General Georges (operational controller of the armies of northeastern France), were to "Limit your operations to defense and reconnaissance." The French were not to be allowed to make bombing attacks. After countless stormy protests, General d'Astier finally received permission at 11:00 A.M. to fly bombing missions against enemy columns "but only over open country."

From the outset the German Luftwaffe succeeded in winning not only air superiority but command of the air over France. Most of the French fighter planes were considerably slower than the German Messerschmitt 109s, and only one fifth of the French fighter groups had planes of equal quality, the Dewoitine 520s.

General d'Astier reported that long before the German offensive, plans had been laid for massive Anglo-French bombing assaults to be launched on enemy panzer units on the very first night after any attack; so on May 10 preparations were made for the operation to follow that evening. Not only all the available Allied bombers in France, but also a large number of RAF bombers stationed in England, were scheduled to take part. But the new orders from General Georges ruled out the operation.

On 11 May 1940, the little Belgian air force sent out 9 aircraft to bomb the bridges over the Albert Canal which the Germans had seized by surprise attack. They missed their targets; 7 of the planes did not come back. At 6:00 P.M. on the same day, 12 modern French LeO-45 night bombers with fighter plane cover attacked three bridges west of Maastricht and German tanks advancing on Tongres. Unsuited to such duty, they inflicted almost no damage, and 1 bomber and 4 fighters were lost. The day after, May 12, British bombers made a suicidal attempt to destroy the Vroenhoven and Veldwezelt bridges, across which the Germans were advancing in dense columns. On their first approach, 4 of the 6 antiquated Fairey Battle bombers were shot down.

One of the British bombers, flown by Flying Officer McIntosh, was burning like a torch when he dropped his bombs and managed to make a per-

Left: A formation of British Fairey Battle bombers with French fighter planes flying cover, shortly before their attack on German pontoon bridges at Sedan.

fect landing. The air crew were captured. A fifth bomber crashed on its return flight. The sixth Fairey Battle came back with its remaining escort of two Hurricane fighters.

The Germans admired the courage of the British pilots but were amazed that their leadership had been slow to deploy them. A German officer said to captured Flying Officer McIntosh: "You British are mad. We took the bridges early Friday morning. You gave us the whole of Friday and Saturday to build up our flak entrenchments all around the bridge, and then on Sunday, when everything was ready, you came here with three planes and tried to blow the thing up." The British attack held up the advance of the German motorized columns across the two bridges, for only 30 minutes.

On May 13 the German 22nd Infantry Division (under Lt. Gen. Count Sponeck) found themselves hard pressed northwest of Rotterdam, where they had made an airborne landing on May 10. Meanwhile the 9th Panzer Division (under General Hubicki) and the 3rd Battalion of the 16th Infantry Regiment (under Lt. Col. von Choltitz) crossed through the city up to the Meuse bridge.

At 12:00 noon on May 14, von Choltitz demanded that the Dutch commanding officer of Rotterdam, Colonel Scharroo, surrender the city immediately, but he refused to negotiate. The German 22nd Infantry Division, encircled on the other side of Rotterdam, pleaded for German air support before the Dutch artillery went into action. The 54th Bomber Wing [*Kampfgeschwader*] under Colonel Lackner was ordered to attack Rotterdam "as scheduled" unless red flares signalled the last-minute capitulation of the city. At 1:25 P.M. German bombers took off in two combat formations; but surrender negotiations began while they were in flight, and the order was sent out for them to return. However, the bombers had already wound in their trailing radio antennas so that they were out of radio contact, and the red flares of the recall signal were visible to only one of the formations through the clouds of smoke from the burning steamship *Stratendam.* Forty-three aircraft turned around, but 57 machines discharged their load—97 metric tons of high-explosive bombs—onto the city. The very first bombs destroyed the main water conduit, making it hard to fight the ensuing fire when rivers of burning fat gushed out of the worst-hit building, a margarine factory. More than 900 people died in this attack.

Allied war propaganda took the destruction of the town center of Rotterdam—following the heavy attacks on Warsaw in September 1939—as an added proof that the German Luftwaffe was being deployed ruthlessly to break morale. This carried the escalation of the air war one step further. The destruction of Rotterdam moved Prime Minister Churchill to cancel the prohibition against the bombing of German cities.

The German offensive at Sedan reached its climax under the protection afforded by the bridgeheads on the Meuse. The main body of German tanks crossed the Meuse via a bridge that German combat engineers had built on the night of May 13th–14th, and continued fighting without respite, supported by German Stukas.

Six RAF Fairey Battles attacked the German pioneer bridges; not one came back. Not far away, 60

British bombers dropped their payloads on German columns that had crossed the Meuse; for 35, it was their last flight. According to British Major-General Spears' account, that evening the RAF had only 206 aircraft in France that were still fit to fly, out of its initial force of 474. More than 40 French, and about 70 British machines including 36 Fairey Battles (that is 60% of the aircraft deployed), were shot down on May 14 by German fighter planes or antiaircraft artillery, during their attack on the pioneer bridges. Not one of the bridges was destroyed. Never again, at any time during the war, did the RAF suffer such a high percentage of losses within a 24-hour period. The desperate attempt of the Allied air forces to stop the German breakthrough, failed on the "Day of Sedan."

On May 11, when Churchill induced his War Cabinet's decision to allow bombing attacks on German territory east of the Rhine, it was realized in London that for the immediate future, bomber planes were the only British offensive weapon which could strike directly at the German Reich. At this time the RAF had only 99 combat-ready long-range bombers. Nevertheless, the British government did not want to stake everything on Douhet's theory that wars could be won by the use of bombers alone. Therefore, it was decided, Bomber Command would continue to be a main offensive weapon; but given Britain's limited industrial capacity, its needs could not claim precedence over those of all the other armed forces.

On 15 May 1940, the Dutch laid down their arms even though their main front was still unbreached. Their surrender was speeded up by the threat of further air attacks on Dutch cities.

On the night of May 15, 99 RAF planes bombed oil refineries and rail installations in the Ruhr district. One aircraft was lost and little damage was inflicted. This night began the British "strategic bombing offensive" that was to last almost exactly five years. But as yet, Bomber Command did not have enough aircraft, navigational aids, bombs and experience to carry out precision bombing on picked targets at night.

Between the 10th and 15th of May, the French fighter planes flew 2,000 missions on which they shot down 273 enemy planes, yet with all their inexhaustible combat readiness they could not change the situation. The Allied bomber formations also failed to ease the strain on the hard-pressed ground troops.

During the Western Campaign the airplane showed itself, for the first time in the history of warfare, to be the most dangerous enemy of the tank. For example, on the 17th and 18th of May General de Gaulle, who had his tank units at Lâon, made a counterattack on the flank of the German tank wedge, the 19th Panzer Corps under General Guderian, as it advanced toward the Atlantic coast, and he was able to achieve a breach. But this initial success was neutralized by the action of German Stuka dive bombers, and the greater part of the French armored vehicles were destroyed.

The French Armée de l'Air suffered more from its fragmentation into many separate commands, than from the lack of an effective strategic concept. Its leaders had no authority over the Army's fighter, reconnaissance and observation planes. The French Commander in Chief never directed air operations personally, and confusion reigned among his staff. Command authority was divided among General Vuillemin, the commander in chief of the air force; General Têtu, the staff liaison between the army and air force; the staffs commanding the various air zones; and the individual army leaders. This fragmentation made it almost impossible for air and ground units to synchronize their operations.

One peculiar feature of the Battle of France was that, apart from the German Luftwaffe's initial strategic missions against Allied air bases, both the German and Allied air forces confined themselves to purely tactical operations. Yet despite the fact that the French pilots were trained primarily for support of the ground troops, no effective tactics had been worked out for such operations. Communications between French army and air force units were almost nonexistent. Besides that, not one French aircraft type was suited to intervene in ground battles like the German Stukas.

On Wednesday 22 May 1940, the RAF evacuated the airfield at Merville, its last base in France. Its aircraft began to operate out of the British Isles, above all over Dunkirk.

The French fliers too saw the inevitability of imminent defeat. One of them was Captain Antoine de Saint-Exupéry, the pilot of a long-distance reconnaissance plane who in civilian life was one of the best-known prose-writers of his time. In his book *Pilote de guerre* (Eng. trans. *Flight to Arras,* 1942), he noted about those final days: "It is the end of May [1940], a time of full retreat, of full disaster. Air crews are being sacrificed the way one would pour glasses of water into a forest fire. How can the danger be weighed to individuals when everything is breaking down? One moment we had fifty long-distance reconnaissance air crews for the whole of

Left: Captain Antoine de Saint-Exupéry, pilot of the 3rd Escadrille of French 33 Squadron, 2nd Reconnaissance Group.

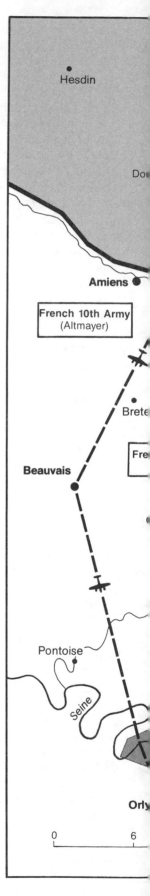

France; fifty air crews of three men each. Twenty-three of them were in our Group, the II/33. In three weeks we have lost seventeen of our twenty-three crews. We have melted away like a lump of wax. Yesterday I said to Lieutenant Gavoille: 'We'll see about that after the war.' And Gavoille answered me: 'Surely you don't think you're coming out of this war alive, mon Capitaine?' "

On Thursday 23 May 1940, General von Kleist's panzer divisions attacked the English Channel coast. Boulogne-sur-Mer fell after bitter fighting. Calais was encircled. Other panzer units reached Lorette. The 7th Panzer Division under Major General Rommel, bypassed Arras on the west and threatened the communication lines of the British troops still fighting there. The French General Staff ordered out reconnaissance planes to bring them a clear picture of the evacuation of Arras and the British retreat. The 3 escadrilles of French 33 Squadron, 2nd Reconnaissance Group were detailed to send one of their aircraft on a reconnaissance flight over Arras. Captain Saint-Exupéry and his crew took over this mission, No. 108 Mission, which would later enter world literature under the name "the Flight to Arras."

" 'Arras.' Right. There in the distance. But Arras is not a town now. Arras is nothing but a glowing candlewick against a blue background of night . . . The ground defenses, which have missed us, readjust their aim. The walls of explosive shells rebuild

Right: The flight to Arras

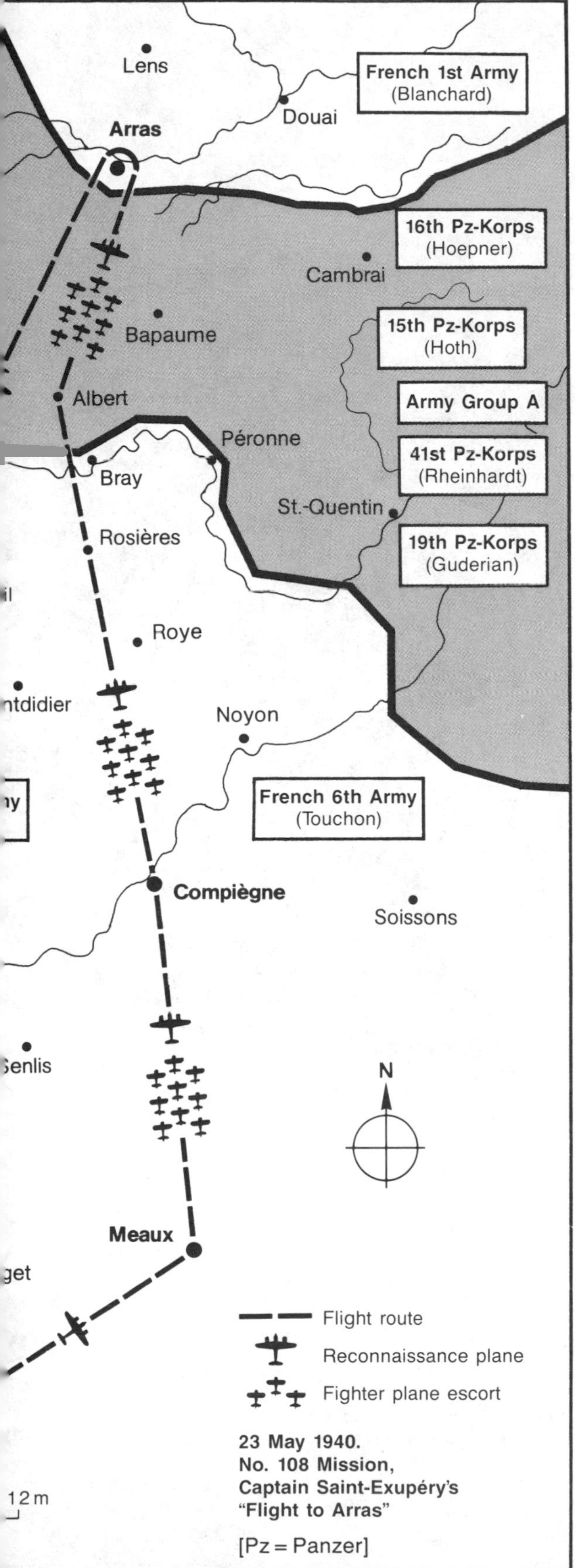

23 May 1940.
No. 108 Mission,
Captain Saint-Exupéry's
"Flight to Arras"

[Pz = Panzer]

themselves at our level. They are not seeking us out, they are hemming us in.

" 'Dutertre, how much farther?'

" 'If we can hold out another three minutes, we'll have made it . . . but . . . '

"How long do I still have to live? Ten seconds? Twenty seconds? The vibrating shock of exploding flak shells hammers at us incessantly. The really close ones make the plane resound like boulders falling into a cart. Then the whole aircraft emits an almost musical sound. A funny sigh . . . "

The duty report of the aircraft's observer, Lieutenant Dutertre, tells us about the flight:

"*No. 108 Mission.* Thursday 23 May 1940. Crew: Capitaine Saint-Exupéry (pilot), Lieutenant Dutertre (observer), Sergeant Mot (aerial gunner). Aircraft: a Bloch 174, No. 24.

"Mission: Medium-altitude reconnaissance with fighter plane support; aerial photographs is possible.

"Air route: Orly – Meaux (rendezvous here with fighter escort), then Compiègne – Rosières-en-Santerre – Bray-sur-Somme – Albert – Arras – Douai and return.

"At Meaux we are joined by escort of 9 Dewoitine 520s; heavy hailstorm over Compiègne; altitude 800 feet [300 meters]. Observations: At Albert, aircraft outside the hangars, some trenches. A short way past Albert, very heavy flak. We fly over the Bapaume area. Long-distance view of Arras, which is under artillery fire. Before Arras we got into a storm and lost our fighter cover, had to descend to 650 feet because of the storm, and came under strong defensive fire from the panzer units 2 miles [3 km] southeast of Arras. Very strong flak fire over the city itself. Our machine received a hit. Fuel tank damaged. Operation suspended, landing at Orly.

"We were able to take a few aerial photographs over Liquemenil – Ferrin – Aubigny (east of Arras) with F 30 cameras.

That same afternoon Göring told the Führer by telephone that it was now "the great task of the National Socialist Luftwaffe" to smash the British troops retreating to Dunkirk. The day after, Hitler ordered the halt of von Kleist's Panzer Group, which had advanced to the outskirts of Dunkirk. He wanted to conserve the armored units for the second phase of the French Campaign. Also, he was relying on Göring's promises that the Luftwaffe could annihilate the encircled British and French troops without aid from the German ground forces.

But things did not turn out as Göring had expected. The Luftwaffe's takeoff bases were too far from Dunkirk, and moreover were blockaded by fog for three crucial days.

On May 30, some 300 German bombers stood ready for combat all day, but could not take off due to low-hanging clouds; and when the weather improved at last and the bombers took off, new problems arose. The little boats of the evacuation flotilla were not the kind of target the Stukas were used to; and besides that, the bombs rammed deep into the dunes along the beach so that the sand muffled the effect of their explosions. But the decisive factor was that the British gained local air superiority over Dunkirk with their Spitfire fighter planes—deployed here for the first time and taking off from bases in England.

On Tuesday 28 May 1940, King Leopold III of Belgium signed the surrender treaty for his army and became a German prisoner-of-war. The Belgian Cabinet, who had fled, formed a government-in-exile in London.

The RAF fighter planes succeeded in covering the retreat of the British Expeditionary Force, so that 225,000 Britons and 112,000 Frenchmen were successfully rescued, even though they had to leave all their arms and equipment behind. Over Dunkirk, the Germans lost command of the air for the first time.

In the first days of June, after the German flying formations had regrouped, they began to make bombing raids on the French hinterland. On the afternoon of 3 June 1940, a Luftwaffe contingent of approximately 300 planes—French sources say 700—carried out what the Germans called "Operation Paula," the bombing of airports and industrial installations around Paris. Luftwaffe General Kesselring stated that in this attack, "over 100 French aircraft were shot down and three or four times that number were destroyed on the ground."

According to French sources, "Operation Paula" was by no means so effective. "In the concentrated attacks on 13 airfields around Paris, only 16 aircraft were destroyed on the ground and 47 damaged. Six runways were temporarily put out of service, 21 vehicles were demolished and 32 ground personnel were killed. However, it proved possible to repair all the assaulted air bases within 48 hours. The 22 railroad stations likewise bombed by the Luftwaffe, were for the most part restored by the following morning, June 4. Of the 15 raided factories, only 3 were seriously damaged. The French fighters brought down 26 German machines while losing only 16."

During one attack, at around 1:30 P.M., French

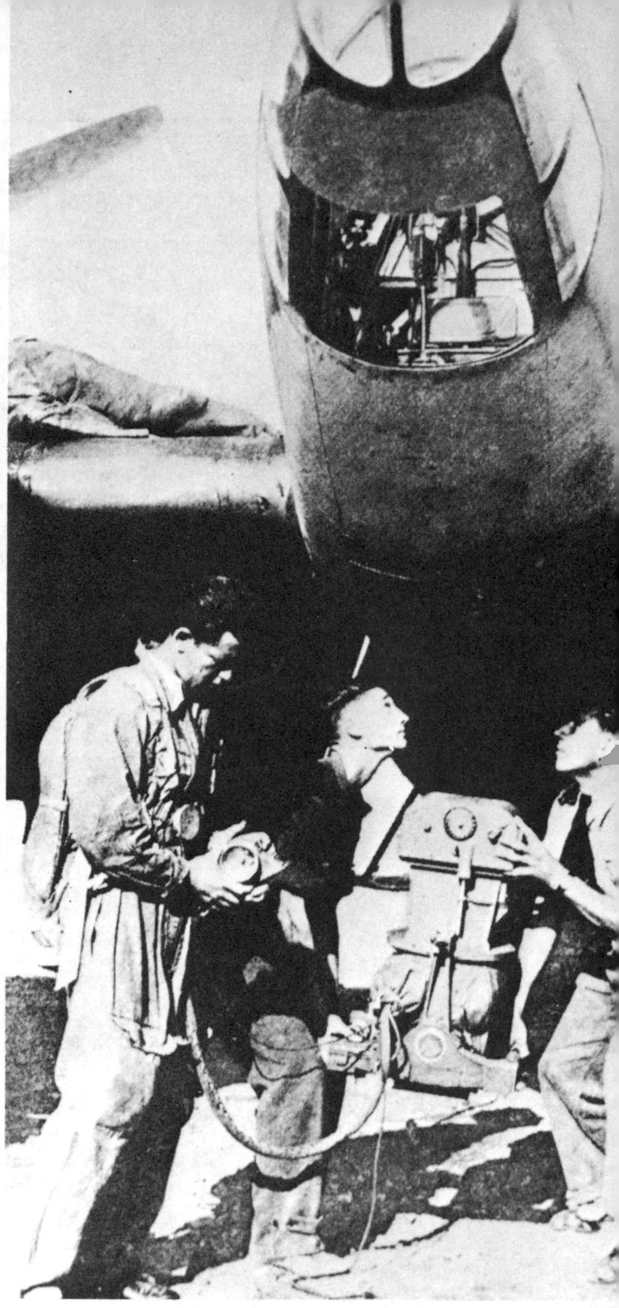

Right: 1 June 1940, Dunkirk: A Lockheed Hudson of RAF Coastal Command on a reconnaissance flight. Clouds of smoke from the burning oil tanks rise over the harbor.

Rotterdam
9th Air Corps
LONDON
NORTH SEA
British Fighter Command
4th Air Corps
Air Fleet 2
Antwerp
German fighter planes
Dunkirk
BRUSSELS
1st Air Corps
Cambrai
Abbeville
Cologne
Frankfurt/M.
Koblenz
2nd Air Corps
8th Air Corps
Amiens
St. Quentin
Guise
Mainz
Laon
Stenay
Air Fleet 3
Saarbrücken
N
Reims
Karlsruhe
5th Air Corps
Metz
Stuttgart
Strasbourg
Augsburg
Basle

27 May–4 June 1940:
The Luftwaffe's operations against Dunkirk
Front lines
Main attack thrust of the German air corps
Air Fleet 2 (4th and 9th Air Corps)
Air Fleet 3 (1st, 2nd, 4th and 8th Air Corps)

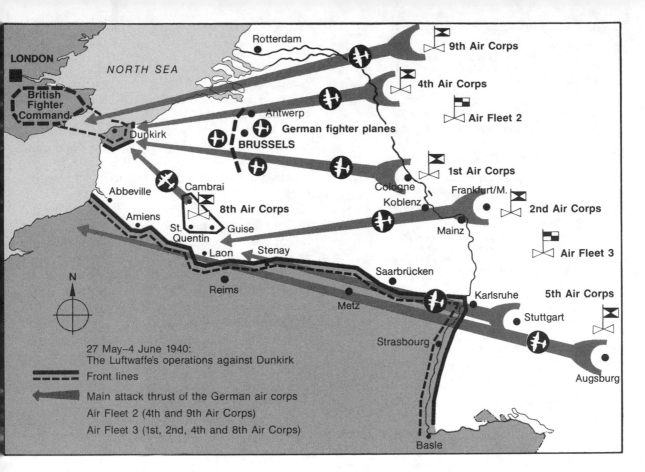

Above: 27 May–4 June 1940: The Luftwaffe's operations against Dunkirk.

Left: A Bloch 174, the most modern French reconnaissance plane. On 31 March 1940, Captain Saint-Exupéry flew this model's very first operation—over Cologne, Düsseldorf and Duisburg.

fighters encountered seven Ju 88 bombers that had just bombed Étampes airfield. One Ju 88 was shot down by a Bloch 152 of 3 Squadron, 1st Fighter Group *[Groupe de Chasse]*. The crew managed to bail out and were taken prisoner. One of them was Colonel J. Kammhuber, commander of 51st Bomber Wing, the "Edelweiss," and later the organizer and commander of German night fighter defense.

On Monday 3 June 1940, Allied troops began their evacuation from Narvik, Norway.

The 5th of June 1940 was the highpoint of French bomber unit operations. A total of 77 bombers of various groups flew a number of assaults, mostly against German armored spearheads and motorized columns on the northern sector of the front. In the afternoon, 2nd Lt. Pomier-Layragues of 7 Squadron, 2nd Fighter Group shot down an Me 109 Bf fighter plane, in an aerial fight over Compiègne. The pilot managed to parachute out. He was Captain Werner Mölders, the famous German flying ace. Mölders, who was captured by an artillery soldier from a nearby French battery, expressed the wish to meet the man who had shot him down; but it was too late. While Mölders was still dangling from his parachute, Pomier-Layragues had his hands full tackling 4 German Me 109 fighters. He succeeded in shooting one down; then Pomier-Layragues him-

9 JUIN 1940
119e Année

EN PAGE 2 :
Le Carnet du « Figaro ».
Les informations étrangères.
Les Spectacles.

L'AÉRONAUTIQUE NAVALE
bombarde les usines des faubourgs
DE BERLIN

L'Amirauté française communique :
Une escadrille de l'aéronautique navale a bombardé dans la nuit du 7 juin certaines usines des faubourgs de Berlin. Tous les appareils sont rentrés à leur base.

French newspaper *Le Figaro*, 9 June 1940: The French Admiralty reports a French bombing raid on Berlin and makes the exaggerated claim that a single Farman 223.4 (the *Jules Verne*) was a whole bomber formation.

self was hit, and crashed with his machine near Marissel. The plane exploded at once and he did not have a chance to bail out.

That day General Vuillemin renewed his entreaties to the British government to send him 10 fighter squadrons at once, and 10 more "as soon as possible." The French air force commander, who was not even making use of all the planes he already had at his disposal, was now asking the RAF to deliver one half of all the fighters it had left—a demand which, as Churchill telegraphed to him that same evening, was "completely insupportable."

The French navy came up with one of the queerest ideas of the French Campaign when they decided to attack Berlin. At 3:00 P.M. on 7 June 1940, one of France's three Farman 223.4 long-range naval reconnaissance aircraft, the *Jules Verne*, was cleared for takeoff at Bordeaux-Mérignac airfield. The four-engined high-wing monoplane, painted dull black, had already logged several missions. At 3:30 the *Jules Verne* rolled up for takeoff carrying a bombload of 2 metric tons. The target: Berlin. This was the first bomb assault of the war made on the German capital. The crew commander was Captain de Corvette Daillière, a former professor of aerial navigation at the École de Guerre. With him flew Paul Comet, an ex-chief navigator of the Air France airline. "At once we set a northern heading for the English Channel. I flew the plane visually; the weather was clear and I was completely familiar with the flight route via Pas de Calais and Holland. We did not meet with a single aircraft; we came under heavy antiaircraft fire only over Sylt. By sunset we were flying over Denmark, some time later the Baltic Sea lay beneath us. When Stettin appeared on our right, we took a southern heading, flew at high altitude over the Mecklenburg lake district, and reached the northern outskirts of Berlin at exactly the appointed time. I got ready to release the bombs and realized that someone had failed to install our bombsight, so I pressed my nose to the glass of the cockpit. Visibility was good, but I could not identify any of the numerous lakes around Berlin and the city lay in complete darkness. Suddenly, as if on command, countless searchlights lit up the night and all calibers of flak opened fire. We circled over the city center for a while, throttled the engines, let them run again full blast, then repeated the process. We wanted to create the impression that a whole formation was over Berlin. Then we turned off toward a northern suburb and dropped our payload there on one of the numerous factories. The attack certainly did not cause any great destruction, but after all we were more concerned with the psychological effect."

The *Jules Verne* then set a course for Leipzig, crossed all of Germany unmolested by either fighter planes or flak, and landed at Paris-Orly at around 5:00 A.M. after a 13½-hour flight of almost 3,000 miles.

Next day the French Admiralty announced: "On the night of June 7–8, a formation of French long-range bombers bombed an industrial quarter in north Berlin as retaliation for the German air attack on Paris. All our aircraft came back."

On Sunday 9 June 1940, after the Allied troops had completed their evacuation out of Norwegian harbors, King Haakon VII of Norway ordered an end to hostilities there. The Germans' "Operation Weserübung"—the occupation of Norway—was completed.

On Monday 10 June 1940, Mussolini issued Italy's declaration of war. His air force, the Regia Aeronautica, comprised a total of 1,796 combat-ready aircraft based in Italy, including 783 bombers, 594 fighters, 268 reconnaissance planes and 151 seaplanes.

At dawn next day, RAF bombers of 202 Wing (under R. Collishaw), stationed in the Western Desert, attacked the chief Italian air base of El Adem in Cyrenaica. A few hours later came the first Italian air raid on Malta. The island's air defense fell to 3 antiquated Gloster Gladiator biplane fighters.

That afternoon Winston Churchill met in Briare

with the French government, who had been evacuated from Paris. To France's desperate pleas that Great Britain throw all its squadrons into the Battle of France, Churchill replied that their sacrifice would mean an end to Britain's own prospects for survival. French government leader Reynaud answered: "History will say that the Battle of France was lost for lack of airplanes," and General Georges added that he considered it "improbable that Great Britain would be attacked, whereas a massive deployment of aircraft on the Marne could alter the position." But Churchill could not be swayed.

Wisely foreseeing that Italy would enter the war against France, the RAF had prepared two airfields near Marseilles where Wellington bombers could make intermediate landings during attacks on industrial centers in northern Italy. But the French government feared that French-based RAF attacks on Italy would result in retaliatory strikes on French cities.

At the same time that Churchill was under pressure to send every last fighter squadron he had into France, Wellington bombers of 99 Squadron were landing on their airfield at Salon (in Provence) to open the offensive against Italy. But General Vuillemin ordered a halt to the operation. When the RAF fliers tried to prepare their takeoff notwithstanding, local French authorities mobilized the population to block the flying fields with trucks, cars and drays of every description, and so prevented the British operation.

On Wednesday 12 June 1940, the battle-ready 1st Wing of the Regia Aeronautica, stationed in northern Italy, took off for its first assault on targets in southern France. Italian Fiat Cicogna bombers and Fiat Cr.42 Falco fighters attacked French seaports. The Italian 3rd Wing was also active and bombed vessels off the French coast.

On June 14 the Allied air force leadership recognized that the Battle of France was lost and ordered virtually all their fighter, bomber and reconnaissance groups to southern France, as the first step in a planned transfer to North Africa.

On the afternoon of Sunday 16 June 1940, the 9th Panzer Division under General Hubicki, which was part of von Kleist's Panzer Group, conquered the small French town of La Charité-sur-Loire. That same evening, German Senior Radio N.C.O. Balzereit of regimental intelligence, went scouting through the railroad site of La Charité and made a surprising discovery inside the freight car of a military transport train: the secret records of the French General Staff! Meanwhile Private 1st Class Kranzer, the member of a neighboring division, found more documents among the almost 15-mile-long lines of transport trains that had piled up due to the destruction of the Loire bridges, and that extended from the La Charité depot to Mesves-sur-Loire. The Germans soon determined that these papers stemmed from the secret archives of the French General Headquarters, and from the Interallied Section of General Gamelin's Office, the storage-house for all the records of top secret conferences between the Allied commanders. They included the plans for the Caucasus bombing operation, along with the target maps and the aerial photographs that MacPhail had taken of Baku and Batum. A short time later, copies of the plans and photos arrived in Moscow via Berlin. The Soviets' knowledge of British plans to attack them, sheds a different light on the distrust that Stalin showed toward Churchill to the very end. Moreover, the British attack plans help explain why Hitler's deputy Hess had some hope of obtaining British cooperation when he flew to Scotland [on a private peace mission] just before Germany's offensive against the Soviet Union.

The South African Air Force (the SAAF), sent 17 Junkers Ju 86 bombers and 10 Junkers Ju 52 and 53m transport aircraft to intervene in the fighting in Italian East Africa. The SAAF won its first victory when it bombed the Italian air base of Yavello (southern Ethiopia) on 19 June 1940. Three Ju 86s and 2 Hawker Hurricane fighters under Captain Truter, successfully shot down a Fiat CR.42. In the first week the Italians lost 15 planes to these attacks.

On 23 June 1940, 17 French Morane fighter planes of 1 Squadron, 1st Fighter Group and 2

The Farman 223.4 *Jules Verne*. This four-engined machine, shown here in its role as an Air France passenger plane, dropped the war's first bombs on Berlin.

Morgenausgabe
10 Pf., auswärts 15 Pf.

Donnerstag, 4. Juli 1940
M

Berliner

Lokal-Anzeiger

Nummer 158

Organ für die Reichshauptstadt

58. Jahrgang

Wöchentlich zwölfmal, Sonntags mit der Bilderbeilage „Die Weite Welt". Bezugspreis wöchentlich 75 Pfennig, monatlich 3,25 Mark. Durch die Post monatlich 3,25 Mark einschließlich 48 Pfennig Postgebühren, hierzu 72 Pfennig Bestellgeld. (Tagesausgabe. wöchentlich sechsmal, Sonntags mit der Bilderbeilage „Die Weite Welt", wöchentlich 50 Pfennig, monatlich 2,20 Mark. Durch die Post monatlich 2,20 Mark einschließlich 35 Pfennig Postgebühren, hierzu 36 Pfennig Bestellgeld). Bestellungen in allen Scherl-Filialen, Postanstalten und beim Verlag. – Bei Ausfall der Lieferung wegen höherer Gewalt oder Betriebsstörung kein Anspruch auf Nachlieferung oder Rückzahlung. Schriftleitung und Verlag Berlin SW 68. Fernsprecher Sammel-Nummer 17 45 71. Drahtanschrift Scherlverlag Berlin. Postscheck-Konto 3111. Für unverlangt eingesandte Beiträge übernimmt die Schriftleitung keine Verantwortung.

Anzeigen-Preise: Die Millimeter-Zeile (22 mm br.) 50 Pfennig (Sonntags 60 Pfennig), Textteil-Zeile (65 mm br.) 4 Mark (Sonntags 4,50 Mk.), Stellengesuche 25 Pfennig (Sonntags 30 Pfennig), eigene Familienanzeigen 20 Pfennig. Kleine Anzeigen: Überschriftswort 66 Pfennig (Sonntags 90 Pfennig), Textwort 33 Pfennig (Sonntags 45 Pfennig), Stellengesuche Textwort 15 Pfennig, in der Überschrift 30 Pfennig. – Bei Anzeigen mit Kennwort (Chiffre) ist eine Kennwortgebühr zu zahlen. – Kennwortgebühr 30 Pf., portofreie Zusendung der Offerten innerhalb Groß-Berlins 40 Pf., nach auswärts 80 Pf. Keine Gewähr für die Aufnahme in bestimmte Ausgaben. Anzeigen-Annahme im Scherl-Haus, Zimmerstraße 35–41 und in den Scherl-Filialen

Der geplante Angriff auf Rußland

Einzelheiten über die verbrecherische Absicht der Westmächte, die Oelgebiete von Baku und Batum in Brand zu werfen – Ein weiterer sensationeller Dokumentenfund

Bereit sein ist alles!

Brandstifter Massigli

Schuld und Sühne

The National Socialist press takes malicious pleasure in reporting Anglo-French preparations for an air attack on the Soviet Union.

Squadron, 2nd Fighter Group, took off to assault the motorized units of General Guderian in the Rhône valley. They intended to raid tanks of the 3rd Panzer Division, but could not find them. Only 2nd Lt. Marchelidon of 2 Squadron, 1st Fighter Group, shot down a German Henschel 126 reconnaissance plane that was flying solo. This was the last French fighter plane victory of the French Campaign.

Below: About 55 undamaged multipurpose Caudron C-445 M Goeland aircraft have fallen into the hands of German troops at this French airfield.

The French took off on their last bomb assault two days after signing an armistice in Compiègne: On the afternoon of June 24, 11 LeO 45s of 6th Bomber Group attacked German pontoon bridges between Moirans and Grenoble. Only 4 machines found their target and their attack was unsuccessful.

One surprising feature of the air war over France is that at the end of battle, the Armèe de l'Air had a larger number of modern combat aircraft than at the beginning of the German offensive. The reason is that despite German bomb assaults, the French aircraft industry managed to work to full capacity between May 10 and the early days of June. Thus according to French sources, 1,131 new aircraft—mostly of modern design and including 668 fighters and 335 bombers—were delivered to French units during this time.

Another baffling fact about the Battle of France is that for reasons that can no longer be determined today, the French did not deploy most of their combat aircraft—not even when the French government and military were pressing England to send its meager fighter plane stores to France.

French air force general d'Astier de la Vigerie reported: "Virtually every evening I myself had to take the initiative to call up the commanders of an army or army group and inform them that I had a certain number of aircraft formations available for the following day which had not been assigned any duty, and to ask whether they had any operations for us to carry out." The reply was always the same: "Thanks very much, but we don't need them."

But the French fighters who *were* deployed fought

with extreme heroism: In 46 days they managed, in spite of everything, to bring down 935 enemy aircraft. In the end these losses forced Göring to postpone launch of the aerial Battle of Britain, which the Germans intended should pave the way for their invasion of the British Isles. The British were granted a six-week lull and did their best to make use of it.

The Franco-German Armistice agreement of 22 June 1940 provided, among other things, that the French armed forces in the unoccupied part of France should be reduced to 100,000 volunteers; that the French would retain a small air force and navy which however were to be neutralized; and that the French government would continue under Marshal Pétain at Vichy.

After the successful evacuation from Dunkirk and the conclusion of the land war operations in France, the RAF changed its offensive tactics against the Reich. In order to sow greater unrest among the German population, British bomber formations now began to raid several targets at the same time, mostly working districts in the large cities. This made it clear to the German leadership that antiaircraft artillery alone was not capable of defending the air space over Germany at night.

These night bombing raids posed many difficulties to the RAF as well. Its main problem was target location and precision aim, especially when increasingly powerful antiaircraft artillery forced planes to attack from higher altitudes, which made pinpoint targeting practically impossible. German fighter planes posed less of a problem because when the RAF night raids began in May 1940, the Germans had no distinct night interceptor units: They had not reckoned on this threat.

Adolf Hitler with his Luftwaffe chief Hermann Göring.

The German Luftwaffe's chief focus was now on training and equipment to repel night attacks. No night interceptor planes existed as yet, so the flak artillery had to fire a relatively ineffective umbrella barrage over targets while the day-fighters flew interception patrol, aided by searchlight batteries. This technique was known as *helle Nachtjagd* (night interception with searchlights) and the day-fighter planes that relied on searchlights to show them their targets, rarely came into position to attack. The first success of *helle Nachtjagd* came on the night of 28 June 1940 when the crew of a German Do 17 – Non-Commissioned Pilot Officer Schwarz, Flight Mechanic Staff Sergeant Born, and Radio Operator Staff Sergeant Palm – succeeded, on their first operation as night destroyers, in shooting down a bomber captured by the searchlights. This was the first of at least 4,000 British bombers that would fall victim to the aerial guns of German night interceptors over the next few years. However, *helle Nachtjagd* was heavily dependent on the weather and was possible only so long as the RAF bombers attacked in weak widespread formations.

With Italy's entrance into the war, the RAF's position in the Mediterranean and East Africa worsened considerably. Sir Arthur Longmore, the commander in chief of the British air force in Cairo, had only 29 squadrons at his command (about 300 aircraft), to cover Egypt, the Sudan, Palestine, Transjordan, East Africa, Aden, Somaliland, Iraq, Cyprus, Turkey, the Balkans, the Mediterranean Sea, the Red Sea and the Persian Gulf. He had a little less than one aircraft for each patch of land the size of Switzerland. Yet at the end of June, despite the

RAF Handley Page Hampden medium bombers. They had a tadpole fuselage [i.e. a deep forward fuselage with a slender tapered tail] that was only 36 inches wide at its widest point.

numerical superiority of the Italian air force, his Blenheim bombers attacked Italian airfields, seaports and troop concentrations, and at night the antiquated Bombays of 216 Squadron – designed as troop-carriers and bomber-transports – made Tobruk their chief target. Gloster Gladiators flew cover to hold off the enemy fighters, and the Lysanders of 208 Squadron pursued every Italian troop movement behind the front.

While these attacks were going on, Italian antiaircraft gunners made a serious blunder. On 28 June 1940, startled by two British Blenheims flying over Tobruk, an Italian antiaircraft battery opened fire on the next aircraft they saw, which crashed in flames. It turned out to be the plane of Air Marshal Balbo, the Italian governor of Libya, a famous aviator and the former commander of the Italian air force; he died in the crash.

1940

July to December

Tuesday 2 July 1940
The *Wehrmacht High Command* announced:

In the course of British air raids on north and west Germany on the night of 1st–2nd July, bombs were dropped on (among other places) Kiel, but caused only slight material damage. Several civilians were killed. A total of 5 enemy aircraft were shot down by flak artillery; besides these, 2 more enemy planes were brought down by German Navy flak during the night attack on Kiel. Three of our own aircraft are missing.

Thursday 4 July 1940, Berlin
The *German News Bureau* reported:

We have learned concerning the attack of the British fleet on French warships in the post of Oran [Algeria], that some of the ships were not under steam at the time of the sudden British assault, and were so positioned in the harbor that they could not bring their heavy artillery to bear. The battleships *Dunkerque* and *Provence,* as well as the combat flotilla leader *Mogador,* now lie burning in Oran harbor. The battleship *Bretagne* was apparently blown up by a British-laid mine as it put to sea. The battleship *Strasbourg,* five flotilla leaders and a large number of torpedo boats and submarines succeeded in fighting their way through the encircling British ships and broke through to the Mediterranean.

Secret Report of the *SS Secret Service* on German internal affairs, No. 102 of 4 July 1940 (extract):

Now that the military actions in France have been concluded and all eyes are directed exclusively on England, the English bombing attacks on the Reich have become the daily topic of conversation [in Germany] . . . The general mood of the [German] populace has not been essentially damaged even now by the enemy air attacks. To some extent these are being treated with humor, for example when people greet each other in the evening by saying "Have a [bomb]-splinter-free night!" . . . All discussion culminates again and again in the wish that we would finally proceed in earnest with our long-heralded retaliatory measures against England. The pitmen from the Ruhr district formulate this wish in the phrase we frequently hear repeated: "It's time that Hermann [Göring] opened up his pigeon loft and let them fly!" [i.e. let his Luftwaffe planes fly].

Saturday 6 July 1940, Vichy
The French *Havas News Agency* reported:

The French Admiralty has announced that because of the British fleet's attack on our naval combat forces which were in the process of disarmament, French naval officers are prohibited from wearing British medals.

Monday 8 July 1940, London
The *Exchange News Agency* reported:

Marshal Pétain's government has published a warning to all British war vessels and aircraft, not to approach the French coast. His naval and aerial combat forces have been ordered (he says) to open fire without previous warning on any British units that appear.

8 July 1940, Algiers
The *Reuters News Agency* reported:

Official confirmation has been received that French fighter planes and coastal batteries shot

down two British aircraft during the attack on the French fleet at Mers el Kebir (Oran).

Secret Report of the *SS Secret Service* on German internal affairs, No. 110 of Monday 29 July 1940 (extract):

V. The economy: The effects of night air raids on industrial production

. . . Thus Dortmund reports a falling-off in mining production there as a result of overfatigue and diminished resiliency. Many personnel say that they have a long way to go to get to the pits, and as a result they have only a short time to sleep at the end of the air raid alert. The consequence is that personnel frequently fall asleep, which is leading increasingly to short shifts. The alertness of personnel is also said to be suffering, so that already additional accidents have occurred.

Daily Keynote from the Reich Press Chief
Wednesday 7 August 1940:

In the matter of air leaflet propaganda, the Minister [of Propaganda, Goebbels] states that he does not expect much to come out of a German air leaflet propaganda campaign in England, because the amount of effort that would go into it would be out of all proportion to the results . . . The Minister admits that the most recent leaflets dropped by the British, are somewhat more dangerous than the earlier ones. He wishes to be informed at once of the exact wording of every new enemy leaflet that appears.

The Battle of Britain

Monday 12 August 1940, London
RAF Headquarters announced:

This morning a series of violent aerial combats involving more than one hundred aircraft took place over the Channel and the southeast coast of England. British fighter planes attacked a strong formation of enemy aircraft that was nearing the English coast, and so far have shot down 5 machines while seriously damaging other German aircraft.

12 August 1940
The *Wehrmacht High Command* announced:

As has already been revealed by a special announcement, German combat aircraft formations attacked the naval harbor of Portland on August 11. Important harbor installations, the jetty, the floating dock and a loading bridge were demolished; oil warehouses were set on fire. Two merchant vessels and one destroyer were badly hit.

12 August 1940, Berlin
The *German News Bureau* announced:

In the first segment of hostilities over the Channel and England on Monday, German fighter and destroyer aircraft have already shot down 22 aircraft according to reports received so far. German losses thus far are 6.

Tuesday 13 August 1940, London
The London *Evening News* reported:

Left: 12 August 1940, the French coast at Cape Gris Nez where the Germans had set up marine batteries. The staff of the German 3rd Air Fleet are seen observing dogfights over the English Channel.

Right: British Hurricane fighters are intercepting a flight of German Heinkel He 111 bombers on their way to attack London. This photo was taken with a monitor film camera built into the aircraft wings.

One of the greatest aerial battles ever to take place, happened this afternoon off the southeast and southern coasts. However, well-informed experts doubt that the present raids represent the beginning of a blitzkrieg against England, and instead believe their true purpose is to reconnoiter the strength of the RAF before the Germans mount even more vigorous air attacks.

13 August 1940, London
RAF Headquarters announced:

On Sunday night to early Monday morning, the "industrial squadrons" of the RAF chiefly attacked petroleum installations in Germany. The raids on each target were carried out by several squadrons at defined intervals, beginning shortly before midnight; the return flight did not start until 3:00 A.M.

13 August 1940, Berlin
The *German News Bureau* reported:

Aerial dogfights are continuing over the southern coast of England. More and more fresh formations of German bombers and dive bombers are flying against the English coast. The German bomber wings, which make their approach in compact formations at a fairly high altitude, are almost invariably escorted by Me 109 and Me 110 fighters. So far it has not once been observed that a German bomber formation was forced by the English to turn around before reaching its target. It has struck our attention that the fighting spirit of the English fighter pilots—especially the Spitfire pilots—has fallen off markedly since yesterday. According to reports received so far, 38 British aircraft were destroyed in aerial combat today (Tuesday) and 15 were destroyed on the ground.

Wednesday 14 August 1940
The *Wehrmacht High Command* announced:

On August 13, German aerial formations made effective bombing raids on the harbor and dock installations in Wallsend, Hartlepool, Bournemouth and Plymouth, and munitions plants in Exeter and Bristol, as well as major fuel storage depots in North Killingham . . .

A large number of violent dogfights took place during the raids in the Channel and on England, in the course of which 74 enemy aircraft were destroyed.

Air Raid Alert in Berlin

14 August 1940, Berlin
The American *United Press News Agency* reported:

Tonight an air raid alert was sounded in Berlin at 1:35 A.M. and ended at 2:22 A.M. This was the third alert in the German capital since the outbreak of war. No explosions could be heard from the vantage point of the United Press offices, nor were any searchlights seen operating. The German Ministry of Propaganda has stated that no details may be released as yet.

RAF Fighter Command headquarters: The general map with its marker tokens shows the momentary positions of the aerial forces.

14 August 1940, London
The *Reuters News Agency* reported:

The southeast of England has repeatedly been the arena of heavy dogfights. This morning more than 300 German aircraft took part in the raids; but the RAF fighters foiled the intrusion of the enemy planes. Dozens of Messerschmitt fighter planes dived from a great altitude to protect their bombers, but the British air defense was so effective that in most cases the enemy wings had to veer off and change course.

Thursday 15 August 1940, Berlin
The *German News Bureau* reported:

English reports claiming alleged losses suffered by the German Luftwaffe during its attacks on British airbases, harbors, munitions plants and convoys, have led to comment by the [German] press in articles with headlines like "England Flees into Numbers Craze" and "Delirium Still Mounting." The [newspaper] *Berliner Börsen-Zeitung* states that in no other way could the English demonstrate so clearly what they are seeking to hide at all costs: that their situation is desperate and that the blows struck by the German Luftwaffe have taught them the meaning of fear. Fear alone (says the *B.B-Z.*) could drive them to rave in this way about the supposed numbers of German and British losses.

Friday 16 August 1940, Berlin
The *German News Bureau* reported:

An authoritative source has informed us that in the course of this afternoon's aerial hostilities, one German aerial formation took off on a special mission. This combat group was deployed against all military and war-related targets immediately surrounding the British capital. The German Luftwaffe will offer proof that no power in the world can prevent it from dropping its bombs anywhere in England that it chooses—even, if it should be necessary, over the City of London.

Saturday 17 August 1940, London
The *Reuters News Agency* reported:

For the first time in the war German aircraft have bombed the suburbs of London, but the actual city of London neither saw enemy aircraft, nor heard the roar of their engines nor of antiaircraft fire. Londoners are quietly going about their work. In the evening the usual crowds are to be seen outside theaters and cinemas, and the parks are packed with strollers who will be very surprised to read in the morning papers what the Germans say about the great air battles over London. The first German report that London's port district had been "very badly damaged," provoked some mirth here; while the later German reports that their planes "danced" over London, that gigantic fires were raging on both sides of the Thames, and that a curtain of smoke lay across the whole of London, gave Londoners much amusement. When the air alert was sounded for the second time in twenty-four hours on Friday afternoon, at an hour when there was busy traffic on the streets, the majority of passers-by entered the air raid shelters in complete composure.

Daily Keynote from the Reich Press Chief
17 August 1940:

The Minister [of Propaganda, Goebbels] reckons that sooner or later the English will give up their present tactic of trivializing [the German air raids] and substitute a new tactic: playing the fiddle of humanitarian sentiment in order to "awaken the world's conscience," for which they will trot out murdered women, pregnant women, old people etc. for inspection. To meet this predictable eventuality, Herr Fritsche and Herr Böhmer [of the Ministry of Propaganda] should have material ready to hand, pictures of the children killed in Freiburg and so on . . .

First-Hand Observation Reports

Luftwaffe Front-Line Bulletin No. 5

Considerations on British Night Interception

The main night fighter planes deployed by the British are the single-seater fighter planes, the Supermarine Spitfire, the Hawker Hurricane and the Bristol Blenheim auxiliary destroyer. The testimony of captured prisoners has revealed that even the oldest-model Blenheims (Blenheim Mk I) have been converted into auxiliary destroyers and deployed in night interception. Single-seater fighters of the Gloster Gladiator type, which formerly were observed handling night interception, have just recently dropped from view. One straight-motor twin-engined aircraft has been observed.

British night fighters have been encountered along the whole length of the east and southeast coasts [of England], as well as sporadically in the hinterland. The focal points of night fighter defense have been over the Humber estuary, The Wash (inlet of North Sea) and the London area. Attacks ensued at all altitudes up to 16,000 feet.

The results of the final pre-war maneuvers told us that the British are not trying to institute permanent night interception zones but wish to deploy night fighters on a variable case-to-case basis, wherever they are needed. Thus the observed light signals on the ground cannot possibly represent the boundaries of night fighter zones but must have a purely navigational significance, for example to mark combat aircraft approach lanes. Such a [variable] system seems highly possible given that during deployment the British fighters are commanded by radiotelephone from ground stations [and so are not confined to patrolling fixed zones], and that antiaircraft artillery operates very sparingly at night [so that there is no risk of its firing on British planes]. It must be assumed that searchlights, antiaircraft artillery and night fighters are controlled from a single command post and that the antiaircraft artillery is deployed only as long as the night fighters cannot possibly have reached the enemy yet. Occasionally the antiaircraft artillery seems to fire leading shots. Cooperation between night fighter plane and searchlight appears to be conducted as follows: The enemy aircraft to be attacked is grasped by a searchlight, then the light briefly flashes a signal so that all the surrounding searchlights beam onto the plane; as a result its crew lose all visibility and the attacking night fighters are not perceived until they open fire. The night fighters attack individually or in combinations of up to three aircraft. When several planes collaborate, they put up position lights [so as not to fire on each other]. Occasionally individual night fighters were observed trying to illuminate the enemy aircraft by use of their own spotlight or landing searchlight.

Information supplied by captured prisoners has revealed that the Bristol Blenheim is the preferred night fighter because of its good visibility and stability. However, the glasswork panelling on the underside of the cockpit results in the pilot being blinded by his own [British] searchlights upon making his attack; this is described as extremely disruptive and dangerous.

It has been determined that during the summer

A British Hawker Hurricane night fighter. At this time it was still slower than the German Messerschmitt Me 109 E fighter-destroyer, so it was deployed to intercept German bombers.

months the nights in England (above all in the north of England) are so bright that aircraft can be seen silhouetted against the northern sky (which is still light) from as far as a mile or more away [2 km]. On dark nights successful attacks on unilluminated aircraft have as a rule been made only when the position of the aircraft was revealed to the enemy by some kind of light source (exhaust flames, position lanterns, interior lighting).

Life Buoy from the General Air Affairs Chief

Luftwaffe Front-Line Bulletin No. 22:

At the instigation of the General Chief of Air Affairs [Göring's aide], Colonel General Udet, the Reich Ministry of Aviation has developed a life buoy for the rescue of German aircraft crews forced to make an emergency sea landing at some distance from the coast. The buoy is designed to shelter the crew until the arrival of emergency rescue vehicles. It is approximately 13 feet long, 8 feet wide and 8 feet deep and on its upper deck carries a tower just under 6 feet high with a signal mast and antenna. The buoy can accommodate 4 men for several days and in an emergency can also receive the crews of several aircraft.

The crew who have taken charge of one of these life buoys are obliged, upon reaching the coast, to report the fact immediately and to cite the number of the buoy, so that the provisions and clothing they have used can be replaced.

In conclusion it should be pointed out that sealing plugs that can be driven in with a mallet have been furnished to seal bullet holes that may arise in the buoy wall. A pump can be used to pump out water that has already penetrated the buoy.

19 August 1940, Rome
The *Italian High Command* announced:

In British Somaliland our troops have broken through the enemy's second line of defense, occupied La Faruk and crossed over. They pursued the enemy, who withdrew to his ships, and also bombed these. A British plane was shot down by Italian fighter planes. An enemy air raid on Kassala (East Africa) caused neither casualties nor damage. Another enemy air attack on the Addis Ababa airfield resulted in 2 dead and 5 wounded; hits were also scored on two hangars that contained only antiquated equipment.

Emergency life buoys for shot-down German air crews. They were suggested by Generaloberst Ernst Udet, Göring's friend and Luftwaffe aide whose tragic suicide inspired dramatist Carl Zuckmayer in his 1946 play *Des Teufels General* [The Devil's General].

Sunday 25 August 1940
RAF Headquarters announced:

A night raid on the City of London has been carried out by two or four German bombers—the exact number has not yet been determined—that made a surprise attack emerging out of low-hanging clouds. Not one military target was bombed; but one business center caught fire so that the London sky glowed bright red. The toll of the injured is slight.

25 August 1940, London
The *Reuters News Agency* reported:

The air alert in London on Saturday afternoon took place during a championship Tottenham football match. The huge crowd tried to outscream the alarm sirens, making a wild noise so as to prevent the match from being broken off. The same sort of thing went on at the greyhound races. Huge ovations greeted the sight of British aircraft.

Monday 26 August 1940
The *Wehrmacht High Command* announced:
On the night of 25th–26th August, a large number of aircraft bombed airplane and munitions factories in Birmingham, Kingston and Coventry . . . That same night, for the first time since war began, several enemy aircraft flew over Berlin and released a number of incendiary bombs along the city limits. In the rest of Germany, random bombs were released at various points over nonmilitary targets. No damage was inflicted either there or in Berlin. One of the aircraft that flew over Berlin was shot down by flak on its return journey.

26 August 1940, Berlin
The American *United Press News Agency* announced:
Shortly after midnight (12:20 A.M.) an air alert was called in the German capital. During the first ten minutes, 10 heavy explosions could be heard in the city center that made the ground tremble. There was persistent audible flak fire, interrupted by heavy explosions that probably came from impacting bombs.

26 August 1940, London
The *Reuters News Agency* reported:
Early on Sunday, dense smoke clouds lay over London. The considerable number of fires is attributed to the fact that German aircraft dropped incendiary bombs inside large collecting bins that opened as they fell scattering the contents far and wide. So far only a few people have been reported with severe injuries.

26 August 1940, Berlin
The American *United Press News Agency* added the following supplementary report:
It has been confirmed here that during yesterday's attack on Berlin, British bombers released not only incendiary bombs but also air leaflets over many parts of the city. The leaflets were collected by the police immediately.

Friday 6 September 1940, Stockholm
Swedish radio announced:
Starting immediately, we will be ending our transmissions at the earlier hour of 10:30 P.M. Transmission time has been reduced because of the effect that night-time radio transmissions have on aerial combat navigation.

Saturday 7 September 1940, Berlin
The *German News Bureau* announced:
As reported, the operation of the German Luftwaffe has already succeeded in substantially weakening the military strength of England at several important points. The British aerial forces are qualitatively and quantitatively inferior to the German to begin with, because they do not have anywhere near such efficient production plants. Even the reinforcements from the USA are by no means extensive enough, and are not arriving fast enough, to seal the developing gaps. Thus marked signs of exhaustion are already apparent in the behavior of the British fighters. Moreover, German Luftwaffe leaders have so far been very sparing in their deployment of bomber and fighter wings, and they still have substantial reserves available with which to intensify the struggle against England.

7 September 1940, Cairo
The *British Middle East Air Force (Egypt)* announced:
Yesterday Italian aircraft made three air raids on Marsa Matruh and inflicted some damage. It is believed that two attacking machines were damaged by British ground defenses. In Palestine on Friday

afternoon, Italian aircraft attacked Haifa. The British air defense went into action and forced the assault aircraft to turn around. There were no casualties and no damage was inflicted. There is nothing to report from the other fronts.

7 September 1940, Rome
The *Italian High Command* announced:

Italian bombers have again bombed oil refineries in the center of Haifa and caused extensive fires. In North Africa our planes bombed the rail line between Alexandria and Marsa Matruh.

Target: London

The following descriptive account appeared in the Nazi newspaper *Völkischer Beobachter,* September 1940:

We climb in and then everything goes off "like

Above: A Ju 88 takes off on a night raid. This most versatile and most produced bomber of the German Luftwaffe (14,676 were built), could not adequately fend off the RAF fighters despite its relatively powerful guns.

Right: This time a German mission has ended in no more than a few artillery-holes. During the Battle of Britain all the German He 111 bomber formations suffered high casualties.

yesterday" again. We maintain a high altitude until we reach the east coast of England, passing alternately through hail and snow showers.

The Tommy soldiers are on the alert. Above and below us fly the cotton swabs of exploding flak shells. The glaring light of searchlights holds onto us briefly. We manage to escape by evasive maneuvers. A [British] night fighter plane flies past right beside us, headed in the opposite direction . . .

Menz was first to recognize the Thames. Large numbers of fires at many points have already joined to form a huge unbroken glow. It must be hell down there. Our heaviest-caliber bombs are released and whistle far below.

The flak fire is getting uncomfortable. The flak cloudlets are damned close. We turn around and fly back. Again we have to pass through the antiaircraft barrage around London. Suddenly there's a hit! Our right engine begins to tremble. The whole machine is vibrating. The engine stops. We are hanging over the center of London. Fortunately we are still fairly high up. Slowly and steadily losing altitude, we sail eastward in glide flight. I have given up hope of our reaching the continent. . . . Only a few hundred feet above the ground, we emerge from the clouds and see the coast.

We are over German territory, and we succeed in making an emergency night landing, setting down our heavy Ju 88 in open country. Our good Ju and a clump of trees both have to fight hard to believe it. We are a bit scratched up ourselves. But we made it after all. Two hours later I am already lying in a military hospital.

Fresh Attacks on London

Sunday 8 September 1940
The *Wehrmacht High Command* announced:

The Luftwaffe attacked the port and city of London in strength for the first time on Saturday afternoon. The raids were a retaliation for the night raids of British aircraft on nonmilitary German targets that have been carried out in increasing numbers in the last few weeks. One single vast cloud of smoke now stretches from the London city center to the mouth of the Thames.

8 September 1940, London
The *Reuters News Agency* reported:

During the German raids of Saturday, the traditional Saturday afternoon matches continued uninterrupted play on various football grounds, despite the fact that the most violent dogfights were going on over the heads of the players and spectators, and that exploding bombs and antiaircraft fire were making a deafening noise. Admittedly the Londoners exposed themselves to serious risk by this behavior. For example, a bomb fell onto the racecourse during a greyhound race where between 5,000 and 6,000 spectators were present. No one was injured, so the race continued.

Daily Keynote from the Reich Press Chief
8 September 1940:

The Minister has provided guidelines for the [German] press's treatment of the grand assault on London which is due to continue for several more days.

1. Strict attention must be paid to maintaining the claim that our attacks are directed solely against military installations. Should civilian targets be hit as well, this is because many military targets lie in the middle of the city of London.

2. Cynical phrases that repeatedly turn up in British reports—like "Today English fliers had an opportunity to practice bomb drill over Nuremberg"—should be heavily underscored by us to show the justification of our retaliatory measures.

3. Even though emphasis must be placed on increased speed [of press releases] just now, the psychological aspects must not therefore be neglected. It is wrong to allude beforehand to the heavy casualties that our raids will cost: we can only talk of very minor casualties, or else give clear exact figures. Likewise it is impossible even to so much as leave open the possibility that German planes have

not dropped their bombs with precision on military targets.

8 September 1940, London
The *Reuters News Agency* reported:

On Saturday night through to the early hours of Sunday, heart-rending scenes took place in London's East End when a bomb fell into the ventilation shaft of an air shelter harboring hundreds of people. The bomb killed a great many women, children and elderly.

Daily Keynote from the Reich Press Chief
Tuesday 10 September 1940:

The British air raids on Berlin and Hamburg on Monday night/Tuesday morning should be played up, magnifying all the details as much as possible, in such a way as to further validate our retaliatory measures in the eyes of the world. Furthermore material from the last few months should be exploited more than it has been so far, to make plain the justification of our measures.

Daily Keynote from the Reich Press Chief
Wednesday 11 September 1940:

The British attack on Berlin on Tuesday night/Wednesday morning should be denounced by the press with blazing indignation as an attack on our national symbols. However, in the interests of good preparation, the press should as a general principle wait until the morning papers to bring out a summarizing view, unless the individual newspapers have already done satisfactory groundwork of their own accord, without the need of a previous press conference.

Saturday 14 September 1940, Berlin
The American *United Press News Agency* reported:

A clear indication of the optimism reigning in Berlin with regard to the outcome of the war, is the fact that during the last few days bets have been concluded all over Germany that the war will end soon. For example, in officer circles it has been wagered that the campaign against England will end successfully at the beginning of October. Journalists, on the other hand, are betting that the war will end on October 15.

This dominant optimism seems partly traceable to the fact that for the last two nights the RAF has not paid a visit to Berlin. Conversation in cafés and on the street also reflects this confident mood.

What Should People Out on the Road Do in an Air Alert?

The German newspaper *Völkischer Beobachter,* September 1940:

The Commander in Chief of the Luftwaffe [Göring] has issued an order of particular significance to the larger cities. An announcement states that the main recourse of people out on the streets, especially streetcar and bus passengers, is the public air shelters indicated by pointer signs. In areas not equipped with public air shelters, it is a clear duty to shelter travellers in private air shelters if any space at all is available.

Monday 16 September 1940, Berlin
The *German News Bureau* announced:

The English report stating that 175 German air-

Left: September 1940. Firemen are desperately fighting the fires in London's Eastcheap district.

Above right: The last moments in the lives of a German He 111 air crew. Seconds later their bomber exploded over London.

craft were shot down on Sunday during the aerial fights over London, bears no relation to the facts. This exaggeration of German losses can only be attributed to the difficult position in which England finds itself as a result of the incessant German air raids which continue without interruption even in bad weather.

16 September 1940, London
The *Reuters News Agency* reported:

Today, when four separate waves of the German Luftwaffe have attacked England so far (4:00 P.M.), the characteristic marks of approaching autumn are making their appearance for the first time. Rain has been pouring down since early morning, and low-hanging clouds and thick fog veils are obscuring visibility. Particularly poor weather conditions are reported from the Channel coast, where gales are raging in some places. The German Luftwaffe seems to be adjusting to the changed atmospheric conditions by flying at higher altitudes than formerly. Moreover, for the first time a change in assault tactics has been observed: Whereas in the past German bombers have flown in long, stretched-out formations, today a dense square formation has been reported which apparently is designed by its impact to force a breach through the fighter plane defense. Each of today's attack waves has displayed this kind of compact formation, followed by loose groups of bomber and fighter planes.

Daily Keynote from the Reich Press Chief
Wednesday 18 September 1940:

1. The Navy has again reported damage to the British aircraft carrier *Ark Royal.* The Minister has ordered the greatest caution to be taken in the treatment of this case so that we are not caught out again [making false damage reports about the *Ark Royal*].

2. By order of the Führer, enemy air raids on Germany should be played up on a large scale in future, even when relatively little damage has occurred. Attention should also be paid to treating raids on other [German] cities as of equal importance to attacks on the capital.

Daily Keynote from the Reich Press Chief
Wednesday 25 September 1940:

The night raid on Berlin should again be played up on a large scale, although care must be taken not to mention any details that would supply the English with important information. Further, events must not be exaggerated so much that Churchill can use the German reports to give the English people the

impression that our attacks on London and British attacks on Germany are more or less balancing each other out.

Over 100 French Bombers Raid Gibraltar

Several Enemy Aircraft Shot Down

26 September 1940
The *Gibraltar Chronicle* reported:

Today the fortress commandant of British-held Gibraltar issued a communiqué about yesterday afternoon's attack:

Today a large number of French aircraft again raided Gibraltar. The alarm was sounded at 2:33 P.M. Shortly thereafter the antiaircraft artillery opened a heavy barrage and the first bombs fell. Several waves of bombers dumped their payloads—mostly from a high altitude—until 4:50 P.M. Over one hundred aircraft were counted; they released approximately 300 bombs of varying explosive calibers. Although the majority fell onto rock or into the sea, houses, streets and the old fortress installations were also hit.

Private homes and government buildings suffered some damage, but the damage to military targets and personal injuries were slight.

Daily Keynote from the Reich Press Chief
Friday 11 October 1940:

The Minister has once again specified the wishes of the Luftwaffe staff leaders that we issue formal denials in all cases when the English claim to have hit military targets, unless the English have hit the corresponding mock installations . . . The Luftwaffe has repeatedly raised objections to the use of expressions like "air pirates" or "night pirates," but on the other hand the Reich Chancellery desires that these expressions be used: Therefore the Wehrmacht High Command [the OKW] should take up the matter with the Führer.

Daily Keynote from the Reich Press Chief
Monday 14 October 1940:

The British raids on Berlin (or other German territory) should not be presented in such an exaggerated form that the reader is bound to get the impression that half Berlin has been destroyed. But by the same token, the destruction in London should not be depicted so as to suggest that London has already been razed to the ground: in each case the possibility of intensified attacks must be preserved.

Daily Keynote from the Reich Press Chief
Tuesday 22 October 1940:

The Minister has reported the results of his trip yesterday to view an air raid shelter destroyed by bombs . . . In addition the Führer has ordered the visiting of air raid shelters, and thus any further discussion is superfluous.

In the aerial operations theater at RAF Fighter Command, the women's auxiliary corps (WAAFs) work at the synoptic table recording the newest positions of British and enemy fighter formations.

Foreign Aircraft over Sweden

Friday 25 October 1940, Stockholm
The Swedish newspaper *Svenska Dagbladet* reported:

Yesterday at 4:00 P.M., a German fighter plane coming from Norway was forced to make an emergency landing north of Karlstad [Sweden]. The non-commissioned officer on board, and the aircraft, were interned by the Swedish military. Major Sundell, the defense staff chief of the Swedish antiaircraft department, stated that around 40 foreign aircraft have already been forced to make emergency landings onto Swedish territory since war began—chiefly due to the work of the Swedish air defense.

Foreign Fliers in England

25 October 1940, London
The British *Air Ministry* announced:

The number of Allied fliers in England has risen markedly. At the moment 8,000 Polish airmen are serving in England, including approximately 3,000 pilots. Of these, 200 flying officers and 2,000 men of other ranks came to England as early as autumn 1939, and another 6,000 men from the Polish air force arrived after the collapse of France. The Czechs have furnished 1,000 airmen including 300 pilots. General de Gaulle commands over 600 French pilots. The Belgian air force is represented by 100 men and the Dutch by 300. These figures do not include the large numbers of personnel from these nations who are now undergoing training. Lastly, England is now the home of the Eagle Squadron of American volunteers which is steadily growing by the arrival of experienced airmen.

25 October 1940
The *Wehrmacht High Command* announced:

In the course of the German Luftwaffe's hostilities against England, Italian air combat formations have taken off from their base in the occupied zone for the first time. Boldly-led raids and well-aimed bombs have enabled them to achieve great success against harbor installations in the eastern parts of the British Isles.

SACCONE & SPEED LTD.
(Established 1839)
130, Main Street Gibraltar
The firm with a Century's experience in
WINES, SPIRITS, CIGARS, CIGARETTES & TOBACCO

VAT 69
"Quality Tells"
LIQUEUR SCOTCH WHISKY

Gibraltar Chronicle
MONTIS INSIGNIA CALPE
AND OFFICIAL GAZETTE.

Vol. CCIV.—No. 31,890. WEDNESDAY, SEPTEMBER 25, 1940. Price One Penny

OFFICIAL GAZETTE

25th SEPTEMBER, 1940.

GOVERNMENT NOTICE No. 214.

THE CURRENCY NOTE ORDINANCE (CAP. 29)

The half yearly statements required under Section 9(1) of the above mentioned Ordinance are published for general information as a supplement to this Gazette.

Colonial Secretary's Office, Gibraltar, 25th September, 1940. (M.P. No. 303/34).
By Command, ALEXR. E. BEATTIE, Colonial Secretary.

POST OFFICE NOTICE.

It is hereby notified for general information that the Scud Hill Sub Post Office is closed until further notice.

General Post Office, Gibraltar, 24th September, 1940. (P.O. Ref. 4/31/72).
H. G. JESSOP, Colonial Postmaster.

POST OFFICE NOTICE.

It is notified for general information that the transaction of business at the public counters will be suspended when incoming overseas mails are being sorted.

2. The enquiry counter will remain open.

3. Business will be resumed immediately the mails have been sorted.

4. After 7.00 p.m. the transaction of business will be confined to the delivery of registered and surcharged correspondence for Private Letter Box holders and the Office will be opened for this purpose, if sorting is not completed before 7.00 p.m., for one hour provided attendance after 10.30 p.m. is not entailed.

General Post Office, Gibraltar, 24th September, 1940. (P.O. Ref. 72/40/2).
H. G. JESSOP, Colonial Postmaster.

GIBRALTAR RAID LASTS 2½ HOURS

4 KILLED, 12 INJURED BY INTERMITTENT BOMBING

Gibraltar's fifth and longest air-raid is described in the following press communique issued by Fortress H.Q. last evening:

"Some twenty or more aircraft of French types, taking advantage of low patches of levanter cloud, began to bomb Gibraltar from a height of about 20,000 feet at 12.45 hours to-day.

"They were engaged by anti-aircraft defences from ships and shore. Bombing continued intermittently for 2½ hours with some low dives below clouds.

"Approximately 100 bombs were dropped, many in the sea. Some damage was done to buildings and roads, and three small fires were started but were soon under control.

"Casualties so far reported are four killed and 12 wounded.

"Damage to the enemy is uncertain but at least one aircraft is believed to have been shot down."

REPRISAL FOR DAKAR, SAYS GERMAN NEWSAGENCY

(Through Reuters Agency)

London, September 24.

The German newsagency, quoting what is said to be a Vichy report, says 120 French warplanes stationed in Morocco heavily bombed Gibraltar as a reprisal for the British bombardment of Dakar.

The agency adds that it is believed in Vichy that Britain is planning a serious campaign in connection with the French colonies.

ALGECIRAS CONTRADICTS PREMATURE REPORT

Berlin, Later.

A despatch from Algeciras to the official newsagency states there is no confirmation of reports that French aircraft bombed Gibraltar.

In Algeciras it is merely known

DAKAR EMISSARIES FIRED UPON

No British Landing Attempted

(British Official Press)

London, September 24.

There is no truth in reports emanating from Vichy that any British landing at or near Dakar has been attempted.

The course of events, which occurred after the arrival of General de Gaulle, is described in the following communique issued by General de Gaulle's headquarters in London.

"Called to Dakar by numerous Frenchmen anxious to continue the fight at his side Gen. de Gaulle appeared with French soldiers and sailors before the fortress.

The naval authorities at Dakar ordered fire to be opened on Gen. de Gaulle's emissaries who had come without weapons in a motor-launch flying the tri-colour and the white flag.

Two of these four emissaries, Captains Dargealiu and Perr[illegible] were seriously wounded.

Later Gen. de Gaulle, having attempted to land his troops peacefully, fire was opened by the Dakar authorities on the French sloop [illegible] vorgnan de Brazza, Commandant Duboc and Commandant Dom.

Several men were killed and many wounded.

Gen. de Gaulle then withdrew his troops and ships, not wanting to be a party to a fight between Frenchmen."

With regard to subsequent developments it is authoritatively stated that operations are continuing.

FRENCH SUBMARINE SUNK AT DAKAR, SAYS VICHY

Vichy, September [illegible]

According to a Havas message from Dakar, two attempts [illegible] were made during the night [illegible] were repulsed.

ENEMY PLANES FAIL TO REACH LONDON

SOUTHAMPTON & BRIGHTON IN LATER ATTACKS

(British Official Press)

London, September 24.

LAST NIGHT'S RAIDS OVER ENGLAND

FOUR HOSPITALS HIT IN LONDON AREA

(Through Reuters Agency)

London, September 25.

London was again the main objective of the attacks made by enemy

A Gibraltar newspaper reports the largest bombing raid the French have made in the war so far.

Saturday 26 October 1940, Rome
The special correspondent of the Italian *Stefani News Agency* reported from the Channel coast:

In the night preceding Thursday 25 October, the Corpo Aereo Italiano began its collaboration with the German Luftwaffe against southeast England. Its aircraft bombed industrial and naval centers of great military importance for more than one hour. They released many metric tons of explosives and caused a number of fires that were fanned by the strong wind. Despite vigorous antiaircraft fire, all the Italian aircraft were able to carry out their missions without losses to themselves.

Raid on the Transport Vessel "Empress of Britain"

Luftwaffe Front-Line Bulletin No. 26

On Saturday 26 October 1940, a Focke-Wulf 200 Condor took off under the command of 1st Lt. Jope (pilot) with the following crew: Lt. Burkhardt, second pilot; NCO Dörschel, flight mechanic; NCO Iwang, 1st radio operator; Airman 2nd Class Mix, 2nd Radio Operator; Dr. Habich, meteorologist, on an armed reconnaissance and weather-scouting mission over northwest Ireland. During this flight a large vessel with 3 smokestacks was sighted west of Ireland. Despite powerful antiaircraft activity which inflicted serious hits on the attacking aircraft after its first assault, the German plane inflicted 2 severe hits on the ship in a total of 4 daring low-level attacks. As the plane was flying away, the ship showed a slight list and was burning along its whole length. Mission "Weather Reconnaissance" was carried out at the conclusion of this success. The assaulted ship burned for 24 hours and the following day its wreck was sunk by a U-boat. The vessel in question was the passenger steamer *Empress of Britain,* which at 42,000 tons was the tenth largest ship in the international merchant fleet and did service as a troop transport vessel.

Monday 28 October 1940, London
The *Reuters News Agency* reported:

The Admiralty has announced that the English steamship *Empress of Britain* has gone down. The vessel was attacked by enemy aircraft and caught fire so that it had to be evacuated. Salvage maneuvers were instituted at once, but when the steamer was taken in tow, it reared up and sank. Of a total 643 persons on board, 598 survivors were brought to land by British war vessels. They included the families of military men and a small number of military personnel. The energetic and effective action of the steamer's antiaircraft defense was largely responsible for the fact that so many people were saved.

The vessel was a 42,000-ton luxury steamer. The British royal couple sailed home on her last year from their trip to Canada and the United States.

Sunday 10 November 1940
The *Wehrmacht High Command* announced:

Our aerial combat formations continued their retaliatory raids on London all day and through the night. Once again they hit a large number of war-related industrial plants.

Tuesday 12 November 1940
The *Italian High Command* announced:

Last night enemy aircraft raided the Italian naval port of Taranto. The antiaircraft artillery in the harbor and on the ships anchored there, emitted strong defensive fire. Only one shipping unit was severely hit. Six enemy aircraft were shot down and a portion of their crews taken prisoner. We can count on 3 more machines being lost [later from damage].

Thursday 14 November 1940, London
The British *Air Ministry* announced:

Today the German Luftwaffe made several unsuccessful attempts to penetrate to London. British fighters put up vigorous resistance enabling them to repel each of the attack waves. Not one bomb fell on London.

14 November 1940, Rome
The Italian *Stefani News Agency* reported:

The Italian Armed Forces Bulletin No. 138 reported on the enemy raid on Taranto on the night of 11th–12th November. Yesterday in the House of Commons, Churchill gave a completely false version of this incident. However, Italian authorities do not think it necessary to reply to this kind of tendentious twisting of the facts.

14 November 1940, London
The British *Air Ministry* announced:

On the night before Thursday, the Italian naval port of Taranto was again bombed by aircraft of the Royal Navy.

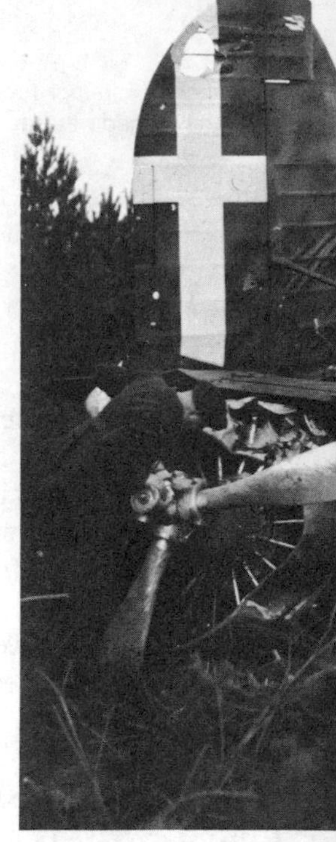

Eastern England, 11 November 1940: The wreck of an Italian air force Fiat BR.20 Cicogna (Stork) light bomber. This ruin befell the first Italian "invasion" of Britain since 429 A.D. when the Roman legions left Britain.

Coventry

Friday 15 November 1940
The *Wehrmacht High Command* announced:

After an improvement in weather conditions, the Luftwaffe was able, on the night of 14th– 15th November, to deal an extraordinarily heavy blow to its enemy in retaliation for the British raids on Munich by a grand assault on important munitions targets in central England. Relay attacks by the powerful air combat formations of Field Marshals Kesselring and Sperrle, were particularly intensive and successful over Coventry, where a number of engine factories and large aircraft accessory plants, as well as other war-related installations, were raided with heavy-caliber bombs causing immense devastation.

15 November 1940, Coventry
The British *Air Ministry* announced:

The night attack [on Coventry] by the German Luftwaffe caused very severe damage especially in the city center. The new enemy tactic was first to release many hundreds of bundled incendiary bombs from a large number of raiders at high altitude; the bombs caused violent conflagrations in the most disparate quarters of the city and directly beside the fourteenth-century cathedral. Twenty minutes later, when members of the Civil Air Guard and the fire brigade were busy fighting the fires and rescuing the people buried in the rubble, more German formations appeared and released a multitude of high-explosive bombs.

15 November 1940, London
The British *Home Office* announced:

The toll of victims of the air raid made on Coventry last night, may possibly reach 1,000. There is very great material damage. Many buildings including the cathedral have been demolished.

The Night over Coventry

Extract from *Flights against England [Flüge gegen England],* published by the High Command of the German Armed Forces (the OKW), 1941:

Quietly our commanding officer gave the pilot his approach instructions: "A little more to the right, still a little more. Fine, now we're in position." We came nearer and nearer. The horrible yet beautiful scene was close enough to touch. Dense smoke rose over the roofs of the city and stretched far into the countryside. We could distinctly see tall flames flickering upward. One particularly large fire among the countless others, showed where an extensive industrial plant must have been badly hit. We were over our target. The antiaircraft artillery fired des-

perately. We were surrounded by the flashes of exploding shells. We could see clearly the vast extent of the fire-centers and the flames licking across large areas of this industrial town. At that moment our bombs too were released. A blow passed through the plane. Down below, the glow of fresh explosions shot up with the brightness of daylight. We were the first machine of a group of German bombers. Others had been there before us, and more followed—until dawn of the new day that would reveal the full extent of the Coventry disaster.

Coventry in Ruins

15 November 1940, London
The American *Associated Press News Agency* reported:

German bombers have destroyed the heart of this formerly peaceful town in the English Midlands in a raid that lasted from the evening dusk until dawn, turned parts of the city into an inferno and left at least 1,000 people dead and injured. Coventry's wonderful and famous red-brown sandstone cathedral is a pile of smoking ruins . . . Throughout the night the narrow streets through which Lady Godiva rode her horse almost one thousand years ago, trembled and cracked under the thunder of the dive bombers, the howling and explosions of the bombs, and the crackling of the antiaircraft artillery.

Saturday 16 November 1940, Cairo
The *British Middle East Air Force (Egypt)* announced:

During Thursday night and early Friday morning, British planes raided Berlin, Hamburg, Bremen and ports from Stavanger, Norway to Lorient in Brittany. The raid on Berlin had already begun by early evening and was carried on for several hours by relief waves of aircraft. It caused a number of serious fires that were visible from a distance of as much as 30 miles away.

Monday 9 December 1940
The *Wehrmacht High Command* announced:

On the night of 8th–9th December, in retaliation for the British air assaults on western German cities, the German Luftwaffe mounted very heavy forces in a grand assault on London and operated in relays from nightfall until morning. Illumination was good and bombers dropped the heaviest caliber bombs on the city and especially on vital supply installations. Huge fires developed at many points which in the course of the night joined to form one huge blazing sea of flame.

9 December 1940, Rome
The *Italian High Command* announced:

Despite unfavorable weather conditions the Regia Aeronautica has bombed military targets at Santa Maura [= the Greek island of Levkas] and the Arta Bay. In East Africa there were enemy air raids on Gallibat and Gherille (Somaliland), resulting in several deaths and injuries.

9 December 1940, Cairo
The *British Middle East Air Force (Egypt)* announced:

Reconnaissance flights have revealed that extensive damage was done during the [British] bombing of Castel Benito near Tripoli on December 7. In the hours leading to Monday morning, British planes raided the Benina airfield [East Africa].

The Fireguard Tower Observers

The Nazi newspaper *Völkischer Beobachter* reported in December 1940:

To oversee where the fire department must lend aid during and after an air raid, every [German] city under air threat now has tower observers and civil air patrols. The tower observer will report the direction and estimated distance of observed fires to the

The firemen of Coventry. The bombing raid on this city was prelude to the turning point in the strategic air war in Europe.

communications center of the local civil air patrol headquarters. But these data would be insufficient for the fire department, because in a city like Berlin, Essen, Stuttgart or Munich the tower observer can rarely indicate exactly what is burning and what is the extent of the fire—two things that it is absolutely essential for the fire department to know. Thus the most important fireguard role is assigned to the civil air patrols.

Daily Keynote from the Reich Press Chief
Monday 23 December 1940:

Once again the British have dropped 5 bombs on Zürich. The Minister emphatically reminds us of his earlier instructions not to praise Switzerland for the furious remarks of the Swiss press regarding the British attacks. It is not in our interests to show gratitude for any protests that Switzerland might happen to make.

Strategy and Tactics

July to December 1940

In the first days of July the newly-assembled British naval formation Force H (under Vice-Admiral Somerville) put out to sea from Gibraltar with the aircraft carrier *Ark Royal,* the battle cruiser *Hood,* two battleships and several cruisers and destroyers, to launch "Operation Catapult," the largest and most successful Royal Navy operation of the war so far—although unfortunately it was aimed against the navy of France, Britain's erstwhile brother-in-arms. The Swordfish torpedo bombers in particular proved their worth in this operation.

Churchill stated that the purpose of Operation Catapult was either to seize and bring under British control as many French vessels as possible, or to put them out of action and destroy them. It was essential to the British that the French fleet should not fall into German hands, for its possession would have more than doubled the striking force of the German Navy after the losses it had suffered in Norway.

Admittedly, Admiral Darlan, the French naval minister, had given orders that no French war vessels were to fall into German hands, but Churchill wanted to avoid any risk that the Germans might violate the terms of the ceasefire agreement and seize the French fleet after all. On Wednesday 3 July the powerful Force H appeared outside the French naval base of Oran (Algeria) and demanded that the French commander, Admiral Gensoul, join Force H or sink his units. At 5:40 P.M., after the time specified in the British ultimatum had run out, the British opened fire. Within 15 minutes the bulk of the French warships had been sunk or put out of action.

The French ships had not weighed anchor, so they made an easy target. The battleship *Strasbourg* and the torpedo-destroyers *Terrible, Tigre* and *Volta* severed their anchors and sailed through the British-laid mines surrounded by the thundering salvos of British ships and pursued by British aircraft. Next day three waves of torpedo bombers from the aircraft carrier *Ark Royal* vainly attempted to sink the *Dunkerque,* which was lying only slightly damaged in Mers el Kebir. By strafing the French motor-torpedo boats loaded with rescued seamen, the British raiders raised French casualties to 1,297 after 977 had gone down on the battleship *Bretagne* alone.

On Thursday 4 July 1940, the first aerial combats between British and French aircraft took place about 30 leagues southwest of Gibraltar. Three French Curtiss Hawk fighters attacked a British Sunderland flying boat (seaplane) that was just then on patrol against German U-boats. The flying boat shot down one fighter and damaged a second.

On Monday 8 July 1940, British torpedo bombers from the carrier *Hermes,* made a torpedo attack on the new French battleship *Richelieu* anchored in Dakar (French West Africa). Winston Churchill stated later that it made a deep impression on all nations that the French Navy was eliminated as a power factor, almost at a single blow, in one powerful operation.

When news of these events reached Vichy, Laval and Darlan demanded that France declare war on Great Britain. Two days later Darlan told the French Cabinet that he had asked the Italian Admiralty to join with him in a naval attack on Alexandria in order to liberate the French fleet encircled there. At the same time he proposed a French raid on the British colony of Sierra Leone in West Africa, and a bombing assault on Gibraltar.

On Wednesday 10 July 1940, as a prelude to the Battle of Britain, the German 2nd and 3rd Air Fleets [Luftflotten], under Air Fleet Generals Kesselring and Sperrle respectively, raided military targets in southern England in force, for the first time. Their main aim was to challenge the British fighter planes to combat.

In mid-July 1940, weeks before the Battle of Britain actually began, Hitler decided to attack the Soviet Union. From then on, the battle in the West lost its priority status in the planning the German high command.

The first effective air defense measure by the Germans was taken on Wednesday 17 July 1940, when Colonel Kammhuber was assigned to build up a night fighter organization. He set up the first German night interceptor division, composed of the 1st Group of the 1st Destroyer Wing [I/Zerstörergeschwader 1] along with night fighter squadrons from various fighter wings. The division was known as the 1st Night Fighter Wing [NJG1 = Nachtjagdgeschwader 1] under Major Falck.

The aircraft warning and radio interception service in Germany was expanded more and more, but Germany never overtook Britain's one-year lead resulting from the early development of radar. Germany extended a network of radar stations from the coast of northern France to the coast of northern Germany and to Berlin, that was known as the *Himmelbett* ("Four-Poster Bed") system, in which each station was equipped to guide one German interceptor to its intruder target. The system functioned even under unfavorable weather conditions and was also known as *dunkle Nachtjagd* [unilluminated night interception, as opposed to *helle Nachtjagd,* the night interception system that lit up the enemy bomber in a box of searchlights and was dependent on clear weather conditions].

The German night fighter units were stationed at Dutch airfields so as to intercept the enemy as early as possible. The division command post was in Zeist near Utrecht.

Not until the end of July did Hitler decide to intensify the air and sea war against Britain. On 2 August 1940 Order No. 17 was issued: "To destroy the RAF and the British aircraft industry, 2. to disrupt the British food supply, and 3. to inflict extensive damage on the British merchant and war navy. The intensified air offensive should be launched by August 5 . . . " This order posed a completely novel task for the Luftwaffe: For the first time it was

The Royal Navy and British torpedo bombers attack the French naval base at Mers el Kebir (Oran) on 3 July 1940.

commanded to operate independently of the other armed forces as prescribed in the theories of General Douhet, and to win a victory that would decide the outcome of war, before the German Navy and Army moved on to Operation Sea Lion, the invasion of England. Instead of making its tried-and-true blitz strikes, it was now asked to make relay bombing raids under powerful fighter plane cover, to engage the British fighter planes in combat, cut them to pieces and thus win command of the air.

The Luftwaffe assembled 14 bomber wings, 8 fighter wings, 4 Stuka dive-bomber wings and 3 fighter-destroyer wings—a total of almost 1,700 aircraft (600 bombers, 700 fighters, 200 Stukas, 200 fighter-destroyers)—in northern France, Belgium, Denmark and Norway.

Opposite the southeast coast of England between the Seine and the Loire, were stationed the formations of the German 3rd Air Fleet (under Field Marshal Sperrle, Paris). The 2nd Air Fleet (under Field Marshal Kesselring, Brussels) stood ready along the Channel opposite southeast England. The 5th Air Fleet (under Col. General Stumpff) was based in Norway, ready to move against the English Midlands.

The 2nd Air Fleet played the principal role. Its fighter planes alone could reach London from their air bases in the Pas de Calais, and under favorable conditions could operate there for about 10 minutes. The fighters of the 3rd Air Fleet, on the other hand, had their bases at Le Havre, and just barely had time to reach the outskirts of London before they had to turn around at once.

England, the summer of 1940: The British mount massive obstacles wherever German airborne troops might land.

At this point, when the German air fleets were waiting for their deployment orders and Hitler was hoping to force Britain to its knees, the German leaders had no notion of the trump cards that England held. Not until their raids began did the astonished Germans learn that the RAF's fighter defenses were controlled by ground radar, which enabled the British each time to concentrate their fighter forces where they were needed. And not until 30 years after the war did the Germans discover another and far more significant secret, the secret of Operation Ultra.

Way back at the end of 1932, a team of three young Polish mathematicians in Poland—J. Rozycki, M. Rejewski and H. Zygalski—during an intensive study of the theory of revolving drums, had successfully unravelled the code of the German cipher machine "Enigma" [that would be used to transmit all the secret signal traffic by which Germany ran its war machine]. But not until the summer of 1939, several months before the German invasion of Poland, did the three scholars bring off their great coup: They built a replica of Enigma. Upon receipt of their secret information, Major G. Bertrand, Chief of a division of the French secret service, travelled to the Polish capital on 24 July 1939. Two British specialists, Commander Denniston and the mathematician "Dilly" Knox, were also there. Two days later they were presented with what was no doubt Poland's most precious pre-war contribution to the Allied cause: two reproduced models of Enigma. One model stayed in Paris, the other went to London where initially it met with a skeptical reception. In August 1939, cryptologists of the British Secret Intelligence Service, the SIS, set up their headquarters at Bletchley Park, an isolated country residence north of London. Here too they set up a remote ancestor of the computer, designed to help them decode intercepted German radio code messages. The Chief of this most secret of all British operations (codenamed Ultra) was Wing Commander F. W. Winterbotham, a friend of Sidney Cotton, who was also responsible for passing on the decoded Enigma messages to Churchill. In a short time, thanks to Ultra, almost none of the intentions of the German Luftwaffe could remain a secret to the Allies. Göring's orders, planned military operations, the strength and position of German aircraft formations, structures of command, and other information, often came to lie on British desks as fast as it reached the Germans. Now Churchill was able

The Ju 88 A, the fast German medium-range bomber that took a 5,500-lb disposable bombload, and in addition had dive brakes that enabled it to make dive attacks.

to follow step by step the German Luftwaffe's preparations for its strike against England. In mid-July, Bletchley Park intercepted an Enigma radio message from Göring to the commanders of the German air fleet commanders in which a mysterious word cropped up for the first time: "Sea Lion," the code name for the planned German landing in Great Britain.

At the beginning of the air battle, England had 52 fighter squadrons (approximately 960 machines), 7 antiaircraft artillery divisions, and 21 operational radar stations that were increased to 40 by October. Air Marshal Sir Hugh Dowding was able to command all the air defense forces directly from a central command post, his headquarters at Stanmore. The air defense forces consisted of four fighter wings of varying squadron strengths. Fighter Command controlled not only the antiaircraft batteries but also the searchlight units, the observer corps and the Balloon Command.

The fighter planes on both sides bore the brunt of battle. The British and German fighters were technically and numerically on a par, but the British radar guidance system gave the British commanders the ability to concentrate their forces where they were needed, and thanks to Ultra, they often knew beforehand which targets the enemy would attack and in what strength.

Into the second half of July, the RAF squadrons still flew in dense formations and only fanned out at the moment of battle; thus only the squadron leaders had a clear field of vision. But a massed squadron is easy to detect from some distance away, so often the German fighters were able to discern their enemy [before being seen themselves], and make a surprise attack. Thus the German fighters won the majority of the early aerial combats.

Saturday 3 August 1940, marked the beginning of the Italian offensive against British Somaliland. The Italian air force won a speedy victory: By Saturday 17 August the British were forced to evacuate the country's capital, Berbera, which was exposed to heavy Italian bomb assaults.

Splintered British aerial forces in Aden, the Sudan and Kenya were for the time being too weak to put up a decided resistance.

On Thursday 8 August 1940, Winterbotham learned—at the same moment as the commanders of the German air fleets—of Göring's deployment orders for the air offensive against England. He alerted Air Marshal Dowding at once.

Göring fixed August 10 as the date for the attack launch, codenamed the "Day of the Eagle." Then, after receipt of more favorable weather predictions, he postponed the launch until 7:00 A.M. on August 13. On Monday 12 August, German Me 110 hunter-bombers and Stukas were already in operation. They made surprise raids on five British radar stations at Dunkirk, Pevensey, Rye, Dover and Ventnor, hoping to create a breach in the British radar system, whose functioning they knew relatively little about. But they failed to hit the transmitter poles, and the stations themselves were well camouflaged in the surrounding countryside. Despite the almost suicidal operations of the German Stukas, British Fighter Command's vital radio guidance system remained intact. Spare radar stations deceived the Germans with their simulated radio traffic.

Right: The aerial Battle of Britain 1940/41

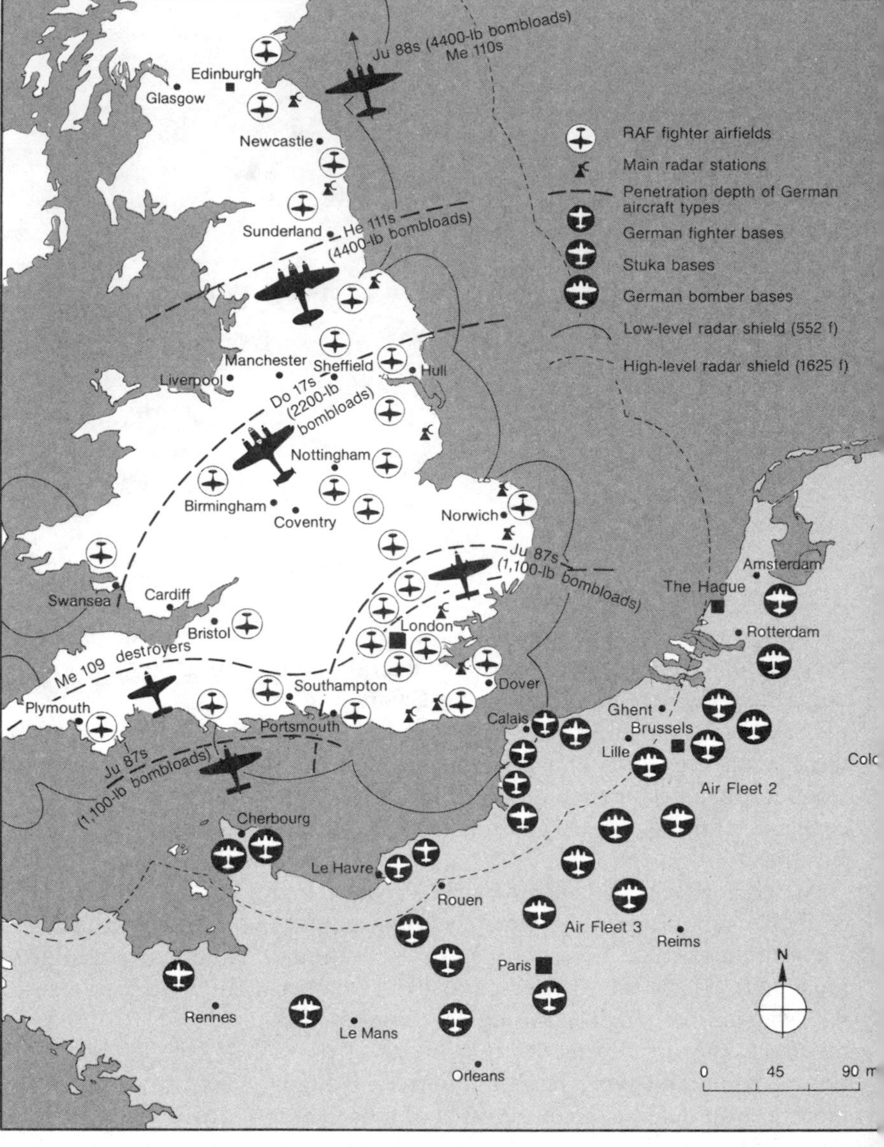

Below right: An Me 109 E-4 that has been forced to land off the steep French coast at Calais when the pilot was only a few hundred yards from an ideal landing field. Its limited range was the Achilles heel of this German fighter.

On the morning of August 13, the Day of the Eagle grand assault was briefly postponed until 2:00 P.M. due to bad weather. But the counter-order failed to reach all the German formations, so the 2nd Bomber Wing (Kampfgeschwader 2) under Col. J. Fink opened the air offensive with raids on Eastchurch and Sheerness. In the afternoon aerial hostilities intensified dramatically when the bulk of the German 3rd Air Fleet (under Field Marshal Sperrle) attacked airfields and port towns in Great Britain. The RAF fighter squadrons were outnumbered three to one, and Göring hoped to gain air superiority within ten days.

That day German bombers flew a total of 485 missions, German fighters approximately 1,000; 34 German planes were lost. Because the Luftwaffe had not drawn any lessons from the RAF defeat over the German Bay on 19 December 1939, they led their day raids on Britain with bombers that were far too weakly armed, and with fighters that although substantial in numbers, had too short a range to provide the bombers with adequate cover.

On Wednesday 14 August 1940, bad weather allowed only isolated nuisance raids initially. The British, who until then had flown in a 3-plane flight formation, now adopted the more advantageous formation—a pack of 4 planes flying in pairs—that the Germans had devised in the Spanish Civil War. This change in British fighter tactics swiftly made itself felt by the Luftwaffe. That day the RAF fighters flew 700 missions in which they lost 13 aircraft, while downing 45.

On Thursday 15 August 1940, the German 2nd, 3rd and 5th Air Fleets carried out a total of 2,119 operations against England with a loss of 55 machines. That day British Fighter Command succeeded for the first time in deploying all three of its wings simultaneously.

On Friday 16 August 1940, 1,720 German raiders attacked targets in Kent, Sussex, Hampshire, and the south coast between the Thames estuary and the Isle of Wight. They lost 45 machines, compared to 21 by the RAF.

Despite their powerful fighter cover, the German bomber wings suffered further heavy casualties during their August 18th raids on Kenley and Tangmere airfields (both of which were largely destroyed), and on Croydon, West Malling, Manston and Biggin Hill: They lost 71 aircraft while the RAF lost only 27 fighters. That day saw the end of the first segment of the Battle of Britain, that had begun on August 8. Starting August 19, the raids on air bases and aircraft industrial plants were extended to the whole of southeast England. Now the British reaped the benefit of the ability that their radar confirmed on them, to deploy their aircraft in heavy concentrations [at selected points]. Lord Dowding routinely held 20 of his 52 squadrons in reserve and could nevertheless meet attacks with superior numbers. When the Luftwaffe failed to realize its plans to lure the British fighters into combat, it began to concentrate its raids on airfields and aircraft manufacturing plants, so as to strike a heavy blow at the British fighter arm as quickly as possible. This second segment of the Battle of Britain lasted until September 6.

When a German air crew inadvertently strayed off course due to bad weather and ended up over London on the night of 24th–25th August, bombs fell on the London city center for the first time, and 9 civilians were killed around St. Giles and Cripplegate. Churchill took this incident as grounds to demand raids on the German capital. On the night of 25th–26th August, 81 twin-engined bombers flew to Berlin, 29 of which reached their targets. Four more British raids followed over the next ten nights.

Hitler replied on 4 September 1940, when he ordered German air assaults to be concentrated on London starting immediately. The Germans had made the crucial mistake of switching from a tactical to a stategic offensive. This gave the British a breathing-space that was most welcome; for despite the effective combination of British radar, Operation Ultra and a well-organized fighter defense, the RAF was in difficult straits, with many of Fighter Command's airfields, fighter-plane radio-control centers and intelligence-gathering centers having been bombed to bits.

Between 13th and 31st August 1940, the Germans lost a total of 252 fighter planes and 215 bombers. British losses were 359 aircraft. Whereas the German air crews of 3 or 4 men to a plane could at best hope to be captured if they were shot down, British pilots of most of the single-seater fighters could bail out over home ground and often were able to return to combat only a few hours after they were shot down.

On the night of 5th–6th September 1940, selected bomber squadrons of the 2nd, 3rd, 26th and 53rd German bomber wings totalling 68 aircraft, carried out the first terrorist bombing raid on London, in which 60 metric tons of bombs were dropped. This first night raid by German bombers on targets in the English capital, marked the beginning of a new phase in the Battle of Britain: the German strategic bombing war on British economic resources.

Left: A British Hawker Hurricane Mk I taking off. During the Battle of Britain this make of fighter shot down more enemy planes than all the other fighters and the antiaircraft artillery put together.

Right: The first RAF raid on Berlin, 25th–26th August 1940. The curving road on the upper right is Charlottenburg Avenue; the bright patches are the beams of flak search-lights.

On September 7 the first German retaliatory grand assault was launched on the East and West Ends of London, with around 300 bombers and 600 fighters taking part. The assault was made under the personal command of Göring from his observation post at Cape Gris Nez in occupied France. The German retaliatory raids continued for 65 days, until November 13.

On the afternoon of September 7, the German fighter planes used a new tactic of flying cover for their bombers. Some of the fighters flew far in advance of the others at an altitude of 26,000 to 32,500 feet [8,000 to 10,000 m], while the rest flew dense cover for the bomber formations, surrounding them on all sides at a distance of about 975 feet [300 m]. This first grand assault on London began the third segment of the Battle of Britain that lasted until 5 October 1940. It was this segment that brought the first clear-cut results: German leaders were forced to accept that their casualties were too high to justify any longer.

Meanwhile the RAF raided the jammed ports of Flushing (Netherlands), Ostend, Dunkirk, Calais and Boulogne, where over 1,000 small river boats lay anchored in readiness for the German Operation Sea Lion, and on 600 more boats upriver at Antwerp. On the night of 12th–13th September alone, 80 barges were sunk in Ostend harbor.

On the night of 14th–15th September 1940 the RAF repeated its raids on shipping targets in the ports between Boulogne and Antwerp. The transport fleet for Sea Lion suffered heavy losses, especially in Antwerp.

On Sunday 15 September, called "Battle of Britain Day" by the English, two German grand assaults marked the climax of the air battle and at the same time concluded its first critical phase. For the first time the RAF deployed all its available fighter units. Almost one quarter of the attacking German raiders – 56 machines – were lost, while 26 British fighter planes were shot down. The German

Lower left: One of the first bombs to strike Greater London during the night raid of 24th–25th August 1940, fell on a suburban movie-theater.

losses were so great that Luftwaffe leaders were now forced to abandon their concentrated daylight grand assaults, and shift to night raids.

Even more crucial was the German failure to win command of the air, which finally led the Germans to give up plans for an invasion. On September 17 Hitler ordered Operation Sea Lion "postponed until further notice."

Given the difficulty of sea transport and the halt to air traffic over France, the only route by which the British could transport needed relief aircraft from England to Egypt, was to send it over the Bay of Biscay to Gibraltar, and from there to Malta. Malta, as a key strategic position in the central Mediterranean, was Britain's "unsinkable aircraft carrier."

But only long-range aircraft were able to make the Biscay-Gibraltar-Malta flight, so on Thursday 19 September 1940, a regular air bridge was opened across Central Africa over which short-range aircraft could be transported to strengthen the units in Egypt. A base was set up in Takoradi, the Gold Coast, where aircraft arriving from England by ship could be equipped and then moved to Cairo via a 4,350-mile route across Nigeria, French Equatorial Africa and the Sudan.

Monday 23 September saw the beginning of Operation Menace, when the British fleet under Admiral Cunningham attacked the French West African seaport of Dakar in an attempt to prepare the landing of Free French Gaullist units. But the French naval forces and coastal batteries remained loyal to the Vichy government and put up a vigorous defense. When they put the British cruiser *Cumberland* out of action and severely crippled the battleship *Resolution,* Churchill broke off the operation.

The Vichy government under Marshal Pétain responded promptly with bombing raids on the British-held base and city of Gibraltar. Six bomber groups of what had formerly been the French Armée de l'Air, and 4 escadrilles of the French naval air arm, received the raid orders on 24 September 1940. The bombers, 64 in all, were stationed at the bases of Oran and Tafaroui in Algeria, and Merknes, Mediouna and Port Lyautey (= Kenitra) in Morocco. Their operation was approved by both the German and Italian ceasefire commissions, and directed by Air Force Brigadier General Tarnier, commander of the French air force in Morocco.

That same day just after 12:20 P.M., the first LeO 45 bomber groups (I/23 and II/23) took off from Merknes airfield and headed for Gibraltar.

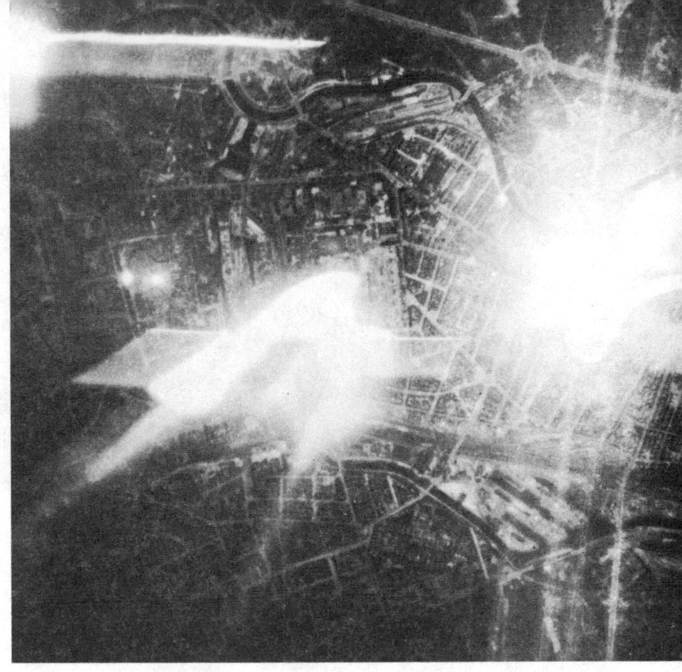

French Lt. Rolland gave the following account: "The distance from our base to Gibraltar was less than 180 miles [300 km] by air. Flying over the Er Reef in clear weather we could see the outline of Europe with the rocky pinnacle of Gibraltar. By 1:00 P.M. we had reached our target. We were flying at an altitude of about 19,500 feet [6,000 m]; the Rock and part of the port lay under a thin cloud layer. The British antiaircraft artillery immediately opened vigorous fire; fire from the battery at the end of the south mole was especially strong. Not one RAF fighter plane appeared. We dropped our payload over the harbor—a number of 1,100-lb, 660-lb and 220-lb bombs—and observed the impacts."

Between 1:30 and 2:15 P.M., a number of French fighter planes were deployed over Gibraltar to protect the French bombers. They included 12 Dewoitine 520 fighters of 3 Squadron, 2nd Fighter Group (Groupe de Chasse II/3) based on Mediouna, 12 Curtiss Hawk fighters from 5 Squadron, 2nd Fighter Group (GC II/5) based on Casablanca, and 12 Curtiss Hawks of GC I/5 based on Rabat. But no RAF fighters were to be seen. Two escadrilles (2B and 3B) from Port Lyautey (Kenitra), with their 12 Glenn Martin bombers, concluded the operation at 4:15 P.M. The French had dropped a total of 41 metric tons of bombs, suffering no losses to themselves; only a few of their bombers bore the punctures of flak splinters.

The next operation against Gibraltar took place on the following day, Wednesday 25 September. The French formation was reinforced by two more bomber groups and two escadrilles. A total of 83 bombers made their run in good weather from 3:00

SETS THE SEAL ON ANY MEAL H·P SAUCE

BLACK OUT ZERO HOUR TO-NIGHT UNTIL 6.9 A.M.

Daily Express

No. 12,579 Monday, September 16, 1940 One Penny

13

Can He Wag His Tail?

SHERLEY'S

R.A.F. smash Goering's Sunday raids on London by 400 planes

175 SHOT DOWN

Another bomb on Palace

5 RAIDERS CRASH ON LONDON

Fifth hospital bombed

SECOND WEEK OF THE BATTLE OF LONDON WAS OPENED BY GOERING WITH FOUR MORE BIG DAY AND NIGHT RAIDS—AND BY THE R.A.F. WITH A SMASHING VICTORY.

This morning it was learned that 175 enemy aircraft, out of 400 sent in many waves, were shot down in the three Sunday daylight raids on London. Thirty R.A.F. fighters were lost, but the pilots of ten are safe.

Again the Nazi murder bombers were sent against Buckingham Palace in a third deliberate attempt to kill the King and Queen. One bomb, which did not explode, damaged the Queen's private apartment.

Vengeance was swift. Almost immediately afterwards the plane which bombed the Palace was shot to pieces in mid-air by Spitfires.

Great air battles were fought out fiercely all the way from the coast to London as big formations of

Spitfires ambush raiders

SPITFIRES and Hurricanes,

A story that must earn a man the V.C.

St. Paul's saved: 1-ton bomb

A MONSTER bomb weighing fully a ton which for three days has been buried near St. Paul's Cathedral in London, exploded yesterday—but not at St. Paul's.

The courage and tenacity of a bomb disposal section under Lieutenant R. Davies saved St. Paul's from being levelled to the ground. Instead the bomb went off harmlessly

STOP PRESS

BERLIN RAID ALARM —GERMAN VERSION

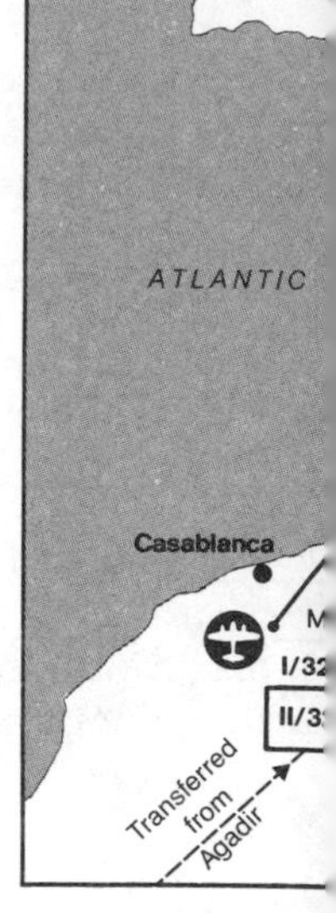

Left: The climax of the Battle of Britain, when 175 German aircraft were shot down on a single day.

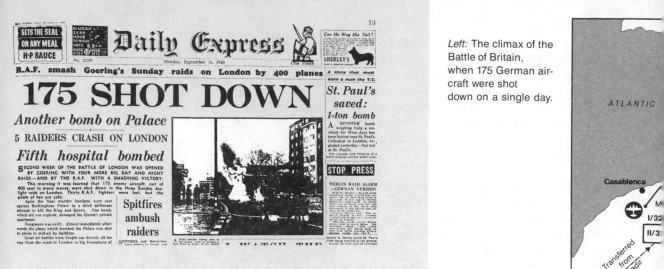

to 4:15 P.M., this time without fighter plane cover. The air crews reported stronger antiaircraft fire than on the previous day. This time too they met no British fighters. The formation dropped 56 metric tons of bombs.

A LeO 45 bomber of French 23 Squadron, 2nd Bomber Group based on Merknes, was shot down by British antiaircraft and crashed into the sea with its air crew under Lt. Court. Thirteen bombers were slightly damaged. Scout aircraft confirmed hits confirmed bomb hits on the base and the harbor installations.

This raid was the largest operation by French bombers since war broke out. At the climax of their bombing raids against the German Army on 5 June 1940, the French had deployed only 77 bombers, some of them antiquated, along the entire area of the front.

On Monday 30 September yet another grand daylight assault was made on London, during which 47 German machines were shot down by fighters and antiaircraft. Twenty British aircraft were lost. After that, German bombers were for the first time being deployed only at night.

In September the Luftwaffe flew a total of 268 missions against London in which it dropped 6,224 metric tons of explosive bombs and 8,546 bomb bins, each containing 36 2-lb incendiary bombs. The RAF, on the other hand, had released only 390 metric tons of explosive bombs over German territory since war began.

The shifting of German bomber raids to the night hours began the fourth phase of the Battle of Britain that lasted from 6th to 31st October 1940.

At first the new assault tactic was successful: German losses to British night interceptors and flak were initially low. The German radio-navigational system also functioned smoothly, even under poor weather conditions. All this changed as soon as the British equipped their antiaircraft and searchlight batteries, as well as their night fighters, with new radar instruments [that increased their efficiency or counteracted the German devices].

For example, by 1 October 1940 the modified G.L. (gun-laying) device was introduced into the British antiaircraft batteries, and for the first time in the history of aerial warfare, antiaircraft guns were shooting at targets whose geometric coordinates could be ascertained by radio direction finding.

On the night of Monday/Tuesday, the 7th–8th October 1940, 30 Wellington bombers of 3rd Group and 12 Whitley bombers of 4th Group RAF Bomber Command attacked the German capital. This was the heaviest raid on Berlin so far, in which 50 metric tons of high-explosive bombs were released. There were 25 dead and 50 wounded, all civilians. Two British aircraft did not return.

On Wednesday 16 October 1940 *Dunkelnachtjagd* (dark night interception) reported its first success: 1st Lt. L. Becker of German 6th Group, 2nd Night Fighter Wing, found and shot down a British bomber on the basis of data supplied by Freya radar equipped with a special direction finding device.

On Tuesday 22 October 1940, units of the Italian Air Corps assembled 75 bombers, 5 long-range reconnaissance planes and 98 fighters at the air base of Épinette at Brussels, Belgium and on October 24 took off for their first operation against Harwich in cooperation with the German 2nd Air Fleet.

At 5:30 A.M. on Monday 28 October 1940 the Italians began their attack on Greece, operating out

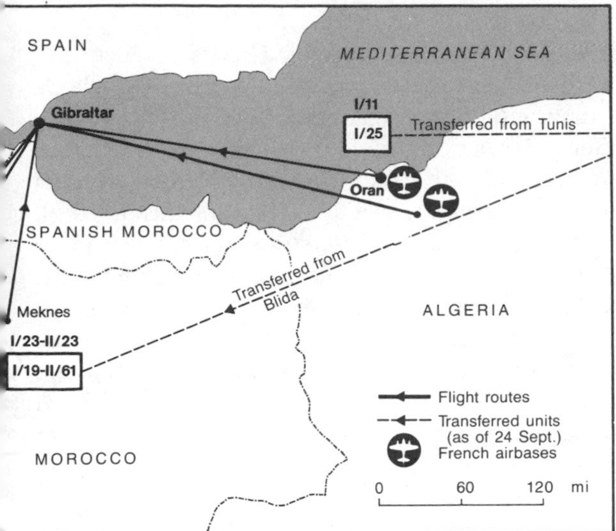

Above: Order of battle of the French aerial forces during their bombing raids on British-held Gibraltar, 24th and 25th September 1940. The numbers refer to the group and squadron (I/11 = No. 11 Squadron, 1st Bomber Group).

of Albania. The Commander in Chief of the Italian aerial forces was General Visconti-Prasca. He had 107 fighter planes, 55 bombers and 25 reconnaissance planes in Albania, and 119 bombers, 20 German-supplied Ju 87 Stukas, 54 fighters and 18 reconnaissance planes ready for takeoff in Apulia (Italy). By contrast the Greek air force had only 44 fighters, 39 bombers and 66 reconnaissance aircraft some of which were out of date.

On Tuesday 29 October 1940, one day after Mussolini's attack on Greece, the British occupied Crete, thereby acquiring a key position in the Mediterranean within bomber range of the important Rumanian oil fields.

During the first three weeks of October, Germany's day and night raids on London were carried out almost exclusively by hunter-bombers. Not until the end of the month did the Luftwaffe once again deploy large units of bombers by night.

In October, 333 bombing raids were made on London in which 7,160 metric tons of high-explosive bombs and 4,735 bins of incendiary bombs fell on the city. So far British civilian losses came to 15,000 dead and 21,000 injured.

Below: A Glenn Martin 167 F Maryland medium bomber of the French 22 Squadron, 1st Bomber Group based on Rabat, before it makes a reconnaissance flight over Gibraltar.

On Friday 1 November 1940, the first large aerial combat took place between Italians and Greeks, and an Italian aircraft was shot down north of Joannina by a (Polish-manufactured) Greek PZL-24, a member of the Greek 21st Fighter Wing.

Next day a Greek fighter plane won an extraordinary victory. After his ammunition had given out, 1st Lt. Marinos Mitralexis (22nd Fighter Wing) rammed his PZL-24 fighter into the tail of an Italian SM.79 bomber. While the stupefied Italians were still floating to earth with their parachutes, Mitralexis landed his damaged machine and then captured the whole air crew.

Sunday 3 November 1940 brought a halt to the series of 57 night raids on the British capital that had begun on 5th–6th September, and that had involved an average of 200 bombers and hunter-bombers apiece. Admittedly, several more attacks of bombers in wing strength were made on London during the first half of November; but by now the coastal cities and the industrial centers in the interior were the preferred German targets.

On Wednesday 6 November, British troops launched their first offensive of the war against the Italians, near Gallabat in the Italian-occupied borders of the Sudan; but the attack was repelled. The weak British motorized troops, trekking across an impassable landscape, came under heavy air attack. A number of Gladiators deployed to support the ground troops suffered grave casualties at the hands of Italian fighter planes. Italian air superiority and the dogged resistance of the Italian army units, forced the British to retreat.

In the morning hours of Sunday 10 November 1940, 7 Hudson aircraft flown by BOAC civilian air crews took off from Gander, Newfoundland under the command of Captain D. Bennett. The planes were being transferred to British Coastal Command, which needed them urgently. After 10½ hours of flying they reached Northern Ireland, thus initiating a regular Atlantic airlift that would continue until the end of the war transporting US- and Canadian-built aircraft to Britain.

On the night of 11th–12th November, British torpedo and bomber aircraft raided the Italian naval base at Taranto which lay at the heel of the Italian boot, 300 miles from Malta. The Italian navy was ready to put to sea, for next day it was due to leave Taranto to bombard Suda Bay in British-held Crete. Shortly after nightfall the first wave of British raiders – 12 Fairey Swordfish carrying auxiliary fuel tanks and commanded by Lt. K. Williamson – took off from the carrier *Illustrious* about 150 miles southeast of Taranto. The second wave under Lt. J.W. Halle – which consisted of only 8 planes due to some mechanical breakdowns – followed one hour later. One machine after another flew through the gap between the barrage balloons and discharged its air-launched torpedoes precisely over the holes in the anti-torpedo nets at a distance of between 1,900 and 2,300 feet from their assault targets. In doing so they flew so low that occasionally the wheels of an aircraft grazed the surface of the water. If they had discharged their torpedoes from a higher altitude, the torpedoes would have shattered on impact. The antiaircraft artillery opened a violent barrage. The Italian battleships stood out clearly against the western sky, illuminated by the moon and by flash bombs. The *Conte di Cavour* received one torpedo hit, the *Littorio* two. Then the second wave of raiders arrived and despite its smaller strength, scored one torpedo hit on the *Caio Duilio* and two more on the *Littorio.* Each British assault formation lost only one aircraft. The three struck battleships sank while lying at anchor. Although the *Littorio* and the *Caio Duilio* were later hoisted up and repaired, they had been put out of action for five or six months, and the *Conte di Cavour* was never returned to service. The bombing assaults on the cruisers and destroyers in the inner harbor were less successful: only two bombs hit a target and these failed to detonate.

British 44-mm antiaircraft artillery at the Princess Royal site on the Rock of Gibraltar, standing by for emergency.

"I have good news for you," Churchill cried in the House of Commons as he brandished the victory despatch, and announced that the balance of naval power in the Mediterranean had shifted.

By an irony of fate, the Italian air force took part that same day in the German bombing offensive against England, on the express wishes of Mussolini. An Italian bomber wing, escorted by about 60 fighter planes, tried to raid British shipping convoys. Eight bombers and 5 fighters were shot down. Churchill remarked that they would have been put to better use defending their navy in Taranto.

The raid by carrier-based torpedo aircraft on the naval base at Taranto put half the Italian battleships out of action and so confirmed the unique importance of carrier-based aircraft in the new epoch of naval warfare. Admiral Cunningham described the raid as an unprecedented example of the economical deployment of air combat units. The admiral did not suspect that his most zealous disciple was then to be found in faraway Tokyo. The British success at Taranto confirmed to Japanese Admiral Yamamoto that he was right in his plan to attack the US naval base at Pearl Harbor using carrier-based aircraft.

Above: RAF night fighters of 85 Squadron standing by. On the right is Squadron Leader Peter Townsend with his German Shepherd Kim.

At 3:00 P.M. on November 14, the code-breakers at Bletchley Park decoded an Enigma radio transmission that made them prick up their ears: The German Luftwaffe was preparing a grand assault on Coventry for the coming evening. There was still time to warn the people or even to evacuate them from the city. Winterbotham contacted the Prime Minister's offices at once, but Churchill was unavailable at that moment and so Winterbotham spoke direct to his personal secretary and told him

Below: A Macchi C.200 Saetta (Arrow). The type was famous for its outstanding maneuverability and at this time was the best Italian fighter plane.

what had happened. "I asked the personal secretary if he would be good enough to ring me back when the decision had been taken, because if Churchill decided to evacuate Coventry, the press, and indeed everybody, would know we had pre-knowledge of the raid and some countermeasure might be necessary to protect the source [of the secret information] which would obviously become suspect." (quoted from p. 60 of *The Ultra Secret*)

The Prime Minister's reply did not arrive at Bletchley Park until late that afternoon: There would be no evacuation and the citizens of Coventry would not be warned, but only the air defense and emergency services should be alerted. Clearly Churchill felt that taking conspicuous defense measures might betray the fact that the British had Enigma.

The grand assault on the British aircraft-engine industrial center of Coventry on the night of 14th–15th November, marked the true launch of the German night raider offensive. The full moon and the calmness of the night made weather conditions ideal for the operation. A German bomber group, the 100th Pathfinder Group, used the German *X-Gerät* radio-beam navigational system to guide them to their target and assured that it was well-illuminated. Their nearness to their takeoff fields (about 240 miles from the target), made it possible for some of the 449 bombers to be deployed twice. British antiaircraft downed only two bombers despite its heavy fire. The British night fighter planes—reinforced by some daylight fighters because of the great brightness over the target zone—were even less effective.

The bombers discharged 503 metric tons of high-explosive bombs, and 881 incendiary bins, over Coventry. The fires could not be brought under control until the following night. For the first time in the war a city center was deliberately reduced to ashes and life was brought to a standstill by the loss of the entire electricity, gas and water supply networks. The price for keeping the Ultra Secret was

Right: The battle-proven British Fairey Swordfish I torpedo bombers made of sheet metal, fabric and plywood, flew the raid on Taranto, and later flew other missions that had a crucial effect on the naval war.

Below left: The British aircraft carrier *Illustrious* (under Rear Admiral Lyster), which took part in the operation against Taranto.

554 dead and 865 injured citizens of Coventry.

This operation also showed the inability of the German air fleet commands to carry out a concentrated raid within a short space of time. The bombardment stretched over ten hours.

While Allied war propaganda treated Coventry as a symbol of German aerial barbarism, British Bomber Command took it as an object lesson that crucially influenced their planning for British area raids on large German cities. It did not escape their notice that the maximum damage could be inflicted by causing extensive fires and fire storms in densely-built city centers.

At the beginning of the third week in November, the Luftwaffe carried out a series of bombing raids on Birmingham. During one of these operations on the night of 19th–20th November, a British Bristol Beaufighter night interceptor fitted with on-board radar and flown by Flying Officer J. Cunningham, succeeded in locating and shooting down a German Ju 88. It was the first aircraft in the history of aerial warfare to shoot down an enemy by using its own airborne radar.

In the late autumn of 1940, the operations of German Focke Wulf 200 Condor long-range bombers operating out of occupied airfields in western France, became ever more menacing in their effects. In November alone these long-range craft sank 18 ships totalling 66,000 tons. At the same time they searched broad reaches of the Atlantic for British convoys and radioed their position to the German U-boats. As a result the U-boats rapidly increased their successes.

On Friday 6 December 1940 in Cyrenaica, a British motorized army of 31,000 men under General Wavell, stormed forward more than 36 miles undetected by the Italian air force. This was the first successful British troop offensive of the war. British Hurricanes, Gladiators and Blenheims flew air support for their ground troops all day, and at night the Wellington and Bombay bombers took over. Soon the British won air superiority, because the Regia Aeronautica had lost its forward airfields near Sidi Barrani and Sollum at the beginning of the offensive.

On the night of 16th–17th December 1940 the RAF flew its first extensive raid on Germany when 134 British aircraft bombed residential districts in the center of Mannheim. They dropped 80 metric tons of explosive bombs and 14,000 incendiary bombs on the city center, with a loss of 10 machines.

In the second half of December the RAF despatched fighter-bombers to initiate its continuous daily raids on France. The first of these operations, called Rhubarb, involved nuisance raids in which British aircraft flew low over the continent bombing any target that presented itself. The first such raid was flown by two Spitfires on Friday 20 December 1940; whereas the first night-time nuisance

Right: 13th–14th November 1940: The layout of the guide beams that, together with *X-Gerät* radiolocation devices, enabled the Germans to bomb Coventry.

A = Rhine intersect beam, where German aircraft fly along the Weser beam
B = Oder intersect beam, where the observers engage the bomb-release mechanism
C = Elbe intersect beam; the target is now only 3 miles away. Target Coventry, where the bombs are released automatically
+ = British Bromide stations for the electronic jamming of the *X-Gerät*

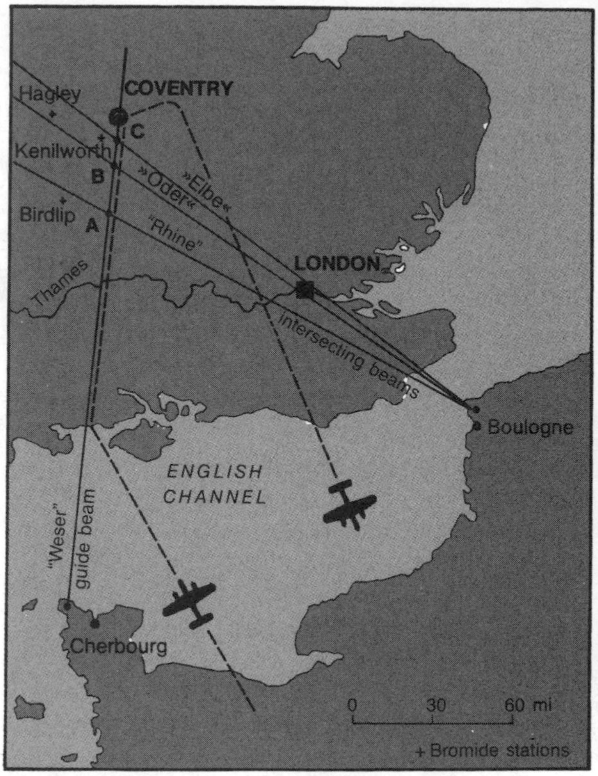

Below: German pilots of the Lion Wing (26th Kampfgeschwader) displaying umbrellas that they later dropped over England. The umbrellas carry jaunty messages to British leaders.

Coventry

Lange(westl.Greenw.) 1°29 50', Breite 52°26 (Mitte Luftbild) 8.6.39

16 200 162 m

Above: Coventry, 16 November 1940, where men of the British Pioneer Corps are helping to clean up the demolished city center.

Left: This aerial photograph of the target was used by German bomber crews in their raid on Coventry on 14th–15th November 1940. The typewritten table at the bottom lists the principal military targets.

raids, aimed to intercept German bombers over their own flight bases, started that night and into the early hours of Saturday morning.

German air operations against English industrial cities continued in December. The main targets now were Southampton, Portsmouth, Birmingham and Manchester.

On the night of Saturday/Sunday, 28th–29th December 1940, the Luftwaffe mounted a retaliatory attack on London with the intention of destroying the business district in the City, which was largely depopulated during the night. Huge fires raged through the City district, all the more unchecked because at the weekend it was almost stripped of fire wardens. The raid was repeated next day. These two raids were the worst that London had suffered so far.

However, to seriously cripple the industrial output of Great Britain would have required the German Luftwaffe to deliver a bombload that far outstripped its capabilities. This failure was the main factor in the fiasco of Germany's strategic air offensive against England. The Battle of Britain had crucial influence on the further course of the war and for the Germans represented an additional proof of the untenability of the Douhet theory.

By the end of 1940, British Bomber Command had flown 36 raids on Berlin. During the comparatively heavy raids made on Germany in December, almost as many British bombers were lost through crew inexperience, navigational difficulties, weather problems, miscalculations of fuel supply, and crash landings, as to German flak or to German night interceptors, which at that time were still few and far between.

A Supermarine Spitfire fighter plane of the Polish 303 Squadron. This fighter-type was the most maneuverable machine to take part in the Battle of Britain and could climb faster than the German Me 109. It was the only RAF aircraft that continued to be produced uninterruptedly for the duration of the war.

1941

January to June

Official Recognition of Aerial Shoot-Downs

9 January 1941
Luftwaffe Staff Office Document 29, No. 54624/40 (5, VII), from the Reich Air Ministry and the Luftwaffe High Command:

Particular events have once again emphasized the importance of absolute accuracy in reporting shoot-downs of enemy aircraft, both in the initial duty reports handed in by the troop after combat and in the petitions for official recognition of air kills: because the first are the basis for evaluating our position and conferring the highest military decorations, whereas the latter involve the historical truth of the war record.

Before shoot-down reports can be passed on they must be keenly and critically examined in verbal interrogation by the aerial formation leader to whom the air kill is reported by the scoring gunner. Additionally, it is the duty of commanders—especially wing commanders—to train their crew to exercise the highest moral principles in making their reports, to guide them in judging which shoot-downs qualify for report, and to supervise them properly in delivering their reports.

As a rule the petitions should be handed on through official channels promptly while memories are still fresh, so that the petition has passed through the various examining headquarters up to the Luftflotte [Air Fleet] level, within three days at most.

Daily Keynote from the Reich Press Chief
Monday 13 January 1941:

The Minister [of Propaganda] sharply censures the layout of the Sunday afternoon papers which in contravention of his express orders, have again given large coverage to neutralist comments concerning the attack on London . . . How (the Minister asks) does the Press intend to show due appreciation for the final victory over England when it comes?

Daily Keynote from the Reich Press Chief
Tuesday 14 January 1941:

The Minister has explained that we must avoid giving air shelters the reputation of being military barracks. This is in fact what is happening due to a multitude of prohibitions and regulations that have merely caused people to feel annoyed and indignant. The Minister suggests that certain absolutely necessary rules of conduct should be displayed in the air shelters in a summarized form as the "Ten Commandments of the Air Shelter."

A Lesson from Experience

Luftwaffe Front-Line Report, February 1941

Regarding diversionary hoaxes on [Allied] ships: A neutral source reports that ships under [German] attack mislead air crews with simulated hits, starting what appear to be fires on board (perhaps produced by pans of tar?), while the ship's crew climb into the boats [as if abandoning ship].

British Barrage Balloons in Sweden

Tuesday 4 March 1941, Stockholm
The Swedish newspaper *Svenska Dagbladet* reported:

Further severe damage has been caused in western

A German Arado Ar 196 seaplane is shooting down an RAF Whitley bomber. Both types of aircraft made a name for themselves—the Arado 196s on 4 May 1940 when they captured the British submarine *Seal,* and the Whitleys, also called "barndoors," when they became the first RAF bombers to fly over Berlin.

Sweden by drifting British barrage balloons.

At the moment approximately 20 British barrage balloons are drifting over Sweden. In Ucklumä a balloon pulled down a factory chimney with its 1,875-foot-long trail rope. Other balloons have destroyed the rigging of fishing boats with their trail ropes. In the rock island-strewn Göteborg area, a number of islands were left completely without electricity because one of the barrage balloons had destroyed the power transmission line.

Canadian Airmen in England

Wednesday 5 March 1941, London
The British *Air Ministry* announced:

A new contingent of fliers trained in Canada has arrived in the London area. They are the strongest aerial detachment to land in Great Britain so far.

Wednesday 19 March 1941
The *Wehrmacht High Command* announced:

On March 16, German reconnaissance aircraft attacked a powerful formation of enemy war vessels consisting of 2 heavy units, 6 cruisers and 2 or 3 destroyers, in the Mediterranean 24 miles west of Crete. Each of the 2 heavy battle units was struck by one air-launched torpedo.

Daily Keynote from the Reich Press Chief
Thursday 20 March 1941:

The remarks of Colonel [Charles] Lindbergh stating that the United States has barely as many combat-ready aircraft as Germany produces in a single week, would (we are told) lend itself well to commentary by the German press and the translating and interpreting service.

Aircraft Made of Coffee Beans?

Sunday 23 March 1941
The American *United Press News Agency* reported:

Lord Forbes, the national export union president, declared that Brazilian scientists have succeeded in finding a new use for their coffee surpluses. After extensive experimentation, it is now possible to produce a substance called "cafelite" from coffee. Lord Forbes said that it is highly durable and possesses extraordinary physical properties. In fact the substance is of such high quality that it can be used to manufacture airplane parts, if not even in the construction of entire planes.

Saturday 29 March 1941, London
The British *Royal Navy* announced:

Significant operations took place in the eastern Mediterranean on Friday when our naval formation under the command of Admiral Sir Andrew Cunningham encountered strong Italian forces. The enemy vessels tried to escape but several of them were brought to battle. It is presumed that so far at least one battleship of the *Littorio* class has received a direct hit, and two enemy cruisers are believed to be badly damaged. The aircraft of the Royal Navy and the RAF carried out raids whose results are not yet known. Greek naval forces also took part in these operations. Further reports will be announced as soon as they come in.

29 March 1941, Rome
The *Italian High Command* announced:

In East Africa, the battle on the northern front continues to rage bitterly at the new positions east of Keren (Ethiopia). Our aerial formations have bombarded British motor truck columns. Our fighter planes shot down two enemy aircraft in aerial combat. In the early hours of Friday morning, British aircraft raided the airfield at Lecce (southern Italy), opening machine gun fire on the installations. There were a number of injuries.

Sunday 30 March 1941, Rome
The *Italian High Command* announced:

We have repeatedly attacked a strong enemy naval unit in the eastern Mediterranean. Despite vigorous enemy antiaircraft fire, an Italian torpedo bomber scored a direct hit on a light cruiser. Aircraft of one German air corps damaged an aircraft carrier and shot down an enemy fighter plane. In East Africa, enemy pressure is continuing on the northern front east of Keren but is being impeded by our violent counterattacks. Our troops have evacuated Dire Dawa in the Harar area (Ethiopia) and moved into new positions without breaking ranks. Italian fighter planes destroyed several aircraft on the ground on the Jijiga airfield (Ethiopia). Two British Hurricanes were shot down in aerial combat. Two Italian aircraft have not returned to their bases.

30 March 1941, Cairo
RAF Headquarters in the Middle East announced:

RAF operations in Eritrea continued on Friday south of Keren. Enemy motorized columns and troops near Asmara (capital of Eritrea) were bombed and fired on by our machine guns.

30 March 1941, Cairo
The *British Middle East Air Force in Egypt* announced on Saturday:

Yesterday in Italian East Africa, British aircraft once again operated forcefully in the Asmara area. In Asmara itself, rail station buildings, railroad cars and motorized columns were hit by repeated bombs. Free French aircraft led an assault on an enemy base between Gondar (Ethiopia) and Asmara and destroyed a large number of military installations with precision-aimed bomb hits.

Monday 31 March 1941, Athens
The *British Air Force in Greece* reported:

On Sunday British bombers made successful raids on Elbasan (Albania) and its environs. Enemy fighter planes tried to stop our aircraft, but gave up the battle after one enemy fighter was brought to crash. Our armed reconnaissance flights in the Tepeleni area of Albania also went off successfully. All British aircraft returned to base.

Daily Keynote from the Reich Press Chief
Monday 31 March 1941:

We must wait for reports of Italian losses in the sea battle in the Aegean Sea [before issuing news about it]. If further reports arrive concerning the British aircraft carrier that we crippled, we must not mention [in press reports] that the carrier in question was once again the *Ark Royal.*

March 1941, Greece: An Italian Savoia Marchetti SM 79 Sparviero (Hawk) on an advanced airfield. These efficient bombers had already seen action in the Spanish Civil War.

A Vickers Wellesley bomber of No. 14 RAF Squadron (based on Port Sudan), at an advanced airfield in East Africa. This machine had one of the widest wingspans of any single-engined aircraft and was the first plane built with a geodetic construction by Dr. Barnes Wallis.

German Stukas Smash the Greek "Metaxas Line"

The following descriptive account appeared in the Nazi newspaper *Völkischer Beobachter,* April 1941:

We have hung out position lights [on our aircraft to keep from colliding], blue-grey shadows have settled over the slopes, and the sun, like a blood-red ball, pushes slowly across the snow-white ridges of the border mountains. We are on course, we rise in a wide arc around the mountain massif and attack. We drop our full bombloads into the enemy positions, one bomber, two, three, four. There is a crackling and flashing. Huge mushrooms of dust and debris mount upward, join together and trail like ominous exhalations through the valley which we penetrate as fast as the wind, then disappear like phantoms just as we appeared . . .

Monday 7 April 1941
The *Wehrmacht High Command* announced:

Along the southeastern front the assault is proceeding according to schedule in dogged fighting. Powerful Luftwaffe contingents have supported the advance of the Army by flying reconnaissance and by raiding enemy columns, positions and transport vehicles. As has already been reported, the fortress installations and other military targets in Belgrade have been raided repeatedly by powerful formations of German combat aircraft, to devastating effect. In particular, the main railroad station in Belgrade, a pontoon bridge over the Danube east of Belgrade, and several transport trains, have been badly hit. A multitude of large fires went on burning into the night and lit up the way for German ground-attack aircraft as they made their fourth attack on the fortress of Belgrade. Further, airfields in central and southern Yugoslavia were bombed to sustained effect and bombarded with aerial guns. A number of their aircraft were destroyed on the ground.

An Airfield Lit by Thirty Torches

The following descriptive account appeared in the *Völkischer Beobachter,* April 1941:

We group above the clouds and then take off a wild daring attack on Yugoslavia's last remaining airfields.

Soon we see the dark ribbon of the Danube shining through the cloud-gaps; the river has overflowed its banks and flooded large areas of country. South of us lies Belgrade. A single German reconnaissance aircraft circles over the city, where flames and columns of smoke in various districts still testify to the might of our grand assaults. We fly west along the Sava river. There is the rail line, over here is the airfield, where our foe has withdrawn with a row of his best machines. Like swarms of hornets our destroyers hurl themselves onto the aircraft parked along the edge of the field. A powerful drama begins. The pilots of the first flight descend to an altitude of 16 to 32 feet, then yank their birds up again, and flashing blue smoke clouds pound incessantly out of the cannons and machine guns hacking the clusters of Blenheims to pieces, setting them on fire so that one after another turns into a giant burning torch whose glow rises into the sky. Thirty modern enemy aircraft are demolished, including 20 British Bristol Blenheims.

Daily Keynote from the Reich Press Chief
Thursday 10 April 1941:

Next the Minister calls our attention to reports about Belgrade. Expressions like "The city is one single heap of rubble, its streets covered with the corpses of women and children" are naturally to be omitted before publication.

Daily Keynote from the Reich Press Chief
Saturday 12 April 1941:

The Minister has ordered that the music of the

German Junkers Ju 86 Z-7 passenger liners of the SAAF (South African Air Force), were converted into bombers and served in 11 and 12 Squadrons, where they fought against Italy in East Africa.

grand Prince Eugen Fanfare and the German national anthem should no longer be played every time a special announcement is made, because then we would have no way left to intensify [the people's mood]. He has reminded us that our broadcast for the ceasefire with France moved the people most profoundly, precisely because [the music played] was unique. Thus the grand Prince Eugen Fanfare and the German national anthem must be played only two or three times throughout the whole Balkan campaign.

Sunday 13 April 1941
The *Wehrmacht High Command* announced:

In southern Serbia our advance proceeded as scheduled, after we overcame local resistance by scattered Serbian troops. Yesterday the Luftwaffe fought with great success against important military targets in the southeast zone. It demolished a total of 39 enemy aircraft on airfields in Bosnia and Herzegovina. In the Belgrade area, transport and supply trains were successfully destroyed by bombing, and march columns were dispersed.

Tuesday 15 April 1941
The *Wehrmacht High Command* announced:

Yesterday the Luftwaffe again inflicted heavy losses in repeated raids on the remains of the Serbian army. Dive-bomber, destroyer and fighter aircraft cut enemy march columns to pieces in the lower Bosnia valley and in the area between the Sava and Drin rivers. Ground-attack aircraft bombed military installations around Sarajevo and scored bomb hits on aircraft stationed on the ground at Mostar airfield. Other Luftwaffe formations blew up Greek troop assemblies at Deskati. In the Lake Prespa area, German fighter planes shot down 6 British Bristol Blenheims. In bomb raids on Piraeus harbor, the Luftwaffe sank four merchant vessels totalling 35,000 tons, badly damaged eight large merchant vessels, and set the harbor installations on fire. During the last two nights, heavy caliber bombs hit a destroyer and 3 large merchant ships in the inlet at Eleusis and outside the port of Piraeus. Another effective high-explosive bomb raid was made on Eleusis airfield.

Thursday 17 April 1941
The *Wehrmacht High Command* announced:

In retaliation for the British air raid on the residential and cultural center of the German capital on the night of 9th–10th April, the German Luftwaffe last night carried out a grand assault on the British capital. A great number of German bomber wings released countless high-explosive bombs of all calibers, and incendiary bombs, uninterruptedly throughout the entire night. Ground visibility was good and the bomb detonations and their effects could be observed with absolute clarity. Large fires had sprung up in the harbor districts, as well as in other city areas, by the time the first German formations flew away; some of the fires joined together to form wide-scale conflagrations. The glow from these huge fires was visible from as far away as the Channel, and some of them even from the Belgian

Left: 3 May 1941, German Dornier Do 17 medium bombers (known as Flying Pencils because of their extreme slimness) during the German victory parade over Athens.

Below right: The Tower Bridge, one of London's symbolic landmarks, shrouded in heavy smoke from fires in the East End.

coast. In future, any British air raid on residential quarters of Germany will be answered by increased retaliation.

Sunday 27 April 1941
The *Wehrmacht High Command* announced:

In a bold aerial assault, paratroops seized the isthmus and the city of Corinth on the morning of April 26. Large numbers of British were taken prisoner; the rest fled south.

Wednesday 30 April 1941
The *Wehrmacht High Command* announced:

During the evening and night hours of 29 April, German bombers and dive bombers made a very effective raid on the port of Valetta on the island of Malta. They scored direct hits on a light cruiser and on antiaircraft positions, wharves and fuel tank depots, and set a destroyer and a large merchant vessel on fire. Additional raids were made on the Lucca and Valetta airfields. The enemy lost two Hurricane fighters in aerial combats over the island. There were no German losses. In North Africa German and Italian dive bombers bombed Tobruk harbor, artillery positions at Fort Pilastro, and fortifications south of Via Balbia, with the heaviest caliber bombs.

British Paratroops

Friday 9 May 1941, London
The British *Air Ministry* announced:

Like all the great powers, Great Britain formed a paratroop corps shortly after the outbreak of war. We now have a large number of paratroops who have completed their training and are ready for action. The paratroops consist exclusively of volunteers who are carefully selected and trained; most of them are aged between 23 and 27 years.

A Dutch Bomber Squadron

Saturday 10 May 1941
RAF Headquarters announced:

Last night a Dutch bomber squadron was deployed for the first time. Up to now Dutch air crews in the Dutch aerial formation, served as reconnaissance fliers. Shipments from the USA have now made it possible to set up the first Dutch bomber wing, which flew its first mission last night against a German Luftwaffe base in Kristiansund, southern Norway.

Sunday 11 May 1941
The *Wehrmacht High Command* announced:

Over the last few nights the British air force has once again deliberately bombed the residential districts of German cities, including the German capital. In retaliation, strong German Luftwaffe forces carried out a major assault on London last night. Ground visibility was good and the British capital was bombed throughout the night by relay waves that dropped high-explosive bombs of all calibers and tens of thousands of incendiary bombs.

Daily Keynote from the Reich Press Chief
Monday 12 May 1941:

I ask you to avoid any sort of cynicism, frivolousness, and puerile or brazen expressions, in broadcast reports about air raids, which destroy immeasurable cultural, economic and also human treasures. Things must be described in a manly, stern and serious way. This is how we can best live up to the mood in [bombed] cities like Hamburg and Bremen.—For the rest, I am firmly convinced that we are fortunate that the bombing raids made on German territory are taking place in the northern part of the Reich and not in the south, and that these severe trials are being borne by hardy Ditmarshers [= people of Schleswig-Holstein] and other Nordic people.

12 May 1941, Cairo
RAF Headquarters in the Middle East announced:

In Iraq, our fliers continued their raids on rebel-occupied airfields and on other military targets. The military barracks and the airfield buildings and motor vehicle park at Mosul (northern Iraq) received more than twelve direct hits. The military barracks at Al Amarah, Ad Diwaniyah, An Nasiriyah, and Ad Daghgharah (all in Iraq) were also damaged. In Abyssinia, fighter planes and bombers of the South African Air Force (SAAF) supported our ground troops in their destruction of the Italian army in East Africa. Two British aircraft did not return from these missions.

Thursday 15 May 1941, Cairo
RAF Headquarters in the Middle East announced yesterday:

On Monday, aircraft of the South African Air Force went into action in Cyrenaica for the first time when the RAF bombed enemy aircraft at Gambut airfield. On Monday night through to Tuesday morning, heavy English bombers overflew the Mediterranean and attacked the German airfield at Kattavia on the isle of Rhodes.

Aircraft of the British Fleet Air Arm took off to attack the Al Amarah military barracks in Iraq, 48 miles from the Persian Gulf. A factory in Al Musayyib, a fuel tank in Rashid and motorized transports were likewise bombed on Tuesday. The SAAF operated without a halt. In Abyssinia their targets were Fort Aba Maela and military positions at Ama Magiihr. In Lekemti aerial machine guns fired on a motorized transport column and aircraft on the ground. Three of General de Gaulle's Free French aircraft raided Gondar airfield (Ethiopia).

Friday 16 May 1941, Baghdad
Iraqi Headquarters reported:

No change on the Western front. On the southern front, three British aircraft released several bombs over an Iraqi city. The ground defenses succeeded in shooting down one Wellington bomber. The Iraqi air force undertook reconnaissance flights over enemy bases and all aircraft returned undamaged. Our aircraft overflew the area around Ar Rutbah and successfully bombed enemy armored vehicles. British aircraft attacked our military barracks but no major damage was done. One enemy aircraft was probably shot down. Our troops in the desert fought throughout the day and are continuing to keep the situation under control.

Saturday 17 May 1941
General Wavell, the British Commander in Chief in the Middle East, announced:

On Thursday the RAF bombed the three Syrian airfields at Palmyra, Damascus and Rayak. Three German Junkers and two other unidentified German aircraft, as well as an Italian Caproni 42, were sighted at Palmyra airfield. We succeeded in seriously crippling three of these machines; a fourth was demolished with incendiary bombs. Regarding [French collaborationist] General Dentz's communiqué, Wavell Headquarters has learned that one morning, 17 German aircraft landed at one Syrian airfield, and 5 at another field, and flew on in the direction of Iraq after refuelling. There is no question of the machines having been forced to make an emergency landing, because the German aircraft were in impeccable condition. It is remarkable that General Dentz's comuniqué makes no mention of the results of the British raid on the airfield at Palmyra.

US Citizens under the British Flag

17 May 1941, London
The *Reuters News Agency* reported:

As was made clear in a report on foreigners in the British armed services, approximately 10,000 US citizens are fighting under the British flag. Most of them are attached to the RAF as pilots, observers and aerial gunners, or assigned to the training camps. Some US citizens have joined the ranks of General de Gaulle's Free French.

17 May 1941, Moscow
The *Soviet Tass News Agency* stated:

Foreign reports that the Soviet Union has authorized the recruitment of volunteer pilots for the Iraqi army, are completely false.

Sunday 18 May 1941, Damascus
The *German News Bureau* announced:

On Friday the Iraqi air force successfully bombed several [British] ships outside the port of Basra (Iraq).

Aldwych underground station in the City of London was used as an air raid shelter for nights on end.

Iraq, May 1941: The desert fortress of Kirkuk north of Baghdad during an RAF bombing raid.

18 May 1941, Cairo
The *British Middle East Air Force in Egypt* announced yesterday:

German aircraft have been fired on by machine guns at Mosul (Iraq). One German plane went up in flames, the others were damaged. We have set oil warehouses on fire at Al Amarah (Iraq). The RAF base of Habbaniya (Iraq) has been attacked by German aircraft, but damage was insignificant and the toll of victims was low. Our operations in Abyssinia were confined to reconnaissance flights and the bombardment of fortified positions.

18 May 1941, Rome
The *Italian High Command* announced:

Our counteroperations against the Allies in North Africa have been completely successful. The enemy has been forced to retreat. Large numbers of prisoners and supplies have fallen into our hands. Our aerial formations have attacked Tobruk. We bombed defense installations, troop assemblies and motor vehicles in the sector west of Sollum and shot down a British bomber and two enemy fighters in aerial combat. British aircraft in the Aegean raided Rhodes, causing insignificant damage. At Amba Alagi in East Africa, our troops have put up heroic resistance under the personal command of the Duke of Aosta. Combat conditions are worsening hourly due to the lack of material, the losses we have suffered and the impossibility of tending and evacuating the wounded. An enemy assault was repelled in the area around Galla and Sidamo (Ethiopia).

19 May 1941, Baghdad
Iraqi Headquarters reported:

Our bombers have attacked British tank units, which have suffered substantial losses in men and material. Our reconnaissance flights over Cineldebbana and other locations have proceeded without incident. Enemy aircraft overflew the area surrounding the capital and released several bombs over the base at Rashid without inflicting much damage.

German Action against Crete

20 May 1941
New Zealand *General Freyberg,* commander of Crete, reported to the headquarters of General Wavell:

At dawn on Tuesday, powerful German forces began heavy assaults on Crete. Large numbers of paratroops jumped onto the island, and according to reports received so far, airborne troops have landed in transport aircraft. British and Greek units have engaged the enemy. A number of German paratroops have been killed and captured. The battles are continuing.

Thursday 22 May 1941, London
The *Reuters News Agency* reported:

Reports this morning state that violent struggles took place on Crete on Wednesday and that often the opposing troops were locked in hand-to-hand fighting. The battle also extended to the mountains and the tableland.

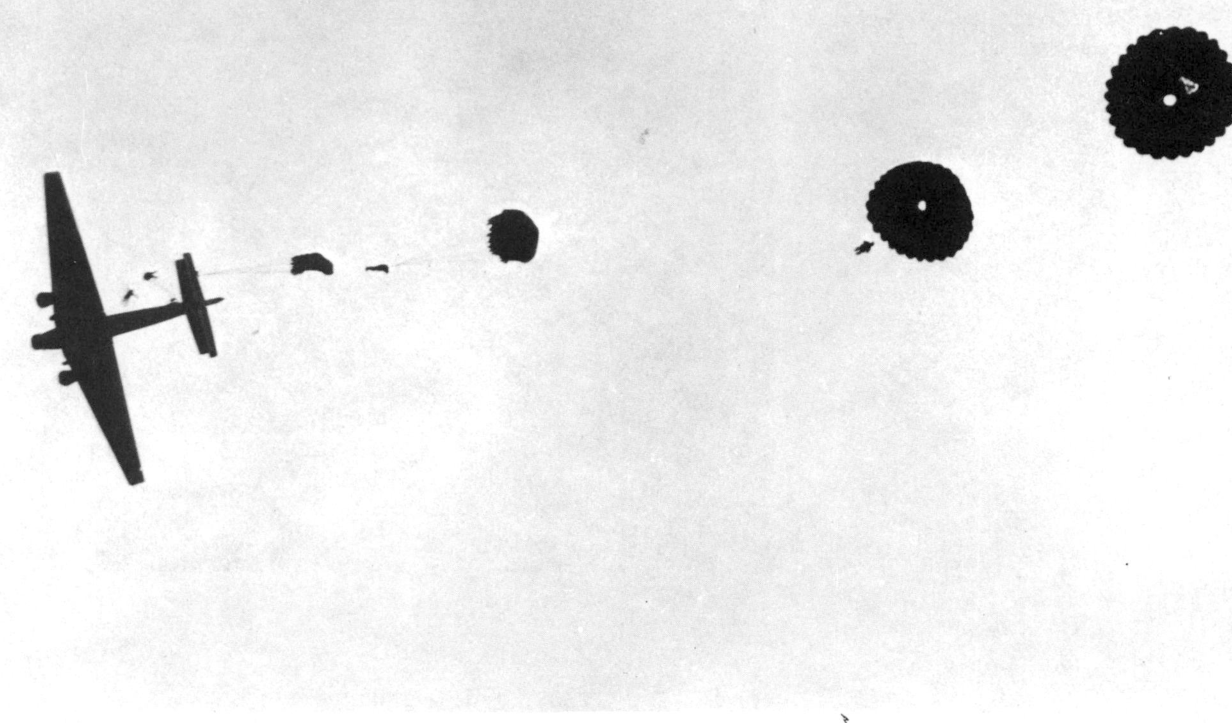

Sunday 25 May 1941
The *Wehrmacht High Command* announced:

Since the early morning hours of May 20, German paratroops and airborne troops have been fighting British army units on the island of Crete. In a bold aerial assault, the Germans conquered tactically important points on the island with the support of German fighter, destroyer, bomber and dive-bomber aircraft. After receiving further reinforcement by army units, the German troops went on the offensive. The western part of the island is already solidly in German hands. The German Luftwaffe smashed the British fleet when it attempted to intervene in the struggle for Crete, drove it out of the sea territory north of the island, sank and damaged a large number of enemy war vessels and won control of the air over the entire battle zone.

Friday 30 May 1941, Cairo
The *British Middle East Air Force* announced:

In Iraq our fighter squadrons flew patrols throughout the day in support of our advancing troops while Italian aircraft tried to prevent them. One of these enemy aircraft was shot down at Khanugah (Iraq). A number of British reconnaissance planes and bombers operated in cooperation with motorized units. We have destroyed the hangars on the airfield at Deir ez Zor in Syria. In Abyssinia, South African aircraft attacked Italian troops still fighting near Gimma. Direct hits were observed on buildings, as were a number of fires. Several Italian motor trucks went up in flames north of Algeh. Forts Azozo and Digya were bombed at Gondar (Ethiopia). In Libya, an enemy bomber wing yesterday undertook an assault on Tobruk; antiaircraft succeeded in shooting down four of them and several others were damaged. Five of our own aircraft failed to return from these operations.

Sunday 1 June 1941, London
The British *Air Ministry* announced:

After twelve days of the bitterest fighting of the war so far, it has been decided to withdraw our forces from Crete. Although the enemy has suffered massive losses of men and material, we would not in the long term have been able to continue successful troop operations on the island without substantial support from the aerial and naval forces.

Approximately 15,000 British troops have already left Crete and arrived in Egypt. However, it must be mentioned that the battle on Crete has taken a heavy toll of our forces. It is believed in London that General Freyberg has left Crete together with our troops. An official report confirms that General Freyberg is still alive.

Monday 2 June 1941
The *Wehrmacht High Command* announced:

The battle for Crete is over. The whole island has been freed from the enemy. Yesterday German troops occupied the last base of the beaten British, the port of Sfakion. German mountain troops fought down the last British resistance in the mountainous country north of Sfakion, capturing 3,000 more prisoners in the process.

The German Luftwaffe effectively supported these final mopping-up actions. In the sea territory between Crete and Alexandria, German bombers demolished a British destroyer with three direct hits as it was travelling with a naval formation.

Taking Crete

The German newspaper *Frankfurter Zeitung,* June 1941:

Many German paratroops ran into the frenzied defensive fire of the British while they were still in mid-air; many encountered bursts of enemy fire even as they vaulted gently, or impacted hard, onto the foreign soil or had just freed themselves from the oppressive hollow of the parachute. When the doors of their planes opened wide and they jumped, it was to land in a raging hell, in the dread of the unknown. But not one of them hesitated, not one kept the comrade behind him waiting. Head over heels they tumbled into the depths below, where the glowing flashes of enemy fire flickered upward out of the grey sand and the scorched stone.

Americans in Greenland

Tuesday 3 June 1941, New York
The American *United Press News Agency* reported:

It is rumored that an American air force unit has already arrived in Greenland, where it is conjectured that they are busy with the preparation of airfields.

Wednesday 11 June 1941
The *Wehrmacht High Command* announced:

German aerial combat formations operating out of newly-won bases in the Mediterranean, have successfully attacked the British fuel tank depots and port installations of Haifa, where they have caused a number of explosions and fires.

Night Flight to Haifa

The following descriptive account appeared in the German newspaper *Völkischer Beobachter,* June 1941:

After a swift run-up that grew more powerful by the second, the aircraft swung into flight. The captain and his observer put the plane on course—on course to Haifa, a journey of well over 1,200 miles over nothing but sea. The hours and miles slipped past. The sea lay barely visible far below our plane, the "Anton Marie." The clock showed that we would be over the target in about thirty minutes. The gunner crawled to his battle post. The glow of the

Upper left: Crete, 20 May 1941: An assault regiment of German paratroopers are making a landing near Heraklion under strong enemy fire.

Published in Canea by Creforce
Editorial Office Fernleaf House Canea
Telephone 460

CRETE NEWS

THE FIRST BRITISH PAPER PUBLISHED IN CRETE

SATURDAY 24 MAY 1941
Sunrise 5.18
Sunset 7.52

Vol 1 No 4 — CANEA, CRETE — Price 2 Drachmas — Free to troops

BATTLE OF CRETE RAGES AROUND MALEME

HERAKLION AND RETIMO IN HAND

Retimo and Heraklion are firmly in our hands and mopping up of small enemy detachments remaining is going on. Heavy fighting is continuing around Malame. On Friday German bombers made a heavy raid on Heraklion but did little damage of military importance.

Sixteen enemy troop carriers have already been destroyed on or near the Maleme aerodrome. Others crashed on landing.

This is the latest news of the battle of Crete. Fuller details of Wednesday night's naval action discloses that the enemy convoy which was smashed by the Royal Navy consisted of one Italian destroyer, two transports and and over forty caiques. The destroyer was the first vessel sighted. Our ships opened fire on her with pompoms. She replied by firing off five torpedoes. Our ships then fired a six inch broadside at her which caused her to blow up. She did not aven have time to fire her guns. One merchant ship was set on fire. Our destroyers then steamed in among the caiques, ramming and sinking them till the sea was full of Germans clinging to wreckage and shouting for help.

Throughout tle se days our naval forces off Gre te have been subjected to heavy and constant attack from the air. One ship was attacked on thirty differn occasions in three days. She shot down three enemy dive bombers.

Mr Churchill made a statement in the House of Commons on Thursday about the battle of Crete. He said »A British naval force intercepted on Wednesday night an enemy convoy making for the island. We sank the destroyer escort, two transport and a number of boats. Today the enemy made further

were three successful counter attacks and the enemy's losses yesterday were even heavier than before.

HESS UNKNOWN

FURTHER

IRAQ SUCCESS

In Iraq the resistance of rebel forces is weakening considerably. It is unlikely that he can hold out much longer, despite the fact that an arms supplies have been sent in to him from French Syria. Many of these arms were collected by General Waygand when he was commander in chief in Syria.

Colonel Colly, most brilliant French commander in Syria, has joined Free French forces. He crossed the border to Transjordania, it was announced from Cairo on Friday.

On arrival he denounced the Vichy policy of supplying arms to the rebels in Iraq. He recalled the first resolve of all French soldiers to defend the Republic and referred scornfully to Vichy's excuses that German planes made "freed landings" on aerodromes in Syria.

Colonel Colly brought the men under his command with him. He did this by ordering a movement to be carried out which was designed to bring them across the frontier.

WE TAKE VICHY SHIP

NAZI AGENTS IN SYRIA

A French oil tanker, en route for Casablanca, in French Morocco has been incepted by British patrols in the North Atlantic.

Mr. Anthony Eden warned Vichy that we will attack Germans even on French territory and hinted that the Germans plan to attack De Gaulle territories in West Africa.

Mr. Eden said that the confused and uneasy explanations put out by Vichy on the policy of collaboration with the Germans could not conceal that Vichy had embarked on a policy of of placing its reserves and empire increasingly at the disposal of a Power which was the enemy, not only of France's former ally but of France herself. Where they acted in any way detrimental to our conduct of the war or assist the enemy's war effort, naturally we must hold ourselves free to attack the enemy wherever he may be found. There could no longer be any distinction between occupied and unoccupied territory in the execution of our military plans.

The negotiations described in Vichy as opening up new phases of action were exemplified by the assistance given the Germans in Syria. Other

A.A. guns since the start of the invasion this week.

AMERICAS WEIGHT

American war production will not reach its peak until the middle or end of next year but American help will become decisive by September

motorcars."

"Those statements were terrible illusions. But the position is improving every day. American industry is

Right: A British military newspaper reports on the crucial battle for Maleme airfield in Crete.

exhaust flames flickered over his face. The coastal surf glowed white. At last the city of Haifa with its extensive port installations etched itself clearly below in the shining white. The flak was still keeping quiet. There was an uncanny stillness. The searchlights too remained dark. Then there was a flicker over there east of the mole. One of our aircraft launched its attack.

For the time it took to draw a breath our aircraft seemed to stick in the air. Then our dive began. The glaring flash of a heavy explosion lit up the jetty down below. The flak fired eagerly as if it were trying to sow flowers in the sky.

The "Anton Marie" flew for home.

War against the Soviet Union

Sunday 22 June 1941, Moscow
Soviet Foreign Minister Molotov made the following declaration in the name of the *Soviet Government*:

At 4:00 A.M. German Fascist and Rumanian forces crossed over our borders without any notification of cause and without a declaration of war. Kiev, Sevastopol, Kovno and other cities were bombed. More than 200 people have been killed or wounded according to reports received so far.

22 June 1941
The *Wehrmacht High Command* announced:

Since the early morning hours of today, we have been engaged in hostilities along the Soviet Russian border. An attempt by enemy aircraft to fly into East Prussia, has been repelled with heavy losses. German fighter planes shot down large numbers of Red bombers. In the struggle against the British Isles, powerful German aerial formations bombed the harbor installations of Southampton last night. Extensive fires broke out in the docks, warehouses and food manufacturing works. Further air attacks were aimed at airfields in northern Scotland and the Midlands. A large British freight vessel was severely damaged by bombs north of Sunderland. Yesterday afternoon a small number of British bombers with powerful fighter cover flew against the French Channel coast. German fighter planes shot down 26 British aircraft in violent dogfights. German flak and naval artillery brought down two more enemy aircraft. [German ace] Lt. Col. Galland won three air victories in these struggles.

Monday 23 June 1941, Moscow
Communiqué No. 1 of the *Red Army High Command* stated:

Early in the morning of June 22, the troops of the German-Fascist Wehrmacht attacked our border forces along the entire line extending from the Baltic Sea to the Black Sea. The enemy Luftwaffe bombed a number of our airfields and villages, but everywhere it encountered energetic resistance from our fighter planes and ground defenses, which inflicted heavy losses on the Hitlerite Fascists. Sixty-five German aircraft were shot down.

23 June 1941
The *Wehrmacht High Command* announced:

In the east the struggles of the German Army and the Luftwaffe against the Red Army are proceeding successfully according to schedule. Very weak forces of the Red Air Force dropped bombs in East Prussia without notable effect. [German ace] Lt. Col. Mölders won his 72nd air victory yesterday.

23 June 1941, Berlin
The *German News Office* announced:

Early Sunday morning 9 Russian Glenn Martin bombers flew into East Prussia and 7 of them were shot down by German fighter planes. In another attempted Soviet raid on military installations in the General Government of Poland close behind the front lines, all but 2 out of 35 Russian bombers were destroyed by German fighter planes.

Tuesday 24 June 1941, Berlin
The *German News Office* announced:

Since early Monday morning the Luftwaffe has continued its successful attacks on Soviet military airfields. Large numbers of Russian aircraft were destroyed on the first day of battle, and we can now report that a great many more aircraft have been shot down on the second day.

24 June 1941, Moscow
The *Headquarters of the Red Air Force* reported concerning the previous day's operations:

Our aerial forces have fought successfully to protect our airfields, towns and military installations. They have fought in the air and supported the counterattacks of the ground troops. In the course of the day 51 enemy aircraft were destroyed by our fighter planes and ground defenses. One enemy plane was forced to land at an airfield near Minsk.

24 June 1941, Berlin
The *German News Bureau* announced:

An attempt by the Soviet air force on Tuesday morning to fly weak forces into East Prussia, has

Eastern Poland on 22 June 1941: Soviet Polikarpov I-16 Rata fighter planes at the forward airfield of a Red Air Force fighter regiment at the time of the German attack on the Soviet Union.

been frustrated by the German air defense. The enemy aircraft encountered such accurate flak fire that they were forced to turn around at once and to jettison their bombs over open country.

Sunday 29 June 1941, Beirut
The French *Havas News Agency* reported:

This afternoon British aircraft bombed and destroyed the residence of the French High Commissioner in Beirut. There were large numbers of dead and wounded.

29 June 1941, Vichy
The *French Government* announced in a communiqué:

The British Fleet has bombed our coastal positions in the Middle East. We have evacuated several of our bases in the mountains of southern Lebanon under cover of artillery fire which inflicted heavy losses on our assailants. Our aerial forces, supported by naval aircraft, repeatedly intervened in the ground fighting, especially around Palmyra (Syria). A British colonel and 40 men were captured.

Monday 30 June 1941, Syria
The *Headquarters of General Wilson* (Allied commander in Syria) announced:

The Allied offensive against Homs (Syria) is making substantial progress. An Australian squadron flying American-model aircraft, shot down a formation of 6 Vichy-French Glenn Martin bombers in aerial combat. The Australians came back without losses to themselves.

Strategy and Tactics

January to June 1941

When the British found devices to effectively jam the German radio navigation system at the beginning of 1941, the Germans began to suffer heavier losses during their aerial operations against Britain, and in January the Luftwaffe was forced to revise its targets once again. Abandoning its raids on industrial centers in the British interior, the Luftwaffe now flew against coastal cities which the German bomber crews could locate in the dark without using radio navigation.

Deployment of the Italian Air Force in support of the German raids on Britain, wound down progressively, and on Friday 10 January 1941 the major part of the Corpo Aereo Italiano returned home.

Between 6th and 13th January 1941, Stuka dive bombers of the German 10th Air Corps (X. Fliegerkorps under General Geisler), operated out of Sicily for the first time against British naval forces in the Mediterranean. On January 10, 60 German Ju 87 and He 111 bombers raided the British aircraft carrier *Illustrious* between Sicily and Tunisia and severely crippled it. Next day the Stukas sank the British cruiser *Southampton* near Malta.

In their battles against the advancing British and their Allies in East Africa, the numbers of Italian fighter planes equipped to ward off bombing raids were melting away day by day. The dense sea and land blockade surrounding Italian East Africa, made it impossible for the Italians to supply their troops with fresh aircraft from Italy. Soon they had no fighters left except for a dozen Fiat CR.42 (Falco) biplanes which although they had outstanding flight characteristics, were powerless against the superior numbers of the British Gladiator fighters. In this desperate situation they seized on an inspiration of Colonel Galante, and transported the needed fighter planes in disassembled pieces inside the spacious fuselage of Savoia-Marchetti SM.82 Canguro (Kangaroo) transport planes whose range made it possible for them to ferry their cargo to East Africa from Libya. By the spring of 1941, over 50 Falco fighter planes had landed in Ethiopia by this method.

A Petlyakov Pe-2 dive bomber is being loaded with bombs. These machines, built in 1939, formed the core of the Soviet bomber formations.

On the night of 10th–11th February 1941, the British carried out the first paratroop mission in their history when they made an amateurish surprise assault on an aqueduct near Monte Vulture (Calabria, Italy). This aqueduct supplied Taranto, Brindisi and Bari with water, and it was hoped in London that its destruction would weaken Italian morale; but the assault ended in a fiasco. Eight officers and 31 soldiers took off from Malta in Whitley bombers and made a parachute landing onto a virtually uninhabited area. After they had fulfilled their mission and were marching toward the coast where a submarine was waiting for them, they were spotted and taken captive. The aqueduct was out of service for only 2½ days.

The first German air offensive against Malta took place in the first half of February 1941. It was carried out by the 10th Air Corps (X. Fliegerkorps under General Geisler), and was intended to make possible the safe transport to Tripoli of the German Afrika Korps under General Rommel. Vice-Admiral Weichold, chief of the German naval command in Italy, proposed that the island should be occupied at once, but his suggestion went unheeded. Later the German armed forces command staff joined Weichold in urging that instead of Crete, the Germans should launch an airborne attack on Malta, which although only 1/26th the size of Crete, was of incomparably greater strategic importance; but their argument too was declined.

After the devastating British naval attack on Italian shipping at Taranto on the night of 11th–12th November 1940, British torpedo bombers dealt another heavy blow to the Italian navy in March 1941. The debacle began with a false victory report from the German Luftwaffe. On Sunday 16 March 1941, 2 He 111 bombers of the German 10th Air Corps went on an armed reconnaissance flight during which they attacked units of the British Mediterranean fleet west of Crete, and after returning to base the air crews reported that they had verified torpedo hits on two heavy naval vessels which they described as battleships. This supposed success meant a substantial reduction of the Royal Navy's strength in the Mediterranean, so German leaders urged the Italian navy to get involved at last and to cooperate with the German attack on Greece that was planned for April 6, by thrusting their vessels forward into the eastern Mediterranean north and south of Crete.

By March 25 the Ultra code-breakers had already intercepted and deciphered the details of this planned operation. In *The Ultra Secret* Winterbotham wrote: "It was fortunate for us that the details of the operation were given [in the Enigma code] to the Luftwaffe which was supposed to provide air cover for the Italian ships; it gave us the complete plan and we were able to pass it to Admiral Cunningham in good time." (p. 66)

On Wednesday 26 March 1941, the Italian navy put out to sea with the modern battleship *Vittorio Veneto* (under naval commander Admiral Iachino), 6 heavy cruisers, 2 light cruisers, and 13 destroyers—under air cover from the German 10th Air Corps. The Italians' intention was to make precision raids on British convoys and the British Mediterranean fleet, so as to cripple British supply routes to Greece from Crete and Egypt. But the hunters turned into the hunted when Admiral Cunningham withdrew his fleet from the battle zone so as to give the impression that he was not expecting an attack. Then,

A disassembled Italian Fiat CR.42 (Falco) biplane inside the cargo compartment of a Savoia Marchetti SM 82 transport aircraft on its way to East Africa.

despite the threat the German Luftwaffe posed to British aircraft, the Admiral sent out a flying boat to scout the area, in order to make it look as if British information about the presence of the Italian fleet in the Aegean came from a reconnaissance plane. On Wednesday 27 March the flying boat sighted 3 Italian cruisers on a southeasterly heading approximately 320 miles west of Crete, and Ultra reports confirmed the sighting. Cunningham ordered British vessels in Alexandria to set sail and then conspicuously left the port carrying his golf clubs in order to mislead enemy agents about his intentions. Later he returned secretly and put to sea at dusk with his 3 battleships, the *Warspite,* the *Barham* and the *Valiant,* the aircraft carrier *Formidable* and 9 destroyers.

At dawn next day an aircraft from the carrier *Formidable* reported an Italian naval formation of 4 cruisers and 6 destroyers heading on a southeasterly course toward the Aegean. This was the advance guard of the far more powerful naval formation under Admiral Iachino.

At 7:45 A.M. a British cruiser formation sighted the enemy vanguard, launched a brief attack, then veered off shortly afterwards and retreated at top speed trying to lure the Italians within range of Cunningham's 3 battleships, which were still about 70 miles to the east. At 11:00 A.M. on 28 March 1941, battle was joined not far from Cape Matapan at the southernmost tip of the Greek mainland.

British torpedo bombers attacking Italian warships during the sea battle off Cape Matapan, Greece on 28 March 1941.

Above right: A Wellington bomber of RAF Coastal Command—a member of the Polish 304 Squadron—in low-level flight along the steep coast of Britain. Its mission: To fight German U-boats and to make patrol flights over the Atlantic.

Below right: The flak (antiaircraft) artillery of Royal Navy units assigned to guard the British coast, were the first line in Britain's air defense.

That afternoon, carrier-borne aircraft from the *Formidable,* and British bombers stationed in Greece and Crete, attacked the Italian battleship *Vittorio Veneto.* Damaged by torpedoes and bombs, she veered off toward the northwest at a speed of 15 knots, the best she could manage. Only the strenuous efforts of the crew prevented the battleship from flooding and got it safely to Taranto. The Italian cruisers formed a protective shield around the *Vittorio Veneto* to screen it from further aerial attack. Then the British carrier-based aircraft turned to bombing the heavy cruiser *Pola.*

In the evening, part of the Italian formation encountered the British battleships *Warspite, Barham* and *Valiant.* A few minutes after the sighting the Italians were under fire from a total of 24 heavy 38.1-cm cannon. The Italians were literally groping in the dark during this night attack, whereas the British were using radar-guided fire. The Italian cruisers *Fiume* and *Zara,* as well as the large destroyers *Alfieri* and *Carducci,* sank without having fired a shot. At dawn the heavily damaged *Pola* also went to the bottom. The Italians lost 5 valuable warships and around 3,000 officers and crew. British losses were: one Fairey Swordfish biplane. With the Battle of Cape Matapan, Britain became the uncontested master of the eastern Mediterranean.

In March the main emphasis of German night air raids on Britain shifted once again to operations against London port installations. For the first time since the night offensive began, the German bomber formations were suffering substantial losses. In March, 43 German combat aircraft were shot down by the British air defense—21 by radar-guided antiaircraft and 22 by night interceptor planes. A new

The City of London. Devastation of a kind that German cities would not experience until 1943, became a daily part of London life in the autumn of 1940.

development had come in radar technology. British night fighter planes were now being equipped with airborne radar, and as a result antiaircraft artillery had ceased to be the most important weapon in the British air defense arsenal.

In the first week of April the German Luftwaffe changed its tactics repeatedly. On the night of 7th–8th April, instead of attacking concentrically on a single target as they had always done in the past, German bombers—several hundred in all—simultaneously raided a large number of targets stretching all the way from the southern coast up to Scotland.

Due to British jamming of their radio navigational aids, German bomber crews increasingly were taken in by British dummy installations. The British had scattered almost 100 mock airfields in among their RAF bases, equipping them with dummy aircraft and simulated runway lighting systems. Another successful bright idea was the use of decoy flares (codenamed Starfish) which the British scattered along the flight route of the German bomber formations, where—if thrown at the right moment—they looked just like the target signal flares set out by German pathfinder aircraft. Mock installations resembling cities were set up and at night were lit by simulated fires; these too attracted enemy formations like a magnet. On the night of 17th–18th April alone, the Germans mistakenly dropped 170 high-explosive bombs, 32 parachute mines and 5,400 incendiary bombs on one such sham installation on Hayling Island in southern England.

Thursday 1 May 1941 was an important date for the German air defense, for this was when the day and night interceptor controls were united under a single command post. German flak units remained under the command of the individual air district headquarters [*Luftgaukommandos*], but in other respects German air defense now made up a single unified military organization.

On the night of 8th–9th May 1941, RAF formations totalling 359 bombers led the strongest mission yet against Germany. Of these aircraft, 317 attacked Hamburg and Bremen.

On Friday 9 May 1941, Radio Berlin reported that on the preceding night German bombers had inflicted heavy damage in the towns of Derby and Nottingham, especially in the Rolls Royce aircraft-engine manufacturing plant. But in reality only two cows and a few chickens had been killed.

In the first ten days of May, the German night air offensive was unexpectedly stepped up. Even the RAF airbases were on the agenda once again. On the night of 8th–9th May, German forces made simultaneous raids on 20 British airfields, and on the night of 11th–12th May, the number was increased to 45 – although as it turned out, two thirds of the airfields hit were dummy installations. This step-up of bombing operations was designed to make it appear that the Germans were preparing to invade England in the spring; but in reality they were trying to camouflage their preparations for the surprise attack on the Soviet Union. The grand assault on London on the night of 10th–11th May 1941, when weather conditions were ideal for the Germans, was the last climactic raid of the Battle of Britain. Five hundred and seven German bombers released 700 metric tons of high-explosive bombs and 2,393 incendiary bomb bins that caused more than 2,000 fires. This last heavy air raid on London inflicted greater devastation than any previous attack. More than 3,000 people were killed or injured. At the same time it was in this attack that the German Luftwaffe suffered its heaviest night-raid losses. Twenty-seven German aircraft were shot down, a toll which previously had been reached only in day raids.

During the ten months of the Battle of Britain, the German Luftwaffe flew a total of some 50,000 operations against Britain and dropped 50,000 metric tons of bombs. It could not have done more, given Germany's industrial capacity, weather conditions and the quality of British air and ground defense.

The German Luftwaffe had now lost the Battle of Britain. The causes for its failure were Germany's lack of suitable well-armed heavy bombers, its lack of long-range fighter planes, and its lack of a purposeful strategy of aerial warfare. Germany did not lose the war when it lost the Battle of Britain; but it could no longer win it.

The Battle of Britain holds a special place in the history of aerial warfare because it was the first battle whose course was determined exclusively by aerial forces. By their victory, the RAF fighter planes prevented Germany from achieving command of the air over England, the first step toward an enemy invasion. This was also the first battle in which the fighter plane, which was an expressly tactical weapon, achieved a strategic victory.

This German poster warns citizens to maintain the blackout because "The enemy can see your light!" All the belligerent nations imposed severe penalties on anyone who failed to observe the blackout regulations.

Beginning in the spring of 1941, despite all Britain's difficulties, it began to deploy substantial aerial forces in the struggle against German U-boat submarines. By April 1941, British Coastal Command already had 110 aircraft equipped with ASV radar (air surface vessel radar), i.e. instruments for the radiolocation of surface shipping. At that time the airborne radar instruments were still highly susceptible to jamming, but they helped to ensure that German U-boats could no longer move about unscathed even at night.

In March 1941, German Luftwaffe formations earmarked for marine deployment were integrated under the "Atlantic Zone Air Commander," Lt. Col. Harlinghausen. Their chief duties were: long range reconnaissance, attack on shipping traffic around southern England, and raids on British ports. Churchill reported in his memoirs that German marine aircraft operations, and especially the operations of the Focke Wulf FW 200 C Condor long-range bomber-reconnaissance aircraft, had a disastrous effect on British shipping. Despite British attempts to combat the Condors, they sank 37 ships totalling almost 150,000 tons in the first two months of 1941. One countermeasure was to install fighter plane catapults on shipping units like the old sea-plane-carrier *Pegasus.* The carrier vessels carried naval fighters to protect British convoys from the infamous German long range bombers. Reportedly at Churchill's inspiration, the British built catapults onto merchant vessels as well. These were known as CAMs for "catapult armed merchantmen." As a rule they had two Hurricane fighters on board which were catapulted into the air when the German Condors made their appearance.

The first CAM ship, the steamship *Michael E,* put out to sea on Tuesday 27 May 1941, but despite the new device it was torpedoed all the same and sank along with its Hurricane aircraft.

Aerial combat between a catapulted Hurricane and a Condor might end in a number of ways, but the pilot, if his craft was hit, always faced a difficult choice: Should he try to get his damaged plane to the coast, which usually was a long distance away, or make an emergency sea landing near the shipping convoy, a course that could be equally hazardous? Often an aircraft would sink within seconds of hitting the water, so as a rule the pilots preferred to bail out with their parachutes rather than try to land their planes; and anyhow, there was no guarantee that an air crew would be picked up by a ship even if they landed close by. In the first place, it was very difficult for a ship's crew to sight a pilot in his inflatable dinghy; and second, a ship that suspected a U-boat was nearby, could not risk stopping for pickups.

The first air kill of a Condor by a Hurricane catapulted from a CAM ship, was made by British Lt. R. Everett based on the steamship *Maplin.* By the end of 1941, CAM-ship Hurricanes had succeeded in shooting down only some 6 German Condor long range bombers over the Atlantic. Following these modest results, the convoy-protector Hurricanes were transferred from CAMs to MACs—merchant aircraft carriers which were a type of mini-carrier. Most were oil tankers that had been stripped of their superstructures and could accommodate up to six sea-going Hurricanes—and sometimes an equal number of Swordfish torpedo bombers—on their improvised flight decks.

On Friday 3 April 1941, an armed uprising took place in Iraq. The 1930 alliance agreement between

Above: A British CAM freighter carrying a Sea Hurricane fighter about to be catapulted into the air.

Left: A German He 111 bomber being loaded with a heavy bomb.

Below: Industry tries to capitalize even on the danger posed by the air war. This British firm is advertizing a good bargain in home air raid shelters.

The Hull TUBULAR INDOOR AIR-RAID SHELTER

An ideal SHELTER at all times—but essential during WINTER months

SLEEP IN SAFETY IN YOUR OWN HOME

We have pleasure in informing numerous enquirers that material has now been made available by the Ministry of Supply for the manufacture of a limited number of these well-known indoor Shelters.

Orders will be executed in strict rotation.

APPLY: LAIRD SECURITIES LIMITED, 149 LEADENHALL STREET, LONDON, E.C.3. (AVEnue 5393)

Iraq and Britain had granted Britain two bases there: Shuaiba south of Basra, and Habbaniya, an important RAF base and training camp in the Euphrates Valley about 48 miles west of Baghdad. It was from Habbaniya that the British had flown their espionage flights over Baku and Batum in March of 1940. In 1941 a coup d'état by the pro-Hitlerite General Rashid Ali el Gailani, overthrew the pro-British regent of Iraq, Emir Abdul Illah. The Soviet Union recognized the new government at once—indeed it was the first to do so—and the German Luftwaffe made plans to set up an airlift to Iraq.

Italy's failed attack on Greece enabled the British to strengthen their position in southeastern Europe. The presence of the British forces in Greece and Crete threatened the Rumanian oil fields and the southern flank of the German forces planning to attack the Soviet Union.

The little Greek air force fought on bravely against the Axis powers. It flew missions in support of the ground troops, secured shipping convoys in the Mediterranean, and protected the disembarkation of the British Expeditionary Force; and using

6 Hurricane fighters supplied by the RAF, it shot down 27 Italian aircraft without losses to itself. All the same it was virtually impossible for Greece to win command of Greek air space.

At 5:15 A.M. on Sunday 6 April 1941, the Germans marched into Yugoslavia without a previous declaration of war and then invaded Greece from Bulgaria. In the invasion, the Luftwaffe deployed Luftflotte 4 (the 4th Air Fleet under Air Fleet General Löhr), comprising 210 fighter planes, 400 bombers and Stukas, and 170 reconnaissance aircraft. Italy had a total of 666 aircraft. At that time Yugoslavia had only 400 aircraft—including 144 fighters, 160 bombers and 40 reconnaissance craft—and Greece had only 80 planes left.

The Luftwaffe opened its attack on Yugoslavia with a bombing raid on the capital, Belgrade. One hundred and fifty bombers and Stuka dive bombers with powerful fighter cover, flew out from their bases in Austria and Rumania. The first strike was made in three waves involving 484 operations. That Sunday Belgrade suffered five heavy air raids and by the end of the day, 17,000 dead lay in the ruins of the capital.

During the air war over Yugoslavia, the Italian air force flew several hundred missions in which it shot down only 4 aircraft while losing 5. One reason for this lack of combat effectiveness was that at no time was there any significant coordination between the Regia Aeronautica and the Luftwaffe.

The Luftwaffe used the same tried-and-true method against Yugoslavia that it had used against other nations: First it demolished the enemy aerial forces in a single massive strike, and then, having achieved complete command of the air, it carried on tactical operations in support of the ground troops.

The assault on Greece was equally successful. On the evening of Monday 7 April, 11 German bombers of the 10th Air Corps (X. Fliegerkorps) attacked the Athens port of Piraeus. One of the bombs hit the British munitions ship *Clan Frazer* causing its 250-metric-ton cargo of explosives to blow up. The explosion devastated the port from end to end and sank 12 ships totalling 51,569 tons, in addition to 60 light sailer boats and 25 motor sailers. Admiral Cunningham, the commander of the British fleet in the Mediterranean, called it a shattering blow. This single direct aerial bomb hit deprived British troops of the only well-equipped transshipment port by which they could maintain supplies and reinforcements. As a result of the German aerial bombing raid, the weak British Expeditionary Force and the Greek armed forces were reduced to a policy of delaying tactics.

In the spring of 1941 there was feverish activity in the special air squadron of German Colonel T. Rowehl. This was a top secret Luftwaffe unit of long range reconnaissance aircraft specially adapted for very high altitude flying. The planes took off from bases in Finland, Bulgaria and what had formerly been Poland, to carry out scout flights over the Soviet Union and take aerial photographs for their bomb target file—all in preparation for Operation Barbarossa, the German attack on the Soviet Union. Inexplicably, since April 1940 Moscow had issued strict orders to Soviet border guard troops, as well as to members of all the other Red Army services, to refrain from shooting at German aircraft that appeared in the skies over Soviet territory. The Soviets looked on passively as their borders were violated by German reconnaissance planes—more than 150 times in the first half of 1941 alone.

Official German files that were taken into custody after the war, make it clear that the Soviets had officially notified the Berlin government of their open policy with regard to German planes. Moreover, on Tuesday 15 April 1941, when a German reconnaissance plane had to make an emergency landing at Rovno in Soviet-held eastern Poland, its crew were allowed to return to Germany without further ado and shortly thereafter their plane was returned to the Luftwaffe. Most remarkably of all, while the German air crew were being checked out at the Soviet military airfield, they were allowed to move about freely and so were able to pursue their observations on the ground.

On the other side of the globe, another air power was also trying to sound out its future enemy in the spring of 1941. A special secret air corps of the imperial Japanese navy, the No. 3 "Kukutai" Corps comprising 3 squadrons of 36 Mitsubishi G3M2 long range reconnaissance aircraft—was set up secretly in Takao (= Kaohsiung) on the island of Formosa. The aircraft, painted a pale grey-blue and bearing no national emblems, had efficient, high-power automatic cameras installed in the fuselage.

"Defend yourselves when attacked, but if you are forced to land you must without fail destroy your aircraft, and if you are captured you must swear that you made a navigational error while on an exercise flight." This is what Captain Kamei impressed on his air crews before their first mission—to scout the harbor fortifications, airfield and military installa-

Greece, April 1941: A P-24 F fighter plane of the Royal Air Force, manufactured in Poland, has made an emergency landing after a fight with a German Me 109.

tions of the US base at Legaspi in the southeast corner of the Philippine island of Luzon.

Very early on the morning of Friday 18 April 1941, a brand-new Mitsubishi G3M2 bearing no national emblems took off from Takao, set a course for Legaspi about 600 miles to the south, and slowly gained altitude.

Lieutenant Nagasi reported about this flight: "Visibility was excellent, up to 40–50 miles. After sighting Luzon we veered off and flew along the coast, taking care to keep outside the territorial waters 15 miles from the shore. Seventy miles east of Polillo Island we ascended to almost 28,000 feet and approached our target. As the camera hatch opened, an ice-cold draught entered the cabin. We crossed the southern cape at Legaspi Bay and flew west. The camera took one photograph automatically every 15 seconds. At the southern end of the bay we took a northern heading and a few minutes later headed east again. We set down on the taxi strip at Takao exactly 8 hours and 50 minutes after takeoff."

The small Greek air force was no match for the German Luftwaffe, so the Luftwaffe dispensed with its customary blitz strike at the opening of the Greek campaign, and immediately began to fly tactical missions in support of the German army. The Greek campaign was a model of effective cooperation between the German army and air force, which proved successful here as it had in the past: Yugoslavia had surrendered after 12 days of fighting on Friday 18 April 1941, and Greece surrendered 6 days later on Thursday 24 April.

The retreat of the British to Thermopylae was a very difficult maneuver, but their stubborn rearguard actions held up the German advance at many points.

On Saturday 26 April 1941, two battalions of the German 2nd Parachute Regiment under Colonel Sturm seized the bridge over the Corinthian Canal after a daring aerial landing. The bridge was undamaged when it fell into German hands, but a stray British antiaircraft shell set off an explosive charge on the structure and it collapsed. This afforded a welcome respite to the retreating British troops, because no strong German heavy-weapons units could follow them for some time. The destruction of the canal bridge did not represent an immediate tactical setback for the Germans, but the debris blocked preparations for the German assault on Crete because the Corinthian Canal was the only safe sea route by which aviation fuel supplies could be shipped to the German transport aircraft intended to carry their airborne troops. By Monday 28 April, the Germans held all of Greece except for the strategically important island of Crete.

On the morning of Wednesday 30 April 1941, the new pro-German Iraqi government ordered approximately 9,000 troops to march on the RAF base of Habbaniya in Iraq and to set up their 28 cannon in artillery positions on the surrounding plateau.

On Friday 2 May the British Flying School Squadron in Habbaniya, armed with Gladiator fighter planes and supported by Wellington bombers from the RAF base at Shuaiba on the Persian Gulf, bombed the Iraqi troops in their positions only one mile away. The Iraqis responded to the raid with a cannon barrage, supported by bombs and machine gun fire from their own aircraft. That same day Rashid el Gailani asked Hitler for military assistance.

Twenty-four hours later the German ambassador in Iraq received orders from Berlin. He was told to obtain permission from the French Vichy government to transport aircraft and equipment to Iraq via French-held Syria. To the surprise of the Germans, the Vichy government not only gave transit permission but immediately transported almost all the French war material stored in Syria, to Iraq. All the same, after four days of non-stop British air raids, the Iraqi troops were forced to leave the high ground around Habbaniya and retreat to Baghdad on the night of Tuesday 6 May.

On Saturday 10 May 1941, the Germans in Athens set Operation Iraq in motion when several Me 110 destroyer aircraft and a number of troop-transport planes flew to Baghdad via Rhodes-Aleppo-Damascus-Mosul. The aim of this operation was to provide aid to the rebel Iraqi generals so as to threaten the flank of the British forces in North Africa. Churchill said later that at that time the Germans actually had an airborne landing troop strong enough to have enabled them to seize Syria, Iraq and Persia with their precious oil fields, so that Hitler's hand could have stretched out as far as India and Japan. No. 4 Squadron of the German 76th Destroyer Wing (Zerstörergeschwader 76 under Lt. Col. Hobein), formed part of the "Junck Special Aerial Force" which was to initiate the planned operation in Iraq. All the German aircraft carried Iraqi national emblems. Colonel Junck reported later: "The force was deployed overhastily with aircraft that were not equipped with tropical kits. Some of them did not even have the maps and charts which were absolutely indispensable for such missions."

To begin with, the British did not notice what was afoot. On May 11, 2 French Morane 406 fighter planes of 7 Squadron, 1st Fighter Group (GCI/7), forced 3 Messerschmitt Bf 110s from 4 Squadron of the German 76th Destroyer Wing to land in the Syrian city of Palmyra because the German planes had crossed French territory without announcing their presence. Next day, May 12, 6 German He 111 bombers under the command of Colonel Junck landed in the Syrian capital of Damascus on their way to Iraq. After a two-day stop they took off for Mosul.

On the morning of Wednesday 14 May, a British reconnaissance plane observed a German Junkers Ju 90 transport aircraft taking off from Palmyra. The reconnaissance plane flew a second mission at noon and determined that several Axis Power transport planes had landed there. Late that afternoon 3 British Blenheim bombers with 2 Curtiss Tomahawk fighters flying cover, made a low-level strafing attack on Palmyra without visible success. This was the first time that Curtiss Tomahawk fighters were deployed in World War II. Next morning, May 15, all the transport aircraft were still safe on the

Right: Inside the cockpit of a Japanese Mitsubishi G3M2 long range reconnaissance plane which is making a secret mission over US bases in the Pacific.

Below: A German He 111 of the Junck Special Unit. A swastika on the vertical fin has been hastily painted over and Iraqi national emblems mounted on the fuselage.

airfield. A second British raid also failed to destroy them.

On Friday 16 May 1941, 3 German He 111s of the special Junck unit, bombed the British airbase at Habbaniya. Then the aircraft of the British Fleet Air Arm raided the Iraqi airfield of Mosul and destroyed one German He 111 bomber and 2 Me 110 destroyers of the Junck force.

Italy joined in by sending a unit of Fiat CR.42 fighters of Fighter Wing 155a to Baghdad. The aircraft were furnished with Iraqi emblems. Due to their delayed arrival they flew only a couple of missions, during which they shot down a British Hawker Hardy general-purpose biplane while losing one CR.42.

The overhasty intervention of the German and Italian air forces in Iraq, continued to be plagued with bad luck. The officer assigned to coordinate German and Italian operations with those of the Iraqi forces – the son of Field Marshal von Blomberg – was retrieved from an airplane in Baghdad with a bullet in his brain, having been accidentally killed by the overeager air defense at the airfield.

Operation Mercury, the conquest of Crete by German paratroops, was not an ordinary airborne troop landing operation but a battle against an enemy who had known about the German plan for several weeks beforehand and who had time enough to do everything possible to thwart it. On Tuesday 20 May 1941, when the German paratroops climbed into their transport planes, they did not suspect that the British knew every last detail of their mission. From the very start, the British communications monitors followed all the coded messages between the Luftwaffe high command and the German military staffs in Greece who were preparing Operation Mercury.

At the express wishes of Churchill, Sir Bernard Freyberg, one of the Commonwealth's most capable generals who had won the highest British decoration for bravery, the Victoria Cross, was appointed Allied commander of the island.

Winterbotham kept Churchill informed about the German coded messages intercepted by Ultra

and told him when the expected airborne invasion of Crete was imminent. The Prime Minister then ordered Winterbotham to pass on all information to General Freyberg as soon as it was received. As a result, Winterbotham said, "Freyberg was in possession of the most detailed plans of an enemy's proposed operation that were ever likely to be available to any commander." (*The Ultra Secret,* p. 68)

From Thursday 15 May onward, the British Mediterranean fleet stayed in the waters around Crete. By May the combined British and Greek troops on the island – 42,640 men of whom 10,258 were Greek – were standing by for emergency and hourly awaited the German assault. Until the actual assault the German leaders were unaware of the strength of the troops in Crete, for German aerial reconnaissance failed to gather an accurate picture of the enemy despite the Luftwaffe's repeated efforts. The Allied defensive positions and troop assemblies were so skillfully camouflaged that they were not visible even on aerial photographs. Low-level scout flights produced no better results.

On Sunday 18 May 1941, 18,000 Italian troops under the Duke of Aosta, finding themselves in a hopeless plight in the East African Desert War, surrendered to the Allies at Amba Alagi, Ethiopia.

German Operation Mercury began at 7:15 A.M. on Tuesday 20 May. The German forces were divided into three groups: West Group under Maj. Gen. Meindl, which made its drop at Maleme; Central Group under Lt. Gen. Süssmann, which attacked the Suda Bay and Khania; and East Group under Maj. Gen. Ringel, which dropped at Heraklion. [Cf. Crete landing map] The overall commander was General Löhr of the 4th Air Fleet. His forces included the 8th Air Corps (VIII. Fliegerkorps under Air Fleet General von Richtofen), the 11th Air Corps (XI. Fliegerkorps under Air Fleet General Student), the 7th Airborne Paratroop Division under Lt. Gen. Süssmann, the reinforced 5th Mountaineering Division under Maj. Gen. Ringel, and reserve forces made up of units of the 6th Mountaineering Division. In addition there were 10 aerial combat groups comprising 493 Ju 52-model transport aircraft, 430 bombers, 180 fighters and 100 gliders.

The actual drop of the first wave of German paratroops went off almost without a hitch and contrary to expectations, losses of transport aircraft were few. Only 7 of the nearly 500 Ju 52s deployed, failed to return to their bases in Greece. But during descent and landing, the paratroops were met by strong defensive fire. Many companies of troops were too widely dispersed; they suffered heavy losses and were virtually incapable of going on the offensive. Thus they failed to capture the important Hill 107 near Maleme airfield which was being defended by New Zealanders. German airborne infantry who made glider landings in the rocky terrain, also met surprisingly vigorous enemy fire and suffered far higher losses than they could have predicted. Instead of carrying out their assignment to secure the landing zone, they were immediately put on the defensive.

Meanwhile the second wave of German paratroop regiments were standing by at Greek airfields, waiting for the return of the transport aircraft that were due to drop them on Crete that same afternoon. But the first wave transports were delayed in arriving back at their takeoff bases and most had to be refueled out of portable fuel drums, which was a painstaking and time-consuming process.

It soon became apparent that the aircraft would be unable to take off at the scheduled time of 1:00 P.M., yet it was no longer possible to relay new orders because British agents had cut all the telephone cables between the transport formations and the German 11th Air Corps. So, the Germans could not shift their preparatory supportive bombing raids to a later time.

Punctually at 3:15 P.M., German bombers around Rethimnon and Heraklion attacked their targets as scheduled – but to no purpose, because the first transport planes carrying the second wave of troops were just rolling up for takeoff when the bombers flew their mission. Only now did it become apparent to the Germans that the huge clouds of dust thrown up by the propellers would make it impossible for a large formation to take off en masse, and thus the groups of transport planes could not form a massed assembly in the air. As a result, the planes were

Above: Crete, 20 May 1941. A crashed German DS 230 cargo glider surrounded by dead airborne landing troops.

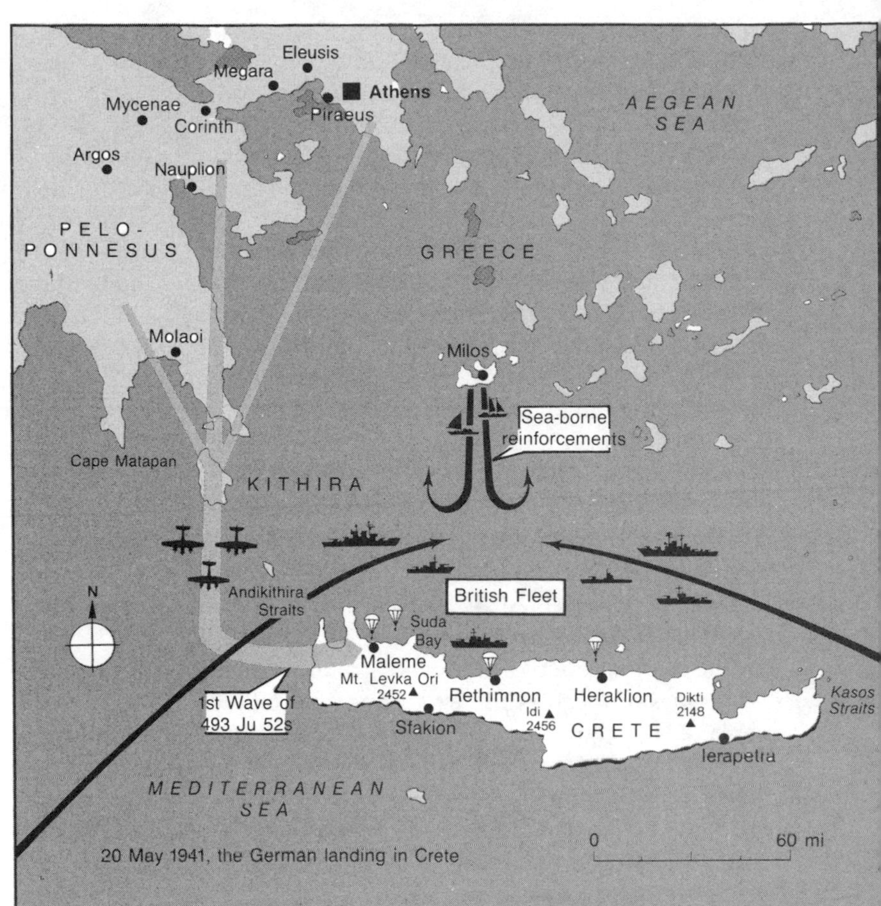

20 May 1941, the German landing in Crete

Right: 20 May 1941, the German landing in Crete

Below: Suda Bay on the northern side of the island of Crete, where British freighters are burning after a German air attack.

forced to approach their drop points individually at intervals causing substantial delay.

Meanwhile General Student, commander of the German 11th Air Corps, was back at his command post in Athens and knew virtually nothing of what was happening in Crete. No radio communications had yet been set up between the Corps and West Group at Maleme or Central Group at Suda Bay and Chania. The only effective German 80- and 200-watt transmitters had been smashed in a glider crash, so the Germans in Athens did not know that the raid on Maleme airfield had miscarried, that many German units had been decimated, that Lt. Gen. Süssmann, the commander of the 7th Airborne Paratroop Division, had crashed in his glider over the island of Aegina, that General Meindl, the commander of West Group, was badly wounded, and that both West and Central Groups, now leaderless, were exposed to strong enemy fire.

The defenders of the island were also prepared for the second wave of German paratroops. Isolated companies dropped in the wrong spots at Rethimnon and Heraklion, were shot to pieces by tanks that loomed up suddenly even before they could free themselves from their parachutes. Thus the attacks on the Rethimnon and Heraklion airfields failed too. Not until evening of that day, May 20, did the Germans in Athens learn of the chaos in Crete. During the night of 20th–21st May, General Student decided to deploy all his remaining forces as fast as possible to seize the most important airfield on the island, at Maleme. The wounded General Meindl was succeeded in his command by Colonel Ramcke, who dropped at Maleme on May 21, took over command of West Group, and went on the offensive with the remains of the assault regiment. By 5:00 P.M. Maleme airfield was in German hands and several Ju 52s had already landed. That same day the first companies of the German 100th Mountain Infantry Regiment landed successfully at Maleme.

Admiral Cunningham now sent a British naval formation to secure the western coast of Crete while light combat vessels – 7 cruisers and 11 destroyers – advanced to patrol both sides of the island. Here they lay in wait to prevent any attempt by the Germans to bring desperately-needed mountain infantry and heavy weapons to the island by boat. At midnight on May 22, British naval forces encountered a convoy of German coastal motor sailers that had left the port of Piraeus carrying a division of mountain infantry troops, and cut them to pieces. Later they attacked a second German convoy carrying about 4,000 mountain infantrymen. At the last moment the bombers of the German 8th Air Corps under General von Richtofen came to their aid.

At 5:30 A.M. on the morning of Thursday 22 May 1941, the Ju 87s of the German 2nd Dive Bomber Wing, the "Immelmann" under Lt. Col. O. Dinort, took off to raid the Royal Navy vessels around Crete. At that time British Task Force D lay 25 miles off the northern coast of Crete, as did also the cruisers *Gloucester* and *Fiji* and the destroyers *Greyhound* and *Griffin.* Heavy near-hits put two gun turrets out of action on the cruiser *Naiad.* The destroyer *Juno* sank within two minutes after receiving a direct bomb hit. Shortly after noon the German bombers sighted the second naval formation. Ten minutes later the battleship *Warspite,* Admiral Rawling's flagship, had been badly hit. The destroyer *Greyhound* sank at 1:00 P.M. after receiving two direct hits. Several flights of Ju 87 Stukas and Me 109 fighter-bombers hurled themselves onto cruisers travelling alone. The *Gloucester* was hit at once. Shrouded in clouds of black smoke, the cruiser circled slowly and sank at around 4:00 P.M. after an explosion inside the vessel. This first air-sea battle in history went on for several days and ended in a decisive victory for the German Luftwaffe.

If the Germans had not had command of the air, the German troops sent to Crete by sea would have been lost. Instead German bombers succeeded in inflicting such substantial losses on the British fleet that it was forced to retreat from the waters north of Crete.

The British sent 12 Hurricane fighters from Egypt to help defend Heraklion. The flak artillery on a British destroyer accidentally shot down 2 of them and chased away 3 others. Four of the other fighters crash-landed or were shot down by the Germans before they could even enter combat.

The fate of Crete was decided in the moment when the Germans deployed their last forces to seize the all-important, fiercely contested airfield of Maleme. Meanwhile, the High Command of the German armed forces made no public mention of the airborne landing operation on Crete until 25 May 1941, after the Germans had successfully occupied the western part of the island surrounding Maleme. On the evening of May 27, the Allied commander General Freyberg received orders to evacuate Crete. The British Navy had paid a heavy toll in its struggle for the island: 2 battleships, the *Barham* and the *Warspite,* as well as the aircraft carrier *Formidable,* and 6 cruisers and 7 destroyers, were badly damaged, while 3 cruisers and 6 destroyers had been sunk.

A British Fairey Swordfish landing on the deck of the aircraft carrier *Ark Royal* after attacking the German battleship *Bismarck* with air-launched torpedoes.

The victory in Crete was also costly to the Germans. Of the 6,580 German paratroopers who had landed on the island, approximately 4,000 ended up dead or missing. Of the 493 Ju 52 aircraft deployed, 271 were destroyed or so badly damaged that they too had to be listed as lost. This was to be the last major German paratroop operation of World War II.

Yet the costly conquest of Crete turned out to be relatively unimportant to Germany, for it accomplished nothing but to improve the defensive position of the Axis Powers in the Aegean.

The important role of the aircraft carrier in naval warfare became particularly clear in the fight against the German battleship *Bismarck* in 1941. Moreover, it was thanks to aircraft equipped with airborne radar that the British were able to sink the German vessel on Tuesday 27 May.

On Sunday 18 May, the battleship *Bismarck* and the German heavy cruiser *Prinz Eugen,* under fleet commander Admiral Lütjens, put out to sea from the Baltic port of Gdynia to raid the Atlantic. As soon as the British Admiralty received news that the German battle group had passed through the Kattegat strait between Jutland (Denmark) and Sweden, it took countermeasures, calling the aircraft carrier *Victorious* down from the northwest along with two battleships, and bringing up the aircraft carrier *Ark Royal* from Gibraltar with a battle cruiser and an ordinary cruiser.

Battle was joined on Saturday 24 May 1941; the battle cruiser *Hood* was destroyed and the battleship *Prince of Wales* was forced to veer off after being badly hit. Two days later, on Monday 26 May, a Catalina flying boat of British Coastal Command discovered the *Bismarck* about 700 nautical miles from Brest, its port of destination. The Catalina was equipped with a recently improved ASV radar device (air surface vessel radar), and this incident offered the first proof of its efficiency.

That same day British Swordfish torpedo bombers from the carrier *Ark Royal*—the bombers too were equipped with ASV radar—attacked the German battleship. The steering rudder of the *Bismarck* was hit so badly that she lost her ability to maneuver and made easy prey for 2 British battleships and several cruisers. Next day, 27 May 1941, the outmatched *Bismarck* was shot to pieces and the burning battleship—the pride of the German navy—was scuttled by her own crew.

In Iraq, Colonel Junck managed to fly 6 additional bombing missions and 7 reconnaissance missions against Habbaniya with his last 3 Heinkel He 111s, all that was left of his "special unit." Their last flight was on May 29.

On Friday 30 May 1941, British troops stood outside the gates of Baghdad. The Iraqi rebel leader Rashid Ali, the German and Italian diplomats in Iraq, and the Grand Mufti of Jerusalem, all fled to Persia. A ceasefire agreement was signed, and next day the pro-British regent of Iraq was reinstated and a new government formed. At the same hour, Berlin ordered Junck's special unit to leave Mosul and transfer back to Rhodes via Aleppo. Only one He 111 successfully completed the desolate journey. That same Saturday, the last Italian fighter planes of 155a Wing landed at Rhodes.

Once the rebellion in Iraq had neared its end, the British turned their attention back to Syria and Lebanon, which were under the control of the Vichy government and posed a threat to the rear of the Allied forces in Egypt and to the important British oil supplies.

Days before the British marched into Syria, violent dogfights took place between British and French aerial forces over Syrian territory. On Wednesday 28 May, the French won their first air victory when Lt. Vuillemin of 7 Squadron, 1st Fighter Group (GCI/7), shot down a British Blenheim reconnaissance plane while he was flying a Morane 406. Alarmed by the presence of the British forces, the Vichy government ordered immediate reinforcements to the French aerial contingent. That same day a group of the most modern French fighters, Dewoitine D.520s, landed in Rayak (Syria). They belonged to 6 Squadron, 3rd Fighter Group (GCIII/6) which had taken off from Algeria on May 24 and flown along the northern coast of the Mediterranean; 2 of the planes were lost over Turkey.

On the morning of Thursday 5 June, 3 British Blenheims raided Aleppo airfield in Syria, where the British had observed a number of Italian CR.42 fighters and SM.79 transport aircraft on the ground. One aircraft and a hangar were demolished. Three French Morane 406 fighters tried in vain to ward off the attack.

On Sunday 8 June, Australian and Indian troops, supported by the First Allied Cavalry Division and small units of Free French as well as 60 RAF aircraft, pushed their way toward Beirut and Damascus. The first operations by British aircraft that day, were raids on the French airbase at Rayak. The British Hurricanes were ordered to destroy the modern Martin 167 Maryland bombers of French 39 Squadron, 1st Bomber Group (GBI/39), which had just arrived at Rayak and by that time had started bombing British columns approaching Quneitra. Next, 5 Tomahawk fighters of the Australian 3rd Fighter Wing raided Rayak, where the French ground defenses took them for French planes because this was the first time they had ever seen a Tomahawk.

On Tuesday 10 June 1941 during a reconnaissance flight over Deraa (Syria), a well-known French pilot, Capitaine Jacobi of 6 Squadron, 3rd Fighter Group, was shot down by the British air defense. That afternoon the air crews of French 7 Squadron, 1st Fighter Group received orders to "drive off small units of the British Navy" that were firing uninterruptedly at the French-held coast; but it turned out that these "small units" were the whole of the British 15th Cruiser Squadron, and the French swiftly halted their operations.

Both the Vichy and the Allied forces received considerable back-up in the course of the fighting. The French increased their fighter plane forces to 159 by bringing in a number of their best and most experienced fighter pilots who had been especially picked for this mission. French squadrons armed with modern Dewoitine D.520s inflicted heavy losses on the British formations because in this war theater the British had no planes of equal quality. The French Martin 167s also kept up an incessant bombardment of British troop assemblies. French relay bombing raids actually held up one British column for several days on its march from Iraq to Palmyra in central Syria.

German He 111 bombers at a forward airfield, waiting for their deployment orders before attacking targets in the Soviet Union.

Syria, June 1941. A Potez 25 TOE reconnaissance plane of the Vichy-French unit GAO 595 based on Palmyra, is flying over a camel patrol.

On the same day that Capitaine Jacobi was shot down – 10 June 1941 – the aerial units of the German Luftwaffe began to form up in preparation for the Eastern Campaign. Its formations included forces from all over occupied Western Europe, Sicily, Greece and Yugoslavia. Only the German air wings in North Africa stayed where they were. Yet despite warnings from other nations that a German invasion of the Soviet Union was imminent, the Soviet press dismissed their alarms as the "ravings of Russia's enemies," and on 13 June 1941, just one week before the German attack, the Soviet TASS News Agency formally denied reports of German troop concentrations along the German-Soviet border.

Stalin's purges of the Soviet officer corps, which

had begun in 1937 with the arrest of General Mikhail Tukhachevski and ended only with Hitler's invasion of the Soviet Union, had claimed countless victims among the Red Air Force high command, including the commander in chief of the air force, J. I. Alksnis; his successor General Khripin; and General J. A. Smuskevitch, who commanded the Soviet aerial forces in the Spanish Civil War using the pseudonym "Douglas" and upon his return was highly decorated and appointed the new commander in chief. General Muklevitch, one of the most senior commanders of the tactical air force, had also failed to survive Stalin's purges.

Despite the example of Germany's successful blitzkriegs, and against the express counsel of the Soviet general staff, large numbers of Soviet airfields had been set up in occupied Poland, the Baltic region and Bessarabia, many perilously near the German border, to reflect Stalin's theory of warfare which emphasized the importance of offensive retaliatory strikes.

Meanwhile the secret Japanese reconnaissance squadrons of the 3rd Kukutai Corps were continuing their missions. After reconnoitering the main Philippine island of Luzon, the Japanese scout aircraft flew over the US base at Jolo Island (Philippines), then took off from Truk Island airfield to get a look at the important US base at Rabaul (New Britain). "In June our squadron was transferred to Tinian [a Pacific island in the Mariannas]. From that base we were ordered to undertake an extremely cautious reconnaissance of the island of Guam. While doing so we maintained a uniform altitude of over 32,000 feet [10,000 meters], which was as high as our machines could go."

But the Americans did not remain unaware of the activities of the 3rd Kukutai. On Monday 16 June 1941, the US government handed in a sharp diplomatic protest to Tokyo, stating that on 11th and 14th June, a twin-engined Japanese military aircraft had flown over Guam at very high altitude. Naturally the Japanese government denied all knowledge of these events. Between April and June 1941, Mitsubishi G3M2s operating out of Formosa, Peleliu (Palau islands), Truk and Tinian photographed British and US bases in the Philippines, New Britain and New Guinea.

After winning the Battle of Britain, British fighter planes rarely had need to fly missions over the British Isles and were now carrying out fighter and nuisance raids over France. When just a few planes were flying random nuisance raids, the pilots called the operation Rhubarb; whereas when several fighter squadrons flew cover for bombers, they jokingly called it a "Circus." Their methods had a questionable success: From the beginning of January to the middle of June 1941, the RAF flew 104 Rhubarb missions and 11 Circuses, in which it lost 33 pilots while shooting down only 26 German aircraft.

On 20 June 1941, a Soviet aerial formation was set up in Moscow for defense of the capital. It was the first of its kind and was known as the 6th Fighter Corps. On Sunday 22 June, civil air raid precautions in Moscow were to be tested "under realistic conditions." Shortly after midnight on 22 June, the Soviet military boards of the Baltic, Leningrad, Western, Kiev and Odessa military districts received a confidential communication from Stalin stating that "a Fascist surprise attack may possibly take place on 22nd–23rd June." Stalin went on to say: "I command . . . that before dawn on 22 June 1941, all our aerial forces including troop carriers, shall decentralize on our airfields and camouflage themselves thoroughly." This order reached the Soviet military district and army staff headquarters before the German attack, but too late to pass it on to all the subordinate troop units in time.

According to Soviet sources, on 22 June 1941 the Red Air Force had at least 18,000 combat aircraft of every variety, approximately one half of which were stationed in the Western military districts. Only one fifth were modern aircraft, and the pilots to operate them were still undergoing training. The German Luftwaffe in the East had a total of 1,945 aircraft of which 1,400 were ready for combat, including 510 bombers, 290 Stukas, 440 fighter planes, 40 destroyer aircraft and 120 long range reconnaissance planes. These forces had been divided up among three of the German air fleets, Luftflotte 1 under General Keller assigned to German Army Group North; Luftflotte 2 under Field Marshal Kesselring assigned to Army Group Central; and Luftflotte 4 under General Löhr assigned to Army Group South.

At 3:15 A.M. on Sunday 22 June 1941, the Germans launched Operation Barbarossa, the attack on the Soviet Union, along the whole line from the Baltic Sea in the north to the Carpathian mountains in the south. The bombers of Air Fleets 1, 2 and 4 were already cleared for takeoff by 2:00 A.M. The most experienced crews were ordered to fly over the Soviet border at very high altitude and to bomb the Soviets' forward airfields in a lightning strike before the actual attack began.

22 June 1941. Germany begins its attack on the Soviet Union using its approved blitzkrieg method, but it soon becomes clear that the Luftwaffe's forces are inadequate to the task. Here we see a flight of Me 110 destroyers (fighter bombers).

This tried-and-true first strike strategy caught many Soviet airbases completely by surprise. The first German wave was immediately followed by a second wave that launched the main attack, in which 637 bombers and 231 fighters attacked 31 Soviet airfields. Late in the morning, approximately 400 bombers flew the next massive strike against another 35 airfields. Thus a total of 66 Soviet airbases were hit, on which about 70% of the entire Red Air Force was stationed.

Soviet historians confirm that approximately 1,200 Soviet aircraft had been destroyed by noon on the first day, 800 of them on the ground. Red Air Force Lt. Gen. Kopets lost 600 of his aircraft without being able to inflict notable losses on the German Luftwaffe, and committed suicide on the second day of the war. Soviet aerial forces in the Baltic zone under Gen. A. P. Ionov, were particularly hard hit because the Luftwaffe's attack surprised them just as many formations were returning from large-scale night exercises.

The air forces of other nations allied with Germany also took part in Operation Barbarossa, contributing a total of approximately 1,000 aircraft. Rumania sent the largest contingent, 423 machines divided into 3 large groups. Finland took part with some 230 fighter planes, 41 bombers and 36 ground-attack aircraft, only some of which were really ready for deployment, and which cooperated closely with the German 5th Air Fleet (Luftflotte 5 under General Stumpff). At the end of July the Comando Aviazione, the Air Command of the Italian Expeditionary Force, sent 3 groups of planes totalling 100 aircraft to operate in the southern sector of the Eastern Front. The Hungarian "Express Corps" contributed one fighter and one bomber regiment and several reconnaissance squadrons which were attached to Luftflotte 4 under General Löhr. Luftflotte 4 also had charge of the "Croatian Air Legion" consisting of one fighter and one bomber group,

Soviet N.C.O. pilot I. Chumbarev, who according to Soviet sources brought down two German planes in one day—an FW 189 reconnaissance aircraft and a Do 215 bomber—by ramming them with his own plane.

50–60 aircraft in all. A Slovakian air regiment also took part in the fighting on the Eastern Front.

Soviet sources testify that due to the absence of Soviet pilots who were either on leave, sick, involved in training courses or out on ferrying flights, "almost half the front-line machines in the five border districts were unable to take off on the first day of the war." Thus on the first day the German Luftwaffe had already won air superiority, and in many cases actual command of the air, in all battle sectors, and this contributed substantially to the success of the German ground troops.

The Soviets were forced to confine their operations to support of the Soviet Army, and made only isolated raids on the German assembly zone. In fact, from time to time a command was issued to Soviet pilots forbidding them to overfly their own front lines. But despite their heavy losses the Soviet aerial forces moved to counterattack. Soviet sources claim that they flew 6,000 missions on June 22 and shot down approximately 200 aircraft in aerial combat.

At the outset, the tactics of the Red Air Force were definitely behind the times. With its antiquated machines that lacked proper radio communications, the only way to give adequate aerial protection to the troops was to fly relay barrier patrols, which demanded the deployment of enormous numbers of aircraft, and when German fighters appeared, the Soviet aircraft had to form up in a full circle to provide each other cover, a tactic which led to heavy losses. In particular, the prescribed tactical order of the Soviet fighter planes caused them difficulty. The fighters flew close together in flight formations of 3 planes each, which cut down on their maneuverability and did not let them afford each other cover; so they made easy pickings for the experienced German fighter pilots.

During the first weeks of the war the Soviet fighters perfected a new aerial combat tactic, aerial ramming. This had first been used by a Russian pilot 27 years earlier on 26 August 1914, when Pyotr N. Nesterov rammed into his enemy Baron von Rosenthal in an aerial dogfight near Lvov in Galicia and made him crash. Nesterov himself did not survive, but the Baron got off with a bad scare.

In June 1941, Soviet fighter pilots S. Y. Sdorovzev, M. P. Shukov, and P. T. Kharitonov used the aerial ramming tactic. When 2nd Lt. Sdorovzev failed to shoot down a German He 111 bomber even after scoring a number of hits, he approached the bomber from the rear and applying his propeller, hacked off his adversary's tail elevator. At his second attempt he got the He 111 to crash. Second Lt. Sdorovzev just managed, with his damaged propeller, to fly the 48 miles back to his base.

After only a short time it became apparent that the Germans were not going to experience the same success with their blitzkrieg tactics as they had in the past. Because of the gigantic extent of the eastern war theater, they had to fly raids on a much broader front than in earlier campaigns, and despite initially good results, this time the Luftwaffe could not be deployed in the same bravura fashion. Once again German leaders fell back on their old battleplan: After its initial successful "strategic" surprise attacks, the Luftwaffe switched to flying "tactical" support for the army instead of taking hold on the air superiority they had won so swiftly and easily and using it for genuine strategic operations. Moreover, the bomber formations, whose chief duty should have been to smash the Soviet communications network in the hinterland and to raid industrial centers, had to be used in direct support of the army, which without the Luftwaffe's cooperation was incapable of combatting the enemy successfully. The attack on the Soviet Union marked the beginning of a multi-front war that the German Luftwaffe could not possibly win.

1941

July to December

Tuesday 1 July 1941
The *Wehrmacht High Command* announced:

In the course of June 30 the Luftwaffe once again inflicted annihilating blows on the Soviet-Russian bomber and fighter formations. On June 30 the enemy lost 280 aircraft in all, 216 of them in aerial combats. German fighter wings led by [air ace] Lt. Col. Mölders and by Major Trautloff particularly distinguished themselves during the fighting by shooting down 110 and 65 planes respectively. At Dünaburg (= Daugavpils in Latvia) the Trautloff Fighter Wing succeeded in destroying all 40 of a 40-plane Soviet attack group. The Mölders Fighter Wing gave equally impressive proof of the superiority of the German Luftwaffe in the region east of Minsk and Bobruisk, where large numbers of enemy formations sought to disrupt the movements of the advancing German troops. Of the approximately 100 attacking fighters and bombers, the Mölders Fighter Wing destroyed 80. In the battle Lt. Col. Mölders won his 82nd aerial victory, Captain Joppien his 52nd.

German Luftwaffe formations have intervened in the ground battle to telling effect. They bombed retreating enemy columns east of Lvov (Ger. *Lemberg*) where these were marching two or three abreast along the same road; inflicted extremely heavy losses on Soviet troops encircled between Bialystok and Minsk; and attacked the enemy in relay waves where he was falling back through Riga (Latvia). Multitudes of armored cars and hundreds of trucks were destroyed during these operations, enemy batteries were silenced and transport trains smashed to pieces.

Tuesday 14 July 1941
The following duty report by *Henri Nannen* describing a bombing attack, was broadcast over German radio:

Release your bombs! and death and destruction rain down. Tense to the bursting point I cling to the panes of the floor bay and watch the bombs being released. Seconds pass. There, a mushroom of smoke and dust is rising up about 150 feet in front of the crossroad, then another, then another, cutting diagonally across the road intersection. Suddenly I can't help giving a shout, because there has been an explosion below us and now a huge red fire is blazing down on the road. We set off for home, watching the flames flashing to the right and left, in front and behind us, where our comrades are at work.

Salvaging the 100th Spitfire

The following descriptive account appeared in the German newspaper *Völkischer Beobachter* in July 1941:

The Sergeant is a leader of rescue and salvage operations along the Channel. A radio call interrupts our conversation. "Seven Spitfires have been shot down. One of them is in my district. Incidentally, it's my hundredth one!" We ride along the narrow, twisting coastal road. Before us lies a Spitfire of the newest design. Its cannon and machine guns have bored into the soil. "Those little devils have had it," the Sergeant remarks. Then he gets down to his real work. "The first thing I have to do" – he explains – "is to look to the pilot. If there is still some way to help him then that's my first duty, unless other soldiers have rushed over before me and taken the necessary steps. If he is dead then I, as the district rescue and salvage leader, am the only one allowed to touch him. The main point is to ascertain his identity. His dog tag and identification papers tell us what we want to know. The deceased's personal possessions are relayed to his relatives via the International Red Cross in Geneva. A record is also made of the burial, so that the fallen soldier's grave can be found even after many years have passed." The Sergeant has completed his "field duty." Meanwhile the shot-down machine is not being neglected. The engineer in charge of the technical investigation tends to the plane, determines its main properties and releases it for salvage. Later the salvage convoy will move in to transfer the crash wreckage to the dismantling plant, which in turn will convey any material that is still usable to its next destination.

Bombs Fall on Moscow

Tuesday 22 July 1941, Berlin
The *German News Bureau* (DNB) reported:

On Sunday night through to Monday morning the German Luftwaffe launched its first grand assault on the Soviet capital. A responsible authority in Berlin confirms that large numbers of bomber wings mounted an extremely vigorous attack. The raids continued several hours without let-up, we believe from sunset until dawn. The German aerial attack on Moscow appears to confirm that the German Luftwaffe has now been successful in setting up takeoff bases inside the conquered Russian territories. These bases are well situated for its bomber missions so that the bombers are now only a few hundred miles from Moscow and can make intensified attacks on the Soviet capital.

22 July 1941, Moscow
The *Soviet Information Bureau* reported:

Yesterday evening Moscow experienced its first air attack of the war. The sirens sounded at 10:00 P.M. after lookout men had reported more than 200 German bombers flying toward Moscow. Soviet night interceptor planes and antiaircraft batteries went into action and succeeded in forcing the bulk of the attackers to turn back before reaching the capital. Only isolated German-Fascist aircraft succeeded in breaking through and released a number of bombs that destroyed dwellings or set them on fire, but no military targets were hit. There were several dead and injured. Night interceptors and antiaircraft guns destroyed 17 German aircraft.

22 July 1941
The *Wehrmacht High Command* announced:

The breakthrough operations of the German Wehrmacht and its allies have broken the Soviet defensive front into disconnected groups. Despite tenacious local resistance and dogged counterattacks, any unified conduct by the enemy is no longer discernible. Operations to smash and annihilate the individual Soviet armed forces groups, are continuing without let-up along the entire Eastern Front. Last night the Luftwaffe attacked Moscow for the first time in retaliation for the Bolshevik air raids on the open capital cities of our allies, Bucharest and Helsinki. Strong German bomber formations with good ground visibility made relay bombing raids on military installations in the Soviet Russian communications and munitions center in Moscow. Direct bomb hits started countless conflagrations and wide-spreading fires in the Kremlin district and around the Moskva river bend. High-ranking Soviet headquarters buildings and government offices have been destroyed or badly hit, as have supply factories.

Wednesday 23 July 1941, Berlin
The *German News Bureau* announced:

The initial reports about the air assault on Moscow reveal that the German air crews who reached Moscow in the second assault wave, could see the sea of flame in the Russian capital while they were still almost 85 miles from Moscow. One of the pilots reports that the conflagrations were as huge and wide-reaching as those he had already viewed in Manchester or Sheffield. He spoke of the strong air defense and said that the incessant muzzle flashes from the antiaircraft artillery could be observed amidst the houses even after they had begun to burn.

Soviet Bombers over Berlin

Saturday 9 August 1941, Moscow
Red Air Force Headquarters announced:

On Thursday night through to Friday morning, Soviet long range bombers attacked Berlin. While several squadrons were carrying out reconnaissance flights over East Germany, one squadron released incendiary and high-explosive bombs over Berlin in retaliation for the raids on Moscow. Severe damage was observed in several quarters of the city. All the Soviet bombers returned to their bases unhurt.

The Soviet Petlyakov Pe-2 light bomber was initially designed and deployed as a twin-engined fighter very similar to the German Me 110 destroyer.

Sunday 10 August 1941, Moscow
Radio Moscow reported:

On Friday evening the Red Air Force made a fresh assault on Berlin in which railway installations and military targets were hit. One Soviet bomber has failed to return so far.

10 August 1941, Berlin
The *German News Bureau* reported:

On the night of 8th–9th August, isolated Russian aircraft flew into German territory. When they attempted to raid Berlin, our flak defense forced them to veer off before they reached the outskirts of the capital.

10 August 1941
The *Wehrmacht High Command* announced:

Operations in the East are continuing as scheduled. Last night German bomber formations made particularly effective raids on munitions plants and traffic and supply installations in Moscow. Countless major conflagrations arose in the city center, and north of the Moskva river bend.

The struggle of the German Luftwaffe against the Soviet aerial forces continued to be extraordinarily successful in the last few days as well, as a result of which the enemy has lost over 10,000 aircraft along the whole of the Eastern Front including the Finnish battle zone, since June 22.

10 August 1941, Moscow
The *Soviet Information Bureau* announced:

Last night a number of Fascist aerial formations attempted to attack Moscow. Only isolated aircraft penetrated to the city center, while most of the machines were blown up by the ground defense and by night interceptor planes. A multitude of incendiary and high-explosive bombs caused numbers of fires in residential districts; however they were quickly extinguished.

Monday 22 September 1941
The *Wehrmacht High Command* announced:

Yesterday the Luftwaffe was particularly successful in its numerous attacks on Soviet shipping. In the Black Sea it sank one cruiser, two destroyers and one antiaircraft gunship, as well as 9 merchant vessels totalling approximately 25,000 tons. Two more ships and two large merchant vessels were set on fire. In the sea territory west of Kronstadt (fortress naval station on the Gulf of Finland), the battleship *October Revolution* and the heavy cruiser *Kirov* received two square hits apiece, and another heavy cruiser received four. In addition, three destroyers, one minesweeper and one gunboat were damaged by square hits.

Shoot-Down in Zone Two-Anton

Night Interception over the German Homeland

The following descriptive account appeared in the German publication *Das Reich* in September 1941:

The slender white fingers of the flak searchlights rise in the far distance. The first flashes of exploding flak shells flicker in the sky. Now, in among them appear bright-colored bead necklaces emitted by the barrels of light cannon.

"Take off!" The cabin windows bang shut. The lookout jumps off the wing in one bound. The fuselage is already trembling in the wind from the racing propeller. The brake blocks are ripped away. We sweep over the concrete runway into the boundless darkness, then we dip into the dense cloud wall and climb and climb.

We have reached the required altitude. Far below us shines the milky grey mass of clouds, clearly defined at many points by the muzzle flashes of the flak guns, the explosions of bombs, the searchlights over my native city and the central core of red-hot fires. Then we too are summoned by the distant radio call. We go hunting [for intruder aircraft]. The moon serves us as a big lamp.

"King" is sitting up front at the control stick. His left hand is on the throttle lever, his right hand on the button that activates the machine guns and cannon. His head darts first to the right, then to the left, his eyes bore into the night.

"There he is up ahead. Do you see him?" Step on the gas. It's a Lockheed Hudson, much slower than we are and it has not detected us. Our black camouflage paint gleams in the silver moonlight. Then we attack: our fighter is pulled up with lightning speed and starts firing out of all its barrels. The hollow roar of the engine is drowned out by the bright rat-a-tat-tat of the aerial guns. For the space of a breath we look on at a dazzling, deadly fireworks, then we rear back before an irresistible force; the Lockheed has made a desperate downswing. We plunge after it. The Tommy [British] pilot must still have control of his machine. He banks skillfully when we bring him to bay again and we get below him in preparation for a new relentless attack. Our brilliant yellow and red, slender tracer trajectories aim at the pot-belly of the British bomber which is just at eye-level with us. The aircraft is not defending itself. Has the gunner already been eliminated? Now little flames begin to sprout along the left wing. "It's on fire, King, it's on fire!" The bomber is still racing for the expanse of cloud, where it might be safe if it gets there undamaged. We mount another attack on our tenacious prey. Before it can dip into the protective cover, a cone of fire appears on the right wing. Flame shoots up as the machine sinks reeling into the white cloud veils.

How ghostly is the meeting with our enemy in the night sky! Abruptly the duck-like profile of a Vickers Wellington bomber appears before us like a black shadow that reveals its shape only after it passes. "I'm going to attack!" says King and sends our machine into a steep climb. But just one pulse-beat before the barrels of our fighter emit their deadly fire, the tail-gun turret of the British bomber flashes overhead, giving out little sparks as if someone were lighting a match a long distance away. At the same time our guns utter a deafening thunder. The white-hot metal must be boring into the belly of our enemy who is spreading his wings out near enough to touch. He has gone past us. Through my headset I hear a kind of wail that seems infinitely far away: "I'm hurt! I can't go on! Get ready to bail out!" At once my hand comes to rest on the emergency lever. Again I look over at the radio operator

Above: This 4-engined long range Soviet bomber built by A. N. Tupolev was prepared for serial production by V. M. Petlyakov, who gave the aircraft its name: the Petlyakov Pe-8.

Below: On 13 August 1941 the Soviet newspaper *Pravda* reported "Soviet bombers over Berlin" and "German bombers over Moscow."

Next page below: A German Messerschmitt Bf 110. Although this type did not prove its worth either as a long range fighter plane or as a fighter bomber, it was successful as a night interceptor.

13 АВГУСТА 1941 г., № 223 (8531) ПРАВДА 3

ЭНЕРГИЧНО ИСПОЛЬЗОВАТЬ МЕСТНЫЕ ПРОДОВОЛЬСТВЕННЫЕ РЕСУРСЫ

Наша страна в результате неустанной заботы партии и правительства о развитии сельского хозяйства и пищевой промышленности располагает достаточно большими продовольственными ресурсами для того, чтобы удовлетворить все нужды фронта и обеспечить снабжение населения. Эти ресурсы можно и надо множить и расширять, всемерно используя богатые возможности, которые имеются буквально во всех краях, областях и районах нашей страны.

Необходимо всемерно использовать местные ресурсы, расходовать продукты экономно, по-хозяйски.

Следует учесть также, что железнодорожный транспорт занят выполнением важнейших заданий, связанных с обороной страны. Поэтому нужно резко сократить перевозки товаров, изыскивать на месте максимум продуктов.

НАЛЕТ СОВЕТСКИХ САМОЛЕТОВ НА РАЙОН БЕРЛИНА

В ночь с 11 на 12 августа имел место новый налет советских самолетов на военные об'екты в районе Берлина.

Сброшены зажигательные и фугасные бомбы большой силы. В Берлине наблюдались пожары и взрывы.

Все наши самолеты вернулись на св… базы. Экипаж самолета, невозвратившегося из предыдущего полета, разыскан и возвр…тился на свою базу.

Попытка налета немецких самолетов на Москв… в ночь с 12 на 13 августа

В ночь с 12 на 13 августа группа немецких самолетов пыталась совершить налет на Москву.

Эффективным огнем зенитных батар… и действиями наших ночных истребител… вражеские самолеты были рассеяны … к Москве не допущены.

НА ОЧЕРЕДНОЙ ПРЕСС-КОНФЕРЕНЦИИ ИНОСТРАННЫХ КОРРЕСПОНДЕНТОВ

to see how he is. The pilot turns his head too. Blood is running over both their faces. King must be badly hurt. A big hole gapes in the glass cockpit to his right. There is a leaden silence. My hands are on the parachute strap. My body is tense. Then come the saving sentences: "My right eye is gone," says King, "but I can still hold the plane under control. I'll try to get you home." The radio operator seems only to have been grazed. Now that the threat of death is past for the time being, we listen as if it were music to the soothing, uniform roar of the engines.

What has become of the Wellington? Has our attack gone for nothing? No, the bomber is badly hit. I see it not far from us, reeling tailward. "King, it's burning! It's crashing over its left wing. It's exploding!" I must have shouted that into my throat microphone at the top of my lungs. I have to repeat it again before they can understand me up front. When King replies—monosyllabic, expressing no joy over his victory—I realize for the first time, with chilling clarity, that our fight is not over yet. Our lives are at stake. Everything depends on him. If the shell fragments have hit the left half of his face as well as the right, and if blood runs into his other eye, we are lost.

The battle is raging with undiminished fury in a wide circuit around our solitary plane, which has already sent out an SOS call. A profound darkness settles over us as we fly underneath the carpet of cloud. Only here and there the muzzle flashes of the flak artillery penetrate the blackness. Bright flames are blazing somewhere in the dark. Our comrades back at our home base must be following our flight and wishing us well with all their might. But only now, when we glimpse the illuminated airfield, do we feel certain that we will master fate. King approaches for a landing. The landing gear comes down with a burst of compressed air. One little hop down onto the sward, then the machine taxies along on smooth wheels and comes to a stop. Later we learn that the last drops of cooling fluid were just running out of the shot-up tank onto the ground.

Twice, then three times King threatens to collapse on our way to the command post. Repeatedly he exerts all his remaining strength to pull himself up while we give him a helping hand. Warm light floods over us as we open the barracks door and walk in. There is complete silence in the bright room: twenty, thirty pairs of eyes rest on the young pilot. He stands tall and erect before his commanding officer with his blond hair in a tangle and a face covered in blood: "Begging leave to report, Sir: Second Lt. King returned from an enemy mission. One positive shoot-down in Zone Two-Anton!"

7 November 1941
Prime Minister Churchill wrote to Marshall Stalin in a personal and secret message:

I can tell you no more about our immediate military plans than you can tell me about yours; but please rest assured that we shall not remain inactive. We are sending our newest battleship the *Prince of Wales,* which can overtake and destroy any Japanese ship, into the Indian Ocean to intimidate Japan, and are assembling a powerful fleet squadron there. I am urging President Roosevelt to intensify pressure on the Japanese and hold them in check so that the route to [the Soviet Asian port of] Vladivostok is not blocked.

The air crew of a Japanese torpedo bomber receiving their final briefing before takeoff.

Air Raid on Hawaii

Sunday 7 December 1941, Washington
The *White House* announced:

Japanese aircraft have attacked Pearl Harbor and all the military and naval installations on the island of Oahu in the Hawaiian Islands.

Monday 8 December 1941, Honolulu
The American *United Press News Agency* reported:

The Japanese air raid began yesterday morning at 8:10 A.M. Bomb explosions and heavy antiaircraft fire alerted the population who at first believed that military maneuvers were in progress. Although the police immediately evacuated the roads and told pedestrians to enter the nearest buildings, thousands of people poured out onto the surrounding mountains to observe the air attack. The Japanese bombers approached their targets at high altitude and then went into dive flight for their attack. They were accompanied by torpedo bombers that attacked the warships lying in the harbor. One eyewitness reports: "Pearl Harbor was covered by thick smoke from the antiaircraft shells; huge black dustclouds rose over the airfield at Hickam Field that could only have come from burning oil tank depots."

Below: Test bench in a German Luftwaffe experimental plant, where a tolerance test is being performed on the landing gear of a shot-down RAF fighter plane.

Honolulu Star-Bulletin 1st EXTRA

8 PAGES—HONOLULU, TERRITORY OF HAWAII, U. S. A., SUNDAY, DECEMBER 7, 1941—8 PAGES ★ PRICE FIVE CENTS

WAR!

(Associated Press by Transpacific Telephone)

SAN FRANCISCO, Dec. 7.—President Roosevelt announced this morning that Japanese planes had attacked Manila and Pearl Harbor.

OAHU BOMBED BY JAPANESE PLANES

SIX KNOWN DEAD, 21 INJURED, AT EMERGENCY HOSPITAL

Attack Made On Island's Defense Areas

By UNITED PRESS

WASHINGTON, Dec. 7.—Text of a White House announcement detailing the attack on the Hawaiian islands is:

"The Japanese attacked Pearl Harbor from the air and all naval and military activities on the island of Oahu, principal American base in the Hawaiian islands."

Oahu was attacked at 7:55 this morning by Japanese planes.

The Rising Sun, emblem of Japan, was seen on plane wing tips.

Wave after wave of bombers streamed through the clouded morning sky from the southwest and flung their missiles on a city resting in peaceful Sabbath calm.

According to an unconfirmed report received at the governor's office, the Japanese force that attacked Oahu reached island waters aboard two small airplane carriers.

It was also reported that at the governor's office either an attempt had been made to bomb the USS Lexington, or that it had been bombed.

CITY IN UPROAR

Within 10 minutes the city was in an uproar. As bombs fell in many parts of the city, and in defense areas the defenders of the islands went into quick action.

Army intelligence officers at Ft. Shafter announced officially shortly after 9 a. m. the fact of the bombardment by an enemy but long previous army and navy had taken immediate measures in defense.

"Oahu is under a sporadic air raid," the announcement said.

"Civilians are ordered to stay off the streets until further notice."

CIVILIANS ORDERED OFF STREETS

The army has ordered that all civilians stay off the streets and highways and not use telephones.

Evidence that the Japanese attack has registered some hits was shown by three billowing pillars of smoke in the Pearl Harbor and Hickam field area.

All navy personnel and civilian defense workers, with the exception of women, have been ordered to duty at Pearl Harbor.

The Pearl Harbor highway was immediately a mass of racing cars.

A trickling stream of injured people began pouring into the city emergency hospital a few minutes after the bombardment started.

Thousands of telephone calls almost swamped the Mutual Telephone Co., which put extra operators on duty.

At The Star-Bulletin office the phone calls deluged the single operator and it was impossible for this newspaper, for sometime, to handle the flood of calls. Here also an emergency operator was called.

HOUR OF ATTACK—7:55 A. M.

An official army report from department headquarters, made public shortly before 11, is that the first attack was at 7:55 a. m.

Witnesses said they saw at least 50 airplanes over Pearl Harbor.

The attack centered in the Pearl Harbor, Army authorities said:

"The rising sun was seen on the wing tips of the airplanes."

Although martial law has not been declared officially, the city of Honolulu was operating under M-Day conditions.

It is reliably reported that enemy objectives under attack were Wheeler field, Hickam field, Kaneohe bay and naval air station and Pearl Harbor.

Some enemy planes were reported shot down.

The body of the pilot was seen in a plane burning at Wahiawa.

Oahu appeared to be taking calmly after the first uproar of queries.

ANTIAIRCRAFT GUNS IN ACTION

First indication of the raid came shodtly before 8 this morning when antiaircraft guns around Pearl Habor began sending up a thunderous barrage.

At the same time a vast cloud of black smoke arose from the naval base and also from Hickam field where flames could be seen.

BOMB NEAR GOVERNOR'S MANSION

Shortly before 9:30 a bomb fell near Washington Place, the residence of the governor. Governor Poindexter and Secretary Charles M. Hite were there.

It was reported that the bomb killed an unidentified Chinese man across the street in front of the Schuman Carriage Co. where windows were broken.

C. E. Daniels, a welder, found a fragment of shell or bomb at South and Queen Sts. which he brought into the City Hall. This fragrent weighed about a pound.

At 10:05 a. m. today Governor Poindexter telephoned to The Star-Bulletin announcing he has declared a state of emergency for the entire territory.

He announced that Edouard L. Doty, executive secretary of the major disaster council, has been appointed director under the M-Day law's provisions.

Governor Poindexter urged all residents of Honolulu to remain off the street, and the people of the territory to remain calm.

Mr. Doty reported that all major disaster council wardens and medical units were on duty within a half hour of the time the alarm was given.

Workers employed at Pearl Harbor were ordered at 10:10 a. m. not to report at Pearl Harbor.

The mayor's major disaster council was to meet at the city hall at about 10:30 this morning.

At least two Japanese planes were reported at Hawaiian department headquarters to have been shot down.

One of the planes was shot down at Ft. Kamehameha and the other back of the Wa-

Turn to Page [illegible], Column 1

Hundreds See City Bombed

Hundreds of Honolulans who hurried to the top of Punchbowl soon after bombs began to fall, saw spread out before them the whole panorama of surprise attack and defense.

Far off over Pearl Harbor the white sky was polka-dotted with anti-aircraft smoke.

Rolling away from the navy base were billowing clouds of ugly black smoke. Sometimes a burst of flame reddened the black masses of the smoke.

Out from the silver-surfaced mouth of the harbor a flotilla of destroyers streamed to battle, smoke pouring from their stacks.

Turn to Page [illegible], Column 1

Names of Dead and Injured

The city emergency hospital reported at [illegible] a list of [illegible] killed and [illegible] injured.

The complete list will be carried later. Here is a partial list:

[illegible]

Schools Closed

All schools on Oahu, both public and private, will remain closed until further notice, Edouard L. Doty, territorial director of civilian defense, announced at 11 a. m. today. This does not apply elsewhere in the territory.

Editorial

HAWAII MEETS THE CRISIS

Honolulu and Hawaii will meet the emergency of war today as Honolulu and Hawaii have met emergencies in the past—coolly, calmly and with immediate and complete support of the officials, officers and troops who are in charge.

Governor Poindexter and the army and navy leaders have called upon the public to remain calm; for civilians who have no essential business on the streets to stay off, and for every man and woman to do his duty.

That request, coupled with the measures promptly taken to meet the situation that has suddenly and terribly developed, will be needed.

Hawaii will do its part—as a loyal American territory.

In this crisis, every difference of race, creed and color will be submerged in the one desire and determination to play the part that Americans always play in crisis.

BULLETIN

Additional Star-Bulletin extras today will cover the latest developments in this war move.

The world's first press announcement of the US war with Japan.

Tuesday 9 December 1941,
Sacramento, California, USA
The American *United Press News Agency* reported:

Military sources have confirmed that on Monday night through to Tuesday morning, several Japanese aircraft overflew the Californian coast west of San Jose, but without releasing any bombs. Early on Tuesday, Japanese aircraft again appeared off the coast and triggered another air raid alert, which lasted one hour. No hostile incidents were reported. US military authorities believe that the repeated appearance of Japanese aircraft indicates the presence of an enemy aircraft carrier in the waters near the US coast.

Wednesday 10 December 1941, Tokyo
Japanese air force officer *Yomiuri* reported:

Weather conditions were very unfavorable for aerial operations that morning. Dark clouds hung low over the South China Sea, so I need hardly say that visibility was very poor. Our aircraft continued its reconnaissance flight sailing low over the Japanese transport ships. We flew along the eastern coast of the Anambas Islands [Indonesia]. Black smoke trails were sighted on the horizon. After careful observation we recognized that it was an enemy naval formation including the vessels *Prince of Wales* and *Repulse.* Our radio operator reported the location of the enemy fleet to our bomber base. Immediately after the report was received, bombers of the Imperial Japanese naval air force took off in large formations despite the bad weather, many of them loaded with torpedoes. Soon our bombers sighted the British Far East fleet, which must have detected our approach and was trying to escape by following a zigzag course behind dense fog clouds, at a speed of 30 knots. The poor visibility resulting from weather conditions prevented us from pursuing the enemy fleet; to the regret of us all, we had to return to our bases. Next morning the engines of our reconnaissance and bomber aircraft were warmed up and ran at full blast. We all took off with the firm determination to annihilate the enemy fleet today. Visibility was better than on the previous day; there was scarcely a cloud in the sky. After a prolonged flight we finally made out the *Prince of Wales* and the *Repulse* a few miles from Kuantan [Malay Peninsula]. Our bombers raced through the antiaircraft fire to attack the two enemy battleships, and our torpedoes struck home, causing white-hot flashes followed by columns of black smoke.

Thursday 11 December 1941, Singapore
The British *Reuters News Agency* reported:

It is officially reported that over 2,000 officers and crew of the sunken vessels HMS *Prince of Wales* and HMS *Repulse* have been rescued. The survivors have been taken to land at Singapore.

11 December 1941, Singapore
The following account was broadcast by radio by *Cecil Brown,* a survivor of the Japanese attack on the British naval Force Z:

Here is an eyewitness account of how the *Prince of Wales* and the *Repulse* ended their career in the South China Sea, 50 miles from the coast of Malaya and 150 miles north of Singapore. The two battleships were sunk by a combined bomb and torpedo raid of extraordinary skill and daring. I was standing amidship on the single deck of the *Repulse* when the first nine Japanese bombers, lined up in a straight row, approached at an altitude of 9,750 feet; they stood out distinctly against the marvelously clear and sunny sky. They flew directly at us, and our flak barked furiously and incessantly. When the machines were right overhead, the first bomb hit the water beside the ship's wall at about the height where I was standing, so close by that the water jet it threw up, soaked us to the skin. At the same time a second bomb hit the catapult deck, exploded, and put our on-board aircraft out of commission. By 11:27 A.M. fire was running through the various compartments and proved extremely difficult to bring under control. Our gunnery crews replenished their ammunition; incidentally they were very cool-headed and cracked jokes every now and then. Bomb fragments had torn a couple of conspicuous, jagged holes in the smokestack not far from where we stood. At 11:40 A.M. the *Prince of Wales* appeared to have been hit and markedly reduced her speed. Then they came to attack us again. "Box barrage!" came the command over the ship's loudspeaker. All the antiaircraft guns fired away for all they were worth. The Japanese flew low, one wave right behind another, completely exposed to our flak and making a good target. A signal went up amid the roar of the heavy guns and the pounding of the light guns: "Man overboard!" Two Japanese bombers were racing toward us. I could see more of them, just with my naked eye; I counted nine in all, the same as the first time. They appeared to be torpedo bombers. They showed admirable daring, coming so close that we could see the heads of the pilots. At 11:48 a plane raced toward our starboard side. It just barely had time to launch a torpedo—an instant later I could already hear our gun crews shouting joyfully that it had been shot down. At 12:15 P.M. the *Prince of Wales* seemed to have come to a permanent stop. I was too busy to follow the attacks made on her, but she seemed to be in very bad straits. Her guns fired non-stop. Firing continued from on board the *Repulse.* At 12:20 P.M. I saw ten bombers heading for us and so far I could not tell whether they were regular or torpedo bombers. One machine circled in closer and closer. Now it was about 1,100 feet from our port side and was turning toward us. I saw the air-launched torpedo splash into the water. The lookout called: "Beware torpedo!" The silvery fish was headed straight for us. Someone said: "He's got us." The torpedo hit us on the port side about 50 feet from where I was standing. It felt as if the ship had run onto a rock. I was hurled a couple of paces across the deck but I did not fall down, nor did I hear any explosion—just a loud cracking sound. We listened. Nothing happened, only one minute later we heard the same cracking sound, this time on the starboard side. After the first torpedo hit we heard a calm order come over the loudspeaker: "Inflate your life jackets." I was busy doing just that when the second torpedo struck the ship, which heeled over so quickly that I had to give up any attempt to inflate my life jacket further. There was no time to lose. Most of the guns had been put out of action by the listing of the ship or by bomb damage. I jumped overboard, leaving the *Repulse* at 12:35 P.M. From the water I had a good view of events on the *Prince of Wales.* She went on firing for a while, then two bombs hit her deck. The Japanese flew in a straight longitudinal row over the vessel as they had done with the *Repulse,* releasing bombs in series of three. Clinging to a piece of furniture, I swam about a mile away and saw the *Prince of Wales* rear up and sink.

11 December 1941, Tokyo
The *Naval Division of the Imperial Japanese Armed Forces Headquarters* announced:

The Japanese navy lost only three aircraft during yesterday's mission over Malayan waters, when it sank the *Repulse* and the *Prince of Wales.*

Strategy and Tactics

July to December 1941

In the Near East the battle between the two former allies, Great Britain and France, continued with undiminished fury. The chief task of the British aerial forces in Syria was to support the ground troops and to fly raids on the French war vessels operating out of Beirut. British fighter planes flew missions in protection of their naval units off the coast of Syria that lay within range of French bombers. The RAF blockaded the French sea supply routes, and just outside Beirut they sank a large transport vessel loaded with ammunition and arms for the Vichy troops; this made clear to the French the hopelessness of their position. Nevertheless the air and ground forces of Vichy France put up a hard struggle against their attackers, and their surrender in Palmyra (Syria) did not come until Thursday 3 July. That same day the last French aerial reinforcements—21 Dewoitine D.520 fighters of 3 Squadron, 2nd Fighter Group (Groupe de Chasse II/3)—landed at the German-Italian airbase on the island of Rhodes, after coming from Tunis via Brindisi and Athens.

During the Syrian Campaign the French deployed

Two British battleships, the *Prince of Wales* (35,000 tons) and the *Repulse* (32,000 tons) try in vain to escape Japanese bombers.

a total of 289 aircraft, 200 of which were machines of the most modern design. They lost 179 of these planes to the RAF, compared to British losses of only 12.

On 3 July 1941, the secret Japanese aerial reconnaissance unit, the 3rd Kukutai, returned to Takao and was disbanded shortly afterward. What the Japanese did not suspect was that the Americans had been keeping busy too: A Consolidated B-24 Liberator of the US Army Air Corps was secretly flying identical spy missions over Japanese airbases in the Marshall Islands and the Carolinas.

Almost all the German bomber formations had now gone into action on the Eastern Front, so during July the Luftwaffe's activities in the West were confined almost exclusively to interceptor missions to ward off raids by the RAF. The beginning of the Russian Campaign brought a decisive turning-point in the development of the German air defense. When a number of German aerial units were transferred to the East, the strength of the fighter plane forces operating in the Western perimeter was reduced to two fighter wings, the 2nd and the 26th Jagdgeschwader. During the first half of 1941, *helle Nachtjagd*—night interception using searchlights to light up an enemy bomber so that the defending fighter could find its target—was still the main defense against British night raids. But in June 1941 this gave way to another more promising deployment tactic.

The introduction of the new Würzburg radar device enabled the Germans to set up a system of overlapping night fighter interception zones, each with a radar station at its center; these were known as *Himmelbett* stations. However, the chain of radar-controlled interception zones, also known as the Kammhuber Line (after the general who designed the German night fighter system), had its weak points: The Würzburg radar devices were still underdeveloped and their range was limited. Often it was not possible to determine the altitude of approaching bombers quickly enough to give the German night fighters a chance to intercept them in time. Meanwhile the British were well aware that the rising losses of their bombers were attributable to the ever-expanding use of radar in the German air defense system.

In the new system of *dunkle Nachtjagd* or *geführte Nachtjagd* (unilluminated or instrument-guided night interception), the German fighters were guided from ground stations without the support of searchlights; because thanks to radar instruments the stations were able to follow the flight paths of both the British bombers and their own fighters, and could direct their pilots where to attack their adversaries. Overlapping Himmelbett zones were set up along the western coast of occupied Europe and around Berlin, along the perimeter of the searchlight barrier. An evaluation and control center was located in each sphere, which had a diameter of approximately 40 miles (65 km), corresponding to the range of a Würzburg radar device. An interceptor-plane control officer [*Jägerleitoffizier*] had control of one night interceptor which he could direct to an enemy bomber that invaded his sphere. The Himmelbett guidance system soon proved quite successful, although it demanded swift reactions from the interceptor-plane control officer.

The Germans tried to supplement this night fighter system by linking it with the flak in combined night interception operations. The technique was practiced around the large cities which had strong flak protection, like Berlin, Hamburg, Kiel, Bremen, Cologne, Düsseldorf, Frankfurt am Main and Munich. If the interceptor-plane control officer judged it worthwhile to deploy a night fighter plane, he would ask the flak commander to order the flak to stop firing in the sector where the fighter was operating.

Two remarkable types of aircraft entered service at virtually the same moment at the end of July 1941: The British de Havilland 98 Mosquito, one of the most versatile planes of the war, and the Focke Wulf FW 190, the best of Germany's conventional fighter planes and the first German fighter with a modern radial engine. Due to its outstanding Rolls Royce engines, the unarmed wooden Mosquito had no need to fear any fighter plane, for it could simply evade and outrun it. The first 50 Mosquitos were deployed as long range photo-reconnaissance aircraft (Mk I model), as night fighters (Mk IIs) or as bombers (Mk IVs).

By now the 18 German bomber wings operating along the Eastern Front had been partitioned further and the precious bombers had turned into an extended arm of the artillery or into close-support aircraft. It no longer seemed possible for them to operate as a concentrated force.

Despite the fact that the Germans had command of the air, and notwithstanding the heavy Soviet losses on the first day of the war, the Red Air Force set up a dogged resistance. According to Soviet sources, their air force flew 47,000 missions between 22 June and 10 July 1941, dropping a total of 10,000 metric tons of bombs, mostly in direct support of Soviet army units.

On the night of 21–22 July 1941, German bombers took off from airfields near Smolensk on a heading for Moscow, and the commander of the Moscow air defense, Maj. Gen. M.S. Gromadin, set off the first grand alert in the Soviet capital. The raid was carried out by 127 bombers flying in several waves, which dropped 104 metric tons of bombs. The Soviet high command, STAVKA, allegedly knew about German preparations for the assault 2 days before it took place, and this explains why German air crews reported that defensive fire over Moscow was even more powerful than over London. But despite the heavy flak fire, only a few Soviet night fighters appeared to fight off the attackers. After this air assault, the Communist Party and STAVKA started to evacuate the families of government members and high-ranking military men from Moscow. General S. M. Shtemenko, the Soviet chief of operations, reports that bombs were frequently dropped near his offices at night, and that consequently the Red Army general staff headquarters was always shifted to the Byelorosskaya subway station in the evening so that the Soviet officers could get on with their work in peace. Later the general staff moved into the Kirovskaya subway station, which had been specially remodelled for the purpose.

On Sunday 3 August 1941, the first aerial victory ever won by a British Hurricane catapulted from a CAM ship, took place when Lt. Robert Everett of 804 Squadron, based on the steamer *Maplin,* shot down a Focke Wulf FW 200 C Condor of German 40 Squadron, 1st Bomber Wing in the North Atlantic. Instead of making a sea landing near his mother ship, the pilot decided to fly the 300 miles to Scotland, and landed there at Loch Earn.

Aircraft of the Red Navy carried out their first Soviet bombing raid on Berlin, in retaliation for the Luftwaffe's operations against Moscow, at 9:00 P.M. on Wednesday 6 August, when 18 Ilyushin Il-4 bombers from the Torpedo Mine Air Wing of the Baltic Red Banner Fleet under Col. Preobrashenski, took off from Kagul airfield on the island of Saaremaa in the Baltic Sea. After a brief assembly over the sea, the squadrons set a heading for Stettin (Pol. *Szczecin,* a seaport in northwest Poland) and reached the German coast at an altitude of 19,500 feet.

In succeeding weeks, squadrons of the 81st Air Division of the Soviet Long Range Air Force, under

Right: The German FuMG 62 radar device, codenamed "Würzburg," had a range of 24 miles (40 km). Starting in the summer of 1941, it was deployed together with the older Freya early-warning radar in the Himmelbett stations of the Kammhuber Line, where it guided German night fighter planes in defending Germany against British night raiders.

Below: Syria, 23 June 1941: The Vichy French airbase in El Quseir during an air raid by the RAF Blenheim bombers of 11 Squadron. On the left we see the nose of an LeO 451, the most modern type of French bomber.

Col. N.I. Novodranov, repeatedly flew offensive raids against Berlin. A group of newly-designed four-engined Petlyakov Pe-8 (TB-7) bombers, commanded by polar flier M. V. Vodopianov, also took part. Besides Berlin, these formations attacked various targets in East Prussia, including Königsberg, Tilsit and Memel.

On Sunday 10 August 1941, aircraft of the Soviet Black Sea fleet, took off on one of the most extraordinary raids of the war, to destroy the strategically important railroad bridge at Cernavoda in Rumania which linked the petroleum region of Ploesti to the port of Constanza. In order to increase the precision of their aim, the two antiquated TB-3 bombers were each fitted with two I-16 Rata fighter planes suspended under their wings; each of the fighters in turn carried two 5,500-lb bombs. Shortly before reaching their target the fighters were released and bombed the bridge in dive flight. After the mission all the aircraft returned to their base on the Crimean peninsula.

Left: On 10 August 1941, this completely antiquated Tupolev TB-3 bomber took off carrying two Polikarpov I-16 Rata fighter planes suspended under its wings; each of the fighters in turn carried two 5,500-lb bombs. The TB-3 was the first 4-engined all-metal cantilever monoplane in the world, and 818 of them were built beginning in 1931.

Below: A Soviet propaganda poster proclaims the alliance between Soviet and British aircraft: The brother-nations are now meeting in the air to bomb Berlin.

ВСТРЕЧА НАД БЕРЛИНОМ
НАЗНАЧИЛИ НАРОДЫ-БРАТЬЯ
НАД ВРАЖЬИМ ГОРОДОМ СВИДАНИЕ.
ОТ ЭТОГО РУКОПОЖАТЬЯ
НЕ ПОЗДОРОВИТСЯ ГЕРМАНИИ!
ХУД. КУКРЫНИКСЫ ТЕМА- И. ЛИВШИЦ ТЕКСТ С. МАРШАК
БЕРЛИН
(TRANSLATION) MEETING OVER BERLIN
THE BROTHER-NATIONS ARRANGED
A RENDEZVOUS OVER THE ENEMY'S TOWN.
THIS HANDSHAKE WILL NOT BE HEALTHY FOR THE GERMANS
Artist: KUKRINIKSY. Theme by I. LIVSHITZ. Words by S. MARSHAK.

In July and August 1941 the Soviets began to deploy their airborne troops—units of the 104th and 212th Airborne Brigades—albeit on a small scale. These troops blew up runway bridges and arms and ammunition depots in the German occupation zone near Kiev. Soviet paratroops were also dropped to carry out reconnaissance and espionage missions. Depending on the mission, they operated in strengths of from 3 to 50 men. After their job was done they either crossed back over the front lines or attached themselves to the larger partisan units that were forming at this time.

On the night of 12th–13th August, Berlin suffered its heaviest British air attack since the outbreak of war when 82 metric tons of high-explosive bombs were dropped over the city. On Friday 15 August 1941, encouraged by the transfer of large numbers of German fighter planes to the Eastern Front, British Bomber Command staged a daring daylight raid which deployed 53 Blenheim bombers against a power-station at Cologne. The bombers had a fighter escort as far as the Dutch coast; but despite diversionary maneuvers by other bomber formations and by fighters, the RAF lost 12 Blenheims in this daylight raid—over 20% of the machines engaged in the mission.

In August 1941 Great Britain decided to lend fighter plane support to the Soviets. This was the first and only time that an RAF unit flew aerial missions against Germany from Soviet territory. British 151st Wing was set up in Leconfield near York, to train Soviet air crews in the assembly, maintenance and operation of the fighters right on the spot. Then Nos. 81 and 134 Squadrons, comprising 39 Hurricanes of model Mark IIB, were shipped to the Soviet Union along with their pilots and ground personnel. The old British aircraft carrier *Argus* transported 24 of the Hurricanes, and the other 15 planes were packed into crates and sent along on other vessels as deck cargo. The convoy put to sea from Iceland on 21 August 1941 and docked at Murmansk on August 28. Here the 24 Hurricanes took off from the *Argus* and landed at Vianga airport about 15 miles away, which served 151st Wing as their main airbase during their stay in the Soviet Union.

Right: August 1941, soldiers of the Soviet 104th Airborne Infantry Brigade before their takeoff in a TB-3.

On Monday 25 August 1941, 4 RAF wings based in Shuaiba and 3 from Habbaniya (Iraq) made a surprise bomb attack on airfields and important military targets in Persia.

It was around this same time that a British pilot managed to capture a German U-boat. On Wednesday 27 August 1941, a Lockheed Hudson bomber of 296 Squadron, RAF Coastal Command, under Squadron Leader J.H. Thompson, attacked German U-boat U 570 under Naval Lt. Col. Ramlow in the North Atlantic despite poor weather conditions. The damaged U-boat, unable to maneuver, drifted along on the surface of the water, and the commander had to surrender to the aircraft. Thompson radioed for support and was sent a Catalina flying boat of 209 Squadron. Two destroyers and several trawlers also turned up at the scene. Next day the U-boat was towed to Iceland and 3 weeks later entered British service as HMS *Graph* under Lt. Colvin.

British and Soviet troops marched into Iran under the pretext of nullifying "the attempt of the Axis Powers to get Persia under their control." Their real concern was to secure a supply route to the Soviet Union, and to protect the wealthy Abadan oil fields. Their very first raid on Ahwaz airbase demolished the little Persian air force with its scant 50 machines. After that British airborne troops occupied the oil fields of Baluchestan. While Hurricane fighters were still patrolling the refineries of Abadan, Wellington bombers raided Persian positions at the Paitah Pass. A ceasefire was signed after four days of fighting, and the Shah of Persia abdicated in favor of his 22-year-old son Reza Pahlevi. By the end of the war, 5 million metric tons of war material from the USA and Britain had been transported via Persia to their ally the Soviet Union.

In late summer of 1941, Great Britain bought 20 of the highly-vaunted four-engined Boeing B-17 C bombers (Flying Fortresses) recently produced by the USA; but the RAF had nothing but bad experiences with them. The B-17 Cs' first war deployment was on Monday 8 September 1941, when they attacked several targets along the Norwegian coast from an altitude of close to 20,000 feet (9,000 meters). But the Germans received radar warning of their presence and sent out Me 109 fighters from 77 Squadron, 13th Fighter Wing (based on Stavanger), which immediately shot down 2 Fortress Is and seriously damaged 3. The remaining British machines veered off. After other fiascos with the B-17 Cs, British Bomber Command concluded that they were completely unsafe, ineffective and unsuitable for use in any serious mission. These aircraft, which were later to become so famous [when they formed the spearhead of the US Army Air Force attack on occupied Europe], were eventually detailed to service in British Coastal Command, and a few were even banished to the Middle East.

On Monday 8 September 1941, the German 51st Fighter Wing (Jagdgeschwader 51 under German ace

of Hitler who wanted to "retaliate" against the British for their bombing raids, the previously shelved A-4 rocket stage development project at Peenemünde was reactivated. This project, which resulted in production of what would come to be known as the V-2 rocket, now received the highest priority classification, so that rocket manufacture was ranked as more important than that of U-boats and fighter planes.

The German bomber groups of the 1st Air Fleet took off from their forward takeoff bases near Minsk on Tuesday 23 September 1941, to raid the heavy Soviet naval units lying in the port and sea roads of Kronstadt. At 8:45 A.M. Nos. 1 and 3 Squadrons of the 2nd Stuka Dive Bomber Wing took off from Tyrkovo advanced airfield. Their targets were the Soviet battleships *Marat* and *October Revolution.* German 1st Lt. H. U. Rudel, who flew a Junkers Ju 86 (T6 + AO), reported later: "We already had the *Marat* in our sights. We raced toward her while she slowly grew enormous. All of her flak guns were now trained on us. I pressed the bomb release on the control stick and pulled our nose up with all my strength. Was there still enough time for

Col. W. Mölders) reported their 2000th aerial victory after the great battles of encirclement between Smolensk and Vyazma.

On Tuesday 9 September 1941, German Air Fleet 1 (Luftflotte 1 under Gen. Keller) opened its offensives against Leningrad, Lomonosov (Ger. *Oranienbaum*) and Kronstadt, paving the way for an attack on these three cities by the German ground troops.

On Thursday 11 September 1941, the British pilots who had been transferred to the Murmansk area with their Hurricane fighters, took off on their first mission. They were about 180 miles into the Arctic Circle, so that the days were only 2 or 3 hours long. During their 11th September patrol flight, the pilots of two of the aircraft managed to get back to their base only by the skin of their teeth because the engines stalled several times due to the poor-quality fuel. Next day 5 Hurricanes shot down 3 Me 109s and damaged one Henschel Hs 126, losing one Hurricane. The British pilot who died in the Hurricane was the only casualty the British unit suffered during their deployment in the Soviet Union. At the end of November the British air crews returned to Britain, and the Red Air Force took over their Hurricanes.

On Monday 15 September 1941, at the instigation

Above left: West Rynham (Norfolk), 6 June 1941: Winston Churchill is observing a US bomber, the B-17 C Fortress I, which proved a disappointment to the RAF.

Above right: 23 September 1941 in the Soviet port of Kronstadt, where a German Stuka flown by 1st Lt. Rudel has just made square hits on the Soviet battleship *Marat*.

Below: The Soviet airfield of Vianga near Murmansk, where a Hurricane 2B of British 151st Wing is preparing to take off.

us to pull out of our dive? I tugged and tugged at the control stick, feeling nothing, just exerting my strength. We accelerated too fast, I could see nothing, I felt a veil come over me, a brief interruption of consciousness unlike anything I had ever experienced. I was not yet clear-headed when I heard Scharnowski's voice saying: "Lieutenant, the ship is blowing up!" Now I looked out, we were flying 9 to 12 feet above the water and I banked gently. There lay the *Marat* beneath an explosive cloud 1,300 feet high. Apparently our bombs had torn into the ammunition room." The big 23,600-ton battleship with its 12 30.5-cm guns and 16 12-cm guns was already badly hit when it received the square hit from Rudel's plane, at which point it broke in two and sank. This was the first time that a battleship had been sunk by a Stuka.

The Luftwaffe continued to be prohibited from attacking strategic targets in the Soviet hinterland, and while German planes went on flying missions in support of their ground troops, the Soviets used their remaining intact railway lines to transport their industrial plants to locations behind the Ural Mountains, where they were out of reach of the German bombers. The transport of Soviet aircraft-manufacturing plants that took place between September and December 1941, was one of the war's most incredible feats of organization and arms management.

The first snowfall on the Eastern Front came on Tuesday 7 October 1941. Hitler ordered the German Central Army Group under Field Marshal von Bock to continue its operations in the direction of Moscow, but the beginning of the mud season thwarted the German advance.

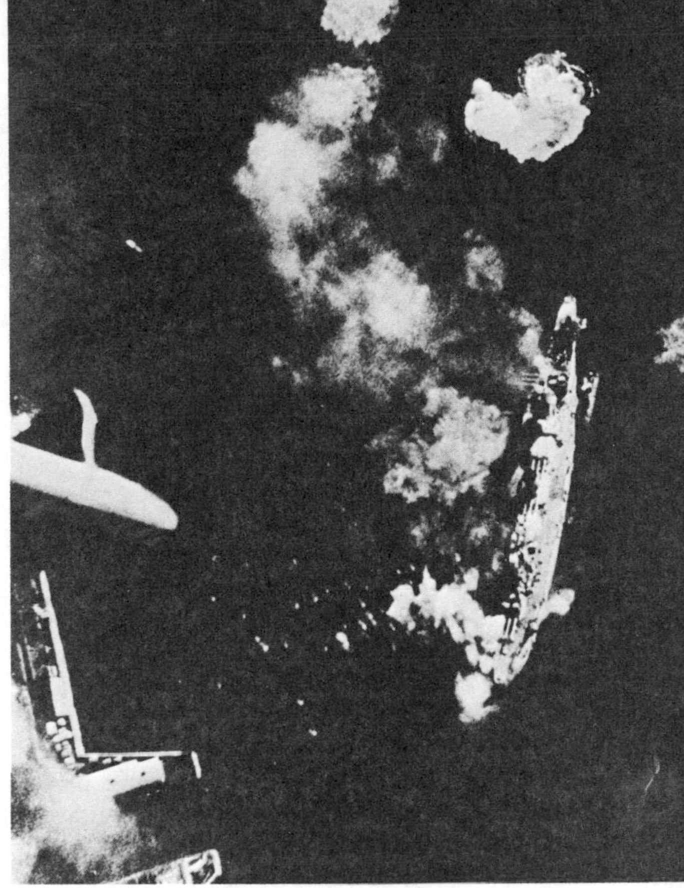

In mid-October, various Soviet governmental agencies including the people's commissariat in charge of the aviation industry, were evacuated from Moscow to Kuybyshev. Stalin remained in the capital and ordered almost 40% of all the Soviet aerial forces to mass in defense of Moscow. As a result, the Soviets succeeded for the first time in winning air superiority for an extended period, along one of the main thrust-lines of the German assault.

On Monday 20 October 1941 the Japanese navy made assembly provisions for a surprise attack on Pearl Harbor in case Japanese negotiations with the USA failed to produce the desired result. The carrier-based dive bombers and torpedo bombers meant to wipe out the US fleet, carried out their final live maneuvers. They had a long tradition of successful air-sea battle to look back to: A Japanese plane had sunk a ship – a German minelayer – way back on 26 September 1914, the first aircraft ever to achieve this. The aircraft involved was a Farman hydroplane.

Since the end of 1940 the German long range night fighter planes of 2 Squadron, 1st Night Fighter Wing had been putting up an effective defense against British Bomber Command. The squadron

used special night fighter versions of Do 17s and Junkers Ju 88s. They operated blind over British bomber bases in southeastern England and attacked the bombers just as their exhausted crews were returning from their missions over Germany and occupied Europe, already down to their last drop of fuel, sometimes damaged by the German air defense, and busy making landing maneuvers; for at this time they made easy prey. In October 1941 the harassed British bomber crews could breathe easily again because Hitler suddenly ordered a halt to the German flights despite their success, and the long range night fighter wing was transferred to the Mediterranean.

The main Italian forces in Ethiopia had surrendered to the Allies in May 1941, but a few bases in the impassable highlands had gone on fighting. The once numerous Italian aerial forces had been wiped out some time ago. Only the defenders of Gondar managed to hide a few Fiat CR.42 fighter planes that had been shipped from the mother country by air freight, and kept them fighting-fit. They mounted a number of nuisance raids against the surprised British troops. Not until October 24 did the British ground defenses shoot down one of these ghost machines.

On the night of 28–29 October 1941, 32 German bombers flew over Moscow. During the air raid a bomb fell onto one wing of the Soviet general staff's alternate headquarters in Kirov Street. Three vehicle drivers were killed, and 15 commanding officers including General A. M. Vassilevski, chief of tactical operations, were wounded.

Between September and November 1941, Bomber Command stepped up its missions against the German capital. The toll of German civilian victims and the damage in residential districts increased. However, the growing effectiveness of the German air defense, and the unfavorable weather conditions, likewise increased the losses to British bombers—especially on the night of 7th–8th November 1941, when 21 bombers out of 169 were lost over Berlin, that is 12.5%. Five days later Churchill called an indefinite halt to British raids on long range targets like Berlin.

On the morning of 15 November 1941, the positions of the German Central Army Group in the Soviet Union were covered with shining frost. The mud season was past and now friend and foe alike were under the command of "General Frost." The second phase of the battle for the Soviet capital began with an attack by the northern flank of the Central Army. The German Luftwaffe faced a new and thorny problem on the Eastern Front: It was not prepared for a winter war and lost much of its effectiveness due to its lack of the necessary equipment.

Above left: Bombs for the next British mission over Germany are rolling out of the depot at the edge of an RAF airbase.

Below: RAF Bomber Command suffered heavy losses at the beginning of November 1941. Here we see the dead British crew of a shot-down Wellington bomber.

On Monday 17 November 1941 General Udet, who had held a high post in charge of air affairs, despaired of developments in the Luftwaffe and shot himself in the head at the age of 45. On the morning of 22 November, the He 111 that was carrying the famous ace Col. Werner Mölders — now 28 and ranked as fighter-plane inspector — to Udet's state funeral in Berlin, broke down due to engine damage, smashed into a factory chimney in the outskirts of Breslau, and crashed.

Tuesday 18 November 1941 marked the beginning of Operation Crusader, the British counteroffensive against the Germans in North Africa. The British Eighth Army under Lt. Gen. Cunningham rolled out of the desert fort of Maddalena and headed toward Tobruk, intending to bring aid to the beleaguered fortress and to occupy Cyrenaica. The British had a total of 1,072 combat-ready aircraft in this war arena. German armored-troop General Rommel had 120 German and around 200 Italian aircraft, and faced insoluble problems in getting supplies because of the German failure to conquer Malta. After only one day the RAF reported virtually complete command of the air over the entire battle zone.

On Wednesday 26 November 1941 (Japanese time) a Japanese aircraft carrier left Hitokappu Bay in the Kurile Islands carrying the combat planes for the bombing of Pearl Harbor. The carrier was escorted by 2 battleships, 2 heavy cruisers, 1 light cruiser, 9 large destroyers, 3 submarines, and 8 tankers and supply ships. The carrier formation, commanded by Vice-Admiral Nagumo, pressed eastward through storm and fog for 11 days without breaking radio silence, and later turned toward the southeast, where it ran into better weather.

On Friday 28 November 1941 the last Italian combat forces in East Africa, under the command of General Nasi, surrendered at Gondar (Ethiopia), where 23,000 men were taken prisoner. By then the Italians did not have one single combat-ready aircraft left.

On the night of 30 November — 1 December 1941, 129 RAF bombers took off to raid Hamburg. Eighty-four of the machines reached their target and dropped 138 metric tons of bombs on the Hanseatic city, losing 13 aircraft in the process. Germany's armaments industry was now becoming increasingly exposed to bomb raids. Meanwhile, the Soviets in the East continued to evacuate all their industrial plants from the European end of the Soviet Union and to transfer them out of German reach behind the Urals. The evacuation which had begun in July, was now nearing completion: a masterly feat achieved in a remarkably short time without imperilling arms development and supply. By December 1941, a total of 1,360 large Soviet munitions plants had been transported eastward in 1.5 million freight car loads. Lt. Gen. S. Ilyushin, commander of the Soviet engineering troops, reported: "At this time the new halls of the largest aircraft manufacturing plant in the Soviet Union were going up in a town near the Volga. The walls of the halls had not yet been raised and the workers did not yet have any roof over their heads, but they were already at work. They did not leave their workplaces even when the temperature sank to 40 degrees below zero. On December 5, 14 days after the arrival of the last transport train, the first Ilyushin Il-2 Sturmovik plane left the plant after its assembly from prefabricated parts that had come along the journey."

The German and Italian supply convoys bound for North Africa continued to suffer catastrophic losses at the hands of the British, so on Friday 5 December Hitler ordered the German 2nd Air Fleet (Luftflotte 2 under Field Marshal Kesselring) to transfer from the central zone of the Eastern Front to Libya and Sicily.

That same day the Red Army defending Moscow went on a counteroffensive and gained ground rapidly. The hard Russian winter reduced the Germans' deployment capability to 30%. The Soviet troops were supported by their new bombers, ground-attack aircraft and fighters, which continued to function even under the most extreme weather conditions. Due to the great number of mechanical breakdowns, the Germans had only about 500 aircraft in the central sector of the 2,100-mile-long Eastern Front, while the Red Air Force had built up its strength to approximately 1,000 aircraft in the Moscow area alone.

On Sunday 7 December 1941 the Japanese made their surprise attack on Pearl Harbor, the chief naval base of the American Pacific fleet. The carrier-based aircraft formation commanded by Vice-Admiral Nagumo, took off at 6:00 A.M. north of the Hawaiian island of Oahu. The first wave of aircraft included 51 dive bombers, 50 horizontal bombers, 40 torpedo bombers and 43 fighter planes; the second wave was made up of 81 dive bombers, 54 horizon-

Above: A Japanese Nakajima B5N1 torpedo bomber takes off from the carrier *Soryu.*

Right center: At Smolensk (occupied Soviet Russia) in November 1941, Germans are using a heating device to try to warm up the engines of their Do 17s.

Next page below: Two burning US battleships, the *West Virginia* and the *Tennessee,* lie side by side after the Japanese bombing raid on Pearl Harbor.

Below right: A Japanese diagram illustrating the special torpedoes with adjustable wooden side fins that the Japanese used at Pearl Harbor—after cribbing the device from the British.

Below: Diagram map of the Japanese attack on Pearl Harbor on 7 December 1941.

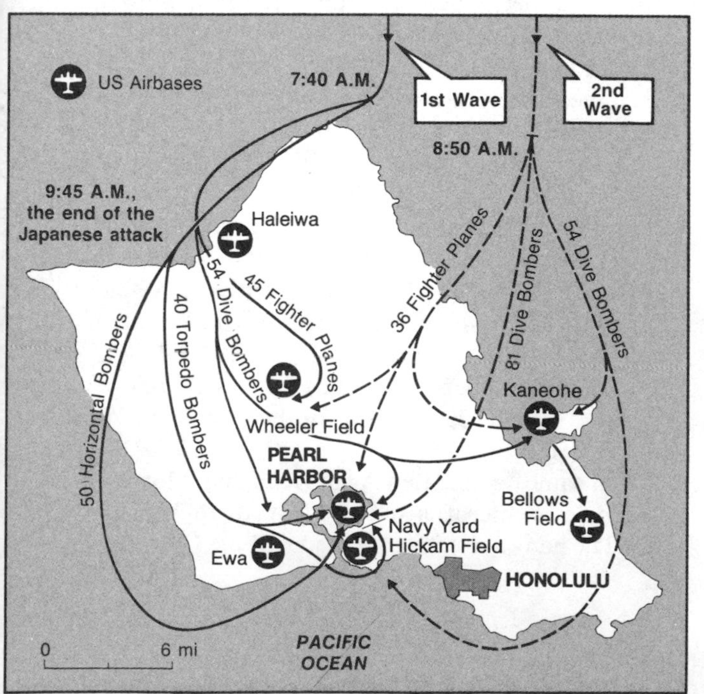

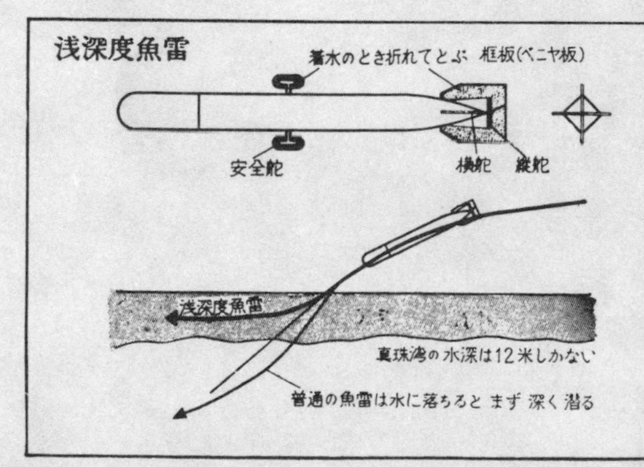

tal bombers, and 36 fighters. So sudden was the attack that the American air defense was almost nonexistent. There were some gunners on hand to man the light antiaircraft guns on board the warships, but the ammunition was locked up in the magazines. Almost all the US aircraft were put out of action by the Japanese raids on Hawaiian airfields. The Japanese fliers sank the battleships *Arizona, California, Nevada, Oklahoma,* and *West Virginia,* the minelayer *Oglada* and the target ship *Utah.* The battleships *Maryland, Pennsylvania* and *Tennessee* were also badly damaged, so that 60% of the US Navy's entire stock of battleships was either sunk or crippled. Bad damage was also inflicted on the light cruisers *Helena, Honolulu* and *Raleigh,* and on 3 destroyers, 1 aircraft carrier and 1 workshop vessel. American casualties were 2,403 dead and 1,178 wounded, and 188 aircraft were destroyed. Japanese losses were 5 torpedo bombers, 15 dive bombers and 9 fighters carrying a total of 55 men. The Japanese forces dropped 138.5 metric tons of torpedoes and bombs. The secret of their success was a special type of torpedo with adjustable wooden side fins that made it possible to predetermine the depth of the charge. The Japanese had picked up this trick from the British during the latter's attack on the Italian naval base at Taranto on 11th–12th November 1940.

The purpose of the Pearl Harbor operations was to secure the sea flank of the Japanese for their advance into South Asia to take over its raw materials. This aim was achieved to some extent in that the US fleet was eliminated; but the attack had been confined to battleships and airfields, which left the giant oil depots and serviceable docks unscathed, and as a result Pearl Harbor could continue to function as a naval base. Moreover, only the antiquated US battleships had been hit. The most important targets, 4 aircraft carriers – which had also been ordered to Pearl Harbor but had been held up by a storm – escaped the attack, and these were to play a crucial role in American conduct of the war. Virtually alone in his views at this early stage, Japanese Admiral Yamamoto said: "This war will cause us great trouble in the future. The fact that we had a small victory at Pearl Harbor, means nothing."

Three days later, on Wednesday 10 December 1941, Japanese aircraft also inflicted a devastating blow on the British Far East naval task force, Force Z, when they torpedoed the battleships *Prince of Wales* and *Repulse,* two of Britain's most powerful vessels. The sinking of these two mighty ships proved that battleships could no longer operate without fighter plane cover against an enemy with strong aerial forces.

On Thursday 11 December 1941, only minutes after Germany had declared war on the USA, an American Lockheed P-38 Lightning fighter plane stationed in Iceland shot down a German Focke Wulf 200 C Condor long distance reconnaissance plane over the Atlantic.

On November 12 a number of ASV-radar-equipped British Swordfish torpedo bombers had managed to survive the sinking of the aircraft carrier *Ark Royal,* and in the second half of December they began to fly patrols against German U-boats which repeatedly penetrated the Mediterranean through the Straits of Gibraltar. On one of these missions they destroyed the U 451 commanded by Naval Lt. Hoffman.

On Sunday 21 December 1941, the German 2nd Air Fleet formations which had been transferred from the Eastern Front to Sicily, began relay wave attacks on Malta. Their main targets were the island's airfields and the flying boat base at Kalafrana. While British Hurricane fighters were busy trying to fend off the German bomber raids, British Blenheim bombers flew counterattacks on Sicilian airbases.

In the period from June 22 to the end of December 1941, the German Luftwaffe lost 758 bombers, 568 fighters and 767 other aircraft on the Eastern Front, while an additional 473 bombers, 413 fighters and 475 other planes were damaged.

The Japanese now began the successful use of their aircraft in massed tactical operations, and deployed a number of carrier-based aircraft formations inside a restricted battle arena. The Japanese navy was able to maneuver freely under the protection of its carrier aircraft, and so could follow up its strategic initiative. At the beginning of the war the Japanese air force was strong and combat-effective and its torpedo bombers in particular were feared adversaries. The climbing ability of Japanese fighter planes was even superior to that of US planes. The greatest mistake of the Japanese was that they used up their best flight personnel and their best aircraft at the very beginning of the war, and waited far too long to train new forces and manufacture modern aircraft.

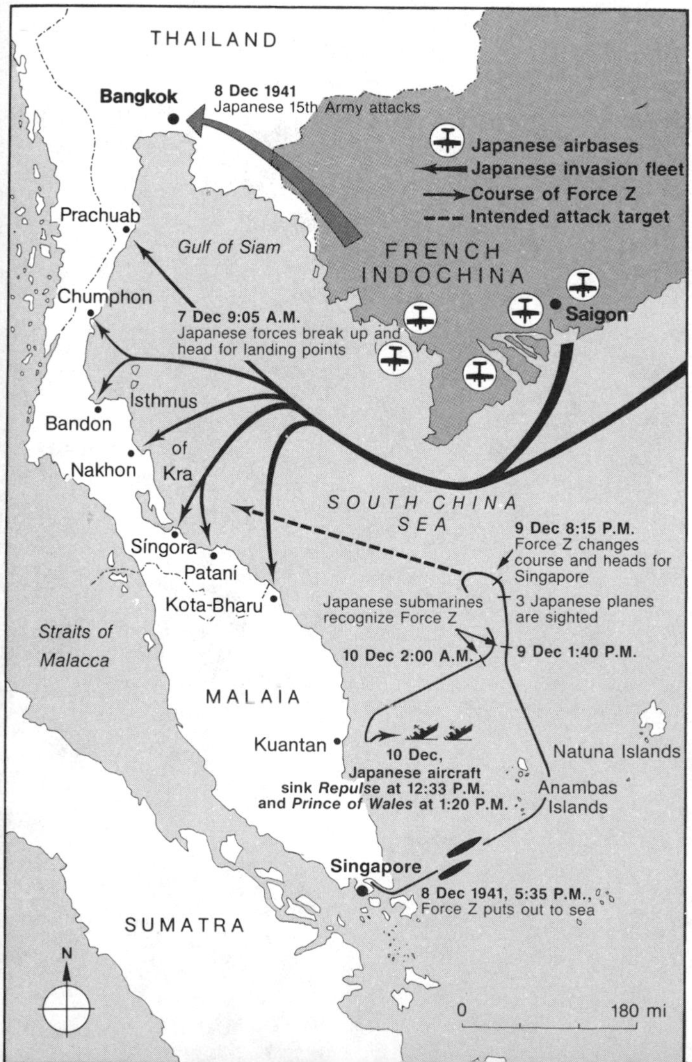

Diagram map showing how the Japanese sank the British naval task force, Force Z – the battleships *Repulse* and *Prince of Wales.*

1942
January to June

Flight into the Troop Pocket

The following descriptive account appeared in the German publication *Das Reich* in January 1942:

A church stands on a hill in the middle of the forest. As we fly over we see that it is completely in ruins. There are German soldiers inside who wave to us joyfully, and we return the greeting by waving our wings. Two minutes before our calculated arrival time we drop to an altitude of 350–500 feet, and see the airfield ahead of us along one corner of the wood. Now cut the gas and turn the flaps, and if the air path ahead of us is clear we will make a clean landing.

We carry away wounded from Demyansk [Soviet encirclement of German troops in USSR]. Most are suffering from frostbite. It is now mid-January and beastly cold; the temperature is around 40 below. On top of that a snowstorm is blowing in from the east. The soldiers on the ground are walking around heavily muffled; the wounded men on the sledges are wrapped up warmly in straw blankets. Icicles hang from the mouths of the shaggy little Russian farm horses. We turn off the engines while we load the wounded into the plane. Everyone must be brought inside within five minutes; then we have to start the engines again because otherwise they will get so cold that we cannot reheat them. It is by no means easy to load up and stow away the wounded in this short a time. People can freeze stiff in no time inside our cold aircraft; but we are prepared for that now and help them in every way we can. They are bedded in straw and well covered with wool blankets. During the flight they are given hot tea with rum or hot nourishing meat broth taken from thermos bottles.

Restricted Material (For Official Use Only)

Report by German Lt. Gen. H. J. Rieckhoff on experience gained during the Luftwaffe's winter flight offensive against the Soviet Union:

Neither the German Army nor the Luftwaffe was equipped for a proper winter campaign when war against the Soviet Union began. The temperatures in Russia in 1941/42 stayed at minus 30 to minus 50 degrees Centigrade for weeks on end, while in extreme cases the temperature reached minus 70. Our real problems occur not when the aircraft are actually in operation, but when we start them up in abnormally low temperatures.

Airframes and landing gear:

The extensive icing-up of wings and tail assemblies that very frequently attacks aircraft on the ground, cannot be removed manually, and greatly inhibits combat readiness. Canvas covers are used to protect smaller aircraft. This is a completely inadequate measure because the covers themselves freeze stiff and are then almost impossible to handle, especially when, as is often the case, there is a violent wind. Closed sheds and hangars are rarely available. The attempt to prevent ice from forming by greasing the wings with water-repellent oils, has failed due to the shortage of lubricant supplies. Thus heating cars remain the most effective, if by no means satisfactory, means for eliminating ground ice. Snow-skid landing gear has proved ineffective except with the Fieseler Storch light courier and communications aircraft, which can be kept combat-ready under any snow conditions by this method. The only thing still needed by the Fieseler Storch is an effective skid brake to increase ground maneuverability. With all

Winter on the Eastern Front meant a never-ending battle by men and machines against the rigors of nature.

other types of aircraft, experiments using rapid-production skids have proved disappointing. The skids can be mounted only when the landing gear is extended and consequently they cause a great loss of speed (25% or more) which is tactically unacceptable. Moreover, it has been shown that depending on its construction and the size of the wheels, landing gear remains completely functional [without skids] when the snow is as much as two feet high.

Flight engines:

Cold disturbance to the engines appears mainly when they are started up. Extremely attentive maintenance and precise observation of the servicing regulations are needed to facilitate a cold start. This is done by feeding a lubricant diluted with gasoline into the engine while starting it up. After about 20 minutes of flight the gasoline additive in the oil has evaporated and the engine runs at normal oil temperature. Disruptions occur in the start-up gear more frequently than in the engines themselves, due to freeze-up of the oil in the gear pipes. If the starter is engaged abruptly, the shaft can even break. As a rule, icing-up of the propellers during flight is not dangerous; but in some cases damage has occurred to aircraft, and injuries to crewmen, from flying chunks of dislodged ice. No experiments have been made to determine whether this could be prevented by heating the propellers.

Aerial instruments:

Our aerial instruments (manufactured by the Siemens and Askania electrical and optical instruments firms) have surprised us by their relatively high insensibility to cold.

Communications equipment:

Aerial communications equipment has proved impervious to cold but on the other hand is very sensitive to moisture.

Fuel:

All fuels are sufficiently cold-resistant. The familiar ethylene glycol makes an effective anti-freeze agent for the cooling water.

Aerial guns:

Problems with the guns are fairly frequent. The usual cause is oil that is insufficiently resistant to cold; occasionally, in the case of electrically-guided weapons, it is water condensation in the circuits.

Bomb armament:

A snow altitude of one meter and above, appreciably dampens the effect of short-fuse high-explosive and fragmentation bombs because the snow muffles the lateral spread of the explosive. Up to 75% of the highly sensitive detonators of the 4.5-lb SD 2 fragmentation bomb fail to function in deep soft snow. On the other hand, hard frozen ground offers such resistance to high-explosive bombs that they very often shatter without detonating. Light fragmentation bombs that fall into the snow and fail to detonate, do produce a secondary effect that we did not initially intend: They act more or less like dispersed land mines that detonate later when touched lightly by people on foot, animals or vehicles. Ever since this characteristic was detected, SD 2s have been deployed frequently to contaminate segments of terrain where we want to impede the enemy's progress.

Air-crew clothing and equipment:

The German sheepskin one- or two-piece flying suit is cumbersome on long marches after emergency landings. Thermal suits have proved even less effective. Attention is required to regulate them; they are also fragile and completely unsuitable in emergency landings. The most practical outfit seems to be a lightweight camel-hair or fur suit with a waterproof lining (no leather or bare pelts). Boots, if fur-lined, must have strong anti-skid soles and sit firmly on the foot. Simple Russian felt boots have proved very effective, whereas the fur boots made for German airmen are unsuitable for marches because they fit too loosely. It is recommended to wear not cotton but light woolen garments underneath the protective clothing. Good gloves, mittens and earmuffs are essential. During strenuous marches, outer garments can occasionally be removed and carried as a bundle or dragged along behind on a flat sledge (*volushka).*

It should be noted that at the same time when the German Wehrmacht is suffering huge casualties due to frost injuries, the Russians punish every man suffering frost injury as if he were guilty of self-inflicted wounds, because the Russian soldier is trained so that he can avoid frostbite despite primitive equipment.

Flying operations:

The bulk of problems and disruptions due to cold ensue when preparing the engines and starting up the aircraft. This results in a disproportionately long period being devoted to flight preparations (up to 5 hours per unit). The long warm-up period rules out short-notice operations where aircraft are needed to support the army; prevents the rapid exploitation of favorable tactical and weather conditions; makes it impossible to deploy an aircraft more than once on the short winter days; and thus makes it difficult to put our aerial power to full use.

American Air Bridge to the USSR

10 February 1942, Washington

The American *United Press News Agency* reported:

Canada and the USA are working together to create an air bridge to Siberia via Alaska and the Arctic zone. Large numbers of airfields are being built along the flight route from the east coast of America, across Canada to Alaska. A regular expedition of tractors, caterpillar towing-vehicles, a mobile sawmill, large numbers of other machines and vehicles, and an army of workmen, had to blaze a trail through 300 miles of wilderness at the beginning of this year, to build the airfield near Watson Lake [Yukon, Canada]. The flight from Alaska to the Soviet Union is made possible by a chain of hitherto secret bases in northern Siberia that continues westward all the way to European Russia. Short-range aircraft will also be able to fly to Moscow over this route. It is believed that US bombers have already been delivered to Russia via Alaska-Siberia.

"Giant White Flowers"

Japanese Paratroop Assault on Palembang (Sumatra)

Tokyo, end of February 1942

Japanese *Lt. Kusoki* reported:

On the eve of the assault on Palembang, the paratroops built a little altar out of parachutes inside their quarters, offered rice wine there according to Shinto rites, and prayed that the parachutes might open safely next day. They did not pray for their own survival, but only that their parachutes would function correctly; they treated the parachutes as carefully as raw eggs, never throwing or stepping on them.

By eight o'clock next morning the preparations were complete. Each soldier had his pistol and his short sword in his belt; each wore a steel helmet, and on his back a yellow-green pack containing his parachute. Each had a reserve parachute hanging on his chest in case the first failed to open. They all formed up with their troop leader, their faces turned in the direction of the Emperor's palace in Tokyo, made their final reverent bows to the palace, and sang the Japanese national anthem. The troop leader issued instructions, told them their target and

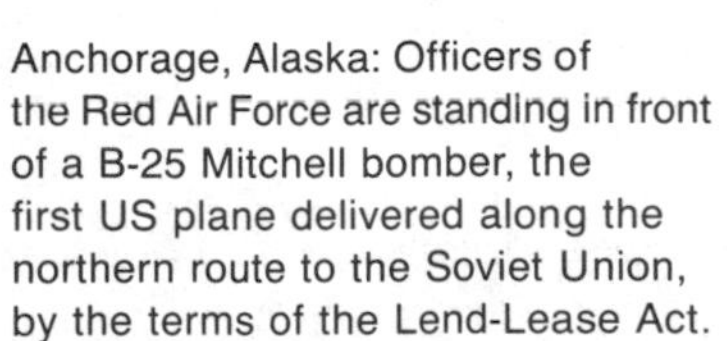

Anchorage, Alaska: Officers of the Red Air Force are standing in front of a B-25 Mitchell bomber, the first US plane delivered along the northern route to the Soviet Union, by the terms of the Lend-Lease Act.

mission, and concluded by saying with a laugh: "Now your lives are in my hands, so come on, let's go." They climbed into the numerous waiting aircraft feeling that they no longer had anything to lose and were ready to give their lives if necessary.

The planes took off at the start signal, among them some that carried no cargo but guns, hand grenades and four days' provisions, and flew south.

Soon Singapore appeared, still wreathed in black smoke rising from the burning oil tanks. The sea with its little islands moved away underneath us, and before we expected it, the pilot called out: "Sumatra dead ahead."

We flew over the mouth of the Musi river and circled around, because our aircraft were now supposed to split into two formations: one was to attack the Palembang airfield, the other the oil refinery. We signalled each other our final greetings above the clouds. One group flew toward the airfield and soon we were again shrouded in black clouds that shielded us completely from the view of anyone down below, so at first we were not fired on. Suddenly we caught sight of the airfield underneath us, clearly recognizable by its long takeoff runway that shone brightly in the sunlight. But before we had time to orient ourselves properly, we saw the first dark figure free itself from the planes flying below us. It was followed by a second, a third. In less than no time the air underneath us was completely filled with giant white flowers gliding slowly and majestically to earth. The aircraft continued to sow an endless stream of huge flowers.

But at the same time defensive fire broke out from the ground. Tracer fire cut a path through the bed of white lilies, sometimes dangerously near to the men dangling under the parachutes.

The first chute landed, trailed for a moment, then slowly crumpled and collapsed. More and more landed. We could see individual jumpers freeing themselves from their chutes, grouping around the troop leader, running to the weapons boxes, tearing them open and opening fire.

By the time we veered away a few minutes later, the field seemed to be strewn with white dots. We knew that the first stage of the assault had been successful; now the battle would begin, and its outcome was no longer in doubt.

From the Diary of the Reich Minister of Propaganda Dr. Joseph Goebbels,
Sunday 1 March 1942:

The British have carried out a night paratroop mission near Le Havre. The mission itself was of negligible importance from a military point of view; only the loss of the Würzburg radar set may cause us some problems. Also, our French coast defenses undoubtedly failed us. Apparently they were sleeping on the job. I expect that the Führer will take appropriate action.

Tips for Fighter Pilots

R. Tilley, American volunteer pilot of the RAF 121st "Eagle" Squadron, offered the following tips to other Allied pilots:

Before takeoff, always note the position of the sun. It could be that you will be shot down over the sea or the desert and that your compass will get destroyed in the crash; then the sun may help to point you in the right direction. Never let your plane climb into the sun. If you really have to fly into the sun, then follow a zigzag path, approaching the sun each time at a 45-degree angle. When circumstances permit, climb as high as you possibly can. A German fighter plane that is hiding under cover of the sun, can dive down on you from above. If this happens, you can curve around him and use the sun to your own advantage. When you detect an enemy, divide your unit into two groups and fly between the sun and the enemy with the two groups aligning themselves more or less one above the other; but the upper group, which to the enemy appears to fly directly into the sun, should stay slightly in the lead. Change your altitude continually: that way, if the enemies see you, they have trouble getting you under their barrels during a banking flight. Always bank your plane into the sun. When you approach an experienced German fighter, keep in mind that he will seldom put all his cards on the table at one go. As a rule the Germans divide their squadrons into flight formations, and each flight keeps the sun at its back; usually they lie in ambush at altitudes of 3,000–5,000 feet. Keep your eye on the sun; that can spare you unpleasant surprises. The Germans often set traps, letting a single German plane fly around on its own like a helpless chicken. Don't fall for it! Half the Luftwaffe is flying around up there under cover of the sun, waiting to pounce on you at the right moment.

Bombs on Paris

Wednesday 4 March 1942, Vichy
The *French Havas News Agency* reported:

Six hundred were killed and 1,000 wounded during RAF bombing of the area surrounding Paris. In Boulogne-Billancourt alone, the toll of the dead was 400. One hundred and fifty to 200 houses were destroyed. The national china manufacturing plant in Sèvres and the Rodin Museum in Meudon were badly damaged. Marshal Pétain has expressed his deep sympathy to the families of the victims. Even before fixing the details of aid measures, Marshal Pétain declared the day of the victim's burial to be a day of national mourning.

The Far East War

Thursday 5 March 1942, Melbourne
The *Australian Air Ministry* reported:

The third attack by Japanese aircraft on Port Darwin [northern Australia] yesterday morning, when approximately 100 planes raided the city and port, was much less massive than the first two raids made during the past two weeks. Prime Minister Curtin has formally denied rumors that the toll of deaths was as high this time as in the first raids.

Malta under a Hail of Bombs

Sunday 8 March 1942, Valetta (Malta)
The British *Reuters News Agency* reported:

German and Italian forces are continuing their non-stop raids on Malta. On Friday two Italian fighters and one bomber were shot down. Another fighter was so badly damaged that it can be counted as lost. During the night of Friday to Saturday, the people of the Maltese capital remained in the air raid shelters for eleven hours. Since the stepping-up of the aerial conflict on 21 December 1941, almost 300 people have been killed on Malta and 4,000 houses have been destroyed.

Secret Report of the *SS Secret Service* on internal affairs, No. 270 of Monday 23 March 1942 (extract):

I. General comments: Reports from western parts of the Reich show that the violent British air raids recently have caused considerable disquiet among the people. A particular source of concern is said to be the release of phosphorus-filled canisters, which cause large fires and make people feel helpless.

Sunday 29 March 1942
RAF Headquarters announced:

On Saturday night leading into Sunday morning, massive British bomber forces attacked large numbers of airfields in France, Belgium and Holland. The main attack was aimed at Lübeck, which waves of heavy and medium bombers carpeted with several metric tons of high explosives. Violent explosions ensued in the port district, near an aircraft plant and amid the shipbuilding installations. Aerial photographs show 40 fires. Twelve British aircraft have not returned.

The fighter pilots of all the belligerent nations had a special personal relationship with their planes: after all, their lives depended on its "whims."

29 March 1942
The *Wehrmacht High Command* announced:

Last night British bombers attacked several towns along the north German coast, chiefly Lübeck. There were a number of civilian casualties. German night fighters, flak artillery and naval artillery shot down 12 of the attacking bombers.

Thursday 2 April 1942
The *Wehrmacht High Command* announced:

Powerful bomber and fighter units made relay

attacks on military installations on the island of Malta; the attacks continued day and night. Square hits on aircraft hangars and sheds, and among aircraft on the field, caused large fires and explosions. British flak positions were put out of action. Direct hits were scored on enemy submarines and destroyers in the port of Valetta. Three British planes were shot down in aerial combat. Italian bombers successfully attacked the British fortress of Gibraltar.

Tuesday 7 April 1942
The *Wehrmacht High Command* announced:
There is strong reconnaissance activity on both sides in North Africa. Bomber and fighter units attacked British airfields in the Marmarica (region of Libya) and along the Egyptian coast, and blew up motor vehicle assemblies southeast of Makale (Ethiopia). German fighters shot down 6 British aircraft in aerial dogfights. Strong formations of German bombers, dive bombers and fighters kept up non-stop day and night raids on military installations on the island of Malta. A British destroyer lying in dock was set on fire.

Wednesday 8 April 1942, Valetta
The *Reuters News Agency* reported:
Yesterday Malta experienced its two thousandth air alert since the outbreak of war, and its heaviest air raid so far. The ground defense set up a powerful defensive barrage. Complete reports have not yet come in, but we already know that 4 enemy aircraft were shot down and 2 damaged; another is presumed destroyed. Last Monday, German bombers, including dive bombers, raided the port and airfields in repeated waves. Air alerts were sounded six times on Tuesday night through to Wednesday morning. Since the incessant attacks on Malta began on 4 December 1941, there has been only one 24-hour period when the air raid siren was not sounded, and only nine nights have passed without an attack.

8 April 1942
The *Wehrmacht High Command* announced:
German forces bombed the British naval base of Alexandria on the night of 6th/7th April; considerable damage was inflicted on the dock installations. Powerful German bomber, dive-bomber and fighter formations led air raids against the port and supply installations of Valetta, the torpedo depot at Kalafrana and British airfields on the island of Malta. Huge fires were started in warehouses, shipyard buildings and factory plants. The British cruiser lying in dock was struck by more bombs.

Thursday 9 April 1942
British Field Headquarters in Libya announced:
This morning the RAF launched large bomber units with strong fighter cover, in a counterattack on Derna airfield (Libya). Several American Curtiss Kittyhawk fighters were also deployed in the attack. The German Luftwaffe operates mainly at night, whereas the RAF is carrying on its operations day and night.

Monday 13 April 1942
The *Wehrmacht High Command* announced:
The continuous day and night raids on military installations and airfields on Malta, have caused further destruction to their targets.

Daily Watchword of the Reich Press Chief,
Friday 17 April 1942:
The Minister says that it is inexpedient to respond to British air raids on Germany with sneering or sarcastic remarks about their ineffectiveness, as this only challenges the British to further raids. Let British propaganda throughout the world quote the effectiveness of their raids: we should respond with silence.

Bombs on Tokyo

Saturday 18 April 1942, San Francisco
Radio Tokyo has made the following announcement: Today the Japanese capital was bombed by enemy aircraft. Allied aircraft are reported to have bombed schools and hospitals in Tokyo and its environs, causing substantial damage. No military targets were hit.

Right: An Italian CRDA Cant Z. 1007 *bis* Alcione (Kingfisher) medium bomber of 15th Group, 16th Bomber Wing, is bombing the Grand Harbour in Valetta, Malta. The strategic importance of Malta made the island one of the most frequently bombed targets of the war.

Below left: Valetta, Malta in April 1942, after one of the Luftwaffe's countless bomb raids. Rescue personnel are trying to save people buried under the rubble.

18 April 1942, Tokyo
Air Defense Headquarters for East Japan announced this evening:

Our antiaircraft early warning service recognized the approach of enemy aircraft so quickly that we were everywhere able to sound the alarm in time. The damage inflicted was slight due to the energetic intervention of our fighters and flak artillery. The imperial family is unharmed. Apart from a few high-explosive bombs, the American aircraft mainly dropped heavy incendiary bombs weighing approximately 4-5 pounds each; these had a negligible effect. We wish to convey our sympathy to the families of the victims. In addition it is reported that aerial machine guns fired on the town of Yokkaichi [island of Honshu] and a village in the prefecture of Makayama. No damage was done in either case.

18 April 1942, Tokyo
The *German News Bureau* announced:

Hundreds of thousands of people stayed out on the Tokyo streets at noon despite the fact that the alarm sirens had been sounded at least one hour before; apparently they assumed that it was a test alarm. But even when the flak started firing, the entire population remained completely calm. Their sense of security increased when Japanese fighter wings began to circle the sky. The city traffic did not slacken despite the relatively high number of attacking planes that were shot down, which shows that Tokyo was not threatened by any serious danger. The nationalities of the attackers are not yet known.

US Aircraft Carrier off the Coast of Japan?

Monday 20 April 1942, London
The British *Reuters News Agency* reported:

Radio messages broadcast under the radio call letters of Radio Tokyo – messages probably intended for Japan's Axis partner, Germany – claim that approximately 100 US North American Na 40 attack bombers made bombing raids on Tokyo and other Japanese cities. Assuming that the report is factual, American naval fliers must have carried out their assault from aircraft carriers, because Na 40 bombers have a range of only 1,600 miles at most. A sortie from aircraft carriers would be highly significant because it would prove that the US fleet has regained complete freedom of action: for surely the US Department of the Navy would not let its aircraft carriers operate off the Japanese coast without a strong protective escort.

Saturday 25 April 1942
The *Wehrmacht High Command* announced:

Our air attacks on military installations and airfields on the island of Malta have continued without interruption. Large numbers of the heaviest caliber bomb hits caused extensive destruction today.

Daily Watchword of the Reich Press Chief, Monday 27 April 1942:

It has been claimed that the British air raids of the last few nights prove the ineffectiveness of switching off German radio transmitters in the evening [so as not to provide signals that can be picked up by British radar], and a proposal has been made to restore German transmitters to use for propaganda and entertainment programs in the evening. This proposal is rejected by the Minister, who points out that he does not want to be held responsible for the success of further British raids. We must assume, he says, that in case of British successes, the Luftwaffe would try to pawn off the responsibility onto him.

The Battle of the Coral Sea

Friday 8 May 1942, Melbourne
The *Headquarters of General MacArthur* announced:

An important air and sea battle is at the moment taking place in the southwestern Pacific. In its initial phases, the Allies have inflicted heavy damage on the enemy while suffering only slight casualties.

8 May 1942, Tokyo
Imperial Japanese Headquarters announced:

The following US vessels were sunk yesterday, Thursday, in the Coral Sea northeast of Australia: the aircraft carrier *Yorktown* (19,900 tons), the aircraft carrier *Saratoga* (33,000 tons), and the battleship *California* (32,600 tons). In addition the British cruiser *Canberra* (9,850 tons) appears to have been either sunk or badly damaged. This has yet to be officially confirmed. The battle with the American and British naval forces is still going on.

8 May 1942
US South Pacific Headquarters announced:

A great sea and air battle is now taking place at the latitude of the Solomon Islands, in the sea territory approximately 480 miles east of New Guinea and 960 miles north of the Australian coast. It is already becoming known as the "Battle of the Coral Sea." Several of the vessels reported damaged, are now on fire. Allied losses can be announced only when it is certain that this will not supply any valuable information to the enemy.

Above right: A Grumman F6F Hellcat is taking off from the US aircraft carrier *Lexington.* Of the total 6,477 Japanese aircraft shot down by American carrier pilots during the war, 4,947 were destroyed by Hellcats, a standard carrier-based fighter plane.

Below right: 18 April 1942, the B-25 Mitchell bombers of Lt. Col. "Jimmy" Doolittle are standing by for takeoff on the deck of the US carrier *Hornet.* The B-25 was America's most-produced two-engined bomber (more than 11,000 were built) and was highly valued for its good flying qualities.

British Issue Formal Denial

8 May 1942, London
A *British Admiralty* communiqué announced:

The report by Japanese headquarters that the *Warspite* or another British war vessel has been damaged in the Coral Sea, is a complete fabrication.

Saturday 9 May 1942, Washington
The American *United Press News Agency* reported:

The American public are waiting in extreme suspense to know the outcome of the naval battle in the Coral Sea. All radio stations, movie houses and theaters have announced that they will interrupt their programs immediately upon receipt of further reports on the course of the battle. Army reports suggest that for the time being, the sea battle in the Coral Sea appears to have ended. The Japanese fleet, which has broken up into three forma-

tions, is now pursuing movements that cannot yet be reported.

9 May 1942, Tokyo
At 3:40 A.M. local time, *Imperial Japanese Headquarters* announced this follow-up report on the results of the sea battle:

The overwhelming Japanese naval victory in the Coral Sea has struck the Allies a devastating blow. The Americans, who had already lost the bulk of their battleships at Pearl Harbor during the first days of the war, could ill afford the additional losses they have now suffered among their remaining capital ships. But worst of all was their loss of two precious aircraft carriers, a blow that has irretrievably paralyzed America's striking power.

Sunday 10 May 1942, Washington
The *US Department of the Navy* announced yesterday evening:

The most recent Japanese reports have made claims about American losses in the naval battle of the Coral Sea. US reports issued so far do not confirm the loss of any US battleships or aircraft carriers. The true toll of the damage will be announced when published reports can no longer prove advantageous to the enemy.

Wednesday 13 May 1942, Valetta
The British *Reuters News Agency* reported:

Reports state that within a 72-hour period between 9th and 11th May, 112 enemy aircraft were shot down or crippled over the island of Malta.

Grandmas Are Flying the World's Heaviest Bombers

Wednesday 20 May 1942, London
The British *Reuters News Agency* reported:

During the worst days of the British Empire—the struggle at Dunkirk—a new policy was begun to release as many men as possible for the armed services and to found a new army. A particular attempt was made to relieve the forces of the RAF, resulting in the formation of the Air Transport Auxiliary Corps. Since then, volunteers have flown new aircraft from the factories to the air force units, and taken on the far more dangerous task of flying damaged but still serviceable aircraft to the repair hangars. This work by volunteer pilots enables pilots of the bomber and fighter squadrons to remain at their posts fighting the enemy. We met several women at one of the bases. The youngest of the female pilots, who flies a giant bomber, has just celebrated her twentieth birthday, and it is amusing to note that her navigator, Mrs. Butler, became a grandmother on the same day, at the age of 44.

Saturday 30 May 1942
The *Wehrmacht High Command* announced:

Since May 25, Luftwaffe formations commanded by General Stumpff, operating in cooperation with forces of the German Navy, have been delivering annihilating strikes on the enemy shipping convoy detected by reconnaissance planes in high northern waters. By the evening of May 25, the Luftwaffe had already flown hundreds of miles to the convoy, where it sank an 8,000-ton merchant vessel and damaged 5 other vessels with bombs. On the following day it again successfully destroyed an 8,000-ton merchant vessel, and set 3 more heavily-loaded freighters on fire. German U-boats have kept the convoy under constant pursuit. It received a particularly severe blow on May 27, when despite a strong defense by the enemy's security forces, German aerial units sank 11 vessels totalling 72,000 tons and inflicted crippling blows on 2 more ships as well as one destroyer. Another 16 vessels were struck and damaged by bombs. This means that the Luftwaffe has sunk 13 of these transport convoy vessels headed for the Soviet Union—a total of 88,000 tons of shipping. Including the 8,000-ton steamship which the Wehrmacht reports was today sunk by a U-boat, enemy losses so far come to 96,000 tons. The remains of the convoy are taking evasive action into the northernmost waters that are still free of ice. We are continuing our pursuit.

The Thousand-Bomber Raid

Sunday 31 May 1942, London
The British *Air Ministry* announced:

Last night more than 1,000 RAF bombers raided industrial installations in the Ruhr district and the Rhineland. Their main target was Cologne. Prime Minister Churchill congratulated Bomber Command on the raid, and said that this operation, in which 1,000 aircraft took part, was only a sample of what now lay in store for all the cities of Germany.

31 May 1942
The *Wehrmacht High Command* announced:

Last night British bombers led a terrorist raid on

the town center of Cologne, causing great damage with high-explosive and incendiary bombs, particularly on residential zones, various public buildings, and among others, on three churches and two hospitals. The British air force suffered extremely heavy losses during this raid, which was directed exclusively against the civilian population. German night interceptors and flak artillery shot down 36 of the attacking bombers. One more bomber was brought down by the naval artillery along the coast.

1 June 1942
RAF Headquarters announced:

The following figures show the extent of the extraordinary forces deployed in the air raid on Cologne: Approximately 1,250 aircraft took part; more than 1,000 of these were bombers; and they also included long-range night fighter planes, that were here deployed for the first time. The plan called for one bomber to appear over a target every six seconds; and every other second, a bomb weighing an average of one ton exploded, so that approximately 3,000 metric tons of high-explosive and incendiary bombs exploded during the 90-minute attack. Thirteen different types of bomber took off from 60 British airfields to raid Cologne. The bombers ranged from the old Handley Page Hampden machines, to the largest and most modern RAF bombers each carrying an eight-ton bombload. About 13,000 men were deployed in the operation, of whom approximately one half were airmen and the other half ground personnel.

The decision to carry out the assault was taken by the War Cabinet, led by Churchill, at the instigation of the RAF Chief of Staff. Although the RAF lost 44 aircraft, the loss quota of barely 4% of the aircraft deployed, was comparatively low.

Air Vice-Marshal Baldwin led the raid and was accompanied by two war correspondents who report as follows: "We had the impression that Cologne had been visited by an earthquake. We could see clearly that the walls of buildings were collapsing not from direct bomb hits but from air pressure, and even more, from the ground vibrations. The chaos in Cologne was indescribable. The ground defenses gradually lost all sense of the direction of the attacks. Most of the RAF losses occurred during approach, and while flying away after releasing the bombs. Machine guns and aerial guns strafed numerous searchlight batteries and flak positions. From the 55th minute of the attack onward, we all had the impression that we were flying over an active volcano."

Bombs Fall on Cologne

The following descriptive account was published by the American *Associated Press* in May 1942:

The moon was on our right, and in the sky ahead of us was a rosy glow. "How long until we get there, Navigator?" "About ten minutes," he replied. "Good, that's all we need to know. The red glow is Cologne. Those chaps have lit themselves quite a

An RAF Short Stirling heavy bomber before a raid on Germany. The Stirling was the first 4-engined Allied bomber, but it failed as a standard bomber because its peak altitude was only 12,000 feet.

fire." The sky was full of antiaircraft projectiles, tracer fire, bursting shells and searchlight beams, so that it looked like a fireworks display at a country fair. The Germans were firing on all barrels. Viewed through the bombsight, Cologne glowed in the dark like the tip of a huge cigarette. Then our plane stood directly over the fires and the pilot ordered: "Bomb bays operational." "Bomb bays operational," came the reply. The pilot spoke again: "Damn it, hold on a minute. There's no point in wasting the stuff on buildings that are already burning. Let's look for a dark spot." Block after block of city buildings blazed up under our aircraft; smoke drifted past the wings, which stood out distinctly against the flames. In the firelight we could make out structural skeletons of white-hot steel. A tiny dark speck appeared on the west bank of the Rhine. "That must be the Elektra steel-wire plant," said the pilot. "Let's have a go at it." We had an anxious moment as we approached the target. Then the bomb-gunner pressed the button and our aircraft zoomed upward, freed of its heavy payload. Jubilant shouts came over the intercom. We had completed our mission. It was a breeze from there back to our home base. Our Short Stirling heavy bomber sent out a call and the control center informed the pilot that he was fourth in line to land; he was told the altitude at which he should circle before landing. The bus carried the cheerful crew to debriefing headquarters, along with other men who had just come back from Cologne. A slender pilot with a sunburnt face and white eyebrows said laughing: "Well, that was the only time I've been glad to be over Cologne—and it was my fifth flight. God, what a nice little fire." "A damned fine sight," others agreed. The debriefing was over, the crews took off to eat a special food allowance of ham and eggs.

Daily Watchword of the Reich Press Chief,
1 June 1942:

The Minister sees the bombing of Cologne as an effort by the British to contribute relief to the Russian forces. Churchill's telegram to the commanding air general, listing the number of bombers deployed, proves—the Minister says—that the quoted figure of 1,250 machines is not correct. All the same, we must not delude ourselves about the number, and we must tell the public clearly and distinctly how high the toll of attacking planes really was.

Secret Report by the *SS Secret Service* on internal affairs, No. 289 of Thursday 4 June 1942 (extract):

I. General comments: The intensified assaults of the British air force on German cities, expecially the terrorist assault on Cologne, have caused dismay throughout Germany; and numerous reports say that they are now the central topic of all conversation and discussion by our national comrades. Many reports—especially from areas that already have been persecuted repeatedly by enemy planes—say that some people seriously fear that the British will continue terrorist raids with the same violence, and will go on to attack other German cities, in order by this means to bring relief to the Soviets, since they lack other means of doing so.

The Battle of Midway

Friday 5 June 1942, New York
A communiqué from US *Admiral Nimitz* reported the following about the Japanese attack on the Midway Islands:

Early this morning, at 6:35 A.M., the Midway Islands were attacked by Japanese aircraft that had taken off from an aircraft carrier. A large number of the enemy planes were shot down.

5 June 1942, Washington
The *US Department of the Navy* announced:

The situation in Dutch Harbor in the North Pacific (Aleutian Islands), is now quiet. The first Japanese air raid on Wednesday was meant primarily to test the strength of our defenses. They dropped high-explosive and incendiary bombs, but as already reported, our casualties were low and material damage was slight. The few fires that developed were quickly put out. Six hours later, our lookouts sighted a second wave of Japanese aircraft, but this time no bombs were released and it seemed to have been no more than a reconnaissance flight. It has not yet been determined where the Japanese planes came from, but it is assumed that they took off from an aircraft carrier.

Saturday 6 June 1942, Honolulu
Admiral Nimitz's Headquarters announced:

For the moment the Japanese have stopped their air raids on the Midway Islands; last night the islands were fired on only by enemy submarine guns. The enemy seems to have decided to retreat while we are continuing to give battle.

Monday 8 June 1942, Washington
The *US Dept. of the Navy* announced:

Admiral Nimitz is continuing his pursuit of the

"We will wipe their cities off the map!" Hitler exclaimed on 4 September 1940 at a Nazi Party rally in the Berlin Sports Palace. He was greeted by cheers; but the German people paid the penalty for his challenge to the Allies.

Japanese naval forces, which are retreating at full steam. Those damaged enemy vessels that cannot maintain full speed, are shrouded in artificial mists and escorted by antiaircraft gunboats. Further investigation reveals that the Japanese have suffered the following losses so far: 3 aircraft carriers sunk; 1 aircraft carrier listing to one side after receiving direct torpedo hits in the bow; 1 battleship in the process of sinking; 2 battleships damaged; 2 cruisers badly damaged and 2 slightly damaged; 1 transport vessel sunk, 2 damaged.

8 June 1942, Washington
The *US Dept. of the Navy* announced:

Admiral Ring, the supreme commander of the US Navy, stated that the larger-scale sea operations underway from Hawaii to the Aleutians, are not yet concluded. It is clear, he said, that the Japanese were planning to seize the Midway Islands. However, the Admiral declined to reveal the strength of the US forces engaged in the Battle of Midway; at the same time he expressed his view that Japan has deployed the main part of its forces in the battle. Furthermore, Admiral Ring emphasized that he did not wish to use the word "defeat" yet, but that in any case the Japanese *had* retreated. Contact with the enemy has been interrupted for the time being due to the extremely bad weather. The situation at Dutch Harbor (Aleutians) is also said to be unclear due to the bad weather.

Tuesday 9 June 1942, Washington
General Arnold, the commander of the US Army Air Force, reported:

The personnel of the US Army Air Force are to be increased to one million men. General Arnold said of his recent visit to England: "It will soon become evident that I did not fly to London to discuss defensive measures. Attacks like those now being made on Cologne and Essen, are only the prelude to aerial operations that the England-based American and British air forces will soon undertake together against Germany. The Axis Powers know that the next six months will either bring them the victory, or mean their ultimate defeat."

9 June 1942, Washington

Elmer Thomas, chairman of the US Senate Budget Commission, announced that the US aircraft industry is manufacturing almost 5,000 aircraft a month.

Strategy and Tactics

January to June 1942

It was the ice-cold, clear and starry night of 4 January 1942. The soldiers of the German Fourth Army, standing south of Moscow, had been listening for hours to the hum of aircraft engines. German guards stood on duty in the biting frost inside the rear-line villages along the Urga river; all the villages were buried in deep snow. Then the guards were dismayed to see the outlines of dozens of parachutes drifting slowly to the ground. Shots rang out. A Soviet paratroop unit of 416 men under Captain I. Starshak, had just landed. Their mission was to occupy Bolshoye Fatyanovo airfield near the town of Yukhnov and secure it until the arrival of the

Soviet airborne troops. This was just one in a series of similar paratroop operations in support of the left flank of the Soviet western front led by Marshal Zhukov, which was waging a winter counter-offensive against the Germans.

On Sunday 11 January 1942, the Japanese led an attack on the Dutch East Indies. A Japanese naval formation under Rear-Admiral Hirose supported the invasion of the oil-producing center of Tarakan (Borneo). Another formation under Vice-Admiral Takahashi, landed at Manado on the northeastern tip of Celebes and was reinforced by paratroops. This was the first airborne landing operation in the Pacific. It was carried out by 28 Mitsubishi G3M medium bombers of the 21st Air Flotilla which dropped 334 naval paratroops onto the island. Their trainers had every reason to be proud of them: for German veterans of the paratroop battle for Crete had passed on their experience to the Japanese paratroops in the autumn of 1941.

The Japanese developed their own special tactics as they advanced from one island to the next. The airfields on one island almost always lay within easy reach of airfields on the next, so that Japanese aerial forces were able to destroy enemy aircraft on the ground and move up by "island-hopping." Carrier aircraft were deployed only in special cases and were kept in reserve for genuine sea battles. Actual troop landings were carried out under protective fire from naval guns, and with aircraft cooperation. Once the troops had set foot on land, airfields were built immediately to pave the way for the hop to the next island.

Britain and the USA agreed on their war plans at the Arcadia Conference in Washington that lasted from 20 December 1941 until 14 January 1942. They reached a fundamental strategic decision: "Germany first"—their primary target was to bring down Hitler's Germany. Great Britain's mission was to intensify bombing raids on Germany so as to create the "second front" demanded by Stalin. The United States pledged itself to set up its own bases in Britain as rapidly as possible, and to start participating in operations during the second half of the year.

After Hitler took over as commander of the German army on 19 December 1941, the German Luftwaffe became steadily more subordinated to the ground troops. Heavy demands were made on its forces to lend direct support on the battlefield; they were spread too thin, and while suffering high casualties they became more and more splintered.

On Sunday 18 January 1942, troops of the Soviet Thirty-Fourth Army under Gen. Bersarin, and the Soviet Eleventh Army under Gen. Morosov, encircled part of the German 2nd Army Corps under Gen. von Brockdorff-Ahlefeld, and the bulk of the German 10th Army Corps under Gen. Hansen, near Demyansk southeast of Lake Ilmen. Approximately 100,000 Germans were surrounded inside an area the size of greater Berlin. Four days later, on 22 January, the German troops garrisoning the city of Kholm were also encircled. The Germans instituted the largest-scale airlift of the war so far, to supply their troops in the pockets of Demyansk and Kholm. The encircled forces received all their supplies by air, including food and large numbers of reinforcements. Initially 100, and later up to 300 metric tons of supplies were flown into the pockets every day until 19 May 1942. Three hundred and fifty German Ju 52 transport aircraft were deployed, and made and average of 500 landings apiece.

The same day that the Germans were encircled at Demyansk, 18 January 1942, marked the launch of the greatest Soviet airborne landing operation of the war. STAVKA, the Soviet high command, entrusted the operation to the 9th Airborne Corps under Gen. A. Kazakin. Two battalions of the 201st Airborne Brigade, and the 250th Airborne Regiment, were transported in four-engined Petlyakov Pe-8 (TB-7)s to a point 24 miles south of Vyazma

near Zhelanya. The aim of the operations was to sever important communications lines to the rear of the German front, especially the Minsk-Moscow military track and the Smolensk-Vyazma railway line. After landing, the paratroop units made contact with the Soviet 1st Cavalry under Gen. Belov which had broken through the German lines, and with the Soviet partisans. On 22 January the Soviet combat group was reinforced with 2,000 men from the 8th Airborne Brigade. At first they concentrated their attacks on Vyazma; then, to the dismay of the Germans, they spent several weeks operating to the rear of the German Army Group Central under Field Marshal von Kluge. Inexplicably, the Soviet Union, which had more than one hundred thousand well-trained paratroops—the strongest paratroop force in the world—never deployed them except in these operations, and in a couple of other, insignificant missions.

On Wednesday 21 January 1942, the German Luftwaffe in North Africa carried out one of its most daring operations: a raid on Fort Lamy, which lay almost 1,500 miles to the south in the interior of French Central Africa. At 8:00 A.M. an He 111 took off with 1,500 gallons of gasoline on board. The pilot was 2nd Lt. Franz Bohnsack, and with him flew desert researcher Capt. Theo Blaich and Maj. Roberto Conte Vimercati, an Italian desert expert. A fourth crew member was a German war correspondent, 2nd Lt. Dettmann, who later reported: "Forward in the gun-pit it was boiling hot like a greenhouse. The Captain and Major Vimercati compared their navigational findings. At 12 noon we overflew the eastern edges of Lake Chad." At 2:30 P.M. the Heinkel dropped its bombs on Fort Lamy. All the center's oil supplies and 400 tons of aircraft fuel were destroyed along with 10 aircraft standing on the takeoff strip.

Second Lt. Dettmann reported: "We had already flown over 70 miles northward but our radio operator and aerial gunner could still see the mushroom cloud hanging in the sky above the explosions. The broad belt of sand dunes lay behind us now. In the west the day was coming to an end. This was the most dangerous time of day for a plane flying in unfamiliar desert regions. The sun seized on the mountains, rocks and sand dunes and transformed them from one moment to the next." They had already been flying for four hours on their return flight, when they noticed that their fuel was running out.

Second Lt. Dettmann reported: "We still had ten minutes left before darkness fell. The last one third of the sun was sinking on the western horizon with a pale yellow, wavering light. The Captain gave the order to land. We swept at low altitude over a landscape interspersed with rock chains, gentle elevations and smooth stretches of Sahara waste. Now the landing gear was fully extended." The aircraft managed to land safely in the desert. Seven days later, Colonel Becker of the German Desert Emergency Air Squadron, flying a Ju 52/3m, finally located the missing crew.

In January 1942 the RAF continued its night-time offensive sweeps, which it flew in broad, loosely-knit formations at spaced intervals. It was no longer possible for the British bombers to evade the German defensive radar-guided interceptor barrier along the Kammhuber Line. They also failed in attempts to fly under the radar barrier at top speed.

Meanwhile the Japanese were single-mindedly and tirelessly pursuing their advance. Tuesday 27 January 1942 was the last day when British bombers

The Battle of Midway: A Japanese bomber has scored a direct hit on the US carrier *Yorktown,* which was sunk by a Japanese submarine a short time later. The carrier was the greatest loss the USA suffered during this crucial sea battle.

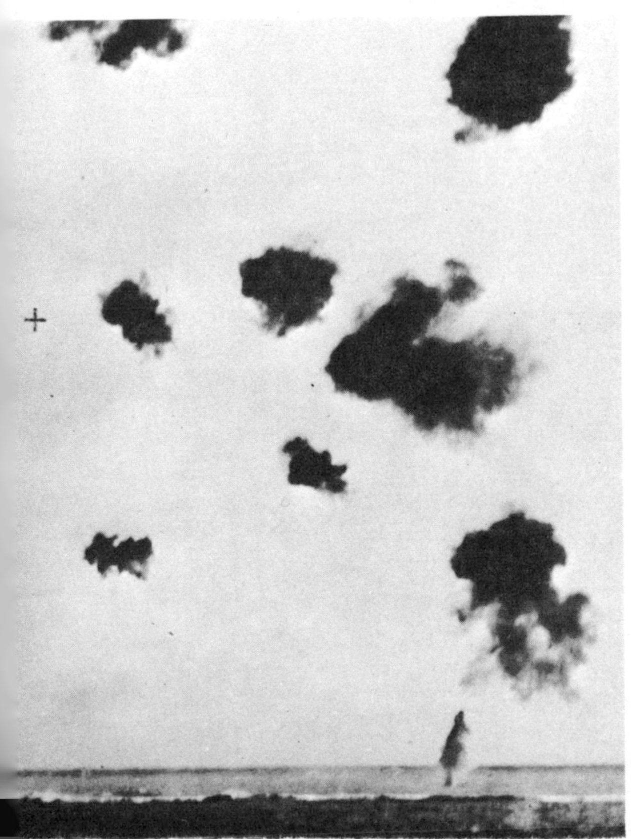

mand, sent to keep the vessels under surveillance, had to fly back to England to repair its defective radar, as did another plane patrolling farther to the east.

Thus, at 10:45 P.M. on 11 February, German Vice-Admiral Ciliax succeeded in getting his heavy vessels out of the port unseen. They were given a protective escort of 6 destroyers, 14 torpedo boats, 3 speed-boat flotillas, 43 mine detectors and sweepers, 21 antisubmarine boats, and 37 other auxiliary vessels. Air cover was provided by 176 fighter planes and fighter-destroyers of the 2nd and 26th Fighter Wings, later reinforced by the 1st Fighter Wing under Fighter-Plane General Adolf Galland. A

Above left: January 1942. Units of the Soviet 9th Airborne under Gen. A. Kazakin, shortly before they took off on the largest Soviet airborne operation of the war.

Below: Spring 1942, the Eastern Front. Around 100,000 German soldiers encircled by the Soviets near Demyansk, were supplied by air for almost 5 months. The success of this supply operation led the Germans into some tragic wrong decisions when they tried to fly in supplies to their troops in the pocket of Stalingrad.

Above right: A Douglas DC-3 Dakota transport plane is landing troops of the Soviet 9th Airborne behind the German front lines. Sometimes the men were dropped into deep snow by slow-flying aircraft flying just above the ground.

and reconnaissance planes flew missions over Malaya. By sunset they had transferred all their aircraft to Sumatra.

After some time raiding the Atlantic, the German battleships *Scharnhorst* and *Gneisenau,* and the heavy cruiser *Prinz Eugen,* were blockaded for almost a year in the French harbor of Brest, where they made a favorite target for RAF bombers. They were attacked and damaged there over 300 times.

Hitler was convinced that the Allies were about to invade Norway, so the Luftwaffe and the German Navy had to protect the Norwegian coast against possible Allied attack. The *Scharnhorst, Gneisenau* and *Prinz Eugen* were to be transferred north for this purpose. "If it should prove impossible for them to make a surprise breakout through the English Channel," Hitler told Admiral Raeder, "the most practical thing would be to dismantle the vessels and use their guns and crews to reinforce our defenses in Norway." German naval leaders, faced with this choice – to risk complete destruction of the precious ships by leaving them in Brest, or to risk trying to get them out past the blockade – decided to try a breakout through the Channel.

On Thursday 11 February 1942, the battleships *Scharnhorst* and *Gneisenau,* the heavy cruiser *Prinz Eugen,* and several destroyers and motor torpedo boats, put out to sea from Brest. This operation, codenamed "Cerberus," was the most daring ploy by the German navy in World War II. Luck favored the Germans. A French agent who was supposed to be keeping the naval formation under surveillance, was not on the job. The British submarine *Sea Lion* (under Lt. Colvin), which was lying in ambush by the whistle buoy at the harbor exit, had to submerge to escape a misguided attack by British bombers. A Hudson reconnaissance plane of Coastal Com-

minimum of 16 German aircraft circled non-stop over the battleships.

The German naval formation in the English Channel went undetected by the dense chain of British coastal radar stations. Not until 10:35 A.M. on 12 February 1942 were the German vessels sighted by a Spitfire pilot, Sergeant Beaumont, when they were already passing Le Touquet. Almost one hour later the staff of RAF No. 11 Group were still hesitating to pass on the news to Air Vice-Marshall Leigh-Mallory because the Vice-Marshal was just then involved in a troop review. Not until 1:16 P.M. did the English coastal batteries open fire, and Admiral Sir Bertram Ramsey ordered out motor torpedo boats, torpedo bombers and destroyers to stop the German combat group; but without success. Fairey Swordfish Squadron No. 285 under Lt. Commander E. Esmonde, attacked the German vessels at the latitude of Gravelines (France); all 6 of the British torpedo bombers were shot down. The German naval formation headed at full speed into the North Sea. More than 240 British Bomber Command aircraft took up pursuit, but in the dismal weather only 40 of them located their target.

The *Scharnhorst* ran into its first mine at the mouth of the Schelde river, and the following night both the battleships hit magnetic mines near the Dutch island of Terschelling. The mines had been laid down previously by the antiquated Hampden bombers of Nos. 49 and 455 Squadrons. This was the only success the British scored in their hunt for the Ghost Armada, which reached its German target ports despite their efforts. The British lost 42 aircraft in the operation.

But the success of Operation Cerberus was not due to lucky accidents alone. The British were still unaware of the main cause for the German victory: the largest radar jamming operation in history so far.

One dozen German jamming stations between Cherbourg and Ostend, abruptly blanketed the British coastal radar stations at 10:00 A.M., when the German vessels were between Fécamp and Dieppe.

The furious British Prime Minister later convened a special commission to punish the culprits supposed responsible for the British fiasco; but the true cause was not discovered. As Churchill wrote later in his memoirs, it was only after the war that the British learned the reason for the disaster: a carefully-prepared plan by General Martini, the chief of German Luftwaffe communications. British personnel (Churchill wrote) had reported nothing alarming and no one suspected that anything unusual was afoot, but on February 12, German jamming measures suceeded in completely blacking out British radar observation of sea routes.

The Channel escape was celebrated with great pomp by National Socialist propagandists. But this acclaim was deceptive, for although the German naval squadron did indeed chalk up a tactical success, Operation Cerberus actually amounted to a strategic retreat that marked an end to German naval operations in the Atlantic Ocean.

A series of significant events in February 1942, made this month the real turning point in the air

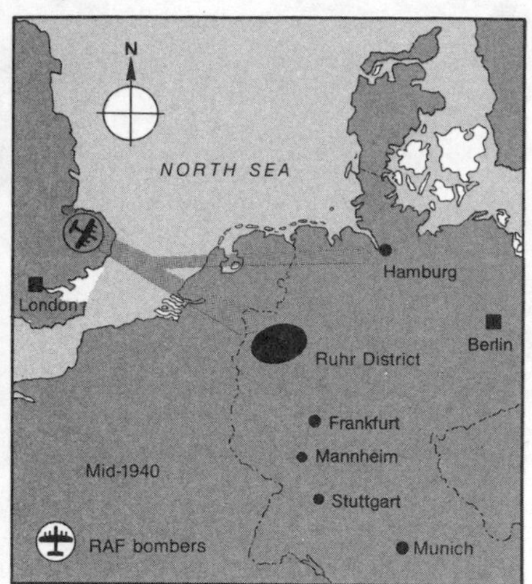

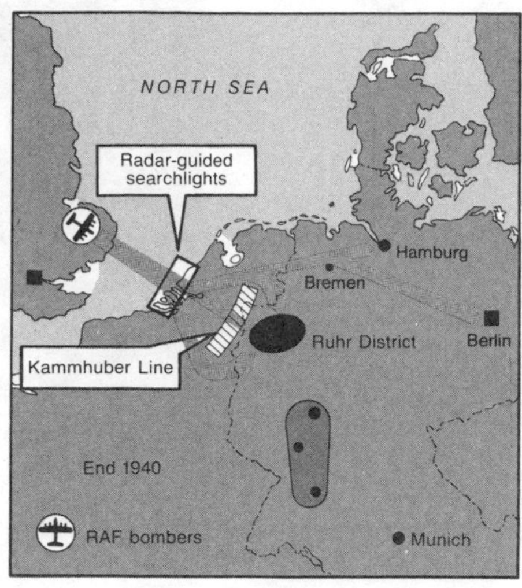

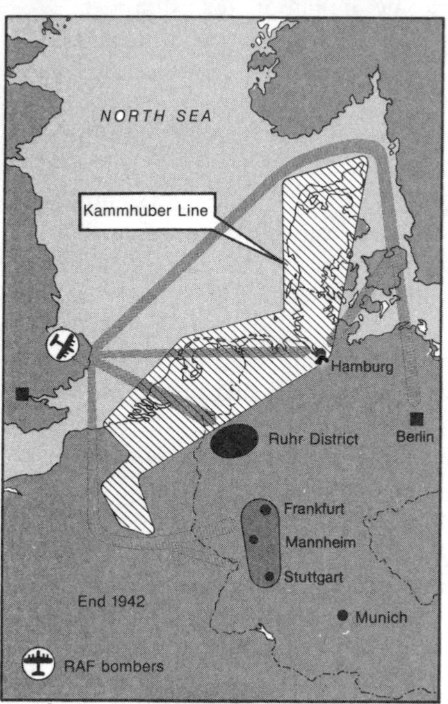

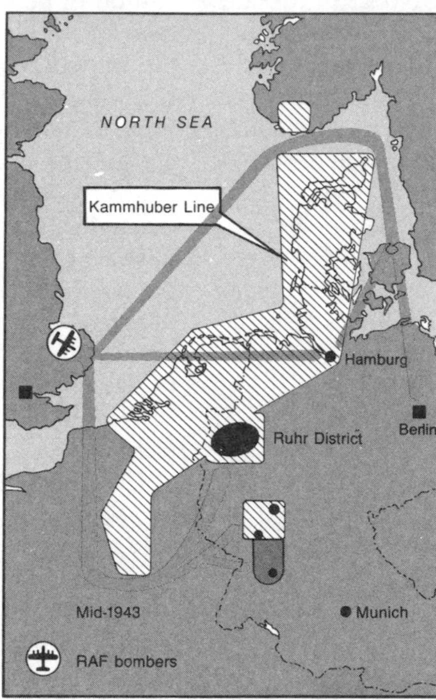

Left: The 4 diagrams show the progressive expansion of the German Kammhuber Line until 24 June 1943, when its radar stations were made ineffective by the British "Window" jamming technique using tin-foil strips.

Right: National Socialist propaganda described it as a great victory when the German battleships *Scharnhorst* and *Gneisenau*, and the heavy cruiser *Prinz Eugen*, made a daring escape from Brest harbor through the English Channel.

Below: Diagram of a Kammhuber Line radar station, mid-1942.

war against Germany. The first fateful decision came on Saturday 14 February, when Churchill and the Air Ministry issued a new order to Bomber Command that proved critical for the course of the air war: From now on, the main aim of British operations was to weaken the morale of the enemy's civilian population and especially of their industrial workers.

That same day, units of the Japanese 38th Division landed on Sumatra north of Palembang, under cover from carrier-based aircraft and of a strong cruiser formation under Vice-Admiral Ozawa. Japanese paratroops landed at the same time.

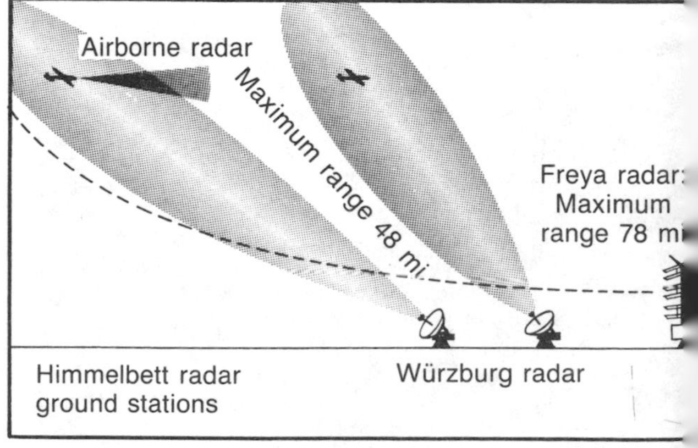

This airborne operation had no parallel in the history of aerial warfare. Never before had so many aircraft violated international law by bearing false national emblems. At 6:00 P.M., approximately 70 aircraft of the American Lockheed 14 WG-3 design which had been built under license before the war by the Tachikawa and Kawasaki firms for the Japanese army, and given the name Ro-Shiki, dropped some 700 paratroops on the island. The aircraft had been painted olive green to look like RAF planes; they carried British national emblems and were almost indistinguishable from British Hudson bombers.

The aim of the operation was to seize the Palembang airfields, and above all the two large refinery plants at Pladyu and Sungai 4 miles east of the city at the mouth of the Komering river, so as to prevent British and Dutch demolition squads from destroying this exceptionally important industrial center before it fell into Japanese hands: for the Allies were just about to retreat from Sumatra.

Sergeant J. Pitter was a member of the demolition squad at Palembang: "Japanese aircraft bombed the airfield from a very high altitude. After they vanished we were free to go on with our preparations to blow up the most important Shell refinery installations in Sungai Gerong. It was about 6:00 P.M. when a large number of planes approached Palembang from the north. We went on with our duties because the lookout reported that the planes were two formations of British Hudson bombers, which we hoped had been sent to support us against the Japanese invasion. There were at least 70 aircraft, some of which flew toward the city while the others headed toward our refineries. We stood next to the massive oil tanks and went on waving to them as they flew along no more than 600 feet or so above us. Suddenly some long dark objects dropped out of the Hudsons, and in a second began to swell up. Only then did we recognize that these were soldiers hanging from varicolored parachutes, floating down toward the refineries. Our antiaircraft guns began to fire like mad. The Japanese had played us a shameful trick."

The assault on Palembang airfield proved successful; but the Japanese gained less than they hoped from their crafty violation of international law. Approximately 16 of the simulated RAF Hudsons—many still full of paratroops—were shot down by the flak artillery posted near the refineries, and the paratroops who landed in and around the installations were wiped out, leaving the Allied demolition units free to finish their mission. When Japanese

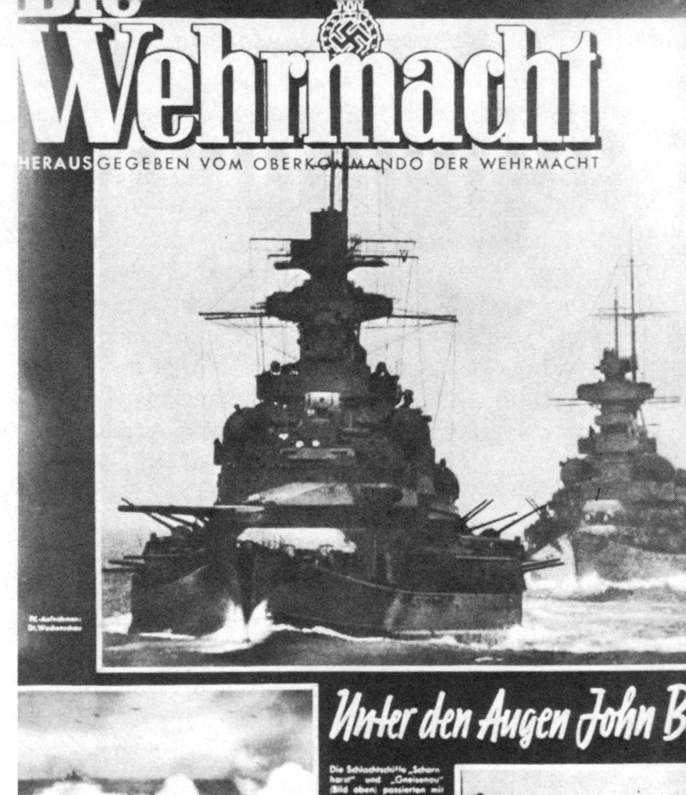
Wehrmacht
HERAUSGEGEBEN VOM OBERKOMMANDO DER WEHRMACHT
Unter den Augen John B

naval forces landed their troops next day, the refineries had turned into a tangled mile-long heap of sheet metal and piping ravaged by fire and explosions.

One week after this operation the Japanese again deployed paratroops, and this time too they used a bluff. On Saturday 21 February 1942, some 25 Douglas DC-3 aircraft built under Japanese license but bearing US national insignia, appeared over the city of Kupang on the Portuguese-owned Pacific island of Timor and dropped 250 troops from an altitude of only 300 feet. This was the first airborne operation carried out by Douglas DC-3s, which later were to become famous—when flown by the other side.

A further escalation of the air war in Europe resulted from the appointment of Sir Arthur Harris as the commander in chief of British Bomber Command on February 22.

Sir Arthur Harris, born in England in 1892, went to Rhodesia as a young man and fought in German East Africa in 1914 before returning to England where he joined the Royal Flying Corps, the forerunner of the RAF. In the thirties Harris defended the Empire, relentlessly leading his bombers in bloody police actions against rebel tribes in Iraq, India and elsewhere. For him, a merciless bombing war against Germany, and indeed all of Europe, also represented a kind of punitive action. He was considered the most committed and most consistent advocate of the Douhet theory. Harris took over Bomber Command just at the time when improved models of aircraft and navigational aids were ready for deployment, so this devotee of the Douhet theory set out to prove that well-equipped strategic bombers could win the war. Immediately upon taking over his post Harris stated that the only international convention that he and his command would feel obliged to honor, was an agreement going back to the Franco-Prussian War of 1870–1871 that prohibited the release of explosive devices from gas-filled airships.

On that same Sunday, another event occurred that was to have major repercussions for the air war over Germany. US Brigadier General Ira C. Eaker reported formation of the first US Army Bomber Command in Europe. The general and six of his aides had arrived at London's Hendon airfield two days before. Their headquarters were set up in an exclusive girls' boarding school in High Wycombe four miles from RAF headquarters, and received the codename Pine Tree. Eaker and his staff at once started their preparations for deployment of the American bomber formations based in the British Isles.

The last in the series of crucial events that took place in February 1942 was Operation Biting, a British airborne operation against a German radar station in France on the Channel coast. At the end of 1941, the percentage of British aircraft being shot down in bombing raids over Europe had increased alarmingly, and Bomber Command worked feverishly to discover the reason for their remarkably high casualties. This was a daunting task, given that almost all the shoot-downs took place over enemy territory. The men in London were convinced that new aircraft radiolocation techniques in use along the Kammhuber Line, were contributing greatly to the British losses; and they left nothing undone to plumb the secret so that they could institute countermeasures.

British radar specialists listened in on German radar emissions, and British air crews were thoroughly interrogated about their experiences after returning from bombing sorties. Reconnaissance planes took aerial photographs of German radar stations, and the French and Belgian resistance movements were asked to supply detailed descriptions of these installations. Statements by shot-down German airmen confirmed that the Germans' new "Würzburg" radar was proving highly effective in the air defense against British night raids. Dr. R. V. Jones, a radar expert and scientific adviser to the British War Office, was asked to discover the secret of the German radar as fast as possible. Then, at the end of November 1941, a high-altitude aerial photograph of a Freya-radar station near the village of Bruneval on the rocky coast 12 miles northwest of Le Havre, was investigated and found to show certain peculiar features that differed from those of previous photos. So Dr. Jones asked Squadron Leader Tony Hill, a pilot whom he knew to be particularly courageous and who belonged to Sidney Cotton's photo reconnaissance unit, to take low-level photographs of the radar station. The aerial photos brought back by Hill, revealed a new device that from the air resembled a parabolic heater. It seemed to be the same device described by interrogated German pilots.

Close observation of the Bruneval area convinced the British that it would be easy to make a surprise raid on the radar station that contained the Würzburg device. The French resistance supplied full data about German security measures, diagrams of the villa where the radar station personnel were quartered, and even amateur film of the surrounding ground. Now preparations for the raid began in London.

A 24-year-old paratroop major, I. D. Frost, was assigned to carry out the mission: "There was no way to attack the place from the sea, so the plan was for us to land on the far side of the station with seven radar experts and then retreat towards it, photograph the radar set and dismantle its most important parts, and finally fight our way down to

the beach where the navy would take us back to England. Our little combat force was to consist of 119 men of all ranks. Professor Jones had even ordered us to bring back German prisoners, including at least one radio operator."

On the evening of February 27, 12 Whitley bombers took off from Thruxton airfield. Each contained 10 soldiers who crouched inside the planes strapped in their parachutes, and began to blacken their faces with camouflage paint. Major Frost was the first to jump. Not a shot was fired; the British surrounded the radar station and stormed the solitary villa.

The whole operation went off like clockwork, due to painstaking preliminary exercises using a realistic life-size model. Frost and his men also had luck on their side. The Germans tried to blow up the Würzburg set but failed because explosives and fuses had been stored separately as a safety measure, and there was no time to combine them. Moreover, the German security force just happened to be on night maneuvers and were armed mostly with blank cartridges. Before giving battle they had to reload with live ammunition.

Meanwhile the British specialists had photographed the Würzburg installation and were dismantling the radar set. In the excitement they sawed off various pieces, and not until they reached England did they realize that the radar set was detachable with a couple of simple hand maneuvers. The British unit fought their way through to the beach, and after some anxious minutes the landing boats arrived to pick them up. They left behind one dead paratrooper and 7 other men who were not able to reach the beach in time.

Above: British Air Chief Marshal Sir Arthur Harris, the new chief of RAF Bomber Command.

Below: 14 February 1942, Palembang (Sumatra): Japanese paratroops jumped out of American-designed transport aircraft that had been camouflaged to look like RAF planes.

The most important prizes seized in the operation were the dipole and frequency-setting parts of the Würzburg set, and several German prisoners including the radio operator "ordered" by Dr. Jones. Now Jones was able to determine the wave-length on which the device operated. What is more, he made a significant discovery: Once the set had been put out of commission by jamming its frequency, it could not be switched to another frequency. The British knew as much about jamming techniques as the Germans. Simple tin foil strips could be dropped that would reflect spurious electromagnetic impulses onto watching radar screens, and their jamming effect was most effective when the strips were cut to half the wave-length of the radar device they were meant to delude. Both British and Germans recognized the effectiveness of the tin foil strips almost simultaneously; the British called their device "Window," the Germans called theirs *Düppel* (radar chaff). Both kept their knowledge strictly secret for

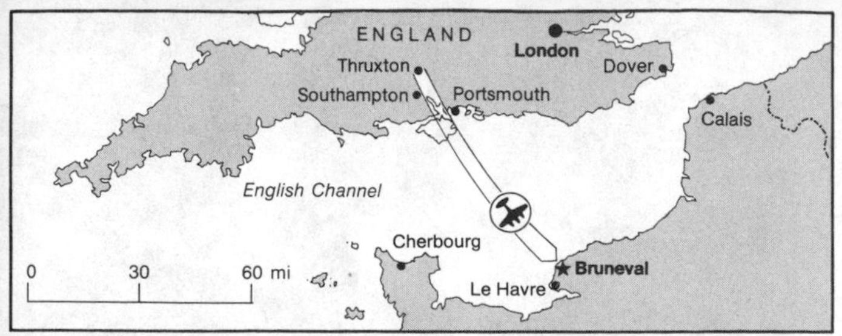

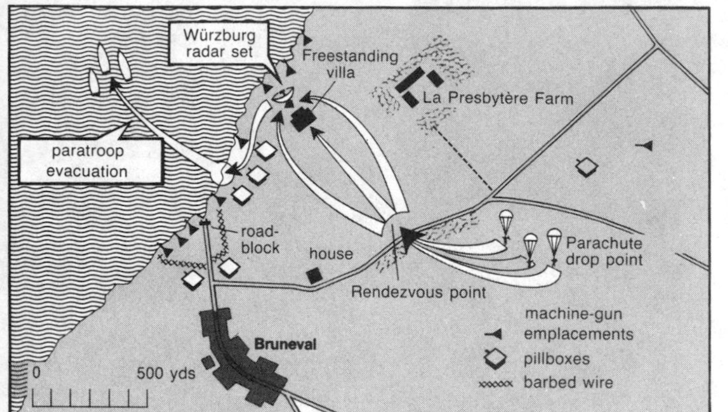

Above: The German Würzburg radar station in Bruneval here shown in a reconnaissance photo made by Spitfire pilot Tony Hill. "One of the classic photos of the air war," was the judgment of Dr. R. V. Jones.

Above left: 27th–28th February 1942, Bruneval, France: Two diagrams of British Operation Biting.

Right: Bruneval on the night of 28 February 1942: A flash photo of the Würzburg radar set captured in Operation Biting.

some time, in their fear that the enemy might use the information.

The British paratroop operation that brought a Würzburg radar set to England, had a significant influence on the further course of the air war. At the same time, it was the most successful and most skillfully conducted British airborne operation of the war.

Operation Biting had one additional effect. The Germans, fearing further attacks on their radar stations, enclosed all their installations in German-occupied Europe inside powerful and conspicuous fences, so that they became immediately recognizable on aerial photographs.

Ironically, not German but French workers were first to feel the sting of Sir Arthur Harris's Bomber Command. On the night of 3rd–4th March 1942, 223 British aircraft dropped 462 metric tons of bombs on the Renault works, an important munitions plant, in Billancourt near Paris. The bombs destroyed two thirds of the plant and interrupted production for months. The British lost one plane. This, the first large-scale operation by Bomber Command under Harris's régime, was, surprisingly, not an area bombing raid but a precision raid. Nevertheless, not only much of the factory was destroyed but also the workers' districts surrounding it; 251 French people were killed.

By early March 1942, three months after the raid on Pearl Harbor, the Japanese had already taken Malaya and all the neighboring islands to the south. They were a good two months ahead of their schedule and had suffered far lower casualties than they had anticipated. The occupation of Burma too went off without a major hitch. In March Japanese troops advanced northward from Rangoon while a strong Japanese naval formation neutralized resistance in the Indian Ocean. The outnumbered and exhausted defenders were driven out of Burma and retreated to India and China.

On the night of 8th–9th March 1942, during a 350-bomber raid on Essen, the RAF made its first large-scale use of the new "Gee" radar navigational aids; one quarter of the bombers were equipped with the device. This raid was also the first in which the British used target illumination tactics and blind bombing devices.

The new Gee device proved a valuable and reliable aid to Bomber Command. Three ground transmitters located about 96 miles apart on British soil, would create a grid of radio beams that extended over the Continent and had a range of almost 400 miles. Receivers on board the British bombers could

then calculate the impulse frequencies coming from the three transmitters, which made it possible to fix the locations of nearby aircraft precisely up to a distance of 6 miles. It was not necessary for a bomber to betray its position by sending out its own radio transmissions. Of course, at this time the Gee system extended only as far as the Ruhr district, and besides being short-range it was still susceptible to jamming. But it brought the bombers so close to their target that the crews could easily make it out by moonlight.

At the end of March 1942 the new head of Bomber Command, Air Marshal Harris, changed his offensive tactics. Instead of deploying several waves of aircraft on each mission, as he had been doing, he despatched strong single formations to carry out area bombing raids. In these raids, large numbers of bombers made concentrated attacks on an area target within the shortest possible time span. This presupposed the ability for several hundred machines to take off and land at the same time, which raised a quantity of logistical problems. The first planned target of British area bombing was Lübeck. The city was easy to locate and approach from the North Sea, and the city center with its predominantly light wooden construction and timbered roofs, was ideal for the purpose. Harris's planning model was the German grand assault on Coventry on 14th–15th November 1940, because of its successful wide-scale use of high-explosive and incendiary bombs. On the clear starlit night of 28th–29th March, the RAF bombed Lübeck. During this first massed raid, 234 aircraft including Wellington, Stirling and, for the first time, Lancaster bombers, released 304 metric tons of incendiary and high-explosive bombs, including liquid incendiaries which were tested here for the first time. Lübeck Old Town burned for 32 hours and was destroyed almost without a trace. Twelve British aircraft were lost. The most important piece of information derived from this raid, was that incendiary bombs caused almost six times as much destruction as high-explosive bombs. The attack on Lübeck marked a turning point in the air war: From now on it would be a war of fire.

Great Britain's leading politicians decided that it would be inappropriate to publicize information about the British air attacks. Air Minister Sinclair said that moral condemnation of the offensive would weaken the morale of the bomber crews.

One of the men in Great Britain responsible for recommending the bombing raids on German cities was Professor Frederick A. Lindemann. Born in Baden-Baden in 1886, he was the son of building contractor Samuel Lindemann. His scientific work in Berlin brought him a chair in physics at Oxford in 1919. In 1921 he met Winston Churchill and became his intimate friend. Churchill made Lindemann his special scientific adviser and later, head of the statistical department with cabinet rank. In 1942 King George VI elevated him to the peerage and he became Lord Cherwell. Hardly a secret committee or advisory staff existed of which Lord Cherwell was not a member, working behind the scenes of politics and science. He was very likely the most successful court politician of our times, and had more direct access to power than any other scientist in history.

Mostly on Lord Cherwell's advice, and guided by his questionable calculations, Churchill initiated an all-out bombing war on German cities. In a note sent to Churchill on 30 March 1942, Lord Cherwell

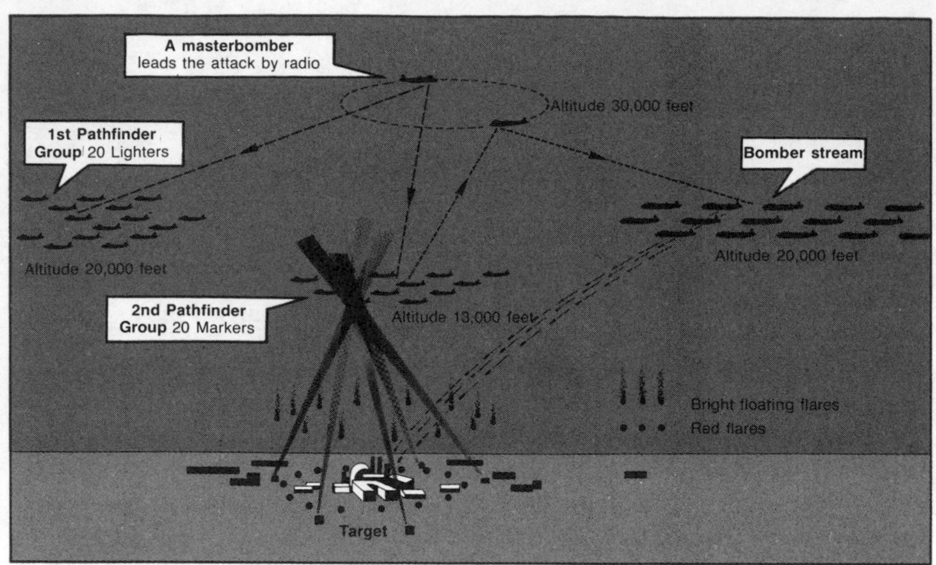

1942: Night raiding tactics of the RAF using Gee radar devices.

offered an analysis showing how every ton of bombs dropped on Germany would make approximately 100–200 people homeless. It had been proved, he said, that the destruction of a person's home had a more shattering effect on his morale than the death of friends and relatives, and the spirit of the German people could be broken by this means. By concentrating all resources on the manufacture and deployment of bombers – the memorandum went on – it would be possible, by the middle of 1943, to destroy 50% of all the homes in the larger cities of Germany, as well as inflicting inevitable damage on factories, traffic lines etc. through the resultant fires; and the effects would be intensified by the collapse of public services. Nevertheless, Lord Cherwell counselled, bombs should be concentrated on German workers' residential districts because, he said, the houses of the better-off classes were too widely scattered and many more bombs would be required to destroy them.

From 2nd to 8th April 1942, the German 2nd Air Corps under General Loerzer, aided by Italian bombers, kept up continuous violent air raids on Malta. The aim of the raids was to soften up the island fortress for an assault. Two destroyers and 4 submarines were sunk in the harbor, and the remaining vessels of the British 10th Submarine Flotilla had to evacuate from Malta in mid-April. British pressure on German convoys was reduced at once, and the more violent the attacks on Malta became, the more German reinforcements got through to Rommel. The ideal moment to take Malta by an air and sea landing, was immediately after the heavy German aerial bombardment; but the Germans missed their chance. Rommel was planning an offensive from the El Gazala front near Tobruk, to the Nile, and demanded the support of all the available German aerial forces in the Mediterranean, [including those earmarked for the conquest of Malta]. In the end he failed to reach his target, the Suez Canal; and his decision had saved Malta from German capture. Once again his supply ships suffered mounting losses that could only end in his defeat.

The RAF's bombing raids on Lübeck and, shortly thereafter, on Rostock, destroyed priceless architectural monuments; so on Tuesday 14 April 1942, Hitler ordered retaliatory terrorist raids on historic cities in England – Bath, Canterbury and Exeter – the so-called Baedeker Raids, [named after the famous tourist guidebooks].

In the spring of 1942 the British 44th Lancaster Bomber Squadron began to make long-range daylight raids and precision raids on important war-industrial targets. One April 17, 12 aircraft tried to bomb the MAN machine manufacturing works in Augsburg, which were producing submarine engines. Seven of the aircraft were lost and the others missed their target.

In April 1942 the Japanese were still moving forward on all fronts, and the last Allied island fortress, Corregidor in the Philippines, was about to fall. Lt. Col. J. H. Doolittle of the United States Army Air Force, decided to bomb Tokyo. This epic raid was carried out by 16 B-25 Mitchell bombers that took off from the US aircraft carrier *Hornet* about 800 miles from Tokyo, and were ordered to fly on to China after the operation because their range would not allow their return to base.

The wings of the Mitchell bombers could not be folded up against the airframe, so all the aircraft had to be stowed on the carrier deck, where they were exposed to bad weather. A Japanese patrol boat sighted the USS *Hornet* on the morning of 18

April 1942, so despite the fact that Tokyo was still almost 800 miles away, and despite the dangerous pitching and tossing of the carrier, Doolittle decided that his planes should take off ahead of schedule.

The pilots on this raid displayed exceptional flying skill. No pilot had ever before taken off from an aircraft carrier flying a B-25, because normally the heavily-loaded B-25s were unable to reach take-off speed along the short deck runway. But the Americans were lucky: all the bombers took off, whereupon the *Hornet* and its companion carrier the *Enterprise* raced at full speed for Hawaii. Thirteen Mitchells dropped their bombs on Tokyo; the other 3 attacked Osaka, Nagoya and Kobe. The aircraft dropped a total of 16 tons of bombs. A large-scale air-raid exercise was just then ending in Japan, and the Japanese mistook the Doolittle formation for stragglers from among the feigned attackers. This enabled the Americans to continue their flight without being recognized after dropping their bombs. But they ran into a bad weather front over China, and 80 crew members had to make parachute landings despite the poor ground visibility. Five died in the attempt, and 8 fell into the hands of the Japanese, who sentenced them to death as war criminals; 3 of these were beheaded while one died in a POW camp.

The 16 tons of fragmentation bombs that fell on Tokyo and the 3 other cities, had little military effect; their value was chiefly psychological. But rarely have so few bombs produced such a dramatic result. The dismayed Japanese military, who had been convinced of the inviolability of Japanese air space, withdrew fighter plane forces from all fronts to provide air defense for their homeland, and the hard-pressed US troops breathed a sigh of relief. Japanese Field Marshal Hajime Sugiyama opened a grand two-army offensive in China which, after weeks of dogged fighting, led to seizure of all the Chinese airfields where American bombers might have landed. But the most far-reaching effect of the Doolittle Raid, was that the Japanese fixed a firm date for the Midway operation which Admiral Yamamoto had been demanding for weeks now. The Japanese thought that by seizing the US-held Midway Islands, they could prevent the repetition of any attacks on the Japanese motherland [and force the US Pacific fleet into a showdown battle that would result in its destruction].

In the USA, the Doolittle Raid gave encouragement and hope to a people who had heard nothing but bad news ever since Pearl Harbor.

On Wednesday 29 April 1942, Japanese forces occupied Lashio (Burma), thus finally severing the Burma Road. Following this, the Allies opened their first great air bridge from Assam to Kunming (China) so that they could supply Chiang Kai-Shek's troops as well as their own bases. Douglas DC-3 Dakotas flew supplies and troops along this 530-mile-long "hump route" straight across the Himalayas, day and night for 3 years.

Luftwaffe losses on the Eastern Front increased rapidly during the winter war in the Soviet Union. From the start of Operation Barbarossa to mid-May 1942, the German Luftwaffe lost almost 3,000 air-

Lord Cherwell (Frederick A. Lindemann). His advice influenced Churchill to initiate an all-out bombing war against German cities.

craft including 1,026 bombers and 762 fighters; around 2,000 aircraft were badly damaged.

A significant change occurred in the Red Air Force in May 1942, when a new chief of aerial administration came in to replace Shigarev. He was the young, energetic General A. A. Novikov, a protegé of Marshal Timoshenko. It was largely due to Novikov that the Soviet air force was preserved from complete destruction under the German onslaught. General Novikov set about building a new strategy and tactics for his forces, and arranged for supplies of modern aircraft to be transported in smoothly.

In May there were 3,164 Soviet aircraft on the Soviet Western Front, of which 2,115 were of modern design. Approximately 3,000 Soviet aircraft took part in the battles near Kharkov in mid-May 1942, against 1,500 German planes.

By mid-April 1942 the Americans had already received intelligence that the Japanese were planning a landing operation in the near future. They had broken the new Japanese naval code weeks earlier, and intercepted radio messages revealing Japanese intentions to attack the chief Allied base of Port Moresby, New Guinea; so Admiral Nimitz ordered all available US naval forces to the southwest Pacific, where they formed into Task Force 17 under Rear-Admiral Fletcher. They included the aircraft carriers *Yorktown* and *Lexington* from Pearl Harbor, which together carried 141 aircraft – 42 fighters and 99 bombers – escorted by two cruiser groups. The other two US aircraft carriers, the *Enterprise* and the *Hornet,* were still heading back to base after the Doolittle Raid. They too were summoned to the Coral Sea, but they arrived too late for the battle.

On the morning of 7 May 1942, Japanese reconnaissance aircraft mistakenly reported having sighted a US aircraft carrier and a cruiser. This prompted Vice-Admiral Takagi to order a grand assault on the vessels and they were both sunk; but they turned out to be merely an oiler and an accompanying destroyer so that the assault hardly paid.

That evening Takagi led a second, smaller raid that was to have devastating consequences for the Japanese: 21 of the 27 attacking Japanese aircraft were lost. Moreover, an American reconnaissance plane mistakenly reported having sighted the main Japanese forces, and as a result, US carrier-based aircraft attacked escort vessels of the Japanese formation that was due to attack Port Moresby. The Japanese light aircraft carrier *Shoho* received a square hit and sank in ten minutes, becoming the first Japanese carrier to be sunk by US aircraft. The presence of American vessels in Australian waters misled the Japanese admiral into changing his plans. He ordered the invasion fleet destined for Port Moresby, to change course so that it could first destroy the Allied fleet.

Next morning the reconnaissance fliers on both sides discovered each other's aircraft carrier formations. Their units were of approximately equal strength: the Japanese had 121 aircraft, 4 heavy cruisers and 6 destroyers; the Americans had 122 aircraft, 5 heavy cruisers and 7 destroyers. The Japanese had the advantage of more combat experience and better torpedoes, whereas the US had a larger proportion of bombers. But the Japanese were girdled by fog that afforded them cover, while the Americans had to fight under a clear sky. Due to the fog, US bombers failed to sight the small Japanese carrier *Zuikaku,* but the carrier *Shokaku* was hit by 3 bombs and forced to veer off. The *Lexington* was hit by two torpedoes and several bombs that set off interior explosions; it was given up for lost and the Americans themselves finished it off with several torpedoes. The small, more maneuverable carrier *Yorktown* escaped with only one bomb hit.

On the afternoon of 8 May 1942, Admiral Nimitz withdrew his carrier formation from the Coral Sea because the threat to Port Moresby had been averted for the time being. The Japanese, convinced that the carrier *Yorktown* had been sunk, also veered off. The large Japanese aircraft carrier *Shokaku* was seriously damaged and put out of service for two months. The carrier *Zuikaku* had lost so many of its aircraft that it too was temporarily out of action.

Tactically, the Battle of the Coral Sea was a Japanese victory because American casualties were much higher than those of the enemy. The sinking of the large aircraft carrier *Lexington* dealt a hard blow to the US Navy. But the US had won a strategic victory, because it had thwarted Admiral Yamamoto's plan to seize Port Moresby. This was the first time that a Japanese invasion plan had been frustrated, and it happened just two days after the surrender of Corregidor, so that it had a significant morale value.

The Battle of the Coral Sea was the first aircraft-carrier battle in history in which the enemy fleets fought without ever coming into sight of each other, and the first battle to be decided exclusively by carrier-based aircraft.

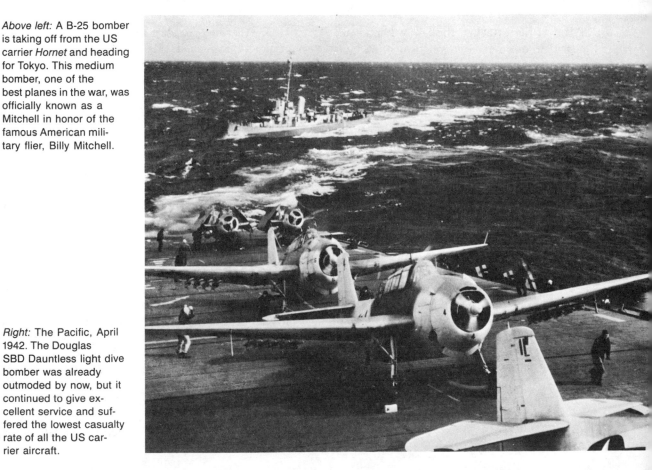

Above left: A B-25 bomber is taking off from the US carrier *Hornet* and heading for Tokyo. This medium bomber, one of the best planes in the war, was officially known as a Mitchell in honor of the famous American military flier, Billy Mitchell.

Right: The Pacific, April 1942. The Douglas SBD Dauntless light dive bomber was already outmoded by now, but it continued to give excellent service and suffered the lowest casualty rate of all the US carrier aircraft.

Left: A burning Japanese Nakajima B5N torpedo bomber is still trying to hurl itself onto a US carrier. It exploded an instant after this photo was made.

Below right: Allied freighter after a German bombing attack.

After Hitler attacked the Soviet Union in 1941, the British, and later the Americans too, began to supply war material to Stalin, shipping it via the North Sea into the harbors of Arkhangelsk and Murmansk. At first Churchill hoped to send one convoy every 10 days, but at no time did that prove feasible. The German Luftwaffe stationed in Norway posed an enormous threat, because the Arctic convoys transporting supplies to the Soviet Union were exposed to German air attack along two thirds of their route, especially in the summer when the pack-ice boundary lay farthest to the south. The operational radius of Allied aircraft that could supply air cover to the convoys, extended only as far as Jan Mayen [a volcanic island in the Arctic Ocean], which left a large unprotected gap from the island northward to Murmansk. But the British Navy had to bow to political demands; so the convoys, rather than halting at their point of maximum risk, were pressed on at top speed. The case of Convoy PQ 16—with its 35 merchant vessels the largest of all convoys so far—clearly shows the relentlessness of their drive.

On Thursday 21 May 1942, a German agent in Reykjavik, Iceland reported that Convoy PQ 16 was putting out to sea. Four days later it was sighted by German aerial reconnaissance.

On Tuesday 26 May 1942, Operation Theseus began in North Africa, an offensive by General Rommel's German-Italian armored army from the El Gazala front toward Tobruk. The German 2nd Air Fleet under Field Marshal Kesselring assembled 542 aircraft; the British Desert Air Force had 604.

On Wednesday 27 May 1942, 101 Junkers Ju 88s of the German 30th Bomber Wing, and 7 Heinkel He 111s of 1st Group, 26th Bomber Wing, attacked Allied Convoy PQ 16 southeast of Bear Island and by nightfall had sunk 7 freighters equalling 36,987 tons, and damaged several other vessels. For almost 5 days the convoy security forces had to fight almost uninterrupted battles with the German torpedo and dive bombers; but the convoy held together and on Saturday 30 May 1942, "reduced in number, beaten and exhausted, but still maintaining strict order," it entered Kola Bay at Murmansk. That day German bombers made their final raid on Convoy PQ 16, but were driven off by the flak fire and by Soviet fighter planes. During the dogfights, the most successful pilot of the Soviet North Fleet, Lt. Col. Safanov, was killed. A total of 32,400 metric tons of war material had gone down with the transporters, including 147 tanks, 77 aircraft and 770 motor trucks.

On the night of 30th–31st May 1942, the RAF made its first "thousand-bomber raid" on the German city of Cologne. This raid marked an epoch in the evolution of the air war against Germany. Only a few days before, public criticism had been voiced in Britain that the bombing war was producing no visible success. Air Marshal Harris decided to convince the skeptics by mounting a grand assault. Coastal Command, aviation training schools, repair-dock workers—all were mobilized to produce aircraft and crews. One aim of the operation was to test the tactic of area bombing on a large industrial city.

On the night of 30th May, 1,047 aircraft took off from 52 separate airfields. Of these, 886 bombers reached Cologne where they released 1,459 metric tons of bombs, two thirds of them incendiaries. High-flying Gee-equipped aircraft attracted the flak fire to themselves, while low-flying aircraft bombarded the flak batteries with fragmentation bombs. In the course of a 90-minute raid, 5,000 fires were set that destroyed 3,300 homes. Casualties were astonishingly low, due in part to the well-built air shelters. There were 474 dead, 5,000 wounded, and 45,000 homeless. Forty British aircraft were lost, that is 4%. The damage was four times greater than had been inflicted in all of 70 earlier raids, employing 2,000 aircraft, put together. The new type of incendiary canister proved especially effective. The last wave of bombers, comprising 200 four-engined machines, dropped high-explosive bombs so as to increase the extent of the area fires and obstruct work to put them out.

That night a new flying tactic was used for the first time: the bomber stream. Previously, bombers had attacked targets singly at space intervals during extended raids, which left the aircraft vulnerable to German air defense. This time they flew in a concentrated stream along the same route, thus swamping the German defenses, and bombed very intensively so that 7 bombers dropped their load every minute; the whole raid lasted only 90 minutes. Harris had calculated that a dense stream of bombers flying at varying altitudes, would make it difficult for the air defense to determine the exact course, and especially the elevation, of individual planes. Even the flak barrage was relatively ineffective against a stream. But the British air crews were less than pleased by the new bomber stream tactic because many bombers returned home with damage to their wings, caused by the release of masses of incendiary bombs from formations flying higher up. The pilots were also concerned about the risk of collision; but actually the risk was only .5%, whereas the probability of being shot down by German air defense while flying in the usual formation flight, was 3 or 4%. So the first thousand-bomber raids using the bomber stream tactic, aimed not merely to achieve greater destruction by the use of a massed formation, but also to show that a bomber stream resulted in lower casualties to aircraft. Raids on Cologne, Essen and Bremen in May and June 1942 confirmed this.

The Cologne raid caused the greatest destruction of any raid so far while costing the RAF only minimal losses. It proved that the Germans' Himmelbett defense system, based on the radar stations of the Kammhuber Line, was inadequate against a grand assault using a tightly-massed bomber stream. In the Himmelbett system, each German night-interception ground station could lead only one fighter plane to a target, so it was useless against masses of bombers. Another flaw of the Himmelbett system was that its radar frequencies could be jammed, making it impossible for the Germans to fix the location of inflying bombers and to guide fighter planes to intercept them. Lt. Gen. Kammhuber responded at once to the new bomber stream tactic by expanding his line with supplementary ground stations. The searchlight cordons were cancelled and the ground defense units reassigned to afford better protection to individual targets. The Germans also took other measures after the thou-

sand-bomber raid. Industry was transferred to central, eastern and southern Germany outside the range of British bombers, to protect Germany's munitions capability. Nazi propagandists were ordered to minimize the effects the massive raids had on German morale.

Japanese Admiral Yamamoto planned to take the Midway Islands by a surprise attack, which had worked for the Japanese at Pearl Harbor, and then to challenge the US fleet to a decisive confrontation. After this, he thought, he could undertake further operations against Hawaii so as to win absolute naval supremacy for Japan.

Midway was one of the smallest atolls in the Pacific and lay halfway between Hawaii and Japan. It had a diameter of only about five miles and surrounded two small islands barely large enough to contain airfields. The two treeless islands held a transmitter, large fuel and munitions stores, a seaplane station, an airfield and other important military installations. At the start of June 1942, Midway was the only strong base the Americans held in the central Pacific west of Hawaii.

On 20 May 1942, Yamamoto radioed a detailed plan of operations to his fleet. Due to a technical breakdown, he had to use an outdated code that the Americans had already cracked. Captain J. J. Rochefort, the US chief of radio reconnaissance on Hawaii, learned in this way of the Japanese admiral's intentions. Yamamoto's radio messages did not specify the invasion point but referred to it only as "the target"; so Rochefort devised a simple but inspired method to get his enemy to reveal the secret. He ordered all Amcrican Pacific bases to radio in damage reports in a code that he knew was already known to the Japanese. Midway reported the breakdown of its water distilling plant, and soon after, Rochefort intercepted a coded message from a Japanese radio station that said: "The target is suffering a water shortage." In this way Rochefort learned the name of the Japanese target, and next day he learned that the Japanese were also planning to attack Dutch Harbor far north in the Aleutians, as a diversionary maneuver [to make the Americans spread out their fleet away from the Midway area].

Yamamoto was convinced that the Americans had lost 2 of their aircraft carriers, the *Yorktown* and the *Lexington,* in the Coral Sea, and that the carriers *Hornet* and *Enterprise* were still in the South Pacific. The US had lost many of its battleships at Pearl Harbor, so Yamamoto thought that there would be little resistance at Midway. Moreover, he believed that US Admiral Nimitz had ordered the bulk of his forces north to ward off the attack on the Aleutians, and he hoped to seize Midway before this formation could return. Yamamoto did not suspect that his adversary had already sent his 3 remaining carriers – the *Yorktown, Enterprise* and *Hornet* – to Pearl Harbor, where repairs to the *Yorktown* were completed in the record time of only three days instead of the estimated three weeks.

Six Japanese aircraft carriers, 7 battleships and 10 heavy cruisers put to sea with their escort units under Yamamoto's command after overhasty preparations; a landing fleet brought up the rear. Another Japanese formation took over the diversionary raid on the Aleutians. The Americans, knowing the Japanese plan of operations, posted their 3 carriers at a distance from Midway and waited for the main Japanese fleet. At the same time the US aerial forces stationed on Midway, also stayed on alert. Meanwhile the Japanese diversionary attack on the Aleutians proceeded as planned on 3 June 1942, under the command of Rear-Admiral Kakuta. The war arena stretched from the Aleutians to Midway atoll, that is from the north to the central Pacific – a distance of over 1,800 nautical miles. The Japanese threw more manpower, vessels and aircraft into this battle than into any so far.

On the morning of 4 June 1942, Vice-Admiral Nagumo sent 108 of his carrier-based aircraft to attack Midway, while a second aerial formation of equal strength stood by to attack any enemy vessel as soon as it was sighted. The first wave took off from the carriers *Akagi, Kaga, Soryu* and *Hiryu.* It inflicted little damage because the Americans, who had prior radar warning, ordered their aircraft on Midway to take to the air and got them off the airfield in time. Rear-Admiral Fletcher, commander of the US naval task force, had concentrated his carriers some distance northeast of Midway. He hoped that the US aircraft at Midway airbase would sight the enemy naval fleet before Japanese planes dis-

Left: The most famous and successful of the RAF's heavy night bombers, an Avro Lancaster, is taking off for the "thousand-bomber raid" on Cologne.

Right: The Battle of Midway.

Below, top: A US Douglas SBD Dauntless dive bomber carrying a 550-lb bombload shortly before attack.

Below, bottom: Heavy German flak guns mounted on low-loader freight cars. Railway flak batteries were particularly maneuverable because they could change position so quickly.

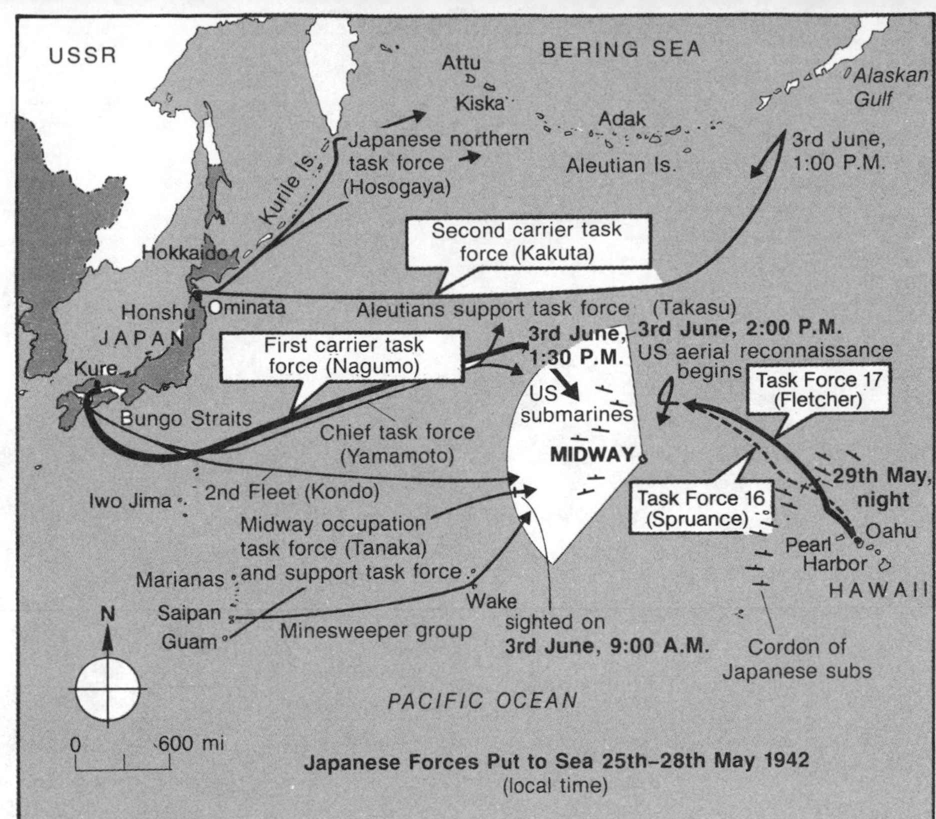

covered the location of his ships. So, while the 4 Japanese carriers under Vice-Admiral Nagumo were busy making their first strike on Midway, US aircraft on the 3 American carriers, under Rear-Admiral Fletcher, got ready to attack the Japanese ships.

Captain Tomonaga, leader of the Japanese bomber formation that attacked Midway, reported in after the first raid. He said that a second Japanese raid would be necessary to eliminate the defensive installations before any attempt at a landing. Meanwhile the Midway-based American aircraft had discovered Nagumo's carrier group and made a counter-raid against it. This caused only slight damage to the Japanese vessels and resulted in several losses to US aircraft; but it may well have been what caused the Japanese vice-admiral to make a fateful decision. Nagumo had been keeping 93 aircraft in reserve on his carrier decks, to use against any American naval forces that appeared. Now he decided instead to replace their torpedoes with bombs and send them to Midway to deal the island a finishing blow. This meant that during the next 60 minutes, the 4 Japanese carriers were completely helpless against an unexpected attack: for while half the Japanese bombers were exchanging their armament, the other formation under Captain Tomonaga, which had just bombed Midway, landed to refuel and re-arm; and all the fighter planes were

in the air to fend off the attacks of the US planes from Midway.

A short time later, Vice-Admiral Nagumo was informed that a group of American ships had been sighted about 280 nautical miles away. At first the Japanese thought they were only cruisers and destroyers, but at 8:20 A.M. a radio message reported that the group included an aircraft carrier. This was unpleasant news for Nagumo: Most of his aircraft were now armed with bombs, not torpedoes, and all his fighters were locked in combat. Moreover, he still had to wait for the last of Captain Tomonaga's bombers to return from their raid on Midway. Meanwhile the American carrier-based aircraft – 3 waves totalling 41 heavy torpedo bombers – approached without fighter cover and attacked the Japanese carriers. Thirty-five US bombers were shot down by fighters or flak without scoring a hit.

At this moment, while the Japanese fighters were still warding off the torpedo bombers, US dive bombers from the carriers *Enterprise* and *Yorktown* appeared on the scene. The first Japanese bombers were just then leaving the hangar decks below and re-emerging onto deck in their elevators. Their bombs had been switched back to torpedoes again so that they could be used against shipping targets. Now the fuel pipes were full and the bombers were surrounded by oil and grease, torpedoes, bombs and aerial ammunition. Thirty-seven American dive bombers dived down on them from a height of 19,000 feet, and no resistance was possible.

The carrier *Akagi,* Nagumo's flagship, was hit by bombs triggering a chain of explosions among the aircraft that had been standing on deck cleared for takeoff. The ship had to be abandoned. The carrier *Soryu* sank in 20 minutes after receiving 3 square hits, and the carrier *Kaga* sank in flames several hours later. The aircraft of the only remaining intact carrier, the *Hiryu,* managed to damage the *Yorktown* so badly that she too had to be abandoned. The 24 US dive bombers led a counterattack on the *Hiryu,* which was badly hit and sank early on the morning of 7 June 1942. The loss of their 4 aircraft carriers forced the Japanese to break off the battle that day. A 12-minute attack at midday on 4 June 1942, decided the outcome of the war in the Pacific. The Japanese successfully occupied the two Aleutian islands of Attu and Kiska, but this could not make up for their disaster. Apart from the carrier *Yorktown,* the USA lost only one destroyer, 307 men and 150 aircraft. Japanese losses were 3,500 dead – 2,155 from on board the carriers – and about 330 planes. Command of the Pacific now passed to the Americans and made it possible for them, two months later, to launch a southwest Pacific offensive at Guadalcanal. Japan's failure at

Left: The Pacific, 6 June 1942. The Japanese cruiser *Mikuma* after an attack by US dive bombers.

Right: An everyday scene in the Pacific war: A US Grumman F6F-3 Hellcat fighter bomber manages only at the last moment to reach safety on the carrier deck.

Below right: On 23 June 1943, the Focke Wulf 190 A-3, flown by German pilot 1st Lt. Arnim Faber, landed at Pembrey (Wales), where it enabled the British to learn many things they did not know about the new German fighter plane.

Below: Torpedo raid tactics 1940/1942

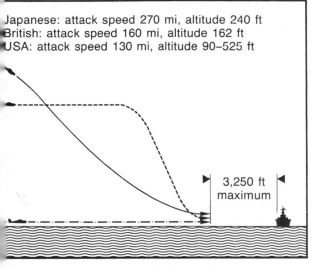

Japanese: attack speed 270 mi, altitude 240 ft
British: attack speed 160 mi, altitude 162 ft
USA: attack speed 130 mi, altitude 90–525 ft

3,250 ft maximum

Midway was the first major defeat it had suffered since the year 1598. The Japanese public, and even the government, were kept in ignorance of the true extent of the débacle.

In June 1942, the first American aircraft appeared over Europe; but their take-off bases were in Egypt, not Britain. On the night of 11th–12th June 1942, 13 Consolidated B-24 Liberator bombers of the US 9th Air Force took off from Fayid (Egypt) on the Suez Canal to attack the Ploesti oil center in Rumania. The whole area was carpeted by thick cloud, so only a few planes were able to make out their target. Shortage of fuel prevented the pilots from returning to Egypt and they were sent on to an alternate base at Habbaniya, Iraq. But only 7 bombers made it to Habbaniya, while 2 of the Liberators made an emergency landing somewhere in Syria, and the other 6 flew into Turkey, where their pilots were interned. This was the first long-range American bombing mission in Europe.

On 18 June 1942 Major-General Carl Spaatz, the commander of the US 8th Air Force, set up his headquarters in Bushy Park near Hampton Court Palace outside London. Spaatz had formed the units of the US 8th Army Air Force in the southern United States. Now Operation Bolero brought their transfer to Great Britain, where the RAF had placed 127 air-

First Lt. Faber's Focke Wulf 190 A-3 is here being carefully researched by the British. The results had a far-reaching influence on British fighter plane construction, especially on the Hawker Tempest II and the Hawker F.2/43 Fury.

bases at the disposal of the US air force commander, General Eaker and his 1,800-man force. The US ground personnel and war material arrived in Britain on the former luxury steamer *Queen Elizabeth.* On 23 June 1942, the first four-engined US bombers took off from North America headed for Britain along the Labrador-Greenland-Iceland-Scotland route (3,600 miles). The fighter planes and lighter aircraft were transported by freight ship. The 8th Air Force planned daylight precision raids on 154 targets in Germany, including U-boat shipyards, docks, ports, aircraft manufacturing plants, munitions factories and traffic junctions. When the RAF objected that losses during daylight raids were unacceptably high, the Americans replied that the British had made the mistake of deploying overly small formations at too high an altitude.

When the new German Focke Wulf 190 fighter planes first appeared along the Channel coast in July 1941, the British pilots thought that the planes must be American Curtiss Hawk fighters captured by the Germans in France in 1941, for the Focke Wulf was the spitting image of the Curtiss Hawk. But then they realized that the FW 190 was German-built and an enemy to be reckoned with.

During Operation Cerberus, the FW 190s of German 3rd Group, 26th Fighter Wing took a devastating toll of the British aircraft. The British War Office decided that they needed to capture one of the German planes – which were faster and more maneuverable even than Spitfires – and bring it back to England to investigate its technology in detail. The chief pilot of the British Vickers aircraft plant planned to make a parachute drop over France, accompanied by a friend, where the French resistance was to aid them in kidnapping a Focke Wulf from a German airbase, much as the Würzburg radar set had been kidnapped in the raid on Bruneval. The date for this top secret operation had been fixed at Tuesday 23 June 1942. But in the end there was no need for the hazardous mission, because several hours before the planned takeoff, an FW 190 landed in Britain of its own accord. German 1st Lt. Arnim Faber, an adjutant of 3rd Group, 2nd Fighter Wing, fought an air duel with a Spitfire of the RAF Polish squadron and when flying away, mistook the Bristol Channel for the English Channel. He flew straight into the RAF base of Pembrey believing that it was a German airbase.

The last grand operation by the RAF during the first half of 1942, miscarried. On the evening of 25 June 1942, 1,006 aircraft of Bomber Command, Coastal Command and the Royal Flying School took off to raid Bremen; but despite the navigational aid afforded by the Gee device, only 713 located the city due, it was said, to the stormy weather and the strong counterwind. The Focke Wulf plant was seriously damaged by the 1,450 tons of bombs dropped that night; but 49 bombers were lost to the German defenses. After this operation the thousand-bomber raids were stopped for the time being.

Sunday 28 June 1942 marked the beginning of the German summer offensive on the Eastern Front. The German 8th Air Corps under Gen. Fiebig supported the attack of the von Weichs Army Group, which moved out from Kursk against the Soviet front at Bryansk under Gen. Golikov. Its Stukas and bombers intervened directly in the battle.

1942
July to December

Thursday 2 July 1942, Constantinople
The Turkish *Exchange News Agency* reported:

The censor authorities have now sanctioned publication of the report that about 3 weeks ago, 2 German paratroopers landed on Turkish soil close to the Russian border. The two Germans belonged to a larger paratroop unit whose mission was to gather information behind the Russian lines and transmit it by radio. The paratroopers, who may have been driven into Turkey by the wind, have been interned.

Friday 10 July 1942
The *Wehrmacht High Command* announced:

Yesterday German combat aircraft and submarines again detected and attacked the remnant of a giant British-American convoy in the North Sea. The convoy still included 3 steamers, with 3 destroyers and 2 guard-ships; all 3 of the steamers were sunk, 2 of them by U-boats. We have kept up successful day and night air raids on airbases on the island of Malta.

Daily Keynote from the Reich Press Chief,
Tuesday 28 July 1942:

The Minister has explained that it is not in the interests of Germany to allow the development of a Second Front. Thus it would be wrong for German propaganda to provoke the enemy into forming a Second Front by (for example) ridiculing the reasons he cites for not doing so. On the contrary, it is in our interests to encourage the British to find an alibi to offer Russia [for not forming a second front in Western Europe], such as the [British] air raids on German cities [which show that the British are already doing what they can to relieve the Soviet Union]. Thus it would be wrong for German propaganda to trivialize these raids.

Secret Report of the German *SS Secret Service* on internal affairs, No. 304 of Thursday 30 July 1942 (extract):

I. General comments: In the past months, fears of a further intensification of enemy air raids was restricted to the urban population, but now they increasingly are spreading to the rural population, who fear not only for their lives, but also the possible destruction of all their property and of the coming harvest. Many of our fellow-Germans are again expressing surprise at our failure to take appropriate retaliatory measures, and fear that Germany no longer controls the air space in the West.

Daily Keynote from the Reich Press Chief,
Sunday 2 August 1942:

The Minister has said concerning the Second Front, that the huge deployment of British aircraft in the bombing of German cities, proves that the British do not intend to make a landing [on the Continent]. [The Minister reasons that] the British air force could not afford the heavy casualties they incur in raiding Germany, if they in fact intended to launch a second front.

Daily Keynote from the Reich Press Chief,
Tuesday 11 August 1942:

The Minister has commented extensively on the bomb-depressed regions after returning from his tour of talks in western Germany. There is [the Minister says] no doubt that the cities of Rhine-Westphalia are having a difficult time right now and

Left: A German flak gunner. Flak artillery and fighter planes were the main elements in the German defense against increasingly heavy bombing raids.

Opposite page: The Nazi authorities in occupied Western Europe did all they could to deter the native population from aiding shot-down Allied fliers. This German notice published in the Netherlands, warns of the death and imprisonment that befell Dutch people who helped the crew of a downed British bomber.

that unfortunately the authorities in Berlin cannot properly appreciate the extent of the problem. He goes on to say that we are not treating the problem of the air attacks in the right way; and he has realized that we have made major psychological errors. We could, he says, profitably learn from the example of the British during the heavy raids on London, who gave the conduct of their people a heroic treatment and turned [the battle of] London into a myth that, there is no doubt, helped greatly to encourage the people and keep up their spirit. The Minister believes first, that German Armed Forces High Command reports must describe the raids much more impressively, and second, that more recognition must be given to the [civilian] population. Thus among other things, he suggests that Iron Crosses be awarded to men and women who particularly distinguish themselves during air raids—and possibly even the Knight's Cross to the especially deserving—and that more coverage in the German press be given to heroic achievements by individuals.

Secret Report of the German *SS Secret Service* on internal affairs, No. 314 of Thursday 3 September 1942 (extract):

I. General comments: Several reports indicate that people are expecting a grand enemy assault virtually every night. Some Germans have taken everything they own to relatives in the country, or divided it among relatives and friends in several different locations, in the hope of salvaging at least a part of their belongings from destruction.

Thursday 10 September 1942
Radio San Francisco reported:

We repeat our report that yesterday morning, an airplane that is presumed to have taken off from a Japanese submarine, dropped several incendiary bombs over the state of Oregon, causing damage in the woods that resulted in several deaths.

Daily Keynote from the Reich Press Chief, Saturday 12 September 1942:

The Minister believes it is time that we take a fundamental position toward the air war. Debate on this extraordinarily important issue must not, he says, be left up to the German people. Millions of Germans are concerned about the worsening air situation in the West and every day ask themselves how it will end. We must [the Minister says] publish a statement, or at least awaken hope that things will change eventually. Perhaps it is appropriate to reveal the full gravity of the situation, and to call to people's attention that the German Luftwaffe cannot be equally strong at every location. So far we have not hit on the right tone about the air war.

Watch Out for Emergency Landings by Enemy Fliers

German official notice dated 9 September 1942:

The crews of enemy aircraft that the German air defense shoots down or forces to make an emergency landing when they fly into German territory, often try to avoid capture as prisoners of war, by skillful camouflage or flight. These attempts succeed mainly at night and when the enemy fliers set down over remote areas, because emergency landings and parachute drops are not easily observable then. Thus we call on the German civilian population for their active cooperation and ask them to stay alert. Anything you observe, however insignificant, may prove of immeasurable value to our national defense.

Anyone who sees anything to do with emergency landings by enemy aircraft and so on, should, in the interests of national security, report it immediately to the nearest armed forces or police authority or gendarmerie.

Sunday 20 September 1942
The *Wehrmacht High Command* announced:

A special announcement has revealed that German forces have won a large convoy battle in the North Sea. After we completely destroyed one giant Allied convoy in the North Sea between 2–7 July 1942, the British, on September 13, made another attempt to lead a giant convoy with a strong naval escort through the North Sea to a Soviet port. The very bad weather conditions, and an ice boundary that allowed [the vessels to pursue] a course far to the north, favored their plan. German combat aircraft and U-boat submarines attacked and smashed this new convoy of approximately 45 merchant vessels, during several days of self-sacrificial fighting. Our combat pilots, fighting under severe conditions, over vast distances, and in poor weather, and meeting strong enemy flak and fighter-plane defenses, sank 25 merchant convoy vessels totalling 177,000 tons. Eight more steamers were so badly crippled that they may be counted as lost. In addition, the Luftwaffe annihilated one destroyer and 2 guardboats from among the escort vessels, and set a second destroyer on fire.

Monday 21 September 1942, London
The *British Admiralty* announced:

German claims of losses to a British convoy in the Arctic have been grossly exaggerated. The British Admiralty is not at this moment in a position to reply to the German reports because they list the names of individual ships. Apparently the enemy claims are meant to provoke a detailed formal denial, which would inform him which Allied vessels are now underway in the Arctic, or already anchored in Murmansk.

Beware Enemy Bombing Raids

The German newspaper *Der Adler* carried the following article in September 1942:

One question that we often hear posed is: If I can hear a bomb whistling, does that mean it is going to hit me? Front-line soldiers have found that when they hear bullets whistle, the bullets do not hit them because by that time they have already flown past. Often people take this fact and try to apply it to aerial bombs, saying that you do not have to be afraid of a bomb you hear whistle or scream, because it will not hit where you are. The old soldier's rule that a whistling bullet does you no harm, is true; but the same does not apply to an aerial bomb.

People should keep in mind that infantry projectiles, and also flat-trajectory shells fired from cannon (e.g. from anti-tank guns), travel faster than the speed of sound. Thus they outrun the gun report and drag their whistle along behind them, so to speak, and consequently no report or whistling sound precedes them.

The sounds come in the reverse order from the usual slow-flying high-angle artillery fire. If you are fired on, the shell impact comes first, then comes the screaming of the missile, and finally the firing report. The aerial bomb is not comparable to a flat projectile; it falls much more slowly at the start. It takes over 10 seconds for it to fall a distance of 1,600 feet, and 25½ seconds to fall 9,750 feet; the bomb will not reach the speed of sound (1,085 feet per sec-

Bekanntmachung.

Wiederholt habe ich die niederländische Bevölkerung davor gewarnt, in irgendeiner Form die Feinde Deutschlands zu begünstigen. Trotzdem ist wieder ein schwerer Fall von Feindbegünstigung vorgekommen. Am 7.8.41 musste auf niederländischem Gebiet ein britisches Kampfflugzeug notlanden. Der unverletzt gebliebenen Besatzung von 6 Mann wurde bei ihrem Bestreben, zu fliehen, Unterstützung durch Niederländer zuteil durch Hergabe von Geld, Nahrungsmitteln und Zivilkleidung.

Noch am gleichen Tage wurden die Engländer gefangen. Die Begünstiger wurden sofort vor ein deutsches Kriegsgericht gestellt. Dieses verurteilte 5 von ihnen zum Tode und 3 weitere zu langjährigen, teilweise lebenslänglichen Freiheitsstrafen.

Den Haag, den 14.8.41.

Gez.: FR. CHRISTIANSEN
General der Flieger.
Wehrmachtbefehlshaber in den Niederlanden.

Left: Radar-supported heavy German flak batteries, combined with searchlights, formed a defensive belt around strategic targets.

Opposite page: Hurricane II D Tank Busters are operating against German tanks west of El Alamein in October 1942. These British fighter planes, which were fitted with 2 Vickers-S 40-mm cannon and two 7.7-mm machine guns, were for some time a "secret weapon." The S-cannon were among the largest-caliber weapons used in RAF aircraft.

ond) until it has fallen a distance of approximately 19,500 feet. Once the bomb has reached a certain fall velocity, it begins to whistle. (The sounds we hear are piercing due to its aerodynamically imperfect shape.) As long as the bomb is falling slower than sound, the whistling noise will precede it, and so is audible at the target point before the bomb itself impacts.

However, it is completely wrong to assume that the duration of a bomb whistle near the target coincides exactly with the time the bomb is falling, because the bomb is always chasing after the sound wave which it approaches at ever increasing speed. No sound follows after the bomb—unlike the case of the projectile that travels faster than the speed of sound.

Can we tell different aircraft apart by their different sound patterns? Many people are certain that they can easily tell the difference between an enemy night bomber and one of our own night fighters, by the sound pattern. There is a lot of truth to this idea. Nevertheless, we should not believe that it is such a straightforward matter to tell our own planes from enemy planes by the sound. In the modern aircraft industry, identical technology is everywhere used to build the same classes of aircraft. A British Rolls Royce Merlin engine has a similar turnover speed and a similar exhaust mechanism to a German Daimler-Benz DB 601 engine, so the sounds they produce are not very different.

Secret Report of the German *SS Secret Service* on internal affairs, No. 328 of Thursday 22 October 1942 (extract):

I. General comments: The address by Reich Minister Dr. Goebbels in Munich has earned considerable attention not only in Munich itself but throughout the Reich. Particularly people in northern and western Germany are pleased because bomb victims who were in southern Germany have said that in the South they are known as the "tough bomb veterans."

British Offensive in Egypt

Saturday 24 October 1942, Cairo
British Middle East Headquarters announced:

Yesterday before dawn, our Eighth Army in Egypt began a showdown offensive in North Africa. The first reports from the front describe the effective results of the heavy Allied air raids made on enemy airfields during the past 10 days to pave the way for the offensive.

Sunday 25 October 1942, Cairo
British Middle East Headquarters announced:

Advanced troops of the Eighth Army broke through the chief enemy positions at several points in the early hours of yesterday morning. We held our territorial gains despite enemy counterattacks. Violent fighting is continuing. During the past 24 hours our aerial forces continued their extremely intensive operations. Our hunter-bombers carried out powerful strafing attacks despite heavy fire from the ground defenses.

25 October 1942, Rome
The *Italian High Command* announced:

After paving the way with intensive artillery activity, the enemy has moved to attack, advancing strong tank and infantry forces in the northern and southern sectors of the El Alamein front. The enemy has been repelled everywhere and has suffered heavy losses particularly in tanks, of which 47 have been destroyed so far. Battle is continuing. The British air force deployed strong units in support of their ground operations, but was beaten back everywhere by the Axis air force, which shot down 15 enemy aircraft in flames.

Sunday 6 December 1942, Cairo
US Headquarters in Cairo announced:

On Friday, Liberator C-24 heavy bombers of the USAAF (US Army Air Force) carried out the first American air attack on Italy. Bombs hit Italian merchant and war vessels as well as port and rail installations in Naples. Bombs of various calibers were very successfully dropped on targets. No enemy fighter planes took to the air. All the bombers returned to base.

Monday 7 December 1942, London
The *British Air Ministry* reported:

On Sunday, approximately 100 RAF bombers took part in an air raid on Eindhoven (Holland). Four hundred fighter planes provided them cover, including the newest model Spitfires, which in addition made diversionary raids over France and Holland. Norwegian, Polish, American, Canadian and one Indian wing, as well as Free French aircraft, took part in the operation. This was the largest daylight operation so far. The main target was the Philips electrical equipment plant in Eindhoven, the largest and most important factory of its kind in Europe.

Thursday 31 December 1942
The *Wehrmacht High Command* announced:

Last night a German long-range bomber formation made a surprise attack on the port of Casablanca (French Morocco) on the Western coast of North Africa. Large numbers of high-explosive and incendiary bombs caused great fires that continued to be visible from long distances as the planes flew away into the desert.

Bombs Fall on Casablanca

War-Log account by the *German Atlantic Fly Command* concerning an armed reconnaissance mission against Casablanca by German 3rd Group, 40th Bomber Wing on the night of 30th–31st December 1942:

Weather at target, 60–80% overcast. Lower cloud edge, 3,000 feet. Fire visibility, 30 miles. Scattered showers. Attack took enemy completely by surprise. Not until departure after releasing bombs did we see 4–5 enemy searchlights, and experience strong,

Opposite page: British Short Stirling bombers proved inadequate and starting in 1943 were deployed only against weakly-defended targets.

Left: A massed formation of German Stuka dive bombers are flying a relief raid in North Africa.

heavy and light flak fire chiefly from naval vessels, badly positioned. Apparently no integrated fire-guidance system. Bombs dropped included: 2 SC 500s, 16 SC 250s, 19 SBC 50s, 4 ABB 500s. Observed bombs impacting on warehouses and freight station rail tracks, saw them followed by explosions and fires. Given the unexpectedness of the assault and the favorable attack weather, we may assume that a high toll of hits were scored on the target. The strong susceptibility of the [German] FW 200 to break down on long approach flights when carrying a heavy bombload, impaired the operation.

Casablanca, 31 December 1942
US General *George S. Patton* reported:

We experienced our first air raid early this morning. Three bombs exploded at 3:15 A.M. and woke me out of a beautiful sleep. I closed the curtains, turned on a light in the center of the room, threw on some clothes and was up on the roof in barely 5 minutes. A cloud carpet spread about 2,500 feet over our heads, it was raining and storming. All our searchlights were busy boring holes in the clouds. The light antiaircraft began shooting like mad, the tracer bullets looked like glowworms. Suddenly there was a giant flash with long octopus arms of flame shooting out of it, made by the signal flares. This firework display gave out a very bright light for 20 minutes, during which nothing happened. Soon after came the persistent crash of a large four-engined enemy bomber that appeared over the building behind us, and was immediately grasped by two questing searchlight beams. At the same time all the antiaircraft guns in the vicinity seemed to start firing. The airplane was literally outlined in tracer fire and in the white light of high-explosive ammunition; but the latter quickly formed into little black clouds. Although the bomber was flying at an altitude of no more than 2,200 feet – or perhaps *because* it was – it was lucky enough to get away without being hit. At least that is what I claim, although other people thought it had been hit. At 4:45 A.M. we heard another bomber behind us, once again a four-engined job. It flew even lower than the first one and likewise was framed in tracer fire and high-explosive projectiles. I am certain that this plane was hit at least twice before it disappeared headed toward Europe.

Strategy and Tactics

July to December 1942

On Wednesday 1 July 1942, the first heavy bomber of the American 8th Army Air Force arrived in Britain by the North Atlantic route. There were shouts of joy at Prestwick airfield, Scotland, as the Flying Fortress B-17E "Jarring Jenny" came in for a landing.

That same day saw the fall of Sevastopol, one of the world's strongest fortresses, on the Crimean peninsula. On 7 June 1942 the German Eleventh Army under General von Manstein mounted an assault on Sevastopol with air support from 7 bomber, 3 Stuka and 4 fighter groups of the German 7th Air Corps under General von Richtofen. The Soviets defended the massive fortress tenaciously, and to subdue it the Luftwaffe had to fly relay attacks on a hitherto unprecedented scale: Over a

three-week period, it flew 23,751 missions in which 20,529 metric tons of bombs were dropped—only slightly less than the 21,860 tons that had been dropped on Britain during the whole of 1941.

Early in the afternoon of 1 July 1942, a German airman, E. Reper of 3 Squadron, 906th Coastal Flying Group, flying reconnaissance seaplane BV 138c, spotted Allied convoy PQ 17 near Jan Mayen island in the Arctic Ocean. The convoy had put to sea on 27 June 1942 headed for the Soviet port of Arkhangelsk, and with its 36 merchant vessels was the largest Allied convoy so far. German agents in Reykjavik quickly reported that it was under way, and both the Luftwaffe and the German navy had time to prepare to fight it. By the following evening the 1st German Coastal Flying Squadron of 406th Group tried—unsuccessfully—to mount a torpedo attack on PQ 17 using their feeble He 115 seaplanes. Then began the biggest convoy battle of the war. German torpedo bombers, dive bombers and submarines made a days-long assault on the convoy, which was abandoned by its protective escort of cruisers and destroyers halfway between Iceland and Arkhangelsk, after the British Admiralty learned that the battleship *Tirpitz* and other heavy German vessels were at sea. Allied aircraft flying cover for the convoy had to turn back, and the merchant vessels were ordered to fight their way through to the Soviet Union individually—through the Barents Sea, which was dominated by German aircraft, naval vessels and U-boats.

On the afternoon of 4 July 1942, pilots of the US 8th Air Force carried out their first mission over Europe. They flew 6 Douglas A-20 Boston bombers placed at their disposal by the RAF. Their mission was to strafe 4 German airfields in Holland; but only 2 of the bombers bombed their targets successfully.

On compte quelques victimes parmi la population indigène

Aucun objectif militaire n'a été atteint

Le Résident général s'est rendu sur les lieux

La nuit dernière, quelques avions ennemis ont survolé Casablanca, et grâce à une violente réaction de la D.C.A., n'ont pu lancer qu'un nombre restreint de bombes sur la ville. On déplore malheureusement un certain nombre de victimes dans la population marocaine et quelques dégâts matériels.

Dès la première heure, le général Noguès, Résident général, accompagné de M. Voizard, secrétaire général du Protectorat et de M. Poussier, chef de la Région, s'est rendu dans les quelques quartiers de la périphérie atteints par les bombes pour examiner la situation. Il a pu constater la rapide et parfaite organisation des secours.

Le Résident général a mis à la disposition du chef de la Région un crédit de 100.000 francs pour apporter une aide immédiate aux familles éprouvées.

Quelques habitations musulmanes dépourvues d'étages ont été endommagées ou détruites par la déflagration des bombes dans les terrains avoisinants. On a malheureusement à déplorer une quarantaine de victimes, marocains pour la plupart.

Les Services de la défense passive sont immédiatement entrés en action et ont fait preuve du plus grand calme et d'un dévouement dignes d'éloges. Des secours en argent et en nature ont été aussitôt distribués aux familles sinistrées par le Résident général qui avait tenu à se rendre sur les lieux accompagné par les autorités locales.

Three Bostons were shot down by flak, and one failed to find its target and returned to base still carrying its bombs.

The British, American and Dutch freight vessels of Convoy PQ 17, scattered in the Barents Sea, were easy game for the German planes and U-boats. Between 5th and 10th July 1942, 130 Ju 88 dive

Above: A French newspaper account of the first bombing raid on Casablanca, resulting in the deaths of Moroccan civilians.

Left: 6 December 1942, Eindhoven (Holland): When the RAF raided the Philips electrical equipment plant with 93 Douglas DB-7 Boston bombers, 15 of the aircraft were lost—that is 16%—and 53 more were damaged.

bombers, 43 He 111 bombers and 29 He 115 seaplanes of the German 5th Air Fleet under General Stumpff, sank 8 vessels; 9 U-boats of the Eisteufel (Ice Devil) Group, sank 9 vessels; and the U-boats finished off 7 more freighters damaged by German air attacks. PQ 17 lost a total of 24 vessels – 143,977 tons of shipping – that were carrying 3,350 motor trucks and jeeps, 430 tanks, 210 aircraft and 99,316 tons of spare parts, rations, armor plates, ammunition and other goods. The German Luftwaffe lost 5 aircraft. Only 12 of the 36 vessels of Convoy PQ 17 reached Murmansk. As a result the British War Cabinet decided not to send any more convoys through the North Sea until the days got shorter.

In the summer of 1942, German Lichtenstein BC airborne radar became fully operational in German night fighter planes. The large antenna structure on the nose – the "antlers" – slowed the aircraft down; but the radar device, with a range of up to 1.8 miles, made it easier for a German night fighter, once the Himmelbett stations had successfully guided it to an enemy aircraft, to make its final run on the target. Lichtenstein radar enabled the Germans to perfect the technique of *Dunkelnachtjagd* (unilluminated night interception) within the framework of the Himmelbett system, and now a fighter-plane control officer could guide several German night fighters to enemy bomber targets at the same time.

On Saturday 11 July 1942, 44 Lancaster bombers of 5th Group, RAF Bomber Command, undertook a long-range daylight raid on U-boat docks in Danzig and Gdynia (Poland). The raid miscarried: Only a third of the bombers, approaching over the Baltic Sea, located their target; German flak shot down 2 of them.

The strength of the Western Allied aerial forces was growing and as a result, had forced the German Luftwaffe to tie down two thirds of its forces in the West by the summer of 1942. Thus fewer and fewer elite German fighter pilots and up-to-date German aircraft were free to be detailed to the Eastern Front. Most of the Luftwaffe's operations during the German summer offensive against the Soviet Union, involved lending direct support to the ground troops. The Soviets too flew no strategic raids, and their low-level ground-attack aircraft – the dreaded, heavily-armed and armored Ilyushin Il-2 Sturmoviks – were a sore plague to the German infantry.

A characteristic feature of aerial warfare on the Eastern Front was that operations were flown at a much lower altitude than in Western Europe, because the airbases on both sides were located close

Norway, July 1942: A German Heinkel He 115 seaplane is cleared for takeoff. Before the war this aircraft had established 8 world records but it was out of date by 1942.

to the front. Also, the short attack runs made it possible for an aircraft to be deployed more than once per day. As a rule the Il-2 Sturmovik ground-attack aircraft attacked in groups of between 4 and 12. The Soviets flew over the front line to one side of their target, then approached it in a rightward extended staircase formation, veered to the left to form a circle, and typically attacked the target while heading toward their own lines, which enabled them, if they were damaged, to pursue a straight course back to safety. In the summer of 1942, the power balance shifted on the Eastern Front: The total number of German aircraft of all types now lay between 2,350 and 2,500 machines so that the Soviet aircraft outnumbered them 3 to 1; and the Soviet fighter planes outnumbered the Germans 4:1. However, the German Luftwaffe still had a technological and tactical edge over the Soviet air forces. Then in July the Red Air Force achieved absolute air supremacy at Voronezh by the Don, the battle ground of German Army Group von Weichs. After receiving reinforcements from the Moscow air force, the Soviet aerial forces on the Don were able to launch counteroffensives.

On Saturday 1 August 1942, the last aircraft of the US 8th Army Air Force had completed their journey from America to Prestwick, Scotland.

On Friday 7 August 1942, 11,000 US Marine Corps troops made a surprise landing on Guadalcanal, the largest of the Solomon Islands, which the Japanese had captured in May 1942. The Japanese underestimated the strength of their enemy and at first sent only limited forces to fight them. The battle for the island dragged on for months. The fate of Guadalcanal hinged on its airfield, which the Japanese had almost finished constructing when the Americans took it on the second day of battle; they renamed it Henderson Field in honor of a Marine flying officer killed over Midway. But the American beachhead surrounding the takeoff runway, remained at risk from the Japanese infantry who kept emerging from the jungle to attack it. The victory at Guadalcanal would fall to the side that gained air supremacy first, because it could then fly in supplies to its fighting troops. On 8 August 1942, 26 Japanese carrier-borne aircraft raided US naval vessels bearing supplies to Guadalcanal. Seventeen of the aircraft were shot down by flak and fighter planes. Two Japanese Aichi D3A "Val" dive bombers were hit while they were still carrying their bomb-loads, and their pilots deliberately crashed into the US transport vessel *G. F. Elliott,* destroying it and forcing the crew to abandon ship. This was the first deliberate suicide attack (kamikaze) by Japanese airmen.

On the night of 9th–10th August, 166 RAF bombers raided Osnabrück (western Germany) and ran into an unpleasant surprise. All their Gee radar devices were put out of action at one stroke by a massive jamming operation: the Germans had developed new countermeasures. The German jamming instruments, code-named "Heinrich," were set up all over Occupied Europe; one was even stationed

Left: A flight of Ilyushin Il-2 Sturmovik low-level ground-attack aircraft, the most famous planes of the Red Air Force. Here is the first, single-seater version.

Opposite page above: The infamous "Christmas trees," colored target-marking flares dropped by RAF Pathfinder Bombers, heralded the fall of death-dealing bombs.

Opposite page below: The radio operator of an RAF bomber in front of a Gee radar-navigational device. The receiver recorded the different frequencies from 3 transmitters in England, which made it possible for an aircraft to fix its location to within 6 miles.

finders were either "finders" or "lighters." Nine miles before reaching the target, the "finder" (the "master of ceremonies") would begin to drop one flare every 30 seconds over the flying lane the bombers were supposed to follow. Meanwhile the "lighters" circled over the target zone where first they dropped flares ("Christmas trees") and then incendiary bombs. Next the finders flew at an angle across the marked line, dropping more flares. The point where the two lines of flares intersected, marked the spot where the approaching bombers were supposed to drop their payloads. A second pathfinder squadron would fly along ahead of the bomber stream to drop additional flares if needed. Thus inexperienced bomber crews had only to follow the pathfinder markings. In the past, many bombers had been lost because it would take 2 hours to channel them all through the strongly-defended target zone; but now it was possible to reduce the time to less than one hour.

At 3:20 P.M. on Monday 17 August 1942, 12 B-17E Flying Fortresses of the 97th Bomber Group (US 8th Air Force) took off on their first mission over Europe, flying with 4 RAF Spitfire squadrons to provide them cover. US Brigadier General Ira Eaker flew with them, in the plane of the Group Commander. A forty-six-year-old, Texas-born, experienced professional aviator, Eaker was the commander of the US 8th Bomber Command – because the term 8th Air Force did not yet officially exist. His plane, suitably, was known as the "Yankee Doodle." The bombers' target was Sotteville-les-

on the Eiffel Tower in Paris. Over the next few weeks, so many jammers came into operation that Gee radar became useless over the whole of Germany and Western Europe. Now the British worked at top speed to complete a new bombing-aid system called "Oboe."

On Saturday 15 August 1942, an important event occurred that changed the course of the bombing war: RAF Pathfinder units were set up, the descendants of the German 100th Pathfinder Group that had fought in the Battle of Britain. These bomber support units, designed to improve British night raiding techniques, were put under the command of Air Commodore D. L. T. Bennett. Bomber Command armed itself for its first grand offensive against German industrial centers and munitions plants. The most able pilots, and the best navigators and bombardiers, flew ahead of the bombers in pathfinder aircraft to locate an area bombing target and mark the place by dropping flares. The path-

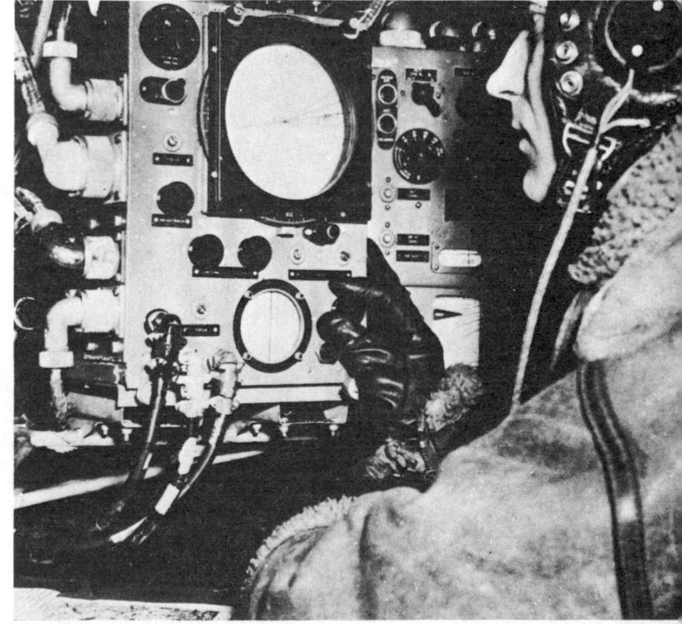

Maj. Gen. Roberts, landed with commando troops and tanks on both sides of the French Channel port of Dieppe. They had strong air cover from B-17 bombers and fighters of the US 8th Air Force, and from the RAF combat aircraft, which flew 2,462 sorties. The Germans repulsed this test invasion in a bloody battle in which the RAF lost 106 planes and the USAAF 8 fighter planes, compared to Luftwaffe losses of only 48 aircraft.

On Thursday 20 August 1942, 4 Soviet long-range air force divisions were transferred from Moscow to the southern front at Stalingrad. That same day the Soviet 287th Fighter Division under Col. S. P. Danilin, went into battle there. This was the first Soviet aerial unit equipped with the new Lavochkin La-5 fighter planes. When strong German aerial forces massed on the southern front, the Red Air Force reinforced its units there too. The Soviets attributed such importance to the Stalingrad front, that the commander-in-chief of the Soviet air force, General Novikov, assumed personal command of all aerial forces deployed along the southern flank. They set out to make relay raids on German airfields, so as to force the Luftwaffe to evacuate their forward bases. In each Soviet fighter division, special groups of particularly successful pilots were formed who

Rouen on the left bank of the Seine, site of a railway switchyard crucial to the supplying of Le Havre. The Flying Fortresses released their 16.6-ton bombload from an altitude of over 22,000 feet. All the bombers returned to base. The main aim of this first operation was to break in the crews. It confirmed that the Americans were right in their ideas about the viability of daylight raids, which both the British and the Germans had abandoned on the grounds that casualties were unacceptably high.

On the night of 18th–19th August 1942, the British tried out their new pathfinder tactics for the first time in a raid on the shipping docks in Flensburg (western Germany). British Mosquitos equipped with Gee navigational and blind-bombing equipment were supposed to mark the area-bombing target with flares, but despite precise theoretical planning, the raid went awry: The Gee devices became non-operational several miles before reaching the city due to German jamming, and the marker flares were dropped in the wrong place.

On Wednesday 19 August, Dieppe was the scene of the largest British operation in Western Europe in 1942. A group of 6,100 men of the 4th and 6th Brigades of the 2nd Canadian Army Division under

Opposite page above: 17 August 1942. The Americans are getting a taste of the air war over Europe as they prepare to raid a French freight railway at Rouen.

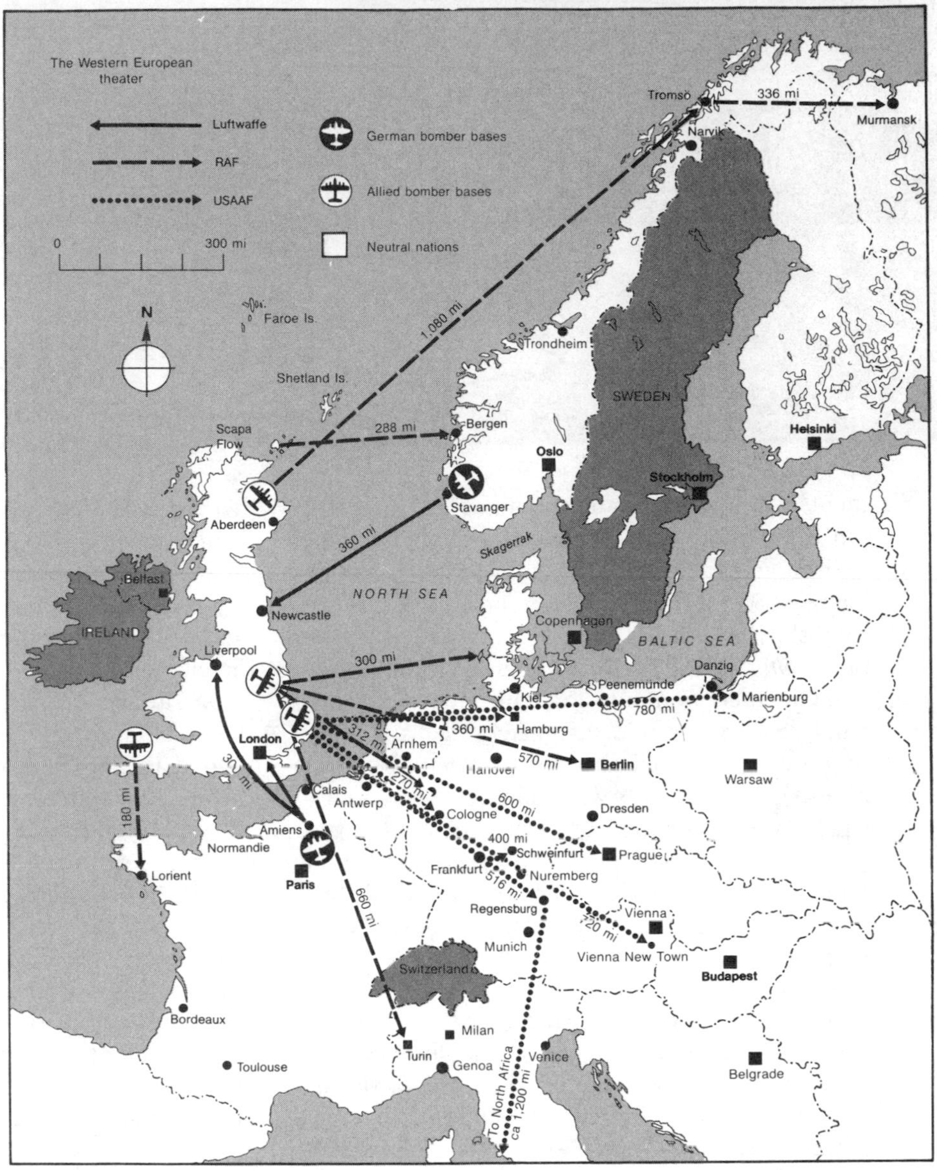

Right: The Western European theater.

Opposite page below: A Soviet fighter squadron taking a noon break. Most regimental commanders worked hard to create the best possible conditions for their pilots.

flew non-guided attacks on whatever German targets they happened to find. The Soviets adopted German fighter plane tactics and deployed their fighters in two pairs of 2 planes each.

Another aircraft carrier battle took place in the Pacific, the first since the Battle of Midway on 3rd–7th June. At 4:00 P.M. on 24 August 1942, aircraft from the US carrier *Saratoga* attacked the Japanese carrier *Ryuju* and scored some 10 bomb hits and one torpedo hit that soon sank the vessel. At the same time Vice-Admiral Chuichi Nagumo ordered dive bombers to take off with fighter cover from the decks of the *Zuikaku* and the *Shokaku*; they dived from an altitude of 16,000 feet onto the US carrier *Enterprise*; it retreated in flames and had to be replaced by the carrier *Wasp*. The Japanese broke off their operation without forcing a showdown, and the Americans chalked up the naval battle as a victory for their side.

In the summer of 1942, both the British and the Germans worked intensively on experiments with tinfoil strips as the best means for jamming enemy radar. But British scientists concluded that the strips could not be used because they might give away the secret to the enemy, and then Britain's radar-based air defense system would become useless. Meanwhile German scientists reached the same conclusion. When General Martini, commander of German aerial intelligence, handed Göring a report about German experiments with radar chaff, the dismayed Reich Marshal ordered the report to be destroyed at once. The Germans actually halted their experi-

Left: A Japanese Yokosuka E 14Y1 seaplane. Pilot N. Fujita, and his observer S. Okuda, flew the first and only bombing raid on the USA in an aircraft of this type.

Opposite page: Sicily, 10 October 1942. Italian Savoia-Marchetti SM. 79 Sparviero (Sparrowhawk) bombers of 2 Squadron are ready to take off for a raid on Malta.

ments with anti-jamming techniques, to keep Britain from finding out about radar-chaff jamming.

In August 1942, while the tinfoil strip concept was being strictly guarded along both sides of the English Channel, the Japanese were serenely dropping *giman-shi* ("tricking paper") virtually every night in their bombing raids on Guadalcanal, to paralyze US radar-guided antiaircraft guns. The idea of gluing thin electrical wires between paper strips approximately 1 inch wide and 30 inches long—equal to one half the wave length of the US gun-laying radar—came from Corvette Captain Hajime Sudo, chief of radar defense for the Imperial Japanese Navy. The strips, dropped in packets of 20 strips each, cut down substantially on Japanese losses in night bombing raids.

Interestingly, neither the Japanese nor the Americans informed their allies about this novel device, and almost one year went by before the British decided to remove "Window," their tinfoil-strip radar-jamming device, from the list of classified materials, and to deploy it over Germany for the first time.

The British air pathfinder unit suffered a second failure on the night of 1st–2nd September 1942, when they tried to raid Saarbrücken but failed to find the target and instead marked out another town with flares. As a result, 120 tons of bombs, including a number of 3.6-ton aerial mines that were here deployed for the first time, mistakenly fell onto the romantic town of Saarlouis almost completely destroying it. After this second failure by the pathfinders, the RAF modified their tactics. Now, two Mosquitos carrying Gee receivers flew ahead to act as guides and to radio to the pathfinder aircraft the positions of searchlights and flak, as well as the locations where marker flares should be dropped to show the way to the bombers that followed. They also corrected inaccurate marking and directed the bomber stream in the role of "master bombers." This method was first tested on the night of 2nd–3rd September in a raid on Frankfurt am Main. Then on 8th–9th September the RAF made another night raid on Frankfurt, but mistakenly dropped both the marker flares and the bombs 12 miles away from the city.

On Tuesday 8 September 1942, a German BV 138 flying boat of the 706th Coastal Flying Group sighted a giant Allied convoy, Convoy PQ 18, comprising 39 freighters and one oiler, at the latitude of Jan Mayen Island. The convoy had an escort of 6 destroyers, one cruiser, and for the first time on the North Sea route, an aircraft carrier: the escort carrier *Avenger,* which carried 12 antiquated Hurricane fighters produced before the war, and several antisubmarine aircraft. Admiral Tovey, the commander of the British Home Fleet, remarked that it was a joke to ask such obsolete aircraft to provide cover for transport vessels filled with modern Hurricanes.

At dawn on 9 September 1942, the Japanese submarine I-25 (2,198 tons) under Frigate Captain Meija Tagami, lay off the coast of the state of Oregon. Inside the repair hangar was a Yokosuka E14Y1 seaplane. The pilot, N. Fujita, one of the youngest Japanese naval officers, pressed his eye to the periscope lens: "I looked out on the coast of Oregon where the mountains were still wreathed in mist and recognized Cape Blanco with its lighthouse. The stormy seas of the past ten days had grown calm again and there was a cloudless sky. 'Captain,' I said, 'it looks good. I think we can carry out our operation today.' 'Fine!' Tagami replied. 'In a couple of minutes you'll make history: you'll be the first man ever to bomb the United States of America.' "

The raid on the USA had been N. Fujita's idea. His proposal to make the raid with a plane based on a submarine, reached Admiral Yamamoto some time in the summer of 1942, just after Yamamoto received a report from the ex-Japanese consul in Seattle advising that the best and simplest way to spread panic among the enemy was to set fire to the abundant forests along the US west coast. Now the young naval flier was about to turn his idea into reality.

"After putting on my flying suit I made my last-minute preparations. I put a couple of locks of my hair, some finger-nail clippings and my will into a small wooden box. In case I did not return from the mission, these 'remains' would be delivered to my wife. Now everything was ready, my observer Okuda was inside the plane and the catapult was lit. We zoomed over the Cape Blanco lighthouse toward the coast and then turned northeast toward the target zone. The sun bathed the eastern sky in red-gold light. When we had travelled about 42 miles, I ordered Okuda to drop the first bomb over the huge forests. We flew another 9 miles eastward and let loose the second bomb. When we reached Cape Blanco again, we veered southwest. Suddenly I saw two freighters. We flew directly over the water's surface to avoid detection. A couple of minutes later we were concealed by the skyline. Only then did we veer off to look for our submarine. Soon we were back on board."

From 13th to 18th September 1942, German bombers of the 30th Bomber Wing, and torpedo bombers of the 906th Coastal Flying Group and of the 26th Bomber Wing, attacked Allied Convoy PQ 18 in the Barents Sea as it was trying to carry supplies to the Soviet Union. The aircraft sank 10 freight vessels (52,908 tons), while U-boats sank 2 transporters and 1 oiler (17,742 tons). The Germans lost 20 aircraft, some of them to fighter planes from the escort carrier.

On Friday 25 September 1942, just a few moments after the air raid sirens sounded in Oslo, the Norwegian capital was shaken by bomb explosions: The Mosquitos of 105 Squadron were carrying out the first of the RAF's famed low-level precision raids on German office headquarters. They raced over Oslo, flying almost as low as the rooftops, before the dismayed eyes of the German ground defenses. Their target was Gestapo headquarters, whose archives and index files contained the names of thousands of Norwegian resistance fighters. The buildings were destroyed with astounding accuracy.

On 29 September 1942, N. Fujita took off for a second bombing raid on the forests of Oregon, this time at night. He struck at the same spot as the first time, 50 miles west of Cape Blanco. This was the last bombing raid made on the USA to this day: Fujita could not make a third sortie, because the sea became too rough for him to take off.

Throughout September 1942, the continuing offensive sweeps by British fighters and fighter bombers against coastal shipping and traffic targets in northern France, Belgium and Holland, kept the German air defenses busy. In the autumn of 1942, British losses in night raids began to increase again: On Monday 28 September, night interceptors of the German 12th Air Corps (XII. Fliegerkorps) shot down their 1,000th British raider.

At the end of September 1942, the British began

الى كل عربي كريم

السلام عليكم ورحمة الله وبركاته وبعد، فحامل هذا الكتاب ضابط بالجيش البريطاني وهو صديق وفيّ لكافة الشعوب العربية فنرجو أن تعاملوه بالعطف والاكرام.
وأن تحافظوا على حياته من كل طارىء، ونأمل عند الاضطرار أن تقدموا له ما يحتاج اليه من طعام وشراب.
وأن ترشدوه الى أقرب معسكر بريطاني.
وسنكافئكم مالياً بسخاء على ما تسدونه اليه من خدمات.
والسلام عليكم ورحمة الله وبركاته

القيادة البريطانية العامة فى الشرق

To All Arab Peoples — Greetings and Peace be upon you. The bearer of this letter is an Officer of the British Government and a friend of all Arabs. Treat him well, guard him from harm, give him food and drink, help him to return to the nearest British soldiers and you will be rewarded. Peace and the Mercy of God upon you.

The British High Command in the East.

Useful Words.

English	Arabic	English	Arabic
English.	Ingleezi.		
English Flying Officer.	Za-bit Ingleezi Tye-yar.	Water.	Moya.
Friend.	Sa-hib, Sa-deek.	Food.	A'-kl.

Take me to the English and you will be rewarded.
Hud-nee eind el Ingleez wa ta-hud mu-ka-fa.

2672/PMEB/2,000-2/42.

Every RAF airman sent over North Africa carried one of these bilingual appeals printed on silk, politely asking aid of any Arabs he might meet if shot down.

to fight the German early warning system, Freya radar, with mass-produced "Mandrel" jamming transmitters that transmitted a broad band of noises and blotted out the Freya frequency: 118–128 megahertz. The Mandrel-equipped Defiant fighters of No. 55 Group approached to within 50 miles of the North Sea coast, where they flew 180-mile-long loops, thus jamming the German early warning system along the coast. Several more British aircraft, also equipped with Mandrel, flew along on every night raid to jam the early warning system farther inland.

US bomber units based in Britain were limited in their operations at first, due to orders that forces of the US 8th Army Air Force were to be formed into the 12th Air Force under command of General Doolittle, leader of the US raid on Tokyo, to serve in Operation Torch, the Allied landing in North Africa that was planned to take place in early November 1942. On October 9, 108 American bombers raided the French city of Lille; 4 were lost. After that the chief mission of the 8th Air Force was to fly cover for the North African convoy vessels of Operation Torch, and to raid German U-boat bases along the French Atlantic coast while the RAF shifted its main offensive thrust to the Mediterranean.

Germany used this respite from Allied bombing to reorganize its air defense. The German day and night interceptor forces, which had so far been separate, were combined, and the combined force divided into 5 fighter divisions under the Luftwaffe Commander Central. Amazingly, the German 3rd Air Fleet (Luftflotte 3) in France had no night fighter planes despite the fact that France was the real forefront of the German defense.

On Saturday 10 October 1942, Field Marshal Kesselring ordered a German-Italian aerial offensive against Malta. Every day from 10th through 19th October, the Axis air forces bombarded the island from morning until sunset, flying between 200 and 270 missions per day. Seventy Axis aircraft were lost, so the operation was halted. The cessation of bombing had dire effects on the later Axis retreat, and on their supply lines. While the Germans and Italians were raiding Malta, the British were preparing a decisive offensive at El Alamein. Their preparatory bombing raids started on October 9 and continued until just a few hours before the offensive began. The targets were Axis airbases, unloading points, transport columns and troop depots in North Africa.

At 9:40 P.M. on the moonlit night of 23 October 1942, 1,200 cannon of the British Eighth Army under General Montgomery, opened the offensive at El Alamein. The German and Italian air forces in the area had 129 bombers, 65 dive bombers, 55 ground-attack aircraft and 123 fighters. Montgomery had over 1,500 aircraft, 1,200 of which were stationed in Egypt or Palestine. Within 2½ hours, the British dropped more than 80 tons of bombs onto Rommel's deployment zone, foiling the planned German counterattacks.

Even more crucial to the outcome of the battle in North Africa, were the strategic missions by the Allied air forces and by British submarines, against Axis supply routes in the Mediterranean.

Allied air attacks sank 30% of the Axis supply

transports in September, and 40% in October. Two thirds of the Axis fuel supplies were lost. In the second half of October the RAF not only flew tactical sorties on the North African battlefield, and raided supply shipping, but also led strategic raids on Italy from its bases in England: its targets were Italian ports and supply depots. Seven hundred British bombers were deployed on these missions. One of the raids took place on 22nd–23rd October, when 100 Lancasters of RAF Bomber Command attacked the port and city of Genoa. Next day, Saturday 24 October, the Lancasters made a daylight raid on Milan; this was the only daylight raid in the series.

In the summer of 1940, after France fell to the Germans, the British set up a secret organization called the SOE (Special Operations Executive), whose mission it was to support and coordinate resistance in the occupied nations of Europe. The SOE's activities included sabotage, intelligence-gathering, political assassination, and the maintenance of radio contact between Europe and London. Groups of agents divided into autonomous sections according to nationality, were organized and trained in SOE training camps, and then infiltrated by air and sea into Occupied Europe. The first SOE members dropped "blind" into western Poland in autumn, 1941. The western Polish border lay just within range of the heavy British Whitley and Wellington bombers. Specially formed RAF squadrons flew night missions to supply weapons, ammunition and explosives to the resistance groups scattered all across the Continent. An extensive apparatus resembling a giant mail-order firm was set up to ensure the punctual delivery of supply containers. The containers had to be dropped by parachute at various isolated drop points, in such a way as to evade the German search squads. Some time passed before the complex system of night delivery began to run smoothly and the "reception committees" all over Europe learned how to order needed goods by radio and then to guide in the supply aircraft using signal flares. By the autumn of 1942, supplies were being delivered in heavy Halifax bombers, by the specially trained crews of 138 Squadron stationed at Tempsford.

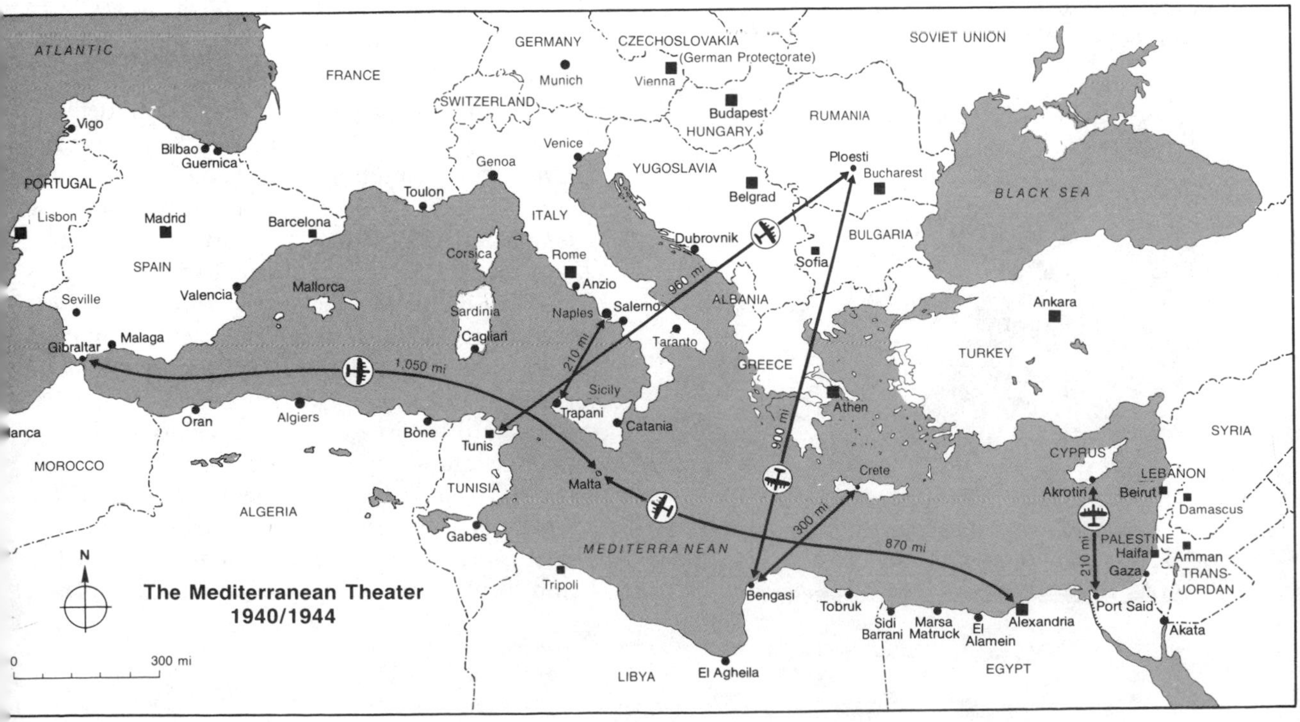

Above: Ringway, a British paratroop training center for SOE agents. This Whitley bomber is being used for training exercises.

The Mediterranean Theater 1940/1944

In addition to its supply runs, the SOE had a special aerial unit, 161 Squadron based at Tangmere on the south Channel coast, which made daring flights between Great Britain and the Continent, dropping off or fetching back SOE agents and members of the French resistance. Westland Lysander MK 5s were the aircraft deployed on these pick-up operations. These sturdy, black-coated machines with their lozenge-shaped, high-set wings and broad "gaiter" chassis, were equipped with a jettisonable long-range fuel tank and a boarding ladder, and were able to land and take off even from country fields. Favorite places for pick-ups were the pastures near Châteauroux, the banks of the Loire, the Dijon area and north of Lyons. Every SOE mission was a flight into the unknown because the pilots never knew who would be waiting for them on the landing strips hastily prepared behind the backs of the Gestapo. The aircraft departure times were transmitted the day before in a coded "personal message" included in the regular daily program of BBC radio. Often the Lysanders had to cross the English Channel or the North Sea two or three times before they could carry out their missions, because bad weather, inadequate ground visibility in the target zone, or attacks by German night interceptors or flak fire, would force them to break off their flight. The end of 1942 saw the development of the so-called S-phone, the forerunner of the walkie-talkie, which allowed radio telephone contact between the inflying aircraft and the reception committee waiting on the ground. Many Lysanders returned from their missions with flak damage or with high-tension wires wrapped around their wheels.

A Type "H" container. The SOE used these containers, which came in 5 variations, to hold weapons that it dropped by parachute to the resistance organizations in German-occupied Europe.

The bloody aircraft-carrier battle that took place at Santa Cruz, east of the Solomon Islands, on 25th–26th October 1942, was only one in a long series of bitter struggles for Guadalcanal. This battle, which put the large carriers on both sides out of action for the time being, began when Japanese General Hayakuta issued a premature victory announcement. His troops had attacked Henderson Field – the important landing strip on Guadalcanal – on October 23, and he assumed that by now they had already seized it. Henderson Field stood in the middle of the overgrown jungle on Guadalcanal Hill and had great strategic importance, because from this vantage point the Japanese could control the sea route from America to Australia. Vice-Admiral Nagumo sent a combined Japanese fleet along the northern end of Guadalcanal so that its carrier aircraft could land on the island as soon as the airfield was in Japanese hands.

US Task Force 16 with the carrier *Enterprise,* and Task Force 17 with the carrier *Hornet,* joined together on Saturday 24 October 1942. The combined naval force, under Admiral Halsey, was ordered to form a wide circle around the Santa Cruz Islands to impede Japanese forces from reaching Guadalcanal. Next day at noon, a US Catalina flying boat sighted 2 Japanese aircraft carriers, but the American forces were unable to locate the Japanese vessels.

On Monday 26 October 1942, "a day of calm sea, gentle south wind and low cumulus clouds," both fleets sent their carrier aircraft into the air. At 6:58 A.M. the first Japanese squadrons took off from the carriers *Shokaku, Zuikaku* and *Zuiho,* and a second formation prepared to follow them. Between 7:30 and 8:15 A.M., the US carriers *Enterprise* and *Hornet* sent up a number of dive bombers on armed reconnaissance. At 8:22 carrier aircraft from the *Shokaku* and the *Zuikaku,* took off for their second attack on the US carrier *Hornet.* Two dive bombers from the *Enterprise* attacked the *Zuiho,* which was forced to retreat in flames. The second Japanese attack wave struck the *Hornet*; and 6 bombs, 2 torpedoes, and 2 shot-down Japanese bombers that crashed into the carrier, turned it into a burning, immobile scrap-heap. Meanwhile US dive bombers seriously damaged the Japanese carrier *Shokaku* so that it had to veer off toward Truk Island. The carrier *Enterprise* was the next Japanese target. Two bombs broke through the hangar deck completely destroying the forward elevator; but the vessel retained its speed and maneuverability.

At 3:00 P.M. Vice-Admiral Nagumo sent a mixed combat unit against the *Hornet* and scored 3 more hits on her by 5:00 P.M.; but the ship chose not to sink even when US destroyers tried to finish her off by driving 9 torpedoes and 400 explosive shells into her hull.

The Americans withdrew their vessels in the evening when a formation of Japanese battleships and cruisers approached. At 1:30 A.M., two Japanese destroyers sent the blazing wreck of the *Hornet* to the bottom. All the US carriers had now been eliminated, and the battleship *South Dakota* and several other vessels were damaged. Two Japanese carriers had been badly hit.

The Japanese were unable to turn the tactical success of their fleet to advantage, for Henderson Field was once again in American hands and the US aircraft destroyed there had been replaced. The outcome of the fight for Guadalcanal was still undecided.

The British had diligently been building up the forces of their Coastal Command; this made it possible for them, in the autumn of 1942, to start deploying large numbers of aircraft against German U-boats. Also, the long-range Allied B-24 Liberator bombers enabled the British to control the North Atlantic, another major step forward in the battle against the U-boats. A network of radar stations grew up along the coasts of Great Britain and Iceland, designed to increase the success of antisubmarine defenses.

In late autumn of 1942, British Bomber Command began to employ a whole arsenal of more or less complex electronic countermeasures to inhibit the performance of German interceptor planes. One was a simple but effective jamming device called Tinsel, which severed the ground-to-air links between German pilots and the night fighter controller. A British airborne radio operator would attack a microphone close to the engine of his plane, then switch his radiotelephone to the same frequency as a German night fighter transmission, and drown out the transmission with engine noise. This jamming device, plus Mandrel, often made it almost impossible for the Germans to guide their night interceptors.

On Saturday 31 October 1942, the Luftwaffe carried out one of its retaliatory Baedeker raids on Britain. That weekend, 68 German FW 190s, with cover from 62 fighters, made a low-level attack on the picturesque town of Canterbury, where they dropped 17.75 tons of bombs.

The Battle of Guadalcanal: A Japanese fighter plane has been shot down by a Mitchell bomber of the 11th US Army Air Force.

The tide turned on the Eastern Front in late autumn of 1942, when the Soviets set up powerful tactical air units to support their ground troops. The Red Air Force bombers flew 93% of their missions at an altitude of about 160 feet, their ground-attack aircraft flew 80% of their missions at altitudes of as low as 35 feet. Unlike the German ground-attack aircraft, which approached at high altitude and then dived to carry out precision raids, the Soviets usually attacked in low-level flight, relying more on the dispersal effect of their aerial projectiles and bombs than on aimed fire.

At Stalingrad, Soviet aerial units operated in massed concentrations as they had done previously at Moscow and Rostov. The German Luftwaffe tried to force a breakthrough by deploying 1,000 aircraft at Stalingrad, half of all its aircraft on the Eastern Front.

The night of 7th–8th November 1942 — four days after Rommel's retreat from El Alamein — saw the beginning of Operation Torch, the Allied landing in Morocco and Algeria under the command of General Eisenhower, whose headquarters were based in Gibraltar. Almost everywhere the Allies encountered resistance from French loyal to the Vichy government. A number of French units that had already fought against the British in Syria, or remembered with bitterness the British raid on the French fleet in 1940, decided to fight back.

At 7:51 A.M. on Monday 9 November 1942, a violent air battle broke out over Casablanca between French fighter planes and aircraft from the US carrier *Ranger*. In a short time the harbor basin was filled with debris. Ten large transport vessels, 3 docked destroyers and 3 submarines were sunk or capsized. By evening a ceasefire had been agreed. But the Allies had failed in their first attempt to land and occupy Tunisia. That same day German troops arrived under orders from Field Marshal Kesselring,

Left: Pitomnik airfield in the Stalingrad troop pocket, where two Ju 52 transport aircraft from the German Blind-Flying School are being unloaded in a temperature of minus 40 degrees Centigrade.

Opposite page: One of numerous Soviet sound detectors set along German flight approach lanes during the Soviet air blockade of the German troop pocket at Stalingrad.

the German Commander South, to foil the Allied attempts at occupation and to cover Rommel's retreat. Alarm units commanded by Col. Harlinghausen, the newly-appointed German air force commander in Tunisia, landed 284 men at El Aouina airfield near Tunis, and they moved forward to form a defensive line, where they were supported by units of the 5th Paratroop Regiment and the 11th Airborne Engineer Battalion. Meanwhile the approximately 25,000-man French Tunisia Division were retreating.

At 7:00 A.M. on Wednesday 11 November 1942, the German First Army under General Blaskowitz, supported by the Felber Army Group under General Felber, crossed the border into the hitherto unoccupied region of France. The Germans called this Operation Anton.

Meanwhile the British landed in Bougie 120 miles east of Algiers, and next day, 12 November 1942, British airborne troops occupied Bône (Algeria), thus forestalling a German paratroop occupation. The Allies now pressed forward to Tunis by land. On November 15, US airborne troops landed at Youks les Bains to lend their support, and on November 16, British airborne units set down in Souk el Arba. Despite these efforts, the Axis powers won the race to Tunisia. The Germans flew in troop reinforcements and even recalled 400 aircraft from the Eastern Front to send to Tunis. The weather also worked to their advantage: Heavy rainfall turned the airfields of North Africa into mud and marsh so that the Allies could not operate there; meanwhile the Axis powers could use their dry taxi strips on Sardinia, which enabled them to bomb Algiers, Oran, Bougie and Bône almost daily.

Shortly before dawn on Thursday 19 November 1942, the Soviets launched a grand offensive north of Stalingrad, from beachheads at Kletskaya and Serafimovich on the Don river. The Soviet 2nd Air Army under Gen. Smirnov, and the 17th Air Army under Gen. Krassovski, provided air cover to the ground troops. Next morning the Soviets attacked south of Stalingrad too, this time with air cover from the 8th Air Army under Gen. Khriukin. On 20 November 1942, the 4 Soviet air armies that were massed along the southern flank of the front near Stalingrad, had a total of 1,916 aircraft including 152 bombers, 561 ground-attack aircraft, 803 fighters and 367 night bombers.

The Soviet troops encircled 20 German and 2 Rumanian divisions totalling 330,000 men, and the German "Fortress Stalingrad" had to be supplied by air for an extended period.

On Wednesday 25 November 1942, the first German cargo plane units began to fly in supplies to the German troop pocket. This duty fell to the German 8th Air Corps (VIII. Fliegerkorps) under Gen. Fiebig.

Feverishly the Germans prepared two large airfields, Tazinskaya and Morosovskaya-West (108 miles west of Stalingrad), from which to fly out supplies to the giant troop pocket. Tazinskaya was equipped to hold 600 transport planes – 11 groups of Ju 52s and Ju 86s. Another 400 transport planes were stationed in Morosovskaya. Spacious storehouses held all the supplies – food, ammunition, clothing and medical aids – that the German Sixth Army would need for months on end. Additional special units were to fly in supplies from other locations: 1 group of FW 200s and Ju 290s from Stalino (= Donetsk,

Ukraine); 3 groups of He 111s from Novocherkask; and Go 242 and Me 323 "Gigant" cargo glider squadrons from Makeyevka (Ukraine); but these units operated only rarely due to the extremely unfavorable weather conditions. There were three airfields inside the troop pocket of Stalingrad [to receive the cargo aircraft], but only two of the taxi strips were actually usable, namely Pitomnik and Bassargino. The weather determined whether the supply planes would fly in a compact formation with fighter cover, or one at a time without cover. The air crews were promised high decorations for making successful landings in the pocket in bad weather. The Udet Fighter Wing, which had suffered heavy losses in the battles of the summer, was detailed to give cover to the transport aircraft as they flew in for landings and took off again. Two squadrons of the Udet Wing were stationed at Pitomnik airfield to ward off Soviet fighters and bombers while the German cargo planes were being unloaded; but it soon became clear that this cover was inadequate. The new wooden-construction, maneuverable Soviet La-5 fighter planes shot down hundreds of the cargo planes that the Germans had gathered together from all their battle fronts, factories and flying schools. Moreover, the German fighters often failed to get off the ground due to fog, snow showers and low-hanging cloud. The Soviet air blockade of the pocket at Stalingrad was the first such operation in World War II. It was directed personally by the commander in chief of the Red Air Force, General Novikov. The bomber and low-level ground-attack aircraft of the Soviet 17th Air Army under Gen. Krassovski, operated out of airfields near the front. The fighter plane divisions of the 8th and 16th Air Armies (under Generals Khriukin and Rudenko respectively), were stationed 30–50 miles from the inner ring of enclosure, where they intercepted German transport planes along their chief approach lanes. Each of these divisions was responsible for maintaining one particular sector of the air blockade. An extensive system of guidance posts led the Soviet fighter planes to the enemy. Soviet aircraft patrolled the approach lanes day and night. Soviet antiaircraft barriers were set up 4 to 6 miles outside the inner ring of enclosure, where they opened fire on the transport aircraft as they were coming in for a landing.

On the night of 6th–7th December 1942, 272 RAF bombers raided Mannheim. It was during this sortie that the British began their concentrated jamming of the German night interceptor defense system. The British Mandrel screen jammed the Freya early warning system along a 180-mile stretch, while Tinsel jamming blotted out the German night fighters' radiotelephonic links. German operations were impeded to such an extent that the German fighters could detect British bombers only after the bombers were already out of range of the German "Giant-Würzburg" ground radar stations. British Bomber Command lost only 9 aircraft (3.3%) in the raid on Mannheim.

In the very first weeks of the Stalingrad airlift, the massed Soviet air defense caused heavy losses among the slow German transport formations that flew with inadequate fighter protection. With mounting frequency, one half or more of the 40- to 50-machine formations would be shot down. One day, only 10% of the 172nd Combat Group came back from Stalingrad.

The high casualties suffered by the slow and almost defenseless German Ju 52 transport planes, made it necessary to halt all massed daylight operations when the skies were clear. Starting on Tuesday 15 December 1942, all the German supply missions were flown at night or when the day was very cloudy. At the same time, the Soviets increased their offensive sweeps against Pitomnik and Bassargino airfields inside the troop pocket, as well as against the German takeoff bases [outside the pocket], took a high toll of aircraft and ground personnel. The

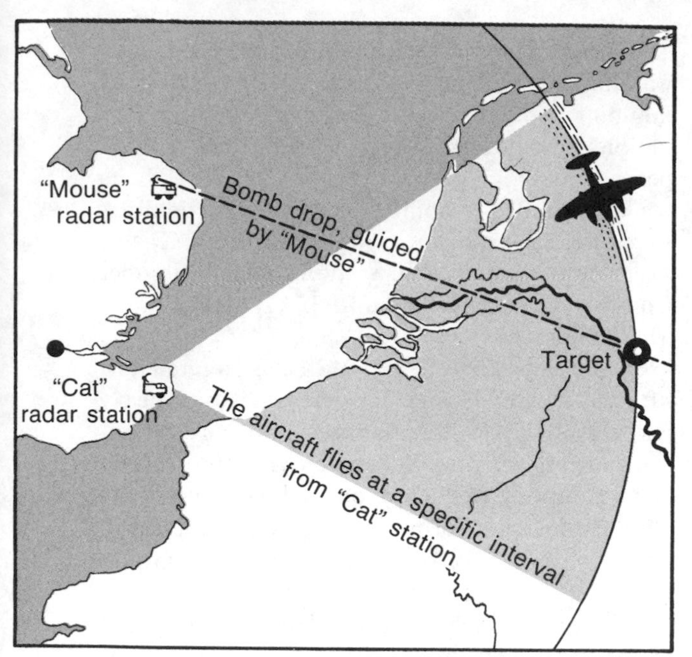

German formations were so decimated that, apart from the special air units stationed at Stalino and Makeyevka, the Germans stopped referring to their aircraft as part of a group or squadron, and classified them only as flyworthy or unflyworthy. Radio defects due to atmospheric moisture, inadequate servicing and explosive damage contributed to breakdowns at the takeoff bases.

In the week before Christmas, the weather turned so bad that only a few German pilots experienced in blind-flying, succeeded in making a landing inside the pocket. Of every 10 planes that took off from Tazinskaya or Morosovskaya, only 6 would reach Stalingrad on an average run, and only 3 or 4 would make it back to their bases.

On Sunday 20 December 1942, 6 British Mosquitos of 109 Squadron, guided by the "Oboe" radar-controlled blind-bombing and navigational aid that was here used for the first time, raided a power plant in Lutterade (eastern Holland). "Oboe" made it possible to achieve a precision strike from a high altitude without seeing the target.

"Oboe"—the abbreviation of "observer bombing over enemy"—was the precision bombing system developed by the British to replace the easily-jammed Gee system. This target-finding radar used two ground transmitters—the "cat" and "mouse" stations—to lead an aircraft to its target by the shortest possible route. When a bomber deviated from course and started veering too far towards the "cat," the pilot would hear a series of dot signals coming through his headphones, and if he strayed too close to the "mouse," he would hear dash signals. As long as he stayed on the right course he would hear a continuous tone. The advantage of "Oboe" was that aircraft could deviate a long way from the arc of the guiding beam if they needed to evade flak or enemy fighters, because the dot and dash signals made it easy for them to find their prescribed course again. The range of the Oboe set was restricted by the curvature of the earth to about 270 miles, but allowed British bombers to raid the Ruhr District as far away as Dortmund. Initially, German attempts to jam Oboe were unsuccessful because the Allied transmitters had various methods to forestall them, for example by suddenly changing the wave length of transmissions just before the attack. The first two Oboe transmitter stations were in Dover and Cromer (Norfolk, England), and each could function both as "cat" and "mouse," so that they could guide two aircraft to their targets simultaneously. When a bomber neared the attack zone, the "mouse" station would transmit a warning signal. The bomber would automatically discharge its bombs or marker flares by blind drop at the point where the radar beams from "cat" and "mouse" intersected. Basically, Oboe was a further development of the German *Knickebein* blind-bombing system used during the Battle of Britain.

On Thursday 24 December 1942, the Soviets launched an offensive toward Kotelnikovo [southwest of Stalingrad]. By early morning their tanks had reached German-held Tazinskaya airfield [from which the Germans had been flying out supplies to their troop pocket]. The gigantic supply storehouse in the village was set on fire. A closed

cloud carpet lay just 65 feet overhead; there was a dense mist and a light snowfall. All the German aircraft had been ordered not to take off unless artillery fire broke out. In the first light of dawn, Soviet tanks rolled up to the airbase and many of the German aircraft soon went up in flames. About 120 aircraft managed to take off at the last minute, but days passed before the escaped remnant could reassemble at Salsk airfield. It was almost 200 miles from here to Stalingrad, and from this distance it was even more difficult to fly in supplies to the pocket.

On the evening of 30 December 1942, 11 FW 200 Condors of 7 and 8 Squadrons of German 3rd Group, 40th Bomber Wing, took off from their base at Bordeaux-Merignac headed for a southern target: the Moroccan port of Casablanca.

A German agent in Washington had informed German intelligence of a meeting to be held in Casablanca between the American and British chiefs

Above: British de Havilland Mosquitos, the most versatile and the safest combat aircraft of the war (only 1 lost per 200 operations). Built almost entirely of wood, Mosquito bombers were so light and thus so fast that they could do without any defensive armament.

Opposite page: Operational tactics of RAF pathfinder aircraft equipped with the "Oboe" blind-bombing device.

Right: Map of the organizational layout of the German air defense against RAF night raids in autumn 1942. Radar and flak stations were designated by animal names like "Drossel" and "Kolibri" ("Thrush" and Hummingbird").

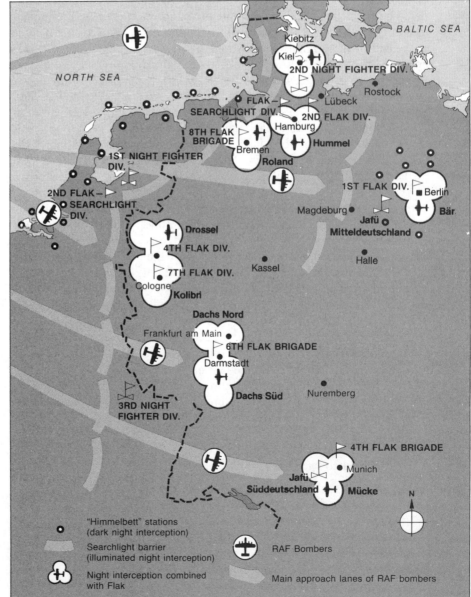

NORTH SEA
BALTIC SEA
Kiebitz
Kiel
2ND NIGHT FIGHTER DIV.
Rostock
Lübeck
FLAK–SEARCHLIGHT DIV.
2ND FLAK DIV.
Hamburg
8TH FLAK BRIGADE
Bremen
Hummel
Roland
1ST NIGHT FIGHTER DIV.
2ND FLAK–SEARCHLIGHT DIV.
1ST FLAK DIV.
Berlin
Magdeburg
Bär
Jafü Mitteldeutschland
Drossel
4TH FLAK DIV.
7TH FLAK DIV.
Kassel
Halle
Cologne
Kolibri
Dachs Nord
Frankfurt am Main
6TH FLAK BRIGADE
Darmstadt
Dachs Süd
Nuremberg
3RD NIGHT FIGHTER DIV.
4TH FLAK BRIGADE
Munich
Jafü Süddeutschland
Mücke
N

"Himmelbett" stations (dark night interception)
Searchlight barrier (illuminated night interception)
Night interception combined with Flak
RAF Bombers
Main approach lanes of RAF bombers

The Focke Wulf FW 200 Condor, a German long-range bomber, was designed as a passenger aircraft and did not meet the specifications for military deployment, but nevertheless proved very successful in the Battle of the Atlantic. A total of 263 were built.

of state and their highest-ranking military authorities. The agent did not know the date of the secret meeting, but the suspicion was that it would be held at the end of the year. To demonstrate the striking power of the German Luftwaffe, 11 four-engined Condors were sent to Casablanca. Eight reached the city where they dropped 7.95 tons of bombs, mostly on the native residential quarters. On their return flight 3 Condors crashlanded in Spain, and one FW 200, the F8 + JR No. 0166, had to land in Seville due to lack of fuel, where it was later turned over to the Spanish Iberia airlines.

In 1942 the British and Americans dropped 53,755 tons of bombs on Germany and the Occupied Zone. Hitler's retaliatory strikes came to only 3,260 tons. The German leadership were forced to recognize that even with the maximum effort, Germany could not have combatted an Allied air offensive successfully that year, because much of the Luftwaffe was tied down on the Eastern Front. Yet, many of the RAF's raids had miscarried, and the range of Allied bombers on daylight raids was limited by their need for protective fighter cover; so the Germans failed to grasp the full seriousness of the threat posed by the imminent Western strategic bombing offensive.

Sir Arthur Harris, the chief of British Bomber Command, said of 1942 that it was a year of preparations; it caused little damage to the enemy but fortified Allied convictions that bombers could be used to beat him.

Churchill admitted that although the British had by now substantially improved the precision of their aim during night-time area bombing, they had not noticeably weakened German war production or the morale of the German civilian population; they had underestimated the strength of the German people.

The Allied raids already had a strongly strategic character, although concentrations on particular target groups were not yet much in evidence. The essential fact is that from 1942 on, the initiative in the air war in Western Europe lay completely with the Allies. Moreover, Allied tactical sorties in support of the ground forces, and missions against Axis supply shipping, also crucially affected the outcome of the war in North Africa and thus in the whole Mediterranean region.

The final tally of results in the 1942 air war against Germany showed that the RAF had made approximately 100 night raids; in 17 of them, more than 500 tons of bombs were dropped. British casualties were 5.6% of aircraft deployed; one bomber was lost for every 40 tons of bombs dropped. The toll of German dead was minimal compared to what it cost the British: It took 3 tons of bombs, and a four-engined bomber with a 6- to 8-man crew, to take one German life. One hundred four-engined bombers were needed to kill 100 civilians, at an average loss of 6 bombers and 40–50 flying crew. Of the civilians killed, 65% were women, children and old people. The effect of the "strategic" raids was correspondingly limited.

1943
January to June

Daily Keynote from the Reich Press Chief,
Friday 8 January 1943:

The debate in England about the British failure to carry out their advertized air raids on German cities, should not lead us to make gloating criticisms, for these might provoke the British, and if then they did in fact come to raid us, the German people might accuse us and our propaganda of being to blame.

Secret Report of the German *SS Secret Service* on internal affairs, No. 349 dated Monday 11 January 1943 (extract):

I. General comments: The terrorist enemy air raids that have now resumed on a regular basis, are lowering morale in the western Reich. The air assaults on various cities, especially in the last few days, have caused considerable depression, above all in the city districts directly affected by the raids. Particularly the women speak almost desperately about the scope of the air raids and the consequent prospects for the future. Throughout western Germany complaints are made that the air raid alert is sounded too late and that flak fire begins immediately after the first siren signal, accompanied simultaneously by the falling of the first bombs. People in the Ruhr District often say they wish that the alarm could be sounded earlier, even if this would mean that sometimes it might turn out to be a false alarm. Women point out that unless the alarm is sounded early, they are not able to dress their children in time and get them and a few necessary items to a place of safety.

Thursday 28 January 1943
RAF Headquarters announced:

On Wednesday the diesel engine plant and shipyards of Copenhagen were the target of a heavy bombing raid by RAF Mosquito bombers. Squadron Leader Edwards, the leader of the raid, reported: "It was one of our most successful operations of the war so far. The sun was shining brightly when we reached Copenhagen and we were able to fly low over the target and drop our time-fuse bombs directly into the factory sheds. By the time we took off for home, the plant was in flames." One Mosquito bomber was lost.

Saturday 30 January 1943
RAF Headquarters announced:

Today at 11:00 A.M., British Mosquito bombers raided Berlin precisely when Reich Marshal Göring was about to address the German people at the German Air Ministry. Our operation, in which only a few aircraft took part, forced Göring to postpone his speech for one hour. This was the first time that British bombers have made a daylight raid on Berlin. The pilots said that the cloud layer prevented them from getting an accurate view of the targets they hit. German air defenses were hardly in evidence, they reported; they were able to detect only 12 flak salvos in the Berlin area.

Monday 1 February 1943
RAF Headquarters announced:

The heaviest British bomber squadrons were deployed in the air raid on Hamburg that took place on the night of Saturday–Sunday. They reached Hamburg in extremely unfavorable weather that led large amounts of ice to form on their wings. Despite the violent whirlblasts, they dropped thousands of incendiary bombs on a 9-mile-long stretch of the port district. In addition, high-explosive bombs dropped in a thirty-minute period, fell on oil refineries, shipyards, warehouses, fuel depots and

Left: Reich Marshal and Luftwaffe commander Hermann Göring is standing with General Adolf Galland, commander-in-chief of the Luftwaffe Fighter Arm with 104 air kills to his credit, in spring of 1943. At this time the German fighter units had to be ready for combat virtually 24 hours a day to ward off the USAAF daylight raids and the RAF night raids.

Opposite page: German bomber crew examining the model of an English city. The lightbulbs show the distribution of marker flares to be dropped by the German pathfinders. Precise planning was needed to carry out night raids on the strongly-defended British industrial centers.

various industrial plants; some of them weighed between two and four tons. The British Air Ministry describes the damage inflicted on Hamburg as "extremely severe." Of the several hundred bombers that took part, only five failed to come back.

Thursday 11 February 1943, Berlin
The *German News Bureau* reported:

By joint order of the Commander-in-Chief of the Luftwaffe, the leader of the Party Chancellery, the Reich Minister of the Interior, and the German Youth Leader, [male] secondary-school pupils are to serve as Luftwaffe Auxiliary soldiers in areas threatened by air raids. Members of the Auxiliary Corps are to continue living in or very near their homes. The military deployment of German youth represents one further step toward the total mobilization of the German people.

Pointers for British Pilots in the Lysander Agent-Pick-Up Operations

Wing Commander C. Wiston, London 1942:

Most of the work that goes into a successful pick-up operation, needs to be done before takeoff. Never rely too much on your own navigational abilities when you are flying a Lysander. You should make careful preparations for every operation regardless of how experienced you may be.

Flight Route Selection

Once you know the exact location of your target, study the map (scale 1:500,000) and look for an outstanding landscape feature near your landing point, maybe a river that you cross to approach the target. Next, review the special flak-emplacement map to see where the German antiaircraft might disrupt your flight. Then work out a route that enables you to fly with the guidance of landmarks and avoid flak emplacements. Look for a clearly visible landmark, for example a coast or a large river, each time you make a turn. Don't forget that the first time you make your approach flight, the reception committee may not be there. It is important that you make a sure identification of the landing place, even if this means having to locate a barn or some similar feature you have seen on the aerial photograph. Regardless of the weather forecast, every time you fly you should be prepared to follow a roundabout route on your return. Your radio equipment could break down, and would you ever feel silly if you didn't have the slightest notion where to go or how to get there. Don't forget that maps often get lost when you are airborne. No map you take with you should be irreplaceable. As a rule you should be sure to take along an old road map in case of emergencies. Before takeoff, spend a few hours sitting comfortably in an armchair reading your maps. You will have a much easier time during the flight if you study the maps thoroughly beforehand. Jot down notes about the landmarks on your route. Try to impress on your mind the shapes and the locations of wooded areas. Note the cities you may possibly overfly, and their nearby landmarks. Take note of the course of coasts and rivers.

Plane Loading

Normally you can transport a maximum of 3

agents although 4 people have been carried without difficulty. You must keep in mind that with a 3- or 4-passenger load, it is not possible to carry parachutes as well. When 4 agents are on board, one sits on the floor, 2 on the rear seat, and one on the hull braces. However, this is not recommended with stout people. The heaviest luggage should be stowed under the rear seat near the plane's center of gravity. Small, important pieces of luggage like moneybags should be attached to the hull braces ready to hand so that they are not forgotten in the plane. Don't entrust anything to the rear fuselage because it is hard to recover luggage that has slipped into the tail section.

Fuel

The more fuel you take along, the heavier the aircraft will be during landing and takeoff. However, it is possible that the reception committee may be delayed and that you will be forced to circle in the air for an hour, or if you get lost, it may take you some time to find your route again. Possibly you may need more fuel than you had anticipated on your return flight, to reach your landing field in Britain. You should have fuel reserves for approximately two flight hours.

Emergency equipment

In case you have to make a crash landing, it is a good idea to have some civilian gear in your plane. You should also take along escape aids in a standard "escape kit," some French money, a revolver and a thermos bottle containing hot coffee or tea. A bottle of brandy or whisky comes in handy. Remove from your pockets anything that might interest the Germans, but don't forget to take along your civilian passport photo: it may prove useful later if you have to get false papers drawn up. It is advisable to wear clothing without tailor's labels, laundry marks or initials. It's very hot inside a Lysander cockpit, so it's better to wear shoes rather than your flying boots. If you have to cross the Pyrenees by foot, you will not have any trouble [while wearing shoes].

Before Takeoff

Make sure if the agent knows how much gear he is supposed to carry and where it should be stowed. He must know how to put on and use a parachute. The same goes for the on-board intercom. He must know the system of emergency warning lights and how the exchange is conducted after landing. As you know, the agent is to remain inside the machine while he hands out his things and accepts the luggage of the returning agent, before he climbs out. On those rare occasions when an agent has experience of night flying, it is useful to give him a map with the route drawn on it. One of our operations failed when a pilot went badly off course and the agent, an experienced French flying officer who knew exactly where they were, could not tell the pilot because the intercom was switched off.

Crossing the Channel

Some pilots recommend that you should overfly the Channel at low altitude, staying if possible underneath the German radar screen. I personally oppose this because you run the risk of being shot at by Royal Navy antiaircraft guns or enemy convoys. Also [if you are flying low] in a heavily loaded plane, you do not reach the necessary flight altitude fast enough to cross the enemy coast with the greatest possible safety. In general it is less dangerous to overfly the French coast at the highest possible altitude, up to 8,100 feet. This gives you a better overview of the situation on the coast and you can avoid being shot at by light flak or machine guns. Also, don't forget that your Lysander is unarmed and completely defenseless, and if you have the bad luck to cross the path of a German fighter, there's nothing to do but pray.

Conduct in the Target Zone

As you approach your landing point, carry out your cockpit drill. This includes switching your signal lamp over to Morse, pressing down arm supports, putting back your blend control. Do not by any means switch on your landing searchlights. You should trace your target by approaching a landmark located approximately 2½–3½ miles from the landing point, because from this distance you can clearly distinguish the marker lights set out by the reception committee. If you do not see the marker lights at your estimated arrival time, circle around and look for them. One of our operations failed because the pilot flew twice on an absolutely straight course over the landing field without seeing the light signals, because they lay directly underneath him. When you have found the marker lights, identify the agreed-on signal. You must be absolutely convinced that it is correct. If anything seems unclear to you, you must not land on any account. There have been cases where the Germans have tried to get Lysanders to land, and the only reason the pilots got away was that they abode strictly by this rule. In one case when the rule was not followed, the pilot came back home with 30 bullet holes in his aircraft and a bullet in his neck. He got away alive only because he landed some distance away from the illuminated track and took off again immediately.

Landing

Make a steep approach in order to avoid trees or other obstacles. You should not set down before reaching the marker light, or farther than 80 feet away from it. During the final seconds of landing make absolutely certain that you use the landing searchlights unless it is a bright moonlit night; but switch them off the moment you touch down. While you are still taxiing to a halt, carry out your cockpit drill in preparation for the takeoff so that you are ready to take off at once the moment you have stopped. At this moment you may be pretty jumpy, but you must on no account forget the mail or the information that you may be given. Pay attention to the "passenger exchange," and take off as soon as you hear the "OK."

The Return Flight

Don't forget that navigation is just as important on the return flight as on the outbound flight, although you can afford a small deviation from course once you are outside the range of the flak and headed into the coast. For your passengers' sake, you must not get shot down on your return flight. Finally, keep in mind that pick-up operations are a perfectly normal form of military transport. Don't pretend to anyone that you are a circus acrobat, because in the past this notion has always led to reduction in the number of the operations.

Tuesday 2 March 1943
Top-secret personal message from *Prime Minister Churchill* to Marshal Stalin:

Last night the RAF dropped over 700 tons of bombs on Berlin in an air raid that is said to have been very successful. We lost 19 out of 302 four-engined bombers.

6 March 1943
Top-secret personal message from *Prime Minister Churchill* to Marshal Stalin:

The weather was unfavorable over Berlin last night, so we dropped more than 800 metric tons of bombs over Hamburg with good success. This is a very large quantity to have been dropped within so short a space of time.

Daily Keynote from the Reich Press Chief,
Friday 12 March 1943:

British threats to intensify the air war should not be published in Germany. The language of German propaganda regarding Britain should under no circumstances sound whining, but must seem tough and composed.

Daily Keynote from the Reich Press Chief,
Saturday 13 March 1943:

The Minister has remarked concerning the air war that the British always know exactly what their bombs have destroyed, whereas we receive no precise reports about [the results of] our air raids. We are too open and honest in our reporting, the Minister says, and spread news where we ought to be making propaganda. The Minister also tells us not to supply data about the destruction of churches, because the data the British supply about the destruction of churches always reveals what success we have had. The percentage of churches destroyed has enabled us to gauge [the amount of] destruction to railroad stations and industrial plants. In future we ought not to supply these sorts of clues to the British. On the other hand, we should naturally publish reports about individual world-famous German cultural monuments that have been destroyed.

A Westland Lysander Mk III Special Duty aircraft built to the specifications of the SOE (Special Operations Executive) with a jettisonable fuel tank and a boarding ladder for the secret agents it would pick up or drop in Occupied Europe. The first pick-up operation was carried out on 4 September 1941 near Châteauroux 150 miles south of Paris, by Squadron Leader John Nesbitt-Dufort of 138 Squadron.

15 March 1943
Secret personal message from *Marshal Stalin* to Prime Minister Churchill:

I have received your messages of the 6th and the 13th March, informing me of the successful British bombing raids on Essen, Stuttgart, Munich and Nuremberg. With all my heart I salute the British aerial forces as they continue to step up their bombing assaults on German industrial centers.

Secret Report of the German *SS Secret Service* on internal affairs, No. 367 of Monday 15 March 1943 (extract):

I. General comments: The excitement of Germans about the "Anglo-American air offensive" is reported to have increased after the raids on Munich, Stuttgart and Essen. The people are very concerned about the raids and are telling each other tales of thousands of dead, tens of thousands of homeless, and of the destruction of big industrial complexes and essential munitions plants in these cities. When German armed forces reports are published, people's primary concern virtually everywhere is "where they [= Allied bombers] were last night"; only secondarily are they interested in the other news. In the areas threatened by air raids, people fearfully ask every day: "Will it be our turn tonight?" Particular disquiet has been caused by the widespread rumors of air leaflets that are said to have been dropped during the raids, which allegedly list a series of particular cities – Berlin, Munich, Nuremberg and several others have been named – that the Allies plan to "level to the ground" or "turn into another Stalingrad" between now and the Führer's birthday.

Extract from the diary of Reich Minister *Dr. Joseph Goebbels,*
Saturday 20 March 1943:

I am suggesting to the Führer that our air raids on England be in future aimed not at the slums but the wealthy districts. My experiences indicate that this is the way to make the deepest impression. The Führer too holds this opinion. Our aerial reprisals will not take place for another five to six weeks, but can then be large-scale. The Luftwaffe itself has been slow and reluctant to adjust to the new course of aerial warfare. The Führer continues to be extremely dissatisfied with the Luftwaffe generals.

Extract from the diary of Reich Minister *Dr. Joseph Goebbels,*
Saturday 10 April 1943:

The British are publishing grand communiqués about the damage they have inflicted in the air war. Their claims are by and large correct. The British espionage service inside Germany functions alarmingly well.

Saturday 17 April 1943, London
The *British Air Ministry* announced:

On Friday–Saturday night, 600 British bombers took part in the largest night operation of this year when they raided two of the most important German munitions plants. Large numbers of Lancaster and Halifax bombers penetrated to the Skoda munitions works in Czechoslovakia. Thirty-seven of the bombers are missing. At the same time another British formation of Wellington, Stirling and Halifax bombers raided munitions plants in Mannheim and Ludwigshafen. Eighteen bombers failed to return from this raid. Our reports say that the two raids were very concentrated and successful.

One bomber pilot who took part in the operation against the Skoda plant, reported: "The 1,500-mile flight over enemy territory was all the more dangerous because the sky was almost cloudless and the bright moonlight put the German night fighters into the ideal position to attack. All the crews knew per-

The German Focke-Wulf FW 190 fighter and low-level ground-attack aircraft, proved their worth both in front-line deployment and in the air defense of Germany.

fectly well that many of them might be making their last flight. To our amazement the outbound flight went off without any obstacle; some dogfights took place only on the return flight. But over the Skoda plant itself we were greeted by numerous night fighters and extremely strong flak fire.

"The Skoda plant, which covered 325 acres, lay clearly visible to us in the bright moonlight. Nevertheless our pathfinder aircraft dropped hundreds of magnesium signal flares which lit up the individual targets—the steel works, the machine sheds, the blast furnaces and forges as well as the assembly shops—as bright as day. Meanwhile the other bomber wings had arrived, and now the bombardment began to devastating effect. Many of the new-model 2- and 4-ton bombs went off inside the plant causing multiple explosions. After only a few minutes, whole rows of factory buildings collapsed, and 25 minutes after the attack began, nothing could be seen of the Skoda plant but a single gigantic sea of flame. Finally a special unit of Lancaster and Halifax bombers carried out low-level precision raids and destroyed five more industrial installations that had gone unscathed at first. We all had the impression that all hell had broken out underneath us."

One of the bomber crews reported concerning the Mannheim-Ludwigshafen raid: "Our unit admittedly was quite a bit smaller than the one that bombed the Skoda works, but we used the heaviest bombers in the RAF. The targets of the operations were machine and electrical plants, as well as a factory that manufactured diesel engines for submarines. Several squadrons succeeded in flying underneath the flak and dropping 2- and 4-ton bombs fitted with time fuses from an altitude of 150 to 500 feet directly into the plant installations. There was considerable ground and air defense. We could only watch as several of our heavy bombers crashed into the sea of houses while flying directly over Mannheim and Ludwigshafen. As we flew away we counted more than 30 large conflagrations and numerous smaller fires."

17 April 1943
Secret personal message from *Prime Minister Churchill* to Marshal Stalin:

You said to me in a recent telegram: "I applaud the bombing raids on Essen, Berlin and other German industrial centers. Every blow that your air forces strike against vital centers in Germany, finds the liveliest echo in the hearts of millions of people all over our land." The commander-in-chief of our bomber crews would very much like to pass this message on to his squadrons, who would truly be delighted to hear it. Will you permit me to do so? There is always the possibility that it might end up being reported by the Press. I personally feel that the effects of this could only be good. What is your opinion?

Sunday 18 April 1943, Stockholm
The Swedish newspaper *Svenska Dagbladet* reported:

The weekend was marked by unusually strong Anglo-American air raids on the Rhineland, and equally remarkable successes by the German defenses. On Friday night through to Saturday the RAF attacked southern and southwestern Germany, especially Mannheim and Ludwigshafen, losing 55 planes, mostly four-engined bombers. This may well be one of the highest, if not the highest, shoot-down records for a single night.

Berlin assures us that the raider formations were no stronger than usual, so the German air defense—mainly reinforced numbers of night fighters operating with improved technical equipment—must be responsible for the high number of Allied casualties. Also, visibility conditions greatly favored the defensive forces. The reason is that now moonlight no longer favors the attacking aircraft but the defenders, so that recently the RAF has preferred to transfer its attacks to clear but moonless nights.

The Battles in Tunisia

Monday 19 April 1943
The *Headquarters of British General Montgomery* announced:

Now, for the first time, a detailed description has been given of the air offensive that preceded our breakthrough of the Mareth Line and our advance to Enfidaville (Tunisia). An RAF staff officer gave this account:

"The Allied air forces had three missions [in the offensive]: First, the fighter squadrons had to form a dense aerial screen above the battle zone and the no-man's-land, to protect our troop movements from enemy reconnaissance planes. General Freyberg's columns were then able to advance toward El Hamma without our troops sighting a single enemy plane.

"The air forces carried out their second task immediately before the [Allied] Eighth Army made its assault, when squadrons of Hurricane tank-buster aircraft with their large-caliber, rapid-fire aerial cannon took off to attack the German tank formations and supply columns. The work of destruction was complete in only 90 minutes. The Spitfires had already cleared the air of the enemy when the Hurricanes, diving to within 35 feet of the ground, plunged down and drove their cones of automatic fire into the massed German troops. In this short time 30 heavy German tanks were annihilated, approximately 60 to 70 medium armored cars were damaged and several hundred vehicles of all types destroyed. Immediately after the Hurricanes had done their work, Boston and Baltimore bombers appeared and completely destroyed the dispersed remnants of the columns. General Montgomery said concerning these operations, carried out under cover from Spitfires: 'Never before has there been such outstanding cooperation between various air force units and ground forces.'

"Finally, the third mission was carried out by the Mediterranean Allied Strategic Air Force under the direct command of General Eisenhower, which operates over the Mediterranean and the supply ports in Italy and Sicily. Long-range bombers and long-range escort fighter planes took off from Algeria, Libya and Malta. These strategic bomber groups inflicted heavy material damage on the Axis powers."

Wednesday 21 April 1943, Moscow
The *Soviet Information Bureau* announced:

Last night Soviet long-range bombers again raided Tilsit. It is reported that a sizeable number of the new Soviet heavy bombers took part in the operation and that major damage was inflicted

A heavy British Handley Page Halifax night bomber of 405 Squadron is being loaded with 1,100-lb bombs. The Halifax and the Avro Lancaster were both standard RAF bombers. A total of 6,176 Halifaxes were built.

Left: A row of Halifax bombers just before takeoff. The "life expectancy" of a Halifax was approximately 6 weeks, during which it would fly an average of 20 sorties; the same was true for its crew. The first five flights were the period of highest risk; they claimed 40% of the casualties.

on Tilsit. The interviewing of pilots has not yet concluded.

Thursday 22 April 1943, Washington
The *US War Department* reported:

The news of the execution of US airmen who fell into Japanese hands last year after raiding Tokyo in planes from the aircraft carrier *Hornet,* has released a wave of indignation in the American public, of a kind that has not been seen in the United States since Pearl Harbor. An official government statement has cited the conduct of the Japanese government as barbarous.

Destruction of a German Air Transport Fleet

Friday 23 April 1943
General Eisenhower's Headquarters announced:

Kittyhawks and Spitfires of the Allied Tactical Air Force, while patrolling the straits of Sicily, discovered just above the sea surface a formation of 20 German Me 323 six-engined large-capacity transport aircraft, escorted by 40 to 50 fighters. The Kittyhawk and Spitfire fighters attacked instantly, and all the transport planes were shot down in an air battle that lasted barely ten minutes; 8 German Me 109s and 2 Italian fighters were also shot down. The giant transporters were on the way from Sicily to Tunesia carrying troops and fuel [for the Axis troops]. It was the first time in this war theater that the German Luftwaffe has deployed its giant transporters, which are very vulnerable due to their great size.

The Night of the Bombs

The German publication *Das Reich* carried the following descriptive article in April 1943:

It was like the aftermath of a battle. Afterward we talked about how quietly we had sat there together while the signals of death went whistling past our ears. [The air raid] lasted barely one hour but it seemed an eternity. Each second wrought more devastation on the city. We were talking with Berlin at the time, while one of us recorded the conversation in shorthand. The voice speaking on the other end of the line was soft and faraway, and had that mysterious vibration produced by a long-distance telephone wire. Sometimes the recording secretary shrugged her shoulders and said that she had not understood what was said because another bomb had just fallen. The whole of the dictation was segmented by these intervals between the bombs; but the secretary went on bravely and her fingers dug into the paper as, with a sigh of exhaustion, she wrote the final period.

During that hour our past lives became concentrated like a rolled-up film when you cannot see how many pictures it contains. We thought about beautiful fleeting things that began to glow until they hurt. Then we smoked a cigarette without tasting it. We walked from one door to another hoping that the racket would subside, but the continuous noise of heavy crashing weights never altered. When the light went out we turned on the emergency light, which put a lot of distance between our large white faces; so all I can remember about the man next to me is his posture, the way his hat sat on his forehead, but not the expression of his features. We felt ourselves becoming more and more estranged, even when we spoke to each other in words that were determinedly meant to sound cheerful. Then we all came back to life when someone cried that our windows were spitting fire, and we dashed forward without a trace of our former paralysis. Suddenly we had overcome the distance created by the emergency lighting, and now each of us stood beside or just behind another, touching him, talking to him, speaking out loud.

There was fire all around us. The sparks danced

across the yard. The men turned on the hoses while we went back inside; we felt as if we had lost something there. Even today, whenever I enter this room I feel that something of mine must have gotten left behind there; but I find nothing. We were on duty that night and could not leave the place, but concern for our loved ones drove us to the telephone. When one of us heard the telephone ring at the other end, he reasoned that it must mean his house was still standing. Each one of us tried to reach home. Some of us gazed wide-eyed when they heard no responsive ring from the earphone.

Fire was racing along the street. Red tongues leaped at the sky. The flames chased up and down the road on the wings of the noisy wind. With a monotonous lamenting sound, staircases, curtains, furniture, fabric, paper and leather collapsed into the blazing blast furnace and turned into ashes. Glass splintered and flew into the street, and an endless train of sparks travelled over the sky. People incapable of saving what had fallen prey to devastation in the last hour, ran searchingly under the spark-strewn arch of the sky, scarcely knowing who they were or what had happened. At the same time high clear sirens signalled the approach of the fire brigades, one after another. They sent high jets of water hissing out of the hoses while timbers broke and trees bent down in the growing conflagration.

As I walked along, a soldier with an amputated arm walked beside me. I felt that there was nothing separating us even though we did not know each other. This night's battle had turned us into soldiers too.

The sun shone next day. We bathed our eyes, which were burning from the smoke and sulfur. Many of the familiar tracks in our life had been shattered. Coming generations would scarcely understand what had happened in this night. We walked along with our hearts like stones inside our chests. Many people went past with tear-stained faces. What formerly had been the impressive façade of a building, now lay on the ground, a heap of sooty stones. Fire still licked the wall hollows sending up bluish smoke. Our churches, including several monuments of medieval architecture with noble soaring towers, had sunk to the ground, dissolved, scattered, turned into a splintered mosaic of the past. Shop buildings, pharmacies, doctors' offices, homes were heaps of debris. Many people were walking around looking for the places where they worked, and found nothing left but the smoking remains of walls. What was left standing, was showered with chalk and mortar dust and blackened by smoke. The rooms of buildings were filled with dry, charred air, with unimaginable filth, with the damp traces of the firemen. As the city came gradually to life, we blew away our own emotional ashes. We put on aprons, took brooms and scouring cloths, poured buckets of water inside the offices, attended to the fires that kept flaring up again over and over, formed chains and passed water-filled vessels along them, carried the furniture of fire-threatened people down to the ground floor, talked about the disaster while we worked, exchanged details of what we had experienced when we returned home, told what had happened to a neighbor woman, to a friend who had nothing left. But in the same breath we talked of how this or that person had been helped. It was understood that everyone had something to offer, one a meal, another a room, another some pieces of clothing.

We saw with amazement that everything that had interested us the day before – a new film, a hat we wanted to have – no longer had the remotest importance. We had given up so much that night: the amenities of a large progressive city, its movie-houses, opera, theater, cafés, the beautiful fashion houses – but we had also given up our claims, our demands, our desires. Suddenly so many things had ceased to mean anything to us: a trip, a fight, a plan. Many of the wall remains were inscribed with big chalk letters written by survivors, saying: "We are all alive and we're living at No. 28 W-Street." Everyone who passed by offered these unknown survivors a mute but heartfelt greeting, the greeting of life. The living wrested triumph out of the dust. They lived and wanted to go on living, despite all the bombs and the cowardly murderers who dropped them.

The Labor Service, the Todt Organization, the armed forces and the SA put their strong hands to work to restore the torn network. They drove trucks, shovelled away debris, blew up blind shells and buildings that were past saving, helped to salvage property spared in the raid, brought the homeless to shelter, and distributed food. The destroyed components of our city machinery were replaced. Running water and gas were restored, the first streetcars began their runs. The owners of burnt-out shops moved new goods into undamaged buildings and shared the premises with the businessmen who were already there. Doctors who had lost their offices brought medical aid to the homeless. Once again there was work for everyone to do.

Efforts at self-help were everywhere in evidence. People whose homes had received only light damage, fetched cardboard and nailed up the window holes. Restaurateurs made rough-and-ready repairs to their damaged premises. Shopowners sold off their remaining goods before they turned to repairing their damaged homes. Many of the homeless managed to leave the city, some of them on their own, others by the efforts of the National Socialist Public Welfare. Schools rapidly set up convoys to transport children into the countryside where they ensured that pupils would be housed in remote areas.

After the hurlyburly of those days, there came a chance to breathe and think things over. Now there was no longer any doubt: We had passed through our baptism of fire. Wherever you looked you saw the grim, resolutely determined faces of people fetching their belongings out of the cellars in baskets and boxes and sheltering them in a place of fragile safety. Already you could buy flowers in the stalls again, blooming bizarrely in the face of the ruins: Italian mimosas and tulips with soft dark red cups. Confirmation ceremonies were very reduced due to the great destruction of the churches. Some candidates were being confirmed in hospitals.

Inquiries multiplied as relatives and friends sent telegrams and urgent phone calls to find out how we were. The post office was the assembly point for thousands of people sending out their good and bad news. The hands and heads of many people were wrapped in bandages.

Sometimes now we pick up a book that talks about spring nights when the stars bud over quiet houses, or a picture that shows us in high spirits, relaxed, happy and young. How long ago that was, we think. The wonder of the ever-changing seasons is still hidden from us. Now we have other things to think about, for we are fighting for our lives. We have no other weapons than our hearts, but they are bright and sharp. So our lives, delayed now and then by painful shocks, are seeking a familiar trail that yet is narrower than before. The opera house is used to distribute food to the homeless. Varicolored buses from many different cities are stitching the torn traffic network together again. Sometimes a bird sings behind our window; the screaming siren may drown out his little song in the next moment. Every night we are ready to ward off the barbarous enemy with the naked blade of our hearts.

Soviet Air Offensive against Germany

Saturday 24 April 1943, Moscow
The *Soviet Information Bureau* announced:

A few months ago, a series of newly-built aircraft plants in the Ural Mtns. began mass production of four-engined long-range bombers. Ever since then, the Red Air Force has been setting up special heavy bomber units. The operations that the four-engined aircraft have flown so far against Königsberg, Danzig and Tilsit, were merely experimental actions to pave the way for the Red Air Force offensive against Hitler's Germany.

24 April 1943, Moscow
The *Headquarters of the Soviet Military High Command* (STAVKA) announced:

On the night of 22–23 April, 200 Soviet long-range bombers took off on a mission against Insterburg in East Prussia. Several military and industrial plants were destroyed during the two-hour raid, and many fires started in the city, accompanied by violent explosions. All but one of our aircraft returned to base.

Fighter Planes Overfly the Atlantic

Friday 30 April 1943, Washington
The *United States War Department* reported:

For some time fighter planes have been crossing the North Atlantic without making any intermediate stops; the conduct of the war has thereby entered a new phase. The long flights are made possible by attaching disposable fuel tanks to Lightning fighters, which substantially increases their range.

Right: The most striking construction feature of the Soviet Petlyakov Pe-8 long-range bombers was the two hand-operated machine-guns in the inner nacelles. Reports said that the plane was being mass-produced, but only 79 were built—approximately the number of heavy bombers lost by the Western Allies on a single day.

Opposite page below: German civilians experiencing the shock of a bombing raid: "Coming generations would scarcely understand what had happened."

Secret Report of the German *SS Secret Service* on internal affairs, No. 381 of Thursday 6 May 1943 (extract):

I. General comments: No apathy is visible [among the German people]. For example, after the heavy raid on Essen on the night of 30 April–1 May, they were observed to be busily at work very early next morning, clearing up the minor damage, and in the afternoon work was going on everywhere in small gardens. The only bad sign is that thefts from bomb-damaged buildings have increased from one attack to the next. Reports from western Germany, and also from other parts of the Reich, indicate that people are saying that the Allied air offensive is a result of the [German] declaration of total war [in which Hitler called for mobilization of German civilians]. This misunderstanding has led to a certain animosity by our people against the Reich capital, from which total war was proclaimed. Characteristic of this attitude is a verse that is already widespread throughout the industrial zone:

Fly on Tommy soldier, it's clear
we're all just miners here.
Fly to Berlin, it's not far:
it's there they wanted war.

Monday 17 May 1943, London
The British *Air Ministry* announced:

The Allied air offensive against Germany has taken on a new aspect with raids on pinpoint targets—as opposed to so-called area bombing. Another positive development in Allied air war strategy—our experts say—is that recently we have increased deployment of the swift Mosquito bomber in night operations. It is believed that this new tactic has caused considerable confusion among the German defenses, because now they are forced to prepare simultaneously for our slower-moving heavy bombers and for the faster lighter Mosquitos. The Mosquitos are so fast that they can escape pursuit by enemy fighters.

For the time being the Allied air offensive is being favored by good weather; thus the raids will no doubt be stepped up this month. RAF spokesman Major Stewart confirms that British Bomber Command alone [i.e. apart from other Allied forces] is able to deploy 400 to 600 heavy bombers per night.

The Dam Raids

Tuesday 18 May 1943
RAF Headquarters:

Wing Commander G. P. Gibson of 617 Squadron reported: "Before takeoff the mood of our crews was very tense, and I am happy to be able to say today that the results achieved have far outstripped our expectations. The bombs we dropped have torn the Möhne Dam in two."

One of the pilots of 617 Squadron stated: "But what our wing commander did not mention is that he was the first one to drop his bomb on the dam with pinpoint accuracy, and then with a complete disregard for death he flew along the dam to draw the flak fire onto himself so that we could continue to destroy the dam without interference. Wing Cmdr. Gibson remained in the field of fire until he was convinced that we had all dropped our payloads. The dam burst after the first square hit, and a column of water close to 1,000 feet high shot into the air. The pressure of the water mass was inconceivable and it carried everything before it until it was no longer possible to recognize the villages that lay in the floodwaters."

18 May 1943, Berlin
The *German News Bureau* announced:

The enemy foreign press are breaking out in sensational speeches about the supposed effects of

British bombing raids on two German dams. The facts are these: The damage done to the two dams has in fact led to serious civilian losses. However, damage to the war economy is comparatively less serious and to some extent can be repaired within a short time. First, the electrical plants fed by these storage lakes supply only a fraction of the total electricity in Germany, and second, the plants served mostly to satisfy peak demands.

Extract from the diary of Reich Minister
Dr. Joseph Goebbels,
18 May 1943:

Last night seriously damaged our side in the air war. The raid by British bombers on our dams was very successful. The Führer is extremely impatient and angry at the inadequate preparations made by the Luftwaffe.

Wednesday 19 May 1943
RAF Headquarters announced:

Yesterday our reconnaissance aircraft overflew the area of the Eder and Möhne Dams several times, and they have determined that damage to the dams was far more extensive than we at first assumed. Their reports have also been confirmed by aerial photographs.

Admiral Yamamoto Is Dead

Friday 21 May 1943, Tokyo
Imperial Japanese Headquarters announced:

Admiral Isoruku Yamamoto, Commander-in-Chief of the Japanese Combined Fleet, died last month aboard an airplane during combat with the enemy. Japan has lost one of its greatest and most able naval commanders. Admiral Yamamoto's name in inseparably linked with the Imperial Navy's great victories in this war, with the annihilation of the American fleet at Pearl Harbor, the sinking of the *Prince of Wales* and the *Repulse,* and with the numerous sea battles that have been successfully fought for Japan all over the Pacific. The Emperor has ordered a state funeral for Admiral Yamamoto and posthumously appointed him Fleet Admiral. Admiral Koga has been chosen as his successor.

21 May 1943, Washington
The American *United Press News Agency* reported:

Radio Tokyo has announced the death of Admiral Yamamoto as he was directing fleet operations on board an aircraft carrier.

Secret Report of the German *SS Secret Service* on internal affairs, No. 385 of Monday 24 May 1943 (extract):

I. General comments: The effects—often greatly exaggerated—of the raid on the Möhne and Eder Dams, have very rapidly become a topic of conversation all over the Reich and have caused great alarm, especially because the Wehrmacht report stated that the loss of life was high. Many Germans are seeking an explanation of how such an attack was possible; they fear that the flak and barrage balloons gave the dams inadequate protection.

Wednesday 26 May 1943, London
The British *Air Ministry* announced:

Early yesterday evening a formation of German FW 190 fighter bombers attempted a surprise raid on a city in southeastern England but was successfully warded off. The German aircraft approached the city in low-level flight, but were intercepted by fighters of a French wing of the RAF and were forced to jettison their bombs aimlessly into the sea. Several dogfights took place between Spitfires and Focke-Wulfs; the French pilots succeeded in shooting down 4 of the German aircraft. Yesterday forenoon, an earlier formation of Focke-Wulf fighter bombers flying with an escort bombed a city in southeast England. In this operation the enemy also lost 4 planes, 3 to antiaircraft guns and one to a British Hawker Typhoon fighter.

Raid on Wuppertal

Sunday 30 May 1943
The *Wehrmacht High Command* announced:

Yesterday enemy plane units attacked the city of Rennes in Brittany and several of our bases on the Atlantic coast, and last night they bombed several western German cities. Heavy damage occurred to buildings. There were civilian casualties, especially in Wuppertal. Present reports indicate that 57 enemy aircraft were shot down, mostly four-engined bombers. Four of our own fighters were lost.

30 May 1943, London
The British *War Office* announced:

The non-stop Allied air offensive against targets in Germany continued on Saturday–Sunday night as RAF bombers carried out a heavy raid on Wuppertal in the Ruhr District. Authoritative sources have described the raid as "very concentrated and successful." Thirty-three of our aircraft have not

King George VI. is visiting 617 Squadron after their raid on the German dams. Wing Commander G. P. Gibson describes the mission using the practice model.

come back. Two German night fighters were shot down. Wuppertal, a city of over 400,000 inhabitants, is the largest center of the German textile industry, but it also contains dyeworks and machine plants including a large ball-bearing plant.

30 May 1943, Berlin
The *German News Bureau* concluded a survey on the civilian damage inflicted by the Anglo-American air force with the warning:

The day will come again when, horror-stricken, they will recognize that National Socialist Germany can never be weakened and bowed down by terrorism, but in the end will strike down every terrorist with his own weapons. Sometimes German mills appear to grind slowly—but they grind exceeding fine.

Thursday 10 June 1943
General Eaker, commander of the US Air Force in the European war theater, stated:

US aerial forces in Great Britain have doubled since March of this year, and will double again by September. By the end of this summer, Allied air might—made up of US bombers for daylight raids and British bombers for night raids—will have grown to such an extent that we can achieve the goal we have set. But even then the war will not be over because it cannot be won by air attacks alone.

Saturday 12 June 1943
US 8th Air Force Headquarters announced:

Late Friday afternoon, more than 200 US B-17 Flying Fortresses and B-24 Liberators made a violent raid on the two German ports of Wilhelmshaven and Cuxhaven, despite meeting a strong air defense. The bombers, which operated without fighter cover, succeeded in dealing a number of square hits to the extensive U-boat bunkers. A sizeable quantity of German fighters were shot down in aerial combats at Wilhelmshaven. Reports from participating air crews are still being checked. The USAAF lost 8 of the more than 200 planes deployed.

12 June 1943, London
The British *Air Ministry* announced:

Last night strong units of Bomber Command aircraft overflew western Germany; their main target was Düsseldorf. Early reports indicate that extensive damage was inflicted. Another bomber formation bombed the city of Münster with good results. Several other targets in the Ruhr District and the Rhineland were also raided. Forty-three bombers failed to return from these operations. One enemy plane was shot down by one of our fighters over Holland.

The Creation of a Tactical Air Force

Monday 14 June 1943, London

It has been officially revealed that reorganization of the RAF has resulted in the creation of a "Tactical Air Force." Its duty is to achieve even closer cooperation with the ground troops. This new air force, commanded by Vice-Admiral J. H. Delbiac, the former RAF commandant in Ceylon, consists of wings made up of all types of aircraft that are suited to lend direct support in the ground fighting. The *Times* newspaper describes this as the most significant reform by the RAF since the war began.

British Raid on Krefeld

Tuesday 22 June 1943, London
The *United Press News Agency* reported:

Official sources say that the raid on Krefeld, an important industrial city and junction for rail traffic heading west from the Ruhr District, was "very heavy and concentrated." This massed operation by heavy four-engined bombers that delivered the largest quantities of bombs dropped so far on a single target, is said to be one of the largest missions ever flown against Germany, the only comparable raid being that made on Düsseldorf on 11 June 1943.

Strategy and Tactics

January to June 1943

The remains of burnt-out and wrecked machines lay piled across Pitomnik, the snowed-over German advanced airfield in the treeless steppes west of Stalingrad.

Victims of the Soviet air blockade and of the merciless weather, they bore witness to the destruction of the German Luftwaffe's best units of transport aircraft. The German airlift to their besieged troops had by now turned into a desperate rescue operation; but it was clear to everyone that they could no longer avert the tragic fate of the encircled German Sixth Army under General Paulus.

At the turn of the year the German transport operations were reshaped when Colonel Förster was replaced by Colonel Morzik, the experienced organizer of the air supply operations to the German troop pocket at Demyansk in the winter of 1942. Once again the entire Luftwaffe was combed for available aircraft. Not only all the aircraft and crews of German Lufthansa airlines, but also industrial transport planes and even Hitler's private courier squadrons were placed at Morzik's disposal. Aircraft arrived carrying civilian crews, with ordinary flight captains and test pilots who had no winter equipment. Experimental aircraft were called up too, some made by the Siemens electrical equipment firm; these contained the first fully automatic three-dimensional autopilot, which so far had been kept top secret. Suddenly all the landing runways were blocked by these aircraft, which had somehow to be reequipped for winter deployment out of the meager stores. The tourist planes also lacked the essential airborne radar equipment, and had no winter safeguards, armament or parachutes. On 6 January 1943, 6 Ju 52s flew into the takeoff bases, the private planes of Göring, Ribbentrop, Ley and other party leaders who had made them available for the Stalingrad airlift.

The numbers of Soviet fighter planes in the Stalingrad area were overwhelming and the Germans could not try to get their transports through when the sky was cloudless. Consequently, when the weather cleared up dramatically in the first week of January, the Germans could make no supply flights for 8 days. Even night flights were full of hazards, because the Soviet flak and searchlight ring had now been reinforced and was claiming increasing numbers of German aircraft. The Red Air Force surrounded Stalingrad with a series of mock airfields with radio beacons on similar frequencies to those of the German fields and with identical airway markings. A number of German aircraft landed there thinking they were inside the troop pocket. The Germans experienced further confusion from incessant night-time offensive sweeps by antiquated Soviet U-2 biplanes that dropped fragmentation bombs and fired their machine-guns at German planes taking off and landing in the pocket. These insidious little aircraft, which the Germans dubbed "sewing machines" because of the rat-a-tat-tat sound of their engines, used to fly along Soviet searchlight beams aimed at the airfields in the pocket.

On Sunday 10 January 1943, a 55-minute-long heavy barrage by 7,000 cannon and trench mortars heralded the beginning of a Soviet offensive on the Don Front led by General Rokossovsky: the Soviets were going to smash the troop pocket at Stalingrad. The Germans just had time to fly out all their specialized Luftwaffe personnel before their two airfields, Pitomnik and Bassargino, both fell. At the same time, Soviet troops advancing to the Caucasus crossed the Manych River and stood outside German-held Salsk. On January 16 the Germans had to evacuate Salsk too. The bulk of the German air transporters at Salsk were transferred to Sverovo airfield and continued their flights to Stalingrad from here.

On 17th–18th January 1943, 118 German bombers raided London, suffering 6 losses. This was the first German night raid on London since 10th–11th May 1941.

An official notice from the German Armed Forces proclaims that at least on paper, German civilians killed and wounded in air raids are to have the same status as soldiers at the front: From now on, dead civilians will be said to have "fallen in battle."

**1083. Änderung der Bezeichnung
für »getötete« und »verletzte« Zivilpersonen
bei Luftangriffen**

Da die Opfer von Luftangriffen unter der Zivilbevölkerung ebenso wie die Soldaten an der Front für Deutschlands Größe verwundet werden oder fallen, ist auch für Zivilpersonen die Bezeichnung »verwundet« oder »gefallen« anzuwenden.

O. K. W./AWA/W Allg./Ob. d. L. Arb. St. LS, 4. 6. 1943
Az. 41 a Nr. 150/43 (1 I C).

Bekanntgegeben.

Der Ob. d. L., 4. 6. 1943,
Az. 41 a Nr. 150/43 (Arb. Stb. LS 1 I C).

L. V. Bl. S. 571

Admiral Isoruku Yamamoto (1884–1943), the commander-in-chief of the Japanese Combined Fleet.

At the beginning of 1943, Allied low-level "tank-buster" antitank aircraft started to operate with increasing frequency over German airbases in Tunisia. Around 200 German Ju 52 and Me 323 Gigant giant transport aircraft remained in Italy and Sicily to fly supplies to the Axis troops fighting at Tunis. German aircraft preferred to land in Tunis and Bizerta (Tunisia) in the daytime because night landings were extremely hazardous. They also made occasional landings in the Tunisian ports of Gabès and Sfax. German casualties were heavy. On 18 January 1943, for example, Allied fighter bombers destroyed 23 Ju 52s on the ground at the Tunis airfield in a single raid. The Germans flew in reinforcements, and even recalled 400 aircraft from the Eastern Front to send to Tunis, which brought some relief to the Soviet armies.

The Anglo-American conference held at Casablanca from 14th to 25th January 1943, resulted in agreements about future Allied operations in the Mediterranean, as well as in publication of a demand for Germany's unconditional surrender. The British and Americans agreed that their air units would fly a "combined bomber offensive" against Germany, aimed at the following targets in the order of their importance:

1. U-boat submarine bases and U-boat manufacturing plants
2. German aircraft plants
3. main traffic junctions
4. oil refineries and synthetic fuel plants
5. ball-bearing plants and munitions plants

So far RAF assault tactics had concentrated on the area bombing of German cities, but the American view was that real success could be achieved only by pinpoint targeting in daylight raids. The plan was for US bombers to attack industrial plants in the daytime and for the RAF to raid residential districts at night. At the end of the conference a communiqué was published that repeated the doubtful tenets of the Douhet theory and justified the terrorist raids on Germany as crucial to the war effort. Air Marshal Sir Arthur Harris, the commander of Bomber Command, said that the last moral inhibitions had been removed at the Casablanca conference and that Bomber Command had now been given a completely free hand.

The top-priority rating given to bombing U-boat installations, resulted from the fact that the Allies had to win the Battle of the Atlantic before they could undertake any large-scale operation against Fortress Europe. Churchill pointed out that up to the end of 1942, German U-boats had been sinking Allied shipping faster than the Allies could build it. In January 1943 the Germans had 235 U-boats on active duty, the largest number so far.

At 8:00 A.M. on Friday 22 January 1943, Soviet units on the Don Front under General Rokossovsky launched their final advance against the German Sixth Army encircled at Stalingrad. Shortly after the attack began, the Soviets seized German-held Gumrak airfield; now the little Stalingradski airfield at the edge of the city was the only link between the pocket and the outside world. At dawn on January 23, German Air Lt. Krausse and his crew took off in the last aircraft left inside the pocket, from a narrow advanced airstrip at the edge of Stalingrad. It was an He 111 with its elevator half shot off and carrying 9 wounded. After that, German cargo aircraft no longer landed but only dropped supply containers to their troops.

That same day the German-Italian armored army evacuated Tripoli and retreated to the Libyan-Tunisian border. Two Axis aircraft wings—one in Sicily, the other in Naples—were detailed to fly supplies to the armored units. Their landing fields in Gabès and Sfax, lacked both ground organization and night-flying facilities. Only the most experienced transport crews dared to land there, and night duty was so hazardous that usually only a solitary aircraft could get through. British fighters based on Malta, attacked the German transport planes over the Mediterranean. The British kept particularly close check on the air space around the Axis takeoff bases at Trapani and Castelvetrano (Sicily).

In the daytime, formations of up to 100 German

Ju 52 and giant Me 323 transporters would fly in a stream with Me 109 fighters or Me 110 aerial "destroyers" flying cover. The stream would be made up of several smaller, close-knit groups of 20 to 24 planes each.

In January 1943 the US 8th Air Force in Britain began to build up a strong fighter plane force to use in defending its bomber formations. The first US P-47 Thunderbolt fighters began to arrive in Britain; but their range extended only to the coast of Holland.

On 27 January 1943, US bombers flew their first mission onto German territory. Sixty-four four-engined B-17 Flying Fortresses and B-24 Liberators made a daylight raid on the U-boat and port installations at Wilhelmshaven, the city that had been the first target of British daylight raids back in 1939. This first American air raid on Germany was carried out without fighter cover and very low casualties were suffered: only 3 bombers were shot down.

On Saturday 30 January 1943, 6 rapid British Mosquito bombers of 105 Squadron based on Bourn, carried out the first Mosquito raid on Berlin; this was also the first daylight air raid on the German capital. Just at noon, two 2-ton aerial mines suddenly fell from an altitude of 30,000 feet, straight onto the radio broadcasting building. The British intended them as a surprise package for Reich Marshal Göring, who was just about to give a radio speech to celebrate the tenth anniversary of Hitler's seizure of power.

By mid-January 1943, 10 Halifax pathfinder bombers of No. 35 Group Bomber Command, and 13 Stirling bombers of No. 7 Group, had been fitted with H2S radar. H2S (an abbreviation of the British codename "Home Sweet Home"), reproduced the profiles of landscapes and cities on the scope. Using this device, British navigators would see German cities displayed as bright silhouettes, and lakes and rivers as darker patches. Pathfinder aircraft were the first to be fitted with the new system, but the plan was for every bomber to carry it by mid-1944. H2S radar proved very important in the later bombing offensives and contributed more than any other radar to the downfall of the German cities, for it made it possible for the bomber formations to obtain an excellent image of the target zone even in darkness and in bad weather, at times when the German fighters might be prevented from takeoff. Once the radar had been developed, a long debate ensued in Britain as to whether it should actually be used; for the British feared that if one of the aircraft carrying H2S was shot down over enemy territory, the Germans could capture the device, reproduce it and use it against the Allies. Then, on the night of 30th–31st January 1943, H2S was used for the first time in a raid on Hamburg. Four-engined pathfinder aircraft equipped with the new radar marked the targets to show the way to the 92 aircraft that followed; 315 metric tons of bombs were dropped on the Hanseatic city with only 5 losses to the British.

The beginning of 1943 saw radical changes in the Red Air Force. Following a reorganization, each Soviet front received its own air army of 700 to 800 aircraft which had enough power to operate independently. In February 1943 the Soviets finally won air supremacy and held it until the end of the war. From 1943 on, the German Luftwaffe had to deploy two thirds of its fighters to defend Germany against the Anglo-American bombers; as a result the numbers of German Luftwaffe planes on the Eastern Front fell to only 20% of the Soviet forces.

On the night of 2nd–3rd February 1943, 137 British aircraft dropped 460 metric tons of bombs on Cologne. Only 5 aircraft were lost on this raid, the second supported by H2S radar. One of the lost

Left: The famous Soviet U-2, one of the most-produced aircraft in the world (30,000 were built), was designed in 1927 by N. N. Petlyakov. Here it is serving as a medical plane (U-2S2).

Opposite page: US Republic P-47 Thunderbolt long-range fighter planes. The Thunderbolt was the most-produced US fighter (15,660 were built) and was also the largest and heaviest single-engined single-seater fighter of the war.

planes, a Stirling pathfinder of No. 7 Group, was shot down by a German night fighter at Rotterdam. Searching through the debris next morning, German salvage specialists found an unfamiliar device in the lower rear fuselage. The device, weighing approximately 330 pounds, was reconstructed in the Telefunken laboratories in Berlin. To their great surprise, German scientists learned that it was a blind-bombing radar that functioned on the 8.7-cm wave length, a frequency that the Germans had up to now deemed unsuitable for such a purpose. It was, in fact, an H2S panorama airborne radar that worked independently of ground transmitters and regardless of poor visibility, and facilitated both navigation and precision bombing – a great advance in the field of radar technology. The Germans built reproductions of the device for their own use and named it "Rotterdam" after the city where they had found it.

The encircled German Sixth Army at Stalingrad sent out their last radio message on Tuesday 2 February 1943; after that communications were cut off. The northern troop pocket under General Strecker surrendered to the Soviets – and the Battle of Stalingrad came to an end. That evening a few German He 111s flew in to drop supply containers over the city, but they could discern no movement in the vast sea of snow-covered debris. Between 25th November 1942 and 2 February 1943 – a period of 70 days and nights – the Luftwaffe had flown in 6,600 tons of supplies to the troop pocket at Stalingrad, a daily average of approximately 100 tons, which was only one third of the planned amount. Their only victory was that they had rescued 34,000 wounded men from certain death or captivity. The price they had paid was the destruction of 495 operating transport aircraft – the equivalent of a powerful air force – and at least an equal number destroyed on the ground. Approximately 1,000 flying personnel had been killed. German General Pickert said later that "During the remainder of the war the German Luftwaffe never recovered from the losses it suffered in the Stalingrad airlift."

In the Pacific the Americans were gradually fighting their way to air supremacy, the first thing they needed before they could open strategic operations against Japan and recover the territory it had seized at the outset of war. The US aerial forces were now strong enough to protect their war and transport ships from Japanese bombers, and they began to intervene in the ground fighting during landing operations. On 8 February 1943, after several major sea and air confrontations, the Japanese finally evacuated the island of Guadalcanal which had been the scene of hard fighting ever since 7th–8th August 1942. The duties of the Allied aerial forces in the Pacific were of even greater moment than in the European war theater, because air supremacy determined naval deployment capability and sea supplies.

550-lb Explosive Bomb of the German Luftwaffe
Length: 5 ft 4 in
Diameter: 1 ft 6 in
Explosive component: 52.2%

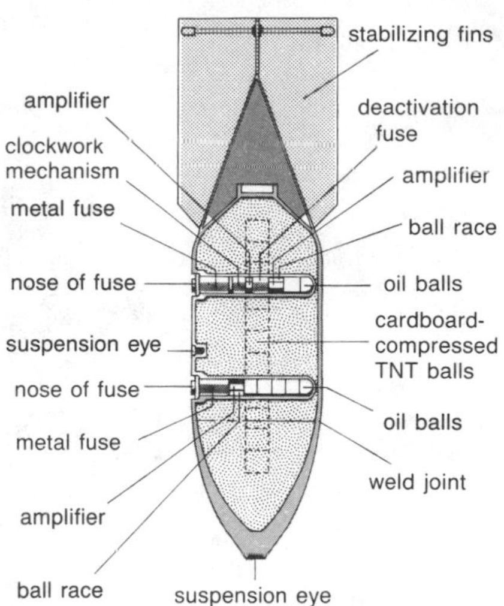

However, on the Asian continent, the Allies confined their aerial operations to support of the ground troops. It was particularly important for them to maintain air supply routes in the impassable regions of Burma and China.

On Thursday 11 February 1943, one week before Goebbels gave a speech in the Berlin Sports Palace issuing Hitler's declaration of "total war," all German secondary-school pupils born in 1926–1927 were called up to serve as Luftwaffe Auxiliary soldiers (flak-helpers). Fifteen- and sixteen-year-old boys took on the task of setting up and manning light, medium and heavy flak batteries. To begin with they were to continue living near home, where supposedly they would go on with their schooling at the same time. Even as fighting soldiers the flak-helpers remained members of the Hitler Youth. They functioned well, in time came to bear the main burden of flak operations in the German air defense, and often suffered heavy casualties. In addition, "flak defenders" were appointed, older boys who worked all day in the factories and at night had to stand guard at the flak emplacements and bring up ammunition during attacks. Heavy work at the emplacements increasingly was performed by another group of "volunteers," most of them Soviet prisoners-of-war who sought in this way to alleviate the misery of their captivity.

All Burma had been firmly in Japanese hands for one year now. When the Japanese had occupied Lashio and severed the Burma Road, they had cut off Chiang Kai-shek's Chinese forces from the supplies coming from the USA. Fortunately for the Allies, the Japanese transferred a large part of their aerial forces to the southwestern Pacific in 1942 to avoid the monsoons that began in May. This gave the Allies on the mainland a comparative respite in which to rebuild their battered aerial forces in this zone. The number-one priority of the British was to reorganize the Indian Army to prepare it for attacks on northern and central Burma; but at the same time they planned a new type of air-and-ground operation on the northern edge of the jungle-covered Burmese war theater, to raise the morale of their troops.

The organizer of the new operations was Brigadier Orde Wingate, the top British expert on the conduct of partisan warfare, who in the thirties had formed Jewish settlers and British soldiers in Palestine into Special Night Squads to combat Arab terrorists. In 1940, Wingate was in Ethiopia leading the guerrilla "Gideon Force" that lent crucial aid to Haile Selassie in liberating his country [from the Italians]. Now Wingate was at work in Burma forming a "long-

Below right: January 1943, a German He 111 is being loaded with "supply bombs" for the German troop pocket at Stalingrad. The Germans managed to airlift only one third of their planned supplies and suffered enormous losses.

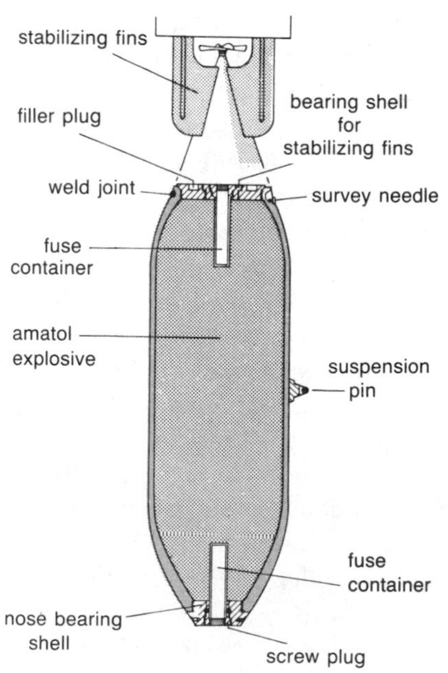

RAF MC 500-lb Explosive Bomb

range penetration group," a commando unit that he named Chindit after a fabulous Burmese monster that was half lion and half eagle, and that was intended to symbolize the close cooperation between ground and air troops. The mission of the Chindits' combined air-and-ground operation was to operate for an extended period behind the Japanese lines, to cut Japanese supply lines, to carry on reconnaissance and to spread confusion. Wingate had an idea that was completely new in the history of warfare: to reinforce and supply a strong mobile troop of over 3,000 soldiers and several hundred pack animals, entirely by air.

On the night of 14th–15th February 1943, Wingate's force—officially called 77th Brigade and made up of British, Indian and Gurkha troops—crossed the Chindwin river in Burma. The brigade, divided into two groups, included experienced RAF pilots who kept in radio contact with the transport plane squadrons, led the air supply operations, reported bombing targets and delivered intelligence about the enemy. Supplies that could not be brought in by aircraft, had to be carried by 1,100 mules and several dozen elephants. In the first three nights, 15th–17th February 1943, RAF aircraft of 31 and 194 Squadrons dropped more than 30 tons of supplies near Myene (Burma); but several containers fell into Japanese hands, including the mail for the soldiers. Thus three days after the operation began, the Japanese already knew what was going on in the hinterland.

At first the Chindits lost considerable time search-

USA 500-lb Explosive Bomb
Length: 4 ft 10 in
Diameter: 1 ft 8 in
Explosive component: 51%

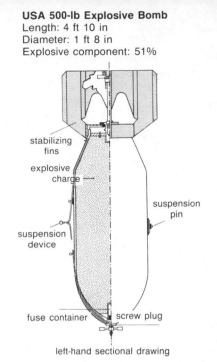

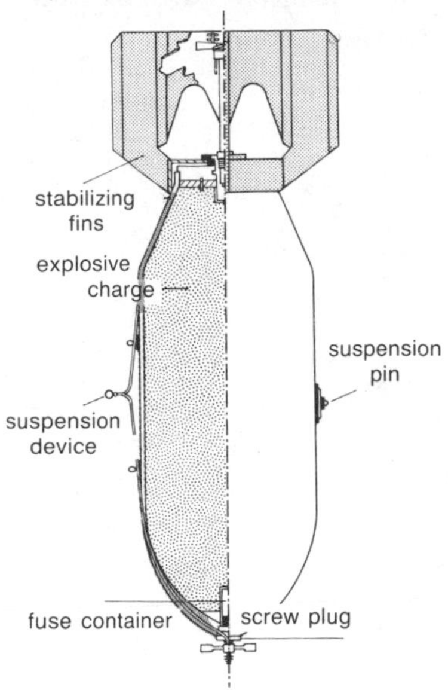

left-hand sectional drawing

ing for suitable clearings in which to receive their supply drops, until they realized that the drops could be made directly into the jungle.

The Chindits' march through the jungle was very taxing to the nerves and demanded unrelenting alertness. Fighting the Japanese patrols took less out of the men than the scarcity of water, the leeches, mosquitos and ticks. They could only light fires half an hour before dawn and just after dusk, and they cut the wood for the fires in an irregular rhythm so that the sound would dissolve away in the jungle. The Chindits took their toll on the Japanese, destroying 4 bridges and cutting at more than 70 points

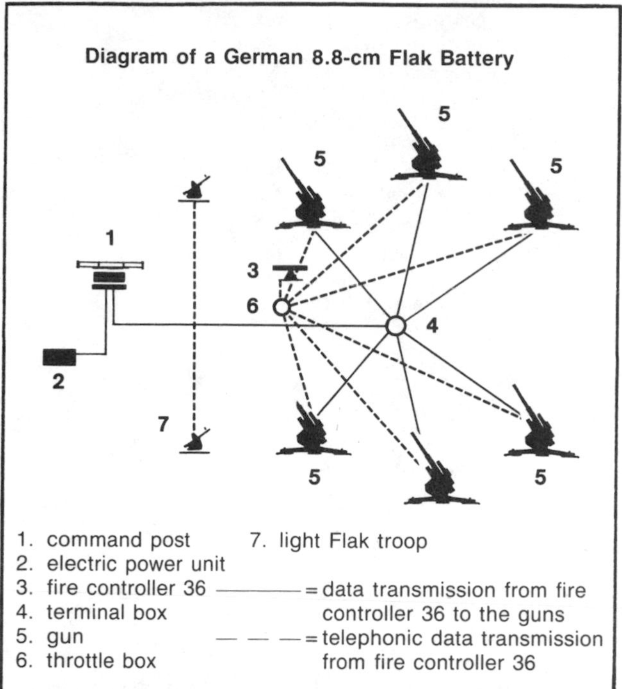

the only railway line leading to Mandalay (Upper Burma).

At 8:58 A.M. on Friday 5 March 1943 a British pathfinder unit comprising 22 Lancasters and 6 Mosquitos—all guided by the Oboe system—dropped their target flares over the Krupp munitions plant in the center of Essen. RAF Bomber Command was beginning a new air offensive against German heavy industry—the "Battle of the Ruhr"—that lasted for four months. Four hundred and twelve bombers (140 Lancasters, 80 Halifaxes, 52 Stirlings and 131 Wellingtons) took part in the opening operation, and 369 of them reached their target. The Essen raid marked another turning point in the bombing war. The Ruhr District was one of the most important industrial centers of Germany, but until now Bomber Command had found it the most difficult target to hit because it was covered by layers of smoke from the blast furnaces that cut down on visibility, and it was also fiercely defended: the Allied bomber crews used to call it "Flak Valley." But now the British no longer needed to have a clear view of the target: Bombardiers had only to follow the target flares in order to drop their payloads in just the right place. Fourteen bombers were shot down; more than 5,000 buildings were destroyed or seriously damaged, and almost 400 people were killed.

At 10:30 P.M. on Saturday 20 March 1943, Montgomery opened an offensive against the Italian First Army in Tunisia. The British Desert Air Force with its Spitfires, Kitty bombers and Hurricane ground-attack aircraft, flew continuous raids to support the ground troop operations. The Axis powers had only 300 aircraft operating against 5,000 Allied planes.

In March 1943 the Battle of the Atlantic entered its decisive phase. This was the worst month of the war for Allied shipping: 43 of their vessels were sunk in a 20-day period. But then in the last week of March, the Allied escort carriers that had been detailed to protect the convoys for Operation Torch, the Allied landing in North Africa, became free to leave the Mediterranean and return to the North Atlantic, and their anti-submarine places returned with them. Once the U-boats had been located, it was now possible to pursue and destroy them.

On Saturday 27 March 1943, the Chindits began their return march from behind Japanese lines in Burma. They slaughtered some of their pack animals and buried unneeded equipment. They laid ambushes and false trails for the Japanese, mined the jungle paths and set some of their mules free to deceive the enemy about their whereabouts. Meanwhile their transport aircraft continued dropping supplies in remote areas to keep the Japanese thinking that their operation was still in progress. More than 300 metric tons of supplies were dropped to them during their mission. Of the original 3,000 Chindits, 2,182 came back. Four hundred and fifty had died in battle; several hundred more had either

That same day US fighter planes shot down 14 German Ju 52 military transport planes over Tunisia north of Cape Bon; 10 more were destroyed on bases in Sicily and 65 were crippled. In the last phase of the battle in North Africa, German transport planes became sitting ducks for the Allied aircraft.

Deeply troubled by the situation in the Solomon Islands, Japanese Admiral Yamamoto decided to undertake personal command of the Japanese air offensive (Operation "I") that began there on Wednesday 7 April 1943. Four Japanese carriers transported approximately 160 fighters and dive bombers to Rabaul (New Britain) and Buka (Papua New Guinea) to reinforce the Japanese 11th Air Force, and that same day the carrier aircraft attacked the US vessels anchored at Tulagi and Lungga (Guadalcanal).

The overwhelming Allied air supremacy in the Mediterranean had almost completely halted German sea and air supplies to Tunisia. On Saturday 10 April 1943, 5 Ju 52s were brought down by Allied fighters; the following day, another 18 heavily-laden transport planes went into the sea, and 18 more Ju 52s the day after that. Losses mounted even when the Germans increased their fighter cover, because the Allics were able to keep increasing the number of aircraft they deployed, including the dreaded American P-38 Lightning long-range fighters.

Above: A German flak battery in February 1943. Male school pupils born in the years 1926–1927 were trained to serve as Luftwaffe Auxiliary troops. Here we see them still wearing the uniforms of the Hitler Youth.

Below right: February 1943. General Arnold, the commander of the USAAF (left) talking with General Chennault, commander of the American Volunteer Flying Group in China, known as the "Flying Tigers." They formed the core of Chiang Kai-shek's Chinese air force and were equipped with Curtiss Tomahawk fighters.

In April 1943, Soviet air raids were aimed mainly

been captured or succumbed to the rigors of the journey. Admittedly this operation had little strategic effect, but it demonstrated that it was possible for troops to survive on airborne supplies; it also showed that British and Indian aerial units could operate in the jungle.

At the end of March, the 8th USAAF in Britain finished setting up their 3 escort fighter groups, which made it possible for them to begin consistent bombing operations. In the light of experience, the Americans had had swiftly to revise their view that the strong armament of their four-engined bombers would allow them to function without fighter escort during daylight raids.

On Sunday 4 April 1943, the Renault plant in Billancourt in the outskirts of Paris was again raided by US bombers; and on Monday 5 April 1943, units of the 8th USAAF bombed Antwerp causing heavy damage to the industrial plants, harbor and the city center. There were 2,130 dead including 300 children.

March 1943: British Brigadier Wingate (wearing tropical helmet) is waiting with his staff for a supply drop in the Burmese jungle.

against the strongly-garrisoned German airfields in the Crimea, and against shipping traffic across the Straits of Kerch to the German beachhead at Kuban (between the Black Sea and the Sea of Azov). The German attempt to widen their Kuban beachhead failed due to Soviet relay bombing raids.

At 5:55 P.M. on Tuesday 13 April 1943, Vice-Admiral Sameijima, the commander of the Japanese 8th Fleet, radioed details about an inspection flight soon to be made by Admiral Yamamoto. He used the highest-level security code due to the importance of the message. His message said that at 6:00 A.M. on April 18, Admiral Yamamoto would take off from Rabaul in a bomber escorted by 6 fighter planes, and would fly to inspect the Japanese bases on Ballale and Shortland islands off the southeastern tip of Bougainville Island. Several US naval monitoring stations intercepted this secret message, and 14 hours later the text had been decoded and was lying on the desk of Yamamoto's opposite number in Pearl Harbor, Admiral Nimitz, the commander of the US Pacific fleet. Nimitz recognized at once the uniqueness of this opportunity to eliminate his most dangerous adversary once and for all. The targets of Yamamoto's visit lay approximately 400 miles from the nearest US airfield, Henderson Field on Guadalcanal, but in order to avoid the radar stations on the Japanese-occupied islands, US aircraft would have to cover a 600-mile stretch in low-level flight over the sea. This posed a major problem because the US Lightning fighters in this area were not equipped to carry fuel for such a prolonged flight.

On Thursday 15 April 1943, the first aerial clash between German and American fighters took place over the mouth of the Schelde river off the Dutch coast at an altitude of over 27,000 feet. Sixty-five American P-47 Thunderbolt escort fighters which had been in the European war theater for only one week, fought 25 German Focke-Wulf FW 190 fighters.

On that same day, April 15, the British chief of staff General Ismay reported to Churchill that the Germans had been conducting secret experiments with long-range rockets. The fact that the British had received five reports of the rocket experiments since the end of 1942, indicated (Ismay said) that the reports were true even if the details were unclear.

On the night of 16th–17th April 1943, 225 RAF bombers raided Mannheim, while at the same time 242 bombers struck at the Skoda munitions works in Pilsen (Czechoslovakia). Due to a navigational fault a large part of the 617 metric tons of bombs dropped in Czechoslovakia, fell on a small town southwest of Pilsen. Bomber Command lost 53 bombers (9%) in the two raids.

On Sunday 17 April 1943, US 8th Air Force bombers with a protective escort of P-38 Lightning fighters, made their first heavy daylight raid on the Focke-Wulf plant in Bremen. Almost half the manufacturing works were destroyed and the rest badly damaged. Thirty FW 190s standing ready for transport, went up in flames. The US bombers suffered particularly heavy losses in this raid—15%.

On the evening of April 17, 4 Liberator bombers landed at Henderson Field on Guadalcanal. They had brought special supplementary fuel tanks to equip the Lightning fighter planes [so that they could make the long flight to intercept Yamamoto]. Now Operation Vengeance, the hunt for Yamamoto, could begin.

At 7:25 A.M. on 18 April 1943, 16 Lightning P-38s of 339 Squadron under command of Major J. W. Mitchell took off from Henderson Field. Their plan was to intercept the Japanese admiral shortly before he landed on the island of Ballale near Bougainville. At 6:00 A.M. Yamamoto took off from Rabaul headed for Bougainville in a Mitsubishi G4M bomber (called "Betty bombers" by the Allies), escorted by another Betty bomber and 6 Zero fighters. His habit of punctuality was the Admiral's undoing. By Major Mitchell's calculations, his planes should cross the path of the Japanese aircraft at 9:35 A.M. The Lightnings split up into 4 flights of 4 planes each. They maintained strict radio silence until the enemy aircraft were sighted.

At 9:30 the Lightnings had reached the southern tip of Bougainville.

At 9:33 they climbed to 20,000 feet. Admiral Yamamoto and his escort appeared with the punctuality of a scheduled passenger liner. When the Japanese Betty bombers sighted the twin-fuselage Lightnings, they made the error of diving down toward the Bougainville jungle, thereby losing the advantage of altitude.

At 9:34, after aerial combat lasting approximately 30 seconds, Yamamoto's bomber exploded in the middle of the jungle 40 miles north of Ballale. Captain T. G. Lanphier: "I sent a long cone of fire into the side of the bomber, more or less at right angles. The right engine caught fire, then the right wing. As I came in range of Yamamoto's aircraft and cannon, the right wing of the bomber broke off."

Admiral Isoruku Yamamoto, the 59-year-old commander-in-chief of the Imperial Japanese Navy and the brilliant strategist of the raid on Pearl Harbor, was the single most prominent victim of the World War II code-breakers, [who had deciphered the original radio message about his flight]. At 11:00 A.M. the Lightnings landed back on Henderson Field, 6 of them badly damaged. Lt. Hine's aircraft was missing. When the body of Admiral Yamamoto was found that same evening, he was still holding his samurai sword in his hand. "There was only one Yamamoto and no one can replace him," said his successor Admiral Koga: "His loss is a terrible blow for us." Japanese headquarters waited one month before publishing news of the crash.

The Americans – in order to give the impression that they were ignorant of the matter – published a deliberate mistake in their reports: They said that Admiral Yamamoto had "died on one of the aircraft carriers."

The state funeral that Yamamoto received was the twelfth such funeral to be held in the thousand-year history of Japan, and apart from Admiral Togo, the victor at Tsushima in the Russo-Japanese War in 1905, he was the only admiral to receive this honor. All the US pilots who had taken part in Operation Vengeance were transferred to the United States for the remainder of the war, where they had to maintain absolute silence. At the time of the operation, no film was available to install in the Lightnings' built-in cameras, so today the question still remains unanswered: Who really shot down Yamamoto? Three pilots claimed the victory: Barber, Holmes and Lanphier.

The German U-boats operating in the North Atlantic were finding their raids on Allied convoys increasingly difficult and costly. Starting in April 1943, Allied carrier aircraft, long-range Liberators and flying boats began to stop up the "Black Hole," the zone of the Atlantic that could not be given fighter cover. At this time, German Admiral Dönitz made an error that was to have grave repercussions: He ordered his U-boats to stay above water while travelling through the Bay of Biscay and to combat attacking aircraft with their flak guns. This tactical error helped British Coastal Command to achieve

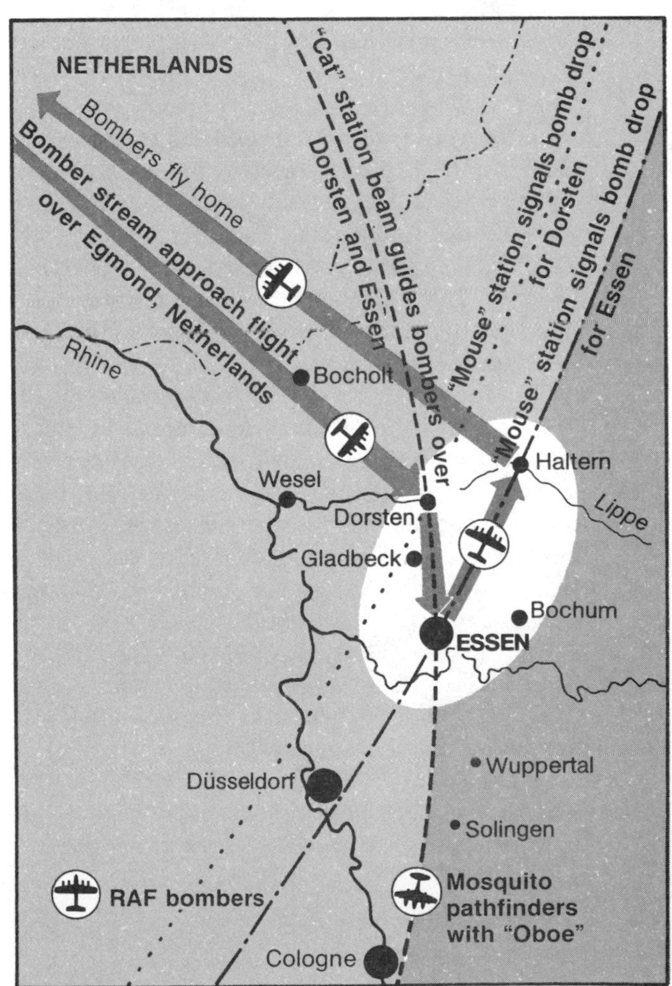

5th–6th March 1943: The RAF begins a new air offensive against the German Ruhr District.

extraordinary successes against the U-boats, which had little chance against the new Allied centimeter-wave radar sets, improved depth charges, and tracking searchlights that could be used to illuminate U-boats at night.

On 18 April 1943, a giant German transport formation of 65 Ju 52s, escorted by 16 Me 109 fighters and five Me 110 aerial "destroyers," took off from Sicily headed for Tunisia. The Allies brought down 24 of the transport planes, along with 9 Me 109s and 1 Me 110. Thirty-five of the Ju 52s, badly damaged, managed to make emergency landings on the Tunisian coast.

On Monday 19 April 1943 the specialists of the British aerial photo-interpreters unit in Medmenham were ordered by the British Air Ministry to use aerial photography to investigate the German "secret rocket" program. Fully 6 years after the Germans built their laboratories and test rigs in Peenemünde, British aerial reconnaissance finally took the new weapons into its target program.

On Tuesday 20 April 1943, Duncan Sandys, Churchill's son-in-law, was officially commissioned to investigate evidence that the Germans were developing a long-range rocket.

On Thursday 22 April 1943, Allied fighters destroyed 16 Ju 52 transport aircraft loaded with fuel north of Tunis. Flying with the Ju 52s were 20 of the last Me 323 Gigant giant transporters available in the Mediterranean zone; 18 of them were shot down. More losses occurred to the Axis Powers during their supply operations to Tunisia than during any other aerial supply operation except the Stalingrad airlift. A total of 400 Ju 52s, Savoia Marchetti SM 82s and Me 323 Gigants were shot down.

But the Ju 52s went on flying despite it all, so long as there was the least possibility of their getting through to land in the narrowing German beachhead in Tunisia. On Monday 3 May 1943, they managed to bring in 40 metric tons of munitions, 68 tons of gasoline, and 3.5 tons of equipment, and on May 4 they delivered another 3 tons of ammunition and 70 tons of fuel. Their sacrifices were in vain. On Friday 7 May 1943, the Allies simultaneously penetrated Bizerta and Tunis. Hitler issued appeals to the soldiers to fight on and ordered them to dig themselves in and hold onto Cape Bon; but all his impassioned slogans were incapable of moving them to let themselves be slaughtered.

At the climax of the Battle of the Ruhr, Air Marshal Harris became alarmed at the steadily mounting losses to the British bombers. Despite the bomber stream tactic, the new navigational devices and the most varied radar-jamming countermeasures, dozens of bombers were failing to come back night after night. Although it was not impossible to replace the lost aircraft, there was a shortage of experienced flying crews.

The success of the German night fighter planes was due to a secret device with which Germany hoped to halt the RAF bombing offensive: Lichtenstein BC. This was the codename of an airborne radar system developed by Telefunken that led the night fighters within range of enemy borders located by Freya and Würzburg radar. When the first four fighters, equipped with massive antler-like radar antennas, arrived at their base at Leeuwarden (Holland) in February 1942, all but one German air crew, that of Air Captain Becker, refused to fly them. Months passed before the other night fighters came to appreciate the advantages of Lichtenstein BC.

The British had spared no effort to uncover the secret of Würzburg radar, and now they devoted

Opposite page: A US Lockheed P-38 Lightning single-seater fighter plane. German soldiers called Lightnings "fork-tailed devils" [due to their unusual forked shape]. The Lightning was the first American aircraft to shoot down a German plane and also the first to raid Berlin. Lightnings destroyed more Japanese planes than any other US land-supported fighter. A total of 9,923 were built.

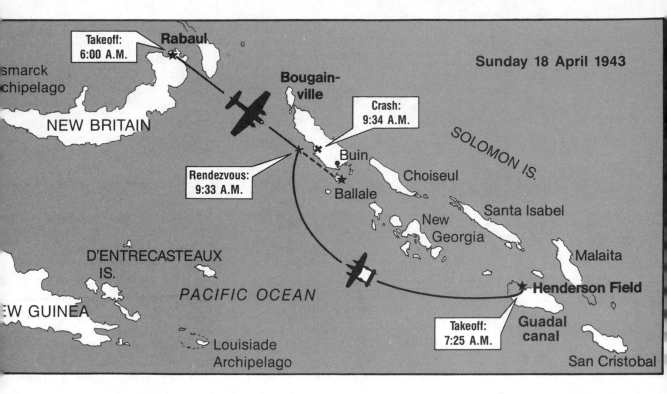

Above: Sunday 18 April 1943: Operation Vengeance, when the Americans shot down the bomber in which Admiral Yamamoto was travelling.

Right: US Air Captain T. G. Lanphier, hero of Operation Vengeance, is being decorated with medals including the Silver Star. Behind him is his P-38 Lightning.

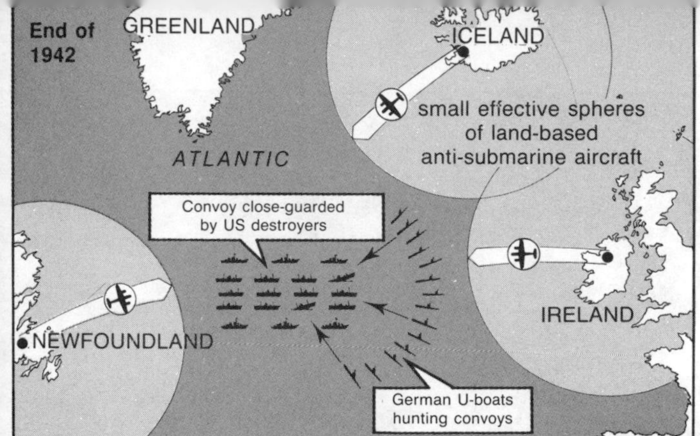

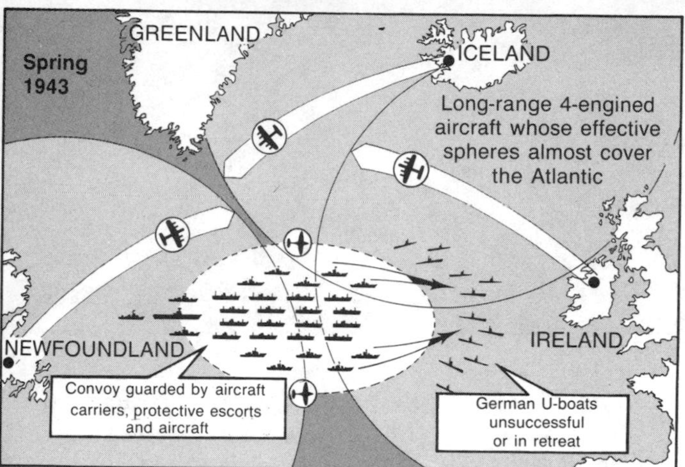

Above: The "Black Hole" in the Atlantic, the hunting ground of the German U-boats in 1942. The Black Hole ceased to exist in spring 1943.

equal zeal to investigating the new German target-locator system. They had learned of its existence through their radio monitoring stations, which repeatedly picked up the codename "Emil-Emil" being passed between the German night fighters and their ground controllers. The British suspected that some unknown type of airborne radar was at work. On 3 December 1942, six months after the investigation began, Dr. R. V. Jones, chief of the scientific branch of the secret service in the British Air Ministry, obtained Churchill's permission to send a Wellington bomber full of measuring instruments to Frankfurt am Main. The plane, the DV-819, was to be used as a decoy in the hope that the crew could find out at least the megahertz frequency of the menacing German radar. The plane was shot down a short distance from the coast of Britain, but the crew were saved at the last minute and reported: "It was 490 megahertz."

In the spring of 1943 the German Kammhuber Line, whose night interception zones stretched from Denmark in the north down to Lake Constance in the south, functioned at its maximum efficiency as it tried to ward off the British bombing offensive against the Ruhr District. In June 1943, the German night fighters shot down 235 enemy bombers, which was the greatest success they had ever scored using the Himmelbett system. Bomber Command reported an increasing decline in the morale of its crews.

But the British were just about to strike a new blow against the German air defenses. At 4:40 P.M. on Saturday 9 May 1943, the radar station of No. 100 German Night Fighter Zone in Grove (Denmark) intercepted a distress call from a German Ju 88, the C-6/R-1 (D5 + EV) of the 3rd Night Fighter Wing (NJG 3). The night fighter had taken off from Aalborg (Denmark) with a three-man crew—pilot 1st Lt. H. S., radio operator Technical Sgt. P. R. and mechanic Technical Sgt. E. K.—on a special mission: to intercept a British Mosquito courier aircraft over the North Sea that was on its way from England to Sweden. Now the plane reported fire in its left engine and a short time later, said that it had to make an emergency sea landing. Lt. Col. von der Pongartz of No. 100 Night Fighter Zone at once ordered a rescue plane to Quadrant 88/41; it sighted 3 empty inflatable rubber dinghies and radioed for a sea rescue speedboat.

At 6:05 P.M. that same day, British Flight Lt. Roscoe, piloting Spitfire BM 515 T of 165 (Ceylon) Squadron and accompanied by another plane flown by Sgt. Scaman, was making a patrol flight along the coast of northern Scotland between Peterhead and Aberdeen when he sighted a German plane.

Flight Lt. Roscoe gave this account: "The plane reported to me by our radar station was about 15 miles from Peterhead, heading west. I flew toward it at top speed to intercept it before it reached the coast. About 5 miles off the coast it changed course and flew south. When I managed at last to cut off its eastward flight path, the plane was already one mile inland. By this time I had identified it as a Ju 88 and was preparing to attack, when suddenly I saw that it had let down its landing gear and was firing a series of red signal flares. Then it began to wave its wings up and down. I came nearer and motioned with my hand for the plane to follow me, at the same time ordering Sgt. Scaman to stay on the other side of it and escort it toward Dyce airfield. At the airfield the Ju 88 again sent out red signal flares, curved around and landed. I followed it until it switched off its engines and halted just

Right: A German Messerschmitt Me 323 Gigant (Giant), one of the largest aircraft of the war. This heavy transport plane, photographed on 22 April 1943, was shot down a moment later by an RAF Martin B-26 Marauder bomber flown by Wing Commander Maydell of 14 Squadron.

Below: A German U-boat shortly before it was sunk. RAF Coastal Command aircraft sank more German and Italian submarines during the war than the Royal Navy. Coastal Command also proved more successful than the Navy in mining German coastal waters.

at the edge of the airfield, and took the three Germans prisoner."

While German Lt. Col. von der Pongartz in Grove was reporting the disappearance of the plane to the 3rd Fighter Wing, the missing German air crew were scrambling out of their D5 + EV at Dyce, a small Scottish airstrip about 15 miles northwest of Aberdeen, just at tea-time. The Ju 88 was at once rolled into a hangar, and Group Captain J. W. Colquhoun, the airfield commander, sent several top-priority coded telegrams to London.

No one at Dyce was aware that this event marked a major coup for the British Secret Intelligence Service, the SIS, in its campaign against the Luftwaffe: German night fighter Ju 88 C-6/R-1, carrying the top secret Lichtenstein BC radar set, was now in British hands. Its German pilot, 1st Lt. H. S., was in reality an SIS agent who had been recruited by his father, a Social Democrat at that time living underground and the former personal adviser of German Chancellor Stresemann who had died in 1929.

Next day, 10 May 1943, a German-speaking RAF interrogation officer arrived at Dyce, and 1st Lt. H. S. gave him a detailed report on the organization, structure and tactics of the German night fighter zones in Denmark, as well as suggestions how Bomber Command could better protect its planes from night interceptors and avoid detection by Freya and Würzburg radar. Air Marshal Harris gained other first-hand tips that only a German night-fighter pilot could know.

On Monday 11 May 1943, Dr. Jones left London and arrived at Dyce to take charge of the Ju 88. Dr. Jones, one of the top British radar specialists who in 1937 had been the first to discover the basic principles of radar-jamming using tinfoil strips, was initiated by H. S. into the secrets of Lichtenstein BC, and ordered a series of test flights.

The national emblems of the Ju 88 (D5 + EV) were painted over and replaced with the RAF badge and the identification codenumber PJ 876; then it flew to the RAF testing center at Farnborough with a Spitfire for escort. Here Squadron Leader Charles Hartley and Wing Commander D. A. Jackson took charge of it. The British wanted to see Lichtenstein radar working under realistic conditions, so they carried out the tests at night and arranged for the German plane to fight a duel with a Halifax bomber. The two planes fought their improvised battle with such zeal that they almost collided. The Halifax could not shake off the German night fighter no matter how it maneuvered; but the experimental flights revealed that the correct use of continuous vertical flight curves—corkscrew curves—made it hard for the pursuer to come into firing position.

The most amazing finding to come out of Dr. Jones' investigation of the German airborne radar system, was that the Window tinfoil-strip jamming technique the British had designed to combat Würzburg radar, also neutralized Lichtenstein BC.

On Wednesday 12 May 1943, the remnants of the German Afrika Army Group under General von Arnim stopped fighting in North Africa, and the Italian First Army under General Messe surrendered the following morning. The fighting in Africa was over.

Now the Allies began their preparations for the invasion of Sicily. Ports, rail junctions and especially airfields in Sicily and southern Italy became the target of heavy bombing raids.

On the night of 13th–14th May 1943, Bomber Command again raided the Skoda munitions works in Pilsen (Czechoslovakia). The RAF crews missed their target just as they had done one month before: 141 of the bombers dropped their 527-metric-ton payloads several miles from the industrial plants. Nine bombers were lost.

After the failure of the German airlift operations at Stalingrad and Tunis, the Luftwaffe's air supply transport system was reorganized starting on Saturday 15 May 1943. It was given the same structure and status as the other branches of the Luftwaffe and the rank of general of military transport aircraft was created. Transport wings were set up and all the aircraft, squadrons, groups and wings received tactical markings.

On the evening of 16 May 1943, 19 British Lancaster bombers took off from Scamton airfield (Yorkshire) on what was probably the most spectacular operation of the strategic air offensive: the night-time precision bombing of the Möhne, Sorpe and Eder Dams. A newly-formed special unit, 617 Squadron under Wing Commander G. P. Gibson, was detailed to carry out this raid, the climax of the Battle of the Ruhr. Before takeoff the pilots—none of them older than 23—were told that their raid would contribute substantially to ending the war.

The Möhne and Sorpe Dams controlled about two thirds of the water-storage capacity of the Ruhr District; the Eder Dam controlled the water level of the Weser and Fulda rivers. If the dams could be destroyed, water supplies for industry, traffic and drinking water in many of the manufacturing plants would fail for a period of months.

The plan was for giant drum-shaped bombs weighing 4 tons and containing 2.5 tons of explosive, to be carried by converted Lancasters and used to blow up the dams. Shortly before they were released, they would be set spinning by an auxiliary engine fitted into the aircraft. Each bomb was to be dropped from an altitude of no more than 60 feet and would have to miss the anti-torpedo nets that secured the dam. It would crash into the steep dam wall and cling to it due to centrifugal force as it slowly sank; then, when it reached a pre-established depth, the explosion would be triggered by a hydrostatic fuse. This bomb-model had been designed by Dr. Barnes Wallis, who had built the famous Vickers Wellington bomber.

The dams lay in deep clefts between the mountains and it was difficult to drop bombs on them from an altitude of 60 feet while travelling at a speed of 220 miles per hour; so the bomber had to approach in dive flight and then, after releasing its payload, to pull its nose up as fast as possible in order to get out of range of the exploding bomb.

Wing Commander Gibson reported: "We veered right between Hamm and Soest to where we could see the hills of the Ruhr. As we passed them, Möhne Lake appeared and then the dam itself, mighty and impregnable. Yet it looked extremely familiar to us, as if we were looking down at the model. The Germans opened fire—that was a terrible moment. We were still several hundred yards from the dam; a special mechanism in our aircraft had already begun to work so that the bomb would be rolling as it fell. There was something weird about the whole operation. My plane seemed tiny to me seen against the great dam. I smelled burnt powder and saw tracer fire whistling past the cockpit. Then I heard the call: 'Bombs away!'

"We were still circling when we saw a giant waterspout shoot up. At first we thought the dam had broken. Then the next bomber came roaring up. When it was only 300 yards from the dam someone called: 'My God, it's been hit!' I saw them manage to drop their bomb before the plane crashed close to the power station. I ordered the next crew to attack. Again there was an enormous explosion that shook the whole surface of the lake. If Dr. Wallis' theory was right, the dam should have broken now; but it did not break until the sixth explosion.

Dyce airfield (Scotland) on 11 May 1943. The nose of a German Ju 88 heavy night fighter, the C-6/R-1 (D5 + EV), now in British hands, holds the stag antenna of a Lichtenstein BC radar. The Himmelbett air defense system required the German night fighters to remain airborne for a prolonged period, so more and more medium-range bombers had to be pressed into service as night fighters: they were the only German aircraft that could carry enough fuel.

"I flew over to the dam and could not believe my eyes. There was a big 300-foot-long tear through which huge masses of water were pouring. The flak had stopped firing. Everything was still, you could hear nothing but the roaring and rushing of the water. We flew on to the Eder Dam. The wall there was hard to see because mist was rising in the valley. The dam was undefended, but nevertheless it cost us one plane and a great deal of effort to get it to collapse."

The surging masses of water swept away villages and isolated farms, bridges and railroad beds, a barracks camp of Ukrainian female laborers, herds of livestock and boats. City districts were flooded and approximately 1,200 people drowned. Not only was there almost no air defense in the area, but there was also no warning system for the event of a raid on the dams; so the chaos was complete.

The most important dam, the Sorpe Dam, remained intact. Two others, the Ennepe and Lister Dams were not attacked. Although the Möhne and Eder Dams were severely damaged, they were repaired in two months, so their destruction did scarcely any damage to industry in the Ruhr. Of the 18 Lancasters that had taken off on the mission, 8 did not return. This high casualty rate—42%—dissuaded the elite squadron from undertaking further missions for some time to come.

The effect of the raid on German morale was considerable and long-lasting despite the speed with which the damage was repaired. It is still a moot point whether the mission was worthwhile. Gibson and his crews had expended 2,500 flying hours in their special training—the equivalent of sending 500 bombers to raid the Ruhr District. No. 617 Squadron, now known as the "Dambusters," was awarded a coat-of-arms bearing a motto borrowed from Madame de Pompadour: "Après moi le déluge"—After me, the flood.

In May 1943 the Battle of the Atlantic reached a crucial turning point. That month 36 German U-boats were sunk in the North Atlantic, 22 of them by Allied aircraft; and during the period of May 17 to the end of September 1943, not one Allied ship was sunk there by the U-boats. On Wednesday 19 May, A Liberator bomber, the T/120 of No. 120 RAF Squadron, sank German U-boat U 954 under Captain Loewe in the North Atlantic. The submarine sank with all its crew, including watch officer Peter Dönitz, the son of the commander-in-chief of the German Navy. Five days later, on Monday 24 May 1943, Fleet Admiral Dönitz wrote: "Losses suffered in the last few days make it especially clear that the submarine war has reached a crisis and that radical measures must be taken." He halted German attempts to fight the North Atlantic convoys. Dönitz ordered all units to retreat, except for a few that were to keep up radio traffic to simulate large formations. This victory in the war against the U-boats was largely attributable to the operations of the Allied aerial forces.

On the night of 23rd–24th May 1943, the RAF made a powerful air raid on Dortmund. Seven hundred and fifty-four bombers dropped 2,042 tons of bombs, badly damaging residential districts and industrial plants. In this raid Bomber Command dropped its one-hundred-thousandth ton of bombs. Air Chief Marshal Harris sent a message to the air

crew responsible, saying: "In 1939 Göring assured the German people that not one single bomb would fall on the Ruhr District. I congratulate you on having just delivered the Reich Marshal his reply: our first one-hundred-thousandth ton of bombs."

On the night of 29th–30th May 1943, Bomber Command flew one of the most significant raids of the Battle of the Ruhr. Six hundred British bombers dropped 1,822 tons of bombs on the Barmen district of Wuppertal. The city burned down almost to the ground. The death toll was 2,450 and around 118,000 were made homeless. Flak and night fighters shot down 33 bombers.

On the night of 31st May–1st June, 3 Me 110 German night fighters attacked a Douglas Dakota DC-3 over the Bay of Biscay; it was the regular Boeing aircraft passenger liner (codenumber G-AGBB) plying its route between Lisbon and London. A couple of machine-gun salvos sent the burning plane crashing into the sea; its passengers and crew were killed. Among the 13 passengers was the world-famous British actor Leslie Howard.

The motive for this attack was the mistaken belief that Churchill was aboard the plane. The Germans knew that Churchill had been in North Africa, and when a German agent in Lisbon turned in a misguided message that he had seen a man resembling the British Prime Minister boarding a BOAC plane at the airport, German fighters were sent out in the hope of bringing down their worst enemy.

At the beginning of June the Soviet army groups had 30 air corps comprising approximately 10,000 first-line aircraft. The aircraft and their equipment displayed a remarkably high level of technology. Most of the Focke-Wulf FW 190s had been transferred from the Eastern Front to defend Germany in the West, so German fighter units in the East were flying mainly Messerschmitt Me 109 Fs. Meanwhile, the Soviet fighter wings were equipped with modern Mikoyan-Gurevich MiGs, Jaks or Lavochkin La GGs. Only a remnant of the once powerful German bomber units were still on the Eastern Front, where for the most part they carried out purely tactical operations.

One of the few exceptions was a strategic operation by bomber wings of the 4th Air Fleet (Luftflotte 4 under Field Marshal von Richtofen) in the first half of June 1943, when they raided the Molotov Collective Combine in Gorki, one of the largest Soviet tank-manufacturers west of the Urals. This sprawling target about 2½ miles square, lay just within range of the German bomber units that had been transferred to Briansk. The Germans hoped to carry out precision bombing using a new homing device, the Lotfe 7 D, which had just been delivered to them. At 8:00 P.M. in the dusk of 3 June 1943, 168 bombers, mostly He 111s of the 3rd, 4th, 27th, 55th and 100th Bomber Wings, took off armed with large numbers of heavy 1.7- to 2.4-ton mine bombs, and fragmentation, high-explosive and incendiary bombs. They used the Moscow transmitter to help them navigate, flying from the south in a wide arc around the Soviet capital so as to avoid the flak barrier. At midnight the 149 bombers that reached the target dropped 224 tons of bombs from an altitude of 13,000 to 20,000 feet. Five of the bombers were shot down by the Soviet air defense. After this came a rapid series of other raids in which the Luftwaffe tried to eliminate the Molotov Combine—which reportedly was producing 800 of the famed Soviet T-34 tanks per week—before the Germans began their summer offensive. On the night following the first raid, 4th–5th June, 128 German bombers dropped 179 tons of bombs on the Combine; two bombers did not come back. The night after that, another 242 tons of bombs were dropped, and only one bomber was lost out of the 154 deployed. On the night of 7th–8th June, 20 bombers raided the plant dropping 39 tons of bombs. German agents reported that as a result, the Molotov works at Gorki were brought to a standstill for six weeks; but in reality the Combine continued production without any interruption.

On the night of 9th–10th June 1943, 109 bombers of the German 9th Air Fleet engaged in a long-range operation against the synthetic rubber combine in Yaroslavl, dropping 190 tons of bombs.

In the period 27th January 1943 to 10 June 1943, the US 8th Air Force carried out a series of heavy raids on German U-boat bases along the Atlantic coast. Brest was bombed three times, Lorient four times, St-Nazaire five times and La Pallice twice. Simultaneously, the RAF bombers concentrated their 300- to 500-bomber night raids on the same targets. In one month they bombed Lorient nine times and St-Nazaire eleven times. Sixty-three per cent of all the American raids, and 30% of the British raids, were aimed against U-boat bases, shipyards and ancillary supply works. The Allies believed that air raids on U-boat bunkers would help to cripple U-boat operations and put some of the boats out of action. Between January and June 1943, RAF and US bombers dropped 11,000 tons of high-explosive bombs and about 8,000 tons of incendiaries on these targets. But the powerful steel and concrete bunkers proved stronger than the bombs: Not one U-boat was put out of action and the U-boat construction program went on unimpeded.

Thursday 10 June 1943 marked the beginning of the "combined bomber offensive" against Germany that the Allies had agreed on in Casablanca—area bombing by the RAF at night and precision raids by US forces during the day. Chief on the new list of priority targets—the "Pointblank Plan"—were aircraft plants and fighter plane bases. The Allies had chosen these fighter-plane targets because, as General Ira Eaker said, German fighter planes were the chief obstacle preventing a step-up of the daylight precision raids. Other important targets of the strategic bombing offensive against Germany were the ball-bearing industry, synthetic fuel and rubber production, U-boat docks, motor vehicle plants, traffic networks and other elements of the munitions industry.

On the night of 11th–12th June 1943, Düsseldorf experienced its heaviest raid of the war. A formation of 693 four-engined bombers guided by pathfinder aircraft, dropped 1,968 tons of high-explosive and incendiary bombs within a period of 45 minutes. Huge fires transformed the city into a sea of flame. Some of the buildings were saved due to a simple artifice: The roof beams were fireproofed with slaked lime so that the incendiaries failed to make them catch fire. Despite this measure, 120,000 people were made homeless. Diversionary maneuvers kept the German night fighters occupied until the bombers were already on their return flight, but the Germans pursued and managed to shoot down 27 raiders.

German 1st Lt. H. S. had landed his Ju 88 night fighter at Dyce on 9 May 1943. Only three weeks later, Dr. R. V. Jones and his team built a special receiver codenamed "Serrate" that enabled RAF night fighters to detect radiation from Lichtenstein BC radar, and thus to turn German night fighters carrying the device into flying targets.

On 14 June 1943, No. 141 Group under Wing Commander J. Braham became the first British

Opposite page: The Möhne Dam in Germany on 17 May 1943, after the raid by 617 Squadron of the RAF. It took five bombs to collapse the dam wall. The destruction of two German dams failed to halt German industry in the Ruhr District as the British had hoped.

Right: Abadan (Iran) in June 1943: A British Supermarine Spitfire fighter plane is being painted with the Red Star of the Soviet Air Force. This was one of the 18,000 aircraft that Britain and the USA sent to the Soviet Union as part of the Lend-Lease Pact. The Spitfire, which was built in 40 different versions, was the most-produced British airplane of World War II.

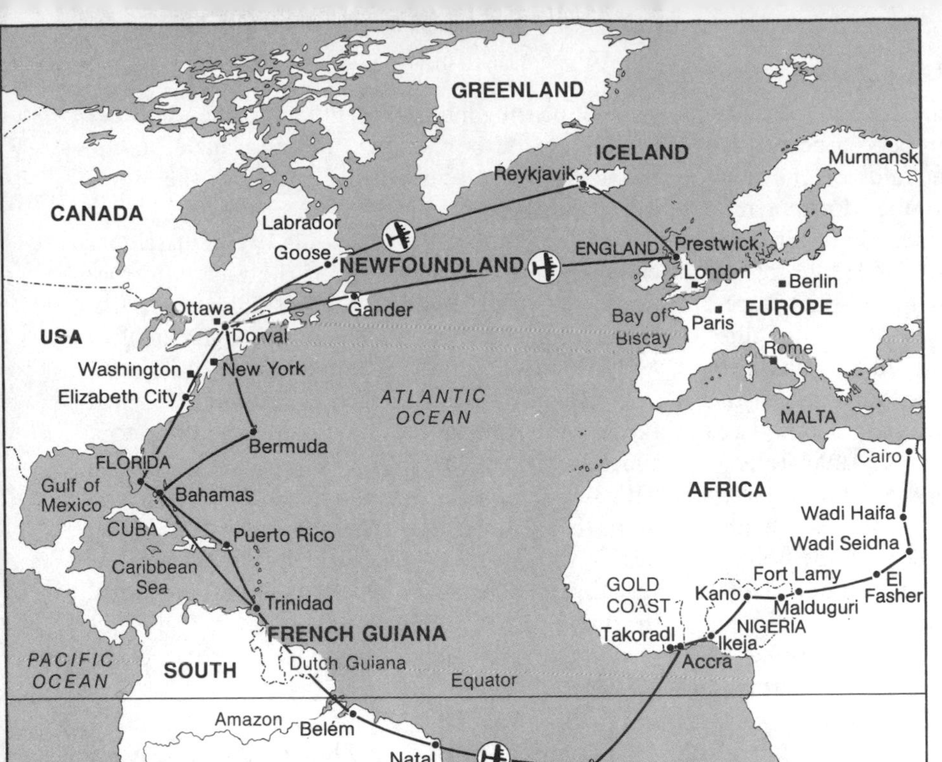

Left: The Atlantic air bridge.

Opposite page: The crew of an Allied high-altitude aerial reconnaissance plane just before reaching their target. The camera, which they will stick out of the fuselage, is kept inside a protective cover to shield it from the cold.

night fighter unit to receive the Serrate device, which had already gone into mass production. Its effects were soon felt: The Lichtenstein BC devices attracted the Serrates, quite literally, the way moths are attracted to a flame; and in June 1943, the Beaufighters of No. 141 Group shot down a total of 23 German night fighters. About half the kills were by W/Cmdr Bob Braham and his crew.

In the summer of 1943, US and Canadian transport aircraft, bombers and even short-range fighters took off with the regularity of freight trains from North America and flew to Great Britain over the Atlantic air bridge, with stop-offs in Newfoundland, Labrador and Iceland.

In mid-June, for the first time, a Dakota FD 900 cargo plane of RAF Transport Command landed in Prestwick, Scotland, the end station of the North Atlantic route, towing a glider. The two planes had taken off together twenty-four hours earlier from Dorval (Montreal). The glider – a Waco CG-4A that the RAF codenamed Hadrian – had been built in a New York piano factory. It carried a full load of urgently needed vaccine and radio and engine parts for the Soviet Union. The pilots, Squadron Leader Seys and Squadron Leader Gobeil, faced no easy task when they undertook to be towed across the Atlantic: "We could not take our eyes off the Dakota and the towrope, which was especially difficult in clouds or at night. We had to stay the whole time in the same position in relation to the tow plane, which kept disappearing from our field of vision. Thank God we had radio contact with our Dakota. Unfortunately there was no heating in the glider, so our teeth chattered with cold during the night or during a prolonged flight through cloud, whereas sunshine changed our cockpit into a hothouse."

Lively air traffic flowed too along the South Atlantic route to North Africa via West Palm Beach (Florida), Trinidad, the mouth of the Amazon, Natal and the Gold Coast. Admittedly this route was longer than over the North Atlantic, but it enabled cargo aircraft to avoid flying over the usually stormy Bay of Biscay to get to the Mediterranean.

On the night of 20th–21st June 1943, the Lancasters of No. 5 Group, Bomber Command, initiated a new type of operation, so-called "shuttle bombing," when they made a long-distance raid on the Zeppelin plant – a manufacturer of Würzburg radar sets – in Friedrichshafen on Lake Constance. During the short summer nights it was impossible for the bombers to get back to their bases in England in the dark, so instead of returning home, the Lancasters flew on to North Africa, where they were overhauled, fueled up and loaded with fresh bombs. Then they started on their return flight to

England, carrying out another bombing raid along the way. Their first shuttle raid was completed on the night of 23rd–24th June, when they hit the Italian naval base of La Spezia. One reason for shuttle bombing—double raids carried out as they shuttled back and forth over Europe—was to confuse the German air defense. But this type of operation presented great problems when it came to servicing the bomber units away from their home bases. In particular, the North African airfields were not equipped to deal with a massive landing by hundreds of heavy bombers at one time. Nevertheless, the British did score an unexpected bonus when they raided Friedrichshafen. Quite unintentionally they had just struck their first blow against the German secret rocket program. The Zeppelin works, which were charted to assemble 300 A-4 rockets per month, were so badly damaged that plans to manufacture the V-2 rocket there had to be abandoned.

Shortly after 12:00 noon on Wednesday 23 June 1943, Flight Sergeant E. P. H. Peek landed his Mosquito at Leuchars airbase (Scotland). He brought a little present with him: the first very clear aerial photos of the entire experimental layout at Peenemünde, with the rocket-launch zone at Test Rig VII. Aerial photointerpretation was the province of the Allied Central Interpretation Unit, the ACIU, located at a country house in Medmenham about 30 miles from London. Some 4 million aerial photographs arrived here every month, and the unit sent out 250 detailed reports to the Allied military staffs and to the Prime Minister every day. It had photointerpreters stationed at every airbase. Immediately after reconnaissance planes had landed, their aerial photographs were developed, examined and interpreted. Approximately 3,000 men and women worked in the ACIU. Twenty-six different sections, each specializing in one particular region, studied the target photos that showed the results of bombing raids. After comparing all the aerial photos made in the last twenty-four hours, they would complete their reports about the movements of enemy ships and troops, as well as about the condition of industrial plants. It was the photointerpreters of Medmenham who discovered the German secret rocket experimental station at Peenemünde.

The photos left the experts in no doubt: they were looking at rockets shortly before firing. The rocket photos were one of the most important discoveries made during the secret-weapons investigation, and were the product of the photoreconnaissance squadron that Sidney Cotton had set up in late autumn 1939.

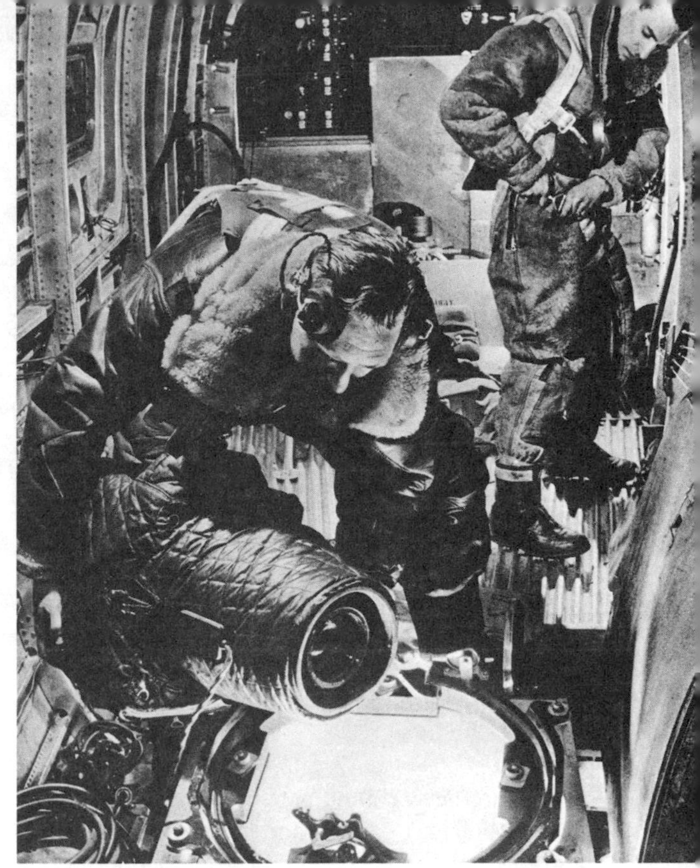

That same evening, on 23 June 1943, Churchill called a staff conference in which the use of Window radar-jamming during British bombing raids, was to be discussed for the first time.

The bomber stream tactic tested in the thousand-bomber raid on Cologne one year earlier, had continued to prove successful, and the toll of British bombers destroyed by collisions with other bombers was low. In the rapid succession of large-scale night raids on the Ruhr District, the marker flares dropped by pathfinder aircraft enabled the following bomber stream to drop their bombs in the record time of 30 to 40 minutes. Neither German night fighters nor German flak could adequately combat the massive stream of bombers pouring through a single night fighter zone. The stream of bombers swamped the Germans' previously successful system of concentrating the fire of several batteries on a single target. The greatest danger threatening the bombers once they were over the target zone, came neither from German night fighters nor from flak, but from other British aircraft that accidentally dropped their bombs on bombers flying lower in the stream.

The Germans were plagued not only by massed raids but also by solo-flying planes. They soon realized that individual Mosquitos, which could hit their targets with great precision, were very hard to shoot down. Because they could not shoot down a

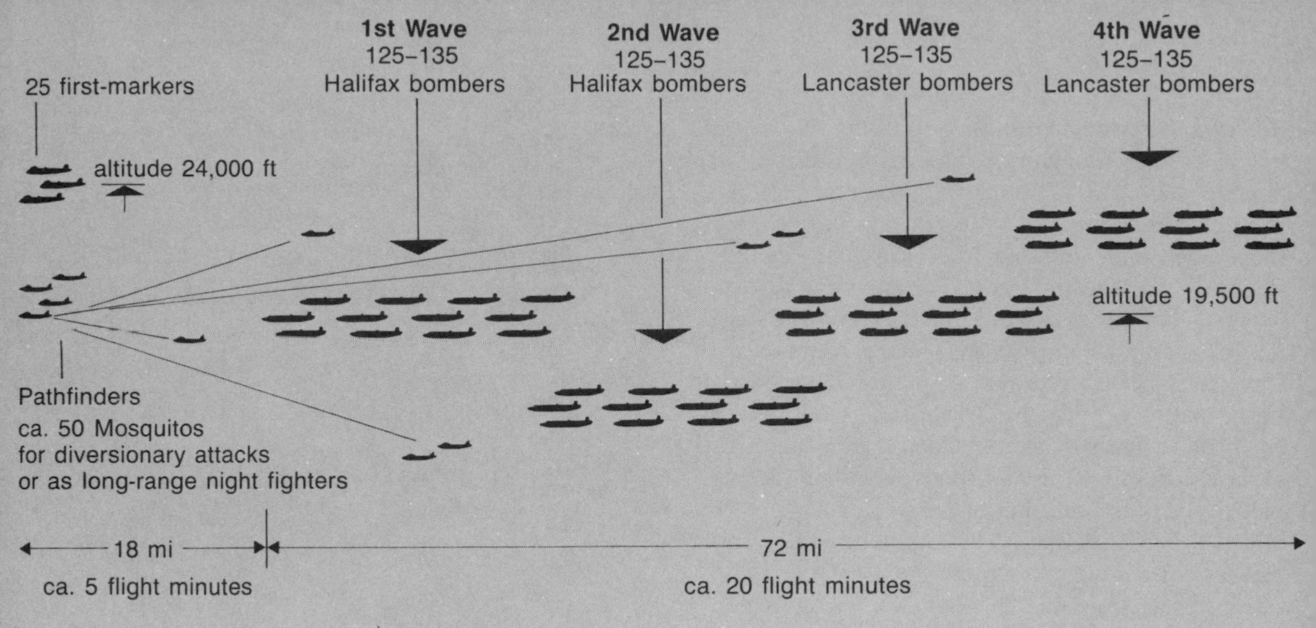

British bomber formation tactics during night raids on Germany in 1943.

Mosquito they were unable to get their hands on an intact Oboe navigational and blind-bombing device, and for some time were unable to develop an effective countermeasure against Oboe. Even Göring expressed amazement at the performance of the British homing devices: "Fog or not, an Englishman can locate a speck of dust if it's on German soil." Hitler believed he had ferreted out the secret of the remarkable precision of aim shown by individual Mosquitos when they raided the blast furnaces of the Ruhr District: He thought that the RAF bombs were guided to the target by infra-red devices and he ordered Field Marshal Milch to investigate this possibility. Meanwhile, the German experts speculated that British agents near the selected targets had set up radio beacons that began to function when they were switched on by a radio beam from the aircraft.

On Monday 28 June 1943, SS Reichsführer Himmler paid his second visit to the military experimental institute at Peenemünde. At 9:15 next morning, the experimental model of the A-4 long-range rocket took off. "A few yards from the ground the unit already showed a deviation," the report stated, and the A-4 crashed close to its takeoff point, at the Peenemünde West airfield. Three aircraft standing there were destroyed when 8 tons of fuel (liquid oxygen with alcohol) exploded and tore a crater 100 feet across in the takeoff runway. But within 55 minutes the technicians had prepared a second A-4 rocket for takeoff. With an ear-splitting roar the rocket climbed and disappeared into the sky and flew 142 miles along the Baltic Sea. Himmler, visibly impressed, reported to Hitler that same evening.

Meanwhile Air Marshal Harris' Battle of the Ruhr rolled on. On the night of 22nd–23rd June 1943, 499 British bombers bombed Mülheim-an-der-Ruhr and Oberhausen. The 1,643 tons of bombs they dropped, caused considerable damage in the cities; 35 aircraft were lost. Two nights later, 24th–25th June, 554 Bomber Command aircraft raided the Elberfeld district of Wuppertal with a loss of 34 machines; the city was almost completely devastated by 1,663 tons of bombs. Of the 1,000-acre built-up area, 962 acres were reduced to rubble. After the raid the city was only a memory of what had been there the day before. The RAF lost 34 planes that night.

Four days later, on the night of 28th–29th June 1943, Cologne became the target of another grand assault by 540 British aircraft; some 1,614 tons of bombs were dropped on the city. This raid concluded the Ruhr offensive which had been going on for four months. During the offensive Bomber Command had launched 18,506 missions with a loss of 872 machines, while 2,126 were damaged (4.7% casualties). Enormous damage had been done; the city centers of Bochum, Dortmund, Duisburg, Essen, Cologne and Wuppertal had been destroyed and burnt out almost completely. Yet the munitions plants in the area went on working anyhow. That month, German fighter-plane production exceeded 1,000 planes for the first time since the war began. But this was a mere fraction of the fighters produced by Germany's foes during the same period.

1943
July to December

Secret report of the German *SS Secret Service* on internal affairs, No. 410 of Thursday 1 July 1943 (extract):

I. General comments: Numerous rumors are spreading about new [German] weapons and defensive devices. Due to the [Allied] terrorist air raids whose effects have intensified even further in recent weeks, and to the fact that we have not yet retaliated, a small number of Germans are expressing doubt as to whether Germany really is still capable of carrying out its advertized reprisals; but the majority believe that the reprisals will in fact take place soon, by the beginning of autumn at the latest.

The Battle of Kursk

Tuesday 6 July 1943, Moscow
A special communiqué from the Soviet Military High Command (STAVKA) reported:

Since the morning of July 5, Soviet troops in the Kursk sector from Orel to Belgorod [= the Kursk salient, a Soviet troop bulge along the central Eastern Front] have been mounting a heavy defensive war against strong enemy infantry and armored forces that have moved onto the attack with the support of large numbers of aircraft.

The enemy attacks have been repelled with heavy losses to the attackers. Only at a few points have small German Fascist formations succeeded in penetrating some way into our positions. Initial, still incomplete reports indicate that 586 German tanks and 203 German aircraft were destroyed on the first day of battle. The fighting is continuing. The Soviet High Command were prepared for the launch of the German offensive.

Wednesday 7 July 1943, Moscow
The *Soviet Information Bureau* announced:

German Fascists stormed our positions all day Tuesday. Despite their attempt to smash our defensive system with strong armored units at Orel and Belgorod, the aggressors made only slight territorial gains. On Monday night leading into Tuesday, the strategic Red Air Force brought powerful forces into the battle and bombed German troops and material concentrations in the Orel and Belgorod zones, dropping large numbers of high-explosive and fragmentation bombs. Two of our aircraft have not come back.

7 July 1943
The *Wehrmacht High Command* announced:

On Tuesday the Soviets led heavy attacks, deploying very strong formations that they had been preparing for weeks, near Belgorod and south of Orel; the attacks failed. Thereupon our troops moved onto the offensive with effective support from the Luftwaffe; they succeeded in penetrating deep into the enemy positions and inflicting extremely severe losses. Our army troops alone destroyed or immobilized over 300 enemy tanks, some of them of the most modern design. Bitter fighting between German and powerful Soviet flying units also took place in the air over the battle zone.

On 5–6 July, 637 Soviet aircraft including a large number of ground-attack planes, were shot down in aerial combat and by German flak artillery; we lost 41 aircraft. Strong Luftwaffe units bombed Soviet supply lines, airfields and rail installations to the rear of the enemy lines, inflicting long-lasting damage.

10 July 1943, a Red Air Force forward airfield east of Novosil [near the Kursk salient]. Bombs are being unloaded; in the background are Soviet Petlyakov Pe-2 dive bombers, which were built of wood like the British Mosquitos.

Thursday 8 July 1943, Moscow
The *Soviet Information Bureau* reported:

On the third day of the German-Fascist grand offensive, the attack became more extensive as fresh reserves were deployed. Today the German formations again made only slight territorial gains which cost them disproportionately heavy losses.

No notable changes have occurred on the Orel Front, but the Germans have succeeded in expanding somewhat the breaches they made at Belgorod. By evening our troops once again occupied their initial front-line positions at almost all points, and Soviet units temporarily cut off by the German armored penetrations were relieved.

The Germans have lost more than 220 tanks, 40 of them Tigers, at this sector of the front alone. Throughout the day bitter aerial combats took place between large formations of aircraft, without either side being able to gain air supremacy. Our Sturmovik low-level ground-attack planes played a major role in smashing the Fascist tank onslaught, as did our new "destroyer" aircraft which fire a new type of antitank shell.

8 July 1943
The *Wehrmacht High Command* announced:

Heavy tank battles took place near Belgorod and south of Orel on Wednesday, resulting in the destruction of more than 400 Russian tanks by German army troops, German flak artillery, and combat and close-combat wings of the German Luftwaffe. We broke through the densely-ranged enemy positions by tenacious fighting in the woods and villages. Combat and close-combat wings of the Luftwaffe supported the assault operations of the German Army, causing the enemy to suffer grave losses of men, heavy weapons and rolling stock.

Saturday 10 July 1943, Moscow
The *Soviet Information Bureau* announced:

Fighting continued all day Friday along the whole front, especially at the focal points of Orel and Belgorod. The Red Air Force flew heavy day and night raids against German material and troop concentrations, close behind the front lines, and against roads, railway lines, airports and river crossings. Numerous violent air battles were fought in which both sides suffered major losses. We have positive information that the Germans have drawn off aerial forces from the other sectors of the Eastern Front, as well as from Western Europe, to make up their squadrons. We located strong concentrations of German aircraft on all airfields from Orel to Belgorod and bombed them heavily with our Sturmoviks.

Landing in Sicily

Sunday 11 July 1943
Allied Headquarters announced:

The aerial invasion of Sicily preceded the sea

Right: 19 July 1943, Ostiense railroad station, a target of the first Allied air raid on Rome.

Below: A Soviet Ilyushin Il-2m3 Sturmovik, shot down during the Battle of Kursk. This was a new twin-seater version of the dreaded low-level ground-attack aircraft. The entire forward fuselage was a uniform armor shell, with rear fuselage and wings of plywood [and other light materials]. The new model carried 2 37-mm cannon and was just beginning to be deployed on the front.

invasion by several hours. Shortly after 10:00 P.M. on Friday evening, the first transport glider planes were released over Sicily, and at 10:30 Allied airborne troops were setting foot on Sicilian soil. Paratroops took up positions behind the enemy's defensive installations.

Monday 12 July 1943, Rome
The Italian *Stefani News Agency* reported:

For military reasons, for the time being we can release only the following facts:

1. All enemy parachutists have been destroyed.
2. So far, all attempts by the British and American troops to penetrate from the Italian coast into the interior, have failed. Extremely violent, uninterrupted and turbulent fighting is continuing, but overall operations suggest that the enemy's hopes will shatter when confronted by hard reality. Italian and German troops, aided by the Sicilian population, are fulfilling their missions as planned, with the greatest calmness and dedication. The troops are resolute, no rash orders are being issued, and the population are not panicking.

Bombs Fall on Rome

Monday 19 July 1943, Algiers
Allied Headquarters in North Africa announced:

Today heavy bombers of the Allied Mediterranean Air Command attacked military targets in Rome and its environs. The air crews were ordered to avoid damaging churches and cultural monuments whenever possible. The main target of the raid was a rail switchyard important to the regroupment of German troops. Warning leaflets were dropped over the city before the raid.

19 July 1943, Rome
The *Italian Military High Command* announced:

The church of San Lorenzo fuori le Mura, one of the seven basilicas of Rome, was completely destroyed today in the massed raid by American aerial forces. The bones of numerous popes rested in the basilica, including those of Pius IX. The enemy aircraft flew over Rome in successive raids starting at 11:15 A.M. The workers' district on the

Tiber was the worst-hit area of the city. Large numbers of dwellings were reduced to rubble; there were heavy casualties. The Campo Verano cemetery also suffered heavy bomb damage.

19 July 1943
Allied Headquarters in North Africa reported in a special communiqué:

A German air convoy consisting of 16 Junkers Ju 52 transport aircraft was sighted by an RAF reconnaissance plane over the Tyrrhenian Sea (north of Sicily) and attacked by RAF fighters shortly afterward. All 16 aircraft were shot down with their cargo of troops and war material.

Tuesday 20 July 1943
Allied Headquarters announced:

The commander of the US aerial forces in Europe has congratulated General Doolittle on the precise and successful US air raid on Rome. It is considered particularly noteworthy that only 5 bombers were lost in the raid, in which more than 500 heavy bombers took part. This was due both to the weakness of the enemy aircraft and to the fact that only a few enemy fighters attempted to intercept the waves of US bombers.

Sunday 25 July 1943, London
The *Headquarters of the US 8th Air Force* announced:

All day yesterday, large formations of USAAF heavy Flying Fortress bombers flew raids against industrial installations in Norway. The Flying Fortresses successfully bombed the aluminum factory of Herüya and the U-boat docks in Trondheim. Air defense was relatively weak. We succeeded in shooting down 17 enemy fighter planes; one of our B-17s is missing. This was the first time that US bombers have operated against targets in Norway.

25 July 1943, Stockholm
The *Swedish Army Staff* announced:

Yesterday afternoon a four-engined B-24 Liberator bomber was forced to make an emergency landing in western Sweden approximately 12 miles from the Norwegian border.

Grand Raid on Hamburg

Extract from the diary of *Reich Minister of Propaganda Dr. Joseph Goebbels,* dated Monday 26 July 1943:

Hamburg during an RAF bombing raid in the summer of 1943. This is one of the last photographs taken of this city district, which a few days later was rubble and ashes.

Last night an extraordinarily heavy air raid was made on Hamburg. It had the most devastating consequences both for the civilian population and for armaments production in Hamburg. This raid has finally blown apart the illusions that many people still had about future enemy aerial operations. Unfortunately we shot down remarkably few of the enemy bombers, only 12 in all out of a total of approximately 500; of course this is a woefully inadequate showing. Regrettably, just two days ago General Weise took the heavy flak guns away from Hamburg to send to Italy. That was the crowning blow.

26 July 1943, London
RAF Headquarters announced:

Last night the RAF carried out major raids against Germany. Rapid Mosquito bombers raided Cologne, while Hamburg was bombed for the third time within a 48-hour period.

Wednesday 28 July 1943, London
The *Reuters News Agency* reported:

Here in London, the present series of air raids on Hamburg is being described as the heaviest ever

suffered by any city. Hamburg has been attacked uninterruptedly day and night since Saturday. Well over 5,000 tons of bombs have fallen on Hamburg in these four days. By comparison, the German Luftwaffe dropped a total of 5,800 tons of bombs on Great Britain during the climax of its raids in the months of September, October and November 1940—that is, approximately the same quantity dropped on Hamburg alone during the past four days.

Extract from the diary of *Reich Minister of Propaganda Dr. Joseph Goebbels,* dated Thursday 29 July 1943:

Last night the heaviest air raid so far was made on Hamburg. Between 800 and 1,000 British bombers appeared over the city. Our air defense succeeded in shooting down only a few, so we cannot claim that the assailants paid for what they did. Kaufmann is giving me a preliminary report on the effects of the British raid. He speaks of a catastrophe of hitherto inconceivable proportions. We are seeing the destruction of a city of millions of people, an event unparalleled in history. The resultant problems are virtually insuperable.

Friday 30 July 1943
RAF Headquarters announced:

On the night of Wednesday–Thursday, British Mosquito rapid bombers repeatedly raided targets in Hamburg. Great fires were still raging in the city that had not yet been extinguished after the heavy raid of the previous night. The German ground defenses had been reinforced and large numbers of fighter planes appeared, but neither could prevent us from carrying out our raid. Our bombers shot down at least 3 enemy aircraft.

Top-secret personal message from *Premier Stalin* to Prime Minister Churchill, dated 30 July 1943:

I have received your message informing me of your successful bombing of Hamburg. I congratulate the British aerial forces and applaud your intention to intensify bombing raids on Germany.

30 July 1943
RAF Headquarters issued the following supplementary bulletin:

Last night Hamburg was heavily bombed for the seventh time in six days. Nine thousand tons of bombs have been dropped on Hamburg within the space of 120 hours. Almost 1,000 heavy British bombers took part in the grand assault under the command of Sir Arthur Harris, the Air Chief Marshal of Bomber Command. The bombers approached in 5 waves and in barely one hour dropped more than 2,000 tons of bombs on the city and its industrial installations. The German Luftwaffe made every conceivable effort to protect Hamburg and deployed more night fighters, flak and searchlights than ever before. As to the consequences of the raid, it is said that it is no longer possible to estimate the number of fires and explosions, and the belief is that war production in Hamburg has been eliminated. Airmen report that the city looks as if it had been struck by an earthquake.

30 July 1943, Berlin
The *German News Bureau* reported:

Last night the enemy again dropped a large quantity of high-explosive and incendiary bombs on the city of Hamburg, causing further severe devastation. There were heavy casualties among the civilian population. Reports received so far indicate that the German air defense shot down at least 43 enemy raiders.

Sunday 1 August 1943, Stockholm

Eyewitness reports in the press unanimously indicate that Hamburg has ceased to exist as a city. "Dante's Inferno is as nothing compared to this hell," stated the captain of a Swedish steamship sunk in the port of Hamburg.

Bombs Drop on Rumanian Oil Center

Monday 2 August 1943, Cairo
The *US Air Force Command* in Egypt announced:

Yesterday a formation of more than 175 B-24 Liberator bombers took off from the Middle East to carry out a heavy daylight raid on the Rumanian oil fields at Ploesti. The bombers approached Ploesti at high altitude, then swooped down on the target in formation to an altitude of about 450 feet, and within the space of one minute dropped their entire bombload of almost 300 tons, in a carpet over the widespread production plant. Time-delay and incendiary bombs were released as well as high-explosive bombs. Then the bombers descended to 65 feet and opened fire on the installations with their aerial guns. The first reports indicate that the seven large refineries suffered particularly heavy damage. The bomber units travelled almost 2,400 miles on their journey from their Middle East bases and back again. This was the longest flight that bombers have made to a target since war began, and also the first massed raid by heavy four-engined bombers at low altitude.

Reliable authorities say that before the raid, the approximately 2,000 Liberator aircrew members had to undergo an intensive, top-secret specialized training, and several weeks were spent in preparing for the raid. The US aerial forces worked with a series of oil specialists to develop a detailed plan of operations. The Liberator air crews spent weeks testing their low-altitude raiding tactics in attacks on Italian bases; the aircraft would fly at their targets just above the treetops at a speed of over 210 miles per hour. The experience gained during these low-level raids, led to the insertion of a special low-altitude bomb-release device in every bomber for use in the raid on Ploesti. A life-scale model of Ploesti with all its refineries and rail lines, was constructed in the Libyan Desert for the bomber crews to use in their training exercises. For days on end they flew over this model city at rooftop level, dropping mock bombs. Nevertheless, the air raid on Ploesti turned out to be difficult because the Germans had installed numerous flak batteries to secure these essential installations. At this time the oil output of Ploesti was approximately 3.5 million tons per year, at least two thirds of which were delivered to Germany and Italy. Ploesti had already been raided three times: once by several Liberators and twice by isolated Soviet bombers. The refineries of an American company suffered the greatest damage. According to the latest reports, at least 51 enemy fighter planes were shot down. Twenty US bombers were lost right over Ploesti. A number of other bombers have failed to return to base.

New Raid on Hamburg

Tuesday 3 August 1943, London
The *British Air Ministry* announced:

Last night strong Allied bomber forces again attacked the city of Hamburg and other targets in northwestern Germany. Thirty bombers did not come back.

Warning to Industrial Cities

3 August 1943, London:

On Monday evening *BBC Radio* broadcast a

Left: A properly laid-out German air shelter could look almost cozy, but provided only limited security against the increasingly massive bombing raids.

Opposite page above: When British hands reached into the RAF target file, it meant death and destruction for the people of the chosen German city. The British drew up detailed plans of a whole operation on the basis of information in these files.

warning to the German-occupied industrial cities of Europe, saying that in future no industrial plant that works for Germany, should consider itself outside the range of the Allied aerial forces as these continue to gather strength.

The Air Raid on Ploesti

3 August 1943, Bucharest
The Rumanian *Rador News Agency* reported:

On August 1 between 1:00 and 4:00 P.M., formations of US four-engined bombers, approximately 125 in all, raided the Rumanian oil region. The violent resistance by Rumanian and German forces, prevented some of the attackers from reaching the target. Casualties include 147 wounded and 116 dead. Of these, 63 of the dead and 60 of the wounded were inmates of Ploesti Prison who were hurt when a burning American bomber crashed into the roof. So far we have determined that 56 bombers were shot down and 6 American airmen captured. The Queen Mother Helene visited the petroleum zone on the morning of August 2; and immediately after the air raid, Marshal Antonescu [= Ion Antonescu, wartime military dictator of Rumania] arrived there accompanied by members of the government.

3 August 1943, Constantinople
The American *Associated Press News Agency* reported:

Of the 8 Liberator bombers that were forced to make emergency landings on Turkish territory on Sunday after the raid on Ploesti, 3 suffered severe damage from enemy fighter planes and flak. The US crew members say that the air defense was very strong. The crews have been interned in Smyrna pending a final decision about their fate.

After the Ploesti Raid

3 August 1943, Berlin
The *German News Bureau* announced:

The enemy air raid on the Rumanian oil district, reported on August 2, is revealing itself to have been a disaster for the attackers. Enemy losses have by now increased to 52 aircraft. Reports from abroad say that 15 enemy bombers have made emergency landings on neutral territory. This means, by our calculations, that more than half of the formation who entered the raid, have failed to return to base.

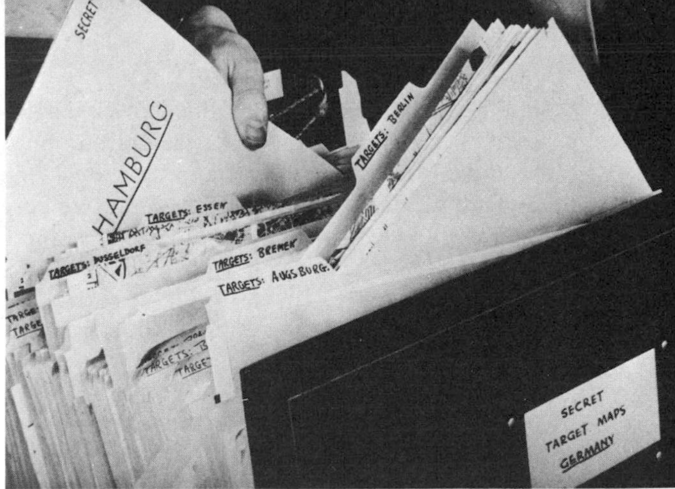

Wednesday 4 August 1943, Sofia
Radio Sofia in Bulgaria reported:

During their return flight from Ploesti, 7 US heavy bombers damaged over Rumania were forced to make emergency landings at various points in Bulgaria. The air crews have been taken prisoner.

Run-Up to the Berlin Raids

4 August 1943, London
The *Reuters News Agency* reported:

After the air raids on Hamburg, authoritative sources believe that other similar operations will be carried out, probably against Berlin. It has been noted that extensive preparations are already underway at a number of new airfields that are used exclusively by heavy four-engined RAF bombers. The predicted raids on Berlin will be mainly RAF night operations. The date of the raids will depend on the length of the nights, which now is increasing by half an hour per week. This means that each week the heavy bombers can penetrate fifty miles deeper into Germany.

In two or three weeks the RAF will be able to reach Berlin just as easily as it can reach Hamburg because Berlin is only 130 miles farther away. In several weeks' time the Americans may also begin daylight raids on Berlin. The 8th USAAF has already made daylight flights into Germany as far as Warnemünde, which is the same as the distance to Berlin.

Sunday 15 August 1943
The *Headquarters of US General MacArthur* announced:

Yesterday a large formation of Allied Liberator bombers led a raid against the Japanese-occupied oil-producing center of Balik Papan on the (Indonesian) island of Borneo. Their flight covered a distance of more than 2,400 miles. The aircraft dropped their bombs over a period of approximately one hour. Despite the active Japanese ground defense and the deployment of large numbers of Japanese night fighters, we succeeded in heavily damaging the refinery installations.

Emergency Landings in Switzerland

Tuesday 17 August 1943, Bern
The Swiss newspaper *Neue Zürcher Zeitung* reported:

Today at midday, two American Flying Fortress bombers made emergency landings in Switzerland: one at 12:48 P.M. in Dübendorf and the other at 2:00 P.M. in Utzendorf (Berne). The two crews of 10 men each have been interned.

Wednesday 18 August 1943, London
The *British Air Ministry* announced:

Yesterday the Allied aerial forces continued their extended daylight raids on enemy targets in France, Holland, Belgium and Germany. A strong unit of Flying Fortresses bombed industrial installations in Schweinfurt, and the Messerschmitt aircraft plant in Regensburg. The latter city is also the distribution center for transports of Rumanian oil. The bombers encountered strong flak, and were repeatedly attacked by some 200 German fighter planes. Of the Allied aircraft deployed on these various operations, 36 Flying Fortresses, one Mosquito rapid bomber and 5 fighter planes have failed to return.

18 August 1943, London
RAF Headquarters announced:

Last night in clear moonlight our bombers undertook a massive raid on Peenemünde approximately 60 miles northwest of Stettin, the largest and most important air research and development institute in Germany. Our aircraft encountered a great many enemy night fighters, several of which we shot down. Mosquito bombers raided targets in Berlin.

US Bombers Fly Back to Base

The US magazine *Stars and Stripes* carried the following descriptive account in August of 1943:

I leaned against the co-pilot's seat and observed our formation. There were now far fewer bombers than there had been at takeoff, and most of them were marked by fire from German fighter planes or flak. Several bombers were limping along on three engines. A number had dead on board, and wounded who were trying to relieve their pain with morphine injections and tablets. All the crew were exhausted by their nine-hour flight at high altitude. We tried to close up our scattered formations.

Flying back over the coast of Holland was a psychological turning point, and the crews whose planes were in good shape could relax a little. Some of them pulled out thermos bottles of coffee and unpacked their sandwiches or smoked a forbidden cigarette. Only the gunners were expected to remain on the alert.

Now our navigational devices were no longer jammed, and we could determine our positions accurately for the first time in hundreds of miles. We switched on our identifying signal so that the RAF fighters and radar stations could recognize the approaching unit as friendlies.

Several bombers had lost fuel from their shot-up fuel tanks. We saw one bomber go down into the sea. A few minutes later a second bomber went down and shortly after, a third. The remaining bombers of our exhausted and beat-up group flew on, throwing overboard any unnecessary weight.

As soon as we crossed the British coast, we ran into the usual picture: The bombers that could barely stay aloft, broke out of formation as if on order and one after another headed for an airfield that lay a mile inland. The tower control officer was definitely on the edge of despair. He wildly fired off every possible color of flare; but he could have spared himself the fireworks display because the returning crews had only one thought in mind and that was to get on the ground as fast as possible. Our thinned-out formation flew on to our own base. There was always a contest on between the squadrons to see which crew would land first after coming back from a raid. The winners were usually the experienced veterans. A few clever pilots reported to the control tower that they were back when they were still a long distance from the airfield, in order to get themselves a better place in the waiting line.

The buses were already waiting to take us to our billets. After we had taken off our parachutes, flying suits and other gear, we dragged ourselves deadtired to interrogation. Holding the welcome-back cigarette and hot tea with rum, each air crew reported on the operation to an intelligence officer.

I looked at the pilot next to me, who seemed upset. It was the usually cocky C., who now looked completely done-in. "Lost somebody?" I asked.

British WAAFs, members of the Women's Auxiliary of the RAF, enthusiastically greet the air crew of a Lancaster bomber returning from a raid on Hamburg.

—"I have a dead radio operator out there," he answered, "and they shot up my bombardier and my technician. My co-pilot passed out, he really needs some time off."

Daylight Raids on Schweinfurt and Regensburg

18 August 1943, London
The *Headquarters of the US 8th Air Force* released further details about yesterday's daylight raids:

Our B-17 Flying Fortresses encountered a strong fighter plane defense over Schweinfurt, but the air crews report that they scored good results and said that the clouds of smoke rising from the extensive fires, spread for a distance of over 20 miles.

Our Flying Fortresses had to wage hard aerial combat for almost one hour before they were able to attack Schweinfurt. More and more German fighter planes kept appearing that had been called up from all over, and the ensuing air battle was the hardest that US bombers have had to fight so far.

It should be noted that unlike all the other branches of Germany's war industry, the ball-bearing plants have not been decentralized. Schweinfurt produces by far the largest percentage of ball-bearings for all types of military equipment, so that the destruction of these plants must lead to a serious decline in production throughout the German munitions industry. This morning, reconnaissance aircraft determined that extensive fires are still burning in the city.

Another giant formation of Flying Fortresses attacked the Messerschmitt aircraft plant in Regensburg. Today our reconnaissance planes learned that the Regensburg plant too suffered considerable damage. Some of the B-17s flew on to North Africa, while the rest of the formation returned to England. We can already predict that in all probability, heavy bombers that take off from England for future raids on southern Germany, will fly on to North Africa rather than returning to England.

Be Sure to Report and Hand In Parts of Enemy Aircraft

German Reich Marshal Göring, commander of the Luftwaffe, published the following appeal in an issue of the Hamburg newspaper, the *Hamburger Anzeiger,* dated 8 September 1943:

Fellow Germans! We have scored significant victories while defending ourselves against the recent powerful day and night enemy air raids. This has resulted each time in our shooting down a large number of enemy bombers, which are lying scattered at wide intervals through the country, and for the most part are in places where our people can find them. Anyone who finds aircraft parts and equipment, must immediately report it to the nearest police or Air Raid Protection authority. Unauthorized seizure or retention of these objects will be severely punished. To avoid accidents, scrap material you find should not be touched, but must absolutely be left to the authorities to dispose of. Scraps of shot-down aircraft, the remains of enemy bomb munitions, and any sort of enemy material found after air raids, is not appropriate matter for souvenir-collectors.

German Bombs Drop on Italian Ships

Friday 10 September 1943, Berlin
The *German News Bureau* reported:

On Thursday German bombers sank an Italian battleship and a cruiser between Sardinia and Corsica. These vessels belonged to an Italian warship formation that had fled from La Spezia and was trying, under orders from the Allied commander-in-chief, to stop German shipping traffic between Sardinia and Corsica.

Wednesday 15 September 1943, Berlin
The *German News Bureau* reported:

The Führer has awarded the Iron Cross, Knight's Cross degree, to Otto Skorzeny, the Army SS Lieutenant who carried out the commando mission to liberate Mussolini.

Extract from the diary of Reich Minister of Propaganda *Dr. Joseph Goebbels,* dated 15 September 1943:

Our liberation of Il Duce is continuing to create a sensation among our enemies abroad. This heroic act has made the deepest impression on the whole world. Virtually no military operation of the war has stirred people so deeply or moved them so much. We have achieved a morale victory of the first order.

Heavy Fighting on Kos

Monday 4 October 1943, Berlin
The *German News Bureau* reported:

A short time ago the Greek island of Kos, one of the Dodecanese islands which lies northwest of Rhodes, was occupied by British troops, apparently aided by troops loyal to Badoglio [= Marshal Pietro Badoglio, who had taken command of the Italian government after Mussolini's overthrow in July]. Since then British aerial forces have been using the island as a base from which to carry out raids on Rhodes. Yesterday morning, several German landing groups succeeded, by determined action, in approaching the coast undetected with their assault and landing boats, and captured all the important military installations on Kos. The surprised enemy offered strong resistance at only a few points and suffered heavy casualties. More than 200 British soldiers were captured. Some British troops fled to the almost inaccessible mountains in the interior of the island. Among the captured equipment were 4 heavy British bombers.

Sunday 10 October 1943, London
The *British Air Ministry* announced:

Yesterday strong formations of Flying Fortress and Liberator bombers penetrated deep into German territory. The main targets of the raid were: the

Above right: A US B-17 Flying Fortress bomber taking part in the raid on Schweinfurt on 17 August 1943. The official caption on the photo claims that 75% of the city's ball-bearing plants were destroyed, but in reality the figure was less than 34%.

Opposite page left: US Consolidated B-24 Liberator bombers are making practice flights near Bengasi airstrip (Libya) before mounting a low-altitude raid on Ploesti, the Rumanian oil fields which were Hitler's largest petroleum suppliers.

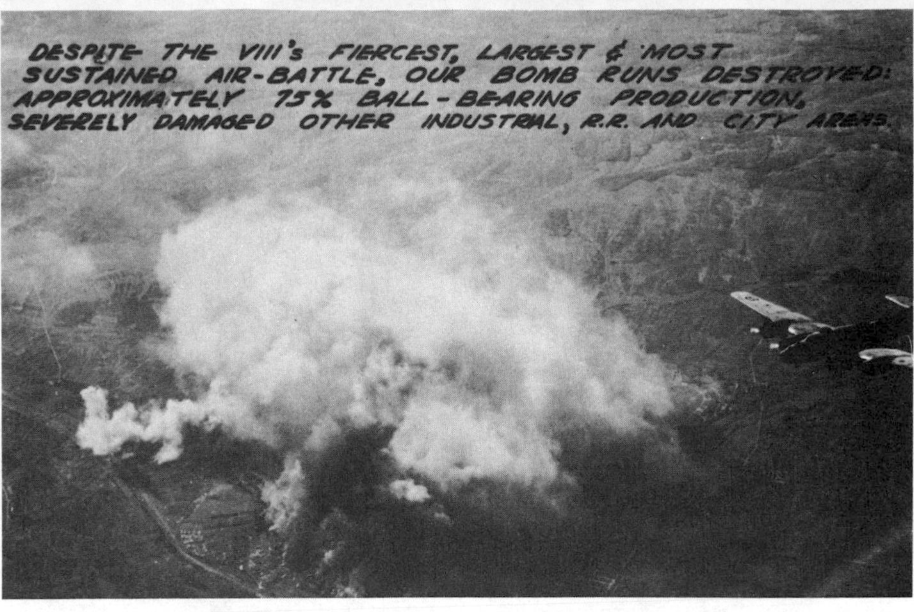

Arado Plant in Anklam (eastern Germany) northwest of Stettin which produces parts for the Focke-Wulf 190 fighter planes; the aircraft assembly plant in Marienburg, East Prussia, one of the largest plants of its kind in Germany; the U-boat docks of Danzig; the docks and port installations of Gdynia in Poland. The US bombers flew without fighter escort and encountered strong resistance, so that violent combats took place over the target zones. The bombers were also attacked by formations of German fighters during their outbound and return flights.

Emergency Landings in Sweden

10 October 1943, Stockholm
The Swedish newspaper *Svenska Dagbladet* reported:

Yesterday afternoon, 5 foreign aircraft – 3 US Flying Fortresses and 2 German Messerschmitt fighters – were forced to make emergency landings in southern Sweden. The Swedish general staff informs us that on their outbound flight the US bombers kept out of Swedish air space and flew eastward south of the province of Schonen (southwestern Sweden). On their return flight they were attacked by German fighter planes and pursued over Swedish territory. Both the Flying Fortresses and their pursuers seem to have become disoriented. Two of the US bombers were set on fire by their crews after landing, while the third fell undamaged into the hands of the Swedish military; the German planes are also undamaged. The crew members, totalling 32 men, have been interned.

A Flying Fortress Lands near Basle

Thursday 14 October 1943, Basle (Switzerland)
The Swiss newspaper *Neue Zürcher Zeitung* reported:

Today at about 3:10 P.M., a US Flying Fortress bomber landed between Aesch and Ettingen. The airmen did not realize that they were on Swiss soil and were extremely glad to hear it. Their reports indicate that they were returning to base after bombing a German city, when they came under heavy fire from German flak and fighter planes. In fact, a flak missile has left a mark larger than a man's head in the fuselage of their bomber. There are also smaller imprints left by exploding shell fragments and machine-gun missiles. As they headed toward base, their engines gradually conked out, and the airmen were forced to make an emergency landing.

Saturday 16 October 1943, London
General Anderson, commander of the US 8th Air Force based in Britain, issued the following statement about the US air raid on Schweinfurt:

We anticipated heavy losses and our expectations have been realized; but the damage suffered by the enemy is far greater. Visibility and weather over the target zone were excellent, and the bombs were concentrated on the industrial nerve-centers. Our initial estimate is that we destroyed at least half of Schweinfurt's ball-bearing plants. This raid will undoubtedly cause a decrease in the production of German tanks, aircraft and guns, and the construction of U-boat submarines will also be affected.

"We saw one bomber going down into the sea. A few minutes later a second bomber went down and shortly after, a third." A shot-up US B-17 is steadily losing altitude.

Saturday 23 October 1943
RAF Headquarters announced:

Last night a large number of RAF wings attacked the Henschel locomotive-engine plant (the largest of its kind in Europe) and the Fieseler plant (the manufacturers of German Focke-Wulf fighter planes) in Kassel, while other formations bombed the city's rail installations. The German Luftwaffe made every effort to prevent the raid but was unable to keep the bomber wings away from the city. Visibility over Kassel was extremely clear and the bombers had an accurate view of their targets. One of the Mosquito pilots reported: "Kassel was a single sheet of flame from which violent explosions were continuously erupting. You could see the smoke up to an altitude of 16,000 feet. We approached the city repeatedly from different directions, but after the raid we found no opportunity to take aerial photographs due to the dense clouds of smoke. The rising wind caused the sea of flame to spread more and more. Now the extent of the destruction in Kassel must virtually match that in Hamburg."

Warning from the Allies

Thursday 18 November 1943
RAF Headquarters announced:

Yesterday for the first time we broadcast over our BBC radio transmitter a list of important military installations in France which will shortly become the targets of concentrated bombing raids by our aerial forces. The broadcast was repeated a number of times. It said that certain industrial centers in France are very important to German war operations, and that it is essential to destroy them in the interests of shortening the war; but to spare the lives of French workers and to give them the opportunity to get to a place of safety in time, the RAF has decided to specify the selected targets beforehand, even though this will give the named installations a chance to reinforce their defenses. The broadcaster emphasized that this prior warning is by no means an attempt to wage a "war of nerves"; for the French will very soon recognize that we are in deadly earnest.

Grand Operations by the Royal Air Force

Friday 19 November 1943
RAF Headquarters reported:

Last night Bomber Command sent to Germany the largest contingent of heavy bombers ever deployed in a single night. It divided up into two formations which operated independently. One formation attacked Ludwigshafen, the other Berlin, which lay under a pall of cloud so that the damage could not be accurately observed. A stream of several hundred four-engined bombers reached the German capital along the Havel river (in eastern Germany), and then split into groups that bombed Siemensstadt, Neukölln, Mariendorf, Steglitz, Marienfelde and other districts of Berlin. Tens of thousands of incendiaries, and 2- and 4-ton high-explosive bombs, dropped on Berlin within a period of barely 30 minutes. The reflection of huge fires lit up the clouds, revealing that severe damage must have occurred in the industrial districts.

A Turning-Point in Air War Strategy

19 November 1943, London

The *British Air Ministry* announced:

More than 2,500 tons of bombs were dropped in the raids on Berlin and Ludwigshafen. Two important targets were raided simultaneously; simultaneous raiding is a new tactic of Bomber Command. Recently the German Luftwaffe has concentrated extremely strong formations of night fighters around probable target zones. Aerial reconnaissance informs Bomber Command of the positions of the German night fighters, and Bomber Command then tries to strike at places where there is inadequate fighter protection. For example, last night the RAF deployed its formations simultaneously over two cities approximately 300 miles apart, so that the German night fighter defenses found it impossible adequately to protect both targets. Naturally these new tactics require the deployment of formations that are as large as possible, because despite everything the German Luftwaffe remains a formidable enemy that is quite capable of warding off twin attacks of limited force.

Heavy Raid on Berlin

Tuesday 23 November 1943, Berlin
The *German News Bureau* reported:

Yesterday evening British bombers raided Berlin. They had no ground visibility because the sky was completely overcast, but the raid was a severe one that caused heavy damage and casualties in many districts of the capital, mainly in workers' districts. It is also reported that irreplaceable art-historical treasures were destroyed, and damage was inflicted on offices belonging to the diplomatic representatives of several neutral nations.

23 November 1943, London
RAF Headquarters announced:

More than 2,000 tons of blast bombs and approximately 150,000 incendiaries were dropped on Berlin [yesterday] in barely 45 minutes. The air crews report that large fires spread through the city and that their glow lit the sky a fiery red. Repeated violent explosions took place that could not be attributed solely to the explosive effect of the bombs.

23 November 1943, Berlin
The *German News Bureau* reported:

At today's foreign press conference, the head of the German Foreign Ministry press division stated his views of the air raid on Berlin last night. He emphasized that the most important thing about the raid had been the reaction of the Berlin population. He was proud to say that Berlin had honored its role as the capital of the Reich. The people had defended their city in an exemplary way, often at risk of their lives. The spokesman mentioned several examples of the self-sacrificial conduct of the populace. There had been much suffering that night, he said; yet there had also been countless proofs of comradeship and unconditional will to serve. The British might believe that they can undermine German morale by destroying German homes and places of culture, but the events of this night bear out that the Berliner will emerge unbowed from these trials, and that faith in our Final Victory cannot be shaken.

24 November 1943
RAF Headquarters announced:

The air raid on Berlin on the night of Monday to Tuesday, was comparable to the heavy grand assaults on Hamburg in summer of this year. Around 2,400 tons of blast and incendiary bombs were dropped on the German capital. The extremely misty weather hindered operations by the German searchlight batteries, so the German flak could only shoot aimlessly. We employed new tactics in this raid. A large number of pathfinder aircraft flew with the bombers to light up particular districts of Berlin, and then to mark the targets with colored flares for each bomber wing. A new type of flare has been developed for this purpose which lit Berlin

7 September 1943, Malta. Three old British Gloster Gladiator I biplane fighters—"Faith," "Hope" and "Charity"—were the sole defense of Malta from Italian bombers for a period of 18 days in June 1940. Here the garrison and citizens are paying honor to the remains of the "Faith."

adequately despite the heavy clouds overhead. For example, the whole of the government office district was clearly discernible in the light of the flares. The RAF planes remained over the capital for 35 minutes in all. Approximately 20 minutes after the first bomb was released, there was a gigantic explosion whose effects were clearly visible from an altitude of over 21,000 feet. On Wednesday, hundreds of British air crews confirmed that they had never seen such a severe explosion or felt such a shock wave, on any previous mission. Experts believe that either a munitions warehouse or a giant gasworks must have blown up. One of our pilots gave this account: "The German antiaircraft started firing about 180 miles outside Berlin, so that we had to fly for a total of 360 miles through a more or less dense barrage, which was hard on the nerves. We saw the explosion too; it was almost unimaginable. Suddenly a blazing light shot up and the horizon turned fiery red. The colored flares from the pathfinders showed us our way as clearly as we could wish. We had no problems as we released more than 50 two-ton bombs on the city center, which the flares had divided into sectors. Only one of our bombs hit down outside the area marked by the flares."

24 November 1943, London
The British newspaper the *Daily Mail* reported:

It has entered the realm of possibility that Berlin may be approaching the end of its days as a capital city, due to the fearful rain of bombs that fell on it Monday night. The RAF has devised means to level targets the size of Berlin. The raid was by far the heaviest that that city has ever experienced.

Extract from the diary of Reich Minister of Propaganda *Dr. Joseph Goebbels,* dated 24 November 1943:

Early in the morning I am already at work. Straightaway Schaub gives me a report on the situation in Berlin, which is very sad. It is inexplicable how the British were able to destroy so much of the capital in one air raid. The Wilhelmsplatz is truly the picture of desolation. It is still blazing from end to end. The Propaganda Ministry [Goebbels' ministry] has mainly been spared . . . Now and then I am able to snatch half an hour's sleep; but then I am called back to work. Large formations of British aircraft are again set on an obstinate course for Berlin . . . The raid begins shortly after the alarm siren. This time there are more blast bombs than incendiaries. Once again it is a first-class grand assault . . . Mines and explosive bombs hail down incessantly on the government district. One after another the most important buildings start to burn. After the raid when I take a look at the Wilhelmsplatz, I find that the ghastly impression of the previous evening has grown even worse. I pass on into the Propaganda Ministry. The offices are burning in two places on the side of the Wilhelmsplatz.

New Raid on Berlin

24 November 1943
RAF Headquarters announced:

Last night Berlin was again the target of a grand assault by the RAF. This time the attack concentrated mainly on the western part of the capital with its three large rail installations: Westend, Bahnhof Zoo and Bahnhof Charlottenburg. The night was clear and there were only a few clouds to hinder visibility, so that operational conditions were far more favorable to the German air defense than on the previous night. From a distance of 30 miles the British air crews could see the fires that have continued to smolder since Monday. Finally in the fire-glow over Berlin they were able to observe many details of the destroyed city districts. The whole complex around the Wilhelmstrasse, the Brandenburg Gate area and the Tauentzienstrasse, Potsdam Square, the Anhalter Strasse and many other building-lined streets have been completely destroyed. On Tuesday night leading into Wednesday, the western part of Berlin suffered more than in all the previous raids. On Wednesday afternoon, Mosquitos flew over the capital and reported having observed well over 200 giant conflagrations.

24 November 1943, Berlin
Today at noon a spokesman for the *German Armed Forces High Command* (the Wehrmacht) stated to representatives of the foreign press concerning the raid on Berlin:

"These terrorist raids on German cities have expanded to such an extent that regrettably we are forced to deploy our retaliatory weapon." However, when questioned by journalists the spokesman expressed no details about the method or date of German retaliatory measures.

Extract from the diary of Reich Minister of Propaganda *Dr. Joseph Goebbels,* dated Thursday 25 November 1943:

Now we are gradually learning again to get used

14 November 1943 near Aesch (Switzerland). A US bomber, the B-17 F (no. 230 831), received many hits from German fighters and flak on its way to raid Schweinfurt, and the air crew decided to make an emergency landing.

to a primitive pattern of life. Mornings in the Göringstrasse there is no heat, no light, no water. One can neither shave nor wash. One has to leave the bunker with a burning candle. At the crack of dawn I get up with the worst headache of my life. I am plagued with headaches non-stop. But what does that matter; it's time to get to work. I drive straight to the office where I can shave and wash . . . Most of the Kaiserdamm [road] is still burning; but the fire department hopes to get the fires under control in the course of the night. Isolated clumps of people flit over the streets making a genuinely ghostly impression. Your heart is wrenched when you drive through areas like this. How beautiful Berlin was once, and how wretched and dilapidated it looks now.

25 November 1943
RAF Headquarters announced:
Although Berlin has already been bombed more heavily than Hamburg, the damage is comparatively less because the built-up area of Berlin is substantially larger. It would take approximately 50,000 to 60,000 tons of bombs to destroy the German capital to the same extent as Hamburg.

Extract from the diary of Reich Minister of Propaganda *Dr. Joseph Goebbels,* dated Friday 26 November 1943:
Your heart is wrenched when you see all that has fallen victim to the air raids . . . At last I have gotten the Führer to allow us two types of air raid siren, at least for Berlin: that is one genuine alarm siren to signal that bomber formations are approaching the city, and a mere warning siren to warn of isolated offensive aircraft. This is essential because I cannot throw a city of four and a half million people into a violent turmoil every evening for the sake of two Mosquitos. So far the Führer has given permission for these two distinct types of air siren only in Berlin; but I hope that they can soon be transferred to other districts as well. Also, in future the radio transmitters will no longer be turned off when individual offensive aircraft fly in.

Fresh Bombing Raids on Berlin

Saturday 27 November 1943, Berlin
The *German News Bureau* reported:
Yesterday evening the British made another terrorist raid on the German capital. Partly for reasons of weather, partly to mislead the German air defense, they chose to make a detour across southwestern Germany. German night fighter planes fought the enemy along his lengthy run-in route, and involved him in heavy aerial combats especially in the Berlin area, with support from German flak guns. Reports received so far indicate that 15 bombers were observed to go down before this new raid began. We are still receiving reports of further shoot-downs.

Extract from the diary of Reich Minister of Propaganda *Dr. Joseph Goebbels,* dated 27 November 1943:

Then I travelled through the damaged areas with Naumann and Schaub. We also stopped at several ration distribution stations . . . The misery one sees is indescribable. It breaks one's heart to see it; but all the same we must clench our teeth [and bear it]. Sometimes one has the impression that the mood of people in Berlin is almost religious. Women walk over to me and make signs of blessing and pray God to keep me safe. All this is very moving . . . The food [being distributed to the people] is praised everywhere as excellent . . . You can wrap these people around your little finger with small tokens of kindness. I can hardly believe that this city led a revolt in 1918. Under my leadership that would never have happened . . . Another grand assault comes due on the city. This time it is not the turn of the city center so much as of the Wedding and Reinickendorf districts; the main target in Reinickendorf is the big industrial munitions plant . . . Back to the bunker in the Wilhelmsplatz. The situation has taken a more threatening turn as one industrial plant after another has gone up in flames. The sky arches over Berlin with a blood-red eerie beauty. I can no longer stand to look at it.

24 November 1943, eight hours after the third RAF grand raid on Berlin. Part of the city center is still burning. The numbers 1 and 2 mark the Kurfürstendamm (road) and the Kaiser Wilhelm Memorial Church.

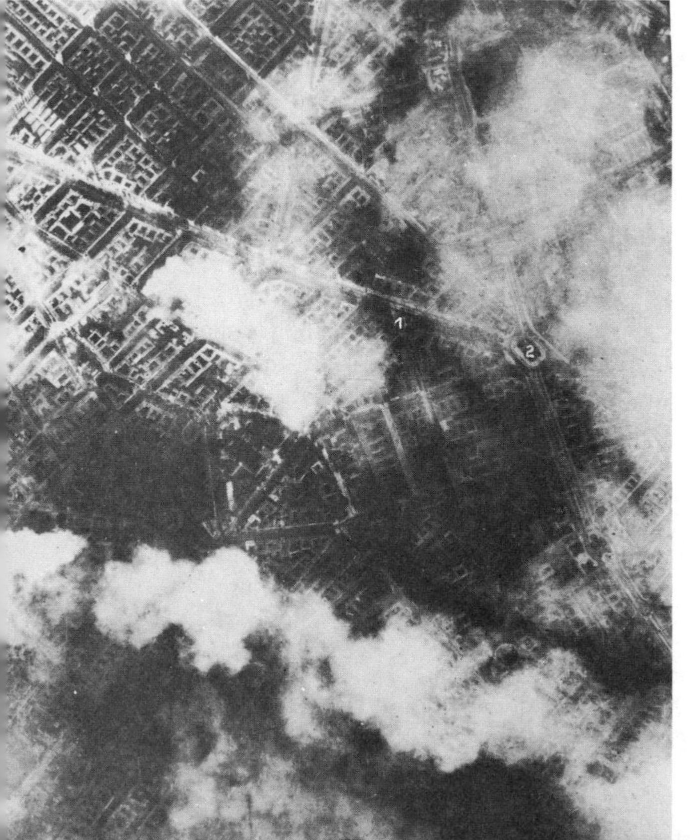

27 November 1943, London
Lord Sherwood, undersecretary of state in the British Air Ministry, stated concerning the air war against Germany:

In the past Berlin expressly ordered Warsaw, Rotterdam and Belgrade to be levelled. In their enthusiasm the Germans even made documentary films of these great deeds of the German Luftwaffe so that they could be suitably admired. Now they are being paid out in the same coin.

The crocodile tears in the eyes of so many Germans can awaken no pity. The blows now being dealt to Germany, are merely just punishment for the crimes that the Third Reich has committed against small nations, their unprotected cities, and minority groups in many states. We can make Germany only one promise: Our blows will increase in power until the military capacity of the Nazi Reich has been broken.

Extract from the diary of Reich Minister of Propaganda *Dr. Joseph Goebbels,* dated Monday 29 November 1943:

I went to Reinickendorf and especially to Wedding [in Berlin]. I took part in a public meal at the Gartenplatz. Male and female workers here received me with an enthusiasm that was as incredible as it was indescribable. Once that was the Reddest [most Communist] part of Wedding, around the Ackerstrasse. I would never have believed it possible for such a change in attitude to take place.

The people made me eat with them, I was lifted onto a box to speak to them. I gave a very passionate and unrestrained talk that spoke to the hearts of the workers. Everyone addressed me in the familiar and called me by my first name. The people wanted to carry me across the square and I managed only with difficulty to prevent them. Women embraced me. I was forced to give out autographs. Cigarettes were handed out; we smoked a fag together. In short, everything was as jolly as an amusement park.

Naturally the destruction is enormous. But as far as the public themselves are concerned, they are taking it in good humor . . . In an extended discussion with Dr. Ley [= Robert Ley, head of the German Labor Front and one of Hitler's inner circle] I considered how we can get the workers to go back to the factories; because for the most part they have not returned there . . . Tobacco is now the most approved luxury; a Berliner will stand on his head for a cigarette.

"Ranger" Mosquito nuisance bombers, painted matt black and equipped with the most up-to-date radar, became a real plague to the Berliners and the citizens of other large German cities.

Friday 3 December 1943, Berlin
The *German News Bureau* reported:

Last night strong German bomber forces raided the enemy supply base at Bari (Italian seaport on the Adriatic) and scored bomb hits that caused lasting destruction to the port area. The incomplete reports we have received so far indicate that 7 freighters were sunk. Two other vessels loaded with fuel or ammunition, exploded after being hit by bombs. Numerous other freighters suffered substantial damage.

A Thousand Bombers over the Rhine-Main Zone

Tuesday 21 December 1943, London
RAF Headquarters announced:

On Monday night leading into Tuesday, RAF Bomber Command sent almost 1,000 heavy bombers to operate over Frankfurt am Main, Mannheim, Ludwigshafen and several other industrial cities of southern Germany. In a period of barely 40 minutes, 2,200 tons of high-explosive and incendiary bombs were dropped on Frankfurt, the chief target. The bomber groups found their targets, which had been marked with flares by pathfinder aircraft. The ground defenses and more than one hundred German night fighters tried to drive the bombers away from Frankfurt, but banks of cloud offered enough cover for evasion. It is believed that the main gasworks in Frankfurt blew up 20 minutes after the attack began. The explosion was clearly perceptible up to an altitude of almost 20,000 feet. One squadron ran under the hail of flak missiles and flew over the main Frankfurt railroad station at an altitude of 975 feet: they raced along the Kaiserstrasse, which a few minutes later had turned into a single sea of flame.

Daylight Operations over Northern France

21 December 1943, London
The *Headquarters of the US 8th Air Force* announced:

In the afternoon the Allied aerial forces continued their air offensive against northern France and the Netherlands; they sent out a total of several hundred aircraft. A large group of US Marauder bombers with a fighter-plane escort, mounted one of their most successful raids, against an unspecified military target. All the bombers returned to base. Later, British Mitchell and Boston bombers took off for further raids on northern France; these too were carried out without any losses. A powerful group of Typhoon and Hurricane rapid bombers raided important military targets in the Pas de Calais.

Wednesday 22 December 1943, London
The British *Air Ministry* announced:

On Tuesday, several hundred American and British medium bombers and fighters left the southeast coast of England to bomb military targets in Northern France in continuous rotation. The main attacks again concentrated on the Pas de Calais region, which had already suffered heavy bombardment the day before. The pilots report that the German ground defense was generally weak, and comparatively few German fighter planes appeared on the scene. A very large quantity of bombs dropped on enemy territory while at the same time pinpoint targeting was achieved.

Thursday 23 December 1943, London
The *Reuters News Agency* reported:

All of a sudden the British public are being presented with slogans like "secret weapon" and "rocket missile." Rumors about the existence of German secret weapons have been circulating for a long time, and invariably the Germans are said to be threatening us with imminent retaliation.

However, discussion of this topic in the press has been strongly circumscribed, and at times caricaturists and humorists have turned the rumors into an object of mockery. But on Wednesday, for the first time, the way seems to have been cleared for technical experts to publish their own opinions concerning the secret weapon. The *Daily Mail,* the *News Chronicle,* the *Daily Herald* and other papers have published articles led by startling headlines like "Day Raid on the Rocket Coast" or "Rocket Guns May Have Been Target of Great Day Raid" or "RAF Raids Rocket Coast."

23 December 1943, London
BBC Radio reported:

On Wednesday the Allied aerial forces continued their powerful daylight raids. Reports from the southeast coast of England say that Allied fighter and bomber squadrons overflew the Straits of Dover all day long, probably on their way to raid military installations in the Pas de Calais. It has been suggested that the raided targets may include the assembly zones of the German "secret weapon," the rocket-firing bases whose existence was reported a short time ago.

Friday 24 December 1943, London
The *Reuters News Agency* reported:

Yesterday the RAF and the US aerial forces continued their intensified daylight raids on the northern French coast. We have reason to believe that in these operations, sites where German rocket-launch ramps are being built in the Pas de Calais, were bombed again.

Saturday 25 December 1943, Berlin
The *German News Bureau* reported:

We have learned that during their raids on residential districts of Germany in the morning hours of December 24, British airmen distributed a great quantity of delayed-fuse explosives timed to blow up on Christmas Eve. The operations of ordnance technicians and other measures, have thwarted their intentions.

Sunday 26 December 1943, London
RAF Headquarters announced:

The air offensive against mysterious targets in the Pas de Calais area, reached its climax on Friday. The headquarters of the US 8th Army Air Force have announced that more than 1,300 aircraft of the 8th USAAF raided "special military installations" in this area along the eastern coast of the English Channel. More US heavy bombers were deployed in these operations than have ever before taken part in a bombing raid over Europe. For hours on end, huge swarms of US bombers and fighters could be seen in the sky above the southeast coast of England; their engine noise drowned out the explosions on the enemy coast. The air crews of the returning aircraft reported that a regular shuttle formed over the Channel. One wing commander stated: "We scored good results. Most of our wings had specific targets to raid, and we saw numerous explosions scattered over a sizeable area."

Opposite page: Munich after an RAF Bomber Command raid on the Old Town. On the left the new town hall is on fire; in the background are the flaming tower of the old town hall and the Holy Ghost church. This remarkably fine color photograph was taken by a tower warden inside the Church of Our Lady.

Strategy and Tactics

July to December 1943

The RAF was reluctant to carry out grand raids on the short, bright moonlit summer nights that were ideal for the operations of the German night fighters.

There was a shortage of twin-engined German night fighters, so earlier in the year German Major Hajo Herrmann had recommended to General Kammhuber, commander of the Luftwaffe fighter arm, that single-engined Me 109 and FW 190 day fighters should join the night fighters in the struggle against the British night bombers. He believed that the day-fighter pilots could detect the RAF bombers by the light of ground fires, searchlights and pathfinder target markers [so that they could intercept them visually, without depending on jammable radar], over the target zone. On the night of 3rd–4th July 1943, 589 British aircraft raided Cologne, and the Germans made their first experiment: they sent 5 FW 190 day fighters and 7 Me 109 day fighters to fight them. The operations of the day fighters were inhibited by exposure to their own flak, but within minutes they nevertheless succeeded in shooting down 12 bombers over the city, using the light of the target flares to sight the enemy.

A total of 30 bombers were shot down that night. The exhaust flames of the British bombers made it easy for the swift and maneuverable day fighters to detect them, and the bomber silhouettes also stood out clearly against the fires, so they were very vulnerable. Major Herrmann had succeeded in devising a new German fighter-plane tactic which was known as *Wilde Sau* (Wild Pig). It was an improvement on the clumsy and complicated Himmelbett system, in which German night fighters had to be guided to the enemy bombers by radar that was susceptible to British jamming. Herrmann's daylight aircraft no longer had to rely on radar [because they intercepted their targets visually]. For 14 months British Air Chief Marshal Harris had been trying unsuccessfully to get Churchill's permission to deploy the Window tinfoil-strip jamming process [in British bombers to counteract German night-fighter radar]. He did not suspect that the new German tactic of *Wilde Sau*—unlike the old Himmelbett system—would prove completely immune to Windowing.

In the early days of July, the Germans finally concluded the preparations for Operation Citadel, their summer offensive on the Eastern Front. However, the Soviet secret service had kept STAVKA, the Soviet Military High Command, fully informed so that they were able to take defensive measures in time. It was a great advantage to the Soviets that the Germans chose to strike at Kursk, where Soviet forces were strongest.

The Germans planned a pincer attack with Luftwaffe support. The Luftwaffe had called up aircraft from almost all sectors of the Eastern Front, and from the fighter forces assigned to defend Germany, and formed them into two main thrusting forces. Luftflotte 4 (under Gen. Dessloch), joined by the 1st Air Force (I. Fliegerkorps under Gen. Pflugbeil) and the 8th Air Force (VIII. Fliegerkorps under Gen. Seidemann), were to cooperate with 2 groups and 3 squadrons of the Hungarian air force and with powerful flak units, to support the German Fourth Tank Army under General Hoth and the Kempff Army Detachment. Luftflotte 6 under General Ritter von Greim, combined with the 1st Air Division (Gen. Deichmann) and the 12th Flak Division (Gen. Buffe), would support the German Ninth Army under Field Marshal Model. The Germans hoped to turn the tide of the war with thirty-three divisions, including 16 armored divisions containing 3,400 armored cars and 1,800 combat aircraft. Back in

The underground headquarters of RAF Bomber Command in High Wycombe about 30 miles from London. The golf course surmounting the installation provided a perfect camouflage.

1941, when the Wehrmacht had first attacked the Soviet Union in Operation Barbarossa, it had deployed a total of 3,580 armored vehicles and 1,945 aircraft. Now an almost identical number of German forces were ranged along a single, relatively narrow sector of the front about 100 miles long.

The German High Command hoped that by launching Operation Citadel, they would regain the strategic initiative and win command of the air. The plan was that the Luftwaffe would destroy the Soviet aerial forces on the ground using blitzkrieg tactics at the start of the attack, gain air supremacy and then support the German tanks.

At 3:00 P.M. on Sunday 4 July 1943, the German artillery opened fire along the south sector of the Soviet defensive lines at the Kursk salient. The German Fourth Armored Army (under Gen. Hoth) launched an attack to seize the range of hills along the front, so as to secure higher positions for the offensive that was to begin on the morning of July 5. Around 800 German aircraft including Stukas, bombers, ground-attack planes and antitank squadrons flew relay flights to help the Fourth Armored break through the strong Soviet defensive field.

At 3:00 A.M. on July 5, the German aircraft assembled for the attack. Then German aerial reconnaissance reported that 132 Soviet ground-attack aircraft and 285 fighters of the Soviet 17th Air Army under General Sudetz, were running in to raid the airfields of the German 8th Air Force (VIII. Fliegerkorps).

A dawn battle began between the Soviets and the fighter planes of the German 3rd Fighter Wing (the "Udet Wing"), and in a short time the Soviets had lost 120 aircraft. The VIII. Fliegerkorps not only succeeded in warding off an enemy air offensive but also gained command of the air in the southern sector. In the course of the day the Germans shot down 432 Russian aircraft with losses of only 26.

Soviet army general Shtemenko, chief of operations of STAVKA, commented: "A report that our fighter planes had been sent to the Kursk salient carrying inadequately trained pilots, led Stalin to conclude that the whole of our fighter forces were good for nothing. Fortunately, the situation did not turn out too badly and it proved possible to exchange the air crews relatively quickly." The Red Air Force sent 3 air armies and 2 fighter divisions into combat, a total of about 3,200 aircraft. Nevertheless it failed to keep the Germans from bringing up reserves, and these in turn prevented the threatened encirclement of the German Ninth Army at Orel. The Luftwaffe fought advancing Soviet tank spearheads, and on 8 July 1943 the new Henschel Hs 129s of the German 4th Antitank Group of the 9th Ground-Attack Wing under Captain Meyer, virtually wiped out a Soviet armored brigade. But the Luftwaffe no longer had the capability it had in the past, crucially to influence the course of the ground battle. In a four-day period which saw the greatest tank and air battle of World War II, the Germans succeeded in penetrating only 10 miles into the 12-mile front in the north, and approximately 30 miles into the 30-mile front in the south at Prokhorovka. The two pincer spearheads of the German attack were still separated by almost 120 miles when the offensive was broken off.

20 December 1943, Pas de Calais (northern France): Douglas DB-7 Boston light bombers of the 9th USAAF are raiding the building sites of launch ramps for German V-1 flying bombs. Three thousand of the 7,385 Boston bombers produced were sent to the Soviet Union.

Saturday 10 July 1943 saw the launch of Operation Husky, the Allied invasion of Sicily. At dawn,

Allied units under the overall command of General Eisenhower landed on the southeast coast of the island. The RAF forces commanded by Air Chief Marshal Tedder, and the US aerial forces under General Spaatz, sent 3,680 aircraft into the battle. The disembarkation of the ground forces followed an airborne operation involving 400 Dakota C-47 transport aircraft and 170 Waco CG-4A cargo gliders.

This first Allied airborne operation verged on failure. Ninety-seven of the British and US gliders were released from their towropes too soon and plunged into the sea with their crews, and another 24 were reported missing; only 12 of the gliders, all British, landed in the target zone. Then strong antiaircraft fire confused the paratroops flying in the Dakota transports, so they jumped too soon and were scattered over an expanse of almost 60 miles. Six of the Dakotas were shot down, and only 73 British paratroops reached their target, the Ponte Grande, an important bridge on the road to Syracuse [which the British wanted to save from being blown up by the Italians]. The Italian coastal divisions offered little more than token resistance, so the British were able to remove the Italian explosive charges from the bridge and, despite an artillery barrage, were able to hold the bridge until that afternoon.

The second airborne wave included 107 aircraft and 17 cargo gliders of the 1st Parachute Brigade which arrived at Sicily on the night of 13th–14th July 1943. They landed in the middle of a battle between the Allied fleet and attacking German Ju 88 Bombers. Fourteen of the Dakotas were shot down with their paratroops.

The Soviets went on the counteroffensive at Orel on Monday 12 July 1943. By that time they already had command of the air. The Red Air Force had gathered 60% of all its aerial forces in the Kursk zone for this grand assault.

On the following day Hitler ordered a halt to Operation Citadel and transferred some of the Luftwaffe's units from the Eastern Front to Italy.

The close of the Battle of Kursk marked a permanent end to German offensive capability on the Eastern Front, and the Red Army held the initiative from now until the end of the war.

Monday 19 July 1943 was the date of the first Allied air raid on Rome. The toll of civilian dead was 166; there were 1,659 injured. That morning 158 B-17 Flying Fortresses from Tunisia and Pantelleria (island between Tunisia and Sicily), and 112 B-24 Liberator bombers based on Bengasi (Libya), raided

the Lorenzo and Littorio rail stations and the Littorio airfield. In the afternoon Ciampino airbase was bombed by the Allies.

Back in May 1942, the London firm Vanesta Ltd. had punctually delivered to Bomber Command the first parcel of Window tinfoil radar-jamming strips, which the British planned to use in the first "thousand-bomber raid." But at the last minute Sir William Sholto Douglas, the head of Fighter Command, had halted deployment of Window because he was afraid the Germans might learn to use Window against his own British night fighters [when they came to raid Britain].

Eventually new British airborne devices were installed in British night fighters which made them immune to Window, so the British were now free to use Window to neutralize the Himmelbett defensive system. At last, at a staff conference on Thursday 15 July 1943, Churchill stated that he would accept responsibility for initiating Window operations. It was decided that Bomber Command would

Heavy RAF Avro Lancaster bombers over the burning city of Cologne. The German day fighter planes of Major Herrmann's *Wilde Sau* system, were able to detect enemy bombers at night by the light of the flames.

start using the tinfoil-strip radar-jamming device on its raids beginning on 23 July 1943.

On the night of 24th–25th July, the Anglo-American "Combined Bomber Offensive" struck its first blow at Germany in an operation codenamed "Gomorrha." The British received reports that flying weather was good and visibility clear. Their target was the city and port of Hamburg.

When the howling of sirens tore the citizens of Hamburg out of their sleep in the early morning hours of Sunday 25 July 1943, no one divined the disaster that lay in store. The British had sent 791 bombers – 347 Lancasters, 246 Halifaxes, 125 Stirlings and 73 twin-engined Wellingtons – on this first raid. The main targets in Hamburg were the districts of Barmbek, Hoheluft, Eimsbüttel, Altona and the port area. Seven hundred and forty-one of the bombers reached the city.

During their run-in on the city each bomber crew dropped one loose bundle of tinfoil strips per minute; each bundle contained 2,000 strips and weighed 1½ pounds, and each was designed to simulate one heavy bomber. Every bundle formed a tinfoil cloud that for approximately 15 minutes mimicked the profile of one aircraft on a German radar screen; so the British were simulating a bomber fleet of some 11,000 aircraft. The German radar-guided searchlights and radar-guided flak (antiaircraft guns) were jammed so that aimed fire became impossible; moreover, the Würzburg radar sets at the ground control stations were neutralized too, so they were unable accurately to guide a single night fighter to the bombers. The Lichtenstein BC airborne radar carried by the German night fighters, also failed completely. As a result, only 12 British bombers were lost on the raid – 1.5%. Twenty-three hundred tons of bombs fell during the 2½-hour raid, and at the end of it, 52 miles of houses were on fire.

That morning Hitler was awakened with news of this heavy bombing raid on Hamburg. During a midday conference he also learned that tinfoil strips had been deployed. His response that same day was to order series manufacture of the A-4 long-range rocket, later known as the V-2 [from the German *Vergeltungswaffe* or "retaliatory weapon"]. He wanted 900 rockets to be produced every month. Albert Speer, the German armaments minister, later wrote [in *Inside the Third Reich*]: "I not only went along with this decision on Hitler's part but also supported it. That was probably one of my most serious mistakes. We would have done much better to focus our efforts on manufacturing a ground-to-air defensive rocket." [English translation quoted from the 1970 Macmillan edition, p. 365]

At midday on 26 July 1943, 122 US Flying Fortress bombers raided Hamburg to disrupt the rescue operations and the work to extinguish the fires. A pall of smoke and dust lay over the city that the sun could not penetrate.

On the night of 27–28 July, 739 British bombers dropped another 2,312 tons of bombs on Hamburg. This second RAF night raid was the heaviest of all: it set 16,000 buildings on fire. One pilot reported after returning to base: "The clouds looked like a blood-soaked cotton swab."

Thousands of individual fires soon joined to form giant area fires. The atmosphere, heated to temperatures of up to 1200 degrees Centigrade, shot upward like a draught in a giant chimney, and pure air along the ground was sucked up in its wake creating a

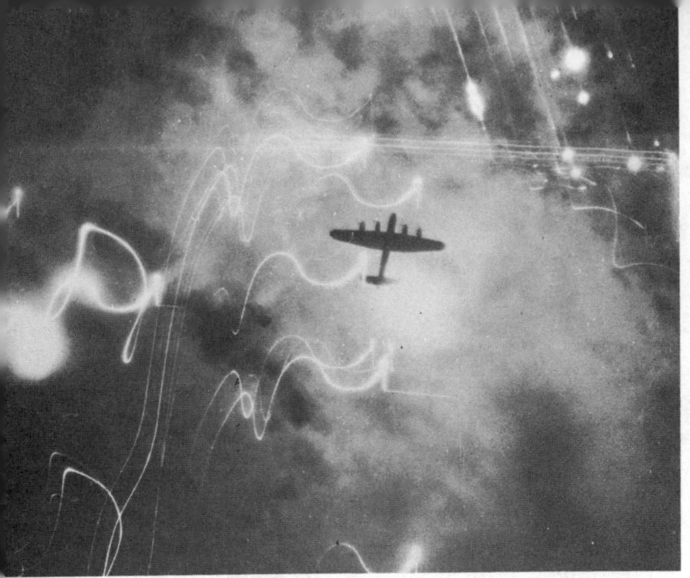

tempestuous firestorm—the first of World War II—which could be seen even from 20,000 feet up. The resultant gale-force winds reached over 70 miles per hour, the trunks of strong trees split and broke, younger trees were bent to the ground like willow rods. Seventy thousand of Hamburg's 100,000 trees were lost to this storm.

Kehrl, the Hamburg police commissioner, wrote a secret report about the storm in which he said: "The only people who escaped death were those who had risked flight at the right moment, or who were near enough to the edge of the sea of flame so that there was some possibility of saving them . . . The overall destruction is so radical that literally nothing is left of many people. The force of the gale tore children out of the hands of their parents and whirled them into the fire. People who thought they had gotten out safely, collapsed in the overwhelming heat and died in seconds. Fleeing people had to work their way over the dead and dying. Seventy per cent of the victims died of suffocation, mostly in poisonous carbon dioxide gas which turned their corpses bright blue, orange and green. So many people died of this poisoning that initially it was thought that the RAF had raided us for the first time with poison gas bombs. Fifteen per cent had died more violent deaths. The rest were charred to a cinder and could not be identified."

On the night of 29–30 July 1943, 726 RAF bombers dropped 2,277 more tons of bombs over Hamburg. Twenty-eight bombers were shot down.

In August 1943, the second Allied air front gained increasing importance. This consisted of Allied planes operating out of North African bases against German-occupied Europe.

At dawn on Sunday 1 August, 178 Liberator B-24 bombers of the US 9th Air Force took off from Bengasi air strip (Libya). One B-24 suffered machine damage at takeoff and collided with a concrete pole. The others formed up to fly across the Mediterranean and hit the Rumanian oil region of Ploesti.

Each Liberator bomber carried a two-ton bombload and needed more than 9 tons of fuel to complete its outbound and return flights, a total distance of approximately 2,100 miles. The plan was for the formation to fly under the German radar screen and to attack the target at treetop level. This low-level raiding would also enable the bombers to attack individual refineries with extreme precision.

An event unique in the history of World War II occurred in July 1943 when the Allies succeeded in breaking the Luftwaffe's weather code and used a decoded German radio message to decide on the ideal date for the raid on Ploesti. The German codes were routinely changed every month, so August 1 was the last day when the Allies could learn about weather conditions at Ploesti by intercepting a German message. But what the US planners of the raid did not know was that German General Gerstenberg, in charge of air defense at this strategically important target, had turned the oil center into the most strongly-defended installation in Europe.

Just one hour after the takeoff, the German air defense at Ploesti already knew that a large formation of US bombers was flying across the Mediterranean headed northeast. They knew this because the Germans had decoded a US radio message addressed to all the Allied air defense zones between Bengasi and Ploesti, informing them of the route to be taken by the bombers and warning the Allied air defense not to fire on the bombers by mistake.

Ten of the bombers crashed due to engine damage during the three-hour flight over the Mediterranean, and another grave incident occurred just before the formation reached the Albanian coast, when the aircraft carrying the operation's chief navigator suddenly went into a spin, flipped over and crashed into the sea. The bomber carrying the deputy navigator made a vain search for survivors and while doing so lost contact with the formation and was forced to head for home. Now that both leaders were missing, a young and inexperienced officer assumed command. The bombers ran into a dense wall of cloud over Yugoslavia. The two forward groups climbed high to fly above the clouds; the other three stayed just high enough to avoid the mountain tops. The first two groups were caught in a powerful tail wind and rapidly increased their distance from the groups following. When the B-24s emerged from the

Opposite page above: Hamburg on the night of the RAF bombing raid of 24-25 July 1943. A Lancaster bomber flying over the Altona district is surrounded by flak tracer fire and falling "Christmas trees," the British target flares. The photo was taken by the crew of another Lancaster flying higher up.

Right: A photo taken in the Altona district of Hamburg on the same night.

mountains into the Danube Valley, the formation was widely dispersed.

To ease navigation the Americans had selected three cities to use as control points; but these looked much alike and the ground fog made it hard to identify them. Shortly before reaching the target, the two leader groups made a disastrous mistake. They took a wrong turn and instead of flying to Ploesti, ended up at the Rumanian capital of Bucharest about 30 miles away, where they strayed into the densest flak belt. The Rumanians discovered the bombers making their low-level run, and this gave the air defenses at Ploesti enough time to prepare for the raid.

When the two leader groups noted their mistake, they turned to approach Ploesti, but from the opposite direction from what they planned. Their new heading led them to cross the paths of the three groups that had been left behind over the mountains. Now the bombers were in a state of chaos over the target, and concentrated flak fire greeted them from all directions.

The bombers swayed under the impact of exploding missiles. One B-24 crashed into a flak battery in flames. The B-24 "Hell's Wench" severed a barrage balloon cable, was hit by 5 flak projectiles and caught fire, but went on to lead its group to the target before it crashed over the refineries. Large numbers of bombers spun into the city streets; one fell onto a women's prison in Ploesti burying many of the inmates under the debris.

While one bomber group scattered to locate its targets, two groups approached from the opposite direction. Seconds later the three groups were weaving in and out of each other's ranks desperately trying to avoid collisions. Meanwhile they were under non-stop attack from German and Rumanian fighter planes.

The rope of a barrage balloon tore off the wing of a Liberator. Another B-24 rammed into a chimney; another could not nose up in time and ran into an oil tank. "We were pulled through the gates of Hell," one of the pilots said later.

The raid on Ploesti was over in 27 minutes. The remaining Liberators set out on the long return flight back to Bengasi, some flying in formation, some alone. Half were damaged and most had dead or wounded on board. Several bombers managed to reach Allied-occupied Mediterranean islands. "We landed on a highway in the mountains of Cyprus," one pilot reported. "I pulled over looking for a place to park, and there was a truck crashing straight into us." Another Liberator just managed with its last gasp to reach an airfield in Sicily and crashed into 7 American P-40 fighter planes at the end of the runway. "No one was hurt, but our crew got a very cool reception." Two Liberators had to make emergency sea landings when they ran out of fuel; two others collided in the air over Bulgaria.

Not until late afternoon did the first bombers begin to arrive back at Bengasi. Most of the airmen were too numb and exhausted to report on their missions. The last Liberator to arrive, had been airborne for 16 hours.

Of the 178 bombers that had taken off, only 11 returned to Bengasi; 54 had been shot down by flak over Rumania and 3 over the sea; others crashed during the outbound and return flights; 7 landed in Turkey. Five hundred and thirty-two flying personnel were lost. The positive consequences of the raid were that oil production at Ploesti was reduced by 40% for a period of two months.

The last raid of Operation Gomorrha took place on the night of 2–3 August 1943, when 425 British bombers dropped 939 tons of bombs on Hamburg with a loss of 30 bombers. British sources claim that only 57 Allied aircraft were lost during the whole series of Hamburg raids.

On 4 summer nights, 3,095 British aircraft (aided by 235 US bombers during the day) had dropped 9,000 tons of bombs on the city of Hamburg. For days afterward the fire-glow could still be seen 120 miles away.

Hitler refused the request of the Hamburg district leader that he come to visit the destroyed city; he even refused to receive a delegation of outstanding air wardens.

Operation Gomorrha, with its total of 9 raids between 24 July and 2nd August 1943, cost the population of Hamburg approximately 55,000 dead and missing, 63 of whom were members of the German armed forces. This toll was 84% of all the Germans who died in air raids in Hamburg, and 13% of the casualties in all of Germany during the war. There were also 600,000 homeless, and 36,000 homes destroyed. Fourteen square miles of built-up area, and almost 300 miles of streets had been burnt out. One hundred and eighty thousand tons of shipping were sunk in the harbor. With all this the damage to industry in Hamburg was less than anticipated: Five months later the city had reached 80% of its former production level.

The four night raids on Hamburg caused more devastation and claimed more victims than Britain suffered throughout World War II.

The Battle of Hamburg was significant for the Allies because it meant they had made a decisive breach in the German defense and had won almost complete air supremacy. The Combined Bomber Offensive that started with Hamburg, marked the beginning of a new phase in the air war against Germany. Its effects brought home to the Luftwaffe leadership the fact that their overriding duty was now the air defense of their own homeland.

According to RAF statistics, the 40 tons of Window tinfoil strips dropped at Hamburg—92 million strips ⅓ inch wide and 1 inch long—saved at least 35 bombers and their crews from certain destruction.

Air Chief Marshal Harris said that the power and effects of the Hamburg raids had surpassed all expectations, and the RAF took these raids as the model for later annihilating attacks on other German cities. Harris presented the King and Prime Minister Churchill with copies of the "Blue Book," a leather-bound album containing aerial photographs of the destruction in Hamburg, and another copy was sent to Stalin.

On Friday 6 August 1943, three days after the final grand raid on Hamburg, Goebbels, deeply impressed by the destruction, announced that except for those actively working in the city, the population of Berlin would shortly be evacuated.

On Friday 13 August 1943, 9 B-24 Liberator bombers of the 5th USAAF took off from Darwin (north Australia) to raid the oil refineries in Balik Papan (Borneo). The 2,400-mile flight took 17 hours, and in terms of time was the longest operation made by Allied strategic bombers in World War II.

On that same day, August 13, Austria experienced its first Western Allied air raid of the war when 61 heavy bombers of the 9th USAAF took off from bases in North Africa to bomb the Messerschmitt aircraft factory in New Vienna. There were 181 dead and 850 wounded.

The stepping-up of US bombing raids on targets in central and southern Germany, led the Luftwaffe leaders to call back their most experienced pilots from all the fronts to defend Germany. The 30th Fighter Division, made up of three wings, was appointed to lead *Wilde Sau* operations. To begin with the air crews had to fly the fighter planes used by the regular fighter units in the daytime. By mid-August the German air defense had over 400 day fighters and almost 100 "destroyer" fighter-bombers. It was impossible to set up additional fighter units because of the shortage of properly-trained personnel, especially pilots. It had become clear that new German pilots were not receiving adequate training; a Luftwaffe pilot would enter combat after only 150 hours of flight training, whereas the Western Allied pilots had 450 hours. More than half of the new generation of German pilots were being shot down before their tenth combat.

Now that the British were deploying Window tinfoil strips on their bombing raids to jam German defensive radar, the German fighter-plane control officers could no longer guide individual fighters

Opposite page below: British "Window" tinfoil radar-jamming strips, whose German counterpart was called *Düppel* (radar chaff).

Above right: Ploesti (Rumania) on 1 August 1943. A heavy US B-24 Liberator bomber flies at chimney-top level over the Rumanian oil refineries.

Below: Firemen at Ploesti are trying to bring the fires under control after the US raid.

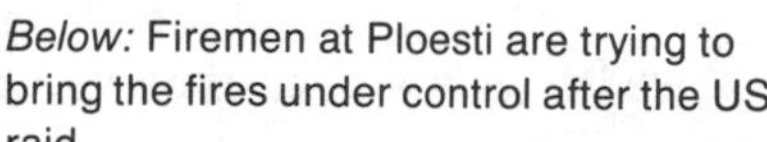

to the bombers by radar as they had done before. Instead the Germans used a "Running Commentary," a continuously updated report of enemy activities transmitted over airborne radio from observation posts not affected by the jamming. The two-engined German night fighter planes used the data supplied by the Running Commentary to locate the bomber stream, but then they had to rely on their airborne radar to help them home in on a target, or to detect the target visually. If a German fighter lost contact with the bomber stream, it would tune back in on the Running Commentary and try its luck again. This tactic was known as *Zahme Sau* (Tame Pig).

The British swiftly developed electronic countermeasures to deal with this new threat. For example, they equipped the Lancasters of 101 Group with ABCs—Airborne Cigars—special transmitters that jammed the frequencies of the German Running Commentary. The German night fighters tried to neutralize the jamming by frequent changes of frequency and by the use of stronger transmitters.

The success of the German night fighters during these weeks depended on how quickly they were released for takeoff, and on the skill of the controller supplying the Running Commentary. The fighters could easily miss the bomber stream if they were deceived by a British diversionary raid or followed the wrong radio beacon and so assembled at a point far removed from the bombers' real target.

Tuesday 17 August 1943 brought an end to what the Germans called Operation Lehrgang, their evacuation of occupied Sicily. German units under the command of the one-armed General Hube, managed to transfer their heavy equipment across the Straits of Messina and into Italy; they even succeeded in taking their mules along. As a result, Germany was able overnight to install a new defensive line in southern Italy.

On 17 August 1943, the anniversary of their first

mission over Europe, the US 8th Air Force took off on an "anniversary raid," a dual raid on the cities of Schweinfurt and Regensburg. This first strategic raid by the US forces was known as Operation Double Strike, but its main target was the ball-bearing industry in Schweinfurt. Instead of concentrating on this target, the raiders made the crucial mistake of dividing up, and 146 of the 376 Flying Fortress bombers attacked a Messerschmitt aircraft assembly plant in Regensburg.

Operation Double Strike was not only the largest US daylight bombing raid since the war began, but at the same time was the US 8th Air Force's first exercise in shuttle bombing. The bombers of the Regensburg formation had been equipped with "Tokyo tanks," that is auxiliary fuel tanks, and intended to fly over Italy to Bône in North Africa after completing their mission.

But their P-47 Thunderbolt fighter escort had to leave them at Aachen (Aix-la-Chapelle) and return to base due to their limited range. The German fighters had been waiting for this moment to swoop down on the bombers. What followed was the largest air battle to take place over Western Europe so far. The battle extended for a long distance, from Belgium and Luxembourg to deep inside the Rhine-Main territory.

The US bomber formations drew some protection from their new type of formation flying. Each bomber group contained approximately 18 aircraft that flew in densely graded echelons forming a "combat box" that enabled them to give each other covering fire.

The German fighters soon realized that they would come under concentrated fire from three machine guns if they tried to attack the Flying Fortresses from the rear or from above; but the bombers were easier to attack from in front. So the Germans flew a parallel course some distance from the bombers, overtook them and built up a lead of about 26,000 feet, and then turned and made a frontal attack. They opened fire from a distance of approximately 2,000 feet, so they would have about two seconds' shooting time before they would have to nose up their planes, fly over the bombers, turn around and repeat the same steps again.

It was in this battle that the Luftwaffe first deployed air-to-air rockets, which were fired by Ju 88, Do 217 and He 111 fighters flying individually or in formation. The rockets flew so slowly that their progress was clearly observable, an especially worrying sight to the US airmen.

One US pilot reported: "We met remarkably violent resistance from enemy fighters. It began as we flew over the Belgian coast, and continued to the border of the Alps. The fighters made frontal attacks from a slightly elevated or somewhat lower position. Attacks by individual aircraft were generally made from the direction of the sun. Several Me 109s were firing large-caliber missiles from cannon mounted underneath their wings. Several crews also reported that rockets were fired. Other fighters dropped packs of 20 to 30 black or brown objects that fell onto the bombers and exploded."

During Operation Double Strike, 59 US Flying Fortresses were shot down and 100 were severely damaged, while 25 German fighters were lost. This anniversary raid was the most serious defeat the US aerial forces in Europe had suffered so far: one out of five crew members was killed. The US 8th Air Force suffered such heavy losses that it deployed no combat aircraft over Germany for five weeks. Meanwhile it confined itself to less important targets in Occupied Europe which lay within range of its escort fighters.

While the beaten-up US aircraft were returning to Britain from their operation at Schweinfurt, RAF Bomber Command was preparing a new operation, "Hydra," planned to take place on the night of 17–18 August 1943. Air Chief Marshal Harris believed it would be one of the most important air raids of the war. The target was the scientific research institute at Peenemünde on the Usedom Peninsula on the Baltic coast, where the Germans were experimenting with V-rockets.

Peenemünde had never been raided before. It was protected by heavy flak guns, night fighters and smoke generators, and lay outside the range of the

"Its power and effects surpassed all our expectations," said British Air Chief Marshal Sir Arthur Harris about Operation Gomorrha, the Allied campaign against Hamburg.

British Oboe beacon-guidance system and the RAF night fighter planes. Thus the RAF bombers—flying without fighter cover—could carry out the mission only on a bright moonlit night.

Operation Hydra was the first night-time precision raid by the main forces of Bomber Command, using target-marking flares and radio instructions issued by a "master bomber" (the "master of ceremonies") circling over the target.

The first target was to be Karlshagen, the residential settlement of the 3,000 scientists and engineers who worked in Peenemünde; then the two large factory sheds and the rocket-development center would be hit.

The master bomber of RAF Group Captain J. H. Searby took off at 9:30 P.M., followed by 597 heavy Lancaster and Halifax bombers. Ahead of them flew a formation of 20 rapid Mosquito bombers, headed toward Berlin along the same route that they had used for their offensive sweeps of the past few days.

The German fighter-plane control stations were surprised at the large number of British bombers reported to be travelling over the North Sea on this bright moonlit summer night, and they believed that a heavy raid on Berlin was about to take place; so fighter planes from all over Germany sped toward the capital. The *Wilde Sau* day-fighter squadrons were also ordered to Berlin for their first large-scale operation. Everything indicated that the RAF was about to suffer even heavier losses than the 8th USAAF had suffered that same afternoon in their anniversary raid.

The 20 Mosquitos dropped vast numbers of target flares to simulate an imminent grand raid on Berlin,

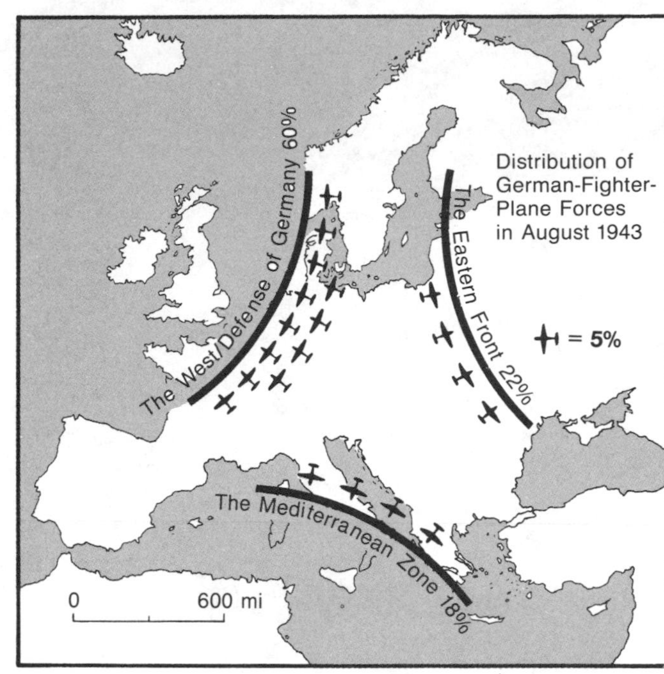

and 203 German fighter planes vainly scoured the sky over the German capital for signs of the expected bombers. Meanwhile the 597 Lancaster and Halifax bombers—undetected by German fighters—made their run-in to the rocket center at Peenemünde. They attacked in three waves, releasing 1,593 tons of explosive bombs and 281 tons of incendiaries.

When the German fighters learned the true location of the attack, some of them succeeded in catching up to the last wave of RAF bombers on their return flight, and shot down 40 of them.

Meanwhile General Kammhuber had been trying for several hours, from his command post in Arnhem-Deelen (Holland), to contact the Himmelbett stations in Germany. Serious damage to electrical cables had separated the command post from the outside world, and approximately 100 German fighter planes were still circling over Berlin vainly waiting for clear instructions from Kammhuber. A number, each on its own initiative, finally decided to land at Brandenburg-Briest airbase. One after another crashed into the planes piling up at the end of the runway, and 34 were completely destroyed. Not until next morning did General Kammhuber learn what had happened during the night. After the war he was told by British intelligence officers that two of the Germans who had been working with him inside the command bunker at Arnhem, had actually been British agents.

After his return home, RAF Group Captain Searby said that the heavy bombs released during

the raid had to all appearances successfully and accurately smashed the target. Then aerial photos of the Peenemünde site were delivered and damage appeared so heavy that the British chief of staff decided, on 19 August 1943, to reject an offer by the US 8th Air Force to carry out a daylight grand assault on Peenemünde; he said that it was unnecessary.

Operation Hydra cost 735 lives. Most of the victims were Russian prisoners-of-war and Polish forced laborers from Trassenheide labor camp. Of the German specialists at the site, 178 were killed, including Dr. Walter Thiel, the head of the rocket-engine division.

"Material damage to the plant is surprisingly small," reported German General Dornberger. All the important installations such as the wind tunnel and the testing fields, were undamaged. The rocket test-rig at Peenemünde-West and the V-1 rocket-development center had not been hit, and work was able to continue without interruption.

Depressed by the raid and before hearing that the damage was relatively minor, General Jeschonnek, Göring's closest aide and for over four years the general chief of staff of the Luftwaffe, committed suicide on the morning of August 19.

After the raid on Peenemünde, the Germans carried out a large-scale deceptive maneuver to keep the enemy thinking that development and production of the secret rockets had been destroyed at a single blow. The debris at the site was not cleared away, and British aerial photographs continued to show that the destroyed worksheds had not been rebuilt. The Germans even changed the official designation of the installation: instead of being called the Peenemünde Army Experimental Institute, it was now called the Home-Artillery Park. These measures so effectively [lulled the enemy into a false sense of security] that the bombers did not return for nine months.

Meanwhile some of the Peenemünde installations were transferred outside the range of Allied heavy bombers. The wind tunnel for breaking the sound barrier, was evacuated to Kochel in Upper Bavaria; firing tests and training courses were now carried out at Blitsna in Poland; and mass production of the V-1 flying bomb and the long-range V-2 rockets (also called the A-4 by the Germans), was assigned to the southern Harz Mountains in central Germany.

Thousands of concentration-camp inmates were driven, at a murderous pace and under inhuman conditions, to dig underground tunnels at Nordhausen in the Harz Mountains where Hitler's secret weapons were henceforth to be manufactured. The

Opposite page above: 17 August 1943. US B-17 Flying Fortress are raiding Schweinfurt. One out of five crew members did not survive this "anniversary raid."

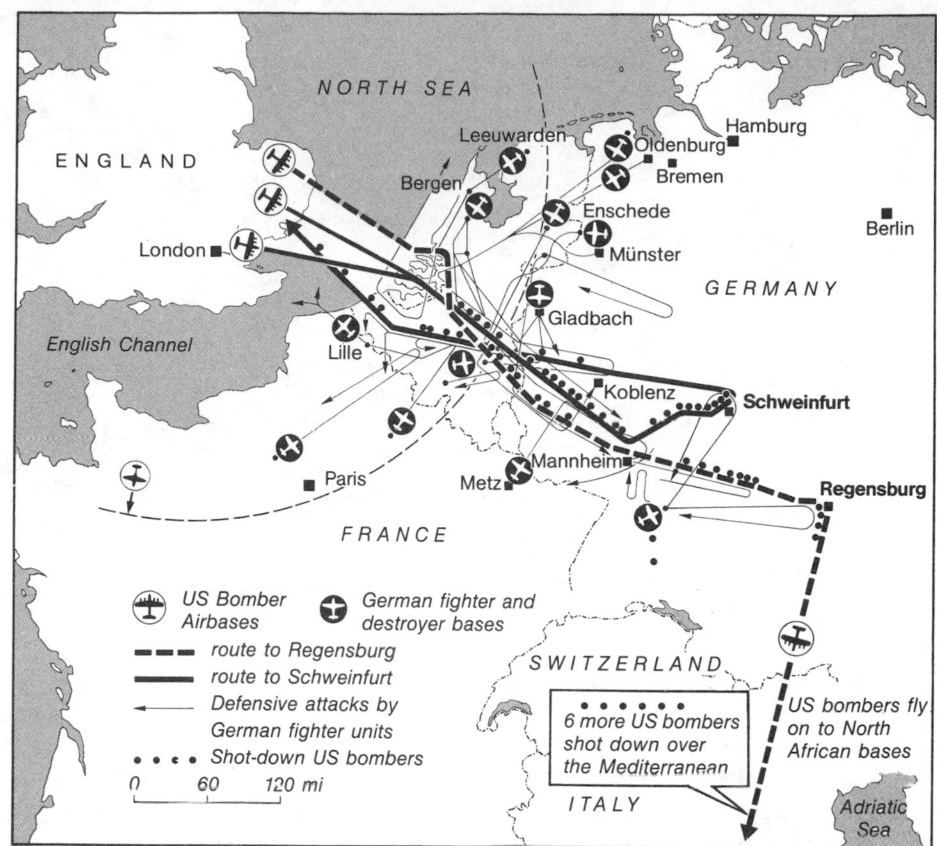

Above right: 17 August 1943. The US 8th Air Force raid on Regensburg and Schweinfurt.

Below: A shot-down US B-17. On the left, standing on the wing, is Lt. Col. E. Mayer, commander of the German 2nd Fighter Wing (JG 2).

so-called Middle Works (codenamed Dora) was a miles-long labyrinth of giant caves and tunnels that cost the lives of thousands of captives to construct.

On Thursday 19 August 1943 the Allied aerial forces began a "round-the-clock" bomber offensive against targets in Italy which was modelled on the Hamburg raids of two weeks earlier. US aircraft bombed Foggia during the day, and on the night of 19–20 August, RAF Wellingtons raided the same target.

On the night of 23–24 August 1943, 727 RAF four-engined bombers – 335 Lancasters, 251 Halifaxes and 124 Stirlings – escorted by 17 Mosquito pathfinders, took off to raid Berlin. Six hundred and twenty-five of the bombers reached the capital where they released 1,765 tons of blast and incendiary bombs. About 35,000 people were made homeless. Fifty-six bombers did not come back. Thirty-three bombers were shot down by German night fighters, at least 20 right over Berlin; and 23 were lost to flak. That night Bomber Command suffered its heaviest losses on any raid so far.

On 24 August 1943, the units of the US 8th Air Force which had bombed Regensburg on August 17 and gone on to North African bases, made their return flight to Great Britain, bombing the airbase of the German 40th Bomber Wing (KG 40) at Bordeaux-Mérignac along the way. But the promising tactic of shuttle bombing now had to be abandoned, because the fine sand of the North African desert airstrips was proving more dangerous than German fighters to the Flying Fortress engines, which were not designed for tropical climates.

In the last week of August 1943, one of the new weapons in Hitler's secret arsenal came into operation. It was a liquid-rocket-propelled, remote-controlled glide bomb built by a Dr. Wagner and equipped with a Walter engine. It carried an 1,100-pound explosive charge and was known as a Hen-

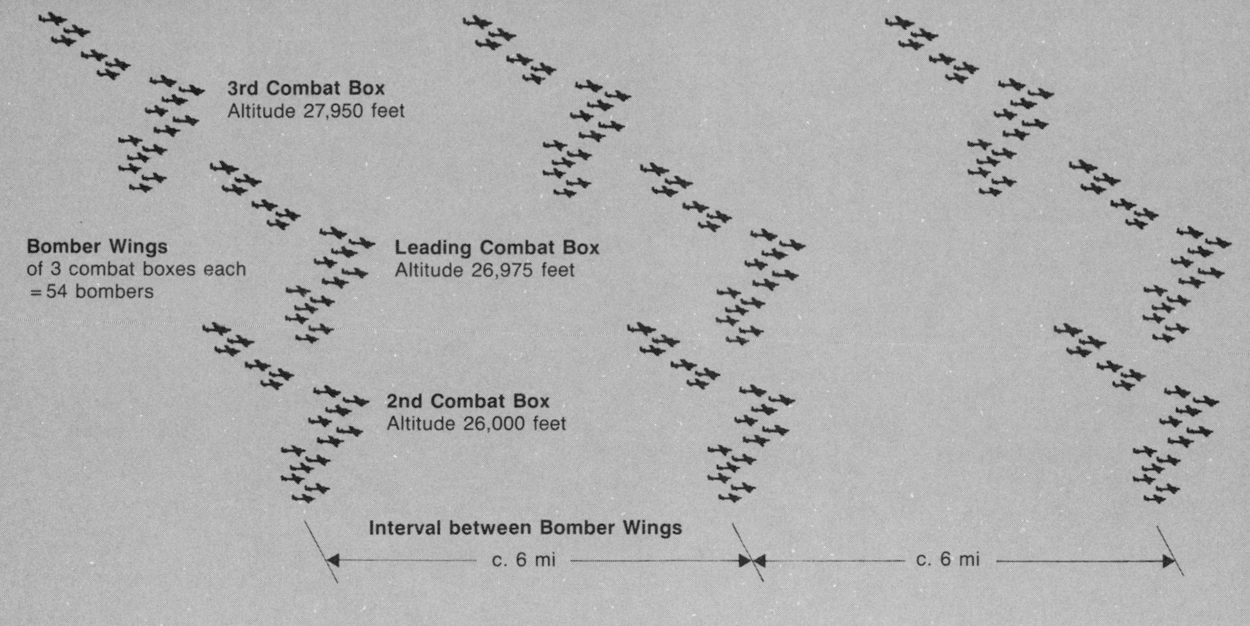

schel Hs 293. The German 100th Bomber Wing (KG 100) was the first aerial unit in World War II to be equipped with remote-controlled offensive weapons. The Hs 293, designed especially for shipping targets, was released and then guided to the target by an observer outside the range of enemy flak, with a pencil-sized "control stick" linked to the radio transmitter.

On Wednesday 25 August 1943, the new weapon was deployed for the first time to relieve the pressure of RAF Coastal Command and the Royal Navy on German U-boats in the Bay of Biscay. Twelve Do 217 bombers of German 2nd Group, 100th Bomber Wing commanded by Captain Molinus, were equipped with Hs 293 glide bombs and ordered to hunt British warships off the northwest coast of Spain. They had an escort of 7 Ju 88 bombers. But the operation was unsuccessful, because only 4 glide bombs came anywhere near their targets. Near-hits were scored on the British sloop *Landguard,* but it suffered little damage.

The captain of another British ship reported: "Off the northwest coast of Spain we sighted a Dornier bomber which was taking care to remain out of range. Then he ran in as if he were planning to attack, but while he was still some distance away he dropped something that looked like a small plane. To our horror, instead of falling it flew straight toward our ship; but before it reached us it veered off sharply and disappeared into the sea."

Two days later, on Friday 27 August 1943, 18 Do 217s of German 2nd Group, 100th Bomber Wing repeatedly fired off Hs 293 glide bombs at a group of British submarines near Cape Finisterre off northwest Spain. The frigate *Egret* (1,200 tons) blew up after receiving two direct hits, and the Canadian destroyer *Athabaskan* suffered heavy damage and had to be towed to Davenport. At the dock, specialists carefully extracted fragments of the bomb.

This successful raid produced an unexpected s. benefit for the German U-boats. The British Admiralty ordered all British vessels in the Bay of Biscay to stay at least 200 miles away from the French coast until a way was found to counteract the glide bomb. Temporarily the German U-boats were free to pass through the Bay of Biscay without having to fear attack from the sea.

On the night of 31st August–1st September 1943, the RAF carried out its next grand raid on Berlin. Nine Mosquito pathfinders and 622 bombers (331 Lancasters, 176 Halifaxes and 106 Stirlings) took part. Only 512 bombers reached the target zone where they released 1,359 tons of high-explosive and incendiary bombs. But due to misplaced target flares, most of the bombs fell some 12 miles from the capital. Forty-seven bombers were lost.

During this raid, German Major Herrmann ensured that his *Wilde Sau* squadrons would have the best possible view of their targets. For the first time, a German bomber unit flew above the British bomber stream and dropped parachute flares to light up the bombers for the German night fighters. The night fighters also used the light from marker flares dropped by the Mosquito pathfinders to home in on their targets.

Major Herrmann suggested that German cities

Opposite page and below: Disposition of the US bomber formations in the 8th USAAF's raids on Regensburg and Schweinfurt. The bombers were ranged in combat boxes.

Right: The German rocket experimental institute of Pëenemunde after the RAF raid on the night of 18–19 August 1943.

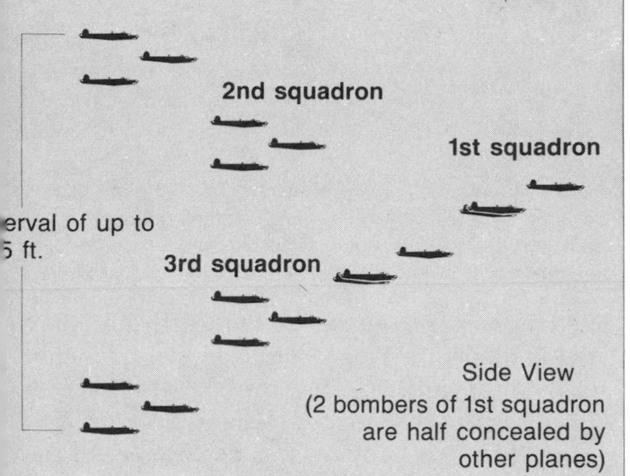

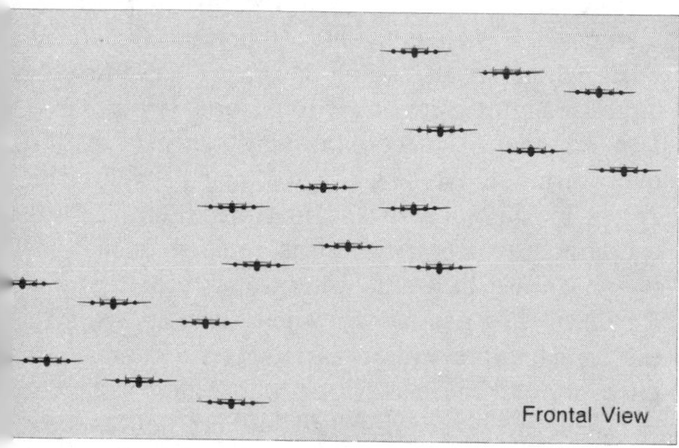

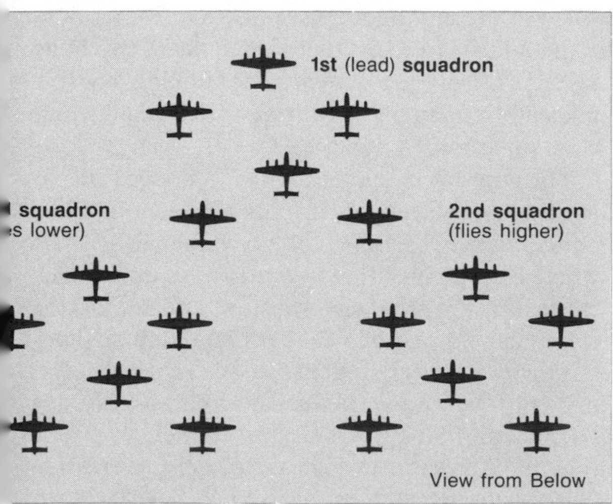

should stop observing blackouts at night because the more brightly lit the cities were, the easier it was for his night fighters to see the enemy bombers; and there was no reason to observe a blackout anyhow, because the RAF bombers did not bomb their targets visually but with radar guidance. But Göring categorically turned down Herrmann's proposal.

The losses to British Bomber Command dropped abruptly by 50% immediately after the first Window operation, but at the end of August 1943, the German night fighter system had improved so that they were able to score 230 air kills within a four-week period. This was only 5 fewer aircraft than they had downed in June 1943, the month of their greatest victories. However, this temporary success only helped to disguise the crisis faced by the German night fighters after the introduction of Window jamming strips.

The *Wilde Sau* tactic had many disadvantages. It increased the risk that the German fighters might fall victim to their own flak. Also, the single-engined day fighters used in *Wilde Sau* could stay in the air for a relatively short time. This frequently resulted in accidents because a number of fighters would run out of fuel simultaneously and all try to land at the nearest airfield at one time. Moreover, the newly-formed night fighter units did not have their own planes but at night had to take over the planes used by the day fighter groups. Naturally, the fighter planes suffered increased wear from having to fly both day and night.

Starting in September 1943, the RAF steadily increased the number of its feint attacks in order to divert the German night fighters from the main bomber unit and to prevent their concentrated deployment over the real target.

In the first days of September 1943, the Soviets launched their largest cargo glider operation of the war. Over a period of 12 nights, a massive supply operation was carried out from Staraya Tropa airfield near Velikiye Luki, in the zone of the Soviet Third Army under General Purkayev. The aim of the operation was to supply partisan units who were needed to support a planned Soviet operation on the Kalinin Front under General Yeremiyenko. Improvised Soviet landing strips were set up in a forest lane west of Idritsa (approximately 300 miles west of Moscow) behind the German Sixteenth Army under Field Marshal Busch. The strips were located at the seam between German Army Group North (under Field Marshal von Küchler) and Army Group Center (under Field Marshal von Kluge).

A total of 35 Soviet gliders took part: Antonov A-7s each carrying one pilot and 7 men, and Gribowski G-29s each carrying one pilot and 11 men. The gliders were towed by Il-4 or SB aircraft. They carried 250 specialists—radio operators, combat engineers, and military and political instructors—to the sites, along with 50 tons of supplies.

Soviet glider pilot A. Piecuch gave this account: "I took off on the first night of the operation with four other rigs. My glider was fully loaded with weapons, ammunition, explosives, the most up-to-date radar equipment, a field printing shop, and even movie projectors. Escorted by 10 fighters, we flew over the German lines without being detected, and after about one hour we sighted light signals at the edge of a forest lake, where our landing strip lay by the shore in the middle of an uprooted clearing. I just managed to halt my glider before reaching a clump of trees. Immediately, as if by magic, a horde of bearded partisans rose out of the ground and dragged our cargo into the woods in a twinkling. I had barely finished smoking my cigarette when they took their axes and chopped my brand-new A-7 glider into kindling. This was a precautionary measure to conceal our operation from German reconnaissance planes, and to make space for more gliders to land here the next night. About two weeks later, when the whole operation concluded, 2 Dakota transport aircraft landed on the forest path and picked up us pilots to carry us back to Staraya Tropa."

In September 1943 the Luftwaffe, following Hitler's instructions, ordered the Volkswagen factory in Wolfsburg and the Fieseler factory in Kassel to begin mass production of the V-1 flying bomb (also known as the Fi-103). The plan was to produce 50,000 of the missiles. Only three months later, in December 1943, the first of them hit London.

Above: A remote-controlled Henschel Hs 293 glide bomb powered by a rocket engine. The Germans delayed deployment of the weapon for more than six months for security reasons.

But Hitler's plans [for mass deployment of the V-1 flying bomb] never got off the ground. In párt this was due to the efforts of a Monsieur Hollard, a humble French mercantile representative from Paris, who managed to halt one of the Third Reich's largest weapons projects for a good six months. Hollard worked as a solitary spy—entirely on his own initiative. No one asked him to spy for the Allies. He did not own a radio transmitter, received no parachute supplies, had no couriers at his disposal. Calmly he shuttled back and forth between Pas de Calais and Berne, where he paid visits to the British military attaché in Switzerland and supplied him with information about military targets in northern France. Monsieur Hollard had already crossed the border in this way no less than 49 times, when at the end of August 1943, a railway worker acquaintance told him that he had heard two building contractors in a Rouen bistro talking about an unusual German building project that would require vast quantities of concrete.

The next day Hollard travelled to Rouen. Dressed in dignified black and carrying a bundle of Bibles under his arm, he visited the city employment office where he explained that he worked for an evangelical institution that gave spiritual aid to working-class men, and asked whether there were any large building sites near Rouen. He was sent to Auffay, a small town about 18 miles away on the Rouen-Dieppe rail line. From here he followed an arterial road until he came to a clearing where several hundred men were building unusual concrete structures.

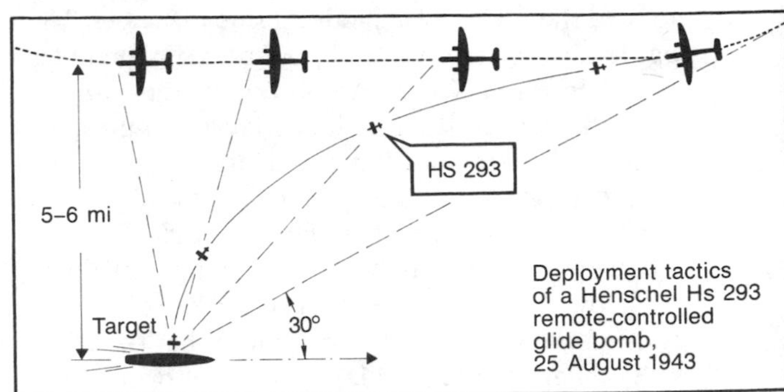

Deployment tactics of a Henschel Hs 293 remote-controlled glide bomb, 25 August 1943

He grabbed a wheelbarrow and mingled among the workers without attracting notice. Most were Dutch and Poles; a few who could speak French told him that they were building garages. Obviously this could not be true because the structures were too small; and besides, what need was there for so many garages in a remote area like this? A concrete strip almost 160 feet long, clearly the base for some kind of launching ramp, particularly roused Hollard's curiosity. Using his compass he discovered, to his surprise, that the concrete strip pointed towards London. He also learned that the Germans kept the work going day and night.

A short time later Hollard crossed the border into Switzerland carrying a sack of potatoes which contained a map-drawing of the suspicious building site.

In September 1943 the months of fine summer weather gradually tapered off. On the night of 6–7 September 1943, 365 British bombers flew to Germany and dropped 1,020 tons of bombs on Munich. Sixteen bombers were shot down.

At 6:30 P.M. on Wednesday 8 September 1943, General Eisenhower announced the surrender of Italy. Immediately the Germans launched Operation Axis, aimed against all the Italian armed forces in Italy, southern France, Sardinia and Corsica, comprising 42 divisions, 4 independent combat groups, approximately 2,000 aircraft (including 600 training aircraft), and strong naval units. The Germans launched 17 divisions, one brigade and some aircraft from Luftflotte 2 to disarm the Italians; but 6 of the divisions and almost all the planes had to be diverted at once to fight the Allied invasion.

Some Italian air crews landed about 300 of their aircraft on Allied airfields and fought against the Germans as "co-belligerent Italian forces"; others chose to fight on the side of the German Luftwaffe.

One of the most successful raids of the war was led by the Luftwaffe against the ships of its erstwhile ally. On the early afternoon of September 9, German troops penetrated the Italian naval base of La Spezia, and Italian Admiral Bergamini left the bay with the battleships *Roma, Italia* and *Vittorio Veneto,* 3 cruisers and 8 destroyers; 3 cruisers and 2 destroyers from Genoa later joined the formation. The declared intention of the Italian vessels was to attack the Allied invasion fleet on its way to Salerno; but in reality it was headed toward Malta to surrender to the British.

Admiral Bergamini's flagship *Roma* (46,215 tons), the pride of the Italian navy, was its most modern battleship and had been in service for less than a year.

The 3rd Group of the German 100th Bomber Wing (KG 100 under Major Jope), stationed in Istres (France) near Marseilles, was ordered to intercept the renegade ally. Shortly after 2:00 P.M., 12 Do 217 K-2 German bombers took off, each carrying one Fritz X (SD 1400 X) glide bomb. This new secret weapon, built by Dr. Kramer of the Ruhrstahl coal and iron company, was on its first deployment. It was a 3,080-lb bomb with great penetrating power, and although it was a drop bomb, its fall trajectory could be corrected using an ultra-wave radio control device.

The Italian naval fleet reached La Maddalena and ran through the Strait of Bonifacio between Corsica and Sardinia, close to the island of Asinara. Then at 3:30 P.M. the lookout reported sighting a number of aircraft.

The German air commander Major Jope said later: "I will never forget the imposing sight of the Italian warfleet as it loomed up beneath us." The Italians thought that the aircraft were Allied planes sent out from Sicily to give them air cover. They realized their mistake only when they saw the bombs falling; then they made desperate evasive maneuvers.

The first bombs missed their targets, but then the

Roma was hit by an FX 1400 glide bomb that perforated the deck and exploded inside the vessel. The battleship's speed dropped by 16 knots. Five minutes later a second FX 1400, dropped from the plane of Lt. Schmetz, hit the foredeck triggering an explosion in the ammunition chambers that tore the *Roma* in two. Admiral Bergamini and the 1,254-man crew went down with the ship. Another FX 1400 swept over her sister-ship the *Italia* and hit down close by, causing a leak to open in the vessel; 800 tons of water streamed into the hull, but the *Italia* still managed to reach Malta under her own steam.

Hitler never learned of the new weapon's unique success. Even Göring, the commander of the Luftwaffe, was not informed that the *Roma* had been sunk by an FX 1400: he was told only that the battleship had been hit by bombs. The German High Command were not fully informed about the incident because General Adolf Galland, the commander of the Luftwaffe's fighter arm, deliberately kept it secret, not wanting to give Hitler any further pretext for increasing bomber production at the expense of the fighter planes.

On Thursday 9 September 1943, in the teeth of strong German resistance, the US Fifth Army under General Clark landed at Salerno with four divisions of troops. Operation Avalanche [the Allied invasion of Italy] had begun, and the British Eighth Army under General Montgomery landed at Taranto.

On Friday September 10, German troops under Field Marshal Kesselring, the commander of the German forces in southern Italy, occupied Rome. The Italian armed forces were disarmed, captured or demobilized.

On the night of 10–11 September, 360 British bombers raided Düsseldorf where they dropped 760 tons of bombs. Thirty planes did not come back.

On Saturday September 11, the 2nd and 3rd Groups of the German 100th Bomber Wing (under Cpt. Molinus and Maj. Jope respectively), carried out several raids on the Allied invasion fleet at Salerno, using remote-controlled glide bombs. They scored a near-hit on the US cruiser *Philadelphia.* One FX 1400 penetrated the forward gun turret of the US light cruiser *Savannah.* The explosion tore a hole in the deck, killed several men and caused considerable damage.

On Sunday September 12, the 11th Air Force (XI. Fliegerkorps) of the German Luftwaffe staged one of the most spectacular surprise airborne commando raids of the war in an operation the Germans called "Eiche" (Oak Tree). Precisely at 2:00 P.M., 9 Fieseler Storch DFS 230 light glider planes landed on an elevated plateau beside the Campo Imperatore hotel in the Gran Sasso mountains of the Abruzzi region of Italy. Inside the gliders were No. 1 Company of the German Paratroop Training Battalion under 1st Lt. von Berlepsch, and the Friedenthal Special Secret Service Squad under Army SS officer Otto Skorzeny. Their mission was to liberate Mussolini, who had been held captive by the Allies since 25 July 1943, [and who had been transferred to this mountain fastness for safekeeping]. They rescued Il Duce and one of the Storchs (flown by Major Gerlach) carried him and Skorzeny to Rome after a bravura takeoff. From here Mussolini was flown via Vienna to the Führer's headquarters.

On Monday 13 September 1943, the 3rd Group of the German 100th Bomber Wing (KG 100) carried out repeated operations over the Bay of Salerno. This time the British light cruiser *Uganda* was severely damaged. German FX 1400 glide bombs narrowly missed the US cruiser *Philadelphia* and 2 British destroyers. They sank the hospital ship *Newfoundland* despite its clearly visible Red Cross markings.

On Wednesday September 15 General Kammhuber, the able commander of the German night fighter arm, was dismissed from his post for disagreement with the Luftwaffe leaders; he was replaced by General Schmid. General Kammhuber was appointed commander of Luftflotte 5 in Norway.

On Thursday September 16, the 3rd Group of the 100th Bomber Wing reported winning a significant victory at Salerno, where 2 FX 1400 glide bombs hit the British battleship *Warspite* and put it out of action for almost a year. The first bomb penetrated the mess-hall decks and exploded in the fourth

Opposite page below: Autumn 1943, Pas de Calais (France). One of numerous firing installations for German V-1 flying bombs is under construction.

Right: 9 September 1943. The most modern Italian battleship, the *Roma*, has just been destroyed in the German Luftwaffe's most effective single operation against a shipping target.

boiler-room. The second FX 1400 fell alongside and tore a great hole in the ship's hull below the waterline. With great difficulty 2 tugboats managed to tow the battleship into Malta.

On Saturday September 18, the German 100th Bomber Wing led its final glide-bomb attack at Salerno and once again aimed at the US cruiser *Philadelphia*; but again they narrowly missed the vessel causing only slight damage.

On the night of 22–23 September 1943, 658 RAF aircraft bombed Hanover dropping 2,357 tons of bombs on the city; 25 bombers were shot down.

In September 1943 the US 8th Air Force carried out a series of unusual night raids in which they dropped leaflets rather than bombs. Approximately 30 Flying Fortresses of 422 Squadron (305th Bomber Group) took part.

The US forces now followed the example of the RAF by equipping their bomber formations with pathfinder squadrons. "Meddo," modelled on the British H2S navigational and blind-bombing device, was among the most important aerial instruments of the US pathfinders. The pathfinders first operated on Monday September 27 in a raid on Emden. They used smoke bombs to indicate the point at which the bombers should discharge their loads.

On Monday September 27 the armored troops of the British Eighth Army under General Montgomery entered Foggia (southeast Italy), securing 13 nearby airfields for the use of the US 8th Air Force. This coup abruptly changed Germany's strategic position, because possession of the Italian airbases placed US bombers within strike range of the important military industrial centers of southern Germany, Austria, Hungary and Rumania. The bases also made it possible for the Allies to supply and reinforce the Yugoslav partisans.

On the night of September 27–28, Hanover was again raided by Bomber Command when 2,196 tons of bombs inflicted heavy damage on the city. Thirty-eight of the 599 attackers were lost.

The RAF continually impressed on its air crews that the war was not over for them if they happened to be shot down. They were told to do everything in their power to avoid capture, or to escape from their POW camps if caught. All flying personnel received basic escape training and were given the obligatory "escape kit" containing maps, a compass, food and money.

A number of escape organizations, founded in Belgium, Holland and France in 1940, made it their duty to save shot-down Allied airmen from the Germans. Well-established escape routes led from eastern Holland across France and the Pyrenees to Gibraltar, or across German-occupied Europe to Switzerland. One of the duties of the SOE, the British Special Operations Executive, was to support the escape organizations. SOE members arranged radio contact with London, checked out the airmen's personal data, and furnished them with false papers and money. German security and counterespionage forces made repeated attempts to infiltrate their agents into the escape organizations and not seldom succeeded.

Hundreds of Allied airmen owed their freedom to the ingenuity of a British journalist and advertizing expert, Major C. C. Hutton, who invented countless technical aids to make it easier for them to escape from German POW camps.

Among Hutton's inventions were tiny compasses concealed inside buttons, rings, pencils and tobacco pipes; maps of escape routes printed on silk and sewed inside jacket linings or boots; slender steel saws for cutting prison bars, which could be concealed in shoelaces; flying boots that could be disassembled revealing a compass, a small saw and a pair of serviceable walking shoes at the bottom, while the upper, fur-lined piece could be turned into a jacket; a miniature radio the size of a cigarette pack; a uniform coat that could be turned into a civilian jacket; and quite ordinary-looking fountain pens that contained a compass, aspirin, a cigarette lighter, a map of Europe, and materials for dyeing a uniform.

The shrewd Major Hutton even set up an extensive charitable organization whose alleged purpose was to relieve conditions for prisoners-of-war. The charity was a camouflage for Operation Post-Box and enabled Hutton to smuggle his escape aids into German POW camps along with the charitable donations. Major Hutton's gadgets came into the hands of captive airmen in the guise of uniform buttons, shoes, chesspieces, even in playing cards and phonograph records.

On Friday October 1, just four days after the British had captured the Italian airfields near Foggia, US Strategic Air Force bombers (under command of General Doolittle) took off from these fields to raid the Messerschmitt aircraft manufacturing plant in New Vienna.

On the night of October 2–3, 273 British Lancasters raided Munich and established a record when they dropped almost 4 tons of bombs per minute on the city in 25-minute period between 10:30 and 10:55 P.M.

In the first week of October, US Thunderbolt P-47 fighter planes fitted with auxiliary fuel tanks were brought in to fly cover for US bombers, making it possible for them to raid with greater safety as far as the line extending from Frankfurt am Main to Hanover and Hamburg. As a result the US 8th Air Force was now able to follow the guidelines of the Pointblank Plan, and at once carried out a series of four grand operations against German traffic centers and the German aircraft industry. On Friday October 8, they led their first grand raid against factories in Bremen-Vegesack, suffering 30 losses. On the night of October 8–9, 457 RAF aircraft dropped 1,667 tons of bombs on Hanover. Almost 6 square miles of the city center were reduced to ashes and 250,000 people made homeless. Yet the Continental Corporation, one of the largest tire manufacturers in Germany and the most important war-industrial plant in the city, was scarcely hit. Bomber Command lost 27 aircraft.

On Saturday October 9, 378 bombers of the US 8th Air Force made its second grand raid, against Gdynia, Danzig and the Focke-Wulf terminal assembly plants in Anklam and Marienburg; 28 bombers were lost.

On Sunday October 10, 236 four-engined bombers of the US 8th Air Force made the third of the four grand assaults, on traffic installations in Münster; 30 bombers were lost.

At the beginning of October 1943, the first Luftwaffe night fighters were fitted with the newest wide-angle FuG 220 airborne radar made by the Telefunken company and codenamed Lichtenstein SN-2, known as SN-2 for short. This device could locate enemy bombers in absolute darkness within a four-mile range and enabled the fighters to home in on their targets. SN-2 functioned on an 85-megahertz frequency, and its great advantage was that it was immune to Window jamming strips. It had only one fairly negligible disadvantage: a wide-branching aerial array that was even heavier than that of the old Lichtenstein BC radar, and that slightly inhibited the aircraft's speed.

Back in August 1943, Göring had given top-priority rating to the development of this new homing device, because the new radar was the technical prerequisite for concentrated mass operations by night fighters using *Zahme Sau* tactics. The old Himmelbett defensive system was now abandoned. Groups of German night fighters were infiltrated into the incoming bomber stream, and were controlled from the ground only until they had homed in on a target using their own airborne radar. These new tactics inflicted heavy losses on Bomber Command and at last enabled the Germans to shift from the defense of localized targets to the defense of larger aerial zones.

The new Lichtenstein SN-2 radar was also immune to the Serrate radio receiver carried by British night fighters, which previously had been able to detect the beacon from German airborne radar and use it to home in on their target. Now the Germans had their own new homing systems that worked according to the Serrate principle and that were known as *Flensburg* and *Naxos* (FuG 227 and FuG 350 radar respectively). They made it possible for the Germans to home in on British airborne radars

Above right: A remote-controlled Fritz X guided bomb. The bombs were both simple and effective, but the lack of suitable carrier aircraft prevented the Germans from deploying them in large quantities.

Below: Compass concealed in a cufflink, one of British Major C. C. Hutton's inventions to help Allied POWs escape German confinement. The lid was screwed on in a way that made it hard to detect the compass.

and to attack the British bomber units without use of ground control stations.

The Germans now had some hope of halting at least the RAF's night bomber offensives. Their hope came not only from the new German radar, but also from a new type of angled gun in the German night fighters. Unlike the wide-receiving SN-2 airborne radar, which had been developed by a whole team of notable specialists, *Schräge Musik* was the invention of one man, a weapons sergeant named Paul Mahle. Mahle, a machine-fitter from Berlin, thought up a device that virtually revolutionized night-time aerial combat. *Schräge Musik* was first installed in the aircraft of 6 Squadron of the 5th Night Fighter Wing and deployed during the British raid on Peenemünde on 17–18 August 1943. One German 2nd Lieutenant was able to shoot down 4 bombers in 29 minutes.

Schräge Musik was a pair of cannon fitted at a 70–80° angle in the rear fuselage of twin-engined fighters, and operated with a reflector sight. In the past the German night fighters had attacked with their rigid forward guns and would come under fire from the four-barreled machine guns in the tail-turrets of enemy bombers. Now they were no longer exposed to this fire, because they could fly underneath their adversary and fire on him from below with their slanting guns. At this time the British night bombers had no mobile armament on the lower fuselage, and the German night fighters could take advantage of the dead angle between the British machine-gun turrets.

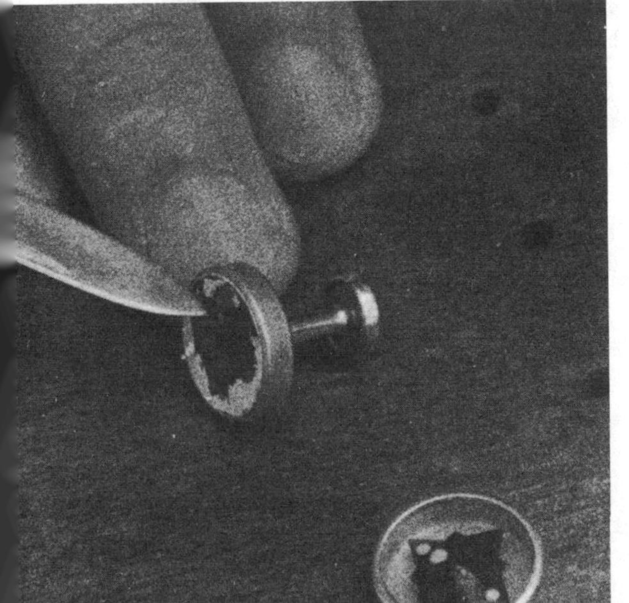

After the German air ministry accepted the slanted gun and it was put into series production, Paul Mahle received a letter of commendation and a prize of 500 marks.

Schräge Musik was in fact a modernized version of a combat technique used in 1916 by Gerhard Fieseler, then a front-line pilot in Macedonia. His friends used to call it "fieseling." With this tactic Fieseler was able to stand up to overwhelming odds and won 21 air kills without receiving a single machine-gun hit. In spring 1918, when Fieseler was a pilot in 38 Fighter Squadron on the Balkans Front, he took a round-turreted Lewis machine-gun from a Bréguet he had shot down, and mounted it in the upper wing indentation of his Fokker D VII, in front of the pilot's seat, so that he could fire it upward at an angle. Each time he attacked he would fly underneath the enemy plane, and his slanted MG rarely missed its target.

On Wednesday 13 October 1943, the new Italian government under Marshal Pietro Badoglio, whose headquarters were in Brindisi in southern Italy, declared war on Germany. The aerial forces of the former Regia Aeronautica were now to fight alongside the Allied forces. They were known as the "cobelligerent Italian forces" and were placed under the command of the "North West African Air Force."

The German aerial forces too had Italian aircraft fighting on their side. On October 23, Mussolini formed a rival Italian government in Salò (northern Italy), and set up a new air force, the "Aviazione della Repubblica Sociale Italiana." It contained a number of torpedo-bomber, bomber and fighter groups.

In mid-October 1943, [the free-lance French spy] Monsieur Hollard had his next rendezvous with the British military attaché in Berne and was asked to investigate mysterious German projects elsewhere as he had done at Rouen. Hollard recruited four assistants and they all rode around on their bicycles scouring the whole of northern France from Calais to Cherbourg. They discovered over 100 concrete structures all lying within a strip of land 180 miles long and 30 miles long, parallel to the coast.

The structures were long, low, narrow, reinforced-concrete bunkers, each curved at one end. Near the bunkers stood 3 rectangular structures and a platform about 32 feet long and 13 feet wide that looked like an inclined launch ramp, with its main axis aimed at the British capital.

The US 8th Air Force, armed with B-17 G bombers, a new version of the Flying Fortress, prepared for the last in the series of 4 grand raids that it carried out within the period of one week in October. The new bombers had a chin turret and 12.7-mm twin machine guns to help ward off the feared German frontal attacks.

On Thursday October 14, two months after the first US raid on Schweinfurt (August 17), 291 US bombers took off to make a second raid on the city's ball-bearing plants. The first German fighter wings zoomed in the moment the US Thunderbolt P-47 fighter escort had to leave the bombers. The Luftwaffe had gathered all its available combat-ready fighter planes in Germany, and recalled several squadrons of Luftflotte 3 (under Field Marshal Sperrle) from their stations in France, to fight the US four-engined bombers. Now battle raged under the brilliant blue sky, and the tactics of the German fighters were so flawlessly coordinated that US pilots wondered if information about the raid had been leaked beforehand.

Despite the new "chin" machine-gun turrets fitted under the noses of the US Flying Fortresses, wave after wave of German single- and twin-engined fighters ran in to attack them with rockets, 20-mm guns and even bombs. The US forces lost 29 bombers before they even reached Schweinfurt. As the bombers made their return flight, 160 fighters swooped down on the thinned-out formations from all directions at once. Non-stop fighting spread across the entire flight route and 32 bombers were shot down. The bombers had to ward off further attacks even after reaching the Channel. Forty German "destroyer" fighter-bombers, 35 night fighters

Heavy German night fighters had two 20-mm machine guns, fitted at a 75-degree angle on the rear fuselage. The Germans called the angled guns *Schräge Musik* (lit. "slanted music," i.e. "hot" music, a pun on the "slant" of the gun).

and almost 300 day fighters took part in the operation; 35 did not come back.

That day came to be known by the US forces as "Black Thursday." The US 8th Air Force lost 60 bombers, 20% of the aircraft deployed. Seventeen bombers crashed over the English Channel and Britain. Only 93 of the bomber force came out completely unscathed.

The series of 4 grand raids that concluded with the raid on Schweinfurt, cost the Americans 148 aircraft and around 1,500 flying personnel.

General Arnold, commander of the US aerial forces, realized that daylight bombers were unable to win command of German air space unless accompanied by a fighter escort. He halted the day raids until the delivery of a new type of long-range fighter plane which could provide cover for the four-engined bombers even over long distances.

Dr. R. V. Jones and his team now came up with a bright idea to meet the growing threat from the German night fighters. With the support of General E. B. Addison, the British chief of aerial intelligence, Dr. Jones built a special extremely powerful radio transmitter in Kingsdown (Kent) that worked on the same frequency as the German fighter-plane control stations. A duplicate control station was installed along with it. Meanwhile all the instructions that the German controllers were transmitting to their night fighters in the Running Commentary, were recorded day after day on wax discs (for at that time the British did not yet have tape recorders), and studied carefully. All this was part of a program of new feint maneuvers to divert the German air defense from Bomber Command's real targets during upcoming British night raids. These maneuvers were codenamed Operation Corona [and involved verbal jamming: German-speaking controllers], including the crew of the Ju 88 that had landed in Britain earlier that year, would imitate the German controllers [on the same frequency] and so lure the German night fighters onto false trails, making it possible for British bombers to raid their targets without interference from the heavy German defenses.

On Thursday October 21, Dr. Jones received word that the Fieseler aircraft factory in Kassel was producing the same secret weapon that had been produced at Peenemünde. Immediately after this report came in, Air Chief Marshal Harris decided to bomb Kassel in what was to prove one of Bomber Command's most devastating raids of the war. Plans were laid to mount the raid on the night of October 22–23, and the Corona [verbal-jamming technique]

Attack from behind and below: The fighter plane rises gently toward the bomber with its guns trained on the bomber fuselage. The tail gunner and the bomb compartment were especially at risk.

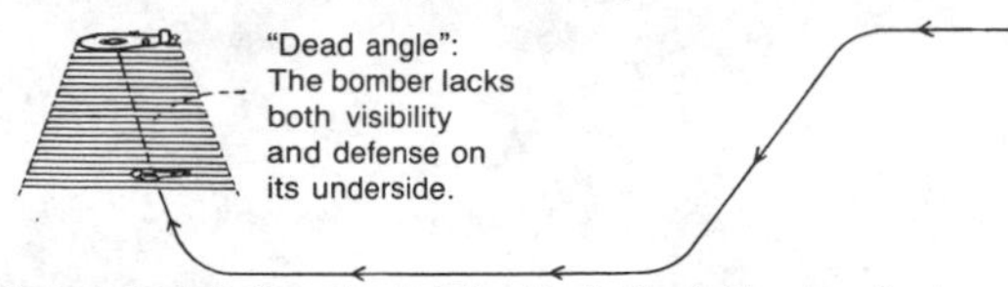
"Dead angle":
The bomber lacks both visibility and defense on its underside.

German attack tactics using *Schräge Musik:* The fighter plane fired from the dead angle underneath the bomber, aiming slanted fire into the wings.

was tried out for the first time.

While 486 heavy bombers headed for Kassel, a group of Stirling bombers carried out a mock raid on Frankfurt am Main, and 12 Mosquitos dropped target flares over Cologne to simulate another raid there. At the same time the simulated German fighter-plane controllers in Kingsdown guided the German night fighter squadrons over Frankfurt and Cologne pretending that they were the main targets. In this way the pathfinders of the main British formation were able, undetected by night fighters, to drop over Kassel the largest concentration of target flares ever used in the war. Incendiary bombs were dropped in such quantities that the entire central part of the city was on fire inside 15 minutes. Only then did the first German night fighters appear at Kassel after their long delay at Frankfurt.

The 1,824 tons of incendiary and blast bombs that fell on the city center of Kassel inside a quarter of an hour, provoked a firestorm like that in Hamburg. Twelve thousand people died in the storm—that is 5½% of the population. Despite the feint maneuvers of the Corona operation, Bomber Command lost 42 planes (9%). Reconnaissance photographs showed that fires were still burning in Kassel 7 days later. "Around 100,000 homes and at least 9 important factories lie in ruins. The Fieseler aircraft factories have been severely damaged by bombs," the British photointerpreters at Medmenham reported.

The Germans now transferred part of their Fieseler plant outside Kassel near to Rothwesten; this delayed mass production of the V-1 flying bomb for months. Goebbels wrote after the raid on Kassel: "It is deeply humiliating to see how the enemy leads us about by the nose on the air front. Every month he devises new methods of attack, and it takes us weeks or even months to deal with them."

The Corona fake controller learned to deceive the German night fighters in many ways, for example by sending out false weather reports to get them to land immediately or to move on to other airfields

A formation of the new US B-17 G bombers with "chin" turrets, escorted by fighter planes emitting white trails of vapor.

farther away. Announcements of ground fog were particularly effective.

The use of fake controllers enabled the British to elaborate new countermeasures as time went on. For example, eventually the Kingsdown transmitter began to broadcast extracts from Hitler's speeches, or German march music, on the frequencies used by the real German night fighter controllers; the jamming sounds would overlay the controllers' instructions and make them incomprehensible to the fighter planes.

The British set up a secret 600-kilowatt radio transmitter, the most powerful in Europe, codenamed Soldiers' Transmitter Calais. On Sunday 24 October 1943 they started to use it to send German-language propaganda broadcasts to the continent to supplement the operations of the earlier-established German Short-Wave Transmitter Atlantic. The operations were supervised by Sefton Delmer. The transmitter studio in Milton Bryan broadcast a regular program aimed at members of the Luftwaffe and was intended to weaken German morale. The broadcasts were supported by the German air crew who had landed their Ju 88 bomber in Britain in May 1943 and who regularly closed the program by inveighing against the British for imposing such impossible conditions on German fighters in their struggle against an overwhelming enemy. The broadcast team had their own wing commander, N. Roffy of Air Intelligence 3, who kept them informed about the most up-to-date technical innovations being used by the German Luftwaffe. Part of the program was a running commentary on the most recent Allied air raids, and included extremely precise details—lists of specific German streets destroyed, the names of individual targets, even the house-numbers of buildings. Of course Germans were strictly forbidden to listen to these broadcasts, but there were many unlicensed listeners who concluded that they were surrounded by on-the-spot British agents who immediately reported the results of British raids back to their headquarters.

Sefton Delmer, supervisor of the propaganda broadcasts, explained that the main source of British reports on the effects of Allied bombing raids, were photos taken by the Mosquitos that flew over the target zones immediately after each raid to photograph the damage. Delmer's friends at Air Intelligence would send him the photos as soon as they were developed and printed. They were delivered to Milton Bryan by motorcycle, and then a special department would do a stereoscopic interpretation. Delmer reported that this team had a whole library of German city maps and guides to help them.

By now the military attaché in Berne had reported to London the results of Monsieur Hollard's investigation of mysterious concrete structures between Calais and Cherbourg. The photo-reconnaissance unit at Benson (Oxfordshire) wanted further data, so the Mosquitos of 541 Squadron took off from Benson on Thursday October 28 to photograph all of northwestern France within a 150-mile radius of London; but bad weather delayed their mission. The weather finally improved on Wednesday November 3, and aerial photos were taken of the sites designated by Monsieur Hollard. The photos reached Medmenham the next day. They revealed large numbers of structures with identical features, including concrete platforms whose central axis always pointed straight at London. All the sites contained one or more sheds shaped like a ski viewed from the side. This special ski-shape helped the searchers to locate other "ski positions." They also discovered giant underground installations with reinforced-concrete walls at least 30 feet thick. One of them, located in Watten (northwest France), was described by US General Brereton as more extensive than any concrete structure in the United States with the possible exception of Boulder Dam.

On Thursday November 11, US aircraft carriers carried out an operation against Rabaul (New Britain). The raiders took off from the decks of three carriers that had just gone into service, the *Essex*, the *Bunker Hill* and the *Independence*. There were now strong land-based US fighter squadrons in the area. They circled over the shipping formation to protect it, so it was possible to deploy all the carrier aircraft on the raid. Sixty-seven Japanese fighter planes, 27 dive bombers and 14 torpedo aircraft took off from Rabaul to fight the Americans, but they were intercepted by American fighters, and lost 33 aircraft to the fighters and flak without scoring any hits.

On Saturday November 13, the German Luftwaffe command received a report from a German agent in Algeciras (Spain) saying that the Allied convoy MKS 30 was leaving Gibraltar headed for Liverpool, and had been joined next day by Convoy SL 139. The new giant convoy contained 66 freighters with cover from the 40th Escort Group, and 7 other vessels including the heavily-armed Canadian antiaircraft cruiser *Prince Robert*.

Meanwhile Air Chief Marshal Harris was preparing a new aerial offensive, the Battle of Berlin which, he wrote to Churchill, would "cost Germany the war." Harris's plan was to reduce Berlin to rubble and ash from end to end. He predicted that his Bomber Command would force Hitler to surrender by 1 April 1944 at the latest.

On the evening of 18 November 1943, the Battle of Berlin began when 402 out of an original 444 bombers reached the German capital, while 325 bombers made a heavy diversionary raid on Ludwigshafen. This was the first time that Bomber Command undertook grand raids on two different cities in a single night. In addition, 13 Lancasters bombed flak positions along the North Sea coast, and 28 Mosquito bombers raided flak around Berlin. The British bomber formations were escorted by large numbers of Mosquito long-range night fighters, which fought German night fighters taking off and landing around Brandenburg.

The marker flares dropped by the pathfinders were almost indetectible due to the closed cloud carpet, and the bomber formations dropped their payloads "blind." It became clear that operations outside the range of Oboe could not have the same targeting precision as raids in the Ruhr District.

Approximately 1,600 tons of high-explosive and incendiary bombs dropped on Berlin that night. The RAF lost 34 aircraft over Berlin and Ludwigshafen, 9 of them over the German capital.

On the afternoon of Sunday November 21, 25 He 177 A-5 bombers of German 2nd Group, 40th Bomber Wing (under Major Mons) took off from Bordeaux-Mérignac airfield. Each was armed with two remote-controlled Hs 293 glide bombs with which to attack the giant Allied convoy SL 139/MKS

Kingsdown (Kent), the sound studio used in British Operation Corona. Fake German fighter-plane controllers would give the German pilots misleading instructions, while phonograph records provided realistic background noises and WAAF stenotypists noted down everything that was said over the air waves.

30, whose course had been reported to the Germans on November 13. The convoy was then about 450 miles north of Cape Finisterre (off northwestern Spain).

The turbulent weather was not ideal for a glide-bomb attack, and mist reduced visibility. As a result the German air crews were unable to locate the bulk of the convoy and devoted their attention to two stragglers, the 4,405-ton freighter *Marsa* and the 6,065-ton *Delius*.

Captain Buckle, commander of the *Marsa,* gave this account: "At 3:39 P.M. our lookout reported a German bomber flying on a parallel course at an altitude of about 6,000 feet. A moment later it released a glide bomb that after falling some 600 to 900 feet, curved to the right and headed for our ship. We managed to make a sharp evasive maneuver so that the bomb crashed into the sea a good 400 feet from the *Marsa* and exploded throwing up a huge waterjet."

The second Hs 293 glide bomb also narrowly missed the freighter. At 4:00 P.M. another 5 He 177s crossed the sky. Captain Buckle reported: "We ran in a circle and then in a zigzag course to escape the bomb. Our Oerlikon rapid-fire cannon was shooting like mad, but to no avail. We saw one of the bombs approach us rapidly; I felt a violent jolt. The bomb tore open the ship's wall near the waterline and exploded in the engine room."

The crew of the *Marsa* were rescued by an escort vessel. The transport vessel *Delius* was also hit, but despite heavy damage managed to reach British harbor. The air crew of Captain Nuss was responsible for the victories over the two steamers.

The German Heinkels were still hunting for the main convoy when they were discovered by a Liberator of 224 Squadron, British Coastal Command while it was out on a U-boat patrol. The British pilot, Pilot Officer Wilson, immediately attacked the German bombers loaded down with Hs 293s. One of the Heinkels, trailing a smoke cloud, disappeared on the horizon; a second was forced to jettison its bombs and depart at low altitude.

The He 177s failed to locate Convoy SL 139/MKS 30 in spite of their special FuG 200 Hohentwiel radar equipment that supposedly could detect any ship within a 50-mile radius. The remaining Heinkels returned to base. Three of the aircraft and 2 crews were missing; one He 177 was heavily and another lightly damaged.

At 8:00 P.M. on Monday November 22, 9 Mosquito bombers marked their targets over Berlin. German flak tried vainly to shoot down the marker flares dropping by parachute. Then the German capital suffered the most devastating air raid it had experienced since the start of the war. Six hundred and thirty-one British and Canadian Lancaster and Stirling bombers released 1,132 tons of blast bombs and 1,334 tons of incendiaries in an attack that went on for two hours. The city center and the Moabit District were hit particularly hard. All the rows of buildings around the Bahnhof Zoo rail station were on fire too. The bad weather was an advantage to the attackers because it prevented some German night fighter squadrons from taking off. Nevertheless, flak and night fighters did manage to shoot down 26 bombers, with losses of 6 German night fighters. On the night of 23–24 November 1943, Bomber Command led its third grand raid on Berlin; 325 Lancasters and Stirlings released 1,334 tons of bombs. Two city districts, Lankwitz and Südende, were very badly hit.

Mosquito formations flew offensive sweeps over Berlin all day on Wednesday November 24, and again on Thursday November 25.

In the period of November 22–26, Roosevelt, Churchill and Chiang Kai-shek held the first Cairo Conference. They drew up guidelines for Allied strategic raids in the Pacific war theater, on Japanese supply lines in China, and on the Japanese motherland. The US 20th Air Force, under the personal command of General Arnold, commander of the USAAF, was appointed to carry out the guidelines.

On Friday November 26, 1,000 combined bombers and fighters of the US 8th Air Force made a heavy daylight raid on the port and industrial district of Bremen.

On the evening of November 26, 407 British Lancaster bombers launched their fourth grand operation of the Battle of Berlin. At the same time a Halifax formation flew to Stuttgart. This time the targets in Berlin were the northern districts of Spandau,

Tegel, Reinickendorf and Siemensstadt.

The RAF successfully confused the German defenses during these two grand raids. The bombers flew first to Frankfurt am Main, drawing most of the German night fighters there; by the time the night fighters left Frankfurt and got to Berlin, the bombers were already on their way home. A number of other night fighters were over Stuttgart, which the British had bombed one hour before Berlin. Despite its diversionary maneuvers the RAF lost 28 bombers over Germany; 2 German night fighters were shot down.

That same day, November 26, 21 He 177s of German 2nd Group, 40th Bomber Wing, carried out a number of operations using remote-controlled Hs 293 glide bombs. This time the target was Allied convoy KMF 26 which was just passing Cape Bougie (Algeria). One bomber suffered engine damage and crashed at takeoff.

After a long flight the German formation sighted the convoy, but ran into strong Allied air cover from 153 Squadron of the RAF, the 350th Fighter Group of the USAAF, and 7 Squadron of the French 1st Fighter Group. During aerial combat the Allied fighters shot down 6 He 177s, including the bombers of Major Mons, the commanding officer, and Captain Nuss.

Not until the He 177s were on their return flight did one of them succeed in sinking a British convoy vessel with a squarely-aimed bomb. It was the troop-transporter *Rohna* (8,602 tons). The swiftly falling darkness and the powerful waves hindered the rescue action, and over 1,000 US soldiers were drowned. Two more bombers of German 2nd Group, 40th Bomber Wing were heavily damaged during landing due to bad weather at their base.

On Sunday November 28, a Mosquito of the British photoreconnaissance unit was flown to Berlin by Squadron Leader Merifield to photograph the effects of the recent night raids. The German capital was covered by a dense cloud carpet as it had been on previous days, so the Mosquito looked for an alternative target on the Baltic Sea coast. It happened to photograph Zemplin, a village 7 miles south of Peenemünde where the German 155st "W" Flak Regiment—the codename for the flying-bomb unit under Colonel Wachtel—was at that moment test-firing V-1 rockets.

Shortly afterward, on Wednesday December 1, a young woman photointerpreter at Medmenham looked at the photos that Squadron Leader Merifield had just taken. Her name was Constance Babington-Smith; she was the daughter of the president of the Bank of England and Churchill was about to dub her "Miss Peenemünde": because it was she who exposed the secret of the so far unexplained concrete structures along the coast of northern France. Looking at the photos of the installations in Zemplin, she found they were identical to those she had seen in many photos of the French installations; and, she reported, on one of the ramps at Zemplin she saw a small aircraft. It was an exciting moment for her, for she had found absolute proof that the emplacements along the English Channel were intended as launch ramps for flying bombs. Just by chance, the magnifying glass she used to decipher the takeoff ramp where the vague outlines of a V-1 rocket were displayed, had been manufactured in Germany, by the Leitz Optical Works in Wetzlar. Miss Babington-Smith said it was their very best product.

On the night of 2–3 December 1943, the RAF made its fifth grand raid of the Battle of Berlin: 401 British bombers released 1,686 tons of incendiary and blast bombs onto the capital. Forty bombers were shot down.

Air Chief Marshal Harris had the ambitious plan

Below right: Heavy Heinkel He 177 Greif (Griffin) long-range bomber was used as a carrier for remote-controlled glide bombs. Of the 1,094 bombers built, over 800 were still standing around unused at the end of the war.

Opposite page above: RAF aerial photograph taken on 28 November 1943, where Miss Babington-Smith discovered a German V-1 flying bomb on a launch ramp (v. white arrow).

to destroy Berlin on the same scale as Hamburg, but he had not reckoned on the capital's extremely tenacious defenses and the fact that it lay outside the range of the Oboe device; moreover it was a more widespread, straggling city than Hamburg.

In their five grand raids on Berlin, 2,212 British bombers dropped a total of 8,656 tons of bombs. More than 2,700 civilians were killed. An estimated quarter of a million people became homeless when almost 70,000 homes were turned into ruins. The RAF lost 123 bombers.

Late in the afternoon of 2 December 1943, 96 German Ju 88 bombers of the 1st and 2nd Groups of the 54th Bomber Wing and the 1st and 2nd Groups of the 76th Bomber Wing, took off from Villaorba and Aviano airfields near Milan to raid Bari, an important port with 250,000 inhabitants on the Adriatic coast east of Naples.

German 2nd Air Lt. Ziegler gave this account: "In late afternoon we took to the air along with two pathfinder aircraft. Our Ju 88 was fully loaded with *Düppel* [radar chaff] jamming strips and flares for marking the targets. It was already dark when we crossed the coast south of Ravenna. We intended to run in on our target from the Adriatic. By Cape Rossa we climbed to 22,000 feet and then to our surprise we noted that the port of Bari was brightly lit as if this was peacetime. We began to drop tinfoil jamming strips, and because the harbor was so brightly lit, we might just as well have dispensed with dropping target flares."

On the evening of December 2, there were in the port of Bari more than 30 Allied vessels whose cargoes of war material and supplies were just then being unloaded. When darkness fell, all the lights in the harbor were switched on carelessly in order to speed up the work of unloading.

German pathfinder aircraft dropped tinfoil jamming strips paralyzing Allied radar, and German bombers appeared over Bari without being noticed. Not until 7:30 P.M. when the bombs began exploding in the harbor, did the antiaircraft guns open fire.

Not one searchlight beam attempted to capture the German bombers; not one barrage balloon was present to protect what at that moment was the most important Allied supply port in continental Europe; and not one Allied fighter plane turned up to help. Never had a bombing mission been carried off so easily; there were no German casualties. Two ammunition boats received square hits and blew up with such force that window-glass shattered within a 7-mile radius. An oil pipeline was hit at the pier, gasoline poured out of the burning tanker and set the oil on fire, and a huge sheet of flame sprang up. All the ships spared so far were now set alight.

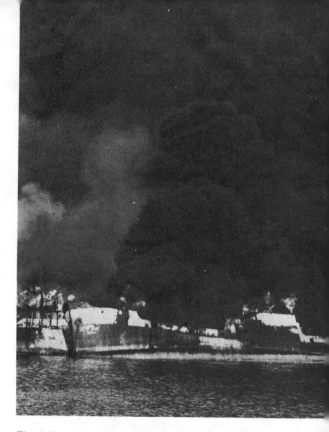

The Italian port of Bari after the German bombing raid of 3 December 1943. Some aspects of the tragedy were kept secret by the Allies for decades after the war.

This raid, which lasted only 20 minutes, was one of the most successful of the war. Never, except at Pearl Harbor, were so many ships sunk at a single blow. Nineteen transporters carrying 73,343 tons of shipping, were destroyed and 7 severely damaged. More than 1,000 guards and seamen were killed. Weeks went by before the port could again work to full capacity.

That part of the disaster was what appeared in the official reports; the other part was kept secret for decades. When the raid began, the freighter *SS John Harvey* lay at the pier; 17 other ships had tied up beside her or were lying at anchor nearby. Along with a cargo of explosive ammunition, the *John Harvey* also carried approximately 100 tons of heavy mustard gas enclosed in bombs each weighing 100 pounds. These were extremely dangerous weapons which violated international law, and which the Allied command wanted to keep in their Italian war-theater arsenal "just in case."

The *John Harvey* was hit at the outset of the raid and sank with her whole crew. The mustard-gas bombs had no ignitor fuses, but a number of them burst and the dangerous substance spread through the harbor basin. Fortunately a large part of it was carried out to sea, but the poisonous gas floating on the surface posed a deadly threat to the survivors of the raid. Many seamen and soldiers were pulled from the poisoned water onto land, but neither the rescue crews nor the rescued men knew anything about the mustard gas. The military authorities at the port were aware of the dangerous cargo on board the *John Harvey,* but in the chaos none of them thought about it. Several of the survivors later remembered having smelled a scent like garlic but no one attributed any importance to it, and no one in the jammed hospitals worried much about the men who, though smeared with oil, were not actually wounded. Still wearing their clothing soaked in mustard gas, they were simply sent to various billets, and not until two hours later did the first of them begin to complain of terrible pains, saying that they felt as if they had sand in their eyes.

Some 12 hours after the raid, authorities at the port discovered several mustard gas bombs and remembered the *John Harvey*'s cargo. At once the hospitals were notified that some of the rescued men might have come into contact with mustard gas. Eighteen hours after the raid, the first death from the poison gas was reported. A total of 617 men had been poisoned; 83 of them died, the last a whole month after the raid. There would have been fewer deaths if the rescue crews and doctors had known that chemical agents were involved and had taken the necessary measures at once.

The fate of the men on the *Bistera* was also kept secret. The *Bistera* had not been damaged in the raid, had picked up 30 survivors and, following orders from the port authorities, steamed toward Taranto. Four hours later, on the open sea, the entire crew started to suffer unbearable pains in their eyes. When the *Bistera* finally reached Taranto 18 hours after the raid, the crew had turned almost completely blind and found it difficult to moor the ship.

The destruction of Bari harbor had another grave aftereffect, coming as it did just a few weeks before the Allies landed at Anzio and Nettuno to open the way to Rome. It was one of the main reasons the Germans were able to hold up the Allied progress longer in this campaign than in any other campaign of the war.

On Friday 3 December 1943 – exactly 48 hours after Miss Babington-Smith discovered a V-1 flying bomb on the launch ramp and the British determined that the ski positions were all launch ramps for unmanned missiles – the "Crossbow" Committee, the body assigned to operate against Hitler's secret weapons, decided to order heavy Allied bombers to raid the ski positions. Based on Monsieur Hollard's reports the Allies estimated that the Germans had 100 launching sites; so a large number of Allied bomber units would be needed to bomb them.

On Sunday 5 December, despite bad weather, the 2nd Tactical Air Force and the US 9th Air Force flew their first raids against the ski positions. US air commander General Brereton said later that every possible effort was made to keep all information about the targets strictly secret so as not to panic the public, and that Prime Minister Churchill himself had ordered the press to designate the targets simply as "military installations."

German Heinkel He 177s armed with remote-controlled Hs 293 glide bombs had suffered heavy losses when they tried to raid Allied shipping in the daytime, so at the beginning of December 1943, 2nd Group, 40th Bomber Wing launched night raids to destroy convoys in the Atlantic and the Mediterranean.

This involved new offensive tactics for the Heinkels. Some of them would drop flares over the convoy while the other bombers released their Hs 293 glide bombs. But the operations required a high measure of coordination between the air crews, which they could not develop without extended preliminary exercises. The night raids proved unsuccessful and were halted.

A new type of US long-range fighter plane, the P-51 Mustang, arrived in Britain, and immediately the USAAF led an operation against Germany. On Monday December 13, 45 Mustang fighters carrying disposable auxiliary fuel tanks that gave them a range of up to 840 miles, escorted a US bomber unit to raid Kiel. The Mustangs circled over the target protecting the bombers from the German fighters. This operation marked the beginning of USAAF daylight raids with long-range fighter cover. The fighters flew ahead of the bombers so that they could intercept the German fighters before they reached their prey.

The result was protracted aerial dogfights which prevented the Germans from advancing against the bomber formations. This deployment of long-range fighters carrying auxiliary fuel tanks, is one example of how a single technical achievement can fundamentally alter the balance of power in aerial warfare.

In mid-December 1943, the Germans finally succeeded in effectively jamming the British Oboe blind-bombing device. German General Weise ordered a jamming transmitter (codenamed *Karl*) to jam the Oboe frequency.

On Wednesday 15 December 1943, the Crossbow Committee urged the US 8th Air Force to fly raids to wipe out the V-1 flying-bomb launch sites. On the evening of December 20, the RAF and the USAAF began a series of heavy air raids on the V-1 launch ramps between the Pas de Calais and the Cherbourg peninsula, and also on giant bunkers that had been discovered at Wizernes (northwest France). They did not realize that the latter were sites for a series of launch ramps that were being built for V-2 rockets.

Before the end of 1943, the Allies raided 83 of the ski positions where they released more than 3,000 tons of high explosive. Despite this heavy bombardment, assembly work at the catapults continued without interruption. Some of the positions were defended by flak or carefully camouflaged. Colonel Wachtel's 155th "W" Flak Regiment did not lose a single man, but the Allied bombs killed 30 French workmen.

On the night of December 20–21, 576 RAF bombers raided Frankfurt am Main, dropping 2,070 tons of blast and incendiary bombs on the city with a loss of 40 bombers. One German air captain, Captain Herget, shot down 8 four-engined bombers.

The last grand RAF raid of the year was aimed at Berlin. On the night of December 29–30, 656 out of 712 British bombers reached the capital and released 2,315 tons of bombs with a loss of 20 bombers. During the Battle of Berlin, in the period from November 18 to December 31, approximately 14,000 tons of bombs had fallen on the city.

At the end of 1943, the progressive deterioration of the weather impaired German night fighter operations. At this time RAF losses were running at no more than 2%; the Germans were losing more than 3% of their night fighters.

In 1943 the RAF and the USAAF mounted 3 major air offensives: the Battle of the Ruhr, the Battle of Hamburg, and the Battle of Berlin. In reality these three battles were a contest between electronic devices, in which the British raced to produce new devices while the Germans struggled to develop countermeasures to neutralize the enemy armament. Yet these three Allied air offensives were unable either to halt weapons production in Germany or to move German workers to go on a massive strike. In short, the offensives were a failure; but no one in Britian drew the logical consequences from this fact. On the contrary, the bombing war became even more harsh and cruel.

German armaments minister Albert Speer later wrote in his book *Inside the Third Reich:* "Actually, as I had early recognized, the war could largely have been decided in 1943 if instead of vast but pointless area bombing the planes had concentrated on the centers of armaments production." (English quoted from the 1970 Macmillan edition, p. 280)

In 1943 the Western Allies dropped 226,500 tons of bombs on Germany and Occupied Europe, while during the same period the Luftwaffe dropped 2,298 tons on Britain, almost half during the last three months of the year. Virtually every night in November and December 1943, the Germans made lightning offensive sweeps over eastern and southern England with a couple of dozen bombers or fighter-bombers—often in low-level flight so as to fly under the radar chain.

Initially, National Socialist propaganda tried to depict the Allied raids as militarily useless, and trivialized their effects; but by the end of the year the preferred approach was concealment or emphasis on the terrorist character of the raids.

In occupied France, Belgium and the Netherlands, almost all the Allied raids were daylight raids. The

North American P-51 Mustang fighter planes surpassed all other US fighters in maneuverability, range and speed. The Mustang was the best and most versatile single seater Allied fighter of the war, and had disposable fuel tanks enabling it to fly cover for bombers raiding from England to as far away as Poland. Mustangs gave the US 8th Air Force air supremacy during its daylight raids. A total of 14,819 were built.

main targets were airfields, port installations, power plants, munitions factories working for Germany, rail switchyards, and the sites where V-1 launch installations were being built.

In late autumn 1943, the air defenses of Germany ran into their first major crisis. The enormous casualties among German flying personnel had to be made up by calling in younger and younger pilots who were inadequately trained for the job. This and the strained military situation impaired the morale and performance of the German fighters.

In 1943 the German fighter arm went through its last major reorganization before the end of the war. The 1st Fighter Corps under General Schmid, comprising the 1st, 2nd, 3rd and 7th Fighter Divisions, was placed under command of General Stumpff's Luftflotte Reich, the air force for the defense of Germany; and the 2nd Fighter Corps, made up of the 4th and 5th Fighter Divisions, was placed under the command of Luftflotte 3 in France, commanded by Field Marshal Sperrle.

Organization was tightened: Day and night fighter operations were merged at the divisional command-post level, and fighter-plane headquarters beneath divisional level were dissolved. All the divisions together had 1,200 day and night fighters at the end of 1943, approximately two thirds of which were reported as combat-ready.

In 1943, the German night-fighter arm had derived fresh impetus from introduction of the *Wilde Sau* system (= detecting the brightly-lit targets visually rather than by radar) and the *Zahme Sau* system (= infiltrating large numbers of fighters into the bomber stream in a given zone when it was making its approach). German flak artillery redoubled its strength despite its losses. Flak was more effective in warding off high-altitude daylight raids, when it could concentrate its forces and deploy large-scale batteries, than at night when it relied on jammable radar.

The German night-fighter arm managed to overcome the crisis it faced in 1943, but the deployment of Window jamming strips dealt a blow to the German antiaircraft artillery from which it never recovered.

By the end of 1943, the USA and Great Britain had already overtaken the tactical and technical lead of the Japanese aerial forces. Most of the veteran Japanese pilots who had completed 300 to 600 hours of flying before war broke out, were now dead, and the younger generation of pilots were inadequately trained.

It became increasingly clear that events in the Pacific theater had taken a decisive turn, and starting in the summer of 1943 the US forces had moved onto the offensive.

1944
January to June

Fresh Raids on Berlin

Monday 3 January 1944, London
The *British Air Ministry* announced:

On Saturday night through to Sunday morning, strong formations of British and Canadian Lancaster bombers carried out an air raid on Berlin, releasing around 1,200 tons of bombs onto the German capital. The operation was shifted to the early morning hours so as to avoid raiding by moonlight. Only isolated German night fighters appeared over Berlin itself during the raid, and during the outbound and return flights the bombers were attacked by only a few enemy aircraft, 2 of which positively were shot down. A German "aerial defensive rocket" was observed for the first time on this operation. The crews report that the rocket, a horizontal flying missile, appeared suddenly and then exploded in all directions. Only 28 bombers were lost on the night operations, an exceptionally low figure.

12 January 1944, Berlin
The *German News Bureau* reported:

One of the greatest air battles of the war took place over Germany yesterday. Last night the German High Command issued a special announcement that according to preliminary figures acquired by nightfall, German fighter planes and antiaircraft guns shot down 123 enemy aircraft; this toll has since climbed to 136 and includes 124 four-engined bombers. Our reports indicate that the Americans suffered higher casualties during their run-in than on their return flight. The number of German fighter planes lost in the air battles has risen to 20.

Left: A "Flying Fortress," the best-known of the American bombers. The photo shows a B-17 G of the 398th Bomb Group of the 8th USAAF. B-17 Gs manufactured after January 1944 were no longer given a camouflage coating because they were lighter and faster without it.

Thursday 13 January 1944, London
The British *Reuters News Agency* reported:

Reports from US airbases are now giving us a more exact picture of Tuesday's great air battle over Germany.

The bombers were escorted deep into Germany by Thunderbolt and Lightning long-range fighters. The new American Mustang long-range fighters were also deployed for the first time on this occasion; they flew with the bombers to just outside the target zone, which was the longest escort flight ever flown by fighters. Strong British and other Allied fighter-plane units escorted the bombers on their return flight over the Netherlands.

All the air crews testify that the German fighters, presumably believing that they were warding off a raid on the capital, attacked with a violence never before experienced. The German Luftwaffe used new tactics and also new armament which are considered responsible for the relatively high American losses.

The bombardier of one US B-17 reported: "On our first run-in to the target we were all alone, and neither antiaircraft nor fighter planes operated against us. Then 18 Messerschmitts arrived. When they got close they changed their formation and stretched out in a perfectly straight line as if they

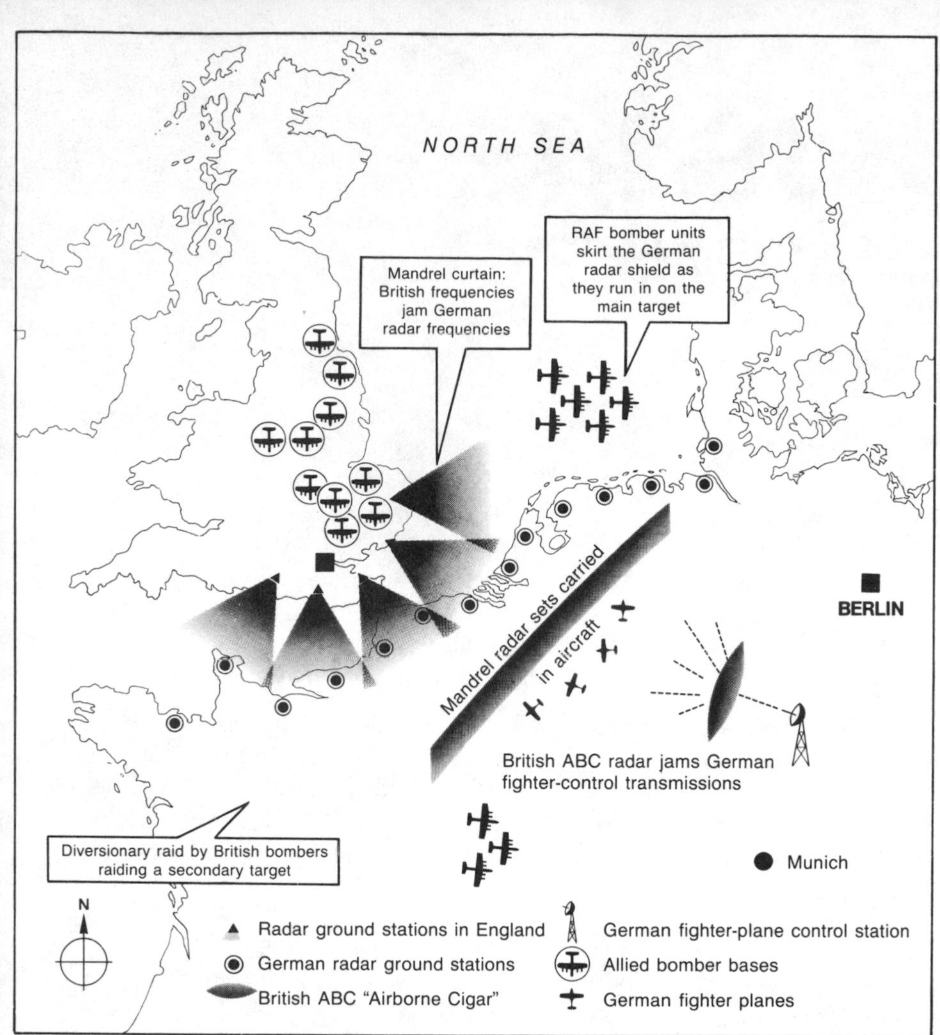

Left: Diagram of RAF night raids on Berlin 1944/1945

Opposite page below: February 1944, a US bomber base command post. At this time the American bombers were stepping up their missions over occupied western Europe, in cooperation with RAF fighter-bombers. Here officers of both air forces are observing operations.

were on infantry drill, then attacked our bombers from the side, firing a simultaneous broadside of rockets which exploded in red and yellow fireballs. After that they all broke formation at once and bombarded us with 20-mm aerial guns. None of us seriously believed that he would get back from the flight alive."

US Long-Range Fighters Are Deployed

Monday 31 January 1944, London
The *British Air Ministry* announced:

The US 8th Air Force has stepped up its deployment of American long-range fighters to combat German Luftwaffe planes during US daylight raids on Germany. This marks a new chapter in the history of the air war. The most recent air battles over Frankfurt and Brunswick, have proved that it is now possible for the bombers to devote themselves to their primary task, while their fighter escort takes over the job of defense. More massive daylight operations now lie ahead, in which the Americans will increase considerably the percentage of Thunderbolts and Lightnings taking part, and the German fighters will have to fight more daytime air combats than ever before.

German Raids on London

31 January 1944, Berlin
The *German News Bureau* reported:

On the nights of 21 and 29 January, more than 600 German aircraft raided targets in London using bombs of every caliber. The arrival of such powerful bomber units caught the British and their air defenses completely by surprise. This explains the low German losses of only 25 aircraft, which is less than 4% of the bombers deployed.

The actual number of aircraft dispatched may have been considerably higher than just stated, because reports by the German Armed Forces High Command indicate that individual British installations outside London were also bombed successfully on the same nights; but it was impossible to obtain details about the targets. The raids may well have been made for special reasons, as was the case with Tuesday's raid on Ipswich. It has been reliably reported that the results of the grand raids on the British capital were satisfactory.

At RAF Bomber Command Headquarters

31 January 1944, London
The British *Reuters News Agency* reported:

For the first time since war began, several press representatives have been admitted to the great Hall of Operations where strategic planning of the air offensive against German industrial targets is carried on.

The walls are covered with the giant maps of 50 German industrial cities which now are targets or will be targets during the coming weeks; these are cities which the Allied commanders believe are of special significance in the present stage of the air offensive. Every map includes a table listing the tonnage of bombs already dropped on the city, and the total weight of blast and incendiary bombs thought to be necessary permanently to destroy the target. Special maps are also provided for each city which give precise aerial-photographic data about the destroyed zones and the progress of German clean-up operations.

Fantastic Reports from Berlin

Tuesday 1 February 1944, London
The *Reuters News Agency* reported:

On Monday Berlin released a report claiming that more than 600 German aircraft raided England on 21 and 29 January. RAF Headquarters describes this as a "fantastic report and one of the most ridiculous exaggerations that Berlin has ever produced."

Reliable official investigations reveal that no more than 90 bombers took part in the January 21st raid, and no more than 30 of these at most, reached the London area. It has also been determined that only a small number of aircraft operated over England on January 29. The damage resulting from the two operations is absolutely negligible in military terms.

Extract from a decree by *SS Leader and Reich Minister of the Interior* [Heinrich Himmler]—Security-Police Central Office—dated 4 February 1944:

Rē: enemy air leaflets and propaganda material picked up by Germans:

In Germany's and Europe's present struggle for survival, our enemies will stop at nothing to bring about the total destruction of the German people. Air leaflets are being dropped to crush both the Front and the Homeland so that they will completely lose all spirit of resistance, and forged entitlement and food-ration coupons are being dropped with the aim of inducing economic chaos.

Apart from the herein-named authorities, and the authorities, officials or employees appointed by them, no government or Party office, organization or person is entitled to keep enemy air leaflets, air-dropped ration coupons, or propaganda food packages, or to collect them as souvenirs or for archival purposes, or to take charge of them, or to requisition them from front-line soldiers or military operational headquarters etc., or to send them to Germany or otherwise dispatch them. The number of those appointed to handle enemy leaflets, is to be kept very small. It is forbidden to reproduce enemy leaflets by making duplicate copies or photocopies. This prohibition applies equally to the offices which deal with enemy leaflets, and to their appointees. Unauthorized transmission of enemy leaflets, or of their contents, and independent use thereof, is prohibited. Violators will be subject to legal prosecution for lending aid and comfort to the enemy.

The local police authorities have exclusive responsibility for the seizure of leaflets, coupons and entitlements of every kind, and of propaganda

packets containing food or luxury goods, that are dropped by aircraft, balloon or other devices. The population should be made aware that those who find and keep forged food-ration coupons, or who pass them on or accept them from others, instead of handing them in or informing someone, will be regarded as economic war criminals and social parasites, and must expect to receive the severest prison sentence or even the death penalty. To deter people from using the forgeries, information should be spread that they differ noticeably from the originals. The features of the forgeries must on no account be made public.

A formation of US B-17 bombers over Germany. The bombardier occupied the most secure position inside a bomber and was comparatively seldom hit by German fighter-plane bullets. He was also close to an escape hatch, and regulations said that he was to be the first to bail out in case of emergency.

Inside a US B-17 Flying Fortress

The US Armed Forces newspaper *Stars and Stripes* carried the following account in February 1944:

Flying in formation at an altitude of 22,000 to 26,000 feet provides quite enough difficulties for an airman, apart from those posed by the enemy.

A bomber crew ascend at enormous speed from sea level to the altitude of Mount Everest. On a long-range flight to Germany the men are airborne for eight to ten hours, every minute of which causes them danger and toil. They must fight for their lives, they may be wounded without any hope of getting proper medical aid, and they must operate safely one of the most complicated machines ever invented.

Every member of the crew from the gunner to the pilot is asked to work fast and accurately, and moreover must do so while wearing extremely cumbersome clothing. Over a woolen undergarment, each man wears an electrically-heated coverall against the fierce cold at 26,000 feet. Then comes the uniform. On top of that comes a sheepskin-lined flying suit in which you can hardly move. But that's not all: to finish off, every man has to fasten on chest and back armor, a thick coat of mail that reaches from neck to pelvis and is designed to protect the men from flak splinters and machine-gun missiles.

Then the crewmen climb into their high sheepskin boots, put on their bright yellow life jackets, belt on their parachutes and finally don thick, electrically-heated gloves. On their heads comes a warm cap followed by a steel helmet.

Their outfit also includes equipment. An airman would pass out in a short time at high altitude without an artificial oxygen supply, so he must drape an oxygen mask around his neck – its pressure on his face later, during the flight, is enough to drive him crazy – and dons a headset and a throat microphone so he can use the radio interphone. The first is jammed over his ears, the second tight around his throat.

The pilot is buckled into his seat, which further confines his freedom of movement, and then he has to get off the ground thirty tons of steel and aluminum loaded with gasoline and explosives.

The tension along the runway starts the moment the gas throttles are moved forward. The speed rises to 90, then 120 miles per hour before the heavy bomber lifts off the ground. The slightest deviation from the runway would make the tires blow up and turn the aircraft into a column of fire and smoke. The whole crew hold their breaths. But the machine does not slip off the runway, it flies.

Now the time has come to put on the oxygen masks so that the rubber slowly digs into the skin. Now comes the moment for the pilot to turn up his radio equipment high enough to drown out atmospheric disturbance and the enemy jamming transmitters. A deafening racket ensues, yet he must not miss a word.

Now the pilot must pay continuous attention to the machines flying above and beside him, holding

the control column with one hand while with the other he regulates the four fuel throttles and the controls of the four variable-pitch propellers; meanwhile his feet press the rubber pedals against the hard spring. In short, he has to keep his place in the formation while the aircraft are speeding along at over 300 feet per second and rearing up and down in the gusting air. Now the gunners inside their revolving turrets begin systematic scanning of the sky for the enemy fighters that may attack the formation at any moment. The sweating navigator begins his ceaseless calculations and checks.

After only two or three hours the pilot has pains in his arms, legs and back; the rest of the crew also feel stiff. The throat microphone begins to chafe tormentingly the tiniest wounds received while shaving; the edge of the life jacket rubs the men's necks raw. As soon as you fly at an altitude of over 22,000 feet, the headset gives out an irritating noise like a circular saw that gets on your nerves. Cold creeps through the thick clothing. The oxygen mask presses down on your face like a strangling hand. Instinctively you would like to loosen it and rip it off, but reason forces you not to.

By your fifth hour of flight at the latest you have to expect German fighters to appear above the bomber formations at any moment and then swoop down on them with screaming engines. But the bombers are escorted by Thunderbolt and Mustang fighters. To the bomber crews their dark, stout and elegantly slender fuselages are more beautiful than the body of the most beautiful girl.

The top gunner signals that you are under attack, calling "Ten Me 109 fighters five o'clock high." The announcement makes your abdomen tighten up, then each of you waits tensely until the rat-a-tat of the top gunner announces the start of combat. From now on everything happens so fast that there is no time to feel afraid. Missiles spray through the wall with a noise like a pneumatic drill.

The right gunner is hit. The co-pilot is ordered to give him first aid. The next few minutes pose many problems for him; the worst is the narrow space. The co-pilot has to loosen his safety-belt, unplug his heater and radio equipment, remove the trunk of his oxygen gear and finally take off the parachute attached to his seat. If the plane is hit during the next ten minutes, the co-pilot will be unable to bail out. He drapes a flask of portable oxygen around his neck, twists his way out of his seat and forces his way back along the plane.

Each fold of his flying suit seems designed especially to catch on every handle, knob, lever and corner, of which there are a great many inside a bomber. He can just barely squeeze past below the upper gun turret, but only if the turret is still; if the gunner swings it around, he may be caught in the gear and injured. The narrow passage beside the bomb bay is full of sharp ribs and reinforcements.

The right gunner is draped unconscious in his turret. A 60-degree-below-zero wind pounds through the opening torn by the fighter guns. The wounded man needs disinfecting powder on his wound and a pressure bandage, and his bleeding leg must be tied up. It is impossible to do this wearing the thick, electrically-heated gloves, so the co-pilot takes them off. If he is skillful and lucky and applies the bandage quickly, he may be able to put his gloves back on in two to three minutes, but even then he will not get off without a souvenir. The air blowing in is cold as Siberia and the couple of minutes without gloves may well mean half a year in a military hospital in the vague hope of saving his fingers. But his buddy's life is at stake so he does not hesitate.

The co-pilot's next problem is to work his way back through the fuselage to his seat again. His oxygen flask is almost empty, and he can only move forward with the greatest difficulty.

Meanwhile the Flying Fortresses are gradually approaching their target. The German fighters and flak have focussed their defense here. The air is filled with explosive clouds from the flak shells. The bomber carries out a number of evasive maneuvers that demand the pilot's whole energy. The crew count the tortured seconds. At last the most

dangerous moment comes, the straight run on the target, and finally the liberating cry "Bombs away!"

The formation turns and heads towards home, and again they face the same problems as on their outbound flight, until the blessed moment when they reach the Channel and are enveloped in the secure protection of the fighter squadrons.

The Six-Ton Bomb

Sunday 20 February 1944, London
RAF Headquarters announced:

British scientists have worked for a number of months to develop new 6-ton bombs to use in raiding special targets, and the bombs were used for the first time on February 18 in a raid on the Gnome-Rhône aircraft-engine works in Limoges. Aerial photographs later revealed that the bulk of the factories were destroyed by the action of the massive explosions. All experiments conducted in Britain so far, show that the bomb produces effects that were scarcely thought possible only a short time ago.

Tuesday 22 February 1944
The British *Reuters News Agency* reported:

It has now been learned that some 2,000 tons of bombs were dropped on Stuttgart during the RAF raid of Sunday night-Monday morning. Only one bomber was lost for every 200 tons of bombs dropped, which is a record low for the RAF.

Wednesday 23 February 1944, London
The *British Air Ministry* announced:

Yesterday US bombers again made powerful raids on aircraft factories and airfields, mainly in Germany. For the first time the 8th and 15th Air Forces carried out simultaneous, coordinated operations from their bases in Britian and Italy respectively. Large formations of Flying Fortresses and Liberators, escorted by Thunderbolt, Lightning and Mustang fighters, bombed the Bernburg, Oschersleben and Halberstadt [eastern German] aircraft plants which had already been bombed on Sunday, as well as other aircraft factories and military targets. In some areas German fighter planes offered violent resistance.

23 February 1944, Berlin
The *German News Bureau* reported:

Strong German Luftwaffe formations bombed the city of London again last night. The Wehrmacht High Command described the operation as a "grand raid." The German wings used the "compass rose" tactic in which they converged on the target from all directions at once, and "line tactics," which German airmen also call flying "single file." These tactics are designed to catch off guard the strong British air defense around London.

Lightning Fighters over Berlin

Saturday 4 March 1944, London
The *British Air Ministry* announced:

Yesterday strong formations of USAAF and RAF aircraft made further daylight raids on Germany and the western occupied zones. A large formation of Flying Fortresses and Liberators, escorted by Thunderbolt and Mustang fighters, bombed targets in northwestern Germany. While this operation was still in progress, US Lightning long-range fighters penetrated to Berlin and raided important military targets. The Lightnings encountered no German fighter planes in the area. This was the first US daylight raid on the German capital.

Heavy US Daylight Raid on Berlin

Monday 6 March 1944, London
US 8th Air Force Headquarters announced:

This morning strong formations of US bombers escorted by large units of long-range fighters, mounted a concentrated raid on targets in Berlin.

Left: A British Lancaster B 11 bomber is being loaded with a 12,000-lb Tallboy bomb. The Tallboys were carried only by Lancasters, the fastest and heaviest RAF bombers.

Right: German Luftwaffe soldiers on fire-fighting duty after an incendiary bomb raid: "There is nothing left to save here."

This was the first large-scale daylight raid by US aerial forces on the German capital. The city was covered by a pall of cloud, but even so, the bombs were observed to destroy planned targets.

All along their flight route our units encountered sizeable resistance from enemy fighters, but our escort aircraft attacked them successfully and shot down 83 German fighter planes for losses of 11. It appeared that the German Luftwaffe had called up numerous fighter-plane units from other war theaters. Many of our air crews believe that 800 to 900 German fighters were operating over the German capital alone; they attacked with the greatest determination.

At first there was very vigorous antiaircraft fire over Berlin, but then it diminished rapidly and finally stopped altogether. The preliminary reports on the results of aerial combats indicate already that 160 to 170 German fighters were shot down.

One pilot reported: "Dogfights took place over the Continent that were completely beyond anything we had experienced before. Hundreds of German fighters tried to bar our bombers from breaking through to Berlin. Clearly we were fighting the elite of the German fighters, who operated with extreme daring and tenacity. Our unit was held in defensive combat for fully 5 hours, but the enemy could not keep us from attacking the German capital.

"We had strict orders to pinpoint our targets, and our photos confirm that we carried out this duty to the letter. We can say that the city districts that suffered most, were those that escaped the night raid by the RAF. One formation of four-engined bombers strayed into a flak belt approximately 2 miles wide and a thousand feet deep, and we could only look on helplessly as 5 Flying Fortresses crashed in flames into the sea of houses in Berlin."

US Bombers Land in Sweden

6 March 1944, Stockholm
Swedish Army Headquarters announced:

Today at noon, 2 US Flying Fortress bombers flew over the coast of southern Sweden and were forced to land by Swedish fighters and ground defenses. In the early afternoon, a third US bomber appeared over Swedish soil, signalled an emergency and landed on an airfield in Schonen. The 3 bombers are almost undamaged. The crews, totalling 30 men, have been interned.

3,000 Aircraft Fly against Berlin

Thursday 9 March 1944, London
The British *Reuters News Agency* reported:

Yesterday the US air force led its heaviest daylight raid on Germany so far. Reliable sources say that some 3,000 aircraft took off to raid Berlin, including more than 1,000 long-range fighters. One of their main targets was the ball-bearing plant in Erkner on the eastern fringe of the city.

The Flying Fortress and Liberator bombers released more than 10,000 blast bombs and 350,000 incendiaries in this operation against the German capital. The more than 1,000 Mustang, Lightning and Thunderbolt escort fighters of the American, British and other Allied air forces, shot down 83 German fighter planes while losing only 16 aircraft. Thirty-eight four-engined bombers have not returned from this raid, the largest daylight operation by US aerial forces so far against a single target. The US bombers and their escort fighters encountered a heavy defense by German antiaircraft as well as by the Luftwaffe. The Germans deployed every conceivable type of aircraft including some training aircraft. Very violent aerial combats took place, although this differed from previous raids in that the German fighters appeared only just before the bombers reached Berlin, and over the city itself. German fighter planes tried to attack the US bombers over Hanover but to a large extent were unsuccessful.

Once it became clear that Berlin was the target, large numbers of German fighter wings took to the air and fought with the fiercest determination.

The scale of this aerial operation may be judged from the fact that a total of 600,000 men took part in the attack and defense on both sides. Approximately 13,000 airmen flew over Berlin, and some 50,000 men were involved in getting the aircraft ready for takeoff on British airfields. The German Luftwaffe deployed approximately 15,000 men, and half a million men and women worked the flak batteries all around Berlin.

9 March 1944, London
The British *Reuters News Agency* reported:

The tactics of the US aerial forces have proved extremely successful in that, despite facing much less favorable geographical conditions, they have achieved what the Germans vainly tried to achieve in the 1940 Battle of Britain: increasingly deep penetration by large compact bomber formations into a strongly-defended enemy zone.

The success of the US bombers is due mainly to the use of large formations of escort fighter planes which take turns protecting the bombers. This system will be crucially important to the further course of the air war.

Friday 10 March 1944, London
The *British Air Ministry* announced:

Yesterday's daylight raid on Berlin was completely different from Wednesday's raid in that no German fighters turned up to fight, and of the strong formations of US bombers and their hundreds of escort aircraft, only 7 bombers and one fighter failed to return to base. As far as has been determined, no German aircraft have been shot down.

The US air crews who took part in the daylight raid on Berlin, say unanimously that antiaircraft fire over the city was stronger than ever before. One of the pilots said: "So many antiaircraft missiles were whizzing through the air that all you had to do was stretch out your hand and you could have caught a couple of them."

Directly over the city center the bombers ran into an extremely dense antiaircraft barrage; they realized that the guns were capable of firing 4 rockets at once. A B-24 Liberator was hit by one of these missiles and crashed over the sea of buildings.

German Radio Broadcasts Hourly Reports on the Air Situation

Tuesday 21 March 1944, Berlin
The *German News Bureau* reported:

Starting today at 6:00 P.M., German radio will be broadcasting reports on the air situation. Both day and night as long as they are on the air, all German radio transmitters will broadcast a report on the current air situation every hour on the hour, and supplementary updates will be transmitted if any change occurs in the situation.

Heavy Losses in Raid on Nuremberg

Friday 31 March 1944, London
The British *Reuters News Agency* reported:

It is reliably reported that the RAF lost 96 bombers in last night's raid on Nuremberg, the highest toll of casualties that it has suffered in any night raid since war began.

Saturday 1 April 1944, London
The *British Air Ministry* announced:

It has been confirmed that the RAF went through the most severe night air battle of the war in its raid of Thursday night–Friday morning. Between 900 and 1,000 Halifax and Lancaster bombers took part in the operations, with the largest number going to Nuremberg.

Several hundred German night-fighter planes—the largest number so far in any one night—repeatedly attacked the bomber formations, which had to fly through some 550 miles of strongly-defended territory to reach Nuremberg.

In many cases the German ground defenses used

Layout of the radar navigational and blind-bombing equipment inside an RAF bomber in 1944.

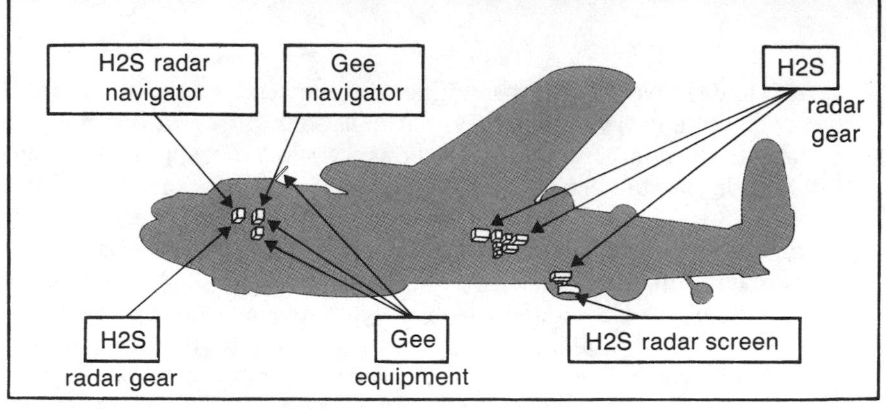

new rocket missiles which climbed into the sky creating broad streaks of light. The air battle over Germany lasted about three hours in all.

The air defense over Nuremberg itself was not as strong as had been anticipated given what had gone before. The bombers arrived at the city in dense succession shortly after 1:00 A.M. Heavy aerial combats raged again on their return flight. The RAF lost 10% of the aircraft dispatched, the heaviest losses it has suffered so far. Ninety-four bombers, 13 of them Canadian, are now reported missing, and not 96 as originally announced.

Daylight Operations over Poland and Eastern Germany

Monday 10 April 1944, London
The *British Air Ministry* announced:

Yesterday the US 8th Air Force led raids against the German aircraft industry, extending its operations as far as Poland for the first time. Strong units of Flying Fortress and Liberator bombers, escorted by Thunderbolt, Lightning and Mustang long-range fighters, bombed German aircraft plants in Gdynia, Poznan and Marienburg (East Prussia).

US Bombers Make Emergency Landing in Sweden

10 April 1944, Stockholm
The Swedish newspaper *Svenska Dagbladet* reported:

Yesterday, Easter Sunday, 11 Liberators and 7 Flying Fortresses returning from northern Germany and Poland, had to make emergency landings in southern Sweden. In several cases the aircraft were forced down by Swedish fighters and antiaircraft guns; regular dogfights ensued. The American planes were undamaged with a few exceptions; one crashed into the sea. The crews have been interned.

Secret Report by the *SS Secret Service* on German internal affairs, dated Thursday 20 April 1944 (extract):

I. General comments: developments in public opinion.

The enemy's new technique of flying in low to strafe railroad trains and Germans working in the fields with his aerial guns, is causing increasing disquiet (for example in Dessau). Farmers, especially women, in areas threatened by air raids, no longer want to farm the fields ever since it became known that enemy airmen are aiming their attacks even against individuals. In the effort to keep themselves "well-informed" [about the location of incoming enemy aircraft], increasing numbers of Germans are monitoring individual flak transmitters once word has spread about the meaning of map grid references.

Air Offensive against the German Rail Traffic System

Sunday 23 April 1944, London
US 8th Air Force Headquarters announced:

Yesterday Flying Fortress and Liberator bombers carried out a heavy raid on the rail installations in Hamm. The bombers were escorted by very powerful contingents of US fighter planes. Besides Hamm, the US 8th Air Force yesterday attacked rail junctions, airfields and military installations behind the devastated Atlantic Wall [of German fortifications]. More than 250 US bombers with a fighter-plane escort, mounted a raid on unannounced targets in northern France. The antiaircraft defense was very intensive but no enemy fighter planes were seen.

The reports of our air crews during the past 24 hours, emphasize the comparative weakness of the German defense. For example, German fighter planes did not reach Munich until a good 20 minutes after the first British bombers arrived there; presumably they had to be called up from bases some distance away. The fact that the RAF nevertheless lost 30 aircraft in the course of the night, is largely attributable to the icing-up of the planes.

The Advance on New Guinea

Wednesday 26 April 1944, London
The American *United Press News Agency* reported:

General MacArthur's present New Guinea offensive is described as one of the most important operations by Americans and Australians against the Japanese positions in the southwest Pacific. The crucial factor in the operations is considered to be the massive concentration of Allied warships, aircraft carriers and aircraft on the island, which represent a major threat to the Japanese in case they try to counterattack. This "clenched-fist strategy" is thought to be the reason why the Japanese fleet has not moved against the Allies.

The London *Times* writes concerning the tactics of the Americans and Australians on New Guinea: "MacArthur's method consists in dispatching fighter-bombers as rapidly as possible to secure the landing troops."

No Losses in the Day Raid on Brunswick

Thursday 27 April 1944, London
US 8th Air Force Headquarters announced:

Yesterday, formations of Flying Fortresses and Liberators raided industrial targets in Brunswick. Not one bomber was lost, and no enemy fighters appeared at any point.

Yesterday confirmed our experience that German fighters do not take to the air when heavy clouds create bad fighting conditions.

Just one year ago it was still thought impossible for massive numbers of bombers to penetrate into the heart of Germany. Later, it was accepted that deep penetration was possible but would involve heavy casualties. Then the casualties gradually dropped due to deployment of long-range fighter escorts.

Yet until now it was still thought impossible for more than one hundred bombers to penetrate as far as Berlin without losing a single plane. The result [of the Brunswick raid] is that command of the air over western Germany now appears to be within our grasp, and has already been achieved when poor weather prevents the German fighters from taking to the air.

Air Leaflet Propaganda

Saturday 20 May 1944
RAF Headquarters announced:

For the first time, information has been released about Allied air leaflet propaganda. We have learned that since the war began, the RAF alone has dropped 1¼ billion leaflets and propaganda brochures over Germany and the occupied zones.

In London a whole series of newspapers are printed to supply information to the occupied countries. For example, Belgium receives the periodical *Courrier de l'Air* just as it did during World War I; the RAF delivers it punctually every Wednesday and Saturday. France gets the newspapers *Revue de la Presse Libre*, *Revue du Monde Libre*, and *Accord*, while the Dutch are furnished with *De Vliegende Hollander* and *De Werwelwind*. The weekly paper *Hvirvelvinden* and the monthly *Vi vil vinde* are airdropped into Denmark.

Norway, Italy, Czechoslovakia, Poland and Luxembourg also have newspapers that appear on a regular basis and that are edited exclusively by exiled journalists. Previously, only air leaflets were dropped over Germany, but recently a weekly containing writings by famous German authors has been printed and dropped there. The latest edition includes an article by Thomas Mann called "Die andere Seite" [The Other Side].

Operations against Java

20 May 1944, Melbourne
Allied South-West Pacific Headquarters reported:

British, American, Australian, French and Dutch aerial forces from the southeastern, southern and southwestern Pacific, have carried out a concentrated raid on [the Indonesian seaport of] Surabaya.

The Japanese naval base was attacked this morning shortly after dawn, by bombers operating from aircraft carriers. Direct hits caused great damage to the naval and merchant-vessel installations, the petroleum refineries and the airfields. The enemy was taken completely by surprise. Ten ships totalling approximately 35,000 tons were hit; one exploded and the others have probably sunk. Two floating docks suffered heavy damage.

The oil refineries in Nonokromo were completely destroyed. Nineteen Japanese at Malang-Tanjong and Perak airfields [Malaysia] were destroyed, 2 more were shot down and numerous aircraft were damaged. Three of our aircraft were lost.

Over 4,000 Aircraft Take Part

Sunday 21 May 1944, London
US 8th Air Force Headquarters announced:

More than 4,000 aircraft took part in yesterday's daylight operations by Allied aerial forces over France and the Netherlands. Over 1,000 US fighter planes of various types flew cover for the heavy bombers.

The RAF and other Allied aerial forces also supported these daylight raids, which continued nonstop from early morning to late evening and were aimed mainly at coastal-defense and rail installations, road junctions, transport columns, small river boats, and German Luftwaffe bases in Pas de Calais.

The air crews report good results and remarkably little activity by German fighter planes. The antiaircraft defense was also significantly weaker than usual. Antiaircraft did not operate at all during raids on a number of targets.

New Tactics in Air Raids on the German Rail and Road Traffic System

Monday 22 May 1944, London
The *British Air Ministry* announced:

Yesterday well over 2,500 aircraft carried on the Allied air offensive against Germany and the western occupied zones. The Allies used new tactics when fighters and fighter-bombers flew in low to attack the German rail and road network and inland shipping. This was the largest deployment of fighter planes in the war so far.

Wednesday 31 May 1944, Stockholm
The Swedish newspaper *Svenska Dagbladet* reported:

The German press has spoken of the Allies' intention to "carry death and destruction wherever human life stirs" and describes their "undisguised murderous terrorism which seeks its victims among the civilian population of town and countryside, and pursues the pedestrian, the traveller or the farmer in the field as well as the child on the playground." The German newspapers add that despite warnings issued by a German government spokesman, "the enemy has continued to step up his homicidal operations." Whatever the conclusions drawn by the

Inside the underground control center—the "opera house"—of one of the 5 fighter-plane divisions defending Germany. Women communications aides projected red and blue dots (= enemy bombers and German fighters respectively) onto the map to mark the positions supplied by the radar stations. The map showed the current position with a time-lag of approximately 1 minute.

German population, "they are a priori fully justified by these facts." The first serious incident which predictably has arisen [from the conduct of the Allies] has taken place in central Germany. So far German authorities have not given full details, but the report in Berlin is that near a central German village during the season of Pentecost, an American pilot who dropped by parachute has been killed by the population before the police authorities could get him to safety.

The people are said to have been stirred up by the fact that American airmen previously strafed and killed local churchgoers with their aerial guns.

In a village in the province of Brandenburg, another American pilot who bailed out by parachute is said to have been killed by the citizens. The report is that the American's fighter plane flew low and shot at farmers on their way home from work and, just outside the village, at a group of playing children; then as he was circling his plane near the village, he was surprised and brought down by a German fighter.

The inhabitants of the village seized the pilot and one of them who knew English asked him why he had fired on civilians. The pilot is said to have replied in a provocative tone, saying that after all there was a war on. The enraged citizens thereupon hurled themselves on the airman and killed him before the police arrived.

US Airbases in the Soviet Union

Saturday 3 June 1944, Moscow
The *US Strategic Air Command, Eastern Zone*

Powerful contingents of US heavy bombers escorted by fighters, have raided targets in Rumania that were selected by our Soviet allies, and then flew on to Soviet bases. The enemy put up a weak air defense; we lost one bomber and one fighter. The Red Air Force supported our operations by raiding an enemy airfield along the route followed by the US bombers, and gave them fighter-plane cover.

The commander of the newly-created US air force headquarters in Moscow, described the landing of American bombers in the Soviet Union as a significant development in the air war against Germany.

Heavy Raids on the Atlantic Wall

Monday 5 June 1944, London
RAF Headquarters announced:

Last night RAF bomber wings raided military targets along the French coast and in Cologne. Shortly after they returned to base, approximately 750 US four-engined bombers with fighter-plane cover, took off early this morning to raid German Wehrmacht installations between Boulogne and Calais. At noon, twin-engined US Marauder bombers escorted by Mustang fighters, likewise raided military targets in northern France. Thunderbolt fighter-bombers made low-level attacks in which they were able to silence the German antiaircraft batteries while meantime the Marauders went on to attack the main targets. Rocket-armed Typhoon fighter-bombers flew successful operations against radio stations near the northern French coast.

Raid on Tito's Headquarters

5 June 1944, Berlin
The *German News Bureau* reported:

In Croatia [= Yugoslavia] an operation against Tito's partisan bands has been carried out successfully. The operation was successful chiefly in its destruction of powerful partisan units, whose effective strength has now been greatly reduced. Most of Tito's personal guard also fell in the surprise German airborne raid.

The Invasion

Tuesday 6 June 1944, London
The *British Air Ministry* announced:

Under the command of General Eisenhower, Allied naval units supported by powerful aerial forces have begun the landing of Allied troops on the coast of France. Heavy air raids preceded the landing.

6 June 1944, Berlin
The *German News Bureau* reported:

We have already captured our first British and American prisoners from the invasion that began in the early morning hours of June 6. They belong to the enemy airborne troops who parachuted down west of the Orne river, and include British from the Caen area and Americans from Cherbourg. To simulate airborne landings east of the Orne, between Yvetot and Le Havre, the enemy dropped life-sized dolls dressed in uniforms which contained explosives and blew up when they were touched.

A US Chance Vought F4U Corsair on a central Pacific island airbase shortly before takeoff. This fighter-bomber, dreaded by the Japanese who called it Whistling Death, did not become operational until 1943. A total of 12,681 were built.

6 June 1944, London
The American *United Press News Agency* reported:

Allied pilots of the fighter-bombers which flew over the invasion zone in late morning, report that they met no resistance in the air; not one German aircraft was seen.

Wednesday 7 June 1944, London
The *British Air Ministry* announced:

Despite the increasing activity by the German Luftwaffe along the coast of France, the Allies continue to command the air space across the entire zone of operations. The ratio of Allied to German aircraft today continued to be approximately 200:1. Although operations were hindered by unfavorable weather, masses of heavy bombers were deployed in the tactical support of Allied ground forces. Medium and light bombers and fighter-bombers also raided German troop concentrations and rail lines and kept up pressure on the enemy. What is particularly important, is that German troops are unable to carry out any large-scale movement without being discovered and attacked by Allied aerial forces.

Portable Takeoff Runways

Wednesday 14 June 1944
The *Reuters News Agency* reported from an advanced RAF airfield in France:

The surprisingly rapid deployment of Allied fighter-bombers in Normandy, is due to portable takeoff runways which have been laid down in the invasion zone. They consist of welded steel plates about 70 feet long and 7 feet wide, which are laid out in a carpet and attached with clamps. Normally a takeoff runway is 3,000 feet long, 150 feet wide and can be completed in 15 hours.

Are American "Superbombers" Raiding Tokyo?

Friday 16 June 1944, Washington
The *US War Department* announced:

The first wings of new US B-29 Superfortress bombers have taken off from bases in India, Burma and China, and have flown a massive raid on an "important target in Japan" from an altitude of 30,000 feet.

German "Secret Weapon" Attacks England

16 June 1944, Berlin
The *German News Bureau* reported:

German Deputy Press Chief Sündermann states that last night a German secret weapon was deployed against England; this marks the beginning of German retaliation.

Sündermann told representatives of the foreign press that the British and Americans may never have believed in the German retaliation, but now they are going to learn that crimes against German civilians and cultural monuments will not go unpunished. Last night London and southeastern England were attacked by the new weapon. It is a completely new, highly effective anti-invasion weapon with an operational strength equivalent to that of a powerful air force.

16 June 1944, London
Herbert Morrison, the British Secretary of State for the Home Department, told the House of Commons:

On Tuesday morning, last night and this morning, the German Luftwaffe dispatched a number of pilotless aircraft against us. In the first raid they caused several deaths, but the attack was inconsiderable. Emphatic countermeasures have been taken.

16 June 1944, Dover

The *Reuters News Agency* reported:

Last night southern England experienced the most extended air raid alert in its history. The entire English Channel coast appeared to be on fire as thousands of British guns of every type laid down a curtain of fire in the path of the approaching German "secret weapons." Vast numbers of searchlights lit up the sky as bright as day. Residents near the coast say unanimously that last night our antiaircraft opposed the enemy with the heaviest and most concentrated fire since the war began.

Observations and Technical Details of the Secret Weapon

16 June 1944, London
The *British Air Ministry* announced:

The first eyewitness reports about the German "secret weapon" have arrived in London. One person compared their incoming flight with a long trail of comets that fell on dozens of targets immediately after reaching southern England. The ensuing explosions resembled huge fires. Eyewitnesses claim that they must have seen either bomber rockets or guided aircraft filled with high explosives, which exploded a few seconds after touching the ground.

The mysterious missiles are said to have flown at unprecedented speeds. Frequently they raced along in groups of two or three, with some flying at an altitude of approximately 3,000 feet, while others flew just above the houses. One witness reported that a number of small towns were simultaneously fired on by machine guns.

RAF fighters took up pursuit of the mysterious aircraft. Flying low, they darted through the ground fire to explode the projectiles before these could fall. Apparently they hit many of the "secret weapons," because numerous reports speak of violent explosions high in the air. An analysis of eyewitness reports received so far, indicates that: 1) The "missiles" travel at extremely high speed. 2) They emit a trail of sparks apparently stemming from exhaust gases. 3) All the missiles follow an amazingly straight flight line.

16 June 1944, London
The British *Home Department* published the following warning:

When the engines of the pilotless aircraft stop sounding and the exhaust flame goes out, this means that the aircraft will explode within 5 to 15 seconds. It is absolutely essential to seek shelter at the approach of the aircraft, particularly because of the dangerous blast wave given off by the explosion.

How to Guard against Low-Altitude Attack Planes

The following article appeared in the German weekly newspaper *Das Reich* in June 1944:

Low-flying US planes appear unexpectedly and are rarely detectible on the horizon. They dip down into valleys, hop over ridges and telegraph wires, exploit every fold in the landscape, and in the city use buildings to screen themselves from the deadly cones of fire sent out by German light antiaircraft batteries. Suddenly there they are; it takes them only fractions of a second to zoom in on moving targets, and then they disappear again. Their success lies wholly in the element of surprise.

So far, low-flying aircraft have appeared in pack and flight strength, in other words never more than 6 aircraft together at one time. They have been single- and twin-engined fighter planes with a velocity of about 360 miles per hour. All the warring powers are building their aircraft to the same aerodynamic specifications, so it is difficult for the layman to tell the difference between enemy fighter planes and German ones.

Two of the aircraft models most frequently used in these long-range fighter-plane sweeps, resemble German Messerschmitt 109 and Focke-Wulf 190 aircraft. The third enemy fighter type that often appears over Germany, is easier to recognize: It has twin engines along the front of twin fuselages, and twin tails.

The aerial guns of all three aircraft types, are rigidly mounted and can fire only in the direction of flight. Thus the whole aircraft must point at the target. The machine guns and aerial cannon have considerable fire-power, but they can emit only a few bursts of fire lasting several seconds; they cannot fire continuously because then the guns would get too hot, triggering automatic controls. The cones of fire released from the two wings—or from the nose in the case of twin-fuselage aircraft—travel at a flat angle. Many projectiles miss the aimed-for target and spray out in a fan. The projectiles have a caliber of 1 to 2 cm. Their penetrating power is not very great. Ordinary stone walls afford adequate protection; but people in the city and country have many other ways to protect themselves.

The approach of low-flying enemy aircraft is reported along the broadcast wires, and immediately a public air alert is sounded. Women, children, old people and persons in frail health should then take shelter exactly as they would in a bombing raid. People working in closed buildings must leave the upper storeys, avoid windows and seek shelter behind the walls of buildings. If you have sufficient prior warning, you should evacuate the street.

If you find yourself on a streetcar or inside a moving vehicle when you hear the rat-a-tat of light antiaircraft or the sound of airplane engines, you should not all panic and run in one direction but should "fan out" (as soldiers say) and head for a number of different building entrances. Don't go on standing there, but either go into the cellar or run to get behind solid walls, and avoid windows. Anyone who is surprised by a strafing attack while he is in a large open area or on a broad highway, would do well to lie down at once.

In Luckenwalde and other towns, women have been killed while crossing the market square. Thus, women should immediately stop making purchases if caught in market areas or waiting outside shops. Strafing planes scatter their fire over groups of people. Strollers and excursionists have been hit and killed on a number of occasions. For this reason it is recommended that you select paths that could provide cover in an emergency, e.g. forest paths. If you lie down in the shadows of trees and bushes, they provide good camouflage from aircraft. Naturally, ditches, earthworks and especially hillslopes make a preferred form of cover, but only if they lie between the pedestrian and the approaching aircraft.

People engaging in water sports should stay close to shores that afford cover, and avoid gathering in groups.

The same considerations should guide the rural population. Before going to work in the open fields, they should dress in a way that enables them to blend in with their surroundings. It is not useful to wear a red kerchief over your head in a field of clover.

German trains are continuing to run. If they were to stop, hold-ups would occur in our traffic network that we cannot afford. If you are forced to travel by business that cannot be postponed, think about places you can take shelter along the way. If a train is attacked en route, you should try to lie down on the floor or move to the side of the compartment away from the approaching aircraft. If the train stops in the station or out on the open tracks, then fan out in all directions. If you cannot get away from the train in time, lie down beside the rail embankment; never mind if your clothes get dirty.

Once you have left the train, do not on any account do what people did in the most recent raids on passenger trains, which was to stand around in groups and wait for the enemy before running and looking for cover. Motionless and well-camouflaged targets hold no attractions for a swift-flying strafer plane, and are hard to detect, whereas people running to escape are a favorite target.

As always, courageous men and women must convince the indecisive, and if necessary must take forceful measures to get careless people to see reason, because the latter can endanger everyone concerned. Once the first attack has passed, remain in a prone position for some time. Strafing aircraft have been known to turn around at 30-second intervals and fly in for another attack.

Inland sailors are not without protection. They can shelter from aerial sharpshooters inside the boat under iron plates or thick planks.

So let's start looking at our immediate environment and our daily travel routes with the eyes of a front-line soldier. Look for possible cover everywhere you go. If you have thought the matter through and trained your eye to look at the landscape, you will act appropriately in case of an emergency.

Air Battle in the Pacific

Tuesday 20 June 1944, Pearl Harbor
The *Headquarters of the US Pacific Air Force* announced:

In a great aerial battle on Sunday, US aircraft destroyed over 300 Japanese planes near the island of Saipan in the Marianas. The Japanese air force tried to mount a massive bombing raid on the US naval fleet off Saipan, but its operation broke down under heavy losses. Only one American ship was slightly damaged.

It is thought that some of the Japanese planes took off from aircraft carriers, and some from nearby island bases. US aerial forces had previously destroyed the most important Japanese airfields on Guam and Rota islands, so it is assumed that many of the Japanese planes must have been based on aircraft carriers. So far no details are known about US aircraft losses.

US infantry landed on Saipan and stormed Aslito airfield at the southern tip of the island, so we have now won our first airbase in the Marianas.

21 American Aircraft in Sweden

20 June 1944, Stockholm
Swedish Army Headquarters announced:

Today 21 American bombers landed or crashed in southern Sweden. Sixteen Liberator bombers landed at close intervals on one airfield near Malmö.

Wednesday 21 June 1944
General Eisenhower's Headquarters announced:

Our troops have seized several launch ramps on the Cotentin Peninsula (northern France) from which the Germans fired off their flying bombs at southern England. Our specialists are now conducting a thorough investigation of the facilities.

21 June 1944, Stockholm
Swedish Army Headquarters announced:

RAF fighter squadrons have reported shooting down more German flying bombs. Since Tuesday the Allies have made a number of successful raids on the flying-bomb launch ramps in northern France. We can now reveal that selected Allied pilots have been practicing aimed bombing on camouflaged mockups of the launch ramps, in preparation for attacks on the German secret-weapon sites.

22 June 1944, London
US 8th Air Force Headquarters announced:

Yesterday morning a contingent of over 1,000 four-engined bombers of the US 8th Army Air Force, escorted by almost 1,000 long-range fighters, led the heaviest raid so far against the German capital and its suburbs. They encountered strong antiaircraft fire over Berlin and its outlying districts. Several bomber groups were attacked by large

Right: The morning of 6 June 1944. A B-26 Marauder of the US 9th Air Force flying over Omaha Beach at Vierville during the Normandy invasion. The beach is covered with landing boats of the American Fifth Corps under General Gerow.

Opposite page below: Amiens (France) on 5 June 1944. By this time almost all the rail installations between Cherbourg and Pas de Calais looked like this rail junction [bombed out by the Allies preceding the invasion].

German fighter-plane contingents, which engaged in aerial combat with the American escort fighters. The latest figures indicate that 21 German aircraft were shot down. Another 16 to 20 German planes were destroyed by American bombers.

22 June 1944, Moscow
The American *United Press News Agency* reported:

The US Air Force Command in the Eastern Zone has announced that on Wednesday, bombers and long-range fighters of the US 8th Air Force took off from Britain and landed at US bases in the Soviet Union. This marks the beginning of US "shuttle bombing" of Germany, in which US planes will fly back and forth between bases in Britain and the Soviet Union.

22 June 1944
The *Wehrmacht High Command* announced:

Last night a powerful unit of heavy German bombers led a concentrated raid on the Russian airfield of Poltava. Thirty enemy aircraft were destroyed on the ground. Large area fires spread through the airfield and fuel sheds.

More US Bombers Land in Sweden

22 June 1944, Stockholm
Swedish Army Headquarters announced:

Yesterday 13 more US Flying Fortresses landed in Sweden due to lack of fuel, or damage to the planes. One bomber was pursued by a German fighter plane right over Swedish territory and forced to make an emergency landing. The German aircraft managed to evade our antiaircraft fire.

German Raids on Britain

22 June 1944, Berlin
The *German News Bureau* reported:

In *Das Reich* [weekly German newspaper], Dr. Goebbels expressed his views about the new German weapon: "Probably this time our enemies will take our predictions more seriously when we say that the present initial stage of our retaliation, is only a prelude to the main event. We will bring new, even more powerful weapons to bear, and once again will do so at what seems to us the most suitable moment."

Daily Keynote from the Reich Press Chief,
dated Saturday 24 June 1944:

The new German weapon has been designated the "V-1." The "V" is an abbreviation of *Vergeltung* [= retaliation], whereas the number 1 means that the present weapon is only the first in a series of retaliatory weapons. The German Press must offer a brief but by no means sensational explanation of the term, the first time that it is used in a report.

US Air Force Operates on the Eastern Front

Wednesday 28 June 1944
Allied Headquarters in Italy announced:

Today Flying Fortresses of the US 8th Air Force took off from bases in the Soviet Union to bomb the southern Polish refinery at Drogobych around 4 miles south of Lvov. Then the B-17s flew on to land in Italy. Not one bomber was lost in this operation.

28 June 1944, Moscow
The American *United Press News Agency* reported:

Yesterday US fighter squadrons took off from Soviet bases for the first time to intervene directly in combat operations along the Eastern Front. Lightning and Mustang formations operated over Lvov and then flew along rail lines toward Krakow, causing two military transport trains to derail and destroying the rail bridge outside Krakow. They succeeded in shooting down 38 German planes in violent dogfights. All the US aircraft returned to their Soviet bases. As a result, Americans now have control of the air space over the triangular zone of Lublin-Krakow-Lvov.

Strategy and Tactics

January to June 1944

The bad weather front over Europe in the first week of January 1944, gave the beleaguered citizens of German cities a brief respite from bombing raids. Nazi security forces, on the other hand, experienced an unexpected increase in their work load at the turn of the year, in an area only marginally related to the air war: They had to investigate the masses of forged food-ration coupons which were being dropped into Germany by the RAF.

These flawlessly-forged ration coupons, which the British produced in various issues, worked particular havoc in the German administration and supply system, as well as putting an additional burden on the police. The color, perforation, paper quality and watermarks of the forged documents were so close to the real thing that the Germans needed special instruments to tell them apart, and a substantial number of ration coupons picked up by the German population, were in fact used to obtain food.

This operation was the result of a collaboration between Sefton Delmer, the British psychological warfare expert, and the Special Operations Executive, who passed on the handiwork to Bomber Command for distribution.

Armin Hull, one of Britain's leading specialists in German typography and printing techniques, was in charge of the SOE's counterfeiting workshop. Sefton Delmer later described how, the moment Hull was informed that the SOE's agents were sending him a shipment of the latest German ration coupons, he would notify his printers and paper manufacturers, and they had to gather at once in his office waiting for the shipment to arrive. If it turned out that the Germans had changed the coupon design and the watermarks, Hull's paper-makers would prepare new sheets of paper while the printers were already readying their offset plates. Work proceeded at an incredible pace. Hull's team became so skilled that only a few days after the German food agencies distributed the original coupons, the RAF was already dropping the counterfeits over Germany.

Despite many special measures and threats of draconian punishment for all those who used forged coupons, the Germans found no really effective way to combat the forgeries, so Dr. Goebbels took charge. He observed that the German printers and paper-manufacturers could not defeat their adversaries by continually altering the ration coupons, so instead he promoted a propaganda campaign claiming that the RAF forgeries were "easily detectible" and would "assuredly bring anyone who used them into the death cell." To support his claims, he had several crude forgeries made up. These were then presented at Party assemblies as evidence of the coarse and shoddy British work-

Left: A German Fi 103 ("V-1") "flying bomb" taking off. It weighed 1.5 tons (1,870 lbs of explosive and 136 gallons of fuel), reached a speed of approximately 390 miles an hour, and took 280 man-hours to build.

Opposite page above: The official Nazi newspaper announces successful flying-bomb raids on England. The bomb was nameless at first; the German armed forces referred to it simply as an "explosive device." Then on 24 June 1944, Dr. Goebbels christened it the "V-1", an abbreviation of *Vergeltungswaffe 1*, "retaliatory weapon no. 1."

Norddeutsche Ausgabe „Freiheit und Brot" **Norddeutsche Ausgabe**

169. Ausgabe / 57. Jahrg. / Einzelpreis 20 Pf. Berlin, Sonnabend, 17. Juni 1944

VÖLKISCHER BEOBACHTER

Kampfblatt der nationalsozialistischen Bewegung Großdeutschlands

Mit neuen Sprengkörpern größten Kalibers

Gegen London und Südengland

Erfolgreiche Gegenangriffe in der Normandie – Weitere Bekämpfung feindlicher Ausladungen

Aus dem Führerhauptquartier, 16. Juni.

Das Oberkommando der Wehrmacht gibt bekannt:

Südengland und das Stadtgebiet von London wurden in der vergangenen Nacht und heute vormittag mit neuartigen Sprengkörpern schwersten Kalibers belegt.

Der vergangene Tag stand in der Normandie im Zeichen erfolgreicher Gegenangriffe unserer Truppen.

Panzerverbände trieben östlich der Orne einen Keil in den feindlichen Brückenkopf. Westlich Caumont sowie südöstlich und südwestlich Carentan warfen unsere Divisionen den Feind zurück und festigten ihre Stellungen. Die feindlichen Verluste waren besonders bei den Kämpfen im Raum von Carentan hoch.

Auch im Raum westlich und nördlich Ste. Mère-Eglise hielten heftige Kämpfe an. Der Feind konnte dort nur geringen Geländegewinn erzielen.

Die Bekämpfung der feindlichen Ausladungen vor dem Landekopf wurde auch in der letzten Nacht durch unsere Luftwaffe erfolgreich fortgesetzt. Sie erzielte Bombentreffer in Schiffsansammlungen und Ausladungen.

Die im Kampfraum der Invasionsfront eingesetzten Bataillone der Freiwilligenverbände des Ostens haben sich bei den schweren Kämpfen voll bewährt und tapfer geschlagen.

Vorposten- und Minensuchverbände haben sich bei der Bekämpfung der Invasionsflotte in zahlreichen harten See- und Luftgefechten sowie bei der unter schwierigen Bedingungen durchgeführten Räumung feindlicher Minensperren und der Verminung feindlicher Schiffahrtswege besonders bewährt.

Bei einem Angriff britischer Bomben- und Torpedoflugzeuge auf ein deutsches Geleit vor Borkum wurden zehn feindliche Flugzeuge durch Sicherungsfahrzeuge und Bordflak zum Absturz gebracht. Ein eigenes Fahrzeug ging verloren.

Vor der niederländischen Küste versenkten Vorpostenboote ein großes britisches Schnellboot und beschädigten ein weiteres schwer.

In Mittelitalien setzte der Feind seine Angriffe mit massierten Infanterie- und Panzerkräften vor allem im Raum nördlich und nordöstlich von Orvieto während des ganzen Tages fort. Die Kämpfe dauern in zwei Einbruchsstellen noch an.

Feindliche Flugzeuge griffen am 15. Juni vor der westfälischen Küste erneut das deutsche Lazarettschiff „Erlangen" an und warfen es in Brand.

An der Ostfront fanden auch gestern keine wesentlichen Kampfhandlungen statt.

Im hohen Norden scheiterten im Kandalakscha-Abschnitt erneut Vorstöße der Sowjets verlustreich für den Feind.

Im Finnischen Meerbusen beschädigten Sicherungsfahrzeuge der Kriegsmarine ein erfolglos angreifendes sowjetisches Schnellboot. Wachfahrzeuge schossen über der Narwabucht neun feindliche Flugzeuge ab.

Vor der Fischerhalbinsel griffen sowjetische Bombenflugzeuge und Schnellboote ein deutsches Geleit erfolglos an. Auch feindliche Küstenbatterien griffen in das Gefecht ein. Ein feindliches Schnellboot wurde dabei schwer beschädigt, zehn feindliche Flugzeuge durch unsere Jäger vernichtet.

Ein schwächerer nordamerikanischer Bomberverband flog gestern in Nordwestdeutschland ein und warf zerstreut Bomben im Raum von Hannover.

Angriffe einzelner britischer Flugzeuge richteten sich in der vergangenen Nacht gegen das rheinisch-westfälische Gebiet.

Deutsche Flugzeuge griffen wiederum Ziele in Südostengland an.

Mit wenigen Worten nur spricht der heutige Bericht des Oberkommandos der Wehrmacht einen Tatbestand an, der das ganze deutsche Volk mit grimmiger Genugtuung erfüllt: Groß-London ist mit schwersten Sprengkörpern aus neuartigen Waffen bombardiert worden. Ein erbarmungsloser Feind hat durch infernalische Terrorangriffe, durch Flächenwurf mit Minen und Phosphorkanistern auf Frauen und Kinder, auf Krankenhäuser und Wohnviertel einen lodernden Haß entzündet.

Er erhält nun die Antwort, die er allein versteht!

Der Stabschef der SA.

Zum 50. Geburtstag Wilhelm Schepmanns

manship "which could not deceive any intelligent German." At the same time he filled the newspapers with reports of the punishment of those "social parasites" who had been caught trying to pass off the RAF coupons as the real thing.

At the end of 1943, preparations were made for a change in the leadership of the US 8th Army Air Force; this became effective on New Year's Day 1944. Lieutenant General Ira C. Eaker, who had commanded the 8th USAAF for over a year, was transferred to Italy to take over chief command of the Allied aerial forces in the Mediterranean. The 8th USAAF was now taken over by Lt. General James H. Doolittle, who had already made a name for himself in the Pacific war.

That same day the Americans set up the United States Strategic Air Forces headquarters in Britain (The USSTAF). Its commanding general was Lt. General Carl Spaatz. USSTAF headquarters included the 8th Air Force and the 15th Air Force, which had been set up in Italy. Meanwhile the US 9th Air Force in Britain, whose targets were all tactical, was assigned separately to Major General Lewis H. Brereton, with his headquarters in Sunning Hill Park, Ascot.

At the beginning of 1944, the German night fighters had the situation more or less under control. Factors contributing to their success were the new Lichtenstein SN-2 airborne radar equipment, which was immune to British Window jamming; the air crews' mastery of new night-fighter tactics; and the new *Schräge Musik* slanted guns. The fighter divisions had their own illuminator squadrons to light up the night-fighter zones.

British Bomber Command realized that the German Luftwaffe had neutralized Window by the end of 1943, and the RAF responded promptly by setting up a special unit, No. 100 Bomber Support Group, under Air Commander E. B. Addison. Its task was to fly in advance of the bomber stream jamming all the German radio traffic and the German night fighters' airborne radar, thus supplementing the activity of British jamming transmitters along the southern and eastern coasts of England.

No. 100 Bomber Support Group was stationed in Bylaugh Hall (Norfolk) and was equipped with American Flying Fortress bombers. The B-17 F and B-17 G Flying Fortresses were painted black [for night camouflage] and had welded-on exhaust pots to screen the exhaust flames that would betray their presence. Radome bubbles were attached under the nose to house and protect the H2S scanners, and a variety of jamming devices were built into the bomb bays.

Each Flying Fortress was equipped with 8 Mandrel jamming transmitters to combat the German early warning radar; each transmitter worked on a different frequency so that together they covered the entire spectrum used by the German radars—Freya, Mammut, Wassermann and Jagdschloss. In addition, all the Flying Fortresses of No. 100 Group carried ABC equipment—Airborne Cigar—with 3 transmitters to overlay the frequencies used by the German fighter controllers. Two highly-trained crew members were assigned to each aircraft to operate the jamming devices.

In the first days of January, the German 4th Air Force (IV. Fliegerkorps under Lt. Gen. Meister) deployed 3 reinforced bomber wings (KG 3, 4 and 5) totalling some 400 machines, and tried to hold up a Soviet offensive on the First Ukrainian Front. Soviet forces under Marshal Vatutin had launched the Front west of Kiev on Christmas Eve 1943. The Germans hoped that massive air raids on Soviet rail stations—which were the Soviets' strategic nerve centers—would weaken the forward thrust of the offensive.

The Soviet fighter plane defenses had by now become much more powerful, and forced German bomber units to limit their raids to strategic night attacks at the rear of the battlezone.

Most of the German operations were nuisance sorties flown by single aircraft which would change their tactics every night. To avoid the Soviet anti-aircraft guns, they would fly over the front lines at an altitude close to 10,000 feet, then choke their engines and continually shift their heading as they dropped down to a low altitude over enemy territory.

The Soviets responded cleverly when they detected large units of German bombers approaching rail targets. They would swiftly transfer their rolling stock to smaller distributing stations and alternative rails, so that even as the German marker flares were drifting downward over the target, the trains were already streaking out of the stations.

The Soviet night fighters were controlled without radar assistance, and so had difficulty locating their targets during German raids. Only the German pathfinder aircraft were exposed to serious attack, whereas the bomber formation in their wake usually went undetected.

Starting on Friday 7 January 1944, the Allied air forces renewed their attacks on the 96 German fly-

Right: Two British Hawker Typhoon fighter planes are looking for a fresh target. Typhoons were among the best low-altitude attack planes of the war. Armed with 4 20-mm guns and 8 rocket projectiles, they flew successful missions against tanks and fortified positions.

Below: 19 June 1944. The largest air battle of World War II, and the one in which the most aircraft were lost, was the "Great Marianas Turkey Shoot," in which the Americans downed 480 Japanese planes. Here a light Mitsubishi bomber crashes in flames right next to a US carrier.

ing-bomb launch ramps in northern France, which they had located with the aid of reconnaissance photos. One quarter of the ramps were damaged; but at the same time the Luftwaffe put almost 10,000 laborers to work and built 50 more simplified, prefabricated launch ramps without being detected by the Allies. The Germans planned to launch their flying-bomb raids from the new ramps.

On January 7 the German air defense at last succeeded in shooting down a Mosquito aircraft near Cleves that carried an Oboe navigational device; the British equipment fell undamaged into German hands. Within 72 hours the Germans had worked out plans for a network of approximately 80 jamming transmitters. As a result, only one week later the precision of Oboe-led bombing operations fell off by one third.

On Tuesday 11 January, 663 four-engined bombers of the US 8th Air Force, escorted by several squadrons of P-51 Mustang long-range fighter planes, carried out raids on aircraft factories in Halberstadt, Brunswick, Magdeburg and Oschersleben. The bad weather hindered the operations of the Mustangs, and as a result the German fighters—some firing Wgr-21 rocket-missiles—were able to shoot down 60 bombers and 5 Mustangs, for 40 German losses.

While the German Luftwaffe leaders were demanding a step-up in fighter-plane production and a shift to defensive armament, Hitler ordered an increase in production of the new Ju 188 and He 177 bombers, in preparation for planned retaliatory raids.

General Peltz of the German IX. Fliegerkorps had been newly appointed to lead offensive raids on Britain, and assembled three reinforced bomber wings in northern France. They totalled 524 aircraft and included Me 410 rapid bombers, and 46 Heinkel He 177 Greif (Griffin) bombers which were forced into battle in an undeveloped state.

Hitler personally had ordered a retaliatory strike against Britain. Codenamed Operation Steinbock (Ibex), it was commanded by Göring and opened with a "grand" raid on London and southern England on the night of 21–22 January 1944. Two hundred and seventy German aircraft took off. The plan was that they would attack in two waves using British bomber stream tactics; but only 95 reached their targets, where they dropped 268 tons of bombs. Sixteen of the aircraft were knocked out. So began a series of nuisance raids on London and southeastern England that would continue until 29-30

May 1944.

Of the German units armed with heavy He 177s, one was 1st Group, 100th Bomber Wing stationed in Rheine west of Osnabrück. A number of the bombers were equipped with two 4,000-lb bombs and two 2,200-lb bombs. The formation assembled over Holland at midnight and crossed the North Sea at an altitude of approximately 26,000 feet, guided by the radio beacon in Noordwijk near The Hague.

Around 25 miles from the English coast, the German radio operators began dropping loose bundles of radar-jamming strips at two-minute intervals. The unit reached Britain north of Orfordness (Suffolk) and headed inland to Newmarket, where German pathfinders had dropped marker flares east of the city. At this turning-point the formation wheeled and flew a beeline south toward London.

The German bombers were equipped with FuG 217 (Neptun) airborne radar, which resembled the British "Monica" warning equipment and signalled the approach of British night fighters. The bombers descended over the City and docks of London, continually shifting their course. Meanwhile the radio operators were dropping large bundles of *Düppel* radar chaff – one every five seconds – to hinder the British radar-guided antiaircraft and seachlight batteries from picking up their targets. After dropping their bombs, the German aircraft continued to maintain low altitude and crossed the Channel at about 2,000 feet. Reaching Boulogne, they flew over Arnhem to their home-base at Rheine.

On the night of 20–21 January 1944, 697 RAF bombers raided Berlin and Kiel, releasing 2,300 tons of bombs and losing 35 bombers.

On the following night, Magdeburg (eastern Germany) suffered its first heavy raid. Five hundred and eighty-five Bomber Command aircraft unloaded 2,025 tons of blast and incendiary bombs; 55 bombers were shot down.

Saturday 22 January 1944 marked the beginning of Operation Shingle, when the 6th Corps of the US Fifth Army under Lt. General Mark Clark, landed near Anzio and Nettuno south of Rome with 9 transporter ships, 226 landing vehicles, 1 oiler and 4 hospital ships.

The heavy He 177 bombers of German 2nd Group, 40th Bomber Wing, and the Do 217s of the 100th Bomber Wing, tried to prevent the Allied landing by deploying FX 1400 and Hs 293 guided bombs.

The US destroyers *Woolsey*, *Frederick C. Davis* and *Herbert C. Jones* used strong JIG jamming transmitters to neutralize the remote control of the guided bombs, and as a result many of the bombs failed to reach their target. Next day, 23 January 1944, the British destroyer *Jervis* became the first vessel at Anzio to be hit by an Hs 293 guided bomb. Despite heavy damage she succeeded in reaching Naples under her own steam.

On the night of 27–28 January, 481 RAF bombers made a run on Berlin. The weather was so bad that people in the German capital did not expect a grand raid; but it came, even though the turbulent conditions caused some Lancasters to collide over the target and crash. A total of 1,761 tons of blast and incendiary bombs were unleashed; 33 bombers were lost.

On Saturday 29 January 1944, German 2nd Group, 100th Bomber Wing, raided the British antiaircraft carrier *Spartan* at Anzio, where it anchored near the coast to fire on enemy aircraft; the 7,181-ton freighter *Samuel Huntington* was also attacked. At 7:05 P.M. an Hs 293 hit the *Spartan*, which shortly thereafter capsized and sank. Almost at the same time an Hs 293 set the *Samuel Huntington* on fire. At around 3:00 A.M. the freighter blew up when the flames reached the munitions and fuel cargo.

Meanwhile units of the IX. Fliegerkorps commanded by Maj. Gen. Peltz, pursued Operation Steinbock, the German "retaliatory strikes" against London and southern England. Throughout the day, small numbers of FW 190 fighter-bombers and Me 110, 210 and 410 rapid bombers would turn up over cities near the English coast. At night He 177 and Do 217 heavy bombers, harried by squadrons of British night fighters, would drop their loads usually quite aimlessly. Compared to the Allied operations, these had the effect of mere pinpricks.

The last January grand raid of Operation Steinbock, was flown by 60 bombers of the IX. Fliegerkorps on the night of 29-30 January against London and south England; 6 bombers were lost.

The Nazi propagandists displayed mastery in upholding the morale of Germans most affected by the bombing war, feeding them nebulous announcements about retaliatory weapons and exaggerating the strength and effectiveness of the German Operation Steinbock raids.

On Tuesday 8 February 1944 at the Supreme Headquarters of the Allied Expeditionary Force

(SHAEF), final plans were laid for Operation Overlord, the Allied invasion of Normandy. The most important operation of the "Overlord Outline Plan" was the establishment of a bridgehead between the Vire and Orne rivers.

On the night of 11–12 February 1944, 15 heavy Soviet bombers tried to sink the German battleship *Tirpitz* with 2,200-lb bombs while it lay in the Alta-Fjord of northern Norway. Only 4 of the aircraft found their target; they scored a near-hit that inflicted only minor damage.

On Saturday 12 February 1944, General Dwight David Eisenhower was appointed supreme commander of the Allied invasion forces. His deputy was British Air Chief Marshal Arthur Tedder; his chief of staff was US General Walter Bedell Smith. The army landing troops would be commanded by General Montgomery, the naval forces by British Admiral Bertram Ramsay, the tactical air force by British Air Marshal Sir Trafford Leigh-Mallory. General Carl Spaatz would continue to command the Allied strategic bomber fleets.

On Sunday 13 February 1944, the bombers of the US 14th Army Air Force (under Maj. Gen. Chennault) raided an important Japanese airbase at Hong Kong.

In London that same day, a new list of top-priority targets was drawn up for the operations of the British-US "Combined Bomber Offensive." German aircraft and ball-bearing manufacturers were declared the number-one targets of Allied strategic air attacks. The second priority were the secret-weapon launch ramps. Third came Berlin and other enemy industrial zones.

On the night of 15–16 February 1944, 806 RAF bombers dropped 2,643 tons of blast and incendiary bombs on the German capital within a 40-minute period, which was the largest load dropped during the Battle of Berlin. The Charlottenburg and Siemensstadt districts were the hardest hit. Forty-three bombers were lost in the operation.

When, on the following day, the British press published optimistic reports about the raid on Berlin, Goebbels made no attempt to contradict, for he wanted to keep Bomber Command believing that Berlin has been so badly damaged that it was no longer a worthwhile target.

On Wednesday 16 February 1944, the German Luftwaffe scored its last success with guided bombs, in a raid at Anzio. The 2nd Group, 100th Bomber Wing sank the US freighter *Elihu Hale* (7,167 tons) and the landing boat LCT-35, which was lying alongside her to receive a transfer of munitions.

On Friday 18 February 1944, Canadian and Australian RAF Mosquitos carried out one of their famous special pinpoint missions in cooperation with the Special Operations Executive. Their aim was to liberate some 700 members of the French Resistance held captive in the prison complex at Amiens in northern France, who were all facing a death sentence.

Nineteen air crews led by Group Captain P. G. Pickard were trained for this special mission, codenamed "Jerycho." They practiced on a realistic mockup of the prison that resembled the target viewed from an altitude of 1,600 feet at a distance of 4 miles.

The Mosquito VI rapid bombers planned to fly in low and place their bombs squarely in the center of the cross-shaped prison building, and were also supposed to collapse part of the prison wall. The guards, surprised by the raid, would seek shelter, and the prisoners, who would have been informed of what was to happen by the SOE, would take advantage of the confusion to make their escape.

At 11:00 A.M. the 3 waves attacked the building complex. In the turmoil 285 prisoners broke out,

500 g Weizenmehl Führergeschenk	500 g Weizenmehl Führergeschenk	500 g Weizenmehl Führergeschenk	500 g Weizenmehl Führergeschenk	500 g Weizenmehl Führergeschenk
500 g Weizenmehl Führergeschenk	Lebensmittelkarte			500 g Marmelade Führergeschenk
500 g Weizenmehl Führergeschenk	4 848758 *			500 g Marmelade Führergeschenk
500 g Weizenmehl Führergeschenk	FÜHRERGESCHENK für Fronturlauber			500 g Marmelade Führergeschenk
500 g Weizenmehl Führergeschenk	500 g Zucker Führergeschenk		500 g Nährmittel oder Hülsenfrüchte Führergeschenk	500 g Nährmittel oder Hülsenfrüchte Führergeschenk
500 g Weizenmehl Führergeschenk	500 g Zucker Führergeschenk	500 g Butter oder Margarine Führergeschenk	500 g Nährmittel oder Hülsenfrüchte Führergeschenk	500 g Nährmittel oder Hülsenfrüchte Führergeschenk

One of the British-forged food ration coupons that the RAF dropped over Germany in great numbers [to undermine German food supplies]. Each square entitles the bearer to 500 grams of a basic foodstuff.

many of whom later fell back into the hands of the German security police. The raid killed more than 100 prisoners, including many criminals, and 50 of the German guards.

Group Captain Pickard and his navigator, Lt. J. A. Broadley, were shot down right after the raid by two German FW 190 fighter planes, when they were about 6 miles from the prison.

On the night of 18–19 February 1944, the German Luftwaffe carried out what the British described as its heaviest raid on London since May 1941. One hundred and eighty-seven aircraft of the German IX. Fliegerkorps under Maj. Gen. Peltz, raided the British capital unloading large quantities of incendiary bombs. Eleven German aircraft were lost.

In February 1944 the US 8th Air Force operating out of Britain, and the US 15th Air Force operating out of Italy, began planned coordinated bombing raids. The first series of large joint operations was planned for the third week in February, because it was expected that weather conditions would have improved by then. The US 8th Air Force supplied 3,300 bombers and escort fighters, the 15th Air Force 500 aircraft. Their objective was German aircraft factories, the number-one-priority target on the Allies' new hit list.

On the night of 19–20 February 1944, despite all its feint maneuvers and jamming measures, the RAF suffered a heavy defeat. Seven hundred and thirty British bombers unloaded 2,290 tons of incendiary and blast bombs on Leipzig, but German night fighters and antiaircraft guns shot down 78 of them while losing only 17 fighters.

On Sunday 20 February 1944, US bombers began their planned heavy daylight raids. Their mission was to level German aircraft factories to the ground within a 10-day period, along with the most important factories. This US air offensive was known as "Big Week."

On February 20, 1,000 four-engined bombers—escorted throughout their route by US and RAF long-range fighters—raided aviation industrial sites in Brunswick, Oschersleben, Tutow, Hamburg and Poznan.

But their main target was the Leipzig plant that manufactured 32% of Germany's Me 109 and Me 110 fighters. The plant had survived the RAF raid of the previous night thanks to the energetic efforts of the German air defense, but they had no remedy against the Americans' massive carpets of bombs.

A total of 3,830 tons of bombs fell on Germany on the first day of Big Week. The German defenses shot down only 7 B-17s and B-24s, and 13 of the escort fighters. This was the greatest strategic operation by the US air forces so far.

The US forces had adopted the RAF's tactic of deploying large formations against a number of different targets at once. This posed an insoluble problem to the German defenses, because the various attack groups were well coordinated and compelled the German fighter units to disperse their forces to fight them.

The German day fighters were no longer able to combat the US formations along a broad front as they had done previously. They altered their tactics and confined their attacks to four-engined bomber formations that lacked a fighter escort. They gathered all the forces they could muster to fight these, and abandoned other targets to the raiders.

On February 20, orders were issued to set up the 200th Bomber Wing (KG 200), the most mysterious unit of the German Luftwaffe. The wing included 1st Group with 3 squadrons, and 2nd Group with 3 squadrons plus a fourth supplementary squadron made up of an experimental unit belonging to the Luftwaffe commander-in-chief, and the "East Zone 11th Transport Unit." Colonel Heigl was appointed commander of the new wing, which was assigned to carry out special secret missions. It was the German cognate of the RAF's Special Duty Squadrons —Nos. 138 and 161 which operated out of Britain in support of the SOE, No. 148 Squadron which handled the same duty in the Mediterranean and Balkans zone, and "C" Flight of 357 Squadron, which did special duty in southeast Asia.

The aircraft of the German 200th Bomber Wing were split up according to the nature of their special duties and distributed throughout Occupied Europe. The squadrons were turned into largely independent detachments, each of which received its orders direct from the wing command staff. KG 200 had several detachments along the Eastern and Western Fronts whose mission was to drop agents and materials behind enemy lines.

For example, on the Eastern Front the KG 200 detachment was a flying unit which, though nominally assigned to Luftflotte 6 (commanded by Gen. Ritter von Greim), was exclusively responsible for deciding which missions it would undertake.

The duties of KG 200 included testing new weapons; preparing and conducting special-weapon strategic bombing raids; and transporting strategically important cargos from Japanese-occupied Manchuria using long-range aircraft.

The Junkers Ju 290 long-range transport plane was the most-flown long-range secret-operational aircraft used in operations extending to the Orient. KG 200 also carried out special transport missions using captured US B-24 Liberator and B-17 Flying Fortress bombers, which the Germans called by the codename Dornier Do 200.

KG 200 had at its disposal the most varied array of aircraft in the Luftwaffe, ranging from 39 different types of Fieseler Fi 156 Storch light aircraft, all the way up to the heavy six-engined giant Ju 390 bomber, and including captured French, Italian and American planes.

KG 200's special hangars were at Finow airbase near Berlin. At Finow the German planes were carefully armed for their secret operations.

The different detachments of KG 200 had girls' names as codenames: "Carmen," "Clara," "Olga," "Toska." Olga Detachment, for example, operated in western Europe including Britain, Ireland and Iceland, and Carmen, based in northern Italy, operated in the Mediterranean.

On Wednesday 23 February 1944, the US carrier aircraft of the 58th Fast Carrier Task Force under Vice-Admiral Mitscher, carried out their first air raid against the Japanese-occupied Mariana Islands. A number of freighters and tankers totalling 45,000 tons were sunk, and 168 Japanese aircraft were shot down.

In July 1943, in the Operation Gomorrha raids on Hamburg, the USAAF and RAF had practiced the "double-blow" tactic, in which both forces struck the same target a number of times in rapid succession. Starting in February 1944 they stepped up their double raids. The USAAF and the RAF complemented each other's efforts; the former would raid first by day and the latter by night. The Allies' main aim by this repeated pounding was to prevent the Germans from salvaging valuable installations that might have been spared in a first attack. Feint maneuvers were used to deceive the German defenses; but a raid intended mainly as a diversion would often itself reach the scale of a heavy raid.

Thc ball-bearing factories of Schweinfurt were the first target of the "double-blow" raids that were soon to become standard procedure. On Thursday 24 February 1944, 266 Flying Fortresses with a strong fighter escort of Mustangs and Thunderbolts, raided

January 1944, Pas de Calais (France). One of the modified, simplified "flying-bomb" launch ramps that the Germans built after Allied air raids destroyed many of the original ramps. They were assembled at high speed from prefabricated parts.

the city with losses of only 11 aircraft.

Less than 12 hours later, on the night of 24–25 February, Bomber Command sent 662 aircraft against Schweinfurt. But in this case the double blow failed, because the British bombers did not get close enough to the target. Twenty-two of them dropped their payloads some 6 miles away, and the other 640 unloaded approximately 2,000 tons of bombs on areas outside the city. The German defenses shot down 33 bombers.

On Friday 25 February 1944, the USAAF halted its Big Week offensive due to sudden weather reverses. During these operations the US forces had dropped 10,000 tons of bombs on targets that manufactured 90% of German aircraft. The US 8th and 15th Air Forces had lost 226 bombers, 28 fighters and 2,600 flight personnel.

The Big Week raids brought about only a temporary reduction in German aircraft production because after the autumn 1943 raids, the Germans had transferred most of their aircraft plants out of the cities. Their main production sites were now inside bombproof installations like tunnels and mines, while preliminary work was done in villages or in Czechoslovakia. Concrete structures were built over installations that could not be shifted at short notice.

In the early months of 1944 the mounting numbers and extended range of US long-range fighters, made them increasingly formidable. The day of the simple escort fighter was now past, and the fighter units of the US 8th Air Force started to use new tactics. The Mustangs, Thunderbolts and Lightnings flew far ahead of the bomber formations at a higher altitude, and then swooped down on the German fighter planes when they formed up to raid the bombers. Frequently the US fighters also made low-level strafing attacks against German airfields.

Just when the Germans seemed gradually to be gaining the upper hand over the British bombers at night, they completely lost command of the air to the Americans during the day.

Starting in March 1944, while continuing their raids on German airfields and industrial targets, the Allied aerial forces began systematic preparations for the invasion. Seventy-nine rail centers in northern France and Belgium and 14 in southern France, were bombed around the clock.

The disruption of rail traffic had dire effects for the Germans. Not only troop and supply transports but also coal and iron supplies were badly hit.

The Allied air offensive against the rail traffic network also produced grave side-effects. Around 18,000 men of the Todt Organization [responsible for large German building projects], had to be drawn away from their work on the defensive Atlantic Wall to carry out necessary repairs to the rail lines.

The destruction of German coastal fortifications, bridges and secret-weapon installations, crippled the Germans later when they were trying to repel the invasion troops.

The effective British night raids on rail centers in France in March 1944, refuted Air Chief Marshal Harris's argument that Bomber Command was unable to bomb targets with the required precision and was therefore compelled to make area-bombing raids on German cities.

On Friday 3 March 1944, the US 8th Air Force had to abandon a planned raid on Berlin due to bad weather, but the P-38 Lightning long-range fighters of the US 20th Fighter Group (under Lt. Col. Hubbard) did carry out a reconnaissance raid; they were the first American planes in World War II to operate over the German capital.

On 3 March 1944 one of the strangest units in the German Luftwaffe, the 1st Eastern Squadron (I. Ostfliegerstaffel) was transferred to Lida airfield near Vilna (Lithuania). This unit consisted of Russian volunteers who flew captured Soviet U-2 biplanes called "sewing machines" in soldiers' jargon. The unit had been set up in Daugavpils (Latvia) in December 1943, and now its members flew operations in the zone of Luftflotte 6 under General Ritter von Greim. The observers on board the antiquated U-2s dropped small-caliber bombs by hand. The aircraft flew every night when visibility permitted them to operate, crossing over the Soviet lines just like their fellow-Russians fighting on the other side, who for a long time had been plaguing the nights of German front-line troops with raids in the identical type of aircraft.

At dawn on 4 March 1944, the Soviets began a spring offensive with a pincer operation against the north flank of German Army Group South under Field Marshal von Manstein. The Soviet First Ukrainian Front (under Marshal Zhukov) launched a grand attack. Twenty-four hours later the tanks of the Second Ukrainian Front (under Soviet General Koniev) rolled forward to link with Marshal Zhukov's troops, thus encircling the German First and Fourth Panzer Armies that were still fighting east of the Dniester river.

Next day, Monday 6 March, the Third Ukrainian Front commanded by Soviet General Malinovsky, also went on the attack and cut off the German Sixth Army under General Hollidt at Kherson. The Luftwaffe now did what it could to improve its co-ordination with the German army in the defensive battles.

Flight communication officers took over from Luftwaffe headquarters the task of distributing German aircraft to the Army and deciding their operations. The actual communication between the fighting troops and the aircraft units was handled by air controllers stationed with the various corps or spearhead divisions.

The Germans lacked special ground-attack aircraft comparable to the Soviet Il-2s, and they could now deploy their Ju 87 dive bombers only at night because their slow speed had led to heavy losses in the spring of 1944; so FW 190 fighter planes were adapted to fly ground attacks.

The use of FW 190s as ground-attack planes in turn influenced German tactics. Instead of directly supporting the ground troops on the battlefield, they flew low-level strafing raids on reserve troops, columns and vehicles up to 30 miles behind the front lines.

18 February 1944. British Mosquitos attack Amiens prison to save Resistance members from the firing-squad.

At the beginning of March 1944, almost one year after his first Chindit expedition, Orde Wingate—now a major-general—prepared the second Chindit expedition behind Japanese lines in Burma. This was to be the largest and longest Allied airborne operation of World War II. Twenty thousand men and 5,000 pack animals took part, and the operation, codenamed "Thursday," went on for five months. Gliders and Dakota transport aircraft dropped thousands of tons of equipment, including bulldozers and heavy road-building gear, onto airstrips in the middle of the jungle.

Wingate's Chindit troops included veterans of the first expedition, Burmese regulars and local tribesmen, but mostly they were British soldiers from ordinary regiments who had no special training or experience in jungle warfare. Moreover, they were reserve troops, often older men who had only recently arrived from Britain.

Wingate, building on the experience of the first expedition, had a number of bases or "strongholds" erected to the enemy's rear. He recommended that they should be situated on a plateau, near villages sympathetic to the Allies and near plentiful water supplies, and should be equipped with a Dakota landing strip and a separate drop zone.

These strongholds resembled Wild West forts. Protected by strong minefields, they became bases for widespread operations by the newly-formed Third Indian Special Forces Division commanded by Wingate. The special troops were detailed to wage guerrilla war against Japanese supply lines, and the plan was that eventually they would support an offensive by Chinese troops in northern Burma led by US General Stilwell.

Wingate's Special Forces even had their own powerful air force, the 1st Air Commando, commanded by the 33-year-old US Colonel P. G. Cochran, a fighter pilot of great ingenuity. It was made up of 11 squadrons including fighter, transport and hospital aircraft, and one squadron of B-24 Liberator bombers.

The night of 5–6 March 1944 marked the start of Operation Thursday. The 77th Infantry Brigade under Brigadier Calvert, and the 11th Infantry Brigade under Brigadier Lentaigne, formed the first wave of airborne troops who took off from Hailakandi and landed some 240 miles away at the "Broadway," "Piccadilly" and "Chowringhee" strongholds. One hundred RAF and USAAF Dakotas reinforced the transport squadrons of the 1st Air Commando under Col. Cochran.

Forty minutes before the gliders took off, a reconnaissance plane delivered aerial photographs showing that Piccadilly Stronghold was buried under felled trees which made it impossible to land there.

Only two weeks before, a photo of "Piccadilly" had appeared in *Life* magazine, so now the British concluded that the Japanese had been tipped off by the photo and had blocked the landing ground; moreover, they might even have laid traps at the other strongholds. Wingate nevertheless decided to detour the operation to "Broadway." At 6:08 P.M. the first Dakotas took off, each one towing 2 Waco CG-4A cargo gliders in its wake.

The 77th Brigade troops under Brigadier Calvert landed at Broadway Stronghold so rapidly that some of the gliders collided, leaving 31 Chindits dead and 30 wounded.

Later it was learned that not the Japanese but only some Burmese woodcutters were responsible for the damage at Piccadilly Stronghold.

The next night the 11th Brigade landed at Chowringhee Stronghold. In just 24 hours the combat engineers at Broadway had levelled out Dakota runways using the bulldozers that had just been flown in. Several hours later the new takeoff runway made it possible to transport the wounded out inside Vultee L-1 (Vigilant) medical planes which resembled Storch light aircraft.

Only 35 of the 61 Waco gliders deployed reached Broadway Stronghold. Gliders made emergency landings at many points in northern Burma; 2 of them even went down directly beside the headquarters of the 15th and 31st Japanese Army Divisions, and 3 near a regimental headquarters in Pyaungbin. This led the Japanese to think they were being invaded.

Artillery, jeeps and even pack animals were flown into the strongholds. On the first expedition the animals' braying had betrayed their presence to the Japanese, so this time their vocal cords were cut before their airplane journey.

Around noon on Monday 6 March 1944, the German capital suffered its first grand daylight raid by American bombers. Seven hundred and thirty B-17s and B-24s of the US 8th Air Force, escorted by 296 long-range fighters attacked Berlin in radiant sunshine dropping 1,500 tons of bombs over the southern districts of the city and the Königswusterhausen radio transmitter. German fighter planes shot down 68 US bombers and 11 fighters while suffering only 18 losses. This first raid on Berlin cost the 8th Air Force more casualties than any other.

By Sunday 12 March 1944, over a period of 6 nights, the British had flown 9,052 men, 1,458 animals, and 242 tons of matériel into Broadway Stronghold.

That same day, 6 Spitfire fighter planes landed at Broadway's first operational airfield, which had just been completed behind enemy lines. The Spitfires were detailed to protect the stronghold from Japanese air attack.

When the full complement of the 77th and 11th Brigades had arrived at their assembly points, they carried out their first mission: to sever the rail line north of Indaw (Burma).

An RAF communications officer was assigned to each Chindit column; he used radio to guide fighter-bombers to targets that were delaying the advance of the Chindits.

The toll of captives testifies to the doggedness with which the Japanese fought: Barely 100 unwounded Japanese were captured in 1944 in all the theaters of war, and only 6 in Burma.

Dakota transport planes of the 1st Air Commando were responsible for supplying the Chindits, and Mustang fighters flew cover. Colonel Cochran had some of the aircraft fitted with hooks which he had designed to tear down Japanese telephone lines. The air supply operation functioned so well that the Chindits were able to rely on it completely: "You can march for a whole day without dragging supplies along, because you know that at 8:00 P.M. on the dot the supplies you want will be dropped at a certain spot."

Many supply goods like uniforms, shoes, canned goods, fodder for the pack animals, and even storage batteries whose electrolyte fluid had been thickened into a jelly beforehand, were simply tipped out of the Dakotas without being attached to a parachute. The first helicopters in the history of warfare were used during Operation Thursday too. They were Sikorsky R-4 Bs, the first series-built helicopters in the world; they had a range of about 75 miles and could travel 75 miles an hour. They were used to transport wounded Chindits out of the strongholds.

The plan was that in the second part of Operation Thursday, the 14th Brigade (under Brigadier Brodie) would be flown into Aberdeen Stronghold; but the stronghold was not yet ready for the landings. The 16th Brigade under Brigadier Fergusson was assigned to go there and build a runway. They made a six-week, 480-mile trek through virtually impassable jungle mountains to reach the Aberdeen site, relying entirely on air supplies throughout their journey.

Along their march, 16th Brigade had to cross the Chindwin river. Gliders flew in bridge-building

February 1944. A formation of B-17 Gs of the 96th Bomb Group, US 8th Air Force, in a bomb run over Germany. Production of B-17 G Flying Fortresses started in July 1943 and they were armed with 13 machine-guns including the chin turret under the fuselage nose. They were the most-produced type of B-17, and were outstanding in their high-altitude performance and resistance to enemy fire. A total of 12,726 B-17s left the works.

materials and assault boats. In just a few hours the 4,000 men and 600 animals had all been transferred across. The bridge material and the assault boats were loaded back into the gliders. Then low-flying Dakotas picked up the gliders and took them back to India.

On Wednesday 22 March 1944, the first 6 gliders landed at Aberdeen Stronghold carrying heavy combat engineering equipment, and began to build an aircraft landing strip in double-quick time. The day after, the first gliders flew in units of the 14th Brigade.

At noon on March 23, Wingate took off from Aberdeen in a Mitchell bomber intending to fly to White City Stronghold, which was under Japanese attack. When his bomber did not arrive on time, a search squad was sent out, and they found the fragments of the Mitchell in the Bishanpur mountains. The cause of the crash was never discovered. All ten men in the plane were killed, and Wingate's body could be identified only by the unusual tropical helmet he wore.

He was replaced by Brigadier W. D. Lentaigne of the 11th Brigade, who was never able completely to fill his loss.

On 22–23 March, 50 Allied air officers broke out of a German prisoner-of-war camp, Air Stalag III in Sagan south of Berlin, through a tunnel and were recaptured. On March 24, Hitler ordered the 50 officers to be shot. Göring lodged a protest to no avail. The Luftwaffe commander-in-chief had ordered that Western Allied airmen should always be treated with honor while they were in the hands of the Luftwaffe, as thousands of former prisoners can testify.

On Thursday 30 March, 795 British bombers took off with orders to destroy Nuremberg. This turned out to be the most costly of the RAF's night raids. Everything went wrong from the start. Weather conditions over the North Sea thwarted attempts at wide-scale diversionary maneuvers. Later it was said that the British made a gross tactical error in launching a grand raid in such weather. The clear, cold moonlit night and the well-defined condensation trails, plainly revealed the course of the bombers. Also, the shifting spring gales led to serious errors in navigation, so that the bombers soon deviated from course and were dispersed.

On the other hand, the weather was more or less ideal for the *Zahme* and *Wilde Sau* operations of the German fighter units. Non-stop fighting took place along a 270-mile span, with more and more night fighters entering the fray as soon as they had determined the bombers' target.

The German twin-engined night fighters had all been fitted with Lichtenstein SN-2 or Naxos Z radar which could home in on the emissions of the bombers' airborne radar, and large numbers of night fighters also carried *Schräge Musik* guns.

The British bomber stream crossed the Rhine between Bonn and Bingen, and then flew over Fulda and Hanau toward Nuremberg. The Mosquitos racing in their vanguard, tried to no avail to conceal the route the bombers would be taking.

The Halifax units suffered the heaviest losses on their bomb run; 30 of the 93 bombers deployed were shot down. Lt. Smith of 467 Squadron reported that he counted 40 burning aircraft between Aachen and Nuremberg, and thought it possible that 50 bombers had been shot down before they could even reach the target.

Another 187 bombers never actually dropped their loads. The pathfinders arrived 47 minutes after the agreed-on drop time, and meanwhile hundreds of bombers had arrived before them and were circling over the target looking out for the pathfinder flares, unable to see through the pall of cloud over the city.

German fighter planes achieved a record that night when they shot down 79 bombers. One crew, Becker and Johanssen of 1st Group, 6th Night Fighter Wing, shot down 7 Halifax bombers.

The German antiaircraft trained 600 searchlights and countless illuminating devices on the cloud-pall over the city, shot away with all its might and set up a barrage in the path of the bombers as they made their run.

The RAF crews were unnerved and dropped their loads at random. Some bombers were driven away by strong wind, and those which were not carrying H2S equipment mistakenly bombed Schweinfurt thinking that they were over Nuremberg.

Ninety-five of the 795 aircraft dispatched never came back; 71 more were badly damaged, 12 made crash landings. A total of 108 bombers were knocked out completely.

The German controllers used new defensive tactics in this operation. The enemy's many feint operations prevented them from guessing the main target of a raid ahead of time, so the fighters now attacked bomber streams along their approach route and no longer while they were already over the target zone.

Damage to Nuremberg was minimal despite the 2,460 tons of bombs that were dropped that night. One factory was partially destroyed and three others only slightly damaged. This was truly a black night for Bomber Command, because apart from its aircraft it lost many of its precious crews. Five hundred and forty-five men were killed, and another 159 airmen — many gravely wounded — fell into German hands. This was the largest number of British airmen ever captured on a single mission. The Luftwaffe lost only 10 planes that night. The citizens of Nuremberg too got off more lightly than might have been expected: 60 civilians and 15 foreign forced laborers were killed.

A slight pause in British operations ensued after the Nuremberg raid, and the tactic of the bomber stream was abandoned. The Nuremberg raid was the last in which the bombers flew in a single giant stream.

On Saturday 1 April 1944, a new phase began in the bombing war. RAF bomber operations were coordinated fully into Operation Overlord, the Allied landing in France planned for the beginning of June. Bomber Command came under the command of SHAEF (Supreme Headquarters Allied Expeditionary Force) and for the next five months Sir Arthur Harris was nominally subordinate to General Dwight D. Eisenhower. During this period the Air Marshal could pursue his offensive against German cities only when his bombers were not needed in raids related to "Overlord."

For a number of weeks the RAF's grand night raids over Germany were almost completely halted, and only the Mosquito nuisance raids continued. But at the same time the daylight raids by the USAAF were stepped up.

March 1944, Burma. Mules with severed vocal cords are being loaded into Dakota transport aircraft and then flown behind the Japanese lines to take part in Operation Thursday.

On Sunday 2 April 1944, the first Boeing B-29 "Superfortress" bomber landed in Calcutta, India. It belonged to 58 Wing, 20th Bomber Command of the USAAF and had flown almost around the world, from the Boeing aircraft plant in Wichita, Kansas to England, and then on to North Africa and the Orient. This heavy bomber weighed 54 tons and had 5 electronically-guided heavy machine-gun turrets; it could carry almost 12,000 pounds of bombs and its range was 3,120 miles. The plan was for Superfortresses to begin the strategic air war against Japan.

On Monday 3 April 1944, a British naval formation commanded by Vice-Admiral H. R. Moore and including the aircraft carriers *Furious* and *Victorious*, 3 cruisers and 5 destroyers, became the base for Operation Tungsten, a raid by 42 British Fairey Barracuda bombers on the German battleship *Tirpitz* lying in the Alta-Fjord in northern Norway.

The first wave of British aircraft, commanded by Lt. Baker-Faulkner, took off at 4:38 A.M. The Barracudas were a new and still secret type of carrier aircraft which could drop their bombs from high altitude or in dive flight, and were also equipped with torpedoes. They were escorted by 21 Corsair fighter planes, 20 Hellcat fighters and 10 Wildcat fighters which bombarded the decks and antiaircraft positions on the *Tirpitz* with machine-gun fire.

Not one German fighter plane appeared in the sky.

At 5:25 A.M. the first attack wave had just completed its run and left the Alta-Fjord when the second wave took off under Lt. Rance. The engine of one Barracuda broke down and it stopped dead in the middle of the deck of the carrier *Victorious*. It was at once tipped into the sea to clear the deck. Another Barracuda crashed right after takeoff and went down with her crew.

The German battleship took 14 hits and was put out of action for three months. The *Tirpitz*'s casualties included 122 dead and 316 wounded, some seriously. Apart from the two Barracudas, the British lost only one fighter plane, which was unable to land on its return flight; but its pilot was able to get out.

Operation Tungsten forced German Admiral Dönitz to come to a serious decision. He had the *Tirpitz* repaired, but ordered it to make no further attempts to raid Allied convoys, because RAF and Royal Navy forces were so overwhelming that the Germans would risk losing their battleship entirely if it continued its missions.

On Tuesday 4 April 1944, the US 20th Air Force was set up to fly strategic bombing raids against Japan, using B-29 Superfortresses that took off from India and China. The commander of the 20th Air Force was General H. H. Arnold, who was at the same time the commander of the entire USAAF.

On the night of 4–5 April, the last unit of the 14th Brigade (under Brigadier Brodie) landed at Aberdeen Stronghold in northern Burma. The Dakotas had flown a total of 463 flights in which they delivered 3,756 men, 609 animals and 274 tons of matériel behind enemy lines.

On Wednesday 5 April 1944, the Allied Mediterranean Air Force based in Italy began its strategic bombing offensive. Two hundred and thirty bombers of the US 15th Air Force raided Ploesti oil zone and German supply lines in Rumania. Other units bombed synthetic-fuel manufacturers and oil refineries in Vienna, Budapest, Blechhamer and Odenthal (Upper Silesia). At the same time P-51 Mustang fighter-bombers of the US 8th Air Force carried out low-altitude raids on airfields around Munich and Berlin.

On the evening of 8 April 1944, a dark grey, four-engined Ju 290 A-9 aircraft of the German 200th Bomber Wing (KG 200) took off from Grigorievka airfield at Odessa (southern Ukraine). The remarkable thing about the flight was that it was headed for Mukden, Manchuria.

Just three weeks before, several Ju 290s based on Mont de Marsan south of Bordeaux, had formed the German 5th Long-Distance Reconnaissance Group and begun to fly wide-ranging missions over the North Atlantic. Now three of these aircraft began to fly non-stop missions for the German munitions industry, in which they fetched raw materials, including the molybdenum essential in certain steel alloys, back to Germany from Manchuria.

The Ju 290 A-9 long-range transporters had been stripped of their armament, except for their nose and tail machine-gun turrets, so that they could carry auxiliary fuel tanks containing thousands of gallons of fuel. They now had a range of almost 5,500 miles. Flying at an altitude of about 38,000 feet, they crossed the Soviet Union and Mongolia undetected, and after some 20 hours of flight they landed at a base near Mukden. On their incoming flight the Ju 290s carried some 4 tons of essential munitions to the Japanese—things like weapon sights and other optical equipment—and next day would make their return flight laden with cargo. They landed back at Mielec northeast of Krakow. From here their precious cargo was transported onward by the fastest possible route.

On Monday 10 April 1944, the Germans were forced to evacuate Odessa and shifted their takeoff base to Mielec too.

On Tuesday 11 April 1944, 6 RAF Mosquito rapid bombers of 613 Squadron under Wing Commander R. N. Bateson, took off on a spectacular new low-altitude raid. This time the target was an art gallery in The Hague.

Once again this precision raid was the work of the SOE. The art gallery contained personnel files on the Dutch citizenry, and the Allies feared that the Gestapo might use them to act against the Dutch underground. As in Operation Jerycho on 18 February 1944, the pilots worked with a detailed mockup of the target district, which enabled them to carry out a successful operation that was timed down to the second.

On Wednesday 12 April 1944, remaining units of the 3rd West African Brigade (under Brigadier Gillmore) landed at Aberdeen Stronghold in north Burma. The first phase of Operation Thursday was now over.

On Thursday 13 April 1944, almost 2,000 US bombers raided Augsburg and other targets in southern Germany. The US 8th Air Force bombed Schweinfurt again at the same time, but again failed to destroy the ball-bearing factories.

German armaments minister Albert Speer later wrote: "At the beginning of April 1944, however, the attacks on the ball-bearing industry ceased abruptly. Thus, the Allies threw away success when it was already in their hands. Had they continued the attacks of March and April with the same energy, we would quickly have been at our last gasp." [English quoted from p. 286 of the 1970 Macmillan edition of *Inside the Third Reich*]

On Friday 14 April 1944, the Allied tactical air forces were placed under the command of General Eisenhower. On the following day, the strategic bombing units of the RAF and USAAF were ordered to bomb transport and traffic targets in Germany in preparation for the invasion. In addition, General Eisenhower now had power to command these units to provide direct support of the land and sea operations. Both the 8th and 9th US Air Forces, and RAF Bomber Command, were now to be used on strategic missions, and also on tactical missions in support of the ground troops, in the planned Operation Overlord.

On Tuesday 18 April 1944, more than 2,000 US aircraft and RAF fighter-bombers flew operations over Germany. Four thousand tons of bombs fell that day, the largest quantity dropped on one day since the outbreak of war. Forty Allied aircraft were lost.

On the night of 18–19 April 1944, 125 bombers of the German 9th Air Force (IX. Fliegerkorps under Gen. Peltz) appeared over London. This was the last grand raid of the German Operation Steinbock and at the same time was the German Luftwaffe's last large-scale raid on the British capital. Five He 177 heavy bombers, 10 new Me 410 rapid bombers, 60 Ju 88s, 29 Ju 188s and 13 Do 217s took part. From now until mid-May 1944, units of the IX. Fliegerkorps continued to raid port cities in southeastern England; approximately 100 aircraft flew on each raid.

On the night of 19–20 April 1944, almost 1,200 RAF bombers raided targets in northern France, Belgium and Germany, dropping approximately 4,500 tons of bombs.

On Monday 24 April 1944, the first Boeing B-29 Superfortress of 58 Wing, US 20th Air Force transferred from India to China. Several transport units crossed the Himalayas carrying supplies for the Superfortress, which needed enormous quantities of fuel and bombs.

That same day, April 24, the US 8th Air Force flew a heavy air raid on the important northern French rail junction at Rouen. Four hundred citizens were killed and 700 wounded. Also on April 24, the US 8th Air Force led concentrated raids against German rail installations; the railroad stations at Koblenz and Hamm were especially hard hit.

On April 24, US pilots established a strange record when 13 US Flying Fortress B-17 G bombers and 1 Liberator B-24 J landed in Switzerland within a 115-minute period—most of them at Dübendorf airfield, Zürich. Scarcely a week passed without some US bombers landing in neutral Switzerland, and the shocked USAAF leaders convened a commission to examine the causes. In most cases, they concluded, the air crews preferred Swiss internment to carrying out further enemy missions.

On the night of 24–25 April, Bomber Command raided the rail stations at Brunswick, Düsseldorf and Munich. The raid took Munich completely by surprise because the British flew over neutral Switzerland from Geneva to Liechtenstein, so the German air warning service was not aware of them in time to give the alarm. Naturally the attacks were not confined solely to rail installations, especially not in Munich, and large parts of the city were destroyed.

On the night of 27–28 April 1944, the RAF mounted a grand raid on Friedrichshafen. No. 3 Squadron of the German 6th Night Fighter Wing (NJG 6) based at Hagenau airfield in Alsace, were called on to intercept the inflying bombers near Nancy. At 12:48 A.M. the 23-year-old German 1st Lt. Wilhelm Johnen, an experienced night fighter pilot, took off in his Me 110 G-4 (No. C9 + EN). His brand-new ultra-modern aircraft carried the top-secret Lichtenstein SN-2 radar and the new slanted guns, and also had two other notable features. Besides the 32-year-old radio operator, 2nd Lt. Joachim Kamprath, there was a third man on board to work the *Schräge Musik* guns, namely their 27-year-old designer Paul Mahle; and at the radio operator's feet lay a briefcase full of top-secret documents concerning the German air network all across Europe, giving details of codes and the daily recognition signs for the coming month of May, which had been taken along contrary to regulations when the alarm sounded so unexpectedly and the fighter took to the air.

Between 18 November 1943 and 31 March 1944—the night of the Nuremberg raid—Bomber Command had lost 1,047 of its planes, three quarters of them to night fighters. This success by the German night fighters was due to their new improved wide-angle Lichtenstein SN-2 airborne radar and to their new slanted guns; but these secret devices inside Johnen's aircraft were about to run a dangerous risk of exposure.

Ever since late summer of 1943, when Lichtenstein SN-2 became operational and showed its immunity to Window jamming strips, British Dr. R. V. Jones and his team had been working to penetrate the new radar's secret. To develop an effective countermeasure he needed to know the megahertz frequency of the new device, but so far none of the

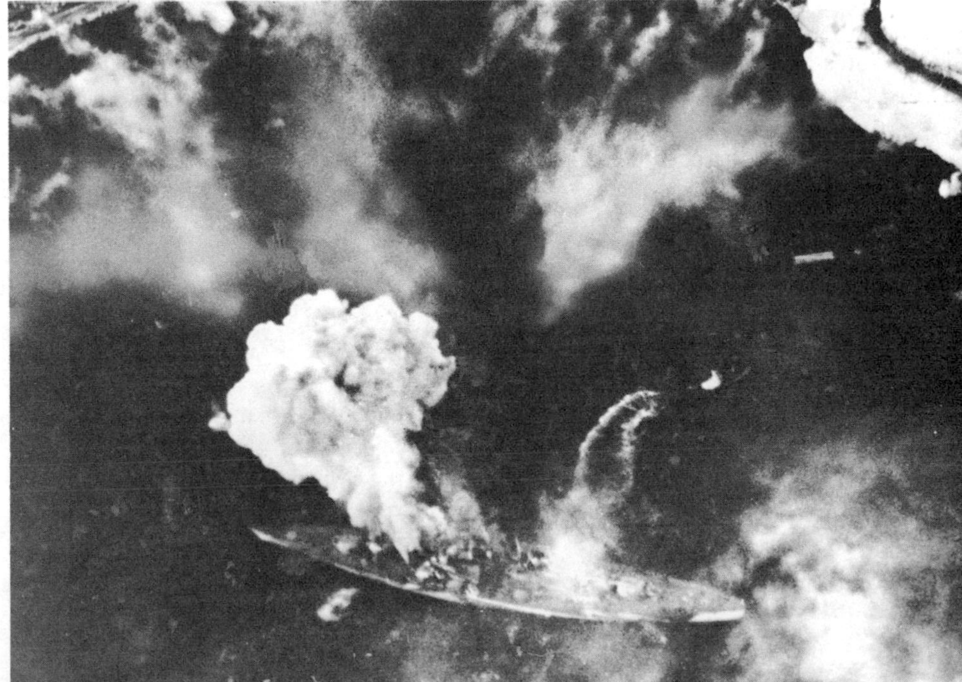

3 April 1944, the Alta-Fjord, Norway. The largest German battleship, the *Tirpitz*, has received 14 hits and been put out of action for 3 months after a raid by Barracudas, the first monoplane torpedo bombers in the British Royal Navy. Two thousand, five hundred and eighty-two of these versatile aircraft were built in all.

fighters equipped with SN-2 had fallen into Allied hands because these fighters had strict orders to operate only over German air space.

First Lt. Johnen had just brought down 2 raiding Lancasters in rapid succession, when disaster struck. Technical Sergeant Paul Mahle gave this account:

"We did not really know where we were because we had already been airborne for a good hour and a half and were flying with our radio equipment switched off, so we had no data on our location. Then things got even worse. Suddenly we were caught by a dozen searchlights that surrounded us with a piercing light . . . I sent out an emergency signal; a green flare shot up from below, the reflectors dimmed, and the airfield lights switched on, signalling us to land. So it had to be Switzerland after all! I too shot off a green signal, which meant "We're going to land!" They answered with green, and switched the airfield lights on and off to say 'Understood!'

"Naturally we had no intention of landing and tried to slip off northward. Instantly all the lights lit us up bright as day again; we had not been able to outwit them. Again I shot off a red flare, but they would not give in until we dropped our landing gear and were unmistakably seen to be heading in to land on the lighted landing runway. Suddenly I saw huge hangars along the edge of the field with rows of aircraft in between. I told Johnen, who then brought us in for a landing.

"The moment the wheels touched the ground, all the lights on the field went out as if in response to a magic wand, and it was pitch-black all around us. Johnen switched on our airborne searchlight, and by its light we recognized dense rows of Flying Fortresses and Liberators. Suddenly a powerful searchlight grasped us in front and blinded us. We sped directly past the American bombers. Johnen braked sharply.

"While we taxied to halt, 2nd Lt. Kamprath tried to trample the equipment in front of his seat with his boots, but this desperate attempt was not very successful.

"We stood still, and suddenly, just as I was dismantling the *Schräge Musik* guns, there came a knock on the cabin roof above my head. I looked up and someone said in German: 'Please get out, you're in Switzerland. You have been interned.' It was a first lieutenant in the Swiss Air Force. We were at Dübendorf airfield in Zürich."

That same night, right after the landing, the Swiss authorities routinely handed over the German air crew's personal data to the German military attaché in Switzerland, who in turn reported to Göring. Göring at once informed Hitler, who ordered the SS leader, Heinrich Himmler, to have the three airmen liquidated. When Göring got wind of the fact that Himmler had been told to send a murder squad into Switzerland, he personally intervened with Hitler, demanding that the three men be allowed to stand an orderly trial and declaring that he "would not allow his airmen to be shot down in a neutral country."

On the morning of Saturday 29 April 1944, Gestapo officers were already knocking on the doors of the families of the Me 110 crew. Scrupulous searches were conducted and all available photos and correspondence of the crewmen were confiscated; then the houses were sealed and the men's families taken to prison.

Even SS officer Otto Skorzeny, the commando expert who had made a name for himself in September 1943 by liberating Mussolini from his internment in the Gran Sasso mountains, was called in on the matter.

Skorzeny gave this account: "On the eve of a double holiday I was sitting along the Wannsee [lake in southwest Berlin] with some old friends, when suddenly I was summoned to the telephone; it was the Führer's headquarters calling. A crazy thing had happened the night before and the news had just come out. A Messerschmitt fighter plane carrying the newest type of night radar had apparently missed its way and landed on a Swiss airfield . . .

"I was ordered to do everything I could, first, to find out whether it had really been a forced landing or whether the crew had deserted. Second, I was to work out proposals about the quickest way to get the equipment back into German possession, or to destroy it. The Reichsführer SS [Himmler] had been called into the matter too and rang me up shortly after, asking for an ongoing progress report.

"The Führer's headquarters attributed the greatest importance to the whole affair. Next day we had to fly a courier aircraft to Berchtesgaden to report and to present both proposals in a written form. Schellenberg and I had dictated the reports to my secretary, who had to give up her free Sunday to do the work." The documents inside the impounded aircraft enabled the Swiss rapidly to penetrate the secret of Lichtenstein SN-2 radar, but they did not reveal it to the Allies.

On the night of 28–29 April 1944, 101 bombers of German 9th Air Force (IX. Fliegerkorps) raided the English port of Plymouth. Do 217s of 3rd Group, 100th Bomber Wing unsuccessfully attacked a British war vessel with Fritz X guided bombs. Two Do 217 Ks were shot down by the British anti-aircraft.

At the start of May 1944, the Allied tactical air forces began massive attacks on rail and road bridges over the Seine south of Paris, and from the Île de France to the Pas de Calais. These bombardments could as well have been meant to isolate the Pas de Calais as Normandy, so nothing betrayed which zone the Allies actually intended to use for their invasion landing.

In the second week of May 1944, the Allies launched an air offensive that at last crippled the German war industry, thus achieving the target the Allies had set at the Casablanca conference in January 1943.

On Friday 12 May 1944, the USAAF began the planned destruction of German synthetic-fuel manufacturing plants. That day, US forces destroyed 60% of the Leuna plant in Merseburg and 50% of works in Böhnau, while factories in Tröglitz and Brüx (near Prague) were destroyed completely.

German armaments minister Albert Speer later wrote: "On that day the technological war was decided. Until then we had managed to produce approximately as many weapons as the armed forces needed, in spite of their considerable losses. But with the attack of nine hundred and thirty-five daylight bombers of the American Eighth Air Force upon several fuel plants in central and eastern Germany, a new era in the air war began. It meant the end of German armaments production." [English quoted from p. 346 of the 1970 Macmillan edition of *Inside the Third Reich*]

The crew of the Me 110 night fighter that had been forced to land in Zürich, were still on involuntary leave in Switzerland. Meanwhile, ceaseless debates were going on behind the political scenes about how this sticky problem could most quickly be resolved while preserving the intricate rules of Swiss neutrality. Time was pressing, because Swiss secret agents in Berlin had learned the alarming fact that Hitler was planning either a bombing raid or a commando raid on Dübendorf airfield to destroy

24 April 1944, Cointrin airfield in Geneva. A US B-17 G bomber with a shot-up engine, one of a number that made emergency landings in Switzerland after an American raid on rail installations in south Germany.

the captured German plane and its precious equipment before the Allies plumbed its secret. But neither Berlin nor any other power suspected that the day after the forced landing, the Swiss had sagely taken the precaution of dismantling the most important parts of the plane's special equipment, and were keeping them at Bouchs, in a strictly guarded underground army depot "until the situation is clarified."

On Friday 12 May 1944, a hastily convened conference took place in a military chamber in Berne. Present were Swiss General Guisan, Colonel Rihner (commander of the Swiss air force and antiaircraft), Colonel Masson (head of Swiss intelligence), Lt. Col. Barbey, Major Primault, and Major Peter Burckhardt, the Swiss military attaché in Berlin who had just left his post to travel home. They all discussed proposals from Hitler and Göring, conveyed to them by Reich Marshal Göring's special envoy, Captain Eggen. The Germans offered to give Switzerland 6 Me 109 G aircraft immediately, and six more one week later, if the Swiss would return the Me 110. Captain Eggen expected their answer in two days' time.

The gravity of the situation was clear to everyone involved: If German bombers or special commandos attacked Dübendorf airfield, it would mean full-scale war with Hitler's Germany.

On the evening of May 12, Major Burckhardt informed Captain Eggen that it was unlikely that the Me 110 CP + EN would be returned. Then Eggen, who had been given full authority by Göring, proposed an alternative: the Swiss could destroy the aircraft on their own soil, at Dübendorf airfield, along with all its equipment. If the Swiss government would comply with this proposal, the Reich Marshal would still honor his offer to give the Swiss 12 Me 109 Gs: six of the fighters would be delivered on the same day that the Me 110 was blown up, and six more would arrive in Switzerland three weeks later.

On the evening of May 17, Colonel Rihner, the commander of the Swiss air force, and Colonel von Wattenwyl, head of the Swiss war technology department, met at Dübendorf airfield, accompanied by their staff officers. Then Captain Eggen arrived, accompanied by an explosives expert named Brand who had come here from Germany especially for the purpose. A short time earlier, the dismantled Lichtenstein SN-2 radar had been fetched from Bouchs military depot and reinstalled inside the night fighter. The profile of the canvas-wrapped Me 110 stood out in the dim light. The plane was rolled out of its hiding place and Captain Eggen carefully inspected the interior. The dully gleaming, almost brand-new fighter was about to make its final journey.

Eventually the Me 110 was towed into the remotest corner of the airfield. Here the explosives specialist Brand supervised Swiss combat engineers as they laid explosive charges in and around the plane. Just as a faraway churchtower clock struck ten, a huge resounding explosion rent the darkness. A pile of twisted, scorched metal and a few official notes wrote an end to the Me 110 affair.

The Me 110's three German crewmembers knew nothing of what had happened in Berne and Dübendorf. Later Technical Sgt. Mahle said: "After our 'cure residence' was over at last, we were taken secretly to the railroad station still dressed in civilian clothes. To our surprise the station was full of rejoicing Germans who wanted to send us off with flowers and music; but the Consul General and the military attaché were there . . .

"On the German side we were received by a couple of Party bigwigs including the National Socialist district leader. The train that was to take us to Berlin was already rolling when a Luftwaffe major forced his way into our compartment with two sub-officers: 'Are you the Johnen crew? Please don't give us any trouble!' They sat down next to us and did not let us out of their sight. Not until we had been delivered to Joseph Schmid, commanding general of night fighters, in Belitz near Berlin, did we learn the whole truth of what had happened to our families and what still awaited us.

"For three days we were grilled by a hastily convened war court, and each of us was interrogated separately until at last everything was cleared up . . . Then at 6:10 P.M. on May 22, we landed at Hagenau. The whole Wing were waiting on the runway and gave a stormy greeting to the prodigal sons, especially when they learned that we were carrying several thousand Swiss cigarettes in our luggage. Our adventure was over."

On Thursday 25 May 1944, Drvar, a small town in Bosnia, became the arena of German Operation Rösselsprung. Its target was to capture Yugoslavian partisan leader Marshal Josip Broz Tito.

Tito, the leader of the Yugoslavian People's Liberation Army, had been plaguing the Germans ever since they occupied the Balkans. Now they wanted to round up Tito and his staff on the day when he was celebrating his fifty-second birthday, suspecting nothing. This carefully-planned opera-

28 April 1944, Switzerland. A German Me 110 G-4 night fighter, No. C9 + EN, has landed at Dübendorf airfield in Zürich carrying the top-secret German Lichtenstein SN-2 airborne radar. The large aerial array on its nose is part of the radar equipment.

tion was the first German paratroop mission to result in failure.

It was planned that the German troops would land in Drvar in two waves. The men belonged to the 500th SS Parachute Battalion, reinforced by the 1st Airborne Regiment, 40 men of the Croatian "Benesch Unit," and the Savadil Troop. The operation leader was SS officer Rybka, the commander of the parachute battalion.

To keep the operation secret as long as possible, the DFS 230 gliders were transferred near to the takeoff bases only the evening before. Then the paratroops and airborne troops moved into the airfields at dawn on May 25.

Operation Rösselsprung began shortly after sunrise with dive-bomber relay attacks on Drvar and its environs. The Germans were hoping that in these assaults they could destroy the radio station of the Yugoslavian High Command, and sever all the telephone connections.

At 7:00 A.M., 314 first-wave paratroops, and the gliders carrying the 340 airborne troops, landed in the Drvar Valley. At first the surprised Yugoslav lookouts thought the descending gliders were German bombers making a forced landing.

Three German paratroop combat groups – "Red" Group with 85 men, "Green" with 95 men, and "Blue" with 100 men – had been ordered to occupy the village of Drvar and, with the aid of the airborne troops, to prevent the Yugoslavian units from breaking out.

German "Panther" Group (100 men) was supposed to raid the "Citadel," the codename for the location of Tito and his High Command. But no one knew exactly where Tito was celebrating his birthday, so the enterprise got off to a bad start.

"Breaker" Group (50 men) was detailed to capture the US military mission, while "Catcher" Group (40 men) overpowered the British and "Stormer" Group (50 men) the Soviet military missions. The plan provided that "Daredevil" Group (70 men) would occupy the "Western Cross" where the army staff radio station was located, and "Stinger" Group (20 men) would seize an important outpost.

The second wave of paratroops (under SS officer Obermeier) and the gliders would land south of the village at 10:00 A.M.

When the first wave landed, there were no Yugoslav units near the "Citadel," the cave where Marshal Tito and his chief staff-members sheltered during the bombardment, but when "Catcher" Group moved against the "Citadel" and tried to occupy the cave entrance, they ran into unexpectedly hard resistance from around 100 guard soldiers.

Meanwhile the Yugoslavs radioed for help, and Allied aircraft took off from Italian bases and appeared over Drvar to "intervene in the battle in unprecedented numbers."

The village itself was now almost completely occupied by the Germans, and the German combat groups launched a concentrated offensive on the cave. Then at 8:00 A.M. an elite unit of over 100 Yugoslav officer cadets appeared in the valley and held up the German flank attack on the "Citadel."

At this point the German second wave landed as scheduled, but they were repulsed by the Yugoslav units near Drvar who by now had been alerted.

Meanwhile Tito and his staff managed to escape. At the last minute they discovered a place at the end of the cave where water had washed through the ceiling. With the aid of a rope they laboriously forced their way one by one through the narrow opening and ended up on the plateau above the cave, where they encountered Yugoslav partisan Aleksandar Rankoviè fighting off the advancing Germans with a small unit of soldiers. At the same time a Tito brigade which had just arrived on the scene, began to encircle the paratroops.

If the German paratroops had made their jump onto the mountain plateau above the cave, Tito would probably have had no chance to escape. As it was, the airborne troops had to content themselves with capturing one of the Marshal's new uniforms that was still in the hands of a Drvar tailor, and a pair of his marching boots. Later both were publicly displayed as victory trophies in Vienna.

SS Lieutenant Rybka, the operation leader, was wounded, and the Fieseler Storch light aircraft that had been meant to fly away with the captive Tito, carried Rybka to the nearest military hospital instead.

Some of the paratroops (under Captain Bentrup) dug themselves in at the nearby cemetery and fought heavy battles against the Yugoslav units all night long.

Next morning, May 26, German aircraft made repeated attacks to relieve the hard-pressed airborne troops, and in the morning hours the remaining Germans were rescued by strong German armored forces moving along the mountain roads to Drvar.

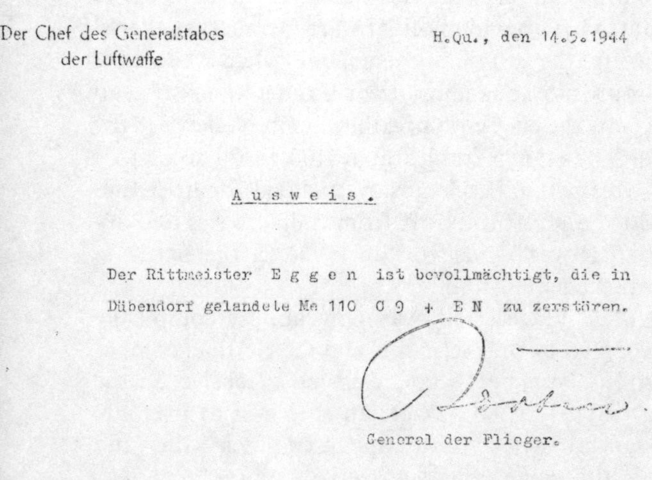
Der Chef des Generalstabes
der Luftwaffe

H.Qu., den 14.5.1944

Ausweis.

Der Rittmeister Eggen ist bevollmächtigt, die in Dübendorf gelandete Me 110 C 9 + EN zu zerstören.

General der Flieger.

German losses in the operation were: 1,153 dead, wounded and missing.

That same day, the operations of Allied fighters and fighter-bombers reached a new peak when over 5,000 machines swooped down on the whole of the rail and road traffic network in northern France, Belgium and western Germany.

On Sunday 28 May 1944, the US 8th Army Air Force raided rail targets in Deutz (Cologne) with GB-1 glide bombs. Each US B-17 E carried two 2,200-lb glide bombs—the product of the Aeronca Works—under the fuselage. The 60 US Flying Fortresses dropped approximately 100 GB-1 glide bombs prematurely, several miles before they reached their target, because of a strong German antiaircraft defense which forced them to veer off. Only a few bombs found the target. This was the first US glide-bomb operation, and it was unsuccessful even though not one bomber was lost.

On 29–30 May 1944, 400 USAAF bombers led heavy raids against synthetic fuel works and oil refineries. German plants in Schwarzheide and Wintershall reported massive hits, and the works at Pölitz near Stettin were put out of action completely for two months on May 29. This was an especially severe blow to the Luftwaffe because the Pölitz hydrogenation plant was their largest producer of aircraft fuel.

On the night of 29–30 May 1944, German Luftwaffe bombers took off for their last raid on London.

This raid marked the end of the Germans' Operation Steinbock, which the British mockingly referred to as a "baby blitz." It had totalled 31 raids, 14 of which were against the British capital. The IX. The Fliegerkorps had lost 329 aircraft.

The fighter-bombers of the USAAF were now making daily low-altitude raids on rail and road junctions in western and southwestern Germany, and on Luftwaffe airfields. German transport, especially rail transport, was seriously disrupted. In the last week of May the German railway lost approximately 500 locomotives to low-level air attacks.

Allied destruction of the rail network in northern France was so successful that Colonel Hoeffner, chief of the German Western transport system, reported to Field Marshal von Rundstedt at the end of May: "We will be unable to transport troops by rail for the first two weeks following the invasion."

Opposite page below: One of the strangest orders issued in the war: German Luftwaffe General Korten has given a cavalry captain written permission to destroy one of the Luftwaffe's best aircraft inside Switzerland.

Right: 22 May 1944, Hagenau in Alsace. Technical Sgt. Paul Mahle (center), still dressed in civilian clothing from his stay in Berne, describes his experiences in Switzerland to his squadron buddies back in Germany.

On Tuesday 30 May 1944, Hitler's secretary Martin Bormann sent a circular to all Nazi Party leaders from the highest to the lowest ranks, demanding that all shot-down Allied airmen be executed without a trial.

Individual acts of violence by Germans against Allied airmen did take place. On the other hand, SS leaders complained that the German people did "not maintain the appropriate detachment from shot-down enemy fliers and showed them a misguided sympathy." SS Leader Heinrich Himmler ordered that this kind of humane behavior should be punished by immediate internment in a concentration camp.

On Friday 2 June 1944, the first shuttle bombing raid took place by US aerial forces flying between Italy and the Soviet Union. US planes of the 15th USAAF landed at Soviet bases, thus initiating Operation "Frantic Joe." General Eaker, the commander of the US Mediterranean air force, led his formation of 130 B-17 Flying Fortresses and 70 P-51 Mustangs as they took off from Foggia airbase in Italy to raid traffic targets in Debrecen (Hungary). After the raid the aircraft landed as planned at airfields in the Ukraine—the bombers at Poltava, the Mustangs at Mirgorod and Piryatin.

On Sunday 4 June 1944, the Allies occupied Rome after Field Marshal Kesselring had declared it an open city.

On Monday June 5, 58 Wing of the US 20th Bomber Command took off on their first operation flying Boeing B-29 Superfortresses. They took off from an airbase near Kharagpur west of Calcutta to bomb rail installations in Bangkok (Siam).

During the period 1–5 June 1944, air raids on Germany slackened; the Allied air forces were now concentrating on preparations for the invasion.

On June 5, Luftflotte 3, the German air force stationed in France and commanded by Field Marshal Sperrle, reported its battle strength. In northern France it had 40 reconnaissance planes, about 80 fighters, 38 fighter-bombers and 110 Ju 88 bombers; in southern France it had 12 combat-ready reconnaissance planes, 24 fighters, and 40 torpedo and glide-bombers. Luftflotte 3 still commanded impressive manpower—approximately 300,000 men including 50,000 in air communications.

On the other side of the English Channel, 2,100 four-engined, 600 twin-engined and 3,500 to 4,000 single-engined aircraft waited for the takeoff signal. The Germans were outnumbered 20:1.

On the night of 5–6 June, the Allied bombardment began shortly after midnight while the landing armada was busy crossing the Channel. In the dawn of June 6, 1,136 RAF Bomber Command aircraft dropped 5,853 tons of bombs and eliminated 10 of the most important German coastal batteries in the Seine Bay between Cherbourg and Le Havre.

At daybreak the 8th USAAF took over the bombing. One thousand eighty-three aircraft dropped 1,763 tons of bombs on the German Atlantic Wall emplacements within a thirty-minute period, just forward of the landing troops. Then a second wave of aircraft attacked individual targets along the coasts, and various inland batteries. On the first day of Operation Overlord, 5 troop divisions were transported to France by sea with strong naval support; and the 3 divisions of General Montgomery's Twenty-First Army Group were transported by air to the Orne estuary, the Calvados coast and the Cotentin Peninsula. Three thousand four hundred and sixty-seven heavy bombers; 1,645 medium, light and torpedo bombers; 5,409 fighters; and 2,306 transport aircraft and gliders took part in the operation. Within a 24-hour period the Allied air forces flew 14,674 missions and dropped 10,395 tons of bombs. The RAF lost 62 aircraft, the USAAF 71. German Luftflotte 3 under Field Marshal Sperrle, led 260 daylight missions and 59 night missions. Only a few German aircraft succeeded in penetrating to the landing beaches.

That same day, June 6, US aircraft of the 15th USAAF based on Soviet airfields in the Ukraine, raided the German airfield of Galatz in Rumania and returned to the Soviet Union a few hours later.

On the night of 6–7 June 1944, heavy He 177 bombers of German 2nd Group, 40th Bomber Wing, took off to raid the Allied landing fleet off the Normandy coast with Hs 293 guided bombs; but strong Allied night-fighter forces prevented the bombers' operations. The Australian 456 RAF Squadron shot down 4 He 177s.

On Wednesday June 7, the British had already begun to build forward airfields in the landing beachhead at Asnelles northeast of Bayeux. They used a new type of steel mesh tracking that could be laid out like a carpet over planed fields.

That day, low-flying Allied aircraft kept up an incessant bombardment of rail lines and motorized columns. One German armored division lost more than 200 vehicles to RAF fighter-bombers within a short period, near Alençon north of Le Mans.

The Allied fighter-bombers used special tactics in their raids on German motorized columns. First they destroyed the armored vehicles at the head and rear of the column, [thus immobilizing all the vehicles]; then using rockets and cannon they systematically fired on the individual vehicles one by one, and on everything else that moved.

Throughout the war, the Western Allied air forces were unexcelled in the tactic of sealing off a battle zone and attacking behind the enemy's front lines.

Belatedly, on June 8 the German codeword "Danger in the West" brought in reinforcements for Luftflotte 3, but the Luftwaffe forces had been plunged into a chaos that led to its total collapse in western Europe. German formations in France were topped up with about 600 fighter planes drawn from the defenses in Germany, and from the Eastern Front and the reserve forces.

Before the fresh German aircraft had even arrived in France, plans for their transfer had to be changed due to the destruction of the German airfields intended to receive them; but some formations were already en route and could not be informed of the changes in time. Many squadrons lost aircraft when they crash-landed at forward airfields that were completely unprepared for landings. Some of the ground personnel had to travel by rail and their arrival was delayed by days or even weeks.

Faced with this chaos, Field Marshal Sperrle decided to concentrate his aerial units in the Pas de Calais because this was the area where German airfields had suffered the least damage; the confinement of the Germans in turn made it easier for the Allied forces to fight them and effectively to shield the landing zone.

Starting on 7–8 June, the bombers of German 2nd Group, 40th Bomber Wing and 2nd Group, 100th Bomber Wing of the IX. Fliegerkorps under General Peltz, started nightly raids in which they mined the Seine Bay. They dropped approximately 3,000 mines in these operations.

On Saturday 10 June 1944, the SOE central office in London received a radio message from one of its agents in Belgium, who reported that a rail-transport train was travelling westward via Ghent, and each of its 33 rail cars was loaded with 3 strange, cigar-shaped, little winged projectiles with gun tubes over the fuselage. The British realized at once that these were flying bombs being taken to their launch sites.

On Sunday June 11, the 15th USAAF formations left their Soviet airbases and returned to Italy. On their return flight they bombed the port of Constanza and the oil depots at Giurgiu (Rumania).

By 12 June 1944, the Allied air forces on the Normandy Front had carried out 49,000 missions in a 7-day period – approximately two thirds of them in tactical support of the ground troops – and unloaded 42,000 tons of bombs, twice as many as fell on Britain in 1941. The Allies had lost 532 planes.

The complete aerial destruction of the main rail lines leading to Caen, prevented the Germans from

28 May 1944, Namur (Belgium). B-26 Marauder medium bombers during the Allied raid on the important Namur rail junction. At this time Marauders were no longer given a camouflage coating, which would have reduced their speed.

bringing up reinforcements.

In the early hours of June 13, the Germans launched Operation Rumpelkammer, the V-1 flying-bomb raids on England. Colonel Wachtel's special unit, known by the codename "115st Flak Regiment," fired the first flying bombs from the new launch ramps at Sâleux (Amiens), aiming at London.

At 4:15 A.M. a sentry at a British aerial observer's station in the southern county of Kent heard a "rushing noise" and saw a "tiny pilotless aircraft" fly overhead, its exhaust pipe emitting orange flame.

It was too late for the British antiaircraft gunners or fighter planes to intercept the strange object. It flew onward "sputtering like an ancient Ford car climbing a mountain," and at 4:18 A.M. impacted in the little town of Swanscombe about 20 miles from its target, London's Tower Bridge.

The second bomb fell in Cuckfield, the third in the London district of Bethnal Green destroying a rail bridge and killing 6 people. These were the night's only casualties. A fourth bomb fell in Sevenoaks, and the rest went down while they were still over the Channel.

An Me 410 reconnaissance plane of Luftflotte 3 was sent out to determine the effects of Operation Rumpelkammer, but was shot down by British antiaircraft at Barking, so Colonel Wachtel received no information about the results of the first flying-bomb raid.

The night of 14–15 June was the first time a flying bomb was shot down by an aircraft. An RAF Mosquito of 605 (County of Warwick) Squadron, flown by Lt. J. G. Musgrave and Sgt. F. W. Samwell, cut down a "doodlebug"—as the British called them—over the Channel.

On Thursday 15 June 1944, after preparatory air raids, the American Fifth Marine Corps under US General H. M. Smith landed on the island of Saipan in the Marianas. Thereupon the Japanese fleet under Vice-Admiral Ozawa left its berth off the Philippine Island of Tawitawi and set sail for the Marianas to halt the US invasion of Saipan, an island of great strategic importance. The US commanders decided not to withdraw their landing fleet, which lay off Saipan, and waited for Vice-Admiral Ozawa to open the attack.

15 June 1944 is one of the crucial dates in the history of the Allied war against Japan. That night 67 B-29 Superfortresses of the 20th USAAF took off from Chung-tu, an airbase in China which had been constructed by vast numbers of coolies. Each Superfortress carried four 550-lb bombs in its fuselage. This was the first US air raid on the Japanese motherland. The target was the Japanese counterpart of the city of Essen in Germany's industrial heartland: the gigantic Javata steelworks on the island of Kyushu, almost 1,500 miles distant from the US airbase in China. Seven Superfortresses were lost, and ten suffered engine damage which forced them to interrupt the operation and return to base.

On the night of 15–16 June, the Germans stepped up their deployment of flying bombs. By noon on June 16, 244 bombs had been fired at London; 45 of them crashed shortly after takeoff.

Early on the morning of June 16, a German reconnaissance plane reported fires in the target zone larger than any that had been seen after IX. Fliegerkorps air raids.

That same day the British began energetic countermeasures. They drew up the Diver Plan, and distributed 192 heavy antiaircraft guns, 246 light guns and 480 barrage balloons over Kent and Sussex.

Eight RAF fighter squadrons were appointed to intercept the flying bombs along the Channel coast.

The five-hundredth German flying bomb took off on Sunday 18 June. One flying bomb crashed into the Wellington Barracks a few hundred yards from Buckingham Palace and killed 121 people including 63 officers and guards. General Eisenhower said that if the Germans had been able to deploy their new weapon six months earlier, the Allied landing probably would have been very difficult and perhaps even impossible.

On Monday 19 June 1944, a bitter sea-air battle took place between Japanese and American forces in the Philippine Sea. The Japanese fleet (commanded by Vice-Admiral Ozawa) had 9 aircraft carriers plus land-based marine air forces. The US 58th Fast Carrier Task Force under Vice-Admiral Mitscher had 15 aircraft carriers.

The Japanese wanted to prevent Allied seizure of the Marianas because possession of the islands would give the Allies naval and air bases less than 1,500 miles from the Japanese motherland, enabling them to raid Japanese industrial centers and to sever Japanese communications with the Philippines and the East Asian continent. Even Tokyo would now lie within range of the B-29 Superfortresses.

In the first hours of 19 June 1944, Vice-Admiral Ozawa's fleet lay southwest of Guam. A beautiful day broke with a radiant blue sky and unlimited visibility.

Japanese reconnaissance planes located the US Fast Carrier Task Force but the Americans did not yet know the position of the Japanese fleet. The Japanese had another advantage too: Their light, unarmored planes had a range 90 miles greater than that of the American aircraft. Thus, the US fleet lay within range of Vice-Admiral Ozawa's fleet while the US carrier aircraft could not yet reach the Japanese.

At 8:30 A.M. the first 64 Japanese aircraft took off from the leading Japanese carriers, the *Chiyoda*, the *Shitose* and the *Zuiho*. At 8:56, 28 more aircraft took off from the main Japanese formation, the carriers *Taiho*, *Shokaku* and *Zuikaku*.

Officer Komatsu, the pilot of one Japanese aircraft, caught sight of a US torpedo as he gained altitude. It had been fired from the American submarine *Albacore* and was headed straight for Vice-Admiral Ozawa's flagship, the carrier *Taiho*. Komatsu crashed his plane into the torpedo to save the carrier.

At 10:00 A.M. a Japanese formation comprising the light carriers *Hiyo*, *Junyo* and *Ryuho*, sent another 47 planes into the air.

At 11:00 A.M. Ozawa ordered his 1st and 3rd carrier formations to send up 114 aircraft. Now 80% of the Japanese carrier aircraft were making runs on the Fast Carrier Task Force, leaving only a dozen fighters to protect the Japanese fleet. The Vice-Admiral had committed a grave error that was to have dire results.

The Japanese pilots launched an eight-hour assault on the US carriers. Most of the Japanese planes were picked up by US radar when they were still 155 nautical miles away. As the Japanese approached, US fighter planes took to the air, and soon heavy dogfights ensued in which the attackers

6 June 1944, Normandy. Fields at the Orne estuary, littered with the Airspeed Horsa gliders that flew British airborne troops into France. A Horsa could carry up to 30 fully-armed soldiers. The main landing gear was discarded after takeoff, and landings were effected using nose and glide wheels. A total of 3,655 were built.

A well-camouflaged Me 109 G for "Gustav" is being prepared for takeoff. The 109 G, first deployed in summer 1942, was the most-built version of the Messerschmitt fighter (70%).

suffered massive casualties.

The US pilots were markedly superior to the less experienced Japanese pilots, who soon had lost 218 aircraft while shooting down only 29 of the enemy.

Only about 40 out of the original 375 Japanese carrier planes, managed even to get near the US task force. By later afternoon of June 19, 401 Japanese land-based and carrier aircraft had been shot down before coming within 60 miles of the US vessels. Only one Japanese aircraft scored a serious hit, on the battleship *South Dakota*, killing 27 seamen; but the *South Dakota* itself was only slightly damaged. The battleship *Indiana* and the heavy cruiser *Indianapolis* received light damage.

Vice-Admiral Ozawa's flagship, the carrier *Taiho*, was hit by a torpedo from the submarine *Albacore*, suffered a violent fuel explosion and six hours later had to be abandoned with large numbers of its aircraft still on board. The Japanese carrier *Shokaku* was torpedoed by the submarine *Cavalla* and soon was wreathed in flames. Both carriers sank at midnight. Ozawa, who did not yet know the extent of the disaster suffered by his aircraft, did not want to give up the fight. During the night his fleet took a northwest heading, bent on picking up added fuel supplies.

On Tuesday 20 June 1944, 1,500 bombers and approximately 1,000 escort fighters of the US 8th Air Force, led heavy raids against the synthetic fuel factories at Hamburg, Fallersleben, Ostermoor, Magdeburg, Misburg and Pölitz, unloading 4,252 tons of bombs. The German air defenses downed 50 bombers and 5 fighters, with losses of 28 German fighters.

That afternoon large numbers of US bombers landed on Swedish airfields. Twelve Liberator B-24 Hs and 4 B-4 Js landed at a single airfield at Bulltofta in Malmö; one B-24 J landed at Klagstrop, and a B-24 H at Röstanga. For these 18 bombers, the war was now over.

At about 3:00 P.M. on Tuesday 20 June 1944, a US reconnaissance plane spied Vice-Admiral Ozawa's fleet.

US Vice-Admiral Mitscher ordered all his dive-bombers and torpedo-bombers to take off even though it was already late afternoon and they could not get back before dark. This meant that the carriers would have to remain lighted until the planes had returned and landed again, and the lights would increase the carriers' exposure to enemy submarines.

Ozawa's fleet was in the process of refueling alongside its oilers when 216 US aircraft approached, and only 35 Japanese fighters came out to meet them.

The Japanese sent up a heavy antiaircraft barrage, but despite this they lost the carrier *Hiyo* and two oilers. The carriers *Zuikaku* and *Chiyoda*, the battleship *Haruna*, and the heavy cruiser *Maya* were damaged. Twenty US aircraft were lost.

When the Japanese carriers that were still afloat,

reported heavy damage on their flight decks, Admiral Toyoda, the commander of the Imperial Japanese Navy, ordered Ozawa to lead the retreat on the night of 20–21 June 1944.

By this time the Japanese had lost three quarters of their deployed aircraft, a total of 480 planes.

The US carriers reported that despite their illuminated flight decks, they had lost 72 aircraft through crash-landings or emergency sea landings. Forty-nine out of the 209 crashed pilots could not be rescued.

The Americans called the battle in the Philippine Sea the "Great Marianas Turkey Shoot." The battle resulted in the almost complete destruction of the Japanese aircraft-carrier force. The way to the Philippines was now open. The Americans were free to continue their landings in the Marianas, and Japan had lost its outermost defensive belt.

On Wednesday 21 June 1944, some 2,500 bombers and escort fighters of the US 8th Air Force attacked the government district of Berlin, and aircraft factories and rail installations in the Berlin area. German fighters and flak shot down 44 heavy bombers.

The attack lasted less than 30 minutes, during which brief time the US forces unleashed 2,000 tons of bombs. While the attack was still going on, 114 Flying Fortresses and 70 Mustang escort fighters turned southward and bombed the Ruhland fuel works in Lower Silesia.

Then the formation took an eastern heading, toward the Soviet Union. A German He 177 long-range reconnaissance plane followed it from Silesia. That evening 73 of the Fortress bombers landed at Poltava base and 41 in Mirgorod, while the Mustang fighters landed at Piryatin. These were the three Soviet airfields that the US forces were using in Operation Frantic Joe.

General Meister, the energetic commanding general of the German 4th Air Force (IV. Fliegerkorps), took only a few hours to organize an improvised blitz operation. He gathered around 200 Heinkel He 111 and Ju 88 bombers of the 3rd, 4th, 53rd and 55th Bomber Wings and sent them on what was to be one of the last German air raids of World War II.

At 11:35 P.M. the US air force command in Poltava was informed by the Soviets that German aircraft had overflown the front lines and were headed their way.

At 12:15 A.M. 80 German bombers flew over Poltava airfield, while the rest went to Piryatin. Flares were dropped over the heavy US bombers, which were lined up along the takeoff runways almost as if this were peacetime and offered a target that it was impossible to miss.

The Soviet antiaircraft opened fire and 4 out of 40 Soviet night fighters took off from a nearby airfield. For almost one hour the German aircraft unloaded their bombs on the US planes, and starting at 2:00 A.M. a number of Ju 88s began strafing raids. This second raid wiped out the entire supply of bombs and the fuel warehouses.

The German formation had destroyed 47 Flying Fortresses, 14 Mustangs and one Jak-9 Soviet fighter without suffering a single casualty. Counting the 44 bombers which had already been shot down while raiding Berlin on June 21, the US forces had now lost a total of 91 four-engined bombers and 14 fighters as the result of a single raid. This was the highest known casualty rate suffered by the USAAF in any operation of World War II. And more bad news was still to come, because 14 more of the US raiders were missing: seven Flying Fortresses and seven Liberators were knocked out when they landed in neutral Sweden around noon on June 21. Operation Frantic Joe was halted until further notice.

The Ju 88s had spent almost half an hour flying in low to bombard Poltava airbase with their aerial guns and SD-2 fragmentation bombs and then took off for home. If their crews had paid closer attention during their return flight in the dawn of June 22, they might have had more to report than merely the successful destruction of the US fuel and bomb depots in Poltava. For today was the third anniversary of Operation Barbarossa, the German attack on the Soviet Union, and Stalin commemorated the event by assembling 166 of his best divisions in the forests of White Russia, under conditions of extreme secrecy. Even as the German bomber units were flying over this region headed west and suspecting nothing, the Soviet troops were waiting for the signal to launch their summer offensive. The offensive came as a complete surprise to the Germans and inflicted on them a defeat that surpassed even Stalingrad. While the last Ju 88s were landing back at base, the Soviet bomber units commanded by General Rudenko were taking off to mount the attack on German Army Group Center under Field Marshal Busch.

On 22 June 1944, German Luftflotte 6 (under General Ritter von Greim) had 40 fighter planes with which to ward off an attack by approximately 7,000 aircraft – the massed forces of 4 Soviet air armies.

By Friday 23 June 1944, 370 German V-1 flying bombs had reached London over a ten-day period.

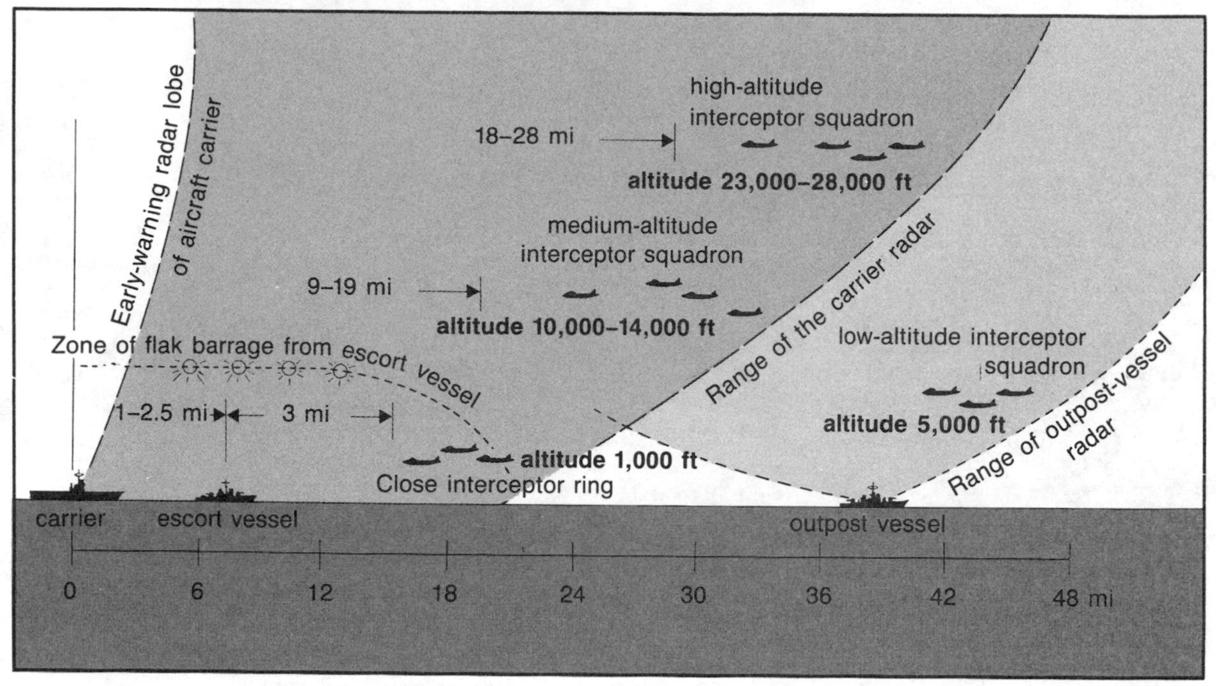

Summer 1944: Radar-screen and air defense layout of a US naval formation in the Pacific.

The British decided to reorganize their air defense once again. Fighter planes were now ordered to intercept the missiles while they were still over the Channel. All the antiaircraft was transferred to the southeast coast. A dense network of barrage balloons rose around London, and more fighter planes patrolled between the antiaircraft battery zone along the Channel coast, and the barrage balloons.

On the night of 24–25 June 1944, a new German weapon was deployed against the invasion fleet in the Seine Bay: "Mistletoe" aircraft (official codename "Beethoven"), also known as father-and-son or piggy-back aircraft. These were composite aircraft, made up of two planes, one riding on the other's back. There were two basic types of Mistletoes. Both used a pilotless Ju 88 bomber as the bottom plane; it carried a large 3.5-ton explosive warhead and was guided to the target by a fighter plane on top. The guide plane on top was either an Me 109, or an FW 190, which would abandon the Ju 88 shortly before it exploded. The Mistletoe composite aircraft were tested at Nordhausen and Peenemünde at the beginning of 1944. In May 1944 they were delivered to a special squadron of German 4th Group, 101st Bomber Training Wing, which was ordered to take off from Denmark to raid the Royal Navy base at Scapa Flow (Orkneys, Scotland). After the Allied invasion, the special squadron was transferred by night-time express transport to St. Dizier in the Pas de Calais. On the night of 24–25 June 1944, 5 S-1 Mistletoes (using Me 109s as guide planes) took off from St. Dizier escorted by Me 109 G fighters. This first raid was a genuine suicide raid, because at the time the whole of northern France was teeming with Mosquito night fighters. The Ju 88 in one Mistletoe rig had to be blown up while it was still making its approach. The other 4 reached the Seine Bay, dropped flares, and by their light raided the ships lying at anchor, without realizing that these were scrap units that were now being used only as breakwaters. The naval bay was fogbound, so the effects of the raid could not be observed. The 5 guide machines returned safely to St. Dizier. Next day the Germans learned that one of the breakwater ships had been sunk. So ended the first and last Mistletoe raid from northern France.

Despite the concentrated Allied air raids on German manufacturing plants, German production reached all-time records in the first half of 1944. The Germans were producing an average of 3,650 aircraft per month. But they could not make use of this substantial capability, because the shortage of pilots and air fuel meant that most aircraft stayed

A German S-2 Mistletoe composite aircraft. On the bottom is a Ju 88 bomber carrying approximately 3.8 tons of hollow explosive; on the top is a Focke Wulf 190 as guide plane. S-1 Mistletoe composite aircraft used a Ju 88 with an Me 109. Approximately 250 Ju 88s were adapted for use as Mistletoe aircraft.

on the ground. In June 1944, the production of synthetic fuel sank to 107,000 tons, which was approximately one third the production of May. It was only a question of months before the German war machine was bound to grind to a halt.

In the Balkans the US 15th Air Force, operating out of Italy, made several grand raids on oil fields in Rumania in the period of March to June 1944. Even the Danube river was mined to stop transport of Rumanian oil to Germany.

At the end of June 1944, a 210-mile-wide breach was torn in the Eastern Front. The Soviet forces streamed west, encircling the remains of 3 German armies.

Luftflotte 6 hastily evacuated its airfields and discontinued its supply flights to the various contingents of cut-off German troops.

Lower, pilotless plane heads for target on autopilot
30° flight angle
Target approach
Rig climbs to attack altitude
Team-rig flight below radar
Upper, piloted plane separates from the team-rig

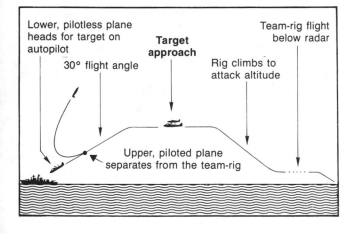

Left: German Mistletoe raiding tactics. Mistletoe composite aircraft were deployed against pinpoint targets when, due to strong defenses, manned aircraft would have little hope of success, and when the explosive charge of normal bombs would have been insufficient to destroy the target.

1944

July to December

Tuesday 4 July 1944
The German *Wehrmacht High Command* announced:

Last night heavy German bombers attacked enemy ship assemblies off the coast of Normandy. Two special landing boats received square hits. Additional hits were observed during unloading.

The battles have become increasingly harsh along the central Eastern Front. The Luftwaffe effectively deployed ground-attack planes in the ground battles, smashed numerous enemy columns and destroyed a number of Soviet tanks, cannon and several hundred vehicles. During the night, German bombers led attacks against several Soviet railroad stations and destroyed large quantities of supplies. Extensive fires and powerful explosions developed, especially at the Borisov rail station.

Heavy Night Bombers Make Tactical Daylight Raids

Saturday 8 July 1944, London
The *British Air Ministry* announced:

The largest deployment of Allied aerial forces so far took place in the 24 hours between Wednesday and Thursday noon. Powerful formations operated day and night over France. The Allies now have such complete command of French air space, that for the first time heavy RAF night bombers could be dispatched on tactical daylight raids with a relatively small fighter escort. This capability has initiated a new phase in the air war that is expected to have devastating consequences for the Germans.

"V-2" Launch Ramps in Holland?

Friday 28 July 1944, London
The *British War Office* announced:

Reports from the exiled Dutch government in London indicate that the newest German secret weapon, known as the "V-2," will be deployed against England from Holland in several weeks' time. The V-2 is said to be a giant heavy rocket weighing 90 tons, a so-called stratosphere missile. The same source suggests that preparations are being made to launch V-1 flying bombs from Holland. The fact that all Dutch males were mobilized in April and May of this year to work on mysterious installations near the Hoek of Holland, substantiates the report.

Field Marshal Rommel in an Accident

The following notice appeared in the Nazi newspaper *Völkischer Beobachter*, dated 3 August 1944:

On July 17, Field Marshal Rommel suffered a motor-vehicle accident in France as the result of an airplane attack; he was wounded and received a brain concussion. His condition is satisfactory and his life is not in danger.

Allied Landing in Southern France

Tuesday 15 August 1944
General Eisenhower's Headquarters announced in a special communiqué:

Today American, British and French forces, supported by the Allied air forces and by the combined American, British and French fleet, landed on the southern coast of France.

16 August 1944
The German *Wehrmacht High Command* announced:

German forces have beaten back a number of attempted enemy landings on the coast of southern France between Toulon and Cannes. Nevertheless the enemy has succeeded in getting a foothold at several points along the coast, where violent battles are now taking place. Enemy airborne troops dropped to the rear of our defensive zone, have been attacked by our reserves. The enemy has lost 23 planes over the western and southern coasts of France in air and sea battles, and to Luftwaffe and naval flak guns.

The Air War Has Been Decided

Swedish Major S. Wennerström stated in the Swedish newspaper *Stockholms-Tidningen*, dated 21 August 1944:

Is this headline premature, which says that the outcome of the air war has been decided? Indeed not, at least where the European war theater is concerned, for the Allied air forces have at last won such overwhelming supremacy in Europe that they can justifiably be said to hold command of the air—and will continue to do so in the foreseeable future. "Command of the air" is a popular phrase stemming from the days when the Germans dominated the air, but technical experts in modern aerial strategy use it too. They would define the term approximately as follows: "Command of the air consists in the ability to prevent any substantial aerial activity by the enemy, and simultaneously to deploy one's own aerial forces without hindrance from the enemy." This is the very thing that the Allies have, for all practical purposes, now achieved.

Victory Is Near!

German *SS soldier-correspondent Joachim Fernau* wrote the following account for the German weekly newspaper *Das Reich*, August 1944:

In half a year at most we will all know what only a few people know today: that this final phase of the war, which broke out on 16 June 1944, held a secret and that in reality the three months of June, July and August had a different face than we all believed. The time we are now going through, is the most dramatic in modern world history. Later ages will one day see plain and clear that it all came down to millimeters and seconds and that split-second timing must have underlain Germany's victory.

So in half a year everyone will know it. The feeling then will be the same as when a raging, noisy, dark night of storm is followed next morning by a day that is completely still, completely clear. Everything, simply everything [is still], there is nothing left that is frightening, that is threatening. The whole of the past night then seems almost incomprehensible . . .

I am writing this article at the Normandy Front and am myself a soldier. Nor am I a stranger to the bombing raids on our German cities; I was in the middle of a bomb carpet in Berlin. I too have known concern about my wife, about illness and poverty . . .

But something strange has happened now that I worked out these thoughts, and now that I find them confirmed at every turn; the fighting and the reports from the East have lost none of their gravity but they have lost all their terror.

Until autumn! Then we will know why we had to make this last great effort; nor is it beyond our energies. Never in this war have we given up when we found ourselves in a critical spot. There is still a final price to pay and we will pay it, with all our means and with all our strength. Truly, victory is very near.

Friday 25 August 1944
The German *Wehrmacht High Command* announced:

Yesterday the Soviets lost 58 aircraft in aerial combats and to German flak artillery. First Lt. Hartmann, squadron captain in a German fighter wing, shot down 11 aircraft, thereby winning his 301st aerial victory, and has been decorated with the oak-leaf cluster to the Knight's Cross degree of the Iron Cross.

Allied Airborne Operation at Arnhem

Tuesday 19 September 1944, London
The *British War Office* announced:

Yesterday large numbers of airborne troops and quantities of supplies continued to be flown into

A German Heinkel 111 H-22 bomber of 3rd Group, 3rd Bomber Wing—renamed 1st Group of the 53rd "Condor Legion" Bomber Wing—has just launched a V-1 flying bomb. Operation Rumpelkammer, the German program to launch V-1s from aircraft, cost many casualties, for often the flying bombs would explode while taking off from the carrier plane.

Holland; the First Airborne have reached their initial targets and taken prisoners.

The armored spearheads of the British Second Army, which are rolling northward from the Belgian border, have made contact with the airborne troops. The Second Army detoured around Eindhoven (Holland) and has travelled 15 miles in 24 hours.

20 September 1944
The German *Wehrmacht High Command* announced:

Enemy airborne forces have landed around Arnhem in central Holland where we are tightening the circle around them with concentric attacks. Our troops, strongly reinforced by German fighter-plane formations, have inflicted on the enemy heavy losses in men and matériel. So far more than 1,700 prisoners have been taken. An enemy armored spearhead is advancing northeastward from Eindhoven. Our troops are counterattacking here too.

Wednesday 27 September 1944
The German *Wehrmacht High Command* announced:

On September 26 we broke the last resistance of the encircled British First Airborne Division at Arnhem. In ten days of bitter fighting, members of all branches of the armed forces, hastily assembled under the leadership of SS Panzer Corps general Bittrick—have totally annihilated a British elite division despite the toughest resistance, and despite the fact that the British flew in additional airborne troops to reinforce the pocket. All attempts by the enemy to relieve the encircled division, came to a bloody end with high losses.

Thursday 28 September 1944, London
The *British War Office* announced:

On Monday and Tuesday nights, the soldiers of the British First Airborne Division were withdrawn across the lower Rhine after putting up a heroic resistance since September 17.

The British division deployed in this operation [Market Garden] numbered 6,500 men (not including the several hundred glider pilots); of these, 2,000 have returned unhurt. Twelve hundred wounded had to be left behind, but an officer who escaped captivity after being taken prisoner, reports that the Germans are giving them fair treatment.

The British Second Army is steadily expanding its corridor as it moves northward through Holland, and is making good progress on the right flank along the Meuse.

The Flying Bombs

Friday 29 September 1944, London
The *British Air Ministry* announced:

Last night over the North Sea, British fighter planes shot down two German Heinkel 111 bombers, which were operating as flying launch ramps for V-1 flying bombs. But the two planes had already launched their V-1s before they crashed into the sea.

Mosquitos and Mustangs in the German Luftwaffe

Wednesday 4 October 1944, London
US 8th Air Force Headquarters announced:

For several days the German Luftwaffe has been using Allied Mosquito and Mustang aircraft furnished with German national emblems. Yesterday a Mosquito flown by Germans was shot down near

Aachen. Aerial combats have taken place over Holland between Allied and German Mustang fighters. These Allied machines which now are in German hands, are aircraft which recently have been forced to land behind German lines.

Sunday 15 October 1944, London
The *British Air Ministry* announced:

Yesterday, a day of clear skies, the RAF and the 8th USAAF undertook heavy daylight raids on targets in Germany. Some of the formations took off from French airfields so they were able to carry heavy bombloads. During the day a total of 6,000 to 7,000 metric tons of bombs fell on Germany, causing vast destruction. The main attack was against Duisburg. Within a short period, more than 1,000 British Lancaster and Halifax bombers, escorted by long-range fighters, dropped more than 4,500 metric tons of explosives bombs and a large quantity of incendiaries on the city, which went up in flames. This was the heaviest air raid that any German city has ever suffered on a single day. The main traffic avenues in Duisburg are blocked with debris. Photographs of the target taken over the bombed city in the afternoon, give the impression that a volcano has erupted.

15 October 1944, London
The *British Air Ministry* issued the following supplementary bulletin:

Last night another 5,000 tons of bombs dropped on Duisburg, surpassing the previous day's record. This was the heaviest air raid in history: Approximately 10,000 tons of blast and incendiary bombs dropped on a single city within a twenty-hour period.

V-1 Flying Bombs

Wednesday 1 November 1944
RAF Headquarters announced:

Yesterday our Mosquitos shot down two German He 111 bombers that were outfitted at V-1 launch ramps. One V-1 hit a packed hotel in southern England, causing many casualties.

US Air Raid on Japan

1 November 1944, Tokyo
Japanese Air Defense Headquarters announced:

Several enemy bombers have appeared over the area between Tokyo and Yokohama. Two planes succeeded in penetrating east of Tokyo at an altitude of 19,000 feet, but Japanese defenses were able to intercept them before a single bomb fell. One bomber was shot down.

Gestapo Headquarters in Denmark Destroyed

Thursday 2 November 1944, London
RAF Headquarters announced:

On Tuesday 31 October, in an extraordinarily daring operation, 4 waves of 6 Mosquito bombers each attacked Gestapo headquarters in Denmark, located in two buildings of Aarhus University. The pinpoint raid was made from an altitude of only 80 feet. Recently the Danish underground reported that the Gestapo had assembled thousands of documents in Aarhus in preparation for a decisive strike against the Danish resistance movement. Several hundred Gestapo officials were reported to have arrived in Aarhus, and were about to go into action after a swift examination of the documentary evidence.

Once this information was received, a mockup of Aarhus University was built in Britain with the assistance of the Danish underground, and the Mosquito pilots practiced flying a precision raid at very low altitude. The most difficult aspect of the raid was that the Mosquitos had to drop delayed-fuse bombs over the target at 2-second intervals before the powerful air defense had time to react, and also the last crew to attack knew that the first bomb dropped would explode in only one minute. The German antiaircraft was in fact completely surprised by the low-flying Mosquitos, and opened fire only after the last squadron had already unloaded its bombs. One Mosquito scraped the roof of a building and barely staggered back to England. Gestapo headquarters were completely destroyed.

The V-2 Secret Weapon

Thursday 9 November 1944, London
The *Reuters News Agency* reported with the advice of military experts:

So far no sign has been seen in England of the V-2 weapon mentioned in German Armed Forces reports. We are prepared to accept that Germany has additional secret weapons, but so far we have had no practical opportunity to confront them. The British Press unanimously believe that German claims about the V-2 are a propaganda substitute for a speech by Hitler due on the 21st anniversary of the abortive Munich Beer-Hall Putsch, which, however, he failed to deliver.

Friday 10 November 1944, London
The American *Associated Press News Agency* reported:

The new V-2 rockets fall like shooting stars, and although they cannot compare with the flying bombs as weapons of terror, they create a huge thundering noise that can be heard six miles away. A man who was less than 50 yards from a V-2 explosion said, "I didn't hear a sound before the blowup—and then I thought the end of the world had come." Many people have said that they heard a double explosion, one accompanying the flash in the sky, and a second when the rocket actually impacted. Publication of reports about the rockets was censored in Britain for a time, but it has now been learned that many people have barely escaped with their lives since the secret "retaliatory weapon no. 2" became operational. Houses, schools, hospitals, churches, pubs and other buildings have been destroyed or damaged in the rocket attacks. Eyewitnesses who have seen them fall, estimate that they are between 30 and 50 feet long.

24 November 1944, Tokyo
Imperial Japanese Headquarters released a communiqué saying:

Approximately seventy aircraft have attacked Tokyo from a very high altitude in a raid lasting 2 hours. Reports received so far indicate that 3 enemy bombers were shot down.

Tuesday 28 November 1944, London
The *British Air Ministry* announced:

One Monday, in favorable weather, the USAAF and the RAF continued their daylight raids on targets in Germany. Approximately 300–400 German fighters, including a number of jet fighters, took to the air in their country's defense and severe aerial combats ensued in which 98 German aircraft were shot down. It is reported that 270 Lancasters made a bomb run on Munich at 5:00 A.M. in clear weather and bright moonlight. The concentrated raid lasted approximately 15 minutes, and 12,000-lb bombs were dropped on a German city for the first time. Previously these largest-caliber bombs had been deployed only in operations against industrial installations or military targets. The German battleship *Tirpitz* was sunk with 12,000-lb bombs this last November 12.

Night Raid on Tokyo

Thursday 30 November 1944, Washington
The *US War Department* announced:

Yesterday US B-29 Superfortresses again raided Tokyo. This was the third US operation against the Japanese capital so far this week.

30 November 1944, Tokyo
Imperial Japanese Headquarters announced:

Yesterday night, relatively small formations of US B-29 bombers stationed on the Marianas, bombed the Japanese capital. The aircraft flew in several waves, unloading their bombs over Toyko and Shizuoka province from a very high altitude and through a dense carpet of cloud. All the fires that broke out in various districts of the city, were extinguished in a short time. No military targets were hit and there was minimal loss of life.

Monday 18 December 1944
The German *Wehrmacht High Command* announced:

At 5:30 A.M. on December 16, after a brief but powerful prefatory bombardment, strong German forces along a broad front of the Siegfried Line have moved onto the attack and in their first assault have overrun the foremost American positions in the Ardennes between Hautes Fagnes and northern Luxembourg. This great offensive battle is now raging, with strong German fighter formations flying cover for the ground troops. The enemy was taken completely by surprise, and details will not be released until later so as to keep him in the dark. By last account our fighters have shot down 48 enemy bombers in combats over the front lines. Luftwaffe flak guns destroyed another 21 aircraft. During the night, strong bomber and night ground-attack aircraft effectively raided enemy troop movements and supply centers.

How the V-2 Is Affecting London

Sunday 24 December 1944, Stockholm
The Swedish newspaper *Svenska Dagbladet* reported:

Portuguese sources say that travellers arriving in Lisbon from Britain in the past few days, are reporting sensational details about the effects of the German retaliatory weapons on the City of London. Three of the Thames bridges have already been destroyed by V-weapons. The travellers, who

It was an unusual spectacle to see a US B-17 bomber meet a B-29 Superfortress in the air. Only by seeing the two side by side does one realize the enormous size of the B-29s, the heaviest bombers of the war.

expressed joy to have escaped the terror of the London bombardment before Christmas, all agree in their impression that the devastation caused by the V-2 weapons is substantially greater than that caused by V-1 flying bombs. The Westminster Parliament buildings have been seriously damaged. Not one building is left standing within a 500-yard radius of Leicester Square. Another large London landmark, Piccadilly Circus, is in ruins. A substantial number of V-2 rockets have exploded right on target in the center of London. Now that thousands of buildings are being destroyed, the population is being evacuated hastily to northern England.

Strategy and Tactics

July to December 1944

The beautiful summer weather of early July 1944, favored air operations in both Western and Eastern Europe. This may help to explain why the Soviets succeeded in smashing German Army Group Center under Field Marshal Busch and penetrating westward with the speed of a blitzkrieg, while in Normandy the Allies still tried in vain to break out of the landing beachhead and extend their forces.

"Our secret weapons are Normandy's apple-tree gardens and thick hedgerows," German staff officers of the 84th Army Corps remarked sarcastically. Indeed, virtually no one on the Allied side had given enough thought to the fact that the Norman hedgerows were not simple rows of bushes but high and solid earth embankments, overgrown with trees and often interspersed with ravines, that could stop even heavy tanks and that afforded ideal cover from aircraft.

In the early hours of 1 July 1944, Allied bombers had laid a carpet of over 1,000 tons of bombs over a single road crossing at Villers Bocage southeast of Caen, yet it had not helped them to speed up their advance.

On Monday 3 July 1944, Field Marshal von Rundstedt, the German Western commander, had a telephone conversation with Field Marshal Keitel, the commander-in-chief of the German armed forces. Keitel asked what conclusions von Rundstedt drew from the situation in Normandy, and von Rundstedt replied: "We should make peace, you fools! What else?" He was replaced by Field Marshal von Kluge.

In July RAF Bomber Command raids on the German V-1 launch ramps and depots in France reached their climax. Very large, 12,000-lb bombs were used, which like the Dambuster bombs deployed in the raids on the Eder and Möhne Dams, had been designed by British engineer Dr. Wallis. The new high-explosive bomb, which exceeded the speed of sound as it fell, was about 20 feet long and was known as a Tallboy.

On Tuesday 4 July 1944, the famed 617 "Dambuster" Squadron flew several raids using Tallboys. The target was the mushroom caves at St. Leu d'Esserent about 30 miles northwest of Paris, an area heavily defended by German flak, formerly the site of mushroom cultivation, where now hundreds of flying bombs were stored instead.

The limestone ceilings of the caves did not give way to the bombing, but Colonel Walter, chief of staff of the German Sixty-Fifth Army, wrote of the bombing raids: "Even men with very strong nerves could no longer be expected to spend any length of time in such caves."

On Thursday 6 July 1944, Winston Churchill stated before the House of Commons that according to his information, by 6:00 A.M. that morning a total of 2,745 V-1 flying bombs had been fired at England and 2,752 civilians had been killed, that is approximately one person for every flying bomb.

On Friday 7 July 1944, 617 Squadron of the RAF

renewed its Tallboy attacks on the mushroom caves of St. Leu d'Esserent.

That same day, the US 8th Air Force carried out several raids on targets in and around Leipzig, deploying almost 1,100 Flying Fortresses and Liberators with Lightnings flying cover; they laid a carpet of bombs across a wide area. The German 9th "Storm" Group, 3rd Fighter Wing, particularly distinguished itself in the defense.

In their attempt to halt the US daylight raids, the Germans tried to use new "storm-fighter" tactics developed by a fighter squadron that had been set up on a test basis in the fall of 1943. Initially part of the 1st Day Fighter Wing (JG 1), the squadron was equipped with armored FW 190 aircraft. The storm pilots flew in as close as they could to the four-engined bomber formations, and opened fire on them while remaining in a densely-graded formation. They were given the choice of ramming their own planes into the enemy bombers to get them to crash and bailing out if they could.

On July 7 an air battle took place in the Magdeburg-Oschersleben-Leipzig area, between US bombers and the German 300th Storm Fighter Wing (JG 300 under Major Dahl). The group, now part of the Udet Fighter Wing, had taken off from a base at Ansbach. In the battle, the German 4th Storm Group, 3rd Fighter Wing, shot down 30 Liberator bombers and 4 escort fighters, the highest number of air kills achieved by a Luftwaffe day-fighter group at any time in the war. The US 8th Air Force also lost several heavy bombers to ramming. A total of 58 US bombers and 24 long-range fighters were shot down that day.

The Allies in Normandy began the unprecedented continuous deployment of heavy bombers in the tactical support of the ground troops. They released bomb carpets onto the foremost German lines, often concentrating on sectors only a few hundred yards wide. These prepared the way for breakthrough attempts by Allied armor and infantry units. The British were the first to use these tactics when their countless attacks on German troops at Caen were halted by strong defensive fire that drew heavy casualties.

On the evening of July 7, the RAF flew one such tactical operation along the northern edge of the city of Caen, in support of British First Corps. To avoid endangering British troops, the bomb carpet was laid 3 to 3½ miles in advance of the British front lines, onto a rectangular strip of land 2½ miles wide and just under a mile deep. Within a 40-minute period, 450 Lancasters had dropped 2,363 tons of bombs. Northern Caen was now in ruins; yet the Germans, whose forces were chiefly north of the bombing zone, suffered few losses. Meanwhile 350 French citizens of Caen had been killed.

At 7:00 A.M. next morning, approximately 2,000 medium and heavy bombers of the US 9th Air Force began carpet bombing of the same segment of the front just bombed by the British. They used mainly blast bombs with contact fuses so as to avoid creating deep bomb craters that would hinder the advance of the tanks.

When the German 84th Army Corps first reported to their Seventh Army headquarters that 1,500 Allied bombers had bombed a sector containing no more than a battalion of German troops, the German commanders refused to believe it. They thought that the report was a flagrant exaggeration and were incensed that a military staff known for its sober and reliable judgments, should have stooped to drawing up "inspired bulletins."

The Allies had by now landed one million soldiers in Normandy; but despite their overwhelming material superiority and the most massive aerial support, they had not succeeded, in over four weeks of hard fighting, in conquering more than 1% of France.

The number of German V-1 flying bombs striking England increased in the first half of July 1944, and on July 10 the British concluded that their anti-aircraft guns could not function with full efficiency because they had to be wary of hitting RAF fighter planes. They then carried out a final regrouping of antiaircraft batteries, transferring all the guns to the Channel coast. The V-1 maintained a constant speed and engaged in no evasive maneuvers, which made it an ideal antiaircraft target; but it proved hard to fight all the same because it flew too high for the light guns and too low for the heavy guns.

On Wednesday 12 July 1944, the RAF brought the Gloster Meteor into service, the first and only Allied jet fighter to become operational during World War II. Number 616 (South Yorkshire) Squadron received the first jets, which were used to help fight the V-1s.

Thursday 13 July 1944 was a special date for RAF Bomber Command—the day when the first German Lichtenstein SN-2 wide-angle airborne radar finally fell into their hands. It was this radar that had been giving the German night fighters their great success since autumn 1943. British Pilot Officer W. D. Raymond reported: "It was shortly after sunrise, at about 4:30 A.M.; the mist still lay over our airbase, Woodbridge in Suffolk, when the sound of engines announced the approach of an aircraft from the North Sea coast about ten miles away. The plane circled several times over the airfield. I took it for one of the Mosquitos which were forever getting lost and straying overhead after returning from their missions in Europe, so I drew my flare gun and fired green flares to signal permission for it to land. The plane seemed to have been waiting for this because it set down immediately and taxied over the runway through the swathes of mist. When I heard the engines switch off, I climbed into the big vehicle we always used to fetch in the crews and drove toward the machine, whose dark silhouette stood out in the fog.

"The first thing that puzzled me was that I saw three crew members coming toward me, whereas a Mosquito has only two men on board. I drove nearer, and there were really and truly three German airmen standing before me, no less surprised than I. I drew my pistol and they surrendered without resistance. I made them give me their weapons and ordered them to walk to the airfield building while I slowly drove along beside them.

"The plane I had taken for a Mosquito in the morning fog, turned out to be the newest type of German night fighter, a Ju 88 G-1, which had become operational only two months earlier and was equipped with every imaginable kind of radio and airborne radar equipment, all completely unfamiliar to us. The aircraft, whose fuselage bore the number 4R+UR, belonged to 7 Squadron, 2nd Night Fighter Wing, and had been assigned to patrol the North Sea. The young crew, who appeared dumbfounded, said that they had only just completed 100 hours of flight training and had flown by compass heading, but by mistake had proceeded in exactly the wrong direction and thought that they were over their own airfield. The lads had been lucky, because when our ground personnel tried to take a petrol sample for testing purposes, there was no fuel left in the tank.

"I immediately notified my superior officer in nearby Ipswich, and a couple of hours later a plane landed at Woodbridge field carrying Wing Commander Jackson, Professor Jones and other specialists."

On the afternoon of that same day, July 13, the Ju 88 was taken to Farnborough where next day Wing Commander Jackson began tests on the aircraft and its equipment. The British Secret Intelligence Service, the SIS, had learned from captured Luftwaffe airmen that in addition to Lichtenstein SN-2, the German night fighters also carried other new airborne radars; but as yet no details were known. Thus until capture of the Ju 88, Bomber Command had no suspicion that their Monica radar, whose bleeps were meant to warn British crews of the approach of German night fighters, had an unintentional side-effect: German Flensburg radar was able to pick up emissions from Monica, so the British device had been leading the night fighters straight to the RAF bombers ever since it was incorporated into the bombers at the start of 1943. Another German radar, Naxos, allowed the night fighters to detect the impulses of the British H2S blind-bombing device, and to locate the bomber streams from a distance of 90 miles.

When Wing Commander Jackson had made his test flights, arrived at these discoveries and reported them to Bomber Command, the horrified Air Chief Marshal Harris ordered all the Monica warning devices removed from the tails of his aircraft immediately. The crews were even ordered to use their basic identification signals only in real emergencies, and the H2S radar equipment was to be switched on only after the bombers were already within range of the German ground radar systems.

But Jackson's most important discovery was that Lichtenstein SN-2, the German wide-angle radar, worked on a frequency of 85 megahertz.

So, the unexpected landing of a Ju 88 G-1 at Woodbridge field took from the German night fighters their last hope of defending themselves successfully against British night raids.

A suburb of Caen (Normandy) in the first week of July 1944, after RAF heavy bombers raided the city in the tactical support of Allied ground troops.

On Friday 14 July 1944, French Bastille Day, the USAAF carried out its largest operation in aid of the French Resistance. Two hundred US B-17s and B-24s—escorted by 60 Spitfires—flew in several waves over a 6-hour period to drop containers of weapons and ammunition over the plateau of Caussée de Loubressac. Fifteen hundred Resistance fighters led by Colonel Collignon secured the drop zone, which was approximately 12 miles square and had been marked with bedsheets. Local peasants carried the supply containers to hiding-places; there were enough supplies to equip at least 7,000 men.

On Saturday 15 July 1944, the US 15th Air Force based in Italy bombed the Ploesti oil refineries. After this heavy raid, the Rumanian oil-production center had been virtually eliminated as a strategic target.

On Monday 17 July 1944, the US aerial forces deployed napalm incendiary bombs for the first time. A jelled, combustible compound of naphtha and palm oil was carried by a number of P-38 Lightning fighter-bombers inside disposable fuel tanks during their raids on the gasoline depots in Coutances southwest of St. Lô in Normandy.

That same Monday, Field Marshal Rommel, commander-in-chief of German Army Group B, was badly wounded during an Allied strafer attack. Early in the afternoon Rommel was with the 1st SS Panzer Corps commanded by SS General Dietrich; at 4:00 P.M. he left to drive to his headquarters at La Roche Guyon. Before his departure Dietrich begged him to avoid the main road and to use a jeep instead of his heavy Horch vehicle; but Rommel refused. Leaving St. Pierre-sur-Dives he took the Livarot-Vimoutiers road. He was accompanied by his aide Captain Lang, by Major Neuhaus and by Sergeant Holke, who looked out for strafer planes. Near the village of St. Foy-de-Montgomery Holke reported two Spitfires nearby. The driver, Sgt. 1st Class Daniel tried to reach a grove of poplar trees; but Spitfire IX flown by Squadron Leader J. J. Le Roux of No. 602 (City of Glasgow) Squadron, who had taken off a short time ago from the newly-installed B 11 forward airfield beside the destroyed German coastal battery at Longues, was already opening fire. Rommel was hit by glass splinters and flying stones and immediately lost consciousness. The badly-wounded driver lost control of the car, smashed into a tree, shot across the road and finally ground to a halt in a flood ditch. Rommel was thrown out. When a second strafer plane appeared, Lang and Holke quickly drew the Field Marshal to cover. Still unconscious, Rommel was taken to the Luftwaffe military hospital at Bernay. Apart from large numbers of shrapnel wounds, the doctors found he was suffering from a severe skull fracture and fractures of the temple and cheekbones. Field Marshal von Kluge, the commander of the German Western armies, now assumed command of Rommel's Army Group B as well.

On Tuesday 18 July 1944, British and American troops launched a powerful offensive in which they began to cross the Orne. This operation was preceded by the most massive Allied tactical air raids so far: More than 2,200 planes, including 1,600 four-engined bombers, unleashed almost 8,000 tons of bombs onto the German positions in Colombelles, a suburb of Caen. Nearly 2,000 of the local population were killed, and 1,300 injured.

By Wednesday 19 July 1944, 412 heavy and 1,184 light British antiaircraft guns, and 200 rocket launchers, stood ready along a 3-mile-wide strip of land between Beachy Head promontory (Sussex) west of Dover, and St. Margaret's east of Dover.

The antiaircraft projectiles were now fitted with the newest type of proximity fuse, the MK 45, a

tiny radar set. If its waves picked up a target within a one-hundred-foot radius, the projectiles would explode automatically. The results were spectacular: Now an average of only 77 antiaircraft shells were needed to bring down a V-1 flying bomb. The US Navy had developed the proximity fuse on the basis of data supplied by Professor R. V. Jones after he had studied Allied aerial reconnaissance photos of the V-1 flying bombs. Thanks to the new fuse, the proportion of V-1s being shot down by British antiaircraft, rose from 43% to 83% within a few weeks.

Above: Woodbridge airbase (England) on 13 July 1944. A Ju 88 G-1 of the German 2nd Night Fighter Wing has landed in Great Britain by mistake, carrying on its nose the large aerial array of Lichtenstein SN-2 airborne radar.

Opposite page above: The strafer pilot who attacked Field Marshal Rommel's car south of Le Havre on 17 July 1944. He was Squadron Leader J. J. "Chris" Le Roux of 602 (City of Glasgow) Squadron of the South African RAF.

Opposite page below: The aerial array of the British "Piperack" jamming set which neutralized German Lichtenstein SN-2 airborne radar. Here we see it installed in the tail machine-gun turret of a B-17 bomber of RAF 214 Squadron, 100 Group.

On Thursday 20 July 1944, General Korten, the Luftwaffe's general chief of staff, was gravely wounded in the attempted assassination of Hitler; three days later he died of his wounds.

On Sunday 23 July 1944, exactly 10 days after the surprise landing of the Ju 88 G-1 in Woodbridge, Bomber Command started dropping a modified version of Window radar chaff during night raids over Europe. These tinfoil jamming strips, developed by Wing Commander Jackson, neutralized the 85-megahertz frequency used by Lichtenstein SN-2 radar.

Meanwhile Dr. Jones and his team worked on a jamming device called "Piperack." Soon it went into rapid mass production and rendered Lichtenstein SN-2 radar completely ineffective.

At 2:30 P.M. on Thursday 27 July 1944, an RAF Gloster Meteor jet fighter of No. 616 (South Yorkshire) Squadron left its airbase at Manston (Kent) to make its first anti-V-1 patrol flight over the Channel; but it met no flying bombs. Shortly after, two more Meteors took off, and Squadron Leader Watts saw a V-1, overtook it near Ashford, and pressed the firing button; but his guns jammed and the V-1 got away.

Chance decreed that the very next day, the German Luftwaffe would deploy for the first time its own new aircraft, the Me 163 B, a rocket-carrying fighter. Seven of these "Comet" fighters were flown by members of 1 Squadron, 400th Fighter Wing (JG 400 commanded by Captain Olejnik), which had been formed in Wittmundhafen out of the 16th Test Unit. JG 400 was assigned to protect the synthetic fuel plants which were vital to Germany.

On Friday 28 July 1944, the US 359th Mustang Fighter Group was escorting a US 8th Air Force unit of B-17 bombers, when suddenly the fighter pilots sighted two vapor trails about 10,000 feet above the bombers; the trails were moving across the sky at a remarkable speed. General Kepner, the commander of the bomber unit, said: "Five German Me 163s were circling over Merseburg in two groups. They coolly carried out a number of attacks on our unit."

That same day, several Me 163s over the city of Wesermünde came out of the sun to attack a formation of B-17s of the 3rd Air Division, and shot down one Flying Fortress. The US P-38 Lightning escort fighters of the 479th Fighter Group, tried in vain to intercept the German rocket-carrying fighters.

On Saturday 29 July 1944, 65 B-29 Superfortresses of the US 20th Bomber Command took off from their base at Chengtu in China, and raided the ironworks in Anshan near Mukden (Manchuria) without suffering any casualties. This was the first successful daylight operation by the 20th Bomber Command. But when 30 B-29s took off from the same base to bomb another target, in Cheng Xian, one Superfortress was shot down by Japanese anti-aircraft guns, and 10 by Japanese fighters.

On Monday 31 July 1944, armored divisions of the US First Army succeeded in making a decisive breakthrough at Avranches, winning strategic victory in the actual invasion zone. Strong Allied fighter-bomber units equipped with rocket missiles, supported the advancing ground troops.

At dawn on 31 July 1944, Antoine de Saint-Exupéry, the 44-year-old French flying major, took off from Borgo airbase on Corsica in an unarmed P-38 Lightning fighter, to take reconnaissance photos of the Grenoble-Annecy area. By 2:30 P.M. that afternoon the French gave up hope of his return because his Lightning had carried only 7 hours of fuel. He had disappeared and was never seen again.

Saint-Exupéry was a thinker, poet, airman, scientist. His investigations of aerial navigation and aerodynamics dazzled the experts by their creative imagination. His aeronautical experiments were adopted into aircraft construction. His unexplained death marked an end to a life that was already entwined with myth.

Among Saint-Exupéry's gear his friends found four manuscripts, one of them the book *The Little Prince*, along with the drawings the author had made to accompany it. The evening before his last flight he wrote a friend: "If I am shot dowr., I will leave the world without regret. I am dismayed by the ant-heap world of the future."

During these weeks of July, the world was falling apart for Germany, and even sleepwalkers could not maintain the illusion that the war would end in a German victory; yet the Nazi propagandists worked on tirelessly, continually refining their techniques. They repeatedly predicted massive German retaliation for the terror bombing, and vague rumors spread about miracle weapons that would decide the course of the war. The articles of SS war correspondent Joachim Fernau, tinged with mysticism and calling on Germans to hold out for a final victory, were printed in all the well-known German newspapers and were particularly influential. Masses of people clung to his die-hard slogans, published in the press and broadcast over the radio. They turned out to be the most successful weapons in

Hitler's secret arsenal, for they made it possible for Germany to prolong for months a war that was claiming devastating losses on both sides, and thus to afford Nazi leaders a brief reprieve.

On Tuesday 1 August 1944, five weeks after the start of the Soviet summer offensive, Radio Moscow reported having smashed 28 divisions of German Army Group Center. The Soviets had taken 158,480 prisoners, including 22 generals. Army Group Center lost a total of 350,000 men. German sources report this as the most costly defeat in Wehrmacht history.

On Wednesday 2 August 1944, Colonel Wachtel's unit, codenamed the 155th Flak Regiment, launched the largest number of V-1 flying bombs ever fired on one day, from the launch ramps in the Pas de Calais. A total of 316 flying bombs were fired at London from 38 catapults. Despite the large numbers of interceptor planes patrolling the Channel, the strong antiaircraft barrage along the coast, and the shield of several hundred barrage balloons, 107 flying bombs reached the British capital that day. At 3:44 A.M. the main target, the Tower Bridge, was hit at last and so badly damaged that all traffic was halted for almost a week. But more serious than the damage to this London landmark was the destruction to the arms factories. Some 40% of the 1,100-lb bombs that the British dropped in their pinpoint raids, were manufactured in factories in Greater London. The V-1s caused such damage that production was seriously threatened, and the British feared that they might have to postpone planned raids on the German rail network.

On Friday 4 August 1944, some 1,200 bombers of the US 8th Air Force raided various German cities near the North Sea and Baltic coasts, including Bremen, Hamburg, Rostock, Wismar and the Arado aircraft manufacturing plant in Anklam. A formation of B-17s bombed the experimental rocket institute at Peenemünde.

That same day the British Gloster Meteor III jet fighter plane won its first aerial victory, when Flight Officer P. J. Dean met a V-1 flying bomb about 3½ miles south of Tonbridge (Kent). His Meteor cannon jammed repeatedly, but the jet could travel as fast as a V-1, so he knocked the flying bomb off course with his wings and made it crash. Several minutes later a second Meteor pilot, Flight Officer J. K. Roger, reported that he too had downed a V-1 near Tenterden (Kent). Starting that Friday, 616 Squadron kept 2 Meteor jets on patrol duty throughout the day; each pair would patrol for half an hour while 2 more waited to take off and replace them.

On the afternoon of August 4, the German 1st Parachute Corps (commanded by General Heidrich), part of the German Fourteenth Army under

Opposite page above: French pilot Antoine de Saint-Exupéry in his P-38 Lightning shortly before taking off on a reconnaissance mission in July 1944, from the advanced airfield of French 33 Squadron, 2nd Reconnaissance Group, in Borgo (Corsica).

Below: The first RAF jet fighter plane, the twin-jet Gloster Meteor III, was the only Allied jet fighter to become operational during the war. This one belonged to 616 Squadron of the 2nd Tactical Air Force.

General von Mackensen, began the evacuation of Florence. They blew up all the Arno river bridges except the Ponte Vecchio.

In the first week of August 1944, the number of flak batteries defending Germany reached their all-time peak: 154 heavy units, 644 medium and light units, 376 searchlight batteries and 57 barrage batteries were in operation. But many of the guns were old and most were suffering from overuse. On an average, a light antiaircraft gun had to fire 4,940 shots to shoot down one four-engined bomber, and a heavy gun needed to fire 3,343 shots. The ammunition for this cost 267,440 German marks [approximately $100,000]. There were now around one million people servicing the guns—soldiers, young Luftwaffe auxiliary troops, prisoners of war, women and young girls. They had permission to fire at any elevation to protect strategically important targets.

Shortly after midnight on 7 August 1944, the German Fifth Panzer Army under General Eberbach carried out a counteroffensive in Normandy that had been planned by Hitler in all its details. Its objective was to cut off the US Third Army under General Patton which had broken through German lines at Avranches. The town of Mortain was occupied by inexperienced US troops who were overcome in only a few hours by the 2nd SS Panzer Division, and the Germans made a 6-mile incursion and continued to advance until dawn when, instead of the 300 German fighter planes promised by Hitler, they were met by British Hawker Typhoon fighter-bombers—able for the first time to fire rockets.

The fighter planes the Germans needed had become entangled in aerial dogfights immediately after takeoff, and most were shot down. Not one German fighter got through to the actual battle zone. The British fighter-bombers annihilated 90 German tanks and 200 motor vehicles within a few minutes. For the first time, rockets fired from fighter-bombers successfully smashed a strong Panzer unit. Field Marshal von Kluge, the commander of the German Western armies, reported to Hitler shortly afterward: "In view of the total domination of the air by enemy aircraft, I see no way of developing any strategy that will cancel their annihilating effect, short of withdrawing from the battlefield." But even a retreat was impossible, as would later become clear.

Simultaneously the RAF deployed four-engined bombers in "tactical" raids in direct support of the ground troops at Falaise; this was the first time that

this had been done at night.

On the night of 8–9 August 1944, Allied aircraft took off from Italian bases for their first weapons and ammunition drops over Warsaw. The underground forces of the Polish Home Army under General Count Bor-Komorowski had broken out in an uprising there on August 1.

On Friday 11 August 1944, US forces completed their reconquest of Guam in the Marianas. Together with the Australians, the American forces had now driven the Japanese out of the Solomon Islands. In a campaign lasting two years, New Guinea had finally been recaptured. Now US forces under General MacArthur prepared to liberate the Philippines.

On Tuesday 15 August 1944, after powerful prefatory bombing raids along the French Mediterranean coast between Toulon and Cannes, Allied forces began Operation Dragoon, their landing in southern France. The landing was made by the US Seventh Army under General Patch, the US Sixth Corps under General Truscott, and the French Second Corps under General Lattre de Tassigny. Around 14,000 airborne troops were flown in from Corsica.

On Wednesday 16 August 1944, armored spearheads of the US Twentieth Corps advanced to Chartres, where they encountered one of the RAF's most extraordinary installations: an Allied fliers' depot behind enemy lines. When the Allied bombing raids paralyzed French rail and road traffic in March 1944, it became increasingly difficult for the SOE to transport shot-down Allied air crews, or airmen who had escaped from German POW camps, to the Spanish border so that they could travel from there to Britain via Gibraltar or Lisbon. So the SOE's central office in London ordered Colonel Boussa, commander of Belgian RAF Squadron, to go to France and set up a catchment camp for escaped Allied fliers between Vendôme and Chartres, where the airmen could take refuge until the successful invasion and liberation of France. The camp was set up in the woods of Frétenal with the help of French Resistance members from the little town of Cloyes.

Tents were obtained and despite the severe rationing, food was supplied regularly from the surrounding area, from as much as 20 miles away. Sentries patrolled continuously to give warning of unwelcome visitors. To avoid air detection, the men camouflaged the tents and all their other gear every morning with fresh branches. For three whole months, from May to mid-August 1944, 152 Allied airmen lived here directly behind the German lines. They passed their time in whispered conversations or playing chess. A woman estate owner living 6 miles away, placed her property at the disposal of sick airmen.

When more and more airmen kept arriving in June 1944, it even became necessary to organize a second camp. Colonel Boussa ordered that none of the men must try to reach the invading Allied troops on his own. On Thursday 17 August 1944, the pilots were taken under the protection of the US armored columns.

That day the Canadian First Army under General Crerar took Falaise and, along with the US First Army under General Omar Bradley, encircled the 125,000-man German Seventh Army under SS General Hausser, and some units of the Fifth Panzer Army under General Eberbach. Now Hitler decided to turn over supreme command of the German Western armies to Field Marshal Model, who replaced von Kluge.

Next day, August 18, Luftflotte 3, the German 3rd Air Force, also acquired a new commander: General Dessloch replaced Field Marshal Sperrle, who in Hitler's opinion was not displaying the necessary readiness for action.

On Sunday 20 August, 127 US four-engined bombers carried out a carpet-bombing raid west of Krakow; the target was the synthetic fuel works near Auschwitz concentration camp. The bomb carpet gravely damaged some of the camp installations killing a number of the camp inmates who were working there. If the Flying Fortresses had dropped their bombloads a couple of miles away, taking precision aim, they could have levelled the Nazi régime's largest "death factory," with its gas chambers and crematoria, and saved countless lives. At least this is what many American Jews maintained at the time; for their leaders repeatedly but vainly appealed to the US War Department to deploy the powerful American air forces against concentration camp targets so as at least to make it harder for the Nazis to annihilate millions of Jews.

On Tuesday 22 August 1944, the German Schenck Unit comprising 9 Me 262 jet bombers, was transferred to Jouvincourt; but only 5 of the planes reached their new base. Four of the turbojet aircraft crashed along the way because the pilots lacked the most basic training. The Luftwaffe had acquired its first jet fighters – the pre-series model Me 262 A-O – in spring 1944 and prepared to test them in combat. But Hitler gave the order that the planes should be used as blitz bombers, a role for which they were completely unsuited because carrying a 2,200-lb bombload, they were no faster than the Allied fighters. When the Me 262 A-2 rapid bomber went into mass production under the name Sturmvogel (Stormbird), some pilots of the 51st (Edelweiss) Bomber Wing were retrained as blitz bomber pilots at Lechfeld. Members of 3 Squadron, 51st Bomber Wing, were formed into the E-51 special unit, named the Schenck Unit after its commanding major. When the Allies landed in Normandy, the Germans planned to have this special unit intervene directly in the fighting along the invasion front.

On Wednesday 23 August 1944, a V-1 flying bomb went down in East Barnet, a northern district of London, and claimed the highest toll of casualties of any V-1 so far: 211 dead and several hundred wounded.

On Friday 25 August 1944, the French Second Armored Division under General Leclerc, and the US Fourth Infantry Division under General Barton, marched into Paris. The German commandant of Paris, General von Choltitz, surrendered to save the city from destruction. Next day General de Gaulle made his triumphal entry into the French capital. While the French were celebrating their liberation, Hitler ordered the remaining 50 bombers of General Dessloch's Luftflotte 3, which had been transferred to Reims, to bomb Paris. When the air raid sirens sounded at midnight, no one in the brightly-lit metropolis thought there was any dan-

US airborne troops next to their Waco CG-4A glider where it landed between Toulon and Cannes on 15 August 1944. This standard US glider could transport 15 fully-armed soldiers and was the most-produced glider of World War II (13,909 were built).

ger. For half an hour the German bombers flew in low, dropping their loads without hindrance, because there was not one single antiaircraft gun left in the city. In no time giant conflagrations sprang up. This was the most severe air raid of the war for the French capital: 213 people were killed, 914 wounded, and 593 buildings were destroyed or badly damaged.

On Saturday 26 August 1944, Operation Thursday in northern Burma, which had started in March 1944 under command of General Wingate, concluded when the last Chindits of the 14th Special Forces Brigade under Brigadier Brodie were flown out of the country.

Throughout their five-month-long battles and marches deep behind enemy lines, the special Chindit forces received constant support from the 1st Air Commando under Colonel Cochran. The Commando had flown more than 3,000 sick and wounded men out of the jungle and dropped in around 2,000 tons of supplies per month.

The antiaircraft battery that had landed at Broadway Stronghold by glider plane, shot down more Japanese planes during this period than all the antiaircraft guns in India and Burma together shot down in the whole of 1944.

On Sunday 27 August 1944, RAF Bomber Command mounted its largest daylight strategic raid on Germany for three years. More than 200 Lancasters with Spitfire escort took off from French bases to raid the synthetic-fuel factories in Homburg-Meerbeck. Not one bomber was lost, yet they inflicted such damage that the factories were knocked out for two months.

On Monday 28 August 1944, Operation Diver—the codename for British defensive measures against V-1 flying bombs—achieved its greatest success when, thanks to their proximity fuses, British antiaircraft guns were able to shoot down 65 out of 97 flying bombs launched against London, while fighter planes shot down 23, and 2 were destroyed by barrage balloons. Of the remaining 7 projectiles, only 4 actually reached London while 3 came down on uninhabited ground.

The Allied troops in northern France were capturing one V-1 launch ramp after another, so by the end of August the numbers of flying-bomb launches were decreasing rapidly.

On the night of 29–30 August, RAF Mosquitos made nuisance raids on Berlin and Hamburg while Bomber Command attacked Stettin (Polish *Szczecin*), releasing 1,341 tons of bombs. Four hundred and ninety-two tons of incendiaries were unloaded on Königsberg, causing virtually the whole of the medieval city center to burn to the ground.

The collapse of the German front in France presented the aerial forces defending Germany with an entirely new situation. They had 20 day fighter groups, 1 night figher wing, and a number of flak batteries in Holland and just inside the German border. Approaching aircraft could still be detected from warning posts in Holland; but the Ruhr District was now almost completely vulnerable to Allied air attack.

The RAF's new electronic countermeasures neutralized the airborne radar of German night fighters, and improvements in Allied navigation achieved at the same time enabled the bombers to carry out raids even in periods of bad weather.

Despite all this, German arms production was at an all-time high in August 1944. More and better weapons than ever before were rolling out of the factories; but they could not avert defeat.

Left: Paris after a German bombing raid on 27 August 1944, after the liberation. The western part of the city was especially hard hit.

Opposite right: Wassenaar, a residential suburb of The Hague, was the site of the mobile launch ramps from which the Germans fired their V-2 rockets at England. Inside the white circle is the Koekoekslaan (avenue): The first V-2 left this point and reached London in 320 seconds (5⅓ minutes).

On the afternoon of 1 September 1944, the last V-1 to take off from French soil arrived in England. It was the 8,564th flying bomb fired at London and southern England. The last of the ground launch ramps had now fallen into Allied hands, so the Luftwaffe stepped up its use of He 111s as flying V-1 launch ramps. Soon more than 100 aircraft were being used on these missions, including a number of Heinkel He 111 H-21s with powerful Jumo-221 engines, an improved version of this basically antiquated bomber. After brief training at Peenemünde and Oschatz, the 3rd Group of the German "Blitz Wing" (3rd Bomber Wing) became 1st Group of the 53rd Bomber Wing ("Condor Legion") and started its operations in mid-July 1944. The planes took off with their flying bombs from Dutch bases at Venlo and Gilze Rijen. By the start of September, large numbers of V-1s had been launched from He 111s; of these, 30 had landed in London, 90 in Southampton, and more than 20 in Gloucester.

To avoid the powerful British antiaircraft, most of the He 111 missions had to be carried out at night; the bombers also had to fly at low altitude in order to stay underneath the British radar screen. When they came within 35 miles of the British coast, they climbed to about 1,500 feet, launched their V-1s and headed back to the Continent, flying just above the water's surface.

At the end of the first week in September 1944, after almost two years of experiments, the German V-2 long-range ballistic missile carrying a 2,200-lb explosive warhead, was at last ready for deployment. On the morning of 6 September 1944, the 44th Test Battery under Major Weber set up a position south of Liège, Belgium, and prepared to fire the first two V-2 rockets at Paris. The long and complicated launch preparations for the first rocket (No. 18 583) were completed at 10:30 A.M. The V-2 lifted off with a loud hiss, but after travelling a few yards suddenly crashed for no apparent reason.

At 11:40 A.M. the second rocket—No. 18 593—was fired with the same result. The problem was a premature disengagement of the fuel supply. Thus Paris was spared the honor of being the first city in history to be fired on by V-2 rockets.

On Thursday 7 September 1944, D. Sandys, appointed by Churchill to deal with the German secret weapons, was asked by the press whether any further threat existed from Hitler's retaliatory weapons now that the Allied troops had overrun the V-1 launch ramps in northern France. He replied that apart from a few parting shots, the Battle of London was over.

At that same hour, SS men were knocking at the doors of elegant villas in Wassenaar, an exclusive, tree-shrouded residential suburb of The Hague. The inhabitants of several streets—Koekoekslaan, Lijsterlaan and Konijnenlaan—were told to evacuate their homes within two hours, leaving their doors and windows wide open. An SS troop installed a tangle of cables over the Rust, En Vreugdlaan and the Rijkstaatweg, close to the houses on the evacuated streets.

Shortly after sunrise on Friday 8 September, a long German motorized column rolled from Cleves toward Wassenaar with a strong SS escort. It included a number of trucks and troop transport vehicles, and camouflaged Meiller trailers—ingenious vehicles that served for transport and at the same time were launch-bases for V-2 rockets—and also armored fire-control vehicles, a testing crew and a radio car. These were the first and second batteries of the German 485th Motorized Artillery Division under Colonel Hohmann, generally known as "North Group" (Gruppe Nord).

The soldiers set up two launch ramps at the two road intersections of the Koekoekslaan (avenue). The rockets were installed on the Meiller trailers about 50 yards apart, and at 6:00 P.M. the start preparations were completed. The target of the two V-2 rockets was the London fire station on Southwark Bridge Road.

At 6:38 P.M. the first of the more than 1,000 V-2 rockets destined to fall on England, took off on its 192-mile flight.

Five minutes later, at 6:43 P.M., the inhabitants of Staveley Road in the London borough of Chiswick, 6 miles from the intended target, were shocked by an explosion "like a clap of thunder followed by the sound of a heavy object rushing through the air." Six houses were completely destroyed, a whole row of buildings badly damaged, three people killed and ten seriously injured. Sixteen seconds later, a similar mysterious explosion took place in Epping Forest (Essex) about 18 miles from the intended target. Several wooden sheds were demolished but there was no further damage. The local citizens could not understand what had caused the explosions, for no one had seen or heard German aircraft or V-1 flying bombs. There were no press statements about the events in Chiswick and Epping. Rumors of a gas-line explosion were not denied. Only a few dozen British scientists, politicians and high-ranking military men knew that the long-feared bombardment by German rockets had begun.

For two months neither the British nor the German government issued any official explanation of the cause of the explosions which had begun to shake southeast England on September 8.

On 7 September 1944, Dutch SOE agents had in fact reported to London the exact location of the V-2 launch ramps in The Hague, but Allied bombing raids were unable to prevent the rockets from continuing to be fired from the area. Even aerial reconnaissance failed to locate the probable sites of launch ramps because, thanks to the Meiller cars, the ramps were now portable, and the German motorized batteries in the dense parkland of Wassenaar were able to move them to a new location for each launch.

The V-2 rocket travelled faster than sound and there was no escaping it because it was immune to radar and arrived at its target before any warning could be issued. Its destructive effects far surpassed those of the V-1. Yet as German armaments minister Albert Speer wrote later [in *Inside the*

Third Reich]: "The whole notion was absurd. The fleets of enemy bombers in 1944 were dropping an average of three thousand tons of bombs a day over a span of several months. And Hitler wanted to retaliate with thirty rockets that would have carried twenty-four tons of explosives to England daily. That was equivalent to the bomb load of only twelve Flying Fortresses." [p. 365 Macmillan edition]

On Monday 11 September 1944, the US 8th Air Force flew Operation "Frantic VI," the sixth American shuttle bombing raid along the route between Western Europe and the Soviet Union. Seventy-five Flying Fortresses, including several 452nd Bomber Group machines which had survived the German raid on Poltava on the night of 21-22 June, were escorted by 64 P-51 Mustangs of the 20th Fighter Group. The formation bombed the Wanderer vehicle and machine factories in Chemnitz (Germany). Only one B-17 and 2 Mustangs were damaged by flak and fighters, but they managed to reach their Soviet bases.

That same day the British Second Army entered Holland, and at 6:55 P.M. units of the US First Army under General Omar Bradley reached Germany north of Trier (Treves). A US 85th Reconnaissance patrol crossed the German border near the Luxembourg town of Stolzemburg, encountering no German resistance.

The advance of the ground troops in turn affected the air war. The mobile Oboe radar stations which now followed in the wake of the fighting soldiers, expanded the range of the blind-bombing device and thus made it possible to carry out precision raids on virtually any target in all of Germany. Another aid to the Allies was the Pluto Pipeline, a group of oil pipes that started in Liverpool and ran along the bottom of the English Channel into the invasion zone, and that was continually extended eastward in the train of the advancing armies. It transported close to 1 million gallons per day and greatly simplified the problems of supplying fuel to the Allied air forces.

On the morning of 12 September 1944, 39 British Lancasters and 2 Liberator bombers (under Group Captain Tait) landed at several separate aerodromes near Murmansk, bringing along their own ground personnel and spare parts. The formation was to wait for favorable weather to raid and sink the German battleship *Tirpitz* lying in the Alta-Fjord, Norway. On Wednesday 13 September 1944, 73 B-17s and 55 Mustangs which had taken part in Operation Frantic VI, flew out of the Soviet Union and back to Italy. En route they attacked munitions plants in Diosgyor (Hungary) and were surprised to meet no enemy antiaircraft over the target.

On the night of 13–14 September 1944, 6 weeks after the outbreak of the Warsaw Uprising, Soviet aircraft began to fly in supplies to support the rebels. Po-2 biplanes of the Krakow Regiment and the Soviet 16th Air Army under General Rudenko, dropped approximately 30 metric tons of food and 20 metric tons of arms and ammunition in Warsaw. Thanks to their special tactics—gliding in to the target with their engines switched off—90% of the supplies got through to the rebels.

On Friday 15 September 1944, 28 Lancaster bombers carrying 12,000-lb Tallboy bombs and commanded by Group Captain Tait, took off from the Soviet airfield of Yagodnik approximately 21 miles from Murmansk. At first they flew south from Inari Lake at an altitude of only 1,000 feet to avoid detection. Twenty minutes before reaching their target, they climbed in attack formation to an altitude of about 11,000 feet. But by this time their target, the battleship *Tirpitz*, had wreathed itself in dense artificial fog, so the unit had to unload their bombs without a clear sight of the target.

One of the first Tallboys hit the foreship on the starboard and exploded inside the hold. The whole ship in front of the armored bulkhead was destroyed, but the *Tirpitz* was still able to maneuver. Two days later the Lancasters returned from Yagodnik to Scotland.

Sunday 17 September 1944, a day of fine weather, saw the beginning of the largest airborne opera-

Above: The V-2 rocket was guided by an electrical beam until burnout. The most sensitive part of the guidance system in the head, was fixed in place only when the rocket was about to be raised on end.

Opposite page left: A V-2 rocket being fueled. V-2s held about 8,720 lbs of fuel—3/4 ethyl alcohol and 1/4 water—along with 10,780 lbs of fluid air as an oxidizer. The fuel burned for approximately 65 seconds; the rocket had a 650,000-horsepower thrust and travelled at a speed of 3,360 mph.

Right: The V-2 rocket was over 45 feet long; its diameter was 5⅓ feet; the empty missile weighed 8,800 lbs; fueled up and ready for takeoff it weighed over 28,300 lbs; the explosive charged weighed only 2,145 lbs.

Below: The first German V-2 rocket to strike England hit this spot on Staveley Road, Chiswick (West London) on 8 September 1944. In the foreground is Mr. W. Harrison who received a head-wound; his wife was killed.

tion of the war so far, Operation Market Garden. Nearly 35,000 Allied airborne troops were involved, almost twice as many as in the Normandy invasion. Three divisions, one brigade, over 1,500 transport and glider aircraft, 1,000 bombers and 1,240 fighters took part. Their aim was to capture key bridge crossings in Holland over the Waal, Meuse and Rhine rivers. Following the establishment of bridgeheads, the tanks of 30th Corps under British General Horrocks would launch a bold operation to cross the Rhine at Arnhem and penetrate the Ruhr District from the north.

The airborne landing took the Germans completely by surprise. The US 101st Airborne Division (commanded by General Taylor) landed between the Netherlands towns of Veghel and Zon; the US 82nd Airborne (commanded by General Gavin) came down south of Nijmegen; and the British 1st Airborne (General Urquhart) dropped at Arnhem north of the Rhine.

Of the 4,603 Allied aircraft that operated over

southern Holland that day, only 73 were shot down by flak. No German fighters were encountered.

That same day Gruppe Nord, the German motorized troop which had been launching one V-2 rocket after another at London from the protective cover of the ancient plane trees on the Oud-Wassenaarse Road, broke off its operations. Now the first and second batteries of Colonel Hohmann's 485th Motorized Artillery Division were hastily transferred to Overveen near Haarlem to avoid being cut off by the Allied airborne troops engaged in Operation Market Garden.

Two battalions of the British 1st Airborne had been ordered to secure the most important bridgehead on the right bank of the Rhine at Arnhem, but they were held up in violent fighting with an SS unit. Only the 2nd Battalion under Lt. Col. I. D. Frost was able to advance through the outlying districts of Arnhem and at 8:30 P.M. reached the strategically vital road bridge. Lt. Colonel Frost, who had led the successful airborne raid on the German radar station at Bruneval in February 1942, sent out a patrol instead of immediately establishing bridgeheads on both sides of the bridge. A single flak gun prevented the troops from advancing further, so Frost occupied a few buildings on the right bank and decided to wait until morning. Next day, September 18, British attempts to cross the bridge were repelled by hard German resistance. Worse yet, all efforts to relieve Frost's battalion failed. German Field Marshal Model, the commander of Army Group B, and General Student, commander of the German 1st Parachute Army, led an energetic defense. German SS forces who happened to be in the area, played a crucial role in the battle. They included the 2nd SS Panzer Corps under SS Bridgadier General Bittrich, the 9th SS Panzer Division (the "Hohenstaufen") under SS Major Harzer, and the 10th Panzer Division (the "Frundsberg") under SS Brigadier General Harmel.

On Monday 18 September 1944, 110 B-17s of the US 8th Air Force, escorted by 148 Mustangs of the 355th Fighter Group, took off on Operation Frantic VII. This was a politically delicate mission preceded by weeks of hard negotiation between Washington and Moscow. The Flying Fortresses were filled not with bombs but with arms and ammunition containers for the Warsaw rebels, who were under hard pressure from the Germans. The troops of the Soviet First White Russian Front stood just the other side of the Vistula, commanded by General Rokossovsky who himself was a native of Warsaw; yet it was not the Soviets who lent the Poles the needed aid. Instead, American planes undertook a ten-hour flight to drop the supply containers over the Polish capital. The US unit crossed Denmark and the Baltic Sea, headed inland at Kolberg and, braving strong flak barrages and pursued by German fighters, reached Warsaw at 1:40 P.M., where they found the city wreathed in clouds of fire. The US planes dropped 1,248 containers from an altitude of about 1,600 feet. Only 10% of them (16 metric tons in all) fell into the narrow strip of the Polish capital still held by the rebels, while most of the supply bombs fell into German hands. German flak shot down one B-17; several others were badly damaged. Two Mustangs were lost to German fighters.

Arnhem (Holland), 17 September 1944. Horsa glider planes carrying British airborne troops descend under German defensive fire.

Next day, September 19, the US planes took off from their bases in the Soviet Union and flew back to Italy, bombing the locomotive engine plant in Szolnok (Hungary) en route. This brought Operation Frantic Joe to a final end.

On Wednesday 20 September, the tanks of 30th Corps under General Horrocks, and the troops of the US 82nd Airborne under General Gavin, captured the undamaged Rhine bridge at Nijmegen. They tried to advance to assist the British 1st Airborne under General Urquhart who were still engaged in hard fighting at Arnhem, but met stiff German resistance and could not get through.

On Thursday 21 September, the Polish 1st Parachute Brigade under General Sosabowski, which

until then had been held back by bad weather, was able to land at Arnhem. Unfortunately their drop zone was on the left bank of the Rhine. In the succeeding nights, only a few dozen Poles succeeded in crossing the raging river and joining up with the remains of General Urquhart's British 1st Airborne who were desperately fighting on at Oosterbeek, a residential suburb of Arnhem.

On Saturday 23 September 1944, the synthetic-fuel works and the rail and road traffic network in Germany became the primary targets of the Allied bomber units and remained so until the end of the war. From that day on, all strategic air raids were aimed at these targets whenever the weather permitted pinpoint targeting.

On Monday 25 September, General Urquhart ordered his decimated British 1st Airborne to break out from Oosterbeek. During the night only 2,398 of the original 10,095 airborne soldiers escaped over the Rhine, whose southern bank had just been reached by the spearheads of General Horrocks' 30th Corps.

An underestimation of enemy strength by Allied intelligence, the unfavorable weather, and especially the immediate intervention of the German 2nd SS Panzer Corps under General Bittrich which was being refitted near Arnhem, gave German troops their last victory of the war. All that remained of the Allied thrust was a narrow 50-mile-long salient which General Horrocks' 30th Corps (part of the British Second Army under General Dempsey) had forged from the front to Nijmegen. This German victory awakened new hope in the foundering Reich, and the Allies did not finally occupy Arnhem until 7 months later, on 14 April 1945.

In the early morning of 25 September 1944, when the situation at Arnhem had stabilized, the first and second batteries of Colonel Hohmann's 485th Motorized Artillery Division rolled back to Wassenaar. That same afternoon they started firing V-2 rockets again.

The amazingly long silence of the Nazi propagandists about the deployment of the new retaliatory weapon, made it possible for Churchill to keep the British people in the dark about the lightning rocket strikes. The British government feared that Londoners and the people of other industrial cities might panic if they knew the truth, and this in turn could negatively affects arms production. Almost 1½ million people had already left London, although this headlong evacuation had slowed dramatically since the V-1 flights abated at the start of September.

The British press cooperated with the government by printing no explanations of the mysterious explosions that were plaguing England day after day. Friend and foe alike kept Britons in ignorance for weeks.

By the end of September 1944, the German Heinkel 111s of 1st Group, 53rd Bomber Wing, had fired off a total of 177 flying bombs at England, mostly in night missions. 1st Group were now taking off from their new bases in Schleswig-Holstein, Oldenburg and northern Westphalia. The German aircraft suffered heavy losses on V-1 launch missions, because they were at risk not only from RAF night fighters but from flying bombs that exploded right after takeoff. In one instance, 12 He 111s failed to return from two successive missions.

The situation changed dramatically starting in September 1944, when the German Luftwaffe began to run out of fuel. In September, monthly production of synthetic gasoline dropped to 7,000 tons, when the demand was for 150,000 tons. The fuel shortage was so acute that when the air raid warning sirens sounded at a Messerschmitt aircraft plant at Obertraubing, the aircraft waiting for delivery had to be towed to cover by horses and oxen.

On Monday 2 October 1944, after 63 days of fighting, the rebel Polish Home Army under General Bor-Komorowski surrendered in Warsaw to a German SS Corps under General von dem Bach-Zelewski.

Number 138 Polish RAF Squadron, a special duty unit, had lost 32 Halifax bombers and 234 crew members flying in supplies to the rebels—that is,

90% of the planes they had flown into Warsaw on 23 separate nights. Two South African squadrons lost 24 of their 33 B-24 Liberators. The losses were all the more tragic because due to the long distance the planes had to fly, they had room for relatively few drop containers, so the rebels received only 40 tons of supplies by air.

On Tuesday 3 October 1944, the German Lechfeld Aerial Test Unit was set up under Major Nowotny, an outstanding 23-year-old fighter pilot. Owing to the vigorous intervention of General Galland, the German Me 262 jets were at last to be deployed as fighters [instead of as bombers as Hitler had wished]. The test unit was made up of two squadrons stationed at Achmer and Hesepe airfields near Osnabrück, a total of 40 Me 262s.

On Wednesday 4 October 1944, 4 Me 262 "Swallow" jet fighters took off from Achmer for the first time. Two were shot down over the takeoff field, and a third was shot down while landing, by Canadian Spitfires of 401 Squadron. The Me 262 required considerable time for takeoffs and landings and was completely defenseless in the process, and Allied fighters took advantage of this weakness.

As a rule, their high fuel consumption allowed the jets to fly only one run. They could be deployed successfully only if the formation was guided precisely to the target, and only if the pilots were experienced. The Lechfeld Unit managed to shoot down some 25 four-engined bombers in a month, but at the cost of 35 jets.

At the end of September 1944, RAF Bomber Command was no longer subordinate to SHAEF, the Allied Supreme Command in Europe, so Air Chief Marshal Harris stepped up large-scale night bombing raids which increasingly extended the punishment to medium-sized and even small German towns.

On Saturday 7 October 1944, the RAF and the USAAF carried out the heaviest day raid on Germany in the war so far. More than 3,000 Allied aircraft operated over Germany simultaneously.

On Thursday 12 October 1944, the first B-29 Superfortress landed on the island of Saipan in the Marianas; its pilot was US Brigadier General H. S. Hansell, Jr. It belonged to the 21st Bomber Command, the twin of the 20th Bomber Command in India and China. The two units were the only American forces armed with B-29s; together they made up the independent US 20th Air Force, and their mission was to conduct a strategic air war against Japan. Their operational commander was Admiral Nimitz, commander-in-chief of the US Pacific fleet.

On Saturday 14 October 1944, 104 Superfortresses of the 20th Bomber Command took off from their base in Chengtu (China) to attack Japanese airfields of the 2nd Japanese Air Force near Okayama (Formosa). They dropped 650 tons of bombs to eliminate the Japanese aerial forces in the area before US forces made their planned landing on Leyte in the Philippines.

On the night of 14–15 October 1944, the RAF deployed 240 Lancasters and Mosquitos against Brunswick and for the first time used fan raid tactics. In order to cover every square yard of the target zone with bomb carpets of uniform density, the bombers flew in from several directions in a fan shape and unloaded their bombs one by one at set intervals.

On Sunday 15 October 1944, the German battleship *Tirpitz* left the Alta-Fjord and entered the northern Norwegian seaport of Tromsö. That same day Egie Lindberg, an agent of the Norwegian branch of the SOE, radioed to London from Tromsö that the *Tirpitz* had anchored there. Admiral Dönitz had ordered the vessel to be turned into a sailing fortress. At Tromsö the *Tirpitz* did not lie under a protective mountain slope as it had done in the Alta-Fjord; there were only low hills nearby. Several flak batteries along the shore and an old Norwegian coastguard ship with a couple of antiaircraft guns on board, were the only air defense present.

On Wednesday 18 October 1944, the report of the Norwegian agent was confirmed: A plane from the carrier *Implacable* had just identified the battleship at its new anchorage 3 miles west of Tromsö. Air Chief Marshal Harris replied that this made the task of the British all the easier, because Tromsö was 100 miles closer than the Alta-Fjord.

On Friday 20 October 1944, US forces under General MacArthur began the reconquest of the Philippines by landing on Leyte. It was extremely difficult for the US troops to get a foothold because the Japanese used destroyers and lighter vessels to bring in reinforcements from neighboring islands, and desperately resisted the American invasion.

During the battles a Japanese pilot crashed his bomber into the Australian cruiser *Australia*, badly damaging it. It hit the bridge, killing Captain Dechaineux and 18 seamen and wounding 54 others.

On Sunday 22 October 1944, the Japanese navy

The world's first serviceable jet fighter plane, the German Messerschmitt 262, built under canvas tents in the woods. When Hitler saw them he said, "At last, a blitz bomber!" and ordered the jet fighters deployed as bombers. Fighter deployment of the Me 262 could not have crucially influenced the outcome of the war but it definitely would have affected the air war over Germany.

launched a three-day grand assault on the US landing fleet off the coast of Leyte. The Japanese fleet included 9 battleships, 4 aircraft carriers, 13 heavy and 6 light cruisers, and 34 destroyers.

On Monday 23 October 1944, Admiral Onishi, commander of the Japanese naval air force on the Philippines, founded the kamikaze ("divine wind") suicide pilot corps. The first kamikaze pilots were recruited from volunteers of the 201st Naval Flying Group stationed at Clark Field about 50 miles north of Manila.

On Tuesday 24 October 1944, Japanese aircraft on Luzon took off to raid a US naval formation, Task Force 38.1 commanded by Vice-Admiral McCain. They were intercepted by US fighters. Only one Japanese plane got through and hit the light cruiser *Princeton* with a 5,500-lb bomb which crashed through the flight deck and exploded inside the hold. The planes standing already fueled on the hangar deck caught fire, the fire exploded the aircraft torpedoes, and this set off a chain of further explosions. Despite attempts by other vessels to put out the flames, the ship continued to burn and had to be abandoned.

As the Battle of Leyte continued, on 25 October 1944 2 kamikaze squadrons under Lt. Yuhiho Seki attacked the Americans and damaged the escort carriers *Santee*, *Suwannee*, *Sangamon*, *Kitkun Bay*, *White Plains* and *Kilinin Bay*. Then Lt. Seki crashed his Zero plane into the flight deck of the carrier *Saint Lo*. Seven massive explosions tore apart the vessel and the entire crew died in the flames. This was the first US escort carrier to be sunk by a kamikaze attack.

In heavy battles between the Japanese and the US Seventh Fleet under Vice-Admiral Kincaid and Vice-Admiral Mitscher's Fast Carrier Task Force 38, US air raids and submarines sank the Japanese aircraft carriers *Zuikaku*, *Zuiho*, *Chitose* and *Chiyoda*, as well as 3 battleships, 6 heavy and 3 light cruisers, and 9 destroyers. The US fleet lost the aircraft carrier *Princeton*, 2 escort carriers, 2 destroyers, 1 escort destroyer and 1 submarine.

The greatest sea battle in history was now at an end. On the Allied side, 216 US and 4 Australian vessels took part in the Battle of Leyte; on the Japanese side, 64 vessels. The Japanese suffered one of their heaviest blows since war began, when four of their aircraft carriers were sunk. After October 26, the Japanese navy offered little resistance.

On Saturday 28 October 1944, the B-29 Superfortresses of the 21st Bomber Command carried out their first operation from Saipan in the Marianas: a raid on Japanese submarine bases at Truk Island in the Carolinas.

On Sunday 29 October, the weather improved and the 36 Lancaster bombers of 9 and 617 Squadrons under Group Captain Tait took off from Lossiemouth (Scotland) headed toward Tromsö, where they made another raid on the *Tirpitz*. They flew over Norway and neutral Sweden to avoid German fighters. Low-hanging clouds prevented them from scoring any hits and they returned to Lossiemouth.

On the last two nights of October, RAF Bomber Command mounted two more heavy raids on Cologne. Some 6,320 metric tons of bombs fell on the cathedral city.

Wednesday 1 November 1944 was an important day for the US aerial forces. For the first time since the Doolittle Raid of 18 April 1942, a US plane flew over Tokyo. It was an F-13, the photo-reconnaissance version of the B-29 Superfortress, flown

by Captain R. D. Steakly, and took off from the Marianas.

On Wednesday 8 November 1944, exactly 2 months after the first V-2 rocket fell on London, Goebbels, the German Minister of Propaganda, told the press that Germany's retaliatory long-range rocket raids on England had begun. Twenty-four hours later, when the British public could no longer be kept in ignorance of the facts, Churchill publicly announced that the Germans were firing rockets at Britain.

In November 1944, a new French aerial unit was formed in western France under the command of General Corniglion-Molinier; it was known as the French Atlantic Air Force (Les Forces Aériennes Françaises de l'Atlantique). The unit was part of the Allied 1st Tactical Air Force and its mission was to raid the "Atlantic fortresses," the fortified German bases on the Bay of Biscay. The special feature of the French unit was that they flew in captured German Ju 88 bombers. The pilots came from 31 Squadron, 1st Aunis Bomber Group, stationed at Cazaux near Cognac.

On Sunday 12 November 1944, 18 Lancasters of 617 Squadron and 20 from 9 Squadron stood ready for takeoff at Lossiemouth; they were about to raid the *Tirpitz* at Tromsö again. They were joined by another Lancaster, flown by Pilot Officer Gavin, whose crew were supposed to film and photograph the raid. At 2:39 A.M. the engines started to roar. Seven of the 9 Squadron aircraft were so badly iced up that they could not get off the ground.

At 9:30 A.M. the Lancasters, commanded by Group Captain Tait, approached the target at an altitude of approximately 14,000 feet.

At 9:40, the "Anton" and "Bruno" gun turrets on the *Tirpitz* opened fire with their 38-mm guns, which fired over the whole zone to disperse the bomber formation. Initially the Lancasters attacked broadside, in flights of three planes each at graded altitudes.

At 9:42 A.M., a number of 12,000-lb Tallboy bombs fell near the vessel, although most were caught by the barrage nets. Two bombs hit the *Tirpitz* on the port side. One destroyed the catapult used to launch the on-board aircraft, then crashed through the armored deck and exploded. The second bomb dug into the "Caesar" gun turret. The other Tallboys scored near hits, and the battleship began to list.

At 9:55 A.M. the *Tirpitz* capsized. The ship's dark bottom rose out of the fjord while the whole of the port side sank under the waves. Twenty-eight officers and 874 crewmen died, while 880 were rescued. Not one of the 30 German "Arctic fighter planes" stationed at nearby Bardufoss under command of Major Erler, turned up to help.

By Monday 20 November 1944, approximately 210 V-2 rockets had reached England, 96 of which hit London. Four hundred and fifty-six people had been killed by the rockets during this time, meaning that each explosion claimed twice the casualties of a flying bomb.

In November 1944 the first US B-29 Superfortresses appeared over Tokyo, and the Japanese in turn mounted an aerial balloon offensive against the US. On Thursday 23 November, children in the state of Montana found a charred and half-destroyed balloon with Japanese printing on it. The remains were investigated at the Naval Research

Berliner Ausgabe

306. Ausgabe / 57 Jahrg / Einzelpr 15 Pf. / Auswärts 20 Pf.

VÖLKISC

Zentralverlag der NSDAP Frz Eher Nachf GmbH Zweigniederlassung Berlin SW 68 Zimmerstraße 88 (Ruf: 11 00 22) Drahtanschrift Eherverlag Berlin Zweigstellen in allen Stadtbezirken von Berlin sowie in Brandenburg (Havel) Adolf-Hitler-Straße 95 (Ruf 2637) Frankfurt (Oder), Richtstraße 63 b (Ruf: 51 29) Potsdam, Charlottenstraße 69 (Ruf 57 93) Zahlungen Postscheckkonto Berlin 4454 Anzeigenschluß 16 Uhr Sonntagsausgabe 13 Uhr am Vortage des Erscheinens Einzelne Nummern können bis auf weiteres nicht nachgeliefert werden

V 2 gegen London

Die erfolgreiche Abwehrschlacht in Kurland
Amerikanischer Großangriff in Lothringen

Aus dem Führerhauptquartier, 8. November.

Das Oberkommando der Wehrmacht gibt bekannt:

Nachdem seit dem 15. Juni der Großraum von London mit nur kurzer Unterbrechung und in wechselnder Stärke unter dem Feuer der V 1 liegt, wird dieser Beschuß seit einigen Wochen durch den Einsatz eines noch weit wirksameren Sprengkörpers, der V 2, verstärkt.

kam es nur zu örtlichen Kämpfen. Die Wucht der bolschewistischen Angriffe gegen unsere Nordfront hat gestern auch im Raume von Autz nachgelassen. Wo der Feind weiter angriff, wurde er zum Teil in Gegenstößen geworfen. Damit ist der von den Sowjets erstrebte Durchbruch in Kurland gescheitert. In zwölftägiger erbitterter Abwehrschlacht haben unsere Divi-

0 50 100 km
Reval

A

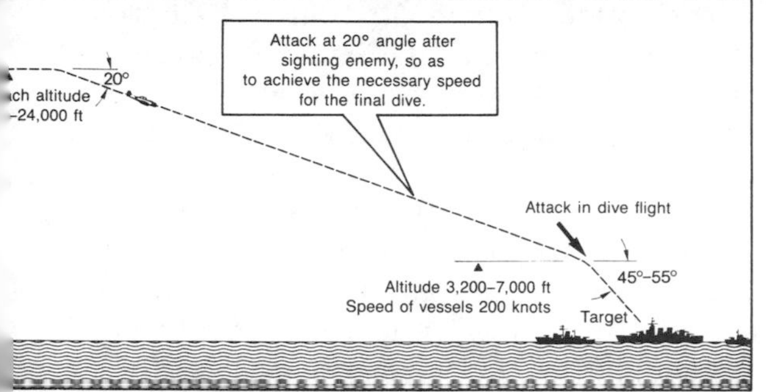

Middle diagram: A Japanese kamikaze raider attacking from high altitude. The pilot had to make sure that his dive angle was not too steep.

Below: Japanese kamikaze using low-altitude raiding tactics. This method required particular skill from the pilots.

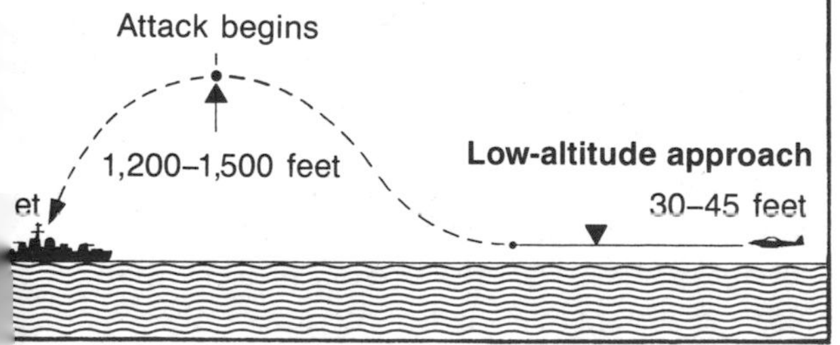

Top photo: Near Tromsö (Norway) in November 1944. The hull of the battleship *Tirpitz*—the pride of the German navy—heaves out of the fjord.

Opposite page above: A hachimaki, the honorary insignia of the Japanese suicide pilots, is tied around a kamikaze pilot's forehead before his mission.

Opposite page below: On 9 November 1944, two months after the Germans began to raid England with V-2 rockets, the German Wehrmacht High Command (the OKW) finally announced the raids in German newspapers.

Institute in Washington, where it was learned that the balloon hull was made of several layers of Japanese vellum glued together with vegetable glue.

The balloons, which were 30 feet in diameter, were designed to cross the Pacific at an altitude of 29,000–35,000 feet because at that altitude, air currents of 90–180 mph would carry them to North America. Each balloon was weighted with 30 sandbags weighing about 7 pounds each, some of which would be jettisoned automatically as soon as the balloon drifted below 29,000 feet. A second tripping device opened a vent that allowed gas to escape when the balloon climbed above 35,000 feet, so that it would then drop down again. Each balloon carried 3 or 4 bombs including one incendiary and several 33-lb shrapnel bombs. They were released automatically after the drop of the last ballast bag, at which time the Japanese estimated the balloons would be over US territory. After the release of the bombs, a special device would destroy the balloon. The self-destruct mechanisms of about one tenth of the balloons malfunctioned, so a large number of balloons were found intact.

The shrapnel bombs posed only a minimal threat; but the incendiaries could easily have set fire to America's forests in the summer months. But the radio and press in the USA and Canada did not report the balloons, so the Japanese were unable to learn anything about the results of their offensive.

On 23 November 1944, D. Sandys told the British government that all attempts by British scientific experts to jam the remote-control system that guided the V-2 rocket, had failed. The German launch ramps were so mobile and easily camouflaged that they provided no tangible targets to the bombers; so, Sandys said, the only recourse for the British was to try to destroy enemy transport routes and communications networks in the launch zones.

On Friday 24 November, the US 21st Bomber Command in Saipan (Marianas) led their first raid on the Japanese motherland. Of 111 B-29 Superfortresses dispatched, 88 reached the Tokyo area; but 17 of these had to jettison their bombloads before reaching Japan.

As the US formation flew along at an altitude of 26,000–32,500 feet, they encountered strong tail winds that increased their speed to over 400 mph. But at the same time, low-lying cloudbanks deprived them of visibility and prevented all but 24 Superfortresses from locating the main target, the Nakajima aircraft factory in Mushashima near Tokyo. About 125 Japanese fighters tried to prevent the operations of the US bombers. One B-29 was rammed and crashed.

The same day Japanese troops under the supreme command of General Okamura, occupied Nanning (China) about 100 miles northeast of the border with French Indochina. At the time Nanning was a US 14th Air Force base. On 17 April 1944, the Japanese had begun a series of offensives to eliminate all US airbases in southern China. The capture of Nanning—an operation called "Ichi-Go"—was the last major Japanese victory.

On Saturday 25 November 1944, a V-2 rocket fell into a crowded Woolworth's store in the New Cross Road in the London borough of Deptford and killed 160 people.

Between 4:32 and 5:50 A.M. on the morning of November 27, RAF Bomber Command raided Munich, unleashing some 784 metric tons of bombs. This was the first raid in which the British deployed against a German city the 12,000-lb Tallboy bombs which they had used to sink the *Tirpitz*. Two hundred and seventy-three buildings were totally destroyed and 332 were badly damaged. The death toll was 180, and 20,000 people were made homeless.

On Monday 27 November 1944, while most of the B-29s of the 21st Bomber Command were away bombing the Mitsubishi aircraft works at Nagoya, their Saipan airbase was bombed by Japanese bombers which destroyed 4 Superfortresses and damaged 13 others.

On the night of 29–30 November 1944, 35 B-29 Superfortresses of the 21st Bomber Command took off from Saipan for their first night raid on Tokyo.

On the night of 4 December 1944, Allied fighter-bombers began low-altitude strafing of the well-camouflaged V-2 rocket launch sites of the German 485th Motorized Artillery Division (Col. Hohmann) in Wassenaar (Netherlands). These missions continued daily until 15 December 1944, but the results were not encouraging: only two of the rockets were destroyed. However, the strafer activity over Wassenaar did force the 485th Motorized Artillery to confine their launch of V-2s to the night hours.

On Wednesday 6 December 1944, the anniversary of Pearl Harbor, the Japanese launched their last airborne operation. At 6:00 P.M., 409 paratroops of the Katori Shimpei unit, flying with a strong fighter escort, jumped from 30 twin-engined "Topsy" transport aircraft over the island of Leyte, near the US airfields of San Pablo, Buri and Bayue. Three of the transport planes landed in the open countryside. They were carrying sabotage troops whose mission was to destroy the headquarters, supply depots and the three airbases of the US 11th Airborne Division. This large and powerful American unit was playing a crucial role in the battles for Leyte, and the Japanese now made a desperate attempt to eliminate it.

The dispersed paratroops sent out identifying harmonica notes, formed up their ranks, and attacked with the battle-cry "Go to Hell, Beast!" Violent battle continued all night between the American and Japanese paratroops. A number of US planes were unable to take off from the airfields and were destroyed; a couple of supply depots were seized by the Japanese troops, and several jeeps and trucks were smashed.

On October 20, when the Americans first began their invasion of Leyte, they had driven the Japanese 26th Infantry Division into the malaria-infested mountains in the interior of the island. Now the Japanese emerged again to attack, but without success.

All the Japanese paratroops were wiped out on Tuesday 12 December 1944, 6 days after their landing. The Americans were surprised to find that few of the fanatical soldiers of the Katori Shimpei unit had been properly trained, and that they carried only makeshift equipment. Each had with him a small bamboo box containing emergency rations—about 750 grams of a white powder which mixed with water would form a sweet broth, and which had to last each man for one week.

At 1:45 P.M. on Friday 15 December 1944, a Noorduyn C-64 light transport plane took off from

Japanese Mitsubishi G3M medium bombers were operational throughout the war. It was these same aircraft that sank the British battleship *Prince of Wales* and *Repulse* back on 10 December 1941.

the US base at Twinwood Farms near the English city of Bedford. It was a single-engined, high-wing monoplane carrying a two-man crew and eight passengers, and its course was set for Paris. Shortly after the C-64 flew over Newhaven and began to cross the English Channel, radio contact with it was lost. On board was Major Glenn Miller, world-famous jazz musician, trombonist and leader of the Moonlight Serenade US Air Force band. He was never seen again.

At 5:30 A.M. on Saturday 16 December 1944, the Germans launched a counteroffensive in the Belgian Ardennes, against the US First Army under General Hodges. The surprise attack began in dense mist and low-hanging clouds in the area between Hautes Fanges and northern Luxembourg. Known by the Germans as Operation Wacht am Rhein (Watch on the Rhine), it was Hitler's last attempt to win back initiative on the Western Front; [but the Americans knew it as the Battle of the Bulge because of the bulge of German troops that penetrated Allied lines]. Twenty-one German divisions under Field Marshal von Rundstedt, commander of Germany's Western armies, tried to break through to reconquer the vital supply port of Antwerp so that they could cut the British and American forces in two, encircling as many as possible.

The German Western air force (Luftwaffenkommando West), under the command of General Schmid, was assigned to secure the offensive from the air with its 1,492 fighters, 171 bombers, 91 ground-attack planes and 40 reconnaissance planes. The Germans marshalled every serviceable plane they could find for the attack, including some old Ju 87 Stukas.

At the same time Colonel Wachtel's 155th W Flak Regiment launched V-1 flying bombs at Antwerp from launch ramps in central Holland, and V-2s were fired at the city too. In the evening one of the rockets hit down in the crowded Rex movie theater near the main railroad station, where it killed 271 people. Isolated V-1s and V-2s also fell on Liège.

On Sunday 17 December 1944, the Germans launched their last paratroop mission, in support of the Ardennes Offensive. To secure the right flank of General Dietrich's 6th SS Panzer Army as it broke out of the Eifel region, a five-company parachute troop from the 6th Paratroop Regiment under Lt. Col. von der Heydte, was ordered to land south of the Hautes Fanges and bar the Eupen-Malmédy road to prevent a possible American counterthrust southward from the Aachen area. This was the first German airborne operation to be mounted at night. The transport aircraft were 32 Ju 52s of 2nd Group, 3rd Transport Wing under Major Baumann, and 35 Ju 52s of a newly-formed transport group under Major Brambach.

The Germans planned the mission for the evening of December 16, but had to postpone it because the truck drivers who were supposed to transport the paratroops to the airfields, were unable to locate the troop billets or the airfields at night. Shortly before the takeoff from Paderborn, Lippspringe, and Senne fields I and II, the aircraft groups were assigned "combat observers" who would be in charge of the operation. To make room for them in the gun pits, the flight mechanics had to stay on the ground, so the pilots lost the support of an important crew-member.

The units took off on December 17, 24 hours later

than scheduled. Further unpleasant surprises lay in store for them. It turned out that the paratroops had secretly stored additional weapons on board in order to be strongly armed when they jumped, and the Ju 52 transport aircraft were carrying more than the permitted weight. One plane of 2nd Group, 3rd Transport Wing, crashed immediately after takeoff due to overloading, and the other planes had difficulty getting off the ground. At first the pilots were baffled, and only later realized what was wrong. The excess weight slowed down the aircraft that had managed to take off.

The Ju 52s met more problems on the final lap of their flight over the enemy zone. They had to fly as low as possible to avoid enemy radar and medium and heavy American antiaircraft; yet the land rose sharply behind Monschau and the troops expected to be caught in downwinds along the slope, so when they jumped, they had to be sure to drop from an altitude of at least 40 feet to be safe. Some planes were unable to maintain the ordered speed and reached the target only after the incendiary bombs used to mark it had already been extinguished. One plane dropped its paratroops over Bonn by mistake, because the combat observer believed the lighted airfield was the drop-point and gave the drop signal without the pilot's knowledge. Another observer also ordered his men to jump prematurely because he saw combat and fires below him and thought they had reached the target.

Several of the young inexperienced pilots were confused because a pair of searchlights that were to have been set up as a halfway marker, had not been installed. Thinking that fires from a heavy RAF bombing raid on Cologne were the marker lights of Bonn's Hangelar airfield, they disregarded navigational calculations and headed on a mistaken course due north. Eight machines in the group lost their way and came under heavy antiaircraft fire around Aachen and Düren; some of their paratroops were unable to bail out of the burning machines.

Another unexpected factor plagued the flight: Contrary to all predictions, the wind velocity was about 36 mph, so that over 100 paratroops were badly hurt on landing at the target and had to be surrendered to the Americans. Of the 870 paratroops dispatched, Lt. Col. von der Heydte now had a force of only 450. To make things worse, when the Ju 52s set out for home, 2 more were shot down by Allied night fighters even after they were already over German territory.

For three days the decimated paratroop unit held the road between Eupen and Malmédy, but their position was hopeless. When they could not make contact with other German units – for the offensive had by now bogged down – von der Heydte ordered his soldiers to disperse and head east individually. Von der Heydte himself, wounded and suffering from pneumonia in a forester's lodge at Monschau, had to surrender to the Americans.

On the same day the ill-fated German paratroop mission began, 17 December 1944, the 509th Bomber Group of the US 20th Air Force was set up on a wide expanse of desert near Wendover, Utah, 120 miles west of Salt Lake City. The 509th Bomber Group, commanded by Colonel Paul W. Tibbets, was a top-secret, completely independent unit whose mission was to make atomic bomb test flights and drop experiments. It had only one combat unit, 393 Bomber Squadron under Major Sweeney, which was armed with a new, improved version of the B-29 Superfortress. The 29-year-old commander, Colonel Tibbets, had distinguished himself as a bomber pilot in missions over Germany, and was assigned to train the group in flight technique.

The bombardiers had to practice dropping bombloads from 30,000 feet. On each exercise they would drop only one 10,000-lb bomb. The B-29 had to be at least 10 miles from the target when the bomb exploded to avoid being caught in the tremendous pressure blast, and the pilots had only 43 seconds to get away. They practiced making a sharp 158-degree turn after dropping the bomb so that they could reach the desired speed while climbing straight up.

The process of building the atomic bomb had been under way since 1941, without the knowledge of the US Congress. Two billion dollars had been spent on the program, codenamed the Manhattan Project, which was given priority over all other military schemes in late summer of 1942. In September 1942, Combat Engineer General L. R. Groves was assigned to lead the bomb-development program. Using untested production techniques, relying solely on equations, theories and scientific ideas, General Groves was supposed to develop a usable weapon from his headquarters at Oak Ridge, Tennessee. Work proceeded on a grand scale. Six hundred thousand people worked on the Manhattan Project, each of whom had to submit a written pledge of secrecy.

After only a few months they achieved a significant success when on 2 December 1942, Italian Professor Enrico Fermi succeeded in triggering the first

The last German paratroop mission took place on 17 December 1944, as part of the German Ardennes Offensive.

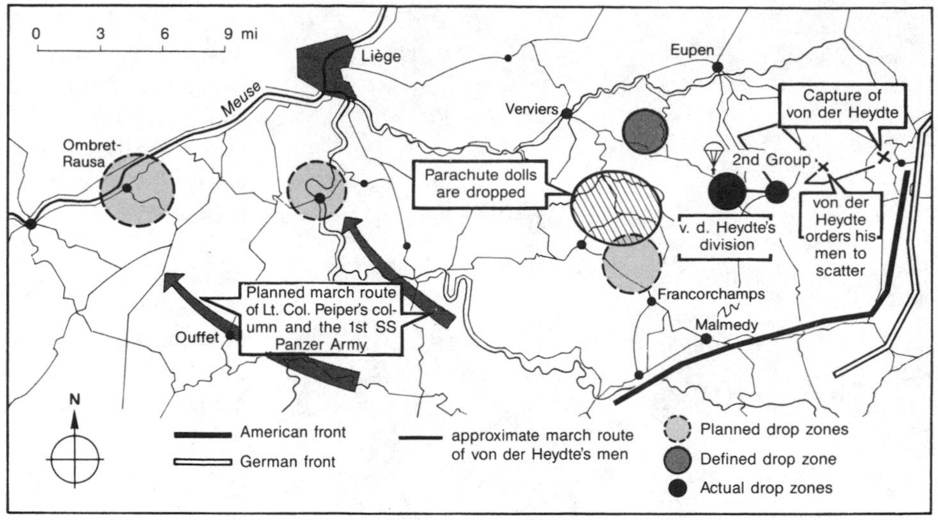

controlled nuclear reaction in a uranium reactor. A research institute was built in the desert at Los Alamos, New Mexico. In March 1943 Dr. J. R. Oppenheimer took over direction of the project. His team included the best physicists in the world, like Niels Bohr, Hans Bethe, Otto Frisch and James Chadwick.

The Allies had swiftly smashed the German Ardennes offensive in the Battle of the Bulge. One factor in their success was "Fido"—"fog investigation dispersal operation," based on the idea Churchill had formed in 1942. Gasoline reactors were set up along the main runways of a number of airfields in Great Britain. They warmed the air causing the ground fog to dissolve so that the aircraft could take off and land more safely.

When the Germans planned their Ardennes offensive, they counted on bad weather to contribute to their success, for they believed that heavy fog would prevent Allied bombers from operating. Unfortunately they knew nothing of the Fido technique. At the start of the offensive Britain was shrouded in dense fog, and only Fido enabled the aerial forces to take off.

On Saturday 23 December 1944, the German Western air force under General Schmid lost 1,088 aircraft. On December 24 Allied planes flew 6,000 missions against German troops and supply routes in the Ardennes.

On Christmas Eve 1944, a group of German Heinkel He 111s of 1st Group, 53rd Bomber Wing, took off on a V-1 raid against Manchester. One of the flying bombs crashed over the city and 17 others went down within a 15-mile radius.

On 25 December 1944, B-25 Mitchells of the US 5th Air Force raided the bases of the 201st Group of the Japanese naval air force at Clark Field near Manila in the Philippines. Seventy-two Zero fighters of Admiral Onishi's special kamikaze unit were destroyed by specially-built shrapnel bombs dropped from low-flying planes.

On the following night, the Japanese bombed the base of the US 21st Air Force in the Marianas, destroying 4 B-29 Superfortress bombers.

On Saturday 30 December 1944, General Groves, the chief of the Manhattan Project, reported to General Marshall, the US general chief of staff, that the first two atomic bombs should be ready by 1 August 1945. They were known as "Little Man" (made with uranium 235) and "Fat Man" (made with plutonium).

On New Year's Eve 1944, the RAF Mosquitos of 627 Squadron carried out another precision raid. This time the target was Gestapo headquarters in Oslo. Forty-four Mosquitos badly damaged the buildings, destroying many German documents.

In 1944, 1,118,580 metric tons of bombs fell on Germany and the German-occupied territories—250,000 metric tons of them on road and rail installations. During the same period Germany dropped 9,151 metric tons of bombs, including the V-1 and V-2 missiles, on Britain. The damage inflicted by the two "retaliatory weapons" was four times what might have been expected from a comparable expenditure on development, production and deployment of other explosives.

German sources claim that by December 31, Germany had fired off a total of 1,561 V-2 rockets, 447

An RAF heavy bomber is taking off from an airfield equipped with "Fido," a fog-dispersing technique. Fifteen of the largest airbases in Britain had this facility since 1942, saving countless lives and aircraft.

at London, and double that number (924) at Antwerp. In addition, 43 had dropped on Norwich and 1 on Ipswich; 25 on Lille in France, 19 on Paris, 19 on Tourcoing, 6 on Arras and 4 on Cambrai; 27 on Liège, Belgium, 19 on Maastricht, 9 on Tournai, 3 on Mons, 2 on Diest; and 13 on Hasselt, Holland.

In 1944, German antiaircraft reported shooting down 2,246 aircraft by day and 325 at night. That year 186,000 Allied bombers and 95,000 fighter-bombers and fighters had been deployed, so German antiaircraft had shot down .8% of aircraft dispatched against them. At night the guns shot down only .65%. During the same period, German day fighter planes shot down 1.2% and night fighters 2.6% of enemy aircraft. Throughout this time Allied aircraft were becoming more resistant to bombardment, their altitude and speed were increasing, and they were systematically jamming the radar that guided German flak fire; also, the Germans failed to develop an effective countermeasure against the bomber steam tactic. As a result of all this, the Germans kept having to increase their consumption of antiaircraft ammunition. Not until the end of 1944, when some German antiaircraft guns began to fire contact fuses, did the number of projectiles necessary to bring down a plane, sink appreciably.

The British continued their tactic of unaimed area bombardment at night, while US bombers flew precision raids to smash German aircraft factories, ammunition plants, traffic junctions, synthetic-fuel plants and refineries. Yet neither of these tactics achieved the Allies' psychological target, which was to break the German will to resist. On the contrary, the destruction of German cities actually intensified the ties between the mass of the people and the Nazi régime. Goebbels took advantage of the fact to fan sentiments of hatred and vengeance, and found that the threats and slogans the Allies used in their air leaflets helped his cause.

By the summer of 1944, Churchill and the British government already realized that the bombing of German cities had been a mistake. Sir Charles Portal, the chief of air staff, ordered Air Chief Marshal Harris to stop the raids on the cities and to begin systematic elimination of the German fuel industry and traffic network. Nevertheless—as the RAF's own official history makes clear—Bomber Command continued to devote its chief energies to raids on German cities, even in this final offensive of the war. In the last 3 months of 1944 alone, more bombs fell on Germany than in the whole of 1943.

By now the British were in fact running the risk of overbombing. In December 1944, 17,113 metric tons of bombs were unleashed on the area in and around Cologne, when RAF specialists advised that 20% of this amount would have been sufficient. Yet these area bombardments had hardly any effect on the German arms industry, for 1944 saw the production of 25,285 German fighter planes, 5,496 ground-attack planes and 1,041 jets. The only thing that kept them from being used was the disastrous precision raiding of fuel manufacturers and of the rail and road network.

1945

January to August

Extract from the *War Logbook of the Commander-in-Chief of the Luftwaffe* [Göring], dated Monday 1 January 1945:

Western front and Germany: Today 600 fighters are ready for combat. After visiting the front, [I] report that despite high losses, the spirit of the men is unbroken and airmen are offering 50–100 marks to take the places of fliers already assigned to combat missions. During the night 57 of our planes raided Bastogne while 155 attacked supply routes, destroying many rail locomotives. Three hundred enemy aircraft raided Oberhausen, 30 Wiesbaden and 70 Berlin.

Grand Raid on Allied Airfields

Tuesday 2 January 1945
The German *Wehrmacht High Command* (the OKW) announced:

On the morning of New Year's Day, powerful wings of German bombers, ground-attack planes and fighters led a surprise strike against enemy airfields in Belgium and Holland. Reports received so far indicate that at least 400 enemy aircraft were destroyed on the ground and 100 more badly damaged. The airfields themselves and their installations were badly hit. Violent dogfights ensued during the raids in which 79 more enemy aircraft were shot down. Thus the enemy in the West lost at least 579 aircraft, probably more.

The Soviet Winter Offensive

13 January 1945
The German *Wehrmacht High Command* announced:

The long-awaited Bolshevist winter offensive has begun on the Vistula Front. After an extraordinarily powerful prefatory artillery bombardment, large numbers of Soviet rifle divisions and armored units advanced along the western front of the Baranow [Poland] bridgehead. Bitter fighting ensued. Secondary attacks south of the Vistula and along the northern Baranow bridgehead, have been repulsed.

The Bombing of Dresden

Wednesday 14 February 1945, London
The British *Reuters News Agency* reported:

German radio reports that last night Dresden was raided by Allied aircraft.

14 February 1945, London
US 8th Air Force Headquarters announced:

Approximately 1,350 US heavy bombers escorted by some 900 long-range escort fighters, today led a daylight raid on Germany. Their chief target was Dresden, which was already bombed last night by RAF bombers.

Soviet Advance toward Dresden

Thursday 15 February 1945, Moscow
STAVKA (Soviet Supreme Headquarters) announced:

Three Soviet armored corps under Marshal Koniev, have made deep inroads in their thrust toward Dresden from Neufalz in the north, Sprottau in the center and Goldberg (12 miles southwest of Legnica) in the south, and are driving 10 to 15 dispersed German divisions before them. The toll of prisoners is rising hourly because the exhausted German troops can no longer bear the strains of

Radio messages from Admiral Nimitz that reached Washington late in the night, say that 4 US bomber wings based on aircraft carriers, are continuing non-stop air raids on Tokyo. Many districts of the Japanese capital are now on fire. The concentration of American warships off the Japanese coast, is described in New York as the "largest armada of all times." The raid on Iwo Jima 720 miles south of Tokyo, is also still in progress. The presumption is that a US landing on Iwo Jima will take place before any invasion of Japan. Possession of the island would make it easier for the US to attack Japan.

a retreat, and also their lack of fuel is paralyzing many vehicle columns. Today at noon our armored spearheads were only about 48 miles from Dresden.

15 February 1945, Stockholm
The Swedish newspaper *Svenska Dagbladet* reported:

Allied air crews who took part in the raid on Dresden, report that in the course of their flight they were able to see fire along both the Western and Eastern Fronts. This is the first time that fire has been seen on both fronts in the course of a single flight. Flying over the Dresden zone, Allied airmen saw—only about 65 miles away—an endless succession of fire columns and explosions along Koniev's front.

Friday 16 February 1945, London
US 8th Air Force Headquarters announced:

Some 200 Flying Fortresses have carried out precision bombing raids on individual targets in Dresden which escaped destruction in the previous concentrated raids. The bomber crews describe Dresden as a "huge smoking heap of debris."

Heavy Air Raid on Tokyo

16 February 1945, Washington
The *US War Department* announced:

At this moment a special aerial unit of the US Pacific fleet is bombing Tokyo. Admiral Nimitz reports that concentrated raids are being mounted on Japanese airfields and other installations of military importance in Tokyo and its environs.

Saturday 17 February 1945, Washington
The American *United Press News Agency* reported:

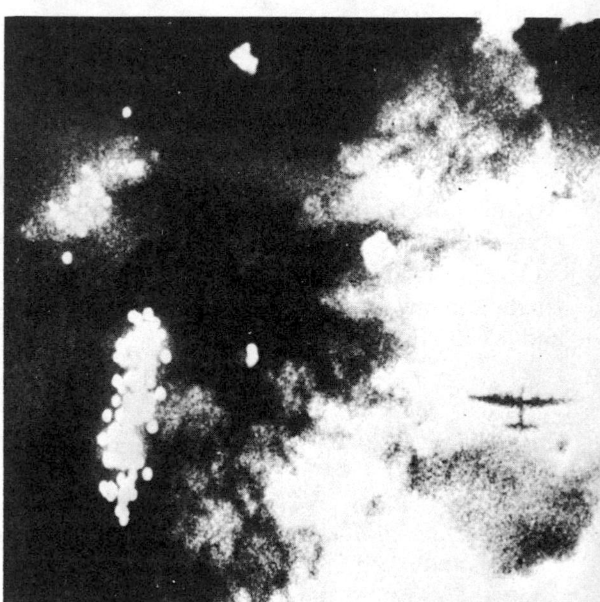

Sunday 18 February 1945, Tokyo
Imperial Japanese Headquarters announced in a communiqué:

The second day of grand raids on the Tokyo area by American carrier aircraft, has resulted in a Japanese defensive victory even greater than that of the first day. One hundred and one enemy bombers were shot down and 28 more were damaged; only 17 Japanese aircraft were lost. Negligible damage was inflicted by the enemy.

German Aircraft over England

Sunday 4 March 1945, London
The *British Air Ministry* announced:

For the first time since June 1944, a number of German aircraft appeared last night over southern

Opposite page above: 1 January 1945, Evère airfield at Brussels after the German 27th Fighter Wing launched Operation Bodenplatte. Belgian firemen are putting out the flames rising from a US plane.

Opposite page below: Dresden on the night of 13–14 February 1945: An RAF Lancaster pathfinder plane flies over the city. The white dots are marker flares.

Right: US B-29 Superfortresses over Japan. These bombers had the world's most powerful engines and were the first mass-produced aircraft with pressurized cabins for the crew. A completely new feature was the remotely-guided armament.

and northern England. Only one plane dropped bombs on London. In the north of England, small-caliber explosive bombs dropped at low altitude damaged some houses. One German aircraft strafed streets with machine-gun fire.

A German strafing attack has also been reported from a city in eastern England. So far 3 German planes have been reported shot down. Faced with a possible renewal of German air raids, the Home Office is considering introduction of a partial blackout. A return to the total blackout of the early war years is unlikely.

Bridge Destroyed at Remagen

Monday 19 March 1945, Berlin
The *German News Bureau* reported:

It can now be revealed that the rail bridge east of Remagen (Germany) has been destroyed by the self-sacrifice of a German pilot who deliberately crashed his plane with its entire bombload into the central pier of the bridge. The pressure of the explosion also badly damaged a pontoon bridge built by the Americans.

Raid on Gestapo Headquarters in Copenhagen

Wednesday 21 March 1945, Stockholm
The Swedish newspaper *Svenska Dagbladet* reported:

This afternoon, 6 British Mosquito bombers led three daring raids on Gestapo headquarters in the Shell House, Copenhagen. Despite intense antiaircraft fire, the building received about eight square hits and burned down completely. The Germans report that widespread damage was done to the center of the city and large numbers of Danes were killed or wounded; but the Danish press, on the contrary, say that the bombs were precisely aimed from an altitude of about 150 feet and hit only the Shell House, whereupon fire spread to only two neighboring buildings which burned to the ground. The toll of the dead including large numbers of Gestapo officers, is still unknown; more victims are still buried in the debris. Supposedly only a small number of Danish hostages were killed inside the Shell House, because resistance fighters had rescued a number of them. The German cruiser *Nürnberg* left the free port of Copenhagen right after the attack because the Germans feared that fresh raids would follow.

A Forward Airfield in the Middle of Berlin

Friday 23 March 1945
Extract from an order to the *German 6th Air Force* (Luftflotte 6):

It is proposed that the Kurfürstendamm [avenue] and the streets between St. Michael's Church and the Wassertorplatz [in Berlin] should be investigated for their suitability as runways for fighter planes and ground-attack planes. Pavement levels must be evened out. Tall buildings that would disrupt air traffic must be taken down.

More than 8,000 Aircraft

23 March 1945, London
US 8th Air Force Headquarters announced:

More than 1,300 Flying Fortress and Liberator bombers of the US 8th Air Force, combined with over 1,000 heavy Halifax and Lancaster bombers of the RAF, and thousands of fighter planes—a total of more than 8,000 aircraft—operated yesterday during daylight hours over the front lines and inside Germany. Several squadrons flew to the Soviet-German front along the Oder, and arrived just in time to help ward off an attack on a Soviet airfield by 5 Focke Wulf 190s. Ten FW 190s were destroyed in the fighting and 3 German jet aircraft are reported to have been shot down.

New Award for Shooting Down Strafer Planes

The German newspaper *Völkischer Beobachter* reported on 24 March 1945:

The Führer has ordered that a decoration be awarded for shooting down enemy strafer planes with small weapons. He emphasizes the extreme importance of shooting down enemy strafers with any means at one's disposal. The commander-in-chief of the OKW (German Armed Forces High Command) will be in charge of issuing the necessary executive decrees.

The Allies Cross the Rhine

Sunday 25 March 1945, London
The *British Air Ministry* announced:

On the night of Friday to Saturday, Montgomery's 21st Army Group launched a grand offensive on the lower Rhine between Wesel and Rees, crossed the Rhine, and thus moved into what Montgomery called the "last round" of the war.

More than 1,500 transport aircraft and gliders dropped troops, war matériel of all kinds, and tanks east of the Rhine and north of the Ruhr District, and in addition flew in the complete outfitting for a military hospital. At the same time, over 1,000 US bombers escorted by 850 fighters, raided German troop assembly areas and especially German airfields, so that the German defensive aircraft were destroyed while they were still on the ground and before they could hamper the airborne operations.

25 March 1945
The *German Wehrmacht High Command* announced:

Yesterday forenoon, British airborne troops landed to the rear of our positions on the lower Rhine. Aerial units which we had been keeping in reserve for such an eventuality, shot down 50 of the 121 gliders before they landed, and attacked the enemy airbornes on the ground. Yesterday around noon, the Americans dropped strong airborne combat teams between the lower Lippe and the lower Ruhr rivers; they too were attacked by German forces from several sides.

Deployment of German Suicide Pilots

11 April 1945
The *German Wehrmacht High Command* issued this supplement to an earlier report:

As already mentioned in the Wehrmacht report of April 8, German fighter units displayed exceptional fighting spirit in warding off American terror-bombing attacks on north Germany on April 7. The German fighters engaged in bitter dogfights in which they broke through the enemy fighter barricade and, disregarding the violent defensive fire from countless aerial guns, sacrificed their own lives by crashing into the four-engined enemy bombers. The American forces suffered heavy losses in encounters that also took a heavy toll of Germans. More than 60 four-engined bombers were destroyed by ramming alone. Some of the German fighter pilots were able to save their lives by bailing out.

Aerial Activity Ends over the Continent

Saturday 5 May 1945, London
The British *Exchange News Agency* reported:

The RAF's 2nd Tactical Air Force, which previously operated in support of Field Marshal Montgomery's troops, has stopped operating temporarily, and will resume its activities later in Norway if it appears that the Germans intend to offer further resistance there. Beaufighter and Mosquito aircraft of RAF Coastal Command, are continuing to operate over the waters between the Continent and the Norwegian coast, where they have attacked a number of fleeing ships that put up strong anti-aircraft resistance.

The War in Europe Is Over

Wednesday 9 May 1945
A special announcement by the *German Wehrmacht*

9 May 1945, Grove airfield, Denmark. The base is jammed with German Ju 88 and (left) Me 110 night fighters that have just fallen undamaged into British hands.

High Command, signed by General Jodl under orders from the German Grand Admiral [Dönitz], said:

At zero hour on 9 May 1945, hostilities by all branches of the Wehrmacht and by all armed organizations or individuals, will cease toward all our enemies and in all theaters of war . . . Also, at zero hour on 9 May 1945, all radio messages from all branches of the Wehrmacht will cease to be broadcast in code.

9 May 1945
The *German Wehrmacht High Command* announced:

Since midnight the weapons have been silent on all fronts. By command of the Grand Admiral, the Wehrmacht has ceased a battle which had become hopeless, thus bringing an end to almost six years of heroic struggle. It gave us great victories but great defeats as well. The German Wehrmacht has made an honorable surrender to a massively superior force.

Göring and Kesselring in Captivity

9 May 1945
General Eisenhower's Headquarters announced:

The US Seventh Army has reported the capture of Göring and Kesselring. According to the reports, Göring says that Hitler sentenced him to death because on April 24 he proposed that he replace Hitler as leader of the German Reich. Göring behaved in a friendly and jovial manner indicating that he felt he had been "liberated."

When Göring was captured, he was wearing only 3 military decorations and a uniform trimmed with gold lace. He was in a relaxed mood and said that he was ready to "supply all desired information honestly and accurately." Then, without waiting to hear the first questions, he emphasized that he had "broken absolutely with National Socialism," and told the story of how he was to have been killed on Hitler's personal orders. "But my connections and precautions proved more effective than Hitler's orders," laughed Göring. "Men in my Luftwaffe did very skillful work. As you see, I was not shot; instead they managed to get me out of Nazi clutches and find me a safe hiding-place."

In Kitzbühel (Austrian Tyrol) where Göring has now been detained, he again revealed his "best side." He attached great importance to being allowed to don his gold-decorated dress uniform with its many rows of medals, and was then eager to let himself be photographed. He continually repeated that he was in the best of health and was absolutely prepared to "cooperate in the difficult task of rebuilding a shattered Europe."

Thursday 10 May 1945, London
A British *Reuters News Agency* correspondent reported:

German Field Marshal Kesselring, in the luxuriously-appointed parlor car of his special train in Saalfelden 60 miles west of Salzburg, told me the three causes which, in his view, had led to Germany's defeat: first, the strategic air raids on the German hinterland; second, the raids by low-flying Allied fighter-bombers; and third, the terror raids on the German civilian population.

Preparations to Invade Japan

Tuesday 17 July 1945, Guam
Admiral Nimitz's Headquarters announced:

By far the largest fleet ever assembled in the Pacific, is now cruising off Japan. Operations have reached the "preinvasion stage." The main aim is to win complete air domination over the Japanese motherland, and to sever all important military communications. Approximately 1,500 carrier aircraft are taking part in current raids on the Tokyo area. As we have already reported, British aircraft and warships are now being deployed against Japan for the first time.

Grand Raids on Honshu

Thursday 2 August 1945, Guam
USAAF Headquarters announced:

Eight hundred and twenty US B-29 Superfortresses have mounted the strongest air raid of World War II on 4 Japanese cities and the Kawasaki oil-production center on the island of Honshu. Six thousand, three hundred and thirty-two tons of bombs were released—that is, 232 tons more than fell on German military installations in Normandy on D-Day (6 June 1944).

US Aircraft Spread the Potsdam Appeal

Sunday 5 August 1945, Guam
USAAF Headquarters announced:

US B-29 Superfortresses have dropped over Japan more than 3 million leaflets publishing the surrender terms demanded [by the Allies] at Potsdam. It has not been announced exactly where the leaflets were dropped, but their number suggests that the citizens of at least 50 Japanese cities have been given the chance to read this proclamation urging them to overthrow their country's warmongers and to surrender.

Explosive Force Thousands of Times that of Bombers

Monday 6 August 1945, Washington
President Truman announced:

Today US bombers dropped a completely new type of bomb, an "atomic bomb," on the Japanese base of Hiroshima. We have spent two billion dollars in the manufacture of these bombs, carrying through a scientific project of enormous difficulty. The Germans too worked on a process for manufacturing an atomic bomb, but their experiments were unsuccessful. The Allies have used the new explosive in response to the Japanese rejection of the Potsdam ultimatum [calling for Japan's unconditional surrender].

Tuesday 7 August 1945, Guam
USAAF Headquarters announced:

US reconnaissance aircraft report that many hours after the atomic bomb was dropped, the entire Hiroshima area was shrouded in a dense, impenetrable cloud of smoke and dust which made it impossible to assess the results. The enemy too have failed to supply any data. Radio Tokyo reported only that yesterday morning at 8:20 A.M. (Japanese time), an attack took place. Hiroshima has 300,000 inhabitants, and experts on the explosive effects of the atomic bomb believe that the city may literally have disappeared from the earth. A single atomic bomb could produce the same effects in Hiroshima as previously could have been achieved only by five raids of 1,000 bombers each, dropping 5,000–6,000 tons of explosive per raid.

The First Japanese Report

7 August 1945, Tokyo
Imperial Japanese Headquarters announced:

The enemy clearly used a new type of bomb in his air raids on the city and prefecture of Hiroshima yesterday. Only a small number of the new bombs were released, yet they caused substantial damage. Investigations of their effects are still in progress.

The Pilot's Report

Wednesday 8 August 1945, Guam
General Spaatz, the commander of the US strategic air forces in the Pacific, announced at a press conference:

Since the first eyewitness reports of an atomic bomb drop over Hiroshima, no technical details have been released about the bombardment. More Superfortresses armed with atomic bombs are in the Marianas standing ready for raids on Japan. Air leaflets will be dropped to warn the Japanese people of the imminent danger of annihilation. The crew of the B-29 Superfortress that dropped the atom bomb on Hiroshima, are still deeply affected by what happened. They tell how a giant mushroom-shaped cloud of smoke shot up 7 miles into the sky and shrouded the entire city of Hiroshima. The pilot, Colonel P. W. Tibbets, said: "We had good visibility as we ran in on our target, the city of Hiroshima. Only Captain Parsons, Major Ferebee our bombardier and I knew what we had dropped. The other crew members knew only that we were going to use a new weapon. We knew that immediately after the drop we had to pull away to avoid the pressure wave, and veered sharply. It is difficult to describe what we saw then. A gigantic smoke cloud shot up at an incredible speed. Where a few minutes before a city lay before us with streets, houses, piers and parks, there was now nothing to be seen. It all happened so fast that we could not see the individual phases of the explosion. All we could feel was the heat of the flash, and the pressure waves following each other in rapid succession; they seemed to us like flak projectiles exploding right next to our plane."

Captain Parsons said: "The bright flash was the first sign that the bomb had ignited. Then I saw a giant mushroom of whirling dust, in which debris was being hurled up to a height of 2½ miles." To the question why Hiroshima had been chosen for

The remains of Hiroshima, a Japanese port with 350,000 people and a center of the shipbuilding, metal and machine industry. It is estimated that the atomic bomb killed one out of three people outright.

the first attack, General Spaatz replied: "Because it is an important industrial city, that's all." The General then repeated his announcement of the new air leaflet campaign which would warn the Japanese people about future attacks with the new weapon.

The Effects of the Atomic Bomb on Hiroshima

8 August 1945
Radio Tokyo reported:

The authorities are busy trying gradually to restore order after the devastating destruction that struck the city of Hiroshima when the new type of enemy bomb was used on Monday morning, and they are not yet able to arrive at a final appraisal of civilian losses. Medical teams drawn from the neighboring districts have been unable even to distinguish the dead from the wounded, much less to identify them.

The effects of the bomb were so fearful that virtually all living creatures, both men and animals, were literally scorched to death by the terrible heat and the pressure from the explosion. All the dead and wounded have been charred beyond recognition. With the houses and buildings destroyed, including medical institutions set up to handle emergencies, the authorities have their hands full trying to lend every assistance possible under the circumstances. The bomb destroyed everything over a wide circumference. Those who were outdoors when it hit, were burned to death, while people indoors were killed by the indescribable pressure and heat. The methods used by the United States in the war against Japan have surpassed in their hideous cruelty those of Genghis Khan.

A Second Atomic Bomb Is Dropped

Thursday 9 August 1945, Guam
General Spaatz's Headquarters announced:

Today at noon (Japanese time), a second atomic bomb was dropped on Nagasaki. The air crew reported good results, but details can be released only after the aircraft has returned to base. In peacetime Nagasaki had 212,000 inhabitants.

Emperor Hirohito Addresses His People for the First Time

Tuesday 14 August 1945, Tokyo
Emperor Hirohito said in a radio address to the Japanese people:

To our good and faithful subjects! After deep reflection on the general course of the world and the present situation of Our Empire, We have today decided to take extraordinary measures to end this situation. We have instructed Our Government to inform the governments of the United States, Great Britain, China and the Soviet Union, that Our Empire accepts the terms of their joint proclamation.

Peace on Earth

The *Münchener Zeitung* (the Allied newspaper for the German civilian population) reported on 15 August 1945:

On August 15 at 1:00 A.M. Central European summer time, Japan simultaneously declared its unconditional surrender in London, Washington, Moscow and [China's wartime captital of] Chunking.

1 January 1945, a burning Spitfire at St. Denis-Westrem airfield (Belgium), the base of 131st Wing of the Polish RAF, during a raid by German fighters of 2nd Group, 1st Fighter Wing.

Strategy and Tactics

January to September 1945

While the Allied fliers were celebrating the New Year in their canteens, German airmen were busy at their bases. On the morning of 1 January 1945, the German Luftwaffe began its last ground operation, codenamed Operation Bodenplatte. The targets of the raids were 13 British and 4 American forward airfields in northern France, Belgium and southern Holland. The exact number of German aircraft that took part in this operation, is unknown. Some sources say that 800 aircraft were dispatched, others as many as 1,500. The official log of the OKW (the Wehrmacht High Command) speaks of 1,035 combat-ready aircraft. All the wings – fighter, bomber and ground-attack – of the German Western air force under General Schmid, were led to the target by pathfinder machines. Operation Bodenplatte took the Allied air forces completely by surprise because their reconnaissance had failed to detect the Germans' westward transfer of their aerial forces, which began on 20 December 1944.

Ground fog impeded the takeoffs, so it took from 7:25 to 9:20 A.M. to get all the planes airborne. To evade enemy planes and radar, the German aircraft had to make their approach at an altitude of under 600 feet, and the crews had to maintain silence. Hitler had ordered the operation to be conducted in absolute secrecy, and as a result the German aerial forces failed to notify the German 16th Flak Division (commander General Deutsch) of their mission. The flak division was protecting the V-1 and V-2 launch sites, and closely guarded the air space through which the German squadrons had to pass. The omission was to have tragic results.

Ten German wings took off as planned. One of them was the 1st "Oesau" Fighter Wing under Colonel Ihlefeld, whose targets were the St. Denis-Westrem and Maldegem airfields in Belgium. At 9:30 A.M., approximately 40 FW 190 fighters of the 1st Fighter Wing flew over St. Denis-Westrem, which had been converted into RAF forward airfield B-61. Two Polish RAF fighter squadrons, Nos. 308 and 317 of 131st Wing, were stationed there, but most of the aircraft of both squadrons were airborne at the time and returned from a routine patrol along the front just when the German fighters were about to fire on the Spitfires and the other British and American aircraft left on the field. Hard dogfights followed in which 6 German and 2 Allied fighters were shot down. On the airfield below, 18 Polish Spitfires, a dozen British and American planes, and several tank trucks full of fuel, went up in flames.

At Brussels-Evère airfield, 85 Allied aircraft including Flying Fortresses, Lancaster bombers, Spitfire and Typhoon fighters, and DC-3 Dakota transports were destroyed by the German raiders. In Eindhoven (Holland) 11 Canadian RAF squadrons lost all their Typhoons. German sources claim that 439 Allied aircraft were destroyed on the ground or shot down in a very short time, while 93 German aircraft were lost to enemy fighters and flak. But soon the German casualties rose to 277, when 184 German planes fell victim to German flak batteries who took them for enemies because they had not been informed of the route to be followed by the low-flying German formations as they returned to base. The disaster was all the worse because the unnecessary victims included 59 highly experienced unit commanders.

During the first two days of January, 570 heavy bombers of the US 8th Air Force raided the Rhine bridges at Koblenz, Neuwied and Remagen. Allied ground-troop resistance to the German Ardennes Offensive had stiffened, and counterattacks by Allied aerial forces against German rear communications helped to brake the offensive. Allied counterattacks expanded to the Cologne-Koblenz-Trier area, and south to Koblenz-Kaiserslautern-Saarbrücken.

On Tuesday 2 January 1945, 15 Japanese aircraft

appeared over Saipan, flew in low and dropped a number of bombs. This was the last Japanese raid on the Marianas.

The victories of the US armed forces in the Pacific were attributable chiefly to the large fleet of aircraft carriers and escort carriers which had rapidly been assembled there, and to the remarkably swift development of the naval air force. On 1 July 1940, the US Navy had 1,700 aircraft; by 1 January 1945, the number had increased to 86,000.

At the beginning of January 1945, the RAF altered its raiding tactics against Berlin. On the night of 3–4 January 1945, Mosquitos started a series of lightning nuisance raids against the German capital which extended into the second half of April. Small units of 35 to 50 aircraft were deployed; as a rule each plane carried one 4,000-lb "Blockbuster" bomb. Often the raids would last less than five minutes, but the Berliners were torn out of their sleep virtually every night.

At this time, the RAF's Halifax and Lancaster bombers directed most of their night raids against rail junctions to the rear of the Ardennes Front, and later attacked the rails throughout Germany.

On Thursday 4 January 1945, five days before US troops landed in Lingayen Bay at Luzon Island (Philippines), Japanese kamikaze units based in the Philippines carried out another raid on the US invasion fleet. The US escort carrier *Ommaney Bay* was sunk; and the battleships *New Mexico* and *California* were damaged, as were large numbers of other vessels.

On the night of 4–5 January 1945, RAF Bomber Command raided the picturesque little French port of Royan, where German Atlantic Wall fortifications were ranged along the city limits. The air crews were carrying out their first enemy mission and their superiors, unaware of the true location of the emplacements, ordered them to bomb the town center where in fact there was not a single German. One thousand six hundred and fifty-one metric tons of bombs—about 200 tons more than had been dropped on Cologne in the first "thousand-bomber raid" back on 30–31 May 1942—turned Royan into a heap of ruins.

The air force staff at Allied Supreme Headquarters who had planned this grand raid, hoped that it would result in the swift collapse of German resistance around Royan. On January 4 a telegram had arrived at the headquarters of the US Sixth Army Group (commander General Devers), which said: "From the air force staff at SHAEF headquarters. Inform all Allied units engaged in that sector, that on 5 January 1945, RAF Bomber Command will bomb the city of Royan with 200 aircraft at 4:00 A.M. and with 100 at 5:30 A.M." It took over four hours to decode the message, register it and pass it on to the French communications headquarters (commander General de Larminat), who could have averted the disaster if the message had not taken so long to reach them. Unfortunately the duty sergeant who received the message was an American who knew no French and could not directly inform the French personnel what the telegram said. The attack was over by the time it was translated.

The 354 Lancasters of the RAF 4th Bomber Group flew in two waves and dropped 1,637 metric tons of blast bombs and 14 metric tons of incendiaries on the city, levelling three quarters of it to the ground. Of the three to four thousand people still living there, more than half were killed or

Opposite page above: January 1945, Lingayen Bay on the Philippine island of Luzon. A Japanese kamikaze plane is deliberately crashing into the escort carrier *Natoma Bay.*

Below: Royan (France), 6 January 1945. The RAF mistakenly dropped on this small French port sixteen times as many bombs as the German Luftwaffe dropped on Rotterdam on 14 May 1940.

buried in debris. The bombs carpeted the residential and business districts while only slightly damaging the strong German defense installations on the outskirts.

The Germans, the intended victims of the raid, gave permission to the French naval fire department at La Rochelle to assist Royan. Meanwhile, French headquarters at first believed that the Germans had carried out the bombing.

On 14 May 1940, when the Germans had mistakenly bombed Rotterdam, they had dropped only 97 metric tons of bombs.

On Saturday 6 January 1945, repeated violent kamikaze attacks were made on the US landing fleet as they approached the Philippines. Ten vessels suffered serious damage. The growing victories of the Japanese suicide pilots forced the Americans to hold back the aircraft carriers that were scheduled to attack Formosa next day.

On Tuesday 9 January 1945, the landing boats of US Task Forces 78 and 79 dropped troops of the US Sixth Army under General Krueger in Lingayen Bay on the coast of Luzon Island in the Philippines, at the same spot where the Japanese had made their invasion landing three years earlier on 21 December 1941. As the landing fleet approached the bay, Japanese kamikazes started an attack that continued non-stop for 8 hours. The attacks were always unexpected because the planes hid among the chains of hills as they made their approach, and also

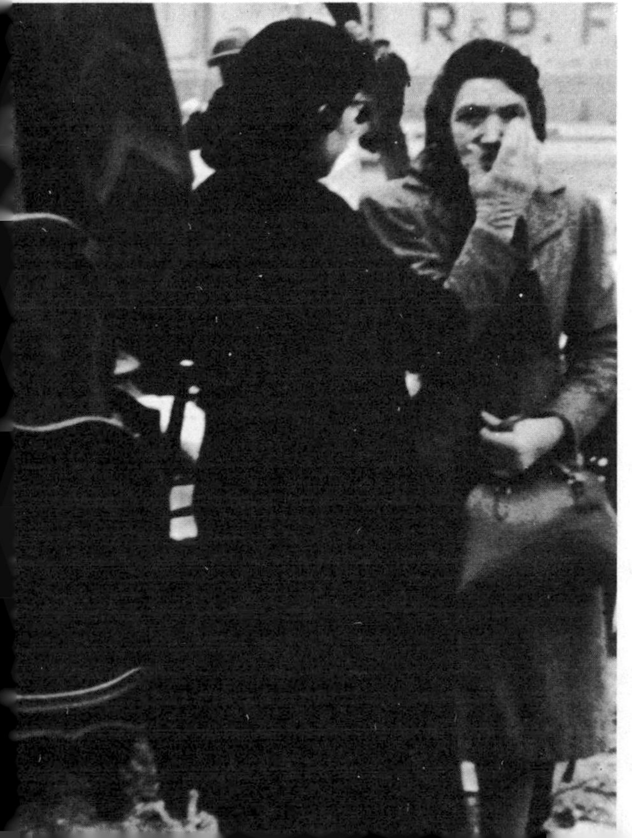

they used radar chaff to jam the US fleet's radar. A number of US ships were hit by the suicide planes. The cruiser *Australia*, for example, took a hit — the fifth she had so far received from the Japanese; but her captain turned down Admiral Oldendorf's offer to let her withdraw from the combat.

The suicide pilots posed a formidable threat compared to the regular pilots. Ordinary Japanese bombers would destroy only one ship for every 6,000 aircraft dispatched, whereas only 722 kamikaze pilots managed to sink 6 vessels. Japanese kamikazes operated most successfully between 6 and 9 January, when they destroyed almost as many US ships as the whole of the Japanese navy.

Friday 12 January 1945 marked the start of the Soviet winter offensive. The First Ukrainian Front under Marshal Koniev advanced from the Baranow bridgehead and overran the weak defensive front of the German Fourth Panzer Army under General Graeser. Next day, January 13, the Soviet Third White Russian Front under General Chernyakhovsky launched an offensive from East Prussia. Finally, on Sunday 14 January the First White Russian Front under Marshal Zhukov started offensives from the Vistula bridges at Magnuszew and Pulawy (Poland), and the Second White Russian Front under General Rokossovsky attacked from the Narev river bridgeheads on either side of Rozan. The Soviet fronts [= army groups] were supported by 4,800 aircraft of the 1st, 2nd, 4th, 6th and 16th Soviet air forces, which were opposed by only 300 German aircraft.

At 4:30 A.M. on 14 January 1945, a V-1 flying bomb exploded near Hornsea (Yorkshire). It was the last of some 1,200 flying bombs launched from the air by Heinkel He 111 bombers of 1st Group, 53rd Bomber Wing. Only one out of ten V-1s came close to hitting its target; the rest fell victim to the Allied air defense or crashed prematurely due to faulty guidance systems.

Starting in mid-January 1945, the Germans began to deploy a new secret weapon, the "Rhine messenger," a surface-to-surface missile developed by two designing engineers (Drs. Klein and Vüllers) of the Berlin steel and machine-manufacturing firm Rheinmetall-Borsig. The *Rheinbote* was a 4-stage rocket whose first and second stages were discarded 6 miles after takeoff, while the third and fourth stages remained linked to the explosive charge. The rocket was about 36 feet long and weighed 3,850 pounds, but it carried only a 44-pound warhead and its range was 132 miles at most. The missile was fired from a wagon platform. One battery in Holland fired about 220 of these rockets at Antwerp.

23 January 1945, a bridge over the Moselle river, destroyed by a bomb during the German retreat from the Ardennes.

On Friday 19 January 1945, B-29s of the US 21st Bomber Command took off from the Marianas on their most important raid so far. Sixty-two Superfortresses dropped 155 metric tons of bombs on the Kawasaki aircraft and engine factories in Kobe near Tokyo. As a result, engine production was reduced by 8% and aircraft production by about 15%.

On Sunday 21 January 1945, 8 kamikaze planes, the Niitaka Group of the Japanese First Air Force, raided the US aircraft carrier *Ticonderoga* (part of Task Force 38.3) and badly damaged it.

On Monday 22 January 1945, Dutch factories near Dordrecht, which manufactured liquid oxygen to fuel V-2 rockets, were destroyed by 4 Spitfire squadrons of the 2nd Tactical Air Force. The British fighter-bombers made several precision raids on the small chemical works, whose activities had been reported to the British by Dutch SOE agents.

The RAF Bomber Command raids on rail targets at Gelsenkirchen, Duisburg and Hanover on the night of 22–23 January 1945, and US 8th Air Force bombing of rail installations at Neuss at midday of January 23, contributed to the increasing decline of Germany's military position. The entire German road network was also under continuous attack. On 22 and 23 January alone, Allied fliers destroyed 6,000 German vehicles while Field Marshal von Rundstedt's armies were retreating from the Ardennes. Lack of fuel was keeping the German Luftwaffe on the ground. Many wings were given fuel for only one squadron mission per day, and often there was not even enough fuel available to transfer German aircraft behind the lines as the German front pulled back.

In January 1945, V-1s continued to be fired at Antwerp and Liège from launch sites in the Eifel (Germany) and in Holland. The 155th W Flak Regiment under Colonel Wachtel launched more than 100 flying bombs per day at the two cities.

Greater London was bombarded by V-2 rockets all through January. In that last winter of the war, people in London and southeastern England experienced a strange mixture of feelings: a happy anticipation of imminent victory, mixed with fear of the dreaded rocket. Everyone knew that there was no protection against it, so this meant that they were on a more or less constant air alert.

The mobile German rocket-launch ramps now circulated not only in Wassenaar but also on the Hague racecourse, in the woods at Leyden and on the Dutch island of Walcheren. The RAF did not try to destroy the ramps with their usual unaimed area raids, but instead sent out Spitfire fighter-bombers; but even these destroyed the surrounding houses rather than the V-2 ramps. It became clear to the British government that Londoners would have no peace until the Allied land forces had occupied the rocket launch zone.

In February 1945 the German 7th Fighter Wing under Colonel Steinhoff, the only Luftwaffe wing armed with Me 262 turbojet fighters, reported that it was ready for deployment. Squadrons of the 3rd Fighter Wing assumed the task of protecting the jet fighters during takeoff and landing. There was one other unit of Me 262 fighters, the 44th Fighter Group, whose commanders included General Galland—the fighter-plane general removed from office by Göring—and several other fighter officers who had fallen into disfavor.

On Saturday 3 February 1945, Berlin experienced its worst air raid of the war so far. That morning 937 B-17 and B-24 bombers of the US 8th Air Force, escorted by 613 Mustang and Thunder-

bolt fighters, appeared out of the densely clouded sky. In a period of 53 minutes they dropped 2,267 metric tons of bombs on the Tempelhof, Schöneberg and Kreuzberg districts and the area around the Anhalter rail station. Five B-24 Liberators, 31 B-17 Flying Fortresses, 8 Mustangs and 1 Thunderbolt were brought down by the German fighters and flak. This was the first US terrorist area raid on residential districts in imitation of the RAF night raids. Two and a half square miles of the city were destroyed, and American sources claim that 23,000 people lay dead under the ruins.

The two US air forces based in England, and the one in Italy, joined with the RAF in a combined strategic bombardment of the target zone between the Rhine, Oder and Po rivers, which was gradually diminishing in size and coming within range of the tactical air forces.

At the start of February 1945, the German Luftwaffe transferred virtually all its air force and flak units to the Eastern Front. This regrouping was intended to stop the Soviet march columns from crossing the Oder. The Luftwaffe even managed to gain air supremacy along the Oder for several days. The main reason for this temporary victory was that the aircraft of the Soviet 6th Air Army were based some distance away and had virtually no weatherproof airfields near the front, whereas the Luftwaffe had bases in Mecklenburg and Saxony from which it could operate even in bad weather.

On the night of 13–14 February 1945, 773 Lancasters of RAF Bomber Command raided Dresden in two waves.

Before the operation, some crews were told that their targets were a large poison gas factory, important munitions factories and Gestapo Headquarters in the city center; others heard Dresden described as an important rail junction of crucial importance to German supplies on the Eastern Front. Only a handful of the airmen knew that Dresden was one of the most beautiful cities in Europe.

The bombers were equipped with every imaginable bombing aid. Most of the crews were already very experienced both in area and precision bombing. Each crew-member was given a large Union Jack printed with the Russian words for "I am British," to be used in case of an emergency.

Since mid-January 1945 there had been no antiaircraft in Dresden, and nothing was left of the former batteries but wooden dummy emplace-

Dresden after heavy Allied bombing raids. It is not known exactly how many were killed.

ments. The guns themselves had been transferred to the steadily advancing Eastern Front to fight Soviet tanks. So far the beautiful city on the Elbe had felt hardly a trace of the air war.

RAF Bomber Command planned to proceed in exactly the same way as in Hamburg. First, blast bombs would be released to shatter windows and roofs so that the incendiaries dropped in their wake would achieve the maximum effect. Only 27 German night fighters took to the air to fight the most terrible of all the air raids on Germany. But the only German plane that flew above Dresden itself was not even a fighter but a courier aircraft belonging to the German Army High Command which had been sent from the Headquarters of German Army Group Center in Josefstadt (Bohemia) to fetch General von Xylander, the chief of the general staff, to Hitler's headquarters in Berlin. This plane was caught in one of the attack waves and lost over the burning city.

Thousands of blast bombs, including hundreds that weighed 4,000 or 8,000 pounds, and almost 650,000 incendiaries – a total of 2,659 metric tons – fell on Dresden that night causing a firestorm similar to that which had destroyed Hamburg two years earlier.

One of the British bombardiers said: "I happened to glance down as the bombs were falling and faced the ghastly sight of a city that was on fire from one end to the other. When the wind drove away the dense smoke clouds, one could see the brightly-lit city of Dresden as if on a city map. The rising heat could be felt even inside my gun pit. The sky had turned bright red, and the light inside the plane was like that of an eerie autumn sunset. I could still see the fires even when I was close to 200 miles from the target."

Over twelve square miles of Dresden were laid waste on this single night. By contrast, throughout the whole of the war the Germans did not succeed in destroying as much as 1½ square miles of London. German General Reinhard, commander of German defense in the Dresden sector, said: "The purely military effects of the raid are negligible – nothing but temporary problems with telephone communications and some delays in rail traffic." Bomber Command lost less than ½% of its aircraft in this, its most successful night raid.

At midday on 14 February 1945, 311 Flying Fortresses of the US 8th Air Force dropped 771 metric tons of bombs on the burning city of Dresden. On this Ash Wednesday the P-51 Mustang escort fighters flew low over the city, strafing people on the clogged arterial roads and the refugee banks along the Elbe. The overcrowded Dresden-Klotzsche airfield was spared again, as it had been in the British raid.

Next day, February 15, 210 B-17s of the US 8th Air Force appeared over Dresden and dropped 461 more tons of bombs into the inferno.

The city was crowded with refugees from Silesia and the toll of the dead cannot be precisely determined, but the German Federal Bureau of Statistics in Wiesbaden claims that it was 600,000; other estimates suggest 245,000. The raid on Dresden neither hastened the advance of the Soviet armies, nor shortened the war. On the day when the Germans surrendered, the destroyed city still lay outside the battle zone.

On 16 and 17 February 1945, airfields and aircraft plants around Tokyo became the targets of the first grand raids by carrier aircraft of the US Fast Carrier Task Force (Task Force 58 under Vice-Admiral Mitscher). On these two days, 2,761 missions were flown. Bad weather hampered operations, but over 200 Japanese planes were destroyed, some in aerial combat but most on the ground. US casualties were the highest since 1942: 60 aircraft shot down by Japanese fighters and antiaircraft. Raids by Task Force 58 carrier aircraft were part of the US preparations for an invasion of the island of Iwo Jima.

On Monday 19 February 1945, after almost three days of uninterrupted air raids and bombardment by the warships of Task Force 51 (under Vice-Admiral Turner), the US Fifth Corps under General Schmidt landed on Iwo Jima, halfway between the Marianas and Tokyo. The battles on the island were among the hardest of the Pacific war.

Opposite page above: 1,112 US 8th Air Force planes raided the city center of Berlin at noon on 26 February 1945. The trails of smoke are from the flares that marked the targets.

Below right: An F4U Corsair fighter plane, trying to take off, crashes into the superstructure of the US carrier *Prince William* on 24 February 1945 – one of the countless incidental tragedies of the air war.

During US invasion operations on Wednesday 21 February, Japanese planes sank the US carrier *Bismarck Sea* and badly damaged the US carrier *Saratoga*.

On Thursday 22 February 1945, the Allied air forces flew relay raids all day against traffic lines inside Germany. This operation, called Clarion, was also meant as a demonstration of Allied strength. That day the air raid sirens howled in every German city. Approximately 9,000 aircraft took off from bases in England, Belgium, France, Holland and Italy to bomb rail junctions, bridges and locomotive depots. Operation Clarion was repeated on the same scale next day. By the end of the operation, 90% of German road and rail centers and transport capability inside Germany had been eliminated.

On Sunday 25 February 1945, Tokyo experienced its heaviest air raid so far when more than 170 Superfortresses of the US 21st Bomber Command based in the Marianas, unleashed 1,667 metric tons of incendiary bombs. Around 28,000 buildings were destroyed and there were heavy civilian casualties.

Until now, American bombing attacks on the Japanese capital had been largely unsuccessful because of the powerful Japanese air defenses. Also, bombs dropped from an altitude of about 32,000 feet lost their precision of aim due to the violent winds that raged at this height, and instruments tended to ice up. Over six per cent of the Superfortresses dispatched against the main Japanese islands were being lost until General Curtis LeMay, commander of the US 21st Bomber Command in the Marianas, evolved new tactics. He reduced operational altitude from 32,000 feet to about 8,000 feet, loaded the B-29s exclusively with incendiary bombs, and shifted operations to the night hours to avoid the full effects of the Japanese antiaircraft. At this lower altitude, the Superfortresses were able to carry three times as many bombs as before.

Between 1:19 and 2:07 A.M. on 26 February 1945, the Allies launched the twenty-seventh in a series of 363 raids on Berlin, aimed mainly at the city center. This raid was even heavier than that of February 3: 1,112 four-engined bombers of the US 8th Air Force, escorted by 700 fighters, released a total of 2,879 metric tons of bombs. Only 13 bombers and 2 Mustang fighters were shot down.

By the end of January 1945, the Soviet First White Russian Front under Marshal Zhukov had already reached the Oder. The Soviet armies built up a strong front along the river, only just under 40 miles from Berlin. In massive and swift advances they seized approximately 120 almost undamaged rail and road bridges over the Oder; only 12 of the bridges were so destroyed that they could not be used again until March 1945. On 1 March 1945, Hitler ordered Lt. Col. Baumbach, the commander of the German special duty bomber wing KG 200 "to attack all enemy passages across the Oder and Neisse rivers." Baumbach, one of the most success-

March 1945, a Japanese balloon has been found in Vancouver, Canada. The balloons took an average of 45 hours to cross the Pacific, at an altitude of 32,000 feet.

ful bomber pilots in the Luftwaffe, "is to deploy all suitable battle resources from all branches of the armed services, weapons and economy and to synchronize their activities to carry out this task."

On the night of 3–4 March 1945, the Germans renewed their nuisance raids on England for the first time in several months. The raids were part of Operation Gisela. German night fighters won their last great victory when over 100 fighters of the 2nd Night Fighter Wing pursued an RAF bomber formation which was returning to base after raiding the artificial-fuel manufacturers at Kamen near Dortmund. Nineteen four-engined bombers were shot down trying to land at their bases, while another 17 were destroyed on the ground.

On Monday 5 March 1945 an American minister, Archie Mitchell of Lake View (Oregon), went on an auto excursion with his wife and five of the community's children to nearby Mount Gearhart. While the minister parked the car, his wife and the children looked for a suitable picnic spot. At that moment one of the Japanese hydrogen-filled balloons carrying an explosive charge, floated to the ground and exploded, killing the woman and the children. These were the only victims of the air war on the US continent and the only victims of the Japanese balloon offensive (command by General Kusaba).

About 9,000 balloons had been launched from Japan since November 1944. Shortly after the Lake View incident the Japanese halted the operations because they could not find either in the American press or in radio broadcasts, any indication that the balloons ever reached the North American continent. They did not suspect that the media had been strictly prohibited from reporting anything about the balloons. Actually 2,000 did reach the West Coast.

On Tuesday 6 March 1945, following Hitler's orders to KG 200 to destroy all bridges over the Oder and the Neisse, one of the unit's He 111s flown by Colonel Helbig, raided the Oder bridges at Görlitz with Hs 293 guided bombs, and scored a hit.

On Wednesday 7 March 1945, the southern flank of the American Ninth Armored Division under General Leonard (a division of Third Corps) successfully crossed the Ludendorff bridge at Remagen, which the Germans had failed to destroy, and reached the eastern bank of the Rhine where they formed a bridgehead.

On Thursday 8 March 1945, 6 Squadron of KG 200 flew its first mistletoe raid on the Oder bridges. At 9:00 A.M., 4 mistletoe composite aircraft took off from Burg airfield at Magdeburg with 2 Junkers Ju 88s and 5 Junkers Ju 188s flying escort, to attack the Görlitz bridges again. One of the mistletoe pilots had to explode his Ju 88 prematurely due to a hydraulic fault. For the first time, German pilots with no experience flying mistletoe raids, had to take off without making any test flights before the mission; but the three pilots flew their raid and reportedly destroyed at least two river crossings over the Oder.

On the night of 9–10 March 1945, the US 21st Bomber Command based on Saipan, Guam and Tinian in the Marianas, flew the heaviest air raid of World War II using conventional bombs. Three hundred and thirty-four B-29 Superfortresses, each loaded with 8 metric tons of napalm bombs, attacked Tokyo. Fourteen B-29s were lost to Japanese antiaircraft.

One US pilot reported: "The weather over the target was better than usual. The first pathfinders located the targets easily and marked them with quick-rising fires a few minutes after midnight. Our three formations flew at low altitude, between 5,000 and 6,000 feet. The fresh wind spread the first fires very rapidly and our B-29s were ordered to bomb in a fan formation so as to create new fires that then joined to form a huge area fire."

Aerial photographs taken on 10 and 11 March show that by this time, 15 square miles of Tokyo had already been destroyed by fire, including 18% of the industrial and 63% of the business districts, and the heart of the overpopulated residential area. Japanese police reports indicate that 267,171 buildings were levelled (one quarter of all the buildings in Tokyo) and that 1,008,000 people were made homeless. The official casualty statistics list 83,793 dead and 40,918 wounded. Radio Tokyo described the raid as "human butchery."

On the night of 10–11 March 1945, 285 Superfortresses of the US 21st Bomber Command in the Marianas, raided the Japanese city of Nagoya. This area bombing raid using napalm bombs had an effect similar to the raid on Tokyo the night before.

On Sunday 11 March, 1,055 Lancasters and Halifaxes of RAF Bomber Command carried out a heavy daylight raid on Essen, unleashing 4,700 metric tons of bombs which destroyed the city almost completely. Allied Headquarters said: "This attack was part of the program to sever rail communications in accord with Operation Rhine Crossing."

On Monday 12 March 1945, Dortmund became the target of the heaviest of all raids on Europe so far: 1,107 Lancaster and Halifax bombers dropped 4,851 metric tons of bombs on the city, which already was almost completely destroyed.

On Tuesday 13 March 1945, the German Luftwaffe threw all the forces it had into an attempt to destroy the Ludendorff rail bridge at Remagen, which the US Ninth Armored Division had seized on 7 March 1945. As the war diary of the German Armed Forces High Command (the OKW) reported: "The Remagen area is drawing American forces to it like a magnet; virtually the whole of the American army is on its way there."

The US seizure of this intact bridge over the Rhine, had come as a surprise even to the American forces: The explosive charges prepared by German engineers to blow up the bridge, failed to go off. Strategists believe that Allied capture of the bridge shortened the war by several weeks.

That day, 360 German fighter-bombers and Me 262 jets, and the world's first jet bombers—Arado 234s of 3rd Group, 76th Bomber Wing—were dispatched in the attempt to destroy the Ludendorff bridge. Recklessly they flew in low to destroy the bridge, which was defended by US antiaircraft guns. "One plane went down to 1,400 feet and dropped a 2,200-lb bomb that did not ignite on the bridge and bounced off the pier into the water" (OKW war diary, entry dated 13 March 1945). Mistletoe composite aircraft were dispatched too, and even 11 V-2 rockets were fired at the bridge; this was the only tactical deployment of the V-2 during the war.

On Wednesday 14 March 1945, the heaviest bomb of the war was dropped to pave the way for the Allied crossing of the Rhine. The 22,000-lb Grand Slam bomb, also known as the Earthquake bomb, was the creation of the same British Dr. Wallis who had designed the Tallboy bombs. A specially-equipped Lancaster I PD 112 bomber of 617 RAF Squadron under Squadron Leader C. C. Calder, dropped the bomb on the rail viaduct at Bielefeld, eliminating this vital communication line for the rest of the war.

Shortly before 11:00 A.M. on Sunday 18 March 1945, the war's heaviest raid on Berlin began. Nine hundred and sixteen Liberators and 305 Flying For-

Tokyo on 10 March 1945. The lightly-built houses burned like straw. One quarter of the city was destroyed after a single air raid.

tresses of the US 8th Air Force, escorted by 632 P-51 Mustang fighters, dropped over 4,000 tons of bombs on the center of the German capital. The government district and the area surrounding the Silesian Railway were the worst hit. Although the raid of 3 February 1945 cost many more dead, this time the material destruction was considerably greater. The Americans lost 48 bombers and 5 escort fighters. Thirty-seven German Me 262 jet fighters of the 7th Fighter Wing, brought down 8 bombers and 5 Mustangs.

Between 18 and 21 March, the US Fast Carrier Task Force under Vice-Admiral Mitscher carried out a series of carrier raids on the main Japanese islands of Honshu and Kyushu. Dive-bombers of the Japanese naval air force, and kamikaze planes repeatedly attacked American aircraft carriers. The *Intrepid* was set on fire by a suicide pilot who crashed beside the vessel, but the fires were put out. The *Wasp* caught fire but was also saved. The *Franklin* received the heaviest damage—724 dead and 265 wounded—and was knocked out of the war. Japan lost 161 aircraft in just two days.

On the night of 19–20 March 1945, approximately 300 Superfortresses of the US 21st Bomber Command in the Marianas, bombed the center of Nagoya, where napalm bombs destroyed the remaining houses. The US grand raids on Tokyo, Osaka, Kobe and Nagoya confirmed the success of the new tactics devised by General LeMay, who three years later would set up the famous Berlin Air Lift.

Within a three-week period, 9,365 tons of incendiary bombs fell on these four Japanese cities destroying a built-up area 50 miles square. Of 1,595 aircraft dispatched, 22 were shot down, which was a loss rate of only 1.4%. Nevertheless LeMay halted the Superfortress raids, because he had run out of his entire supply of 10,000 tons of incendiaries.

On Wednesday 21 March 1945, after the US carriers of the Fast Carrier Task Force (No. 58 under Vice-Admiral Mitscher) were sighted south of Kyushu, Admiral Ugaki of the Japanese 5th Air Force ordered the first deployment of Ohka suicide aircraft—Yokosuka MXY-7 Ohka (Cherry Blossom) piloted bombs. Eighteen Mitsubishi G4M bombers carrying Ohkas under the fuselage, took off from Kanoya airbase; but 150 US Hellcat fighters from the American carrier-escort force, intercepted the Japanese formation long before it reached its target and shot down all but one of the slow Mitsubishis before the Ohkas could be deployed.

On Saturday 24 March 1945, the Allied 21st Army Group under Field Marshal Montgomery crossed the Rhine on either side of the city of Wesel. Their plan was to surround the Ruhr District in the north and advance the bulk of their forces to the lower reaches of the Elbe river. This movement was accompanied by a large-scale airborne operation, the most successful such Allied operation of the war. The American 17th Airborne and the British 6th Airborne Divisions landed north of the Lippe river. Nine hundred and three US and 669 RAF paratroop-transport aircraft and 1,326 gliders were escorted by 679 fighters of the US 9th Air Force and 213 RAF fighters. At the same time, 1,252 fighters of the US 8th Air Force patrolled western

Opposite page: A 22,000-lb Grand Slam bomb, the heaviest of the war, also known as the Earthquake. It was about 25 feet long and exceeded the speed of sound during its fall.

Right: A piloted Japanese flying bomb, the Yokosuka MXY-7 "Ohka" (Cherry Blossom) suicide aircraft. Once this rocket plane had disengaged from its carrier at an altitude of about 25,000 feet, it would dive at the target at a 50-degree angle.

Below: US paratroops land on the eastern bank of the Rhine on 25 March 1945.

Germany and 900 fighters of the 2nd Tactical Air Force helped to secure the drop zone. Also, some 3,000 Allied medium and heavy bombers were operating out of bases in Great Britain, Italy and France, demonstrating their supremacy.

The Allied airborne force numbered approximately 14,000 troops. They met only minor resistance, for the German Luftwaffe scarcely put in an appearance. Only German antiaircraft put up a stiff defense in some places, and according to German reports, shot down 60 gliders and 38 other aircraft. Further Allied losses occurred due to the failure of many parachutes to open, and a number of gliders caught fire on landing when the gasoline in their cargo of jeeps ignited. These accidents claimed almost as many victims as the fighting with the German ground troops, whose strength Montgomery had overestimated.

The greatest obstacle to the advance of the Allied armored units was not German troops but the debris of the destroyed cities, which were subjected to another inordinate bombing raid on the eve of the operation. The debris clogged the roads and held up the troops.

That same day, the US 15th Air Force based in Italy carried out its only raid on Berlin. One hundred and fifty B-24 Liberators from Foggia, escorted by P-51 Mustang fighters, dropped some 450 tons of bombs on the German capital.

On Monday 26 March 1945 after extremely hard fighting, the resistance of Japanese troops on Iwo Jima came to an end. The Americans chose to occupy the island because the Japanese had been using it as a base for fighter planes which intercepted the Superfortresses of the US 21st Bomber Command on their way from the Marianas to raid the main Japanese islands. Iwo Jima now became a base for US long-range fighters. The importance of the island base can best be seen from the fact that by the war's end, 2,251 aircraft carrying 24,761 crew had been able to make emergency landings there when returning from missions over Japan. Without this base, many of the planes would surely have been lost.

At 7:20 A.M. on the morning of 27 March 1945, a single V-2 rocket fell on a residential block in Stepney (East London), killing 130 people. Several hours later the last V-2 struck the Kynaston Road in Orpington (Kent). A total of 1,115 V-2 rockets had landed in England – 517 in London, 537 in other cities, and 61 along the coast – killing 2,724 people and severely injuring 6,467.

Two days later, on Thusday 29 March, the last

Left: March 1945, Assam, the "Hump Route" corridor at the feet of the Himalayas. A Curtiss C-46 Commando transport plane is coming in for a landing.

Opposite page: The US carrier *Hornet* during a raid by Japanese kamikaze planes. (Painting by D. Shepler)

V-1 flying bomb landed in England, in Datchworth near Sittingbourne (Kent). Between 13 June 1944 and 29 March 1945, 9,200 flying bombs had taken off from the launch ramps in France, Belgium and Holland and from He 111 bombers, all aimed at England. More than 1,000 V-1s had crashed immediately after takeoff. Of the V-1s that did not crash on their own, 3,957 were destroyed before landing—1,847 by fighter planes, 1,878 by antiaircraft and 232 by barrage balloons. Those that landed killed 6,139 people and seriously wounded 17,239.

Approximately 12,000 V-1s fell on various cities in Belgium, some 8,000 of them on Antwerp.

At 7:15 A.M. on Saturday 31 March 1945, 6 mistletoe composite aircraft of KG 200 (the German 200th Special Duty Bomber Wing) took off from Burg field at Magdeburg, to raid the Oder river bridges at Steinau in Silesia. Over Waldenburg they joined up with an escort unit of 24 German fighters from nearby Schweidnitz, which protected them from Soviet fighters. Three of the mistletoes had to be blown up en route due to technical faults, but three reached the target and damaged the rail bridge at Steinau so badly that it was unusable for many days.

The 31st of March 1945 was a record day for the Allied aerial "Hump Route" across the Himalayas. Three years had passed since 8 April 1942, when US Colonel W. D. Old and his transport plane had opened the longest regular supply line of the war. Every day without fail, Curtiss C-46, DC-3 Dakota and B-24 Liberator aircraft of the US air transport command, supported by the US 14th Air Force, flew supplies between Assam and Kunming in southern China (a vital supply point at the end of the Burma Road) for the forces of Chiang Kai-shek and for the US 20th Bomber Command. The Hump Route was the only link between China and the Western Allies until the Ledo Road was cut from India through the mountains of Burma in January 1945, again making the Burma Road a vital supply route.

In March 1945, the Hump Route fliers reached a peak when they transported 94,300 tons of supplies; one aircraft landed at the Kunming airfields every 90 seconds. By contrast, between 25 November 1942 and 2 February 1943, German aircraft transported a total of about 6,600 metric tons of supplies into the pocket of Stalingrad. By the end of the war, approximately 615,000 metric tons of supplies and 315,000 reinforcement troops had been flown in over the Hump Route.

While the US forces continued the bombing of Japan from their bases in China and the Marianas, the US Navy followed the strategy of "island-hopping." Each island they conquered made it possible for the US 21st Bomber Command to fly safer and more frequent raids along the Tokyo route. At the same time the Americans yielded more and more to the temptation to turn into ashes as many of the Japanese wood-and-paper cities as they could.

In the last week of March the carrier aircraft of the US Fast Carrier Task Force (No. 58 under Vice-Admiral Mitscher), and of a British carrier group (No. 57 commanded by Vice-Admiral Vian, part of the Pacific fleet under Vice-Admiral Rawlings), led relay bombing raids to pave the way for the next island hop. The Americans had now set their sights on Okinawa.

On Sunday 1 April 1945, the American Tenth Army under General Buckner landed on Okinawa,

one of the Ryukyu islands, along with the amphibious Third Corps under General Geiger and the Twenty-Fourth Corps under General Hodges. The island of Okinawa, about 66 miles long and 5 miles wide, was a large enough site on which to build several airfields for medium bombers. The invasion fleet comprised 318 combat vessels and 1,139 auxiliary vessels. Almost 600,000 men took part in the operation, codenamed "Iceberg." It was the largest landing operation of the Pacific war.

The landing itself met little opposition because the Japanese – the Thirty-Second Army under General Ushiyima – had dug themselves into the southern hills and prepared for a long tenacious combat: for Okinawa was the last bulwark in the Japanese defensive belt. Surprisingly, only 2 men died during the seizure of Tontan and Kadena airfields. Seventeen American, 4 British and 18 US escort carriers supported the landing with a total of 1,900 aircraft. The Japanese brought about 6,000 planes to combat this aerial armada; but most of the pilots lacked the necessary training so the Japanese force was not effective. The real threat lay in the massive deployment of kamikaze planes by the 1st Japanese Air Force.

The aim of the suicide pilots was to attack the Allied fleet directly off the coast in waves of 300–400 aircraft at a time, so as to ward off the landing. The fact that the kamikazes took off from their own motherland, the island of Kyushu only 330 miles away, further stimulated their will to self-destruction. The suicidal Kikisui (Floating Chrysanthemum) operations involved 1,456 sorties aimed to destroy the large combat vessels; but they did not succeed in sinking a single aircraft carrier.

Thursday 5 April 1945 marked an end to the deployment of V-2 rockets, which since 27 March 1945 had been aimed exclusively at Antwerp, Brussels and Liège.

Friday 6 April 1945 was the beginning of Kikisui-1, a new grand raid by 335 kamikazes against the Allied landing fleet. Three hundred and forty-four Japanese dive-bombers and torpedo-bombers also took part in the operation. Many of the aircraft were intercepted but about 200 reached the target zone. The US vessels opened such strong antiaircraft fire that 38 of their own crew-members were killed by falling antiaircraft shrapnel. The Japanese aircraft sank only the minesweeper *Emmons*, one landing boat, the ammunition transporters *Hobbs Victory* and *Logan Victory* (7,607 tons each), and the destroyers *Bush* and *Colhoun* which were out on radar patrol away from the other vessels and were the first to feel the full wrath of the kamikazes. Of 699 Japanese aircraft dispatched, only 3 came back.

At 3:00 P.M. that same day, a Japanese task force under Vice-Admiral Ito sailed out of the port of Tokuyama to make a suicide raid on the landing fleet. The formation included the largest super-battleship in the world, the 69,000-ton *Yamato*, which had 9 of the heaviest (45.7-cm) guns in history; it was commanded by Rear-Admiral Ariga. The task force also included the light cruiser *Yahagi* and 8 destroyers. The Japanese had procured 2,500 tons of oil for the *Yamato*, the last fuel available in Japan, which was just enough to get it to Okinawa. The formation was ordered to beach and fire every shell it had at the Americans.

In April the Allies' air supremacy over all Germany became absolute command of the air, and the German armaments industry virtually ceased to exist. On Saturday 7 April 1945, the US 8th Air Force flew a number of missions in which bombers escorted by long-range fighters, raided airfields and rail installations. One giant unit of 1,300 B-17s and B-24s escorted by 850 fighters, flew a raid whose main target was Dessau. The amazed crews were attacked there by a German suicide squad: the four groups of the German "Elbe Special Unit" which had been set up near Magdeburg several weeks earlier and which carried out their first and last grand mission that day. The unit's founder was that same Colonel Herrmann who had devised the *Wilde Sau* strategy which had cost the British such heavy losses in their night raids on German cities. His younger fighter pilots, who had received only the barest minimum of training, were ordered to "open fire from extremely close up, shoot down at least one four-engined bomber, or if necessary destroy it by ramming." This tactic was the logical development of the ramming attack already practiced by Germans in July 1944. The German suicide squads were based at airfields near Stendal and Gardelegen (eastern Germany).

Today it is not known to which units the pilots formerly belonged, or how they came into the suicide unit; it is assumed that they were volunteers. In any case, some of them came from the 300th and 301st *Wilde Sau* fighter wings. Different sources claim different numbers of fighters taking part in the attack on US bombers on April 7; some say that 120 Me 109 Gs and FW 190s were involved, others 183 fighters. Me 262 jet fighters of the 7th Fighter Wing, and the 1st Group of the 54th (J) Bomber Wing escorted them to fight off the US Mustangs.

Between Uelzen and Celle, at an altitude of just under 36,000 feet, the German suicide planes hurled themselves at the leading units of US bombers with such ferocity that the US escort fighters were powerless against them. German reports claim that some 50 German fighters and several Me 262s succeeded in moving in close to the bomber flights. In the 45-minute air battle – the last large air battle over Europe – 51 US planes were destroyed (according to German sources) – for 131 German losses. American reports on the other hand, say that only 8 bombers were lost and that 100 German fighters were shot down, 59 of them by Mustangs. What is certain is that only 15 German fighters of the Elbe Special Unit returned from this mission, codenamed "Werewolf." Seventy-seven German pilots were killed; the rest managed to bail out in time.

That same day, 7 April 1945, the carrier aircraft of Vice-Admiral Mitscher's US Task Force 58 intercepted the Japanese task force of Vice-Admiral Ito off Okinawa. Three hundred and eighty-six US bombers, torpedo-bombers and fighters attacked the Japanese formation in waves. At 12:41 P.M. the *Yamoto* was hit by two bombs near the mainmast. Four minutes later a torpedo struck her on the forward port side. At 2:23 P.M. the giant ship exploded. Of the 2,767-man crew, only 23 officers and 246 seamen were rescued. The light cruiser *Yahagi* and 4 destroyers shared the fate of their flagship. Japanese losses totalled 3,665 dead. The Americans lost 12 crewmen and 10 planes. The last major Japanese naval operation was over.

Meanwhile the Superfortresses of the US 21st Bomber Command based in the Marianas, were raiding Japanese aircraft-engine factories near Tokyo and Nagoya. Their precision attacks from high altitude (over 30,000 feet), resulted in severe damage to the targets. For the first time, their P-51 Mustang fighter escort from the US 7th Fighter Command, took off from a base on the island of Iwo Jima.

On the night of 7–8 April 1945, RAF Stirlings of 38th Group dropped two battalions of French parachutists – including both regular soldiers and members of the French Resistance – into Holland south of Groningen. The aim of the paratroops was to support the advance of the Canadian Second Division.

Opposite page above: April 1945. A US Navy F4U Corsair is attacking Japanese emplacements on Okinawa with air-to-surface rockets.

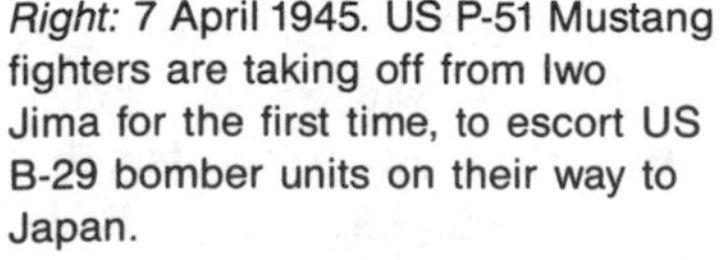
Right: 7 April 1945. US P-51 Mustang fighters are taking off from Iwo Jima for the first time, to escort US B-29 bomber units on their way to Japan.

On Sunday 8 April 1945, the German special-duty aerial unit KG 200 undertook its longest mistletoe mission. The target was a strategically vital rail bridge over the Vistula in Warsaw 210 miles to the east. Five mistletoe composite aircraft with FW 190s as guide planes, took off at dawn from Rechlin airfield in Mecklenburg. The antiaircraft guns along the banks of thc Vistula opened fire so vigorously that the raiders were unable to raid their target with precision. None of the mistletoes hit the bridge, although the 5 FW 190 guide planes all returned safely.

On Tuesday 10 April 1945, the US 8th Air Force responded to the suicide raid by the German "Elbe Special Unit" three days earlier, by launching relay raids on all known Me 262 jet fighter airfields in northern Germany. The jet airbases at Parchim, Oranienburg, Briest, Rechlin and Burg [all in East Prussia] were badly damaged. A short time later, all the Me 262 units that were still intact, were ordered to transfer to southern Germany and to the German Protectorate of Czechoslovakia.

On 10 April 1945, an Arado Ar 234 B-1 German jet reconnaissance plane took off from Sola airfield in Stavanger (Norway). The plane took photographs of Scotland and landed back at Sola 2½ hours later. The German Luftwaffe had just ended its last mission over Britain.

That same day, Japanese forces in China launched a new offensive whose main objective was to seize the airfields of the US 14th Air Force at Chinkiang about 300 miles southwest of Hankow (Wuhan). Operation Kikisui-2 began on April 12 with 143 kamikazes, a strong fighter escort and 9 Ohka suicide bombers taking part. That day a manned Ohka flying bomb succeeded for the first time in sinking a ship, the US destroyer *Mannert L. Abele*.

On Monday 16 April, the Mustangs of the US 7th Fighter Command took off from their base on Iwo Jima to carry out their first independent operation. They attacked Kanoya airfield on the Japanese island of Kyushu with bombs and aerial guns.

Also on April 16, at 4:00 A.M., the Soviet First Ukrainian Front under Marshal Koniev and the First White Russian Front under Marshal Zhukov mounted a grand offensive from their bridgeheads on the Oder and Neisse rivers. Their combined armies – 18 in all – were ordered to encircle and take Berlin. Seven hundred and forty-three bombers of the Soviet 18th Air Army led a massive strike against the German defensive lines along the Seelow Heights east of the city. At the same time 668 bombers and ground-attack aircraft of the Soviet 2nd Air Army were dispatched against the positions of the German Fourth Panzer Army on the Neisse river.

That day in London, General Carl Spaatz, commander of the US strategic air forces in Europe, declared an end to the strategic air war. Virtually all the military problems facing the Western Allies had been resolved. The German traffic network had been smashed, the railroads had almost completely halted activity, and the end of the war was just around the corner.

On Tuesday 17 April 1945, aerial combat on the Oder Front reached its climax when, after the Soviet breakthrough, the German Luftwaffe gathered all its remaining forces to support the German ground troops. On the northern sector of the Oder Front, the Northeast Luftwaffe under General Fiebig had 1,433 aircraft; in the south General Ritter von Greim commanded the 791 aircraft of Luftflotte 6. The 2nd, 4th, 16th and 18th Soviet air armies – 7,500 combat aircraft in all – gathered against the German capital, and the Soviet First White Russian Front was supported by a special aerial unit of 800 long-range bombers.

On Friday 20 April 1945, 150 B-17s and B-24s of the US 8th Air Force mounted their last strategic raid on Berlin, badly destroying rail installations in the suburbs of Marienfelde and Lichtenrade. The air crews reported scattered flak fire. US P-51 Mustangs shot down 5 German fighters without losses to themselves.

At 2:00 A.M. on Saturday 21 April 1945, RAF Mosquitos of 109 Squadron flew a nuisance raid on Berlin. This was the Western Allies' last operation of the war over the German capital. Several hours later, at 11:30 A.M., the first Soviet shells began to hit the Hermannplatz. Berlin had become a frontline city. In the city center, large numbers of buildings already damaged by bombs collapsed under the artillery fire.

At 2:30 P.M. Hitler, Field Marshal Keitel and Admiral Dönitz met inside Hitler's underground bunker beneath the Chancellery. Dönitz was ordered to evacuate his camp at Lobetal and retreat to Schleswig-Holstein. The Luftwaffe's staff headquarters in Werder near Potsdam were also dissolved, at which Hitler commented that "All the

Soviet Il-2m3 Sturmovik ground-attack planes over the Spree river, Berlin, on 22 April 1945.

Luftwaffe leaders are to be hanged at once."

That same day the last passenger plane to leave Berlin took off from Tempelhof Airport with nine passengers on board, headed for Stockholm.

On Monday 23 April 1945, a telegram arrived at Hitler's Chancellery bunker from Göring, who was then at Berchtesgaden, asking whether Göring might immediately assume full leadership of the "Reich." If he received no answer by 10:00 P.M., he said, he would assume that Hitler had been deprived of his freedom of action. What Göring failed to add was that he intended to fly to Paris the following day, April 24, to negotiate a ceasefire with General Eisenhower at Western Allied headquarters. Hitler smelled betrayal, dismissed Göring from all his posts, and ordered the state police to arrest him with his family and staff. "If the Allies get close to Berchtesgaden," Hitler said, "they are all to be liquidated."

At midday on Tuesday 24 April 1945, Lancasters of RAF Bomber Command flew their last grand operation in Europe in World War II. The target was Hitler's residence on the mountain estate at Berchtesgaden. At 7:30 A.M. 318 Lancasters, flying at an altitude of 10,000 feet, dropped around 1,181 metric tons of bombs on the estate; this was roughly the same quantity of explosives dropped on England by all the V-2 rockets put together. The air crews reported strong flak fire, but only one plane was damaged and there were no losses.

The master of the house, at whom this raid was directed, had been shut up for weeks inside his bombproof bunker under the Chancellery in Berlin. Only now, 10 days before the armored spearheads of the US Seventh Army under General Patch reached Berchtesgaden, did the RAF give Hitler and his associates a taste of what the air war was like. Even at his "Wolf's Trench" headquarters in East Prussia, Hitler had always been allowed to work in peace; no Western Allied or Soviet airplane had ever tried to raid it.

A second bombing raid was flown by the US 8th Air Force on that same day, which was the day when the American 69th Division met and shook hands with the Soviet 58th Guard Division at Torgau on the Elbe. US B-17s and B-24s dropped a total of 638 tons of bombs – approximately as many as were dropped during the German raid on Coventry on 14–15 November 1940 – on the Skoda factories in Pilsen. Arms production at this most important industrial center in Czechoslovakia was no longer of any use to the dissolving German Wehrmacht, but it was still central to the economic structure of Czechoslovakia.

At 1:00 P.M. on 25 April 1945, the spearheads of the Soviet Fourth Guards Tank Army under General D. D. Lelyushenko met Marshal Zhokov's Second Guards Tank Army and the right flank of Zhukov's Forty-Seventh Army, at Ketzin northwest of Potsdam. Berlin was now encircled on all sides. Meanwhile the Soviet 16th Air Army raided the German capital twice, with 1,486 aircraft taking part in the operation.

On the evening of April 25, the noted German female test pilot Hanna Reitsch, then at Kitzbühel in the Austrian Tyrol, received a message from General Ritter von Greim asking her to come to Munich immediately to carry out a special mission. En route she learned that von Greim had been summoned to Hitler's side in Berlin. After an eventful flight they both reached Berlin's Gatow airbase.

Starting on 26 April 1945, the RAF and the USAAF gradually tapered off their area bombing raids on German cities, because more and more often they were mistakenly dropping their bombs over towns already occupied by Soviet forces.

That same day, RAF Bomber Command started to fly in relief supplies to the people of German-occupied Holland; the airlift was called Operation Manna. The Allied High Command held discussions with A. Seyss-Inquart, the German high commissioner of the Netherlands, and with General Blaskowitz, the German commander of "Fortress Holland," after which the Germans allowed the Allies to begin dropping food and clothing for the Dutch into Rotterdam, The Hague and other parts of Holland still occupied by German forces.

The commandant of Berlin, General Weidling, called for supplies, and a number of Me 109 fighters and Ju 52 transport aircraft tried to drop supply containers over the city center; but only one fifth of the packages could be recovered from the vast heap of ruins. The few remaining German tanks and 8.8-cm flak guns were out of ammunition, so at around 10:00 A.M. on April 26, 2 Ju 52s landed near the victory column in Berlin. The trees in the Berlin animal park and the lampposts of the main avenue had to be cleared away to create a sufficiently broad landing lane. The planes brought armor-piercing ammunition which was unloaded under sweeping fire from Soviet artillery. Wounded men were carried out from a military hospital to be flown out by the planes. Only one managed to take off; the other barely got off the ground, grazed a building with its left wing, and crashed. The defenders of Berlin had gained 6 metric tons of supplies including 16 antitank rocket launchers.

Hanna Reitsch and Ritter von Greim were now at Gatow airfield, but the Fieseler Storch light aircraft that was supposed to fly them into the German capital, was destroyed by a shell. A second Storch, the last one left, was finally cleared for takeoff at 6:00 P.M.

Hanna Reitsch said: "I had no experience flying front-line enemy missions, so von Greim wanted to pilot the plane himself. Standing behind his seat before we took off, I tried to see whether I could reach the gas pedal and the control stick over his left shoulder so that I could operate them in case of an emergency. The plane took off easily. We

Right: Allied Operation "Manna" in Holland at the end of April 1945: This time the planes dropped boxes of canned goods instead of death-dealing bombs.

Opposite page below: A German Fieseler Fi 156 Storch light aircraft has crashed in the Berlin zoo park on 5 May 1945. This was the same plane that brought Hanna Reitsch and Ritter von Greim into the city on April 25.

flew just above the treetops to evade the enemy fighters which turned up all over the sky. But then a hellish gunfire broke out that seemed to be aimed exclusively at us. I was right. The ground beneath us was crawling with Russian tanks and soldiers.

"I could see the faces of the Russians clearly; they were shooting at us with everything they had, with rifles, tommy guns and tank guns. To the right, left, above and below us floated small, deadly explosive clouds; then suddenly there was a fearful cracking sound. I saw a yellowish-white flame lick up beside the engine and at the same time I heard von Greim cry that he was hit. An explosive tank missile had crushed his right foot.

"Reacting almost mechanically, I reached over his shoulder and gripped the gas pedal and control stick and tried to hold the plane on a defensive course. Meanwhile the wounded man lost consciousness and collapsed. The air was still filled with innumerable explosions, so powerful that I could hardly hear my own engine. Missiles impacted against the plane. I saw with horror that fuel was running out of both wing tanks. There was bound to be an explosion any second, and I could not understand why it did not happen. The Storch continued maneuverable, and I remained unwounded. I was painfully concerned for the wounded man, who now and then recovered consciousness for a moment and then tried with incredible energy to regain control of the stick; but again and again it slid out of his hand.

"We were now approaching the radio tower. Fumes, smoke, dust and an intense sulfur smell

became even denser and more pungent, but the gunfire gradually tapered off. Apparently we were now flying over German-occupied parts of the city. I flew toward the radio tower, but I could hardly see anything from there. Now my practice flights over Berlin stood me in good stead. I did not have to look around to check possible sources of danger; it was enough that I knew the compass heading to the flak bunker. To the left lay the main avenue and the victory column. I set down the plane just in front of the Brandenburg Gate; there was almost no gas left in the tank.

"The area seemed dead and deserted. Uprooted trees, broken branches and chunks of concrete lay everywhere. A terrible sense of dread emanated from them. There seemed to be nothing here left alive. With great effort I helped the general, who had regained consciousness, out of the plane, which could be identified and shot at from above. He sat down at the side of the road."

The two finally reached the Chancellery, where Hitler promoted Ritter von Greim to the rank of Field Marshal and appointed him the new commander of the Luftwaffe, replacing Hermann Göring.

In the early dawn of 29 April 1945, Ritter von Greim and Hanna Reitsch were ordered to fly out of Berlin. An Arado 96 light training plane, the only flyworthy aircraft left in the capital, stood in a garage beside the main highway, 400 yards of which were still free from the enemy. Göring's wounded successor was laboriously brought into the plane under continuous Soviet fire. A German sergeant took off with his two passengers and at 3:00 A.M. they landed at Rechlin airfield in Mecklenburg.

On Sunday 29 April 1945, German Army Group C under General von Vietinghoff, the Tenth Army High Command under General Herr and the Fourteenth Army High Command under General Lemelsen, surrendered in Italy to the Allied forces under General Alexander.

That same day Hitler married Eva Braun in the Chancellery bunker and signed his private and "political" testament, in which he expelled Göring and Himmler from the Nazi party and appointed Admiral Dönitz—then in Plön (Schleswig-Holstein)—President of the Reich.

On the morning of 30 April 1945, the 4 remaining mistletoe composite aircraft of the German 200th Special-Duty Bomber Wing (KG 200) took off from Peenemünde to raid the Oder river bridges at Tantow east of Prenzlau. One explosive plane had to be separated from the FW 190 guide plane and jettisoned right after takeoff due to technical problems. The other 3 composites attacked their target at 9:00 A.M., without success.

That Monday, 30 April 1945, at 3:30 P.M., Hitler committed suicide.

On Tuesday 1 May 1945, Berlin stood in flames. Heavy fighting raged around Unter den Linden, the Wilhelmstrasse, the animal park and the zoo. The Chancellery was stormed and captured.

At this same time in Burma, the British were fighting along what they called the "narrowest salient in the war." Two British units, 33rd Corps

under General Stopford and 4th Corps under General Messervy, set out to take Burma as fast as possible in order to cut off the powerful, still intact Japanese army from its safe retreat route to Siam. The greatest enemy facing the British was not the fanatically fighting Japanese but the forces of nature: The monsoon period was imminent, which would transform the roads into strips of mire and worst of all, turn the airfields into giant marsh holes, halting air operations. By April 29 the vanguard of the Indian 17th Division had already reached the city of Pegu approximately 36 miles north of Rangoon, and threatened the southernmost Japanese retreat route. The Japanese tenaciously defended the rail line and the bridges over the Rangoon river. In the afternoon a deluge of rain signalled the onset of the monsoon. The forward airfields became unusable, vehicles and tanks were tied down on the roads.

Lord Mountbatten, the commander of the Allied armed forces in southeast Asia, was determined to take the Burmese capital before the monsoon. He ordered a battalion of Gurkha paratroops to drop into the approach roads to Rangoon and pave the way for Operation "Dracula": a landing by the Indian 26th Division under General Chambers (part of General Christison's 15th Corps) from the sea on both sides of the Rangoon river about 25 miles south of the capital. A British reconnaissance plane flew over the city and saw giant white letters painted on the roof of Rangoon prison saying, "JAPS GONE, BRITISH HERE." On Wednesday 2 May 1945, the powerful Indian 26th Division made their landing in rough sea and pouring rain, with the support of 224 Group of the RAF under Air Vice-Marshal the Earl of Bandon. But fate decreed that neither the tanks of the Indian 17th Division nor those of the 26th Division would take Rangoon. This achievement fell to a Mosquito pilot, the only man in the war to take a capital city all on his own.

At 12:16 P.M., Wing Commander A. E. Saunders of No. 110 RAF Squadron took off from Yoari on a reconnaissance flight to Rangoon. He saw several figures waving white flags at Mingaladon airfield about 7 miles north of the city and came in to land on a runway; too late he saw that it was damaged, so his plane crashed. The men with the white flags were soldiers of the pro-Japanese Indian National Army, and they accompanied the Wing Commander when, undismayed, he set out to march from the airfield into Rangoon. In the city he discovered that the Japanese, assuming that the arrival of the monsoon would make any Allied landing impossible, had abandoned their garrison on April 26 and withdrawn to defend Pegu. Saunders located several hundred Allied prisoners who had been waiting to be freed for more than three years, requisitioned a sampan, sailed down the river and reported to General Chambers—who was sailing up the river toward Rangoon with the Indian 26th Division—his successful capture of the Burmese capital.

That same day, 2 May 1945, the defenders of Berlin surrendered. The Soviet forces had lost 527 aircraft in capturing the city.

On the night of 2–3 May 1945, the RAF flew its last raid on Germany when 125 Mosquitos of 608 Squadron dropped 174 metric tons of bombs on the harbor at Kiel. The air crews met no opposition. All the aircraft came back, some to Wyton airfield in Huntingdonshire: the same airfield from which Blenheim bombers had taken off five years earlier for the first British operation over Germany, the raid on Wilhelmshaven. Tactical bombing raids continued even in the final days of the war, until, as Churchill said, it became difficult to drop bombs in the path of the troops without endangering the Russians.

On Friday 4 May 1945, all the German forces in Holland (commander General Blaskowitz) surrendered; so did Field Marshal Busch's forces in northwestern Germany and the Frisian islands, and General Lindemann's in Denmark. The surrender was signed by Admiral General von Friedeburg at Field Marshal Montgomery's headquarters on the Lüneburg Heath.

Göring freed himself from arrest on Sunday 6 May 1945 and sent a message from Berchtesgaden to Admiral Dönitz, saying that it would be best if he, Göring, and not General Jodl, would handle the negotiations with Eisenhower—"from one Marshal to another." "I know," Göring wrote, "that the British and Americans would rather deal with me than with any of Germany's other political leaders." Dönitz did not reply to this message.

On Monday 7 May 1945, General Jodl signed the joint surrender of the German armed forces at the headquarters of General Eisenhower in Reims. The surrender became effective at 12:01 A.M. on 9 May 1945.

On 7 May 1945, RAF Coastal Command flew its last raid against a German submarine when a Catalina flying boat of 210 Squadron (pilot Lt. K. Murray) located a U-boat that had stopped dead between the Shetland islands and Norway, and recorded engine noises showing that the U-boat must be in distress. The Catalina dropped a series of depth charges. The boat was the U 230 under 1st Lt. Emmerich, and it radioed later that it was badly damaged. On Wednesday 9 May 1945, the U 230 went down with all her crew off Bergen, Norway.

At 8:30 A.M. on Tuesday May 8, Major Hartmann, the commander of German 1st Group, 52nd Fighter Wing, took off from the wing's forward airfield at Brod (Czechoslovakia) on his 1,405th enemy mission. Hartmann, who with his 351 aerial victories was the most successful fighter pilot in the world, wanted to see "how far away the Russians are from here." He flew his Me 109 G in the direction of Brünn. Eight Soviet Jak 11 fighters were circling over the burning city and unsuspectingly performing acrobatic maneuvers. Hartmann attacked one just as it was flying a loop, and shot it down. This was his 352nd air kill and probably was the last made by the German Luftwaffe.

At noon two Soviet fighters flown by G. A. Lobov, the commander of the Seventh Guard Division, and by Captain Svidirov, ran into a solo-flying He 111 and shot it down. This ended the operations of Soviet fighters in the air war over Europe.

Operation Manna was closed down on 8 May 1945. The bombers of the USAAF and the RAF had dropped a total of 6,600 metric tons of food and clothing into Holland.

On Wednesday 9 May 1945, Field Marshal Keitel, General Stumpff and Admiral General von Friedeburg again signed a joint surrender agreement, in the name of the German armed forces, at Soviet headquarters at Karlshorst, Berlin.

On the morning of May 9 after the war in Europe was over, US P-38 L "Lightning" destroyer aircraft and Soviet Il-2m Sturmoviks of the Soviet 951st Aerial Assault Regiment, combined in the first joint tactical operation by Eastern and Western Allied ground-attack aircraft. The target was a column of German armored vehicles near St. Pölten in Austria. The day before, General Balck, the commander of the German Sixth Army, had reached an

Opposite page above: British General Sir Frank Messervy presents Wing Commander A. E. Saunders with a Japanese officer's sword as a souvenir of his single-handed capture of Rangoon.

Right: Allied aircraft at an airfield near Celle, Germany, on 15 May 1945. Operation Exodus transported hundreds of thousands of former Allied POWs back to their native countries.

agreement with US General M. C. Bridge at Bridge's headquarters in Kirschdorf, allowing the Sixth Army to escape Soviet captivity by withdrawing westward and surrendering to the Western Allies.

General Balck said: "Now it turned out to be worthwhile that we had economized ruthlessly on fuel. It was decided that the Fourth SS Panzer Corps would go to the British at Kärnten, the Third Panzer Corps via Liezen to the Americans, and the two mountain troop divisions across the mountains to Upper Austria." When the Third SS Panzer Division of the Fourth SS Panzer Corps withdrew by rapid march from Soviet units of the Third Ukrainian Front under Marshal Tolbukhin who were advancing around Vienna, and headed toward Kärnten, two flights of Il-2ms and 4 US Lightnings, whose pilots knew nothing about the pact between the German and American generals, tried to halt the motorized columns, but failed as General Balck reported: "When, on the evening of May 9, Russian tanks appeared at Liezen, the bulk of the German Sixth Army had already been taken prisoner by the Americans, and the rest had already surrendered to the British army."

That afternoon the Red Air Force carried out its last operation of World War II in Europe when a Douglas C-47 of the Soviet 19th Special-Duty Aerial Regiment, flown by Captain A. Taimetov, took off at 2:00 P.M. from Tempelhof Airport, Berlin, headed for Moscow. On board were the original surrender documents signed by the German armed forces, and the flags of German units captured in the battle for the German capital.

The Allied bombing offensives in Europe were very costly. The US 8th and 9th Air Forces lost almost 45,000 fliers between them; the Americans

The end of the air war in Europe. Most German cultural shrines had been turned to rubble and ashes like the Old Town in Nuremberg.

lost 79,265 airmen in all. RAF Bomber Command lost 47,293 crew, 1,570 ground personnel and 7,122 aircraft. The RAF as a whole lost 79,281 men and 22,000 aircraft. The build-up of the Allied aerial forces was a long-drawn-out affair, so that 83% of the bombs dropped on Germany, fell in the last two years of the war.

In retaliation for the 71,172 metric tons of bombs (including the V-weapons) that the German Luftwaffe dropped on Britain during the war, the Allies released a grand total of 1,996,036 metric tons of bombs on Germany and occupied Europe. Of this vast load of bombs, 55.8% fell on cities and traffic installations, 30.5% on military targets such as U-boat bases, airfields and V-weapon sites; 9.3% on chemical factories; 1.8% on aircraft plants; and 2.6% on factories such as ball-bearing plants, and on U-boat yards. Until 1944, most of these bombs fell in area bombing raids.

In the last year of the war, the Allies unloaded 477,000 metric tons of bombs on Germany while

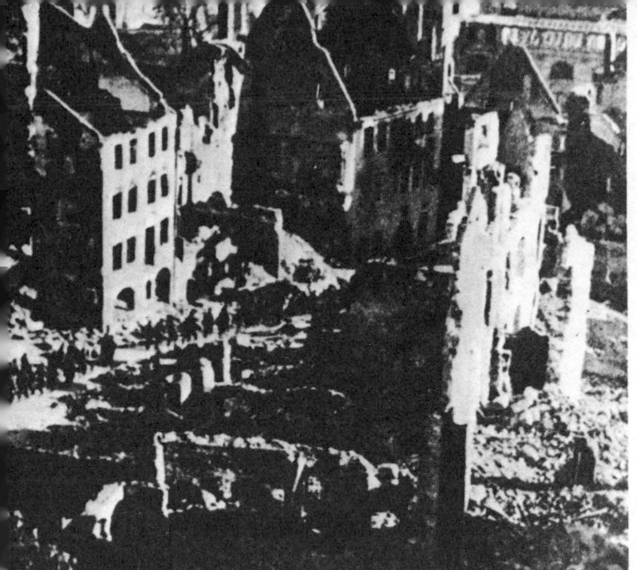

the Germans dropped 761 metric tons on Britain, including the V-weapons. During the last 36 hours of the war, 14,000 metric tons fell on Germany.

According to figures compiled by the German Federal Bureau of Statistics (Wiesbaden), 593,000 civilians died in Germany during World War II. The bombs destroyed approximately 3,370,000 dwellings and 7.5 million people were made homeless. The most frequently bombed city was Berlin. The Allies' strategic bombing raids forced the Germans continually to increase their production of fighter planes (78% of total aircraft) instead of the bombers (11%) which they could have used to bomb Britain.

The Soviet Air Force pursued its own theory in the air war. Soviet tactics were to coordinate the operations of the aerial forces with those of the ground troops, so 46.5% of all missions by front-line aircraft were flown in support of the army. The Soviets did not have many strong bomber units so they flew few strategic bombing raids. Of the 215,000 operations by Soviet "long-range aerial forces," only 7,394 were flown over the German hinterland.

German fighter planes shot down a total of approximately 70,000 aircraft, 45,000 of them on the Eastern Front. On the German side, 103 individual fighter pilots shot down more than 100 enemy aircraft, and 13 of them over 200. Major Barkhorn had 301 air kills to his credit, and Major Hartmann 352. The Germans lost around 55,000 fighter and destroyer aircraft. Between 1 September 1939 and 28 February 1945—the last day for which we have reliable statistics—44,065 German pilots and other crew members died, 28,000 were wounded and 27,610 captured or missing. The original goal of the Allied advocates of the Douhet theory, to bring down the Third Reich without the need for a land offensive, could not be achieved. On the contrary, the effect on German morale of even the heaviest air raids, was not at all what had been universally anticipated before the war. The terror bombing stiffened the will to resist rather than weakened it. On the other hand, success in all important military operations depended on air supremacy, and thus it was the aerial forces that ultimately decided the war's outcome. The Allies succeeded in defeating Germany only by deploying their air forces in conjunction with the advancing ground troops.

While surrender terms were still being negotiated with the Germans, RAF Bomber Command was already preparing a new operation codenamed "Exodus." Almost all flyworthy Lancaster and Halifax bombers took part, as did Dakota transport aircraft. Their mission was to bring back thousands of liberated prisoners of war. In the three weeks following the surrender, RAF aircraft successfully ferried over 140,000 British soldiers back to Britain.

On Monday 14 May 1945, over 470 Superfor-

Right: The Japanese supersubmarines 1.400, 1.401 and 1.14, adapted for use as underwater aircraft carriers. They were intended to launch an air raid on Panama Canal.

Opposite page below: Dübendorf airfield, Zurich, in May 1945, where an entire aerial armada of Flying Fortress and Liberator bombers—186 US heavy bombers—had made emergency landings during the war. Switzerland did not release them again until after the surrender of Japan.

tresses of the US 21st Bomber Command on the Marianas, raided Nagoya in broad daylight with incendiary bombs. Ten B-29s were lost. The raid was repeated by 450 Superfortresses on the night of 16–17 May; only 3 B-29s failed to return. Nagoya burned almost to the ground after these two raids.

On the night of 23–24 May 1945, 550 Superfortresses dropped 750,000 phosphorus incendiaries over Tokyo in the heaviest bombardment of Japanese home territory so far; and on the night of 25–26 May, Tokyo was again the target of 500 US bombers. By now, half of the built-up area had been destroyed, leaving homeless many of the city's six million inhabitants.

On Tuesday 29 May, the advance detachment of the US 509th Bomber Group under Colonel Tibbets had landed on Tinian island in the Marianas to set up a base for 339 Squadron under Major Sweeney, which was to take off from there on an atomic bombing mission over Japan.

At the end of May 1945, final preparations for a special secret mission were taking place at the aerial operations division of Imperial Japanese Headquarters. The secret operation was intended to shatter the USA like the raid on Pearl Harbor: It was a bombing raid on the Panama Canal. The plan was born right after the Doolittle Raid, the first US raid on Tokyo back in April 1942. Ever since, Japanese strategists had been determined to launch a counterstrike against the USA. At the instigation of Admiral Yamamoto, a series of giant class I-400 submarines were ordered, each able to carry 3 special-duty aircraft. These 5,223-ton submarines, with a range of 37,500 nautical miles, were twice as large as the largest vessels in the US Navy and could remain at sea for 4 months without added fueling. A catapult stretched from the spacious cylinder-shaped hangar in the starboard hold, forward to the bow.

The aircraft built to take off from the submarines were twin-seater Aichi M6A1 Seiran seaplanes specially designed for the Panama Canal operation. The Seirans were all equipped with German Daimler-Benz DB 601 A 1,400-horsepower engines and were designed as the world's first "throw-away" airplanes, which would drop off the crew after the raid, be ditched beside the submarines and sink at once. To help insure that the raid on the Canal came as a surprise, the Japanese planned to attack not from the east but from the Caribbean Sea on the west. The four submarine aircraft carriers would launch their 12 Seiran aircraft shortly before daybreak. A twenty-five-year-old pilot, Lt. Atsushi Asamura, was assigned to lead the operation, which was planned for mid-July 1945. The plan was to drop bombs and torpedoes on the canal gates and other nerve-centers of the Panama Canal. As soon as the crews had been taken back on board and the aircraft sunk, the submarine motherships would submerge as rapidly as possible.

Above: A Japanese Aichi M6A1 Seiran seaplane built especially for the planned raid on the Panama Canal.

Opposite page above: The planned route for the Panama Canal raid.

Opposite page center: Japanese kamikaze pilots awaiting their suicide mission. In the background is a Mitsubishi G4M2 bomber with an Ohka piloted flying bomb attached under the fuselage.

The Seiran unit had been formed on 15 December 1944 and was known officially as the 613th Air Corps. Its commander was Captain Ariizumi, an officer of the 1st Japanese Submarine Flotilla to which the giant submarines belonged. The new unit was under the overall command of the Sixth Fleet in Kure. Two of the best-known members of the newly-formed Seiran Corps were officers N. Fujita and S. Okuda, both of whom had been involved in the first and only previous air raid on the USA, from Submarine I-25 on 9 September 1942. The Yokosuka E14Y1 that they had used on that raid, was also a direct ancestor of the Seirans.

The Seiran and submarine crews began minutely-prepared exercises on 2 April 1945. It was determined that 1,760 pounds was the heaviest bombload the Seirans could risk carrying on their cata-

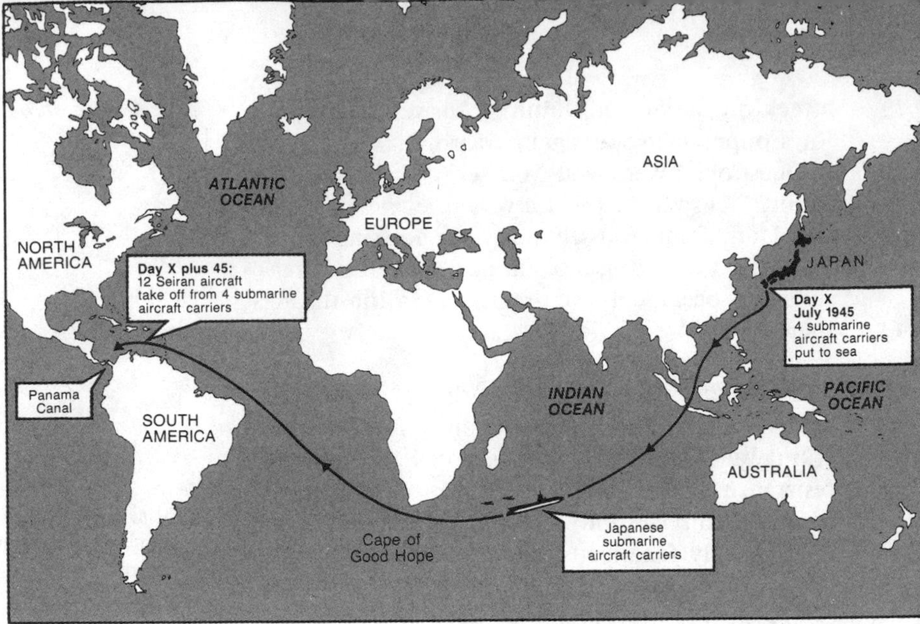

pult takeoff. The hangars had been camouflaged with dummy chimneys to disguise the huge submarines from US reconnaissance planes.

One RAF unit began its work only after the war: EASSU, the Enemy Aircraft Separation System Unit. From its chief airbase at Fuhlsbüttel in Hamburg, the unit distributed captured Luftwaffe aircraft to Germany's former adversaries. EASSU made sure that the planes were flyworthy and delivered them direct to France, Holland, Belgium and Czechoslovakia. Most of the planes were turned over to the British experimental institute at Farnborough.

In June 1945, several groups of RAF Bomber Command set to work getting rid of the RAF's stores of leftover bombs. For weeks on end they unloaded bombs into the target zone, Cardigan on the east coast of Wales. This body of water was the scene of the most protracted bomb drop in history. It was considered inexpedient to store the RAF's excess bombs, so they landed – without detonating fuses – on the bottom of the sea.

On Tuesday 5 June 1945, 470 Superfortresses of the US 20th Bomber Command unloaded 3,000 tons of incendiary bombs on Kobe, Japan. That day units of the US Fifth Fleet in the Philippine Sea were caught in a heavy typhoon. Many warships, including 4 battleships and 4 aircraft carriers, were badly damaged. A total of 36 vessels were sent to the repair docks, and 150 aircraft were lost. This was not the first time that the American aerial forces had suffered grievous losses due to bad weather. Six months earlier, in December 1944, the US 20th Air Force had lost 150 planes to a hurricane, while 3 destroyers were sunk and 4 escort carriers badly crippled.

On Monday 11 June 1945, the first Superfortress of US 393 Bomber Squadron (under Major Sweeney), part of the 509th Composite Group (under Colonel Tibbets), landed on Tinian island in the Marianas. This first B-29 was accompanied by several scientists whose job it was to prepare the atom bombs for deployment.

In mid-June 1945, a Soviet interrogation squad, including five male officers and one woman, arrived at the Palace Hotel in Bad Mondorf (Luxembourg), the American detention camp for prominent Nazi prisoners-of-war. Among the first to be interrogated was the former head of the Luftwaffe. On June 17 he stated for the record: "Göring, Hermann Wilhelm, 52 years old, Reich Marshal, commander-in-chief of the German Luftwaffe."

Question: "What was your attitude to Germany's

Opposite page above: Tokyo, July 1945. The people are being evacuated after heavy American air raids.

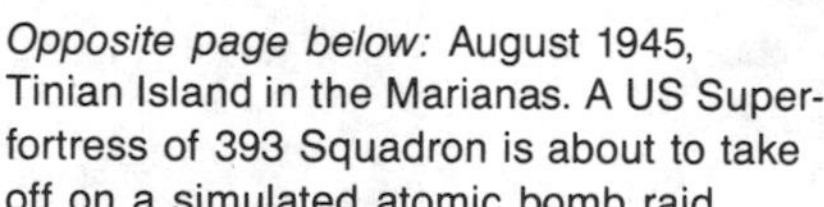

Opposite page below: August 1945, Tinian Island in the Marianas. A US Superfortress of 393 Squadron is about to take off on a simulated atomic bomb raid.

attack on the Soviet Union?" Answer: "I was always opposed to war against Russia."

Question: "Were you yourself on the Eastern Front?" Answer: "I spent a very brief time in Russia. I am familiar with only one Russian town: Vinnitsa. I did not go to Vinnitsa for military reasons but because I was interested in the theater there."

On Friday 22 June 1945, Admiral Nimitz reported an end to organized Japanese resistance on Okinawa; but there were isolated pockets of resistance where Japanese soldiers continued to defend themselves until the end of the war, fighting not only fanatically but with great skill. The battle for Okinawa was the bloodiest and most costly operation in the Pacific. The greatest losses suffered by the American and British navies there, were due to kamikaze pilots who sank 36 ships—none larger than a destroyer—and damaged 368 including 10 battleships, 13 aircraft carriers, 5 cruisers and 67 destroyers. A total of 4,907 Allied seamen and airmen were killed and 5,000 badly wounded. Nowhere, not even at Pearl Harbor, did the US Navy suffer such heavy losses as at Okinawa. British Task Force 57 under Vice-Admirals Rawlings and Vian, which had just left Sydney, took part in the battle with the carriers *Indomitable*, *Victorious*, *Formidable* and *Indefatigable*. The British carriers proved especially valuable because their flight decks—unlike the wooden start decks of the American vessels—were armored, and so offered more protection from kamikazes. Japan lost 7,830 aircraft, including 1,900 kamikazes.

The battles at Okinawa contributed substantially to the defeat of the Japanese air force and what was left of the Japanese naval fleet. The US 21st Bomber Command planned to use the conquered island as a base from which to launch Superfortress raids on Japan, but this proved possible only on the last night of the war.

On Monday 25 June 1945, Operation Post Mortem began in Grove (Denmark). Six weeks after the war was over, German officers and men under General Boner, communications commander of the fighter division Luftflotte Reich, moved into their former control center, accompanied by British radar experts. Among the British officers was that same Wing Commander Jackson who had made experimental flights in the two German Ju 88 night fighters captured by the British in 1943 and 1944. Now that the war was over, RAF wanted to find out how its radar countermeasures had affected the German air defenses, by recreating actual battle conditions. Almost the whole of the former German air defense network in Denmark, with its 10 large radar stations, was harnessed to test the effects. For nine days all the British jamming techniques were evaluated, with RAF aircraft serving as mock enemies in the maneuvers. British specialists learned that the RAF's countermeasures had forced the Germans to control their night fighters very loosely. If the night fighters' airborne radar was jammed, their crews simply had to trust to luck to find their targets. When Window jamming strips were dropped, the German controllers had no way of judging the true strength of a bomber formation. The most important discovery the British made during Operation Post Mortem was that the German controllers were unable, due to RAF countermeasures, to distinguish between real and mock raids. At the end of the operation British units dismantled the German radar stations, sending large numbers of radar sets to the USA, Britain and France.

On 25 June 1945, Imperial Japanese Headquarters halted preparations for the Japanese 1st Submarine Flotilla to attack the Panama Canal, and issued new orders: In view of the American threat to the main Japanese islands, the 12 Seiran aircraft were ordered to find a suitable opportunity to launch a kamikaze raid (Operation Hikari) against US aircraft carriers; but the surrender came before the operation was carried out.

The annihilation of Japanese cities had been continuing with undiminished violence. All raids followed the same pattern: Each time some 500

Superfortresses, loaded with 3,000 tons of incendiary bombs, would operate with an escort of Mustang fighters. Now that the bombers no longer met any enemies in the air, the fighters were free to fly in low and strafe cities with their machine guns. American losses were barely 2% of aircraft dispatched.

On Monday 2 July 1945, some 600 B-29 Superfortresses dropped 4,000 tons of incendiary bombs on large Japanese cities. The effects were indescribable. Japanese morale collapsed after these grand incendiary raids, especially when the 21st Bomber Command began to drop leaflets announcing the date of the next raids. Eight and a half million people fled out of the cities, and arms production dropped overnight. On that same July 2, Japanese radio announced that 6 million people were being evacuated from Tokyo. Everyone was to leave the capital except for 200,000 essential personnel.

When the war ended in Europe, the Japanese government decided to ask the Soviets to mediate ceasefire negotiations between Japan and the Americans, and applied to Y. Malik, the Soviet ambassador in Japan, for assistance. But the Soviets did not reply, and finally on July 12 Tokyo sent a radio message to the Japanese ambassador in Moscow instructing him to contact the Soviet government directly. The Americans had known the Japanese radio code for a long time and learned the contents of the message at once.

On Monday 16 July the first atom bomb was exploded successfully on the rocky desert testing ground of Los Alamos near Alamagordo (New Mexico). The enormous explosion was audible throughout the southwestern United States. Shortly after, newspapermen in the nearby city of Albuquerque received an explanation from the military authorities: "This morning an ammunition depot blew up in a remote area of the air force experimental testing fields. We have learned that light phenomena and pressure waves were observed within a 216-mile radius."

That same day measures were taken to step up the bombing offensive in the Pacific. The US 8th Air Force was transferred there from Europe and combined with the US 20th Air Force (i.e., the 20th and 21st Bomber Commands) to form the US Army Strategic Air Forces in the Pacific (USSTAF), under supreme command of General Carl Spaatz. General LeMay took over provisional command of the US 20th Air Force, replacing General Arnold. The US 8th Air Force under General Doolittle, whose 2,118 aircraft had been flown directly from Britain across the Atlantic and on to the Pacific, was now to lead raids against Japan.

On Friday 20 July 1945, 10 US Superfortresses of 393 Squadron of the 509th Composite Group under Colonel Tibbets, took off from Tinian (Marianas) on their first mission against Japan. Each plane carried a single heavy bomb, and each headed for a separate target. The Japanese air defenses soon got used to solo-flying B-29s carrying 10,000-lb bombs that they dropped from an altitude of 30,000 feet. The 10,000-lb Blockbuster bombs had a fall curve similar to that of an atom bomb. In fact 393 Squadron was making simulated atomic bomb raids and gaining experience that would help Colonel Tibbets to decide on the target to be destroyed at X-hour.

On Wednesday 25 July 1945, Truman made his most significant decision as president: He signed the order to deploy the atomic bomb against Japan if it rejected the Potsdam ultimatum calling for

Japan's unconditional surrender. The order left Washington immediately by plane and was received by the 509th Composite Group on Tinian. Next day the USA and Britain presented their ultimatum to Japan.

On Thursday 26 July, the atomic bomb case arrived at the island of Tinian on board the cruiser *Indianapolis*. The explosive material to be used was Uranium 235, which, unlike plutonium, had not yet been tested. Part of the uranium was shipped to Tinian on the same vessel, and the amount needed to make up the critical mass was transported to the island by a Douglas C-54 Skymaster. When the Skymaster made its intermediate landing at a Hawaiian airbase, the crew had a wrangle with the authorities because airbase regulations would not allow such a large plane to cross the Pacific carrying a cargo that weighed only one metric hundredweight (110 pounds); they insisted that the plane be fully loaded.

Meanwhile the Japanese ambassador in Moscow was trying desperately to move the Soviet foreign minister, Molotov, to mediate with the Americans.

On Saturday 28 July 1945, high-ranking military officers still had the upper hand in Tokyo, and the Japanese government announced in a radio message its rejection of the Potsdam ultimatum.

In July 1945, three times as many bombs were dropped on Japan as in March—approximately 100,000 tons. Meanwhile the Americans had heavily mined Japanese coastal waters to paralyze Japanese shipping traffic. Approximately 1¼ million tons of Japanese shipping were sunk, and traffic in coastal waters came to an almost complete standstill.

Above right: 16 August 1945. The war over, pilots at a Japanese fighter base await further orders.

Below left, upper photo: "Little Boy," the Hiroshima bomb, was 10 ft. long, about 2½ ft. in diameter, and weighed about 10,000 lbs. Its destructive power was equivalent to over 40 million tons of TNT.

Below left, lower photo: "Fat Man," the Nagasaki bomb, was over 10 ft. long, five ft. in diameter, and weighed about 11,000 lbs.

On Thursday 2 August 1945, 800 US B-29s mounted the strongest air raid of World War II when they released 6,000 tons of phosphorus incendiary bombs on four Japanese cities and on the oil-production site of Kawasaki. They met no Japanese fighter planes and only weak antiaircraft fire. Approximately 80,000 Japanese died in this raid.

In all, 260,000 Japanese died in the 8-month US bombing offensive on Japan. Two hundred and fifty square miles of city containing two million houses, were reduced to ashes in 66 different towns.

On Friday 3 August 1945, Admiral Nimitz confirmed that US B-29 Superfortresses had mined all Japanese and Korean harbors, thus completing the blockade of Japan.

On Monday 6 August, the heavily-loaded Superfortress atomic bomber "Enola Gay," commanded by Colonel Tibbets of the 509th Composite Group and named after Tibbets' mother, rolled across Tinian airfield. The takeoff at 2:45 A.M. was touch and go because the Enola Gay was thousands of pounds overweight. Instead of the usual 8-man crew, it carried 12; its fuel tanks contained 1,400 gallons; and the atomic bomb weighed a good 5 tons. Three B-29s had taken off before the Enola Gay to act as weather observers, and reached their targets long before it got there. At 7:09 A.M. the air raid sirens sounded in Hiroshima, but by now the Japanese had grown accustomed to seeing single American bombers flying overhead at very high altitude and the all clear was sounded at 7:31. This first B-29 was the "Straight Flush," a weather plane. At 7:25 it radioed its weather report to Colonel Tibbets adding: "Advise go Target One." When Tibbets had decoded the message, he said to his navigator van Kirk: "It's Hiroshima." The first atomic bomb was dropped on Hiroshima at 8:15

A.M. It destroyed 80% of the city, killing 92,167 people and injuring 37,425.

On Wednesday 8 August 1945, the Soviet Union declared war on Japan, and at 12:10 A.M. (local time) on the night of 8–9 August, the Red Army launched a three-pronged offensive against the Japanese Kwantung Army in Manchuria. The offensive was led by 3 Soviet army groups, the First Trans-Baikal Front under Marshal Malinovsky, the Second Far-East Front under General Puryakev, and the Sixth Guards Tank Army under General Kravchenko.

The Soviet forces totalled 80 divisions, including 6 cavalry divisions, 2 armored divisions, and 4 mechanized armored corps. The First Trans-Baikal Front under Marshal Malinovsky commanded the 12th Air Army; the First Far-East Front under Marshal Meretskov commanded the 9th Air Army; and the Second Far-East Front under General Puryakev commanded the 10th Air Army. The People's Republic of Mongolia, whose troops were fighting along with General Pliyev's Soviet aerial group, supplied one aerial division. General Pliyev's group also included the 350th Fighter Regiment. The Soviets had a total of 3,446 planes taking part in operations against the Japanese Kwantung Army in Manchuria. The Soviets also had a Pacific fleet totalling 1,547 vessels.

On Thursday 9 August, a US Superfortress under Major Sweeney dropped the second atomic bomb, this time on Nagasaki. There were 40,000 dead and 60,000 wounded.

The US had now used up its store of atomic weapons, but of course the Japanese government did not know this. Statements made by the crew of a shot-down Superfortress led the Japanese to believe that a third atomic bomb was due to be dropped on Tokyo in the next few days.

On Wednesday 15 August 1945, the Tenno, the Japanese emperor, addressed his people for the first time over the radio. He explained the hopelessness of Japan's situation and stated why he had taken steps to end the war. People in the Japanese cities sank to their knees in front of the loudspeakers. In Tokyo wounded airmen committed mass suicide outside the Imperial Palace. The last kamikaze pilots crashed into the sea. The pilots of Atsugi airbase staged a rebellion, flying their planes over the Imperial Palace—a hitherto unimaginable act

August 1945. Two children rescued from the inferno after the atom bomb was dropped on Nagasaki.

which in Japan was equivalent to religious blasphemy—and dropping air leaflets in which they cursed the traitors and proclaimed that the battle would be carried on until the end.

On Thursday 16 August 1945, Emperor Hirohito ordered all the Japanese armed forces to cease fire. Two days later, on Saturday 18 August, American reconnaissance planes still encountered Japanese fighter planes resisting over Tokyo.

On Monday 20 August 1945, Soviet paratroops landed at Mukden (Manchuria); at the same time units of the Sixth Guards Tank Army under General Kravchenko marched into the city.

On Wednesday 22 August, Soviet airborne troops landed in Port Arthur and Dairen in the Kwantung territory on the Liaotung peninsula of Manchuria, and on Sakhalin Island and the Kurile Islands. Soviet Li-2s, a version of Douglas DC-3 Dakotas, took over transport of the airborne troops. The Soviet paratroops occupied airfields and disarmed the Japanese garrisons. By the end of August, Manchuria and North Korea were in Soviet hands.

On Wednesday 29 August, the US 11th Airborne Division began the occupation of Japan. For the first time in the 2,500-year history of Japan, there were foreign troops living inside its territory.

This was also the first time in history that a country had surrendered without any portion of its own territory being seized. In this sense the American air force won a momentous victory, for it was General LeMay's bombing offensive in the Pacific that ultimately forced Japan to its knees. On the other hand, the bombing offensive was not really an independent operation; instead its success depended on the operations of the land and naval forces. Japan's weak military position was also intensified by its weak economic foundation. Japanese aircraft production could not keep up with that of the USA, and thus could not continue to afford protection to the Japanese merchant fleet. The most important sectors of Japanese arms production broke down when the US interrupted Japanese sea supply lines, completely cutting off the supply of raw materials—oil, iron ore and bauxite.

Approximately 392,000 people died in Japan as a result of the air war, and there were 500,000 with all degrees of injury. Two hundred and twenty million buildings were destroyed and 9.2 million Japanese were made homeless. The Japanese air forces lost a total of 60,422 aircraft.

Many military theorists believe that the dropping of the atomic bombs brought about the surrender of Japan. On the other hand, US Admiral Leahy, an adviser to presidents Roosevelt and Truman, said that the deployment of these barbaric weapons at Hiroshima and Nagasaki made no concrete contribution to the war against Japan, because the Japanese had already been defeated by the effective American sea blockade and conventional air raids and were prepared to surrender. Scientists and others, Leahy said, wanted to try out the new weapon because of the vast sum—two billion dollars—that had been put into the project.

At 10:30 A.M., Japanese time, on the dull and rainy day of Sunday 2 September 1945, Japanese Foreign Minister Shigemitsu and Japanese general staff chief Umezu signed Japan's unconditional surrender on board the US battleship *Missouri* anchored in Tokyo Bay. General MacArthur and other representatives signed for the Allies.

It was exactly six years and one day since German Stuka dive-bombers had opened their attack on Poland.

Translator's Note

It should be noted that the excerpts from original documents (newspapers, military records, etc.) which form the first part of each chapter, and the first-hand accounts of battle situations by participating soldiers, are in many cases not direct quotations but accurate summary-paraphrases of lengthier material drawn from many languages. The summaries as they appeared in German, have then been translated into English in this abbreviated form. It is suggested that readers seeking additional detail, refer to the original source for the unabridged text.

There are several exceptions to this rule. All quotations from F. W. Winterbotham's *The Ultra Secret* (London 1974) and from the standard English translation of Albert Speer's *Inside The Third Reich* (New York 1970) appear in their full and complete form. Churchill's remarks to the House of Commons of 27 September 1939, are also quoted in full from the Commons' records.

A great number of military ranks and unit designations from a variety of languages appear in this book. These have been translated roughly into their English equivalents because it was felt that it might tax readers to leave them in the original, necessitating continual reference to an extended glossary. Most notably, the terms for German air force units such as *Staffel*, *Gruppe*, *Jagdgeschwader*, *Kampfgeschwader*, *Fliegerkorps*, etc. which frequently appear in German in war histories, have been translated into English. For further detail concerning German military terms, the reader is referred to the section on the structure of the belligerent air forces at the end of the book. Also, Arabic numerals have been used almost throughout, rather than a combination of Arabic and Roman as is standard in some histories.

Jan van Heurck

Structure of the Belligerent Air Forces

Australia
End of 1939
Royal Australian Air Force (RAAF).
12 groups with 246 aircraft (including 164 front-line machines), 250 officers, 3,179 sub-officers and crew.
Deployment:
Europe, Near East, southwest Asia, the Pacific.
Most successful fighter pilot:
Wing Commander C. R. Caldwell – 28½ air victories.

Belgium
End of 1939
The national defense commander headed the air force; subordinate to him was an air defense commander who in turn directed a commander of the air force and an anti-aircraft commander. In spring 1940 the air force had 3,000 men and 180 front-line aircraft. Structure: 1 close-reconnaissance regiment (3 groups), 1 fighter regiment (3 groups), 1 long-range reconnaissance and bomber regiment (2 groups). Each group had 2 active squadrons and 1 reserve squadron.
Deployment:
The German offensive in May 1940, the Battle of Britain 1940/41, West Africa, the Western Front 1944/45.
Most successful fighter pilot:
Major Count I. du Monceau de Bergendal – 8 air victories.

Brazil
Start of 1940
The army and navy air forces were combined to form an independent service of 2,280 men and approximately 200 aircraft of various types.
Deployment:
Battle of the Atlantic, in which Brazilian aircraft sank German submarine U-199 under Capt. Kraus on 31 July 1943; 1 fighter group assisted US 12th Air Force in Italy starting on 14 October 1944.

Bulgaria
End of 1939
The air force was being built up under command of the aviation chief of the war ministry. In 1940 the Bulgarian air force had over 130 planes divided into 8 groups (*orliaks*).
Deployment:
Home defense and Eastern Front. One fighter division fought on the side of the Soviet Union starting in September 1944. The Bulgarian air force was too weak to support Bulgaria's own ground troops, so it was reinforced by the Soviet 189th Ground-Attack Division and the 288th Fighter Division.
Most successful fighter pilot:
Lt. S. Stoyanov – 14 air victories.

Canada
1939
Royal Canadian Air Force (RCAF).
In September 1939 the Canadian air force had 8 groups of front-line aircraft and 12 auxiliary groups, totalling 5,061 men and 270 aircraft. Canada was also a training center for the RAF and for the exile air forces of various nations that fought in the RAF. By 1 April 1945, 131,553 airmen had been trained here.
Deployment:
Europe, North Africa, Battle of the Atlantic.
Most successful fighter pilot:
Flight Lieutenant G. R. Beurling – 31⅓ air victories.

China *(forces of Chiang Kai-shek)*
1939
Air force undergoing reorganization. Supreme command was held by the national air commission. At the start of 1942, US Brigadier General C. L. Chennault set up the American Volunteer Group (the Flying Tigers), which in 1943 was expanded to form the US 14th Air Force. In November 1943 the Chinese-American Composite Wing was formed; it contained fighter and bomber groups and was under the tactical command of the USAAF and the organizational command of China. It received 1,378 aircraft through Lend-Lease.
Deployment:
Home defense, Burma.
Most successful fighter pilot:
Colonel Liu Chi-Sun – 11⅓ air victories.

Croatia *(nominally independent Yugoslavia)*
July 1941
The Croatian air force numbered 4 groups under command of General Kren. In autumn 1941, 2 groups known as the Croatian Legion (German commander: Maj. Ratmann; Croatian commander: Maj. Graovatz) were deployed along the central sector of the Eastern Front where they cooperated with the German 3rd (Blitz) Bomber Wing, suffering heavy losses. In Croatia itself the air force fought for Germany against the partisans. On 21 May 1942, two crews fled to join Tito's partisan troops where they founded the air force of the Yugoslavian People's Liberation Army.
Deployment:
Eastern Front, the Balkans.

Most successful fighter pilot:
Lt. C. Galik – 36 air victories.

Czech Lands *(Bohemia, Moravia and other territories of Czechoslovakia seized by Germany, as distinct from nominally independent Slovakia)*
March 1939
When German troops invaded on 15 March 1939, the air force had 1,514 aircraft including 566 front-line planes. Some airmen escaped to Poland. Shortly before war broke out, 477 Czech pilots were evacuated by sea from Poland to France where they fought as part of the Armée de l'Air. After the surrender of France some of them reached Great Britain. On 12 July 1940 the Czech 310th Fighter Squadron was set up as part of the RAF; later 2 more Czech fighter squadrons and 1 bomber squadron were formed.
Deployment:
France, Battle of Britain, Europe, Western Front 1944/45.
Most successful fighter pilot:
Lt. R. Rezny – 32 air victories.
On 3 May 1944 the independent Czech 128th Fighter Squadron was set up in the Soviet Union as a skeleton unit for the air force of the Czechoslovakian People's Republic to be set up after the Allied victory.

Denmark
End of 1939
The army air force was under the command of the war department, the navy air force under the command of the navy department. The army air force had two branches: the Seeland air force (1 reconnaissance squadron, 1 reconnaissance and bomber squadron, 1 fighter squadron) and the Jutland air force (1 reconnaissance squadron, 1 fighter squadron). The navy air force had 1 sea-reconnaissance squadron, 1 fighter squadron, 1 torpedo and bomber squadron. The forces totalled approximately 800 men and 110 aircraft.
Deployment:
After the German occupation of Denmark, some pilots flew in the RAF and others formed a fighter squadron in Sweden.
Most successful fighter pilot:
Colonel Kaj Birksted – 8½ air victories.

Finland
End of 1939
The air force was under command of the war department and tactically subordinate to the army commander. It had 3 regiments including 2 reconnaissance squadrons, 2 fighter squadrons, 1 naval fighter squadron, and 4 sea squadrons, totalling approximately 2,500 men and 200 aircraft.
Deployment:
The Winter War 1939/40; fought against Soviet Union 22 June 1941 to September 1941, and against Germany starting in October 1944.
Most successful fighter pilot:
First Lt. E. Juutilainen – 94 air victories.

France
End of 1939
The reorganization initiated in 1936 had not been concluded by 1939/40. The French air force, the Armée de l'Air, was under command of the air ministry. The air force general staff chief was also aircraft inspector general and general staff chief for air defense. The home air force (the Aviation Métropole) was divided over 4 aerial zones, each of which had 2 tactical districts and 2 air divisions or independent air brigades to cover them. The naval air corps (the Aéronautique Navale) was under command of the navy and was distributed across 4 regions; the planes included carrier aircraft which were carried by warships, and coastguard aircraft. The reconnaissance wings were attached to the ground troops or to the navy, and had individual commanders who represented them with the various army and navy commanders. The French overseas air force was the Aviation Coloniale. In March 1940 (according to French sources) the French air forces at home and abroad comprised 150,000 men with about 1,200 fighter planes, 800 reconnaissance planes and 1,300 bombers.
Deployment:
The 1939/40 campaign. After the truce agreement with Germany, some pilots and aircraft remained in Vichy France and North Africa, while others withdrew to England. The Free French air units under General de Gaulle fought in Europe, North Africa, the Near East and the Soviet Union (the Normandy-Neman Wing). In 1943 a new French tactical air force was formed. Using US and RAF aircraft, it participated in the fighting along the Western Front in 1944/45.
Most successful fighter pilot:
Captain M. Albert – 23 air victories.

Germany
1939
The air force – the Luftwaffe – was an independent service branch. Hitler became commander-in-chief of the combined German armed forces – the Wehrmacht – on 4 February 1938. The commanders-in-chief of the army, air force and navy were his direct subordinates. The air force was divided into air fleets (Luftflottenkommandos) with headquarters in different geographical areas: Luftflotte 1 Berlin, Luftflotte 2 Brunswick, Luftflotte 3 Munich, Luftflotte 4 Vienna, and the Königsberg Luftwaffenkommando. This territorial structuring of the Luftwaffe fitted in with the army's division into general commands. There were 10 district air headquarters in all.

In 1941 a central air defense command was formed under the "Luftwaffe Commander Central" (Luftwaffenbefehlshaber Mitte). Each Luftflotte (regional air fleet) contained units of each type of aircraft – fighters, bombers, reconnaissance, etc. – and also had its own antiaircraft artillery and communications units; thus, each Luftflotte represented a "mini-Luftwaffe." The strength of a Luftflotte ranged from 200 to 1,300 aircraft. There were also 6 air divisions, which came to be known as Fliegerkorps (air corps), that the various Luftflotten could call on for service but that could also operate independently of a Luftflotte. The strength of an air division or Fliegerkorps ranged from 200 to 750 aircraft.

The largest German tactical unit was the *Geschwader* or "wing" ("group" in British usage). A *Geschwader* contained 3 *Gruppen* ("groups," or "wings" in British usage) each with 27 aircraft plus 9 reserve machines. In addition each *Geschwader* also had 1 group squadron (*Gruppenstaffel*) comprising 9 aircraft plus 3 reserves. So, each *Geschwader* or wing totalled 120 planes. A *Gruppe* in turn was divided into 3 squadrons (*Staffeln*) of 9 aircraft and 3 reserves each, so a *Gruppe* equalled 36 planes. A *Staffel* (squadron) was made up of 3 *Ketten* (flights) of 3 planes each, plus 3 reserves: total 12. On 1 September 1939 the Luftwaffe had 370,000 men and 2,785 front-line aircraft.
Deployment:
Poland, Norway, the Western Campaign, the Battle of Britain, the Balkans Campaign, North Africa, Near East,

Mediterranean, Battle of the Atlantic, Eastern Front, Italy, defense of Germany.
Most-produced aircraft:
Messerschmitt Bf 109 – 35,000 were built; also was the most-built fighter plane in history.
Most successful fighter pilot:
Major E. Hartmann – 352 air victories.
Most successful ground-attack pilot:
Colonel H. U. Rudel. In 2,530 missions he destroyed 519 tanks and over 800 motor vehicles.

Great Britain

End of 1939
The Royal Air Force (RAF).
The RAF was an independent branch of service under command of the Air Ministry. The commander-in-chief was King George VI.; the air staff chief was his deputy. The RAF was composed of the Home Command, the Overseas Command, and the Fleet Air Arm which was under command of the navy. The Home Command included Bomber Command, Fighter Command, Coastal Command, Army Cooperation Command, and Flying Training Command. The largest tactical unit was the group, made up of 9–24 squadrons. The median unit was the wing with 2–3 squadrons. One squadron had 6–18 aircraft. When war broke out, Great Britain claimed a total of 2,327 aircraft at home and abroad, not including reserves.
Deployment:
France, Battle of Britain, East and North Africa, Balkans, Mediterranean, Near East, southeast Asia, the Pacific, Battle of the Atlantic, the Soviet Union.
Most-produced aircraft:
Supermarine Spitfire – 22,884 were built.
Most successful fighter pilot:
Group Captain J. E. Johnson – 38 air victories.

Greece

Start of 1940
The army and navy air forces were under command of the air ministry. The army air force had 3 air regiments of 2 squadrons each; the navy air force had 2 squadrons. The forces totalled 3,250 men and approximately 126 aircraft.
Deployment:
The Italian-Greek war theater, Albania, the German invasion. After the German occupation of Greece, some air personnel evacuated to the Near East where 2 fighter groups and 1 bomber group were formed and flew with the RAF.

Hungary

1940
The air force had 2 fighter regiments, 1 reconnaissance regiment and 1 bomber regiment, totalling 4,300 men and 326 front-line machines.
Deployment:
Home defense, Yugoslavia, Eastern Front; fought on Axis side.
Most successful fighter pilot:
Lt. D. Szentgyorgyi – 34 air victories.

India

1939
In addition to its role in British Overseas Command, India had its own air force consisting initially of 1 squadron with 230 men. By 1944 it had 10 squadrons – fighter, bomber and reconnaissance – totalling 30,000 men.
Deployment:
Air defense of India; Burma, Siam, and patrol duty and anti-submarine warfare in the Indian Ocean.

Iraq

1940
The Iraqi air force was trained by the RAF and included 3 fighter squadrons, 2 bomber squadrons and 1 reconnaissance squadron containing 35 British and Italian front-line aircraft. When the anti-British, pro-Axis usurper Rashid Ali el Gailani rebelled and came to power, the Iraqi air force started, on 2 May 1941, to fly bombing missions against the RAF base at Habbaniya. In mid-May 1941 the Iraqi air force received reinforcements from the German Luftwaffe, in the form of the Junck Special Unit – 6 He 111 bombers of 4 Squadron of the General Wever Bomber Wing, and 3 Me 110 "destroyer" planes of 4 Squadron, 76th Destroyer Wing. Italy sent Iraq the 155th Squadriglia (squadron) of CR-42 fighters. By the time the rebellion ended on 30 May 1941, 21 Iraqi planes had been lost in the air and on the ground.
Deployment:
Bombing raids on British bases; reconnaissance flights.

Italy *(kingdom of)*

Start of 1940
The air force was an independent service branch under command of the air ministry. It had 2 air corps totalling 4 air divisions and 1 air brigade. The army air force had 3 regiments and an additional 4 independent groups containing 24 squadrons. The naval air force had 3 regiments, 6 independent groups and 4 coastal units, with 20 reconnaissance squadrons. Italy had 32 mixed squadrons in East Africa. In the summer of 1940 the air forces totalled 101,400 men including 6,340 pilots, and 3,296 aircraft of which 1,796 were ready for combat.
Deployment:
France, the Mediterranean, East and North Africa, the Battle of Britain, the Balkans, Near East, the Eastern Front.
Most successful fighter pilot:
Major A. Visconti – 26 air victories.

Italy after the surrender:

1943
203 Italian planes landed on Allied bases and formed the Co-Belligerent Air Force which fought against Germany. Supplemented by US and RAF planes, it formed 1 bomber regiment, 1 fighter regiment, 1 naval regiment and 1 transport regiment.

In autumn 1943, a Fascist air force, the Aviazione della Repubblica Sociale Italiana formed in northern Italy. It included 2 fighter groups, 1 fighter squadron and 1 torpedo-bomber group, all of which fought alongside the Luftwaffe against the Allies.

Japan

Start of 1941
The air force was not an independent arm but was subordinate to the army and navy. The army air force was commanded by the Emperor. It was divided into air divisions; these were divided into air groups which were made up of smaller combat units that in turn contained air companies. The navy air force was in several branches: carrier aircraft (distributed among 9 carriers), 1 air force and 13 coast guard units. At the start of December 1941 the army air force numbered approximately 1,600 front-line aircraft and the navy air force approximately 1,700 front-line aircraft.
Deployment:
Southeast Asia, Indian Ocean, the Pacific, home defense.

Most-produced aircraft:
Mistsubishi A6M Zero – 10,938 were built.
Most successful fighter pilot:
Sub-officer H. Nishizawa – 103 air victories.

Netherlands
1 May 1940
The air force was an independent branch of service made up of the army and navy forces. The navy air force was under admiralty command, the army air force under command of air defense headquarters. The home air force included 1 air brigade with 3 regiments (24 squadrons) and 124 front-line aircraft. The navy air force had about 50 planes. In the colonies (the Dutch Indies) the Dutch had 24 squadrons totalling 240 aircraft. Total strength: 3,500 men.
Deployment:
The German offensive in May 1940, the Battle of Britain, the Battle of the Atlantic, southeast Asia, the Pacific, Europe.
Most successful fighter pilot:
Capt. C. Vlotman – 4 air victories.

New Zealand
1939
Royal New Zealand Air Force (RNZAF).
The air force had 3 squadrons for air defense; 4 more squadrons were being set up when war broke out. The force included 1,160 men and 43 aircraft.
Deployment:
Starting on 27 March 1940, deployment was in Great Britain and West Africa; played decisive role in the defense of Malaya and the battles in the Pacific.
Most successful fighter pilot:
Wing Commander C. F. Gray – 27⅗ air victories.

Norway
April 1940
The air force was divided into the army and navy forces, both of which were commanded by the defense ministry. The army air force had 47 aircraft including 7 fighters; the navy air force had 32 aircraft and about 300 men. After the surrender some Norwegian airmen fought with the RAF.
Deployment:
Norway April/May 1940, Battle of the Atlantic, Europe, Western Front 1944/45.
Most successful fighter pilot:
Capt. S. Heglund – 14½ air victories.

Poland
Spring 1939
The air force was not an independent branch of service but an army adjunct. Its main duty was to fly reconnaissance for the headquarters of the commander-in-chief (Marshal Rydz-Smigly) and for the commanders of the tactical army groups. Hence the predominance of reconnaissance planes in its make-up: 54% reconnaissance, 36% fighters and 10% bombers. The air force was under command of the war ministry; a small navy force of 25 planes was under the tactical command of the navy. Originally the air force had 2 groups of 3 regiments each. The regiments resembled the German air fleets (Luftflotten) in that they were made up of squadrons (Pol. *eskader*) that varied in number and type (reconnaissance, fighter and bomber squadrons). In June 1939 a reorganization took place in which the regiments were dissolved and 37% of the squadrons were attached to the military commander-in-chief while the other squadrons were distributed among the 7 armies and operational groups. The C-in-C's forces were formed into 1 fighter brigade (the Brygada Poscigowa) with 5 squadrons, assigned to the air defense of Warsaw; 1 bomber brigade (Brygada Bombowa) with 9 squadrons; 1 reconnaissance squadron, and 4 liaison units of 3 planes each. When war broke out, the air force numbered about 14,000 men and 463 combat-ready front-line aircraft. After the defeat, about 7,500 men escaped through Hungary and Rumania to France, where they fought in the Armée de l'Air until the French surrender. The majority evacuated to England and joined the newly-formed Polish RAF Squadron or other RAF units.
Deployment:
September campaign 1939, French campaign, Battle of Britain, Europe, North Africa, Near East, Battle of the Atlantic, Western Front 1944/45.
Most successful fighter pilot:
Wing Commander S. F. Skalski – 21 air victories.
In July 1943, the Polish Warsaw Fighter Regiment was formed in the Soviet Union, a skeleton unit for the air force of the People's Republic of Poland to be formed after the Allied victory.

Rumania
Start of 1941
The air force commander controlled both the army and navy air forces. The army air force consisted of 1 fighter flotilla (3 fighter regiments of 3 groups each), 1 bomber regiment (3 daylight bomber groups and 1 night bomber group), and 1 mixed regiment (4 reconnaissance groups, 2 fighter groups). The navy air force had 1 multi-duty naval air flotilla consisting of 1 reconnaissance squadron, 5 bomber and 2 fighter squadrons. The forces totalled about 5,900 men and 600 aircraft.
Deployment:
Eastern Front, home defense (especially the oil-production zone). Beginning on 23 August 1944, some squadrons flew alongside the Soviet air force against Germany.
Most successful fighter pilot:
Captain Prince C. Cantacuzene – 60 air victories.

Siam *(Thailand)*
1939
The air force was an independent arm containing 5 groups (3 fighter, 1 bomber and 1 reconnaissance group) and totalling 195 planes, most supplied by the USA.
Deployment:
Beginning in September 1940, after the Japanese occupation of French Indo-China, sporadic air raids on Japanese bases in Laos and the rest of Indo-China. After the Japanese invaded Siam on 7 December 1941, some pilots withdrew to neighboring British colonies and later fought in RAF units.

Slovakia *(nominally independent Czechoslovakia; see also Czech Lands)*
Summer 1939
The Slovakian air force was formed with the support of the German Luftwaffe and consisted of the 1st Regiment containing 6 fighter, reconnaissance and bomber squadrons equipped with former Czech aircraft. In September 1939, 1 bomber squadron took part in the Luftwaffe's raid on the Polish city of Tarnopol. In November 1941 1st Regiment was transferred to the Eastern Front but was withdrawn again a few weeks later. In 1942 and 1943 several squadrons equipped with German, Italian and French aircraft fought in the Caucasus and the Crimea, while a number of crews deserted to the Soviet Red Army. At the begin-

ning of 1944 the Slovakian air force had about 350 aircraft, 78 of them front-line, and about 4,000 men. On 29 August 1944 during the anti-German Slovakian revolt, most of the crews defected to the Soviets. An improvised air group was formed at Tri Duby airfield from which it led raids against the German Luftwaffe and shot down 7 aircraft. The Slovakian air force was dissolved when the revolt was defeated in October 1944.

Soviet Union
1940
The air force was not an independent service branch but was subordinate to the army and navy. The Red Army air force was controlled by an air force commander subject to the People's Commissar for National Defense. The Red Navy air force was under the direct orders of the people's commissar of the navy. In 1940 the army air force was divided into long-range aircraft, front-line aircraft, army and corps aircraft. There were also defensive air forces assembled by air force commanders in the various military districts, and formed into air divisions. There were independent bomber and fighter divisions as well as mixed divisions containing light bomber, fighter and ground-attack regiments. The composition was 59% fighters, 31% bombers, 4.5% ground-attack aircraft and 5.4% reconnaissance planes. In spring 1941 the Soviet Union had 18,000 planes and 200,000 air personnel including 20,000 pilots.

After war broke out between Germany and the Soviet Union, the army air force was formed into air armies, one independent long-range strategic unit and one defensive fighter command. The air armies were given 75% of all aircraft, divided into air brigades or corps, and later into divisions. The air armies included fighter, bomber and ground-attack units; each air army was under command of a particular ground army and was confined to tactical operations in support of the ground troops. The same was true of the long-range strategic unit, a kind of reserve force attached to STAVKA (the Soviet High Command) which would be temporarily assigned to support a particular air army and its ground army in a focal fighting zone (such as Kursk in 1943).

The basic unit was the regiment. A fighter regiment had 4 squadrons, a ground-attack regiment had 5 squadrons, and a bomber regiment 5 squadrons. A squadron numbered 12–15 machines. The smallest unit was the flight (3 planes).

The Soviet navy air force served the Baltic, North Sea, Black Sea and Pacific fleets. Each Soviet fleet had 2 or 3 air regiments made up of mixed fighter and bomber brigades.
Deployment:
Poland, Winter War in Finland (1939/40); Eastern, Central and Northern Europe, the Balkans, Far East.
Most-produced aircraft:
Ilyushin Il-2 Sturmovik – 36,163 were built.
Between 1941–1945, the Soviet Union received 18,000 planes from the USA and Britain through Lend-Lease.
Most successful fighter pilot:
Colonel I. N. Koshedub – 62 air victories.

Union of South Africa
1939
South African Air Force (SAAF).
When war broke out, the SAAF had 104 aircraft and 1,560 men.
Deployment:
East Africa, Battle of Britain, North Africa, Battle of the Atlantic, Balkans, Mediterranean (where in September 1944 the SAAF comprised one third of all RAF forces), Europe, Western Front 1944/45.
Most successful fighter pilot:
Squadron Leader M. T. Pattle – 51 air victories.

USA
1939
The air force was not an independent arm; organizationally and tactically it was subject to the army and navy. It was divided into the US Army Air Corps (USAAC) under the Department of War, and the navy corps under the Department of the Navy. The US Navy Air Corps (USNAC) was attached directly to the navy, but some naval forces belonged to the US Marine Air Corps (USMAC). The largest tactical unit of the USAAC was a wing (2–4 groups each containing 2–5 squadrons). Reconnaissance and bomber squadrons had 13 planes each, while fighter and ground-attack squadrons had 28 planes each. In the naval air force, a squadron included from 6 to 18 machines depending on type (fighter, bomber, etc.). The US Coast Guard air force, like RAF Coastal Command, was organizationally under the command of the Treasury Department while the US Marine Air Corps was responsible for outfitting and training. By mid-1941, the Army Air Corps had about 6,700 planes and the navy corps about 3,000.

On 20 June 1941, the US Army Air Corps changed its name to the US Army Air Force (USAAF) and was placed under command of General Arnold. The USAAF acquired its own general staff and became an independent arm of the US armed forces.
Deployment:
The Pacific, southeast Asia, China, Europe, North Africa, the Battle of the Atlantic, the Western Front 1944/45.
Most-produced aircraft:
Consolidated B-24 Liberator – 18,188 were built.
Most successful fighter pilot:
Major R. I. Bong – 40 air victories.

Yugoslavia *(Kingdom of)*
Start of 1941
The air force was not an independent arm but was under command of the army and navy. The army air force, commanded by the war ministry, was divided into 3 brigades containing 4 bomber regiments, 3 fighter regiments, and 1 reconnaissance regiment. The navy air force, commanded by the navy, had 3 groups containing 7 squadrons. The forces totalled approximately 10,800 men and 930 aircraft, 400 of them front-line.
Deployment:
The German-Yugoslavian war of April 1940; about 25 planes were evacuated to Egypt where they flew with the RAF.

Yugoslavia *(People's Republic)*
1942
On 21 May 1942 the Yugoslavian People's Liberation Army under Marshal Tito had 2 planes. In mid-July 1944, the RAF gave Tito one fighter group of Italian planes from the Balkan Air Force, and at the end of 1944 he received a second group. Starting in autumn 1944, the Soviet Union supported Tito's partisan army by sending in the 235th Air Division, 1 fighter regiment and 3 ground-attack regiments.

The Principal Air Attacks on Germany 1940–1945

1940

Date	Bombers	Target	Bomb-load
12 Jan	RAF	Westerland (island of Sylt)	
12 May	RAF	Aachen Dortmund Essen Hamm Hanover	
8 Jun	1 France	Berlin	2 t
18 Jun	RAF	Bremen Hamburg	
26 Aug	29 RAF	Berlin	22 t
8 Oct	42 RAF	Berlin	50 t
16 Nov	127 RAF	Hamburg	
16 Dec	45 RAF	Berlin	
17 Dec	134 RAF	Mannheim	100 t
21 Dec	23 RAF	Berlin	

1941

Date	Bombers	Target	Bomb-load
11 Feb	189 RAF	Hanover	
2 Mar	108 RAF	Cologne	
24 Mar	RAF	Berlin	
9 Apr	RAF	Kiel	
9 May	317 RAF	Bremen Hamburg	
11 May	110 RAF	Hamburg	
13 Jun	RAF	Bochum Duisburg	445 t
3 Aug	RAF	Hamburg Kiel	
8 Aug	Soviets	Berlin	
9 Aug	Soviets	Berlin	
12 Aug	54 RAF	Cologne	
13 Aug	RAF	Berlin	82 t
30 Aug	101 RAF	Frankfurt am Main	91 t
13 Sep	111 RAF	Frankfurt am Main	135 t
30 Sep	72 RAF	Hamburg	85 t
21 Oct	92 RAF	Bremen	140 t
24 Oct	64 RAF	Kiel	64 t
1 Nov	76 RAF	Hamburg	93 t
8 Nov	169 RAF	Berlin	
10 Nov	RAF	Hamburg	
1 Dec	84 RAF	Hamburg	138 t
8 Dec	54 RAF	Aachen	54 t
12 Dec	43 RAF	Cologne	58 t
28 Dec	132 RAF	Düsseldorf	126 t
29 Dec	60 RAF	Hüls/Krefeld	60 t

1942

Date	Bombers	Target	Bomb-load
11 Jan	91 RAF	Wilhelmshaven	116 t
16 Jan	52 RAF	Hamburg	72 t
22 Jan	RAF	Bremen	
29 Jan	39 RAF	Münster/ Westphalia	38 t
12 Feb	38 RAF	Mannheim	67 t
14 Feb	RAF	Cologne	
8 Mar	135 RAF	Essen	226 t
9 Mar	120 RAF	Essen	221 t
10 Mar	134 RAF	Essen	225 t
14 Mar	104 RAF	Cologne	160 t
26 Mar	192 RAF	Essen	300 t
29 Mar	234 RAF	Lübeck	304 t
6 Apr	212 RAF	Cologne	313 t
9 Apr	168 RAF	Hamburg	250 t
11 Apr	185 RAF	Essen	227 t
12 Apr	178 RAF	Essen	269 t
14 Apr	105 RAF	Dortmund	136 t
15 Apr	110 RAF	Dortmund	142 t
18 Apr	113 RAF	Hamburg	173 t
24 Apr	468 RAF	Rostock	442 t
5 May	34 RAF	Stuttgart	54 t
7 May	54 RAF	Stuttgart	93 t
31 May	886 RAF	Cologne	1459 t
2 Jun	726 RAF	Duisburg Essen	1235 t
4 Jun	132 RAF	Bremen	246 t
7 Jun	195 RAF	Emden	393 t
9 Jun	120 RAF	Essen	294 t
23 Jun	195 RAF	Emden	392 t
26 Jun	713 RAF	Bremen	1450 t
3 Jul	263 RAF	Bremen	511 t
22 Jul	250 RAF	Duisburg	577 t
26 Jul	252 RAF	Duisburg	547 t
1 Aug	470 RAF	Düsseldorf	907 t
10 Aug	166 RAF	Osnabrück	457 t
12 Aug	102 RAF	Mainz	270 t
13 Aug	110 RAF	Mainz	310 t
28 Aug	222 RAF	Kassel	513 t
29 Aug	38 RAF	Nuremberg	85 t
3 Sep	200 RAF	Karlsruhe	
7 Sep	185 RAF	Duisburg	491 t
11 Sep	360 RAF	Düsseldorf	760 t
20 Sep	RAF	Munich	
23 Nov	222 RAF	Stuttgart	335 t
7 Dec	272 RAF	Mannheim	425 t

1943

Date	Bombers	Target	Bomb-load
13 Jan	101 RAF	Essen	326 t
17 Jan	145 RAF	Berlin	367 t
18 Jan	111 RAF	Berlin	356 t
22 Jan	52 RAF	Essen	179 t
27 Jan	64 USAAF	Wilhelmshaven	109 t
31 Jan	92 RAF	Hamburg	315 t
3 Feb	137 RAF	Cologne	460 t
4 Feb	126 RAF	Hamburg	344 t
12 Feb	137 RAF	Wilhelmshaven	421 t
15 Feb	207 RAF	Cologne	513 t
19 Feb	181 RAF	Wilhelmshaven	596 t
20 Feb	302 RAF	Wilhelmshaven	783 t
26 Feb	278 RAF	Nuremberg	749 t
27 Feb	372 RAF	Cologne	1014 t
2 Mar	251 RAF	Berlin	610 t
4 Mar	344 RAF	Hamburg	913 t
5 Mar	369 RAF	Essen	1200 t
9 Mar	292 RAF	Nuremberg	782 t
10 Mar	217 RAF	Munich	567 t
12 Mar	267 RAF	Stuttgart	802 t
27 Mar	387 RAF	Duisburg	945 t
28 Mar	329 RAF	Berlin	873 t
30 Mar	213 RAF	Berlin	587 t
4 Apr	317 RAF	Essen	983 t
9 Apr	304 RAF	Duisburg	846 t
10 Apr	99 RAF	Duisburg	321 t
15 Apr	365 RAF	Stuttgart	801 t
16 Apr	215 RAF	Dortmund	278 t
17 Apr	225 RAF	Mannheim	
17 Apr	USAAF	Bremen	
21 Apr	304 RAF	Stettin	782 t
27 Apr	499 RAF	Duisburg	1450 t
1 May	251 RAF	Essen	840 t
5 May	495 RAF	Dortmund	1436 t
13 May	517 RAF	Duisburg	1599 t
14 May	378 RAF	Bochum	1055 t
14 May	108 USAAF	Kiel	250 t
17 May	19 RAF	Möhne, Eder and Sorpe Dams	
24 May	724 RAF	Dortmund	2042 t
26 May	686 RAF	Düsseldorf	1959 t
28 May	493 RAF	Essen	1442 t
30 May	644 RAF	Wuppertal	1822 t
12 Jun	693 RAF	Düsseldorf	1968 t
15 Jun	165 RAF	Oberhausen	573 t
17 Jun	179 RAF	Cologne	656 t
22 Jun	661 RAF	Krefeld	1956 t
23 Jun	499 RAF	Mülheim Oberhausen	1643 t
25 Jun	544 RAF	Elberfeld	1663 t
26 Jun	424 RAF	Gelsenkirchen	1291 t
29 Jun	540 RAF	Cologne	1614 t
4 Jul	589 RAF	Cologne	1808 t
9 Jul	255 RAF	Cologne	1614 t
10 Jul	373 RAF	Gelsenkirchen	1304 t
14 Jul	161 RAF	Duisburg	342 t
22 Jul	250 RAF	Duisburg	577 t
25 Jul	741 RAF	Hamburg	2300 t
26 Jul	122 USAAF	Hamburg	
26 Jul	599 RAF	Essen	1948 t
28 Jul	739 RAF	Hamburg	2312 t
28 Jul	54 USAAF	Hamburg	
30 Jul	726 RAF	Hamburg	2277 t
30 Jul	245 RAF	Saarbrücken	567 t
31 Jul	228 RAF	Remscheid	693 t
1 Aug	470 RAF	Düsseldorf	907 t
3 Aug	425 RAF	Hamburg	939 t
17 Aug	230 USAAF	Schweinfurt	
	146 USAAF	Regensburg	
18 Aug	597 RAF	Peenemünde	1874 t
23 Aug	427 RAF	Leverkusen	1690 t
24 Aug	625 RAF	Berlin	1765 t
28 Aug	621 RAF	Nuremberg	1671 t
31 Aug	616 RAF	Mönchen-Gladbach	2272 t
1 Sep	512 RAF	Berlin	1359 t
4 Sep	295 RAF	Berlin	906 t
6 Sep	546 RAF	Ludwigshafen Mannheim	1463 t
7 Sep	365 RAF	Munich	1020 t
11 Sep	360 RAF	Düsseldorf	760 t
23 Sep	658 RAF	Hanover	2357 t

Date	Bombers	Target	Bomb-load
28 Sep	599 RAF	Hanover	2196 t
30 Sep	312 RAF	Bochum	1318 t
2 Oct	240 RAF	Hagen	1103 t
2 Oct	273 RAF	Munich	958 t
4 Oct	501 RAF	Kassel	1544 t
9 Oct	457 RAF	Hanover	1667 t
9 Oct	378 USAAF	Anklam	
		Danzig	
		Marienburg	
10 Oct	236 USAAF	Münster	
14 Oct	291 USAAF	Schweinfurt	
19 Oct	349 RAF	Hanover	1697 t
21 Oct	285 RAF	Leipzig	1085 t
23 Oct	486 RAF	Kassel	1824 t
3 Nov	400 USAAF	Wilhelmshaven	
4 Nov	527 RAF	Düsseldorf	2234 t
18 Nov–3 Dec	2166 RAF	Berlin (5 raids)	8656 t
4 Dec	527 RAF	Leipzig	1382 t
13 Dec	1462 USAAF	Bremen	
		Hamburg	
		Kiel	
17 Dec	450 RAF	Berlin	1815 t
21 Dec	576 RAF	Frankfurt	2070 t
24 Dec	338 RAF	Berlin	1288 t
30 Dec	656 RAF	Berlin	2315 t
1944			
2 Jan	386 RAF	Berlin	1401 t
3 Jan	311 RAF	Berlin	1116 t
6 Jan	348 RAF	Stettin	1118 t
11 Jan	663 USAAF	Halberstadt	
		Brunswick	
		Magdeburg	
		Oschersleben	
15 Jan	472 RAF	Brunswick	2005 t
21 Jan	697 RAF	Berlin	2300 t
		Kiel	
22 Jan	585 RAF	Magdeburg	2024 t
28 Jan	481 RAF	Berlin	1761 t
29 Jan	596 RAF	Berlin	1954 t
29 Jan	806 USAAF	Frankfurt	
		Ludwigshafen	
31 Jan	489 RAF	Berlin	1961 t
16 Feb	806 RAF	Berlin	2643 t
20 Feb	730 RAF	Leipzig	2290 t
20 Feb	1000 USAAF	Brunswick	3830 t
		Leipzig	
		Oschersleben	
		Tutow *et al.*	
21 Feb	552 RAF	Stuttgart	1990 t
24 Feb	266 USAAF	Schweinfurt	
25 Feb	662 RAF	Schweinfurt	2000 t
26 Feb	528 RAF	Augsburg	1728 t
2 Mar	503 RAF	Stuttgart	1739 t
6 Mar	730 USAAF	Berlin	1500 t
8 Mar	540 USAAF	Berlin	
9 Mar	330 USAAF	Berlin	
16 Mar	813 RAF	Stuttgart	2609 t
19 Mar	769 RAF	Frankfurt	3068 t
23 Mar	816 RAF	Frankfurt	3116 t
25 Mar	726 RAF	Berlin	2496 t
27 Mar	677 RAF	Essen	2834 t
31 Mar	755 RAF	Nuremberg	2460 t
13 Apr	2000 USAAF	Augsburg	
		Schweinfurt *et al.*	
18 Apr	2000 USAAF	Cuxhaven	
		Oranienburg	
		et al.	4000 t
28 Apr	RAF	Friedrichshafen	
8 May	500 USAAF	Berlin	
8 May	300 USAAF	Brunswick	
12 May	600 USAAF	Mannheim	
21 May	RAF	Duisburg	2000 t
20 Jun	1500 USAAF	Fallersleben	
		Hamburg	
		Magdeburg	
		Ostermoor	4252 t
21 Jun	2500 USAAF	Berlin and environs	2000 t
11 Jul	1150 USAAF	Munich	2430 t
13 Jul	1260 USAAF	Munich	2650 t
16 Jul	1078 USAAF	Munich	2180 t
19 Jul	350 USAAF	Munich	890 t
25 Jul	614 RAF	Stuttgart	1957 t
26 Jul	600 RAF	Stuttgart	1903 t
29 Jul	612 RAF	Stuttgart	1940 t
13 Aug	RAF	Brunswick	1275 t
13 Aug	RAF	Rüsselsheim	964 t
26 Aug	RAF	Darmstadt	556 t
27 Aug	611 RAF	Kiel	
		Königsberg	2381 t
30 Aug	363 RAF	Stettin	1341 t
	133 RAF	Königsberg	492 t
12 Sep	234 RAF	Darmstadt	869 t
13 Sep	209 RAF	Stuttgart	781 t
13 Sep	RAF	Frankfurt	1556 t
16 Sep	RAF	Kiel	1448 t
22 Sep	USAAF	Kassel	1517 t
25 Sep	USAAF	Frankfurt	988 t
27 Sep	USAAF	Cologne	1113 t
3 Oct	USAAF	Nuremberg	1038 t
5 Oct	USAAF	Cologne	649 t
6 Oct	USAAF	Berlin	810 t
14 Oct	1063 RAF	Duisburg	4500 t
14 Oct	1000 USAAF	Cologne	
15 Oct	1005 RAF	Duisburg	
16 Oct	638 RAF	Wilhelmshaven	2198 t
19 Oct	135 USAAF	Mainz	
		Mannheim	2025 t
20 Oct	583 RAF	Stuttgart	2425 t
22 Oct	955 RAF	Essen	4522 t
24 Oct	RAF	Essen	3719 t
27 Oct	597 RAF	Cologne	2699 t
30 Oct	761 RAF	Cologne	3937 t
1 Nov	541 RAF	Cologne	2383 t
2 Nov	922 RAF	Düsseldorf	4468 t
4 Nov	549 RAF	Bochum	2323 t
9 Nov	277 RAF	Wanne-Eickel	1315 t
12 Nov	228 RAF	Dortmund	1122 t
12 Nov	245 RAF	Hamburg-Harburg	913 t
15 Nov	177 RAF	Dortmund	904 t
16 Nov	1188 RAF	Düren	2703 t
18 Nov	291 RAF	Münster	1694 t
19 Nov	309 RAF	Wanne-Eickel	1519 t
22 Nov	237 RAF	Aschaffenburg	1360 t
26 Nov	RAF	Munich	784 t
27 Nov	RAF	Freiburg	
29 Nov	RAF	Essen	1147 t
29 Nov	RAF	Dortmund	1618 t
1 Dec	RAF	Duisburg	2270 t
3 Dec	RAF	Hagen	1802 t
4 Dec	RAF	Heilbronn	1241 t
		Karlsruhe	2297 t
6 Dec	RAF	Soest	1857 t
7 Dec	262 RAF	Giessen	1193 t
11 Dec	USAAF	Frankfurt	882 t
12 Dec	USAAF	Darmstadt	1188 t
13 Dec	RAF	Essen	2354 t
16 Dec	303 RAF	Ludwigshafen	1547 t
17 Dec	243 RAF	Ulm	1292 t
17 Dec	291 RAF	Duisburg	1767 t
17 Dec	180 RAF	Munich	903 t
22 Dec	207 RAF	Pölitz	
30 Dec	337 RAF	Scholven-Buer	
1945			
2 Jan	RAF	Nuremberg	2067 t
6 Jan	561 RAF	Hanover	2365 t
6 Jan	149 USAAF	Cologne-Kalk	1092 t
7 Jan	RAF	Hanau	1653 t
7 Jan	RAF	Munich	2175 t
17 Jan	291 RAF	Magdeburg	1060 t
17 Jan	USAAF	Paderborn	1031 t
3 Feb	937 USAAF	Berlin	2267 t
3 Feb	400 USAAF	Magdeburg	
5 Feb	238 RAF	Bonn	
5 Feb	589 USAAF	Regensburg	
13 Feb	773 RAF	Dresden	2659 t
14 Feb	311 USAAF	Dresden	771 t
14 Feb	294 USAAF	Chemnitz	718 t
14 Feb	340 USAAF	Magdeburg	811 t
15 Feb	210 USAAF	Dresden	461 t
15 Feb	671 RAF	Chemnitz	
16 Feb	263 USAAF	Regensburg	559 t
20 Feb	439 USAAF	Nuremberg	2000 t
22 Feb	373 RAF	Worms	
22 Feb	349 RAF	Duisburg	
23 Feb	369 RAF	Pforzheim	1551 t
26 Feb	1112 USAAF	Berlin	2879 t
2 Mar	406 USAAF	Dresden	
4 Mar	500 USAAF	Ulm	
10 Mar	153 RAF	Scholven-Buer	755 t
11 Mar	1055 RAF	Essen	4700 t
12 Mar	1107 RAF	Dortmund	4851 t
15 Mar	576 USAAF	Berlin	
16 Mar	RAF	Würzburg	
18 Mar	1221 USAAF	Berlin	4000 t
22 Mar	200 RAF	Hildesheim	
25 Mar	606 RAF	Hanover	
		Münster	
		Osnabrück	
30 Mar	345 USAAF	Bremen	
		Hamburg	
		Wilhelmshaven	2849 t
3 Apr	RAF	Nordhausen	
7 Apr	1300 USAAF	Dessau	
9 Apr	RAF	Kiel	2634 t
10 Apr	RAF	Plauen	1139 t
14 Apr	298 RAF	Kiel	1905 t
14 Apr	364 RAF	Potsdam	1751 t
20 Apr	150 USAAF	Berlin	
25 Apr	415 RAF	Wangerooge	2176 t
25 Apr	318 RAF	Berchtesgaden	1181 t
3 May	125 RAF	Kiel	174 t

Sources:

The Strategic Air Offensive against Germany 1939–1945, H.M.S.O., London, 1961.

The US Strategic Bombing Survey, Washington, D.C., 1946.

Dokumente deutscher Kriegsschäden, ed. by the Bundesministerium für Vertriebene, Flüchtlinge und Kriegsgeschädigte, Bonn, 1958/62.

Index of Important Places and People

Italicized numbers indicate photographs, italicized words indicate bodies of water. *See also* place names in the list of the most important air raids on Germany 1940–1945.